BEHAVIOR SCIENCE BIBLIOGRAPHIES

EUROPE: A SELECTED ETHNOGRAPHIC BIBLIOGRAPHY

by

Robert J. Theodoratus

HUMAN RELATIONS AREA FILES PRESS
New Haven
1969

BEHAVIOR SCIENCE BIBLIOGRAPHIES

EUROPE: A SELECTED ETHNOGRAPHIC BIBLIOGRAPHY

by
Robert J. Theodoratus

HUMAN RELATIONS AREA FILES
New Haven, Connecticut
1969

Robert J. Theodoratus is Associate Professor of Anthropology at Colorado State University, Fort Collins, Colorado. His Ph.D. in Anthropology was received at the University of Washington (1961), Seattle. His field research has been among the Wenatchi-Methow Indians in eastern Washington and the Greek immigrants in Tacoma, Washington.

Library of Congress Catalog Card Number: 75-87851

CONTENTS

PREFACE

In the period following World War II, one example of the growing scope of anthropological interests has been the ever-increasing interest in the ethnic groups, especially peasant villages, of Europe. Prior to this, with the possible exception of the work of Conrad Arensberg, this region seemingly was the near exclusive domain of the folklore-oriented European ethnologist. Today, with an ever-growing amount of field research going on in Europe, with more and more anthropology departments offering courses on the "peoples of Europe, " and with the increased use of data on Europe in cross-cultural research, a major problem has been the absence of a general ethnographic bibliography of Europe. This is not to say that there are no bibliographies: there are, but they are structured so as to be of relatively little value to most sociocultural anthropologists. A few examples are the scattered references in various national bibliographies, the short bibliographic articles in localized European ethnological and folklore journals, and the large, biannual Volkskundliche Bibliographie, which has been published since 1921 in Switzerland and Germany. Even the latter volumes, although they are outstanding, are very uneven in their coverage, have many incomplete references, and are so organized (as to the subjects and time-spans covered) as to render them awkward for use by anthropologists. In organizing the references by ethnic groups, I hope to make this volume of greater service to students and scholars in the social sciences and humanities.

Area coverage: All of Europe is included, with the exception of the Caucasus Mountain region and the Finno-Ugric and Turkic peoples of the eastern and northeastern regions of the European part of the Soviet Union. In addition, because of their European cultural affinities and also because they are omitted from other bibliographies, the following areas are also included: Cyprus, Iceland, the Azores, the Canary Islands, the Cape Verde Islands, and Tristan da Cunha.

Time period covered: The sources are almost entirely for the modern historical period, with the primary focus upon the nineteenth and twentieth centuries. For Medieval Europe, only outstanding sources highly relevant to the ethnologist are listed, e.g. George Homans, English villagers of the thirteenth century. This is not to imply that much of the earlier material (or materials on earlier periods) is neither relevant nor of value. The basis for its exclusion is that these data are thin, are rather limited in their scope, and have for the most part been incorporated as comparative data in more recent works.

In evaluating sources for inclusion, a varying set of criteria had to be employed. For some groups, e.g. the Germans, French, and Italians, on whom there is a wealth of published materials, a much higher standard of selection had to be employed than for the Estonians, Albanians, or Icelanders, for whom many sources had to be included which are either very thin or of a poor quality, in order to provide a balanced coverage. For such peoples as the English, the Irish, and the Scots, a larger number of sources were included because of their potential value to students and scholars not only in anthropology but in such fields as literature, history, rural sociology, local government, etc.

Another major problem was that of materials written in non-Western European and lesser-known languages. In general, only very important sources in languages such as Finnish, Latvian, modern Greek, or Bulgarian are included. The exceptions to this are for the Scandinavian languages, Hungarian, and Rumanian, for there are surprisingly more scholars (beyond their own national boundaries) who are competent in these languages than is commonly supposed.

A final selection problem, often quite puzzling to the American-trained anthropologist, is that of the European terms or labels that are applied to certain categories of materials or fields of inquiry. These labels have often led American researchers into overlooking vast bodies of potentially useful ethnographic materials. The most common is the use of the term "folklore" among scholars in Europe—especially in Britain and France—where it refers primarily to studies of the folkways or customs of European peoples. Thus if a scholar were to write about the traditional customs in a French village it would be "folklore"; if he were to describe the customs of an African people, he would use the term "ethnography." A similar pattern is true over much of the rest of Europe, the best example being the German distinction between Volkskunde and Völkerkunde, the former referring to a folk ethnography of a European people and the latter referring to studies on non-European peoples. In a similar sense, the Greek term laographia is used by Greeks for studies of modern Greek folk life.

Asterisks: The most important or useful references for each ethnic group are marked with asterisks. This is done primarily as an aid to nonspecialists in the area, above all to individuals engaged in cross-cultural studies.

Acknowledgments: This bibliography is the result of the aid and encouragement of so many individuals and groups over an eight-year period that it is difficult to know where to begin. First I wish to thank my former professors at the University of Washington for their encouragement of my interest in European ethnology when I was a graduate student there, the anthropology faculty and my students when I was teaching at Sacramento State College, and my fellow faculty members in sociology and anthropology at Colorado State University. In addition this work could never have been accomplished without the aid and continued cooperation of the HRAF staff; especially that of George R. Bedell, Frank W. Moore, Timothy J. O'Leary, and Elizabeth P. Swift. Mrs. Celia Allee, a Work-Study student at Sacramento State College from 1964 to 1966, checked most of the monograph references in the catalogues of the Library of Congress and the British Museum. At Colorado State University, Professor Evan Vlachos carefully checked and added to the sources on Greece, as did Professor Joseph Sardo for the sections on Italy and Sicily. The Colorado State University Faculty Improvement Committee provided two grants for the years 1966-1967 and 1967-1968, which enabled me to do much of the final work on this bibliography. Also I wish to express my sincere thanks to the following libraries, schools, and research institutions for their help in providing added information and help on various sections of this bibliography: the School of Scottish Studies at the University of Edinburgh, the Bibliothèque Nationale (Paris), Bibliothèque Nationale Suisse—Schweizerische Landesbibliotek, Bibliothèque Nationale (Luxembourg), the British Museum, the Manx National Trust, the National Library of Ireland, the National Library of Wales, the Statsbiblioteket i Århus (Denmark), the Akademii Nauk Estonskaja SSR, Institutum Litterarum Estonicum (Stockholm), and the Dansk Folkemindesamling (Copenhagen).

In addition to the above, I must express my gratitude for the patience and help of my wife, Kay; my sister, Professor Dorothea J. Theodoratus; and the many librarians and library workers who made this bibliography possible.

December 1968   Robert J. Theodoratus

ABBREVIATIONS FOR JOURNALS

A.A.   American Anthropologist.

B.J.S.   British Journal of Sociology.

J.A.F.L.   Journal of American Folklore.

J.A.I.   Journal of the Anthropological Institute of Great Britain and
            Ireland. Later became J.R.A.I. (see below)

J.R.A.I.   Journal of the Royal Anthropological Institute of Great Britain
            and Ireland.

M.A.G.W.   Mittheilungen der Anthropologischen Gesellschaft im Wien.

R.D.T.P.   Revista de Dialectología y Tradiciones Populares.

R.T.P.   Revue des Traditions Populaires.

S.A.f.V.   Schweizerisches Archiv für Volkskunde.

S.W.J.A.   Southwestern Journal of Anthropology.

Z.d.V.f.V. Zeitschrift des Vereins für Volkskunde.

Z.f.A.A.   Zeitschrift für Agrargeschichte und Agrarsoziologie.

Z.f.E.   Zeitschrift für Ethnologie.

Z.f.V.   Zeitschrift für Volkskunde

Z.f.Ö.V.   Zeitschrift für Österreiches Volkskunde.

GENERAL BIBLIOGRAPHIES

Bonser, Wilfred. A bibliography of folklore. London, The Folk-Lore Society. 1961. 15, 126 p. (Bibliography of articles in the first 80 years of the Folk-Lore Society's journals.)

Conover, Helen F. Introduction to Europe. Supplement, 1950-1955. Washington, Library of Congress, Reference Department. 1955. 6, 181 p.

Introduction to Europe. A selective guide to background reading. Washington, Library of Congress, Reference Department. 1950. 6, 201 p.

Krauss, Friedrich Salomon. Die Volkskunde in den Jahren 1897-1902. Erlangen, F. Junge. 1903. 180 p.

The Museums Association. Bibliography for students. London, The Museums Association. n.d. (1967?) 43 p. (See section of folk life and local history.)

Ripley, William Z. A selected bibliography of the anthropology and ethnology of Europe. A supplement to "The races of Europe." New York, D. Appleton. 1899. 10, 160 p.

Thomas, Northcote W. Bibliography of anthropology and folklore, 1906, containing works published within the British Empire. London, David Nutt. 1907. 72 p.

Uhlrich, H. Eine Übersicht über volkskundliche Veröffentlichungen der Jahre 1956 und 1957 zum Theme "Arbeit und Wirtschaft." Deutsches Jahrbuch für Volkskunde. 4(1958): 539-550.

Volkskundliche Bibliographie für das Jahr. (Various editors over the years: Eduard Hoffman-Krayer, Paul Geiger, etc.) Berlin and Leipzig. W. De Gruyter. 1921-1939. (For years 1917-1934.) Continued as Bibliographie Internationale des Arts et Traditions Populaires. 1939-1957 to date.

Winchell, Constance. Guide to reference books. 8th ed. Chicago, American Library Association. 1967. 12, 741 p.

Aberg, F. A. The early plow in Europe. Gwerin. 1, no. 4 (1957): 171-181.

Aleksandrov, Vadim A., et al., eds. Narody evropeĭskoĭ chasti SSSR. 2 vols. Moskva, Nauka. 1964.

Anderson, Poul. Forms and names of heddles. Folk-Liv. 14-15(1951): 60-85.

Anderson, Robert T. Changing kinship in Europe. Ph. D. dissertation in anthropology. Berkeley, University of California. 1956. 2, 156 p.

*Anderson, Robert T. Changing kinship in Europe. Kroeber Anthropological Society Papers. 28(1963): 1-48.

Anderson, Robert T., and Gallatin Anderson. The indirect social structure of European communities. A. A. 64(1962): 1016-1027.

Anderson, Robert T. The replicate social structure. S. W. J. A. 18(1962): 365-370.

Baines, Anthony. Bagpipes. Occasional Papers on Technology. 9. Oxford, Pitt-Rivers Museum. 1960. 140 p., 78 fig., 16 pl.

Behrend, H. Die Aufhebung der Feldgemeinschaften. Neumünster, Washholtz. 1964. 149 p.

Beijer, G. Rural migrants in urban setting; an analysis of the literature on the problem consequent on the internal migration from rural to urban areas in 12 European countries, 1945-1961. The Hague, M. Nijhoff. 1963. 14, 327 p.

Benvenuti, Bruno. Farming in cultural change. Assen, Van Gorcum. 1962. 20, 462 p.

*Bernatzik, Hugo A. Die neue grosse Völkerkunde. 3 vols. Frankfurt/Main, Herkul Verlagsanstalt. 1954. Vol. 1: 15-277.

*Biasutti, Renato. Le razze e i popoli della terra. 4 vols. Torino, Unione Tipografico-editrice Torinese. 1959. Vol. 1: 1-375.

Blum, Jerome. The European peasantry from the fifteenth to the nineteenth century. Washington, American Historical Association. 1960. 30 p.

Boberg, Inger M. Folkemindeforsknings historie i Mellem- og Nordeuropa. (The history of folklore research in central and northern Europe.) Copenhagen, E. Munksgaard. 1953. 382 p.

Boissonnade, Prosper. Life and work in medieval Europe. London, Kegan Paul, Trench, Trubner; New York, A. A. Knopf. 1927. 395 p.

Bossert, Helmuth Theodor. Volkskunst in Europa. Berlin, E. Wasmuth. 1926. 12, 46 p., 132 pl.

Bossert, Helmuth Theodor. Peasant art in Europe. London, E. Benn. 1927. 44 p., 132 pl. (Reprinted. London, Simpkin Marshall. 1938. 55 p., 120 pl.)

Burgess, Ernest W., ed. Aging in western societies. Chicago, University of Chicago Press. 1960. 492 p.

*Buschan, Georg, ed. Illustrierte Völkerkunde. Vol. 2, pt. 2. Europa und seine Randgebiete. Stuttgart, Strecker und Schröder. 1926. 24, 1154 p., 708 illus.

Calmet, Dom Augustin. Dissertations on the apparitions of angels, demons, and ghosts, and concerning the vampires of Hungary, Bohemia, Moravia, and Silesia. Translated from the French. London, M. Cooper. 1759. 14, 370 p. (Many later editions.)

Carrier, Else H. Water and grass. A study in the pastoral economy of southern Europe. London, Christophers. 1932. 11, 434 p.

Chadwick, Hector Munro. The nationalities of Europe and the growth of national ideologies. Cambridge, The University Press. 1945. 8, 209 p.

Chiva, I. Rural communities: problems, methods and types of research. Paris, UNESCO. 1958. 52 p.

*Coon, Carleton S. The races of Europe. New York, Macmillan. 1939. 16, 737 p., plates.

Cooper, James Fenimore. Gleanings in Europe. 2 vols. New York, London, Oxford University Press. 1928. 34, 395; 432 p.

Count, Earl Wendel. 4,000 years of Christmas. New York, Rider. 1953. 95 p.

Darby, H. C. The clearing of the woodland in Europe. In William L. Thomas, ed. Man's role in changing the face of the earth. Chicago, University of Chicago Press. 1956: 183-216.

Dickinson, R. E. The West European city: a geographical interpretation. London, Routledge & Kegan Paul. 1951. 18, 580 p.

Dominian, L. The frontiers of nationality and language in Europe. New York, Henry Holt. 1917. 18, 375 p.

Douglas-Irvine, Helen. The making of rural Europe. London, George Allen & Unwin. 1923. 224 p.

Dovring, Folke. Land and labour in Europe 1900-1950; a comparative survey of recent agrarian history. The Hague, M. Nijhoff. 1956. 8, 480 p.

Edmonson, Munro. Kinship terms and kinship concepts. A.A. 59(1957): 393-433.

*Erixon, Sigurd. Regional European ethnology. Folk-Liv. 3(1938): 263-294.

Erixon, Sigurd. Folk-life research in our time. Gwerin. 3(1962): 275-291.

Erixon, Sigurd. European ethnology in our time. Ethnologia Europaea. 1(1967): 3-11.

*Ethnologia Europaea. Paris. 1(1967):--

Evans, E. Estyn. Transhumance in Europe. Geography. 25(1940): 172-180.

*Études Rurales. Paris, Mouton. 1(1961):--

Findlay, William M. Oats, their cultivation and use from ancient times to the present day. Aberdeen University Studies. 137. Edinburgh, Oliver & Boyd. 1956. 207 p., illus.

Fleure, Herbert J. The peoples of Europe. London, Oxford University Press. 1922. 110 p.

Fleure, Herbert J. Peasants in Europe. Geography. 28(1943): 55-61.

Fleure, Herbert J. What is a peasantry? John Rylands Library, Manchester, Bulletin. 21(1937): 387-405.

Folk-Liv. Uppsala, Sweden, Royal Gustavus Academy for Ethnological and Folklore Research. 1(1937):-- (Annual)

Habenstein, Robert W., and William M. Lamers. Funeral customs the world over. Milwaukee, Bulfin Printers. 1960. 973 p.

Handlin, Oscar. The uprooted. Boston, Little, Brown. 1951. 310 p. (Chapter 1 on peasant life in Europe.)

*Houston, J. M. A social geography of Europe. London, Gerald Duckworth. 1953. 271 p., 29 photos, 47 maps. (Revised ed. 1963.)

Hultkrantz, Åke, et al. International dictionary of regional European ethnology and folklore. Vol. 1. General ethnological concepts. Copenhagen, Rosenkilde and Bagger. 1960. 282 p.

Huxley, Julian S., and A. C. Haddon. We Europeans. London, J. Cape. 1935. 299 p., illus.

International Secretariat for Research on the History of Agricultural Implements. National Museum. Research on ploughing implements. The conference in Copenhagen, 1-5 June 1954. Copenhagen, Nordlundes Bogtrykkeri. 1956. 170 p.

Jacobeit, Wolfgang. Möglichkeiten einer verstärkten internationalen Zusammenarbeit auf dem Gebiet der europäischen Agrarethnographie. In Gyula Ortutay and T. Bodrogy, eds. Europa et Hungaria. Budapest, Akadémiai Kiadó. 1965: 137-146.

Karutz, Richard. Die Völker Europas. Stuttgart, Franck'scher Verlag. 1926. 127 p., illus.

Kelly, Walter Keating. Curiosities of Indo-European tradition and folk-lore. London, Chapman & Hall. 1863. 12, 308 p.

Kriss-Rettenbeck, Lenz. Das Votivbild. München, H. Rinn. 1958. 185 p.

Kriss-Rettenbeck, Lenz. Bilder und Zeichen religiösen Volksglaubens. München, Callwey. 1963. 186 p., 414 photos.

Krüger, Fritz. El mobilario popular en los países romanicos. Coimbra, Faculdade de Letras da Universidade de Coimbra. Instituto de Estudios Românicos. 1963. 6, 933 p., illus.

La Landelle, Gabriel de. Moeurs maritimes. Paris, L. Hachette. 1866. 8, 440 p.

Laos. Stockholm, Almqvist & Wiksell. 1 (1951):--

Latham, Robert Gordon. The nationalities of Europe. 2 vols. London, W. H. Allen. 1863.

Lawson, J. European folk dance, its national and musical characteristics. London, Pitman. 1955. 12, 244 p.

*Le Play, Pierre Guillaume Frédéric. Les ouvriers européens. Études sur les travaux, la vie domestique, et la condition morale des populations ouvrières de l'Europe. 2d ed. 6 vols. Tours, A. Mame et fils. 1877-1879. (1st ed. 1855.)

Le Play, Pierre Guillaume Frédéric. The organization of labor in accordance with custom and the law of the Decalogue; with a summary of comparative observations upon good and evil in the regime of labor, the causes of evils existing at the present time and the means required to effect reform; with objectives and answers, difficulties and solutions. Translated from the 2d French edition. Philadelphia, Claxton, Remsen & Hoffelfinger. 1872. 23, 417 p.

Leroy, Olivier. La lévitation. Paris. 1928. 387 p.

Meillet, A. Les langues dans l'Europe nouvelle. 2d rev. ed. Paris, Payot. 1928. 12, 495 p.

Onians, R. B. The origins of European thought about the body, the mind, the soul, the world, time and fate . . . Cambridge, The University Press. 1951. 17, 547 p.

Peattie, Roderick. Mountain geography; a critique and field study. Cambridge, Mass., Harvard University Press. 1936. 14, 257 p.

Rapport, Angelo S. Superstitions of sailors. London, S. Paul. 1928. 287 p.

Redfield, Robert. Peasant society and culture. Chicago, University of Chicago Press. 1956. 8, 163 p.

Reinsberg-Düringsfeld, Ida von. Hochzeitsbuch. Brauch und Glaube der Hochzeit bei den christlichen Völkern Europa's. Leipzig, J. G. Bach. 1871. 272 p.

Ripley, William Z. The races of Europe. A sociological study. New York, D. Appleton. 1899. 32, 624 p.

Runeberg, Arne. Witches, demons and fertility magic: analysis of their significance and natural relations in West-European folk religion. Helsingfors, Commentationes Humanarum Litterarum. 14, 4. 1947. 273 p.

*Salaman, Redcliffe Nathan. The history and social influence of the potato. Cambridge, The University Press. 1949. 24, 685 p., 32 pl.

Sanders, Irwin T. Characteristics of peasant societies. In Edmund de S. Brunner, et al. Farmers of the world. New York, Columbia University Press. 1945: 37-45.

Sandklef, Albert. Singing flails. Folklore Fellows Communications. 136. Helsinki, Suomalainen Tiedeakatemia. 1949. 76 p. (Threshing floor construction, flailing traditions, etc.)

Schechtman, Joseph B. European population transfers, 1939-1945. New York, Oxford University Press. 1946. 11, 532 p.

Sjoberg, Gideon. The pre-industrial city, past and present. Glencoe, Ill., The Free Press. 1960. 353 p.

Slicher van Bath, Bernard Hendrik. The agrarian history of western Europe A. D. 500-1850. London, Edward Arnold; New York, St. Martin's Press. 1963. 9, 364 p.

Sociologia Ruralis. Assen, Van Gorcum. 1 (1960):--

Summers, Montague. The history of witchcraft and demonology. London, Kegan Paul, Trench, Trubner. 1926. 15, 353 p.

Summers, Montague. The geography of witchcraft. London, Kegan Paul, Trench, Trubner; New York, Knopf. 1927. 11, 623 p.

Summers, Montague. The vampire in Europe. New York, E. P. Dutton. 1929. 4, 329 p.

Summers, Montague. The werewolf. New York, E. P. Dutton. 1933. 14, 307 p.

Summers, Montague. The physical phenomena of mysticism, with especial reference to the stigmata, divine and diabolic. New York, Barnes and Noble. 1950. 262 p.

Thompson, G. B., comp. Spinning wheels. Belfast, Ulster Museum. 1964. 52 p., illus.

Thorpe, Harry. The green village in its European setting. In Alan Small, ed. The fourth Viking congress. Edinburgh, Oliver and Boyd. 1965: 85-111. (Village greens.)

Thrupp, Sylvia L. ed. Changes in medieval society: Europe north of the Alps, 1050-1500. New York, Appleton-Century-Crofts. 1964. 13, 324 p.

Thut, I. N., and Don Adams. Educational patterns in contemporary societies. New York, McGraw-Hill. 1964: 27-47. (Chapter on education in the fifteenth century.)

Warriner, Doreen. Economics of peasant farming. London, Oxford University Press. 1939. 208 p.

Weiser, Francis Xavier. Handbook of Christian feasts and customs: the year of the Lord in liturgy and folklore. New York, Harcourt Brace. 1958. 366 p.

Wiese, Leopold von. What is European culture? B.J.S. 11(1960): 1-9.

Wildhaber, Robert, et al. Osterbrauchtum in Europa. S.A.f.V. 53(1957): 61-198.

Wolf, Eric. Peasants. Englewood Cliffs, N.J., Prentice-Hall. 1966. 100 p.

Zeitschrift des Vereins für Volkskunde. 1891-1928. Became, Zeitschrift für Volkskunde. 1929--

Bonser, Wilfred. A bibliography of folklore. London, The Folk-Lore Society. 1961. 15, 126 p.

Aubrey, John. Miscellanies. London, E. Castle. 1696. 179 p. (Many later editions.)

Bertram, James Glass. Harvest of the sea; a contribution to the natural and economic history of the British food fisheries — with sketches of fisheries and fisher folk. London, J. Murray. 1869. 519 p.

Bertram, James Glass. The unappreciated fisher folk, their round of life and labour. London, W. Clowes and Sons. 1883. 8, 83 p.

Blount, Thomas. Tenures of land & customs of manors. London, Reeves & Turner; Bernard Quaritch. 1874 and 1909. (First edition in 1679, with many later editions.)

Brand, John. Popular antiquities of Great Britain, comprising notices of the movable and immovable feasts, customs, superstitions and amusements past and present. Ed. from materials collected by John Brand, F.S.A., with very large corrections and additions by M. Carew Hazlett. London, J. R. Smith. 1870. (Many other editions of this work.)

Burgess, Ernest W., ed. Aging in western societies. Chicago, University of Chicago Press. 1960. 492 p.

Burke, John F. British husbandry; exhibiting the farming practice in various parts of the United Kingdom. 3 vols. London, Baldwin and Cradock. 184

Carrier, Elsé H. The pastoral heritage of Britain; a geographical study. London, Christophers. 1936. 11, 293 p.

Dorson, Richard M. Folklore and folklife studies in Great Britain and Ireland: introduction. Journal of the Folklore Institute. 2(1965): 239-243.

Evans-Wentz, Walter Y. The fairy-faith in Celtic countries. London, Frowde. 1911. 552 p. (Reprinted. New Hyde Park, N.Y., University Books. 1966.)

*Frankenberg, Ronald. Communities in Britain; social life in town and country. Harmondsworth and Baltimore, Penguin Books. 1965. 313 p.

Gair, G. R. Some types of British haystacks and their distribution. Folk. 1(1937): 181-187, map, tables.

Garner, Frank Harold. The cattle of Britain. London, Longmans. 1944. 158 p., plates.

Garner, J. F. The role of the mayor in Britain. Journal of Local Administration Overseas. 2(1963): 16-23.

Gomme, Alice Bertha, Lady. The traditional games of England, Scotland, and Ireland, with tunes, singing-rhymes, and methods of playing according to the variants extant and recorded in different parts of the kingdom. 2 vols. London, David Nutt. 1894-1898. (Reprinted. New York, Dover Publications. 1964.)

*Great Britain. European conference on rural life. National monographs drawn up by governments. United Kingdom. Geneva, League of Nations. 1939. Series of League of Nations Publications. European Conference on Rural Life. 19. 81 p., illus.

Hazlitt, William C. English proverbs and proverbial phrases. London, Reeves and Turner. 1907. 30, 580 p.

Hazlitt, William C. Faiths and folklore of the British Isles. 2 vols. Bronx, N. Y., Benjamin Blom. 1965. (Many earlier editions.)

Heaton, Nell. Traditional recipes of the British Isles. London, Faber & Faber. 1951. 215 p.

Hennell, Thomas B. Change in the farm. Cambridge, The University Press. 1934. 10, 201 p.

Higgs, J. W. Y. Folk life and classification. Handbook for Museum Curators. Part C: Permanent Collections, Archaeology & Ethnology, Section 6. London, The Museums Association. 1963. 58 p.

Hone, William. The every-day book: or, the guide to the year: relating the popular amusements, sports, ceremonies, manners, customs, and events, incident to the three hundred and sixty-five days in past and present times; being a series of five thousand anecdotes and facts; forming a history of the year, a calendar of the seasons, and a chronological dictionary of the almanac; with a variety of important and diverting information, for daily use and entertainment. 2 vols. London, W. Tegg. 1878. (Other editions.) (Reprinted. Detroit, Gale Research Co. 1967. 1719, 1711 p.)

Hone, William. The year book of daily recreation and information: concerning remarkable men and manners, times and seasons, solemnities and merry-makings, antiquities and novelties, on the plan of the Every-day Book and Table Book: or everlasting calendar of popular amusements, sports, pastimes, ceremonies, customs & events. London, W. Tegg. 185_. 1644 cols. in double columns. (Reprinted. Detroit, Gale Research Co. 1967. 1645 p.)

Hornell, James. British coracles and Irish curraghs. London, B. Quaritch. 1938. 12, 5-41, 261-304, 74-83, 148-175, 153-159. (Consists of a series of articles reprinted from Mariner's Mirror. 1936-1938.)

Hornell, James. Water transport. Origins and early evolution. Cambridge, The University Press. 1946. 15, 307 p., 45 pl. (Especially see pp. 111-147.)

Jessen, Knud and Hans Helbaek. Cereals in Great Britain and Ireland in prehistoric and early historic times. Det Kongelige Danske Videnskabernes Selskab. Biologiske Skrifter. Vol. 3, no. 2. Copenhagen. 1944. 68 p.

Lancaster, Lorraine. Some conceptual problems in the study of family and kin ties in the British Isles. B.J.S. 12(1961): 317-333.

Latham, Robert Gordon. Ethnology of the British Isles. London, J. van Voorst. 1852. 8, 260 p.

Lavergne, Léonie de. The rural economy of England, Scotland, and Ireland. Edinburgh and London, W. Blackwood and Sons. 1855. 400 p.

Lethbridge, T. C. Herdsmen and hermits. Celtic seafarers in the northern seas. Cambridge, Bowes and Bowes. 1950. 146 p., pl., 27 fig.

Martin, W. British fish and fisheries. London, The Religious Tract Society. 1850. 6, 192 p.

Middleton, D. The British. London, Secker & Warburg. 1957. 284 p. (The American edition has the title: These are the British.)

Pückler-Muskau, Hermann Ludwig H. fürst von. Tour in England, Ireland, and France in the years 1826, 1827, 1828, & 1829. With remarks on the manners & customs of the inhabitants, and anecdotes of distinguished public characters. Philadelphia, Carey, Lea & Blanchard. 1833. 16, 499 p.

Robertson, J. Uppies and doonies. Aberdeen, Aberdeen University Press. 1967. 239 p. (Folk football.)

Saville, J. Rural depopulation in England and Wales 1851-1951. London, Routledge & Kegan Paul. 1957. 16, 253 p.

Shanas, Ethel, Peter Townsend, et al. Old folks in three industrial societies. New York, Atherton Press. 1968. 16, 478 p.

Smelser, Neil J. Social change in the industrial revolution; an application of theory to the British cotton industry. Chicago, University of Chicago Press. 1959. 12, 440 p.

Spicer, Dorothy G. Yearbook of English festivals. New York, Wilson. 1954. 298 p.

Strutt, Joseph. Glig-gamena angel-dead. Or, the sports and pastimes of the people of England; including the rural and domestic recreations, May-games, mummeries, pageants, processions, & pompous spectacles, from the earliest period to the present time. London, T. Bensley. 1810. 49, 357 p., pl. (Many later editions.)

Strutt, Joseph. A complete view of the dress and habits of the people of England, from the establishment of the Saxons in Britain to the present time. 2 vols. London, H. G. Bohn. 1842.

Spence, Lewis. The fairy tradition in Britain. London, Rider. 1948. 374 p.

Thomson, David. The people of the sea. London, Turnstile Press. 1954. 9, 214 p. (Seal lore.)

Vale, Edmund. The mail-coach men of the late eighteenth century. London, Cassell. 1960. 19, 300 p., illus., maps. (Reprinted. New York, Kelley. 1968.)

Weather lore. Compiled and arranged by the late Richard Inwards; ed., rev., and amplified for the Royal Meteorological Society by E. L. Hawke. 4th ed. London, Rider, for the Royal Meteorological Society. 1950. 251 p., 10 illus.

Bonser, Wilfred. A bibliography of folklore. London, The Folk-Lore Society. 1961. 15, 126 p. (Covers the first 80 years of the society's publications.)

Chope, R. Pearse. Index to the folklore in the transactions of the Devonshire Association, vols. 1-9. Exeter, Southwoods. 1929. 50 p.

———

Adams, William Henry Davenport. Witch, warlock, and magician. Historical sketches of magic and witchcraft in England and Scotland. London, Chatto & Windus. 1889. 428 p.

Addison, W. English fairs and markets. London, Batsford. 1953. 8, 199 p., illus.

Addy, Sidney Oldall. The evolution of the English house. London, S. Sonnenschein; New York, Macmillan. 1898. 28, 223 p., illus., plans, maps. (2d ed. London, G. Allen & Unwin. 1933. 252 p., illus., plans, maps.)

Ah, Chin-le. Some observations upon the civilization of the western barbarians, particularly of the English. Translated by J. Y. Smythe. Boston, Lee & Shepard. 1876. 302 p.

Alford, Violet. An introduction to English folklore. London, G. Bell and Sons. 1952. 8, 164 p., 4 pl.

Allo Isichei, E. From sect to denomination in English Quakerism, with special reference to the nineteenth century. B.J.S. 15(1964): 207-222.

Andrews, William. Bygone England: social studies in its historic byways and high-ways. London, Hutchinson. 1892. 258 p.

Andrews, William. Legal lore: curiosities of law and lawyers. London, W. Andrews. 1897. 280 p.

Andrews, William. Bygone punishments. London, W. Andrews. 1899. 311 p.

Andrews, William. Curious epitaphs. London, W. Andrews. 1899. 241 p.

Andrews, William, ed. Bygone Northhamptonshire. London, Simpkin, Marshall, Hamilton, Kent; Hull, W. Andrews. 1891. 232 p.

Andrews, William, ed. Bygone Lincolnshire. 2 vols. Hull, Brown and Son; London, Simpkin, Marshall, Hamilton, Kent. 1891. 10, 247; 256 p.

Andrews, William, ed. Bygone Derbyshire. Derby, F. Murrey; Hull, W. Andrews; London, Simpkin, Marshall, Hamilton, Kent. 1892. 256 p.

Andrews, William, ed. Bygone Essex. Colchester, F. Forster; Hull, W. Andrews; London, Simpkin, Marshall, Hamilton, Kent. 1892. 267 p.

Andrews, William, ed. Bygone Leicestershire. London, Simpkin, Marshall, Hamilton, Kent. 1892. 264 p.

Andrews, William, ed. Bygone Yorkshire. Hull & York, A. Brown and Sons; London, Simpkin, Marshall, Hamilton, Kent. 1892. 267 p.

Andrews, William, ed. Bygone Warwickshire. Hull, W. Andrews. 1893. 284 p.

Andrews, William, ed. Bygone Cheshire. Chester, Phillipson & Golden; Hull, W. Andrews; London, Simpkin, Marshall, Hamilton, Kent. 1895. 253 p.

Andrews, William, ed. The lawyer, in history, literature, and humour. London, W. Andrews. 1896. 276 p.

Andrews, William, ed. Bygone Durham. London, W. Andrews. 1898. 297 p.

Andrews, William, ed. Bygone Hertfordshire. London, W. Andrews. 1898. 283 p.

Andrews, William, ed. Bygone Norfolk. London, W. Andrews. 1898. 290 p.

Andrews, William, ed. Bygone Hampshire. London, W. Andrews. 1899. 242 p

Andrews, William, ed. Bygone Middlesex. London, W. Andrews. 1899. 248 p

Andrews, William, ed. Bygone Northumberland. London, W. Andrews. 1899. 268 p.

Anson, Peter Frederick. The call of the cloister; religious communities and kindred bodies in the anglican communion. 2d rev. ed. London, S.P.C.K. 1964. 16, 641 p.

Anthony, Sylvia. The child's discovery of death. London, Kegan Paul. 1940. 16, 231 p.

Ashby, Mabel Kathleen. Joseph Ashby of Tysoe, 1859-1919; a study of English village life. London and New York, Cambridge University Press. 1961. 302 p.

Ashton, John. Chap-books of the 18th century; with facsimiles, notes, and introduction. London, Chatto & Windus. 1882. 16, 486 p. (Reprinted. Bronx, N.Y., Benjamin Blom. 1965.)

Athol, Justin. Shadow of the gallows. London, J. Long. 1954. 224 p., 6 pl.

Atkinson, F. Oatbread of northern England. Gwerin. 3, no. 2(1960): 44-45.

Atkinson, F. Yorkshire miners' cottages. Folk Life. 3(1965): 92-96.

Atkinson, John Christopher. Forty years in a moorland parish; reminiscences and research in Danby in Cleveland. London and New York, Macmillan. 1891. 11, 457 p.

Bailey, John. General view of the agriculture of the county of Durham . . . London, Board of Agriculture. 1810. 412 p.

Bailey, John, and George Culley. General view of the agriculture of the county of Northumberland . . . 3d ed. London, Sherwood, Neely & Jones. 1813. 20, 361 p.

Bailey, John, and George Culley. General view of the agriculture of the county of Cumberland . . . London, Board of Agriculture. 1794. 51 p.

Baird, Thomas. General view of the agriculture of the county of Middlesex . . . London, Board of Agriculture. 1793. 50 p.

Baker, William Pearson. The English inn. London, Oxford University Press. 1953. 224 p.

Balfour, M. C., collector. (Edited by Northcote W. Thomas.) Examples of printed folk-lore concerning Northumberland. County Folk-Lore. Vol. 4. London, The Folk-Lore Society. 1904. 180 p.

Banks, Joseph Ambrose, ed. Studies in British society. New York, Thomas Y. Crowell. 1968. 220 p.

Banks, Joseph Ambrose, and Olive Banks. Feminism and family planning in Victorian England. A study of the influence of the feminist movement on the birth rate in Victorian England. Liverpool, Liverpool University Press. 1964. 12, 142 p.

Banks, Olive. The attitudes of steelworkers to technical change. Liverpool, Liverpool University Press. 1960. 10, 152 p.

*Baring-Gould, Sabine. Old country life. London, Methuen. 1890. 10, 358 p. (Primarily on Devon.)

Baring-Gould, Sabine. An old English home and its dependencies. London, Methuen. 1898. 336 p.

Baring-Gould, Sabine. Songs of the west: traditional ballads and songs of the west of England, with their traditional melodies. 5th ed. London, Methuen. 1913. 247 p.

Barley, Maurice W. The English farmhouse and cottage. London, Routledge & Kegan Paul. 1961. 21, 297 p.

Baron, George. Society, schools and progress in England. London and New York, Pergamon Press. 1966. 228 p.

Barrett, W. H. Tales from the Fens. London, Routledge and Kegan Paul. 1963. 20, 203 p.

Barrett, W. H. More tales from the Fens. London, Routledge and Kegan Paul. 1964. 17, 150 p.

*Bennett, Henry Stanley. Life on the English manor; a study of peasant conditions, 1150-1400. Cambridge, The University Press. 1956. 364 p.

Bennett, Henry Stanley. The Pastons and their England; studies in an age of transition. Cambridge, The University Press. 1922. 20, 289 p.

Bennett, W. The Pendle witches. Burnley, Public Library. 1957. 32 p.

Bensusan, Samuel L. Latter-day rural England. London, E. Benn. 1928. 221 p.

Beresford, Maurice. The lost villages of England. London, Lutterworth Press. 1954. 446 p., 15 maps and diagrams, 18 tables. (Reprinted with corrections 1963.)

Billingsley, John. General view of the agriculture of the county of Somerset. London, Board of Agriculture. 1794.

Billson, Charles James. Examples of printed folk-lore concerning Leicestershire and Rutland. County Folk-Lore. Vol. 1. London, The Folk-Lore Society. 1895. 153 p.

*Birch, Anthony Harold. Small-town politics. A study of political life in Glossup. Oxford, Oxford University Press. 1959. 6, 199 p.

Bishton, J. General view of the agriculture of the county of Salop. Brentford, London, Board of Agriculture. 1794.

Blakeborough, Richard. Wit, character, folklore, and customs of the North Riding of Yorkshire. London, Henry Frowde. 1898. 22, 485 p. (2d ed. London, Rapp & Sons. 1920. 519 p.)

Bloom, Alan Herbert V. The farm in the fen. [An account of the author's reclamation of derelict land in the Fens.] London, Faber & Faber. 1944. 192 p.

Bloom, Alan Herbert V. The Fens. London, Robert Hale. 1953. 325 p., illus.

Bloom, James Harvey. Folk lore, old customs and superstitions in Shakespeare land. London, Mitchell Hughes and Clarke. 1930. 7, 167 p.

Bonham-Carter, Victor. The English village. Harmondsworth, Penguin Books. 1952. 249 p.

*Booth, Charles, ed. Labour and life of the people. 2 vols. in 3. London and Edinburgh, Williams and Norgate. 1891. (London)

*Booth, Charles, ed. The aged poor in England and Wales. London and New York, Macmillan. 1894. 527 p.

*Booth, Charles, ed. Life and labour of the people in London. 9 vols. London and New York, Macmillan. 1892-1897.

*Booth, Charles, ed. Life and labour of the people of London. 1st. series: poverty. 4 vols. London and New York, Macmillan. 1902.

*Booth, Charles, ed. Life and labour of the people of London. 2d. series: Industry. 5 vols. London and New York, Macmillan. 1903.

*Booth, Charles, ed. Life and labour of the people in London. 3d. series: religious influences. 7 vols. London and New York, Macmillan. 1902.

*Booth, Charles, ed. Life and labour of the people in London. Final volume. Notes on social influences and conclusions. London and New York, Macmillan. 1902. 451 p. (Reprinted 1903.)

*Bott, Elizabeth. A study of ordinary families. Recherches sur le famille. 1 (1956): 29-68. (Family life in London.)

Bourne, George. See George Sturt.

Bovill, E. W. English country life 1780-1830. London and New York, Oxford University Press. 1962. 266 p.

Boys, John. General view of the agriculture of the county of Kent . . . 2d ed. London, Richard Phillip. 1805. 23, 293 p.

Bracey, H. E. English rural life: village activities, organisations and institutions. London, Routledge & Kegan Paul. 1959. 14, 272 p.

ENGLISH

Bradfield, N. Historical costumes of England from the eleventh to the twentieth century. London, Harrap. 1958. 184 p.

Brand, John. Observations on the popular antiquities of Great Britain; chiefly illustrating the origin of our vulgar and provincial customs, ceremonies, and superstitions. Revised and greatly enlarged by Sir Henry Ellis. 3 vols. London, G. Bell & Sons. 1900-1902. (There are many editions of this work, the earliest being for 1777.)

Briggs, Asa. Victorian people, some reassessments of people, institutions, ideas and events. London, Odhams Press. 1954. 317 p.

British Journal of Sociology. Vol. 1 (1950-)-- London, Routledge and Kegan Paul for the London School of Economics.

Brodrick, George C. English land and English landlords. An enquiry into the origin & character of the English land system with proposals for its reform. London, Cassell, Petter, Galpin. 1881. 8, 500, 14 p. (Reprinted. New York, Augustin M. Kelley. 1968.)

Brown, T. The folklore of Devon. Folklore. 75 (1964): 145-160.

Buck, A. The countryman's smock. Folk Life. 1 (1963): 16-34.

Burke, John F. Farming for ladies; or, a guide to the poultry-yard, the dairy and piggery. London, J. Murray. 1844. 18, 511 p.

Burke, John F. British husbandry; exhibiting the farming practice in various parts of the United Kingdom. 3 vols. London, Baldwin and Cradock. 1834-1840.

Burke, Thomas. The English inn. New York and London, George H. Doran. 1927. 24, 401 p. (Reprinted. New York and London, Longmans, Green. 1931. 11, 186 p.)

Burne, Charlotte Sophia, ed. Shropshire folk-lore: a sheaf of gleanings. London, Trübner. 1883.

Burnett, John. Plenty and want: a social history of diet in England from 1815 to the present day. London, Nelson. 1966. 296 p.

Caird, James. English agriculture in 1850-51. 2d ed. London, Longmans. 1852. 27, 550 p.

Calthrop, Dion Clayton. English costume 1066-1830. London, A. & C. Black. 1963. 12, 463 p.

Carbery, Mary, and Edwin Grey. Hertfordshire heritage. London, J. Green. 1948. 158 p.

Cardus, Neville. Cricket. New York and London, Longmans, Green. 1930. 9, 177 p.

Carr, Philip. The English are like that. New York, C. Scribner's Sons. 1941. 356 p.

Chamberlayne, J. H. From sect to church in British Methodism. B.J.S. 15(1964): 139-149.

Chambers, Sir Edmund Kerchever. The English folk-play. Oxford, The Clarendon Press. 1933. 248 p.

Chambers, Jonathan David. Nottinghamshire in the eighteenth century: a study of life and labour under the squirearchy. London, P. S. King & Son. 1932. 11, 377 p.

Chambers, Robert. Book of days, a miscellany of popular antiquities in connection with the calendar, including anecdote, biography, & history, curiosities of literature and oddities of human life and character. 2 vols. Edinburgh, W. R. Chambers; Philadelphia, J. B. Lippincott. 1863-1864. (Many later editions.)

Chesser, Eustace. The sexual, marital and family relationships of the English woman. London, Hutchinson's Medical Publications. 1956. 36, 642 p.

Christian, Roy. The Country Life book of old English Customs. London, Country Life Publishing Co. 1966. 124 p., 128 photos.

Christie, Mabel Elizabeth. The evolution of the English farm. London, G. Allen & Unwin. 1927. 376 p.

Claridge, John. General view of the agriculture of the county of Dorset . . . London, Board of Agriculture. 1793. 49 p.

Clark, Alice. Working life of women in the seventeenth century. London, George Routledge and Sons. 1919. 7, 328 p. (Reprinted. London, Frank Cass. 1968.)

Clark, John. General view of the agriculture of the county of Brecknock . . . London, Board of Agriculture. 1794. 55 p.

Clark, John. General view of the agriculture of the county of Radnor . . . London, Board of Agriculture. 1794. 41 p.

Clark, John. General view of the agriculture of the county of Hereford . . . London, Board of Agriculture. 1794. 79 p.

Clarke, Joseph Norman. Country gleanings from the Lincolnshire Wolds. London, Batchworth Press. 1954. 191 p.

Clarke, R. Rainbird. The flint-knapping industry at Brandon. Antiquity. 9(1935): 38-58, plate.

Cobbett, William. Cottage economy . . . London, W. Cobbett. 1826.

*Cole, George D. H., and William Postgate. The common people. 1746-1938. London, Methuen. 1938. 10, 671 p., maps, charts. (2d ed. 1946. 10, 742 p., maps, charts.)

Coleman, Stanley Jackson. Gloucestershire lore. Douglas, Isle of Man, Folklore Academy. 1954. 13 p.

Coleman, Stanley Jackson. Bedfordshire lore. Douglas, Isle of Man, Folklore Academy. 1954. 13 p.

Collier, Price. England and the English from an American point of view. London, Duckworth. 1910. 434 p.

Cooper, James Fenimore. England, with sketches of society in the metropolis. 3 vols. London, R. Bentley. 1837.

Corbridge, Sylvia Lovat. It's an old Lancashire custom. London, Dobson; Toronto, Saunders. 1952. 149 p.

Coulton, George Gordon. The medieval village. Cambridge, The University Press. 1925. 8, 603 p.

Coulton, George Gordon. Life in the Middle Ages. 4 vols. Cambridge, The University Press. 1928-1930.

Coulton, George Gordon. Medieval panorama; the English scene from conquest to Reformation. Cambridge, The University Press; New York, Macmillan. 1938. 14, 801 p.

Coxhead, J. R. W. Smuggling days in Devon. Exmouth, The Raleigh Press. 1956. 82 p.

Coxhead, J. R. W. Old Devon customs. Exmouth, The Raleigh Press. 1957. 101 p.

Coxhead, J. R. W. Devon traditions and fairy tales. Exmouth, The Raleigh Press. 1959. 122 p.

*Crichton, Ruth **Mary**.   Commuters' village; a study of community and commuters in the Berkshire village of Stratfield. Dawlish, Devon, David & Charles Mortimer. 1964. 112 p.

Crossing, William. (Edited by B. le Messurier.) Crossing's Dartmoor worker. Neston Abbot, David and Charley Kelly. 1967. 163 p.

Cunningham, Allan. Traditional tales of the English and Scottish peasantry. 2 vols. London, Taylor and Hessey. 1822.

Cunnington, C. W., and P. Cunnington. Handbook of English costume in the eighteenth century. London, Faber and Faber. 1957. 443 p., illus.

Curle, Adam. Kinship structure in an English village. Man. 52(1952): 242.

Curle, Adam. Some psychological factors in rural sociology. Tribus. 4/5(1954-1955): 250-255.

Curtis, L. P., Jr. Anglo-Saxons and Celts. A study of anti-Irish prejudice in Victorian England. Bridgeport, Conn., University of Bridgeport Press. 1968. 11, 162 p.

Dale, J. R. The clerk in industry. Liverpool, Liverpool University Press. 1962. 10, 118 p.

Darby, Henry Clifford. The draining of the Fens. Cambridge, The University Press. 1940. 19, 312 p.

Darby, Henry Clifford. The medieval Fenland. Cambridge, The University Press. 1940. 17, 200 p.

Davidson, T. Elf-shot cattle. Antiquity. 30(1956): 149-155.

Davie, W. Galsworthy, and E. G. Dawber. Old cottages, farmhouses and other stone buildings in the Cotswold district. London, B. T. Batsford. 1905. 13, 72 p., 100 pl.

Davis, Richard. General view of the agriculture of the county of Oxford . . . London, Board of Agriculture. 1794. 39 p.

Davis, Richard. General view of the agriculture of the county of Wilts . . . London, Board of Agriculture. 1794. 163 p.

Dawber, Edward Guy. Old cottages and farmhouses in Kent and Sussex. London, B. T. Batsford. 1900. 10, 28 p., illus.

Dawber, Edward Guy. Old cottages, farm-houses, & other stone buildings in the Cotswold district: examples of minor domestic architecture in Gloucestershire, Oxfordshire, Northants, Worcestershire, etc. London, B. T. Batsford. 1905. 13, 75 p., illus.

Defoe, Daniel. A tour through England and Wales. 2 vols. London, J. M. Dent & Sons. 1935; New York, E. P. Dutton. 1935. (There are many other editions of this work.)

Defoe, Daniel. Religious courtship: being historical discourses on the necessity of marrying religious husbands and wives only . . . with an appendix shewing the necessity of taking none but religious servants . . . Glasgow, J. and M. Robertson. 1789. 6, 274 p. (Another edition, entitled: Religious courtship, or marriage on Christian principles; being a guide in the selection of a companion for life. Cincinnati, Applegate. 1853. 270 p.)

Defoe, Daniel. Conjugal lewdness; or, matrimonial whoredom. A treatise concerning the use and abuse of the marriage bed. Gainesville, Florida, Scholars' Facsimiles. 1967. 14, 8, 406 p. (Original edition 1727.)

Demiashkievitch, Michael John. The national mind: English, French, German. New York and Cincinnati, American Book Co. 1938: 3-178.

*Dennis, Norman, et al. Coal is our life: an analysis of a Yorkshire mining community. London, Eyre & Spottiswood. 1956. 255 p.

Devenish, Dorothy. Wiltshire home. A study of Little Durnford. London, B. T. Batsford. 1948. 10, 116 p.

Dickson, R. W. General view of the agriculture of Lancashire . . . rev. ed. London, Board of Agriculture. 1815. 653 p., index.

Donaldson, James. General view of the agriculture of the county of Northampton . . . to which is added an appendix, containing a comparison between the English and Scotch systems of husbandry. Edinburgh, London, Board of Agriculture. 1794. 68, 19 p.

Dorson, Richard M. Folklore studies in England. In Richard M. Dorson, ed. Folklore research around the world. Bloomington, Indiana University Press. 1961: 16-26.

Douch, Robert. Customs and traditions of the Isle of Portland, Dorset. Antiquity. 23(1949): 140-152.

Drake-Carnell, Francis John. Old English customs and ceremonies. London, B. T. Batsford. 1938. 8, 120 p.

Driver, Abraham, and William Driver. General view of the agriculture of the county of Hants . . . (General view of the agriculture of the Isle of Wight . . . by the Rev. Mr. Warner — postscript to the survey of Hampshire. In a letter ... . from A. Young.) London, Board of Agriculture. 1794. 108, 16 p.

Drummond, Jack Cecil, and Anne Wilbraham. The Englishman's food; a history of five centuries of English diet. London, J. Cape. 1939. 574 p., pl.

*Durant, Mrs. Ruth Lazarus. Watling: a social survey on a new housing estate. London, P. S. King & Son. 1939. 14, 128 p.

Duruz, R. M., and E. E. Crane. English bee boles. Bee World. 34 (1953): 209-224. (Reprinted as: National Beekeeping Museum Pamphlet No. 1. Bromeley, Kent, Bee Research Assoc. 1953. 16 p., 8 fig.)

Dutton, Ralph. The Victorian home, some aspects of nineteenth-century taste and manners. London, B. T. Batsford. 1954. 206 p.

Edwards, Henry (of Hoxton). A collection of old English customs, and curious bequests and charities, extracted from the reports made by the commissioners for enquiring into charities in England and Wales. London, J. B. Nichols & Son. 1842. 8, 267 p.

Elton, Charles Isaac. A treatise on commons and waste lands. London, Wildy and Sons. 1868. 23, 333 p.

Emerson, Ralph Waldo. English traits. New York, T. Y. Crowell. 1899. 23, 248 p. (Many other editions.)

Ernle, Rowland Edmund P., Baron. The land and its people: chapters in rural life and history. London, Hutchinson. 1925. 257 p.

*Ernle, Rowland Edmund P., Baron. English farming, past and present. 5th ed. London and New York, Longmans, Green. 1936. 16, 559 p.

Escott, Thomas Hay S. England: her people, polity and pursuits. 2 vols. London, New York, Cassell, Petter, Galpin. 1880. 10, 625 p.

Escott, Thomas Hay S. Society in the country house. London, T. F. Unwin. 1907. 511 p.

Evans, Edward Payson. The criminal prosecution and capital punishment of animals. London, W. Heinemann. 1906. 10, 384 p.

*Evans, George Ewart. Ask the fellows who cut the hay. London, Faber and Faber. 1956. 250 p.

*Evans, George Ewart. The horse in the furrow. London, Faber and Faber. 1960. 292 p., illus. (East Anglia: folk life, agriculture, horses.)

*Evans, George Ewart. The pattern under the plow. Aspects of folk-life in East Anglia. London, Faber and Faber. 1966. 269 p.

Exeter. University. Survey Committee. Devon and Cornwall: a preliminary survey. A report issued by the survey committee of the University College of the South West. Exeter. Exeter, A. Wheaton. 1947. 318 p., 38 fig., 13 maps.

Fairfax-Blakeborough, J. Yorkshire village life, humour, and characters. London, A. Brown. 1955. 172 p.

Farey, John. General view of the agriculture and minerals of Derbyshire. 3 vols. London, Board of Agriculture. 1811-1817.

Feasey, H. J. Ancient English holy week ceremonial. London, T. Baker. 1897. 247 p.

*Firor, Ruth Anita. Folkways in Thomas Hardy. Philadelphia, University of Pennsylvania Press. 1931. 8, 357 p. (Printed Ph.D. dissertation.) (Reprinted. New York, A. S. Barnes. 1962.)

Firth, Raymond W., ed. Two studies of kinship in London. London, Athlone Press. 1956. 96 p.

Fletcher, G. S. Popular art in England. London, Harrap. 1962. 78 p., illus.

*Fletcher, Ronald. The family and marriage in Britain. 2d ed. Harmondsworth and Baltimore, Penguin Books. 1966. 250 p.

Folk-Lore. London, The Folk-Lore Society. 1 (March 1890): --

Folk Lore Journal. London, The Folk-Lore Society. Vols. 1-7. 1883-1890.

Foot, Peter. General view of the agriculture of the county of Middlesex, etc. London, Board of Agriculture. 1794. 56 p.

Fordham, Montague Edward. A short history of English rural life from the Anglo-Saxon invasion to the present time. London, G. Allen & Unwin; New York, C. Scribner's Sons. 1916. 16, 183 p.

Fordham, Montague Edward, and T. R. Fordham. The English agricultural labourer: 1300-1925. London, Labour Publishing Co. 1925. 63 p.

Fox, Sir Cyril, and Lord Raglan. Monmouthshire houses: a study of building techniques and smaller house plans in the 15th to 17th centuries. Part I, medieval houses. Cardiff, National Museum of Wales. 1951. 114 p., illus.

Fox, John. General view of the agriculture of the county of Monmouth, etc. Brentford, London, Board of Agriculture. 1794. 43 p.

*Frankenberg, Ronald. Communities in Britain. Social life in town and country. Harmondsworth and Baltimore, Penguin Books. 1966. 313 p.

Frankenberg, Ronald. British community studies: problems of synthesis. In Michael Banton, ed. The social anthropology of complex societies. London, Tavistock Publications. 1966: 123-154.

*Franklyn, Julian. The Cockney. A survey of London life and language. London, Andre Deutsch. 1953. 14, 332 p.

Fraser, Robert. General view of the agriculture of the county of Devon . . . London, Board of Agriculture. 1794.

Fried, Albert, and Richard M. Elman, eds. Charles Booth's London. A portrait of the poor at the turn of the century, drawn from his "Life and labour of the people of London." New York, Pantheon Books. 1968. 39, 342 p.

Fuller, Margaret D. West country friendly societies: an account of village benefit clubs and their brass pole heads. Lingfield, Published by the Oakwood Press for the University of Reading. 1964. 174 p.

Fussell, George Edwin. Farming systems, from Elizabeth to Victorian days in the North and East Ridings of Yorkshire. York, Castle Museum. 1944. 42 p.

Fussell, George Edwin. Village life in the 18th century. Worcester, England, Littlebury. 1947. 84 p.

Fussell, George Edwin. From Tolpuddle to T.U.C., a century of farm labourers' politics. Slough, England, Windsor Press. 1948. 150 p.

Fussell, George Edwin. "High farming" in southwestern England, 1840-1880. Economic Geography. 24 (1948): 53-73.

Fussell, George Edwin. "High farming" in the north of England, 1840-1880. Economic Geography. 24(1948): 296-310.

*Fussell, George Edwin. The English rural labourer; his house, furniture, clothing & food from Tudor to Victorian times. London, Batchworth Press. 1949. 14, 160 p.

Fussell, George Edwin. More old English farming books from Tull to the Board of Agriculture, 1731-1793. London, Crosby Lockwood. 1950. 7, 186 p.

Fussell, George Edwin. "High farming" in the east Midlands and East Anglia, 1840-1880. Economic Geography. 27(1951): 72-89.

Fussell, George Edwin. The farmer's tools, 1500-1900: the history of British farm implements, tools and machinery before the tractor came. London, Melrose. 1952. 246 p., 110 illus.

Fussell, George Edwin. Local variety in British farm carts and waggons. Geographical Magazine. 29(1956): 254-260.

*Fussell, George Edwin, and Kathleen R. Fussell. The English countrywoman; a farmhouse social history, A. D. 1500-1900. London, Melrose. 1953. 321 p.

*Fussell, George Edwin, and Kathleen R. Fussell. The English countryman, his life and work, A.D. 1500-1900. London, Melrose. 1955. 172 p.

Garbett, Cyril Forster. In the heart of South London. London and New York, Longmans, Green. 1931. 8, 152 p. (The poor.)

Garnier, Russell Montague. Annals of the British peasantry. London, Sonnenschein. 1895. 16, 460 p.

Gaskell, P. Artisans and machinery: the moral and physical condition of the manufacturing population considered with reference to mechanical substitutes for physical labour. London, John W. Barker. 1836. 16, 399 p. (Reprinted. London, Frank Cass. 1968.)

Gibbs, J. Arthur. A Cotswold village or country life and pursuits in Gloucestershire. London, John Murray. 1898. 431 p.

*Glass, D. V., ed. Social mobility in Britain. London, Routledge & Kegan Paul. 1954. 7, 412 p.

Glass, Ruth. The social background of a plan. A study of Middlesbrough. London, Routledge & Kegan Paul. 1948. 14, 268 p.

Gomme, Lady Alice Bertha. The traditional games of England, Scotland and Ireland, with tunes, singing-rhymes, and methods of playing according to the variants extant and recorded in different parts of the kingdom. 2 vols. London, David Nutt. 1894-1898. (Reprinted. New York, Dover Publications. 1964.)

Gomme, Sir George L. Primitive folk-moots; or open-air assemblies in Britain. London, Sampson Low, Marston, Searle & Rivington. 1880. 11, 316 p.

Gomme, Sir George L. Folk-lore relics of early village life. London, E. Stock. 1883. 11, 246 p.

Gomme, Sir George L. On archaic conceptions of property in relation to the laws of succession; & their survival in England. Westminster, Nichols and Sons. 1887. 20 p.

Gomme, Sir George L. The village community. London, W. Scott. 1890. 11, 299 p.

Gooch, William. General view of the agriculture of the county of Cambridge . . . London, Board of Agriculture. 1813. 303 p.

Goody, Jack. On nannas and nannies. Man. 62 (1962): 179-184.

*Gorer, Geoffrey. Exploring English character. New York, Criterion Books. 1955. 7, 328 p.; London, Cresset Press. 1955. 483 p. (English edition better.)

*Gorer, Geoffrey. Death, grief and mourning in contemporary Britain. London, Cresset Press. 1965. 8, 184 p.; Garden City, N.Y., Doubleday. 1965. 34, 205 p.

Gorer, Geoffrey. English character in the twentieth century. The Annals of the American Academy of Political and Social Sciences. 370 (March 1967): 74-81.

Graham, Stephen. London nights. London, Hurst & Blackett. 1925. 278 p. (The London poor.)

Gras, Norman Scott B., and Ethel Culbert. The economic and social history of an English village. Harvard Economic Studies 34. Cambridge, Mass., Harvard University Press. 1930. 15, 730 p. (Crawley, Hampshire.)

Gray, H. L. English field systems. Cambridge, Mass., Harvard University Press. 1915. 568 p.

Grey, Edwin. Rothamsted experimental station; reminiscences, tales and anecdotes of the laboratories, staff and experimental fields, 1872-1922. Harpenden, E. Grey. 1922. 155 p.

Grey, Edwin. Cottage life in a Hertfordshire village. St. Albans, Fisher Knight. n.d. [1935]. 253 p.

Griggs, Messrs. General view of the agriculture of the county of Essex . . . London, Board of Agriculture. 1794. 26 p.

Grimshaw, I. G. When I was a boy in England. Boston, Lothrop, Lee & Shepard. 1931. 160 p.

Gurdon, Lady Eveline Camelia. Examples of printed folk-lore concerning Suffolk. County Folk-Lore. Vol. 1. London, The Folk-Lore Society. 1893. 202 p.

Gutch, Mrs. Examples of printed folk-lore concerning the North Riding of Yorkshire, York and the Ainsty. County Folk-Lore. Vol. 2. London, The Folk-Lore Society. 1901. 447 p.

Gutch, Mrs. Examples of printed folk-lore concerning the East Riding of Yorkshire. County Folk-Lore. Vol. 6. London, The Folk-Lore Society. 1912. 27, 235 p.

Gutch, Mrs., and Mabel Peacock. Examples of printed folk-lore concerning Lincolnshire. County Folk-Lore. Vol. 5. London, The Folk-Lore Society. 1908. 28, 437 p.

*Haggard, Sir Henry Rider. Rural England; being an account of agriculture and social researches carried out in the years 1901 & 1902. 2 vols. London and New York, Longmans, Green. 1902. (Reprinted 1906.)

Haggard, Sir Henry Rider. The poor and the land; being a report on the Salvation Army colonies in the U.S. and at Hadleigh, England . . . London, New York, and Bombay, Longmans, Green. 1905. 157 p.

Haggard, Sir Henry Rider. Regeneration; being an account of the social work of the Salvation Army in Great Britain. London, Longmans, Green. 1910. 264 p.

Hair, P. E. H. Bridal pregnancy in rural England in earlier centuries. Population Studies. 20(1966): 233-243.

Hameron, Philip Gilbert. French and English. A comparison. Boston, Roberts Brothers. 1891. 23, 480 p.

ENGLISH

Hardwick, C. Traditions, superstitions and folklore (chiefly Lancashire and the north of England). Manchester, A. Ireland; London, Simpkin, Marshall. 1872. 19, 306 p.

Harland, John, and T. T. Wilkinson. Lancashire folk-lore: illustrative of the superstitious beliefs and practices, local customs and usages of the people of the County Palatine. London, Frederick Warne. 1867. 12, 308 p.

Harland, John, and T. T. Wilkinson. Lancashire legends, traditions, pageants, sports, etc., with an appendix containing a rare tract on the Lancashire witches, etc. London, Edinburgh. 1873.

Harper, E. B. Sociology in England. Social Forces. 11 (1933): 335-342.

Harrisson, Thomas Harnett. Britain revisited. London, Victor Gollancz. 1961. 285 p.

Hartland, Edwin Sidney, ed. Examples of printed folk-lore concerning Gloucestershire. County Folk-Lore. Vol. 1. London, The Folk-Lore Society. 1892. 58 p.

Hartley, M., and J. Ingilby. Yorkshire village. London, J. M. Dent. 1953. 8, 319 p., illus.

Hasbach, Wilhelm. A history of the English agricultural labourer. London, P. S. King & Sons. 1908. 16, 470 p.

Hassall, Charles. General view of the agriculture of the county of Monmouth . . . London, Board of Agriculture. 1812. 142 p.

*Havinden, Michael A., and P. D. Wood. Estate villages. A study of the Berkshire villages of Ardington and Lockinge. London, Lund Humphries. 1966. 214 p.

Hawker, James. A Victorian poacher. Edited and introduced by Garth Christian. London, Oxford University Press. 1961. 22, 114 p., illus. (Leicestershire)

Hayward, Arthur L. The days of Dickens. A glance at some aspects of early Victorian life in London. London, Routledge & Kegan Paul. 1926. 14, 280 p. (Reprinted. Hamden, Conn., Archon Books. 1968.)

Heath, Francis George. The English peasantry. London, F. Warne; New York, Scribner, Welford and Armstrong. 1874. 8, 271 p.

Heath, Francis George. British rural life and labour. London, P. S. King & Sons. 1911. 11, 318 p.

Heath, Richard. The English peasant. Studies: historical, local and bio-
graphic. London, T. Fisher Unwin; New York, The Century Co. 1893.
8, 382 p.

Hecht, J. Jean. Continental and colonial servants in 18th century England.
Northampton, Mass., Department of History, Smith College. 1954. 4,
61 p.

Hecht, J. Jean. The domestic servant class in eighteenth-century England.
London, Routledge & Kegan Paul. 1956. 240 p.

Henderson, William. Notes on the folk-lore of the northern counties of
England and the borders. . . London, Longmans, Green. 1866. 27,
344 p. (A new edition with many additional notes. London, The Folk-
Lore Society. 1879. 17, 391 p.)

Hennell, Thomas. The countryman at work. London, Architectural Press.
1947. 80 p.

Henrey, Mrs. Robert. Bloomsbury fair. London, J. M. Dent. 1955. 231 p.

Hewett, Sarah. Nummits and crummits: Devonshire customs, characteristics,
and folklore. London, T. Burleigh. 1900. 6, 219 p.

Hibbert-Ware, Samuel. Illustration of the customs of a manor in the north
of England, during the fifteenth century, with occasional remarks on their
resemblance to the incidents of ancient Scotish tenures. Edinburgh. 1822.

Hillier, J. Old Surrey water-mills. London, Skeffington. 1951. 287 p.,
illus.

Hilton, R. H. A medieval society. The west midlands at the end of the
thirteenth century. New York, John Wiley & Sons. 1966. 10, 305 p.

Hinchy, F. S. North east Dorset. Towns and downs. Blandford Forum,
Dorset Bookshop. 1957. 127 p.

Hinchy, F. S. Dorset days. Blandford Forum, Dorset Bookshop. 1960.
148 p.

Hinchy, F. S. Blandford today and yesterday. Blandford Forum, Dorset
Bookshop. 1960. 197 p.

Hoare, Geoffrey. Caldey. An isle of the Severn Sea. London, H. F. & G.
Witherby. 1936. 126 p.

Hodgen, Margaret T. Glass and paper: an historical study of acculturation.
S. W. J. A. 1(1945): 466-497.

*Hodgen, Margaret T. Change and history. Viking Fund Publications in Anthropology No. 18. New York, Wenner-Gren Foundation. 1952. 324 p., 25 maps.

Hole, Christina. Traditions and customs of Cheshire. London, Williams and Norgate. 1937. 13, 214 p.

Hole, Christina. Haunted England; a survey of English ghost-lore. London, B. T. Batsford. 1940. 8, 183 p.

Hole, Christina. English custom and usage. London, B. T. Batsford. 1941. 8, 152 p.

Holland, Henry. General view of the agriculture of Cheshire . . . London, Board of Agriculture. 1808. 375, 2 p.

Holt, John. General view of the agriculture of the county of Lancaster . . . London, Board of Agriculture. 1794. 114 p.

*Homans, George Caspar. English villagers of the thirteenth century. Cambridge, Mass., Harvard University Press. 1941. 14, 478 p. (Reprinted. New York, Russell and Russell. 1960.)

Hornell, James. The significance of the dual-element in British fishing boat construction; derivation and distribution. Folk-Liv. 10 (1946): 113-126.

Hoskins, William George. Industry, trade & people in Exeter, 1688-1800, with special reference to the serge industry. Manchester, Published for the University College of the South-West of England by the Manchester University Press. 1935. 189 p.

Hoskins, William George. The heritage of Leicestershire. Leicester, E. Backus. 1946. 13, 88 p.

*Hoskins, William George. The Midland peasant; the economic and social history of a Leicestershire village. London, Macmillan. 1957. 322 p.

Hoskins, William George. Devon and its people. Exeter, A. Wheaton. 1959. 175 p.

House, J. W. North eastern England: population movements and the landscape since the early 19th century. Newcastle, Durham University Press. 1960. 66 p.

Hueffer, Ford Madox (Ford, Ford Madox). The soul of London. A survey of a modern city. London, Alston Rivers. 1905. 16, 175 p.

Hudson, William Henry. A shepherd's life. Impressions of the South Wiltshire downs. New York, E. P. Dutton. 1921. 14, 338 p. (Many other editions of this volume.)

Ingham, Alfred. Cheshire: its traditions and history; including a record of the rise and progress of Freemasonry in this ancient province. Edinburgh, Pillars & Wilson. 1920. 370 p.

Innes, R. A. Barns and workshops. West Yorkshire Folk Museum. 5th ed. Halifax, Halifax Museums. 1966. 31 p., illus.

Innes, R. A. Shibden Hall. West Yorkshire Folk Museum. Halifax, Halifax Museums. 1966. 20 p., illus.

Jenkins, John Geraint. The English farm wagon: origins and structure. Reading, Reading University Museum of English Rural Life. 1961. 248 p., illus.

Jennings, Humphrey, and Charles Madge. May the twelfth: mass-observation day-surveys, 1937, by over 200 observers. London, Faber & Faber. 1937. 15, 431 p.

Johnson, Arthur Henry. The disappearance of the small landowner. Oxford, The Clarendon Press. 1909. 164 p.

Jones, M. D. Cerne Abbas: the story of a Dorset village. London, Allen & Unwin. 1952. 143 p.

Jones, Sidney Robert. The village homes of England. London, The Studio. 1912. 8, 162 p., illus.

Jones, Sidney Robert. English village homes and country buildings. New York, C. Scribner's Sons. 1937. 120 p., illus.

Kazantzakis, Nikos. England: a travel journal. New York, Simon and Schuster. 1966. 284 p.

Kendall, Paul Murray. The Yorkist age. Daily life during the War of Roses. London, Allen & Unwin; New York, Norton. 1962. 524 p.

Kent, Nathaniel. General view of the agriculture of the county of Norfolk . . . London, Board of Agriculture. 1794. 56 p.

*Kerr, Madeline. The people of Ship Street. London, Routledge & Kegan Paul. 1958. 7, 215 p. (Liverpool)

King, Joseph. Peasant arts. A handbook of the peasant arts of the Haslemere Educational Museum. Haslemere, The Educational Museum. 1927. 108 p., illus.

Klein, Josephine. Samples from English cultures. 2 vols. Vol. 1. Three preliminary studies: aspects of adult life in England. Vol. 2. Child rearing practices. London, Routledge & Kegan Paul. 1965. 447, 250 p.

Kocher, Paul Harold. Science and religion in Elizabethan England. San Marino, Calif., The Huntington Library. 1953. 12, 340 p.

Kohl, J. G. Ireland, Scotland, and England. (Translated from the German.) London, Chapman and Hall. 1844. 4, 248 p.

Kosminsky, E. A. Studies in the agrarian history of England in the thirteenth century. (Translated from the Russian.) London, Oxford, Blackwell. 1956. 398 p.

Kuper, Leo, ed. Living in towns. London, Cresset Press. 1953. 11, 370 p.

Lambert, Margaret, and Enid Marx. English popular art. London, Batsford. 1951. 8, 120 p., illus.

Lancaster, Lorraine. Kinship in Anglo-Saxon society. Pts. 1 and 2. B.J.S. 9(1958): 230-250, 359-377.

Leatham, Isaac. General view of the agriculture of the East Riding of Yorkshire, and the Ainsty of the city of York . . . London, Board of Agriculture. 1794. 68 p.

Leather, Ella Mary. The folk-lore of Herefordshire. Hereford, Jakeman & Carver. 1912. 28, 286 p.

Leeds City Museum. Guide book to the Abbey House Museum. 2d ed. Leeds, Leeds City Museum. 1964. 16 p., 4 pl.

Levi, Leone. The economic condition of fishermen. London, W. Clowes and Son. 1883. 48 p.

Lewis, Roy. The boss: the life and times of the British business man. London, Phoenix House. 1961. 287 p.

Lewis, Roy, and Angus Maude. The English middle class. New York, Alfred A. Knopf. 1950. 11, 360, 13 p.

Lewis, Roy, and Angus Maude. Professional people in England. Cambridge, Mass., Harvard University Press. 1953. 7, 284 p.

Lindsay, J. Seymour. Iron and brass implements of the English house. London and Boston, The Medici Society. 1927. 11, 211 p., pl. (Reprinted. London, Alec Tiranti. 1964.)

*Littlejohn, James. Westrigg: the sociology of a Cheviot parish. London, Routledge and Kegan Paul. 1964. 164 p.

Liverpool. University. Department of Social Science. The dock worker. An analysis of conditions of employment and industrial relations in the port of Manchester. Liverpool, Liverpool University Press. 1956. 8, 284 p.

Lloyd, Albert Lancaster. Folk song in England. London, Lawrence & Wishart. 1967. 433 p.

Lovett, Edward. The child's doll, its origin, legend, and folk-lore. London, Evans Bros. 1915. 16 p.

Lovett, Edward. Magic in modern London. Caterham Valley, Surrey, the author. 1925. 100 p.

Lovett, Edward. Folk-lore and legend of the Surrey hills and of the Sussex downs and forests. Caterham Valley, Surrey, the author. 1928. 39 p.

Lowe, Robert. General view of the agriculture of the county of Nottingham . . . London, Board of Agriculture. 1794. 128 p.

Lynd, Helen Merrell. England in the eighteen-eighties; toward a social basis for freedom. London, Oxford University Press. 1945. 9, 508 p.

McGregor, O. R. Divorce in England, a centenary study. London, Heinemann. 1957. 220 p.

McKenzie, Robert, and Alan Silver. Angels in marble. Working class conservatives in urban England. Chicago, University of Chicago Press. 1968. 10, 295 p.

Madariaga, Salvador de. English, Frenchmen, Spaniards; an essay in comparative psychology. London, Oxford University Press, H. Milford. 1931. 19, 256 p.

Madge, Charles, and Tom Harrisson, eds. Britain by mass observation. Harmondsworth, Penguin Books. 1939. 246 p.

Malcolm, William. General view of the agriculture of the county of Surrey . . . London, Board of Agriculture. 1794. 95 p.

Manley, V. S. Folk-lore of the Warminster district of West Wilts. London, Warminster, Coates. 1925. 40 p.

*Marcus, Steven.   The other Victorians: a study of sexuality and pornography
in mid-nineteenth century England. New York, Basic Books. 1966. 292 p.

Marris, Peter. Widows and their families. London, Routledge and Kegan
Paul. 1958. 21, 172 p., 7 tables.

Marsh, David Charles. The changing social structure of England and Wales
1871-1951. London, Routledge & Kegan Paul. 1958. 14, 266 p.

Marshall, Sybil. Fenland chronicle. Cambridge, The University Press.
1967. 7, 280 p.

Martin, Ernest Walter. Heritage of the west, etc. [Essays on the folklore
and history of the west of England.] London, Heath Cranton. 1938. 191 p.

Martin, Ernest Walter. A wanderer in the west country. London, Phoenix
House. 1951. 223 p.

Martin, Ernest Walter. The secret people. English village life after 1750.
Being an account of English village people, their lives, work and development through a period of two hundred years, etc. London, Phoenix House.
1954. 319 p.

Martin, Ernest Walter. Where London ends; English provincial life after
1750, being an account of the English country town and the lives, work
and development of provincial people through a period of two hundred
years. London, Phoenix House. 1958. 312 p.

Martin, Ernest Walter. The book of the village. London, Phoenix House.
1962. 9, 149 p.

Martin, Ernest Walter. The book of the country town. London, Phoenix
House. 1962. 8, 152 p.

*Martin, Ernest Walter. The shearers and the shorn: a study in the life of a
Devon community. London, Routledge and Kegan Paul. 1965. 250 p.

Mayhew, Henry. London labour and the London poor: the condition and
earning of those that will work, cannot work, and will not work. 3 vols.
London, C. Griffin. 1861.

*Mayhew, Henry. London labour and the London poor: a cyclopaedia of the
condition and earnings of those that will work, those that cannot work,
and those that will not work. 4 vols. London, Griffin, Bohn. 1861-1862.
(Reprinted. New York, Dover. 1968.)

* Mayhew, Henry.   The criminal prisons of London, and scenes of prison life. London, Griffin, Bohn. 1862. 634 p.

Mayhew, Henry.   (Edited by Peter Quennell.) Mayhew's London. Being selections from "London labour and the London poor" by Henry Mayhew. London, William Kimber. 1951. 569 p.

Mayhew, Henry.   (Edited by Peter Quennell.) London's underworld; being selections from "Those that will not work," the fourth volume of "London labour and the London poor." London, Spring Books. 1958. 427 p.

Mayhew, Henry.   (Edited by Peter Quennell.) Mayhew's characters. Selections from "London labour and the London poor." London, William Kimber. 1951. 336 p.

Mayhew, Henry.   The street trader's lot, London: 1851; being an account of the lives, miseries, joys & chequered activities of the London street sellers as recorded by their contemporary H. Mayhew and now recalled for the edification of the public by Stanley Rubenstein . . . London, Sylvan Press. 1947. 23, 169 p.

Mearns, Andrew.   London and its teeming toilers: who they are, and how they live. Facts and figures suggested by recent statistics of the census and Charities Commission. London, Warren Hall and Lovitt. 1885. 7, 65 p.

Middleton, John.   View of the agriculture of Middlesex . . . London, Board of Agriculture. 1798. 597 p.

[Millin, George.] Life in our village. 3d ed. London, Cassell. 1891. 192 p.

Mills, Enid.   Living with mental illness: a study in East London. London, Routledge & Kegan Paul. 1962. 196 p.

Mingay, G. E.   English landed society in the eighteenth century. London, Routledge & Kegan Paul. 1963. 10, 292 p.

Mitchell, Marjorie Edith.   The child's attitude to death. New York, Schocken Books. 1967. 6, 162 p.

Mitford, Mary Russell.   Our village, sketches of rural character and scenery. 2 vols. London, H. G. Bohn. 1856-1857.

Mitford, Mary Russell.   Sketches of English life and character. Chicago, A. C. McClurg. 1910. 320 p.

Mitford, Nancy, ed. Noblesse oblige; an enquiry into the identifiable characteristics of the English aristocracy. New York, Harper. 1956. 156 p.

*Mogey, John M. Family and neighborhood: two studies in Oxford. London, Oxford University Press. 1956. 16, 181 p.

Monk, John. General view of the agriculture of the county of Leicester . . . London, Board of Agriculture. 1794.

Montague, Joel Benjamin, Jr. Class and nationality: English and American studies. New Haven, College and University Press. 1963. 246 p.

Moody, F. W. Oatbread. Transactions of the Yorkshire Dialect Society. 8(1949): 20-30.

Morton, Henry Canova V. The call of England. London, Methuen. 1928. 11, 206 p.

Morton, Henry Canova V. What I saw in the slums. London, The Labour Party. 1933. 48 p.

Moser, C. A., and Wolf Scott. British towns: a statistical study of their social and economic differences. Edinburgh, Oliver & Boyd. 1961. 169 p.

Moss, Fletcher. Folk-lore: old customs and tales of my neighbors. Didsbury, The Old Parsonage. 1898. 16, 332 p. (Cheshire)

Murray, A. T. Farm labor and social legislation in England. Foreign Agriculture. 2(1938): 249-266.

Murray, Adam. General view of the agriculture of the county of Warwick . . . London, Board of Agriculture. 1813. 187 p., index.

Museum of English Rural Life. Guide to the Museum of English Rural Life. Reading, Museum of English Rural Life. 1955. 16 p.

My secret life. 2 vols. New York, Grove Press. 1966. 63, 2432 p. (Sexual memoirs of a Victorian gentleman circa 1840-1882.)

Nettel, Reginald. Sing a song of England: a social history of traditional song. London, Phoenix House. 1954. 14 plates.

Nevinson, Henry W. The natives of England. New York, A. A. Knopf. 1931. 19, 249 p.

Newman, L. F. The rural craftsman and his tools. Cambridge Antiquarian Society, Proceedings. 39 (1938/1939): 5-28, illus.

Nicholls, Sir George. A history of the English poor law. 3 vols. London, John Murray. 1898. (Reprinted. New York, Augustus M. Kelley. 1967.)

Nicholson, John. Folklore of East Yorkshire. London, Simpkin, Hamilton, Kent. 1890. 12, 168 p.

Oliver, Basil. Old houses and village buildings in East Anglia, Norfolk, Suffolk & Essex. London, B. T. Batsford. 1912. 21, 100 p., illus.

Oliver, Basil. The cottages of England. London, B. T. Batsford. 1929. 24, 91 p., 99 pl.

*Orlans, Harold. Stevenage. A sociological study of a new town. London, Routledge & Kegan Paul. 1952. 15, 313 p. (Also published as Utopia Ltd. New Haven, Yale University Press. 1953.)

Orwin, Charles Stewart. The open fields. Oxford, The Clarendon Press. 1938. 12, 332 p.

Paget, Henry Luke. Home life in England. London and New York, Longmans, Green. 1910. 7, 96 p.

Paget, J. Otho. Memories of the shires. London, Methuen. 1920. 7, 224 p.

Palmer, Alfred Neobard. The town, field and folk of Wrexham in the times of James the First. Wrexham, A. N. Palmer. 1884. 48 p.

Parkinson, Richard. General view of the agriculture in the county of Huntingdon . . . London, Board of Agriculture. 1813. 351 p.

Parkinson, Thomas. Yorkshire legends and traditions as told by the ancient chronicles, her poets, and journalists. London, Eliot Stock. 1888. 12, 244 p. (2d series. London, Eliot Stock. 1889. 10, 246 p.)

Peake, Harold. The English village. The origin and decay of its community. An anthropological interpretation. London, Benn Bros. 1922. 251 p., illus., maps, pl.

Pear, T. H. Psychological aspects of English social stratification. Bulletin of the John Rylands Library. 26, no. 2. 1942. 27 p. (Reprinted as a separate publication. Manchester, Manchester University Press. 1942. 27 p.)

Pearce, Joseph Pearce. Ancient Liverpool, a popular excursion in the "good old days" when eggs were six a penny and when you could rent a cottage in Castle Street for five shillings a year. 3d ed. Liverpool, Philip. 1946. 34 p.

Pearce, Joseph Pearce. Lancashire legends. Liverpool, Charles Wilson. 1947. 7, 160 p.

Pearce, William. General view of the agriculture in Berkshire . . . London, Board of Agriculture. 1794. 74 p.

Peate, Iowerth C. Severn eel-traps. Man. 34 (1934): 153-154.

Pike, E. Royston. "Hard times." Human documents of the industrial revolution. New York, Praeger. 1966. 368 p.

Pinchbeck, Ivy. Women workers and the industrial revolution, 1750-1850. London, Routledge & Kegan Paul. 1930. 10, 342 p.

Pitt, William. General view of the agriculture of the county of Stafford . . . London, Board of Agriculture. 1794. 168 p.

Pitt, William. General view of the agriculture of the county of Northampton . . . London, Board of Agriculture. 1809. 320 p.

Pitt, William. A general view of the agriculture of the county of Leicester; to which is annexed, a survey of the county of Rutland. 2 parts. London, Board of Agriculture. 1809. 401, 10; 182 p.

Pitt, William. General view of the agriculture of the county of Worcester . . . London, Board of Agriculture. 1813. 428 p.

Plimsoll, Samuel. Our seamen. An appeal. London, Virtue. 1870. 128 p.

Plowman, D. E. G., W. E. Minchinton, and Margaret Stacey. Local social status in England and Wales. Sociological Review. n.s. 10 (1962): 161-202.

Plymley, Joseph. General view of the agriculture of Shropshire . . . London, Board of Agriculture. 1803. 366, 2 p.

Pomeroy, William Thomas. General view of the agriculture of the county of Worcester. 2 parts. London, Board of Agriculture. 1794.

Porter, Enid. Folk life and traditions of the Fenns. Folk-lore. 72 (1961): 584-598.

Powell, Chilton Latham. English domestic relations 1487-1653. A study of matrimony and family life in theory and practice as revealed by the literature, law and history of the period. New York, Columbia University Press. 1917. 274 p.

Priest, St. John. General view of the agriculture of Buckinghamshire . . . London, Board of Agriculture. 1810. 8, 412 p.

Quennell, Peter. See Henry Mayhew.

Randell, Arthur R. Sixty years a fenman. Hatboro, Penn., Folklore Associates. 1966. 126 p., photos.

Read, D. H. Moutray. Highways and byways in Hampshire. London, Macmillan. 1908. 17, 444 p., illus.

Reynolds, Myra. The learned lady in England, 1650-1760. Boston and New York, Houghton Mifflin. 1920. 489 p. (Reprinted. Gloucester, Mass., Peter Smith. 1964. 489 p.)

Rham, William Lewis. The dictionary of the farm. London, C. Knight. 1844. 12, 576 p.

Rhodes, Gerald. Town government in South East England. London, London School of Economics. 1967. 75 p.

Ringwood, M. Some customs and beliefs of Durham miners. Folk-Lore. 68(1957): 423-425.

Robin, Gerald D. The executioner: his place in English society. B. J. S. 15(1964): 234-251.

Robins, F. W. The smith: the traditions and lore of an ancient craft. London, Rider. 1953. 160 p.

Rose, Walter. The village carpenter. Cambridge, The University Press; New York, Macmillan. 1937. 21, 146 p.

Roth, H. Ling. Hand card making. Bankfield Museum Notes. Series 1, No. 11. Halifax, England, Bankfield Museum. n. d. 12 p.

*Rowntree, Benjamin Seebohm. Poverty, a study of town life. 2d ed. London and New York, Macmillan. 1902. 22, 452 p. (City of York) (Reprinted. London, Macmillan. 1910. 21, 426 p.; also London and New York, T. Nelson & Sons. 1913. 496 p.)

*Rowntree, Benjamin Seebohm. Poverty and progress: a second social survey of York. London and New York, Longmans, Green. 1941. 20, 540 p.

*Rowntree, Benjamin Seebohm. Portrait of a city's housing, being the results of a detailed survey in the city of York 1935-9. London, Faber and Faber. 1945. 54 p.

*Rowntree, Benjamin Seebohm. Poverty and the welfare state: a third social survey of York dealing only with economic questions. London and New York, Longmans, Green. 1951. 5, 104 p.

Rowntree, Benjamin Seebohm, and George Russell Lavers. English life and leisure; a social study. London and New York, Longmans, Green. 1951. 482 p.

Rowntree, Charles Brightwen. Saffron Walden, then and now. [Saffron Walden]. 1952. 107 p.

Rudge, Thomas. General view of the agriculture of the county of Glouces- ter . . . London, Board of Agriculture. 1807. 407 p.

Rudkin, Ethel H. Lincolnshire folklore. Gainsborough, Beltons. 1936. 102 p., 5 pl.

Rural Industries Bureau. The blacksmith's craft. London, Rural Industries Bureau. 1952. 108 p., 226 pl., 35 fig.

Sackville-West, Victoria. The Land. London, William Heinemann; New York, George H. Doran. 1926. 107 p. (Poetry, but very good on folk life in Kent. Many later reprints.)

St. Leger-Gordon, Ruth E. The witchcraft and folklore of Dartmoor. Lon- don, Robert Hale. 1965. 192 p.

Sayce, R. U. Food in the highland zone of Britain in the 18th century. Folk-Liv. 12/13 (1948/1949): 199-207.

Sayce, R. U. Milking and dairying. Ethnological notes about some every- day things. Montgomeryshire Collections. 52 (1952): 120-154, 21 fig.

Scrope, William. Days and nights of salmon fishing in the Tweed; with a short account of the natural history and habits of the salmon, . . . London, J. Murray. 1843. 17, 298 p.

Seebohm, Frederic. The English village. London, Longmans, Green. 1883. 21, 464 p.

Seebohm, Mrs. Mable Elizabeth. The evolution of the English farm. rev. ed. London, Allen & Unwin. 1952. 356 p., illus.

Sharp, Cecil J. English folk song; some conclusions. Revised by Maud Karpeles. London, Methuen. 1954. 21, 143 p.

Simpson, Alan. The wealth of the gentry. 1540-1660. East Anglian studies. Cambridge, The University Press; Chicago, University of Chicago Press. 1961. 7, 226 p.

Slater, Gilbert. English peasantry and the enclosure of common fields. London, Constable. 1907. 13, 337 p.

Slater, Gilbert. Poverty and the state. London, Constable. 1930. 7, 480 p.

Slater, Gilbert. The growth of modern England. London, Constable. 1939. 17, 642 p.

Small, A. The villages of the Howe of the Mearns. Folk Life. 4 (1966): 22-29, maps.

Smith, A. Notes on the folk-life of the East London child. Folklore. 69 (1958): 39-42.

*Stacey, Margaret. Tradition and change: a study of Banbury. Oxford, Oxford University Press. 1960. 231 p.

Stanyer, Jeffrey. County government in England and Wales. London, Routledge & Kegan Paul. 1967. 12, 116 p.

Stephens, Henry. The book of the farm; detailing the labors of the farmer, steward, hedger, cattle-man, shepherd, fieldworker and dairymaid. 3 vols. Edinburgh and London. 1844.

Stevenson, William. General view of the agriculture of the county of Surrey . . . London, Board of Agriculture. 1809. 607, 8 p.

Stevenson, William. General view of the agriculture of the county of Dorset . . . London, Board of Agriculture. 1812. 487, 5 p.

Stewart, Cecil. The village surveyed. London, E. Arnold. 1948. 171 p., illus., map.

Stone, Thomas. General view of the agriculture of the county of Huntingdon . . . London, Board of Agriculture. 1793. 35 p.

Stone, Thomas. General view of the agriculture of the county of Bedford . . . London, Board of Agriculture. 1794. 51 p.

Stone, Thomas. General view of the agriculture of the county of Lincoln . . . London, Board of Agriculture. 1794. 108 p.

Storms, G. Anglo-Saxon magic. The Hague, Martinus Nijhoff. 1948. 9, 336 p.

Strutt, Joseph. The sports and pastimes of the people of England: including the rural and domestic recreations, may games, mummeries, shows, processions, pageants & pompous spectacles, from the earliest period to the present time. London, T. Tegg. 1831. 67, 420 p. (Many other editions of this work.)

Sturt, George. The Bettesworth book: talks with a Surrey peasant. London, Duckworth. 1910. 332 p.

*Sturt, George. Change in the village. London, Duckworth; New York, George H. Doran. 1912. 309 p. (Reprinted. London, Duckworth. 1955. 15, 206 p.)

Sturt, George. William Smith. Potter and farmer, 1790-1858. London, Chatto & Windus. 1920. 9, 230 p.

Sturt, George. A farmer's life, with a memoir of the farmer's sister. London, J. Cape. 1922. 208 p.

*Sturt, George. The wheelwright's shop. Cambridge, The University Press. 1923. 12, 236 p., 32 illus. (Reprinted. 1934.)

Sturt, George. A small boy in the sixties. Cambridge, The University Press. 1927. 16, 240 p.

Sturt, George. The journals of George Sturt "George Bourne," 1890-1902; edited with an introduction by Geoffrey Grigson. London, The Cresset Press. 1941. 15, 235 p.

Sturt, George. The journals of George Sturt 1890-1927. 2 vols. Cambridge, The University Press. 1967. 8, 453 p.; 5, 454-915 p.

Sutcliffe, Halliwell. By moor and fell. Landscapes and lang-settle lore from West Yorkshire. London, T. Fisher Unwin. 1900. 6, 360 p.

Tavener, L. Ellis. The common lands of Hampshire. Winchester, England, Hampshire County Council. 1957. 7, 123 p., maps, illus., photos.

Taylor, J. Neufville. Guide to the Severn fishery collection. Gloucester, Gloucester Folk Museum. 1949. 16 p., 4 pl. (2d ed. 1953. 24 p., pl.)

Taylor, J. Neufville. Guide to the collection of bygone agricultural implements. Gloucester, Gloucester Folk Museum. 1950. 19 p., 4 pl.

Taylor, J. Neufville. Elver fishing on the river Severn. Folk Life. 3 (1965): 55-60.

Tebbut, C. F. Bluntisham-cum-Earith, Huntingdonshire; records of a fenland parish. St. Neats, P. C. Tomson. 1941. 198 p.

Tebbut, C. F. Huntingdonshire folklore. St. Neats, Tomson and Lendrum. 1952. 51 p.

Tebbut, C. F., and R. U. Sayce. Fenland eel-traps. Man. 36 (1936): 129.

Thirsk, J. English peasant farming: the agrarian history of Lincolnshire from Tudor to present times. London, Routledge & Kegan Paul. 1957. 15, 350 p.

Thiselton-Dyer, Thomas F. British popular customs, present and past; illustrating the social and domestic manners of the people: arranged according to the calendar of the year. London, G. Bell and Sons. 1876. 520 p.

Thiselton-Dyer, Thomas F. English folk-lore. London, Hardwicke & Bogur. 1878. 8, 290 p.

Thiselton-Dyer, Thomas F. Folk-lore of Shakespeare. London, Griffith & Farrar; New York, E. P. Dutton. 1884. 526 p.

Thiselton-Dyer, Thomas F. The folk-lore of plants. New York, D. Appleton. 1889. 328 p.

Thiselton-Dyer, Thomas F. Old English social life as told by the parish register. London, E. Stock. 1898. 6, 257 p.

Thompson, Francis Michael L. English landed society in the nineteenth century. London, Routledge & Kegan Paul; Toronto, University of Toronto Press. 1963. 13, 374 p.

Thut, I. N., and Don Adams. Educational patterns in contemporary societies. New York, McGraw-Hill. 1964: 139-171. (Chapter on "English education: encouraging voluntary schools. ")

Tille, Alexander. Aus Englands Flegeljahren. Dresden and Leipzig, C. Reissner. 1901. 11, 408 p.

Townsend, Peter. The family life of old people: an inquiry in East London. London, Routledge & Kegan Paul. 1957. 300 p., 63 tables.

Tuke, John. General view of the agriculture of the North Riding of Yorkshire . . . London, Board of Agriculture. 1794. 120 p.

*Tunstall, Jeremy. The fishermen. London, MacGibbon & Kee. 1962. 294 p., pl. (Hull fishermen.)

Tunstall, Jeremy. The advertising man in London advertising agencies. London, Chapman & Hall. 1964. 228 p.

Udal, John Symonds. Dorsetshire folk-lore. Hertford, S. Austin & Sons. 1922. 11, 406 p.

Vancouver, Charles. General view of the agriculture in the county of Cambridge . . . 2 pts. London, Board of Agriculture. 1794. 219 p.

Vancouver, Charles. General view of the agriculture of the county of Essex . . . London, Board of Agriculture. 1795. 213 p.

Vancouver, Charles. General view of the agriculture of the county of Devon . . . London, Board of Agriculture. 1808. 472, 2, 3 p.

Vancouver, Charles. General view of the agriculture of Hampshire, including the Isle of Wight . . . London, Board of Agriculture. 1813. 520 p.

Vinogradoff, Sir Paul. Villainage in England. Oxford, The Clarendon Press. 1892. 13, 464 p.

Vinogradoff, Sir Paul. The growth of the manor. London, S. Sonnenschein; New York, Macmillan. 1905. 7, 384 p.

Vinogradoff, Sir Paul. English society in the eleventh century: essays in English mediaeval history. Oxford, The Clarendon Press. 1908. 12, 599 p. (Reprinted 1968.)

Wade, John. The black book: an exposition of abuses in church and state, courts of law, municipal corporations, and public companies; with a précis of the House of Commons, past, present and to come. New ed. London, E. Wilson. 1835. 32, 683, 12, 132 p.

Wailes, Rex. Windmills in England: a study of their origin, development and future. London, Architectural Press. 1948. 8, 48 p., illus.

Ward, Conor K. Priests and people. Liverpool, Liverpool University Press. 1961. 12, 182 p. (A Catholic parish in Liverpool.)

Warren, Clarence Henry. A Cotswold year. London, G. Bles. 1936. 213 p.

Warren, Clarence Henry. Happy countryman. London, G. Bles. 1939. 255 p.

Warren, Clarence Henry. England is a village. London, Eyre and Spottiswoode. 1940. 12, 250 p.

ENGLISH

Warren, Clarence Henry. Corn country. London, B. T. Batsford. 1940.
7, 136 p.

Waugh, Edwin. Sketches of Lancashire life and localities. London,
Whittaker. 1855. 260 p.

White, Richard Grant. England. Without and within. Boston, Houghton
Mifflin. 1881. 12, 601 p.

*Williams, James Eccles. The Derbyshire miners. A study in industrial and
social history. London, Allen & Unwin. 1962. 933 p.

Williams, William Morgan. Kinship structure in an English village. Man.
52(1952): 143-144.

Williams, William Morgan. Kinship and farming in west Cumberland. Man.
56(1956): 21-24.

*Williams, William Morgan. Gosforth: the sociology of an English village.
London, Routledge & Kegan Paul; Glencoe, Ill., The Free Press. 1956.
246 p.

Williams, William Morgan. The country craftsman; a study of some rural
crafts and the rural industries organization in England. London, Routledge
& Kegan Paul. 1958. 214 p.

*Williams, William Morgan. A west country village, Ashworthy: family,
kinship and land. London, Routledge & Kegan Paul. 1963. 22, 228 p.

Williamson, H. Life in a Devon village. London, Faber & Faber. 1952.
288 p.

*Willmott, Peter. The evolution of a community. A study of Dagenham
after forty years. London, Routledge & Kegan Paul. 1963. 14, 153 p.

*Willmott, Peter, and Michael Young. Family and class in a London suburb.
London, Routledge & Kegan Paul. 1960. 202 p., 47 tables.

Wilson, Bryan R. Sects and society: a sociological study of three religious
groups in Britain. London, Heinemann; Berkeley, University of California
Press. 1961. 397 p.

Wilson, Edward M. Folk traditions in Westmorland. Journal of the Folklore
Institute. 2(1965): 276-293.

Wingfield-Stratford, E. C. The squire and his relations. London, Cassell.
1956. 424 p.

Withington, Robert. English pageantry: an historical outline. 2 vols. Cambridge, Mass., Harvard University Press. 1918-1926. (Reprinted. New York, Benjamin Blom. 1963.)

Wo Chang, pseud. England through Chinese spectacles. London, The Cotton Press. 1897. 291 p.

Woods, K. S. Rural crafts of England. A study of skilled workmanship. London, George G. Harrap. 1949. 267 p., 166 fig.

Wright, Arthur Robinson. English folklore. London, J. Cape; New York, H. Smith. 1931. 122 p.

*Wright, Arthur Robinson. British calendar customs. England. Vol. 1: Movable festivals. London, The Folk-Lore Society. 1936. 16, 212 p.

*Wright, Arthur Robinson. British calendar customs. England. Vol. 2: Fixed festivals. January-May, inclusive. London, The Folk-Lore Society. 1938. 11, 272 p.

*Wright, Arthur Robinson. British calendar customs. England. Vol. 3: Fixed festivals. June-December, inclusive. London, The Folk-Lore Society. 1940. 11, 333 p.

Wymer, Norman. English country crafts. London, B. T. Batsford. 1946. 11, 116 p., 145 illus.

Wymer, Norman. Village life. London, Harrap. 1951. 192 p.

Wynn, Margaret. Fatherless families. A study of families deprived of a father by death, divorce, separation or desertion before or after marriage. London, Michael Joseph. 1964. 212 p.

Young, Arthur. General view of the agriculture of the county of Suffolk . . . London, Board of Agriculture. 1794. 92 p.

Young, Arthur. General view of the agriculture of the county of Lincoln . . . London, Board of Agriculture. 1799. 455, 1 p.

Young, Arthur. General view of the agriculture of Hertfordshire . . . London, Board of Agriculture. 1804. 236, 2 p.

Young, Arthur. General view of the agriculture of the county of Norfolk . . . London, Board of Agriculture. 1804. 532, 20, 2 p.

Young, Arthur. General view of the agriculture of the county of Essex . . . 2 vols. London, Board of Agriculture. 1807. 400, 450 p.

ENGLISH

Young, Arthur. View of the agriculture of Oxfordshire ... . London, Board of Agriculture. 1809. 362 p.

Young, G. M. Victorian England: portrait of an age. London, Oxford University Press, H. Milford. 1936. 213 p.

Young, M., and H. Geertz. Old age in London and San Francisco. B. J. S. 12 (1961): 124-141.

*Young, Michael D., and Peter Willmott. Family and kinship in East London. Routledge & Kegan Paul. 1957. 232 p. (Reprinted. Harmondsworth and Baltimore, Penguin Books. 1962. 221 p.)

Zweig, Ferdynand. Labour, life and poverty. London, Victor Gollancz. 1949. 12, 201 p.

Zweig, Ferdynand. Men in the pits. London, Victor Gollancz. 1949. 177 p.

Zweig, Ferdynand. Women's life and labour. London, Victor Gollancz. 1952. 190 p.

Black, George F. A list of works relating to Scotland. New York, New York Public Library. 1916. 1233 p.

Hancock, P. D. A bibliography of works relating to Scotland 1916-1950. 2 parts. Edinburgh, Edinburgh University Press. 1960. 244, 370 p.

Mitchell, Sir Arthur, and C. G. Cash. A contribution to the bibliography of Scottish topography. 2 vols. Edinburgh, Edinburgh University Press. 1917. (Vol. 1 by place. Vol. 2 by subject.)

Adam, F. The clans, septs, and regiments of the Scottish highlands. 6th ed. rev. Edinburgh, W. and A. K. Johnston and G. W. Bacon. 1960. 12, 623 p.

Adam, M. I. 18th century highland landlords and the poverty problem. Scottish Historical Review. 19 (1921): 161-179.

Aiton, William. General view of the agriculture of the County of Ayr . . . Glasgow, London Board of Agriculture. 1811. 19, 725 p.

(Alexander, William). Notes and sketches illustrative of northern rural life in the eighteenth century. Edinburgh, David Douglas. 1877. 6, 221 p.

Anderson, James. An account of the present state of the Hebrides and the western coasts of Scotland: in which an attempt is made to explain the circumstances that have hitherto repressed the industry of the natives . . . Edinburgh, G. Robertson; London, C. Elliot. 1785. 165, 452 p.

Anderson, James. General view of the agriculture and rural economy of the county of Aberdeen. Edinburgh, London Board of Agriculture. 1794. 181 p.

Anderson, John. Prize essay on the state of society and knowledge in the highlands of Scotland. Edinburgh, W. Tait; London, C. Tait. 1827. 176 p.

Anson, Peter F. Fishing boats and fisher folk on the east coast of Scotland. London and Toronto, J. M. Dent and Sons; New York, E. P. Dutton. 1930. 15, 294 p.

Anson, Peter F. Scots fisherfolk. Banff, published for the Saltire Society by the Banffshire Journal. 1950. 11, 166 p.

Argyll, 8th Duke of (George Douglas Campbell). Crofts and farms in the Hebrides. Being an account of the management of an island estate for 130 years. Edinburgh, David Douglas. 1883. 83 p.

SCOTLAND

Arnot, Robert Page. History of the Scottish miners. London, George Allen and Unwin. 1956. 446 p., plates.

Banks, F. R. Scottish border country. London, Batsford. 1951. 8, 152 p., 83 illus., 2 maps.

*Banks, Mrs. M. Macleod. British calendar customs. Scotland. Vol. 1: Movable festivals. Harvest, March Riding and Wapynshaws. Wells. Fairs. London, The Folk-Lore Society. 1937. 19, 202 p.

*Banks, Mrs. M. Macleod. British calendar customs. Scotland. Vol. 2: The seasons. The quarters. Hogmany. January to May. London, The Folk-Lore Society. 1939. 12, 253 p.

*Banks, Mrs. M. Macleod. British calendar customs. Scotland. Vol. 3: June to December, Christmas. The yules. London, The Folk-Lore Society. 1941. 12, 266 p.

Barbour, John Gordon. Unique traditions chiefly of the west and south of Scotland. London, Adams; Glasgow, Thomas D. Morison. 1886. 255 p.

Barr, J. Old people's island (Coll, Scotland). New Society. 150 (August 12, 1965): 5-7.

Barrow, G. W. S. Rural settlement in central and eastern Scotland. Scottish Studies. 6 (1962): 123-144.

Beatson, Robert. General view of the agriculture of the county of Fife. Edinburgh, London Board of Agriculture and Internal Improvement. 1794. 5, 37 p.

Beckwith, Lillian. The hills is lonely. London, Hutchinson; New York, Dutton. 1959. 207 p., illus. (Hebrides.)

Belsches, R. General view of the agriculture of the county of Stirling . . . Edinburgh, Board of Agriculture and Internal Improvement. 1796. 64 p.

Bethune, Alexander, and John Bethune. Tales of the Scottish peasantry. London, Hamilton, Adams. 1884. 351 p.

Beveridge, Erksine. North Uist, its archaeology & topography, with notes upon the early history of the Outer Hebrides. Edinburgh, W. Brown. 1911. 26, 348 p.

Black, George F. Scottish charms and amulets . . . Edinburgh, Neill. 1894. 433-526 p., 7 illus. (Reprinted from the Proceedings of the Society of Antiquaries of Scotland. Vol. 27.)

Black, George F. Some unpublished Scottish witchcraft trials. New York, New York Public Library. 1941. 50 p.

Black, George F. A calendar of cases of witchcraft in Scotland 1510-1727. New York, New York Public Library. 1938. 102 p.

Blundell, Frey Odo. The catholic highlands of Scotland. 2 vols. Edinburgh, Sands. 1909, 1917.

Brand, John. A brief description of Orkney, Zetland, Pightland-Firth & Caithness. Edinburgh, G. Mosman. 1701. 6, 1, 159 p.

Brennan, Tom. Reshaping a city. Glasgow, House of Grant. 1959. 221 p. (Glasgow.)

Brown, Peter Hume. Scotland before 1700, from contemporary documents. Edinburgh, D. Douglas. 1893. 19, 368 p.

(Buchan, Alexander). A description of St. Kilda, the most remote western isle. Edinburgh. 1727. 48 p. (Other later editions.)

Buchan-Hepburn, George. General view of the agriculture and rural economy of East Lothian. Edinburgh, Board of Agriculture and Internal Improvement. 1794. 164 p.

Buchanan, Donald. Reflections on the isle of Barra. London, Sands. 1942. (Reprinted 1943. 239 p.)

Buchanan, John L. Travels in the western Hebrides: from 1782 to 1790. London, G. G. J. & J. Robertson. 1793. 11, 251 p.

Budge, Donald. Jura, an island of Argyll: its history, people and story . . . Glasgow, John Smith & Son. 1960. 15, 206 p.

Burns, Robert. The songs of Robert Burns and notes on Scottish songs by Robert Burns by James C. Dick. Together with annotations of Scottish songs by Burns by Davidson Cook. Hatboro, Penn., Folklore Associates. 1962. 48, 536, 54, 134, 21 p.

Burns, Robert. The merry muses of Caledonia. Collected and in part written by Robert Burns. New Hyde Park, N.Y., University Books. 1965. 66, 326 p.

Burns, Robert. A plea for the poor of Scotland, and for an enquiry into their condition: being the substance of two lectures, read before the Philosophical Institution of Paisley, February, 1841. Paisley, A. Gardner. 1841. 36 p. (Not the poet.)

Burt, Edward. Letters from a gentleman in the north of Scotland . . . 2 vols. London. 1754. (Another ed. 1755. 2 vols. 8, 362 p.)

*Caird, J. B. The isle of Harris. Scottish Geographical Magazine. 67 (1951): 65-100.

*Caird, J. B. Park: a geographical study of a Lewis crofting district. Nottingham, Geographical Field Group, Geography Department, University of Nottingham. 1958. 6, 80 p., 11 maps and diagrams.

Caird, J. B., and H. A. Moisley. Leadership and innovation in the crofting communities of the Outer Hebrides. Sociological Review. 9(1961): 85-102.

Cameron, Joy. Slavery in Scotland. The Scots Magazine. 76 (1962): 348-353.

Campbell, J. L. The late Fr. Allan McDonald, Miss Goodrich Freer and Hebridean folklore. Scottish Studies. 2(1958): 175-188.

Campbell, John Francis. Popular tales of the west highlands orally collected. (Gaelic and English.) 4 vols. Edinburgh, Edmonston & Douglas. 1860-1862

Campbell, John Francis. Leabhar na feinne. Vol. 1. Gaelic texts. Heroic Gaelic ballads collected in Scotland chiefly from 1512 to 1871 . . . London, printed for the author by Spottiswoode. 1872. 36, 224 p.

Campbell, John Francis. More west highland tales; transcribed and translated from the original Gaelic by John G. McKay . . . 2 vols. Edinburgh, Oliver and Boyd. 1940, 1960. 40, 540; 384 p.

Campbell, John Gregorson. Clan traditions and popular tales of the western highlands and islands. London, D. Nutt. 1895. 20, 150 p.

*Campbell, John Gregorson. Superstitions of the highlands and islands of Scotland. Glasgow, J. MacLehose & Sons. 1900. 20, 318 p.

*Campbell, John Gregorson. Witchcraft and second sight in the highlands and islands of Scotland. Glasgow, J. MacLehose & Sons. 1902. 12, 314 p.

Campbell, John Lorne. The book of Barra; being accounts of the island of Barra in the Outer Hebrides, written by various authors . . . London, G. Routledge & Sons. 1936. 11, 326 p.

Campbell, Margaret S. Hunting folk songs in the Hebrides. National Geographic Magazine. 91 (1947): 249-272.

Carmichael, Alexander. Carmina Gadelica, hymns and incantations with illustrative notes on words, rites, and customs, dying, and obsolete: orally collected in the highlands and islands of Scotland. 2 vols. Edinburgh, printed for the author by T. and A. Constable. 1900. (2d ed. 5 vols. Edinburgh, Oliver and Boyd. 1928, 1928, 1940, 1941, 1954. 36, 336; 16, 384; 24, 398; 48, 368; 24, 404 p.)

Celoria, F. Notes on lore and customs in the district near Portnahaven, Rhinns of Islay, Argyll, Scotland. Folk-lore. 76 (1965): 39-47.

Chambers, Robert. The popular rhymes of Scotland. 3d ed. Edinburgh, W. & R. Chambers. 1858. 6, 357 p. (Many other editions.)

Chambers, Robert. Scottish jests and anecdotes. Edinburgh, W. Tait. 1832. 7, 468 p.

Collier, A. The crofting problem. Cambridge, The University Press. 1953. 191 p.

Coull, James R. The island of Tiree. Scottish Geographical Magazine. 78 (1962): 17-32. 7 figs.

Coull, James R. Melness, a crofting community on the north coast of Scotland. Scottish Studies. 7 (1963): 180-198.

Crawford, Iain A. Kelp burning. Scottish Studies. 6 (1962): 105-107.

Crawford, Iain A. Contributions to a history of domestic settlement in North Uist. Scottish Studies. 9 (1965): 34-63. 3 plates.

Cregeen, Eric R. Flailing in Argyll. Folk Life. 3 (1965): 90.

Cregeen, Eric R. Recollections of an Argyllshire drover, with historical notes on the west highland cattle trade. Scottish Studies. 3 (1959): 143-162.

Cregeen, Eric R. The changing role of the House of Argyll in the Scottish highlands. In Ioan M. Lewis, ed. History and social anthropology. London, Tavistock Publications. 1968: 153-192.

Crosland, Thomas W. H. The unspeakable Scot. London, G. Richards; New York, G. P. Putnam's Sons. 1902. 3, 215 p.

Curwen, E. Cecil. The Hebrides; a cultural backwater. Antiquity. 12 (1938): 261-289.

Curwen, E. Cecil. The significance of the pentatonic scale in Scottish song. Antiquity. 14 (1940): 347-362.

SCOTLAND

Dalyell, John Graham, 6th bart. The darker superstitions of Scotland. Edinburgh, Waugh and Innes. 1834. 700 p.

Darling, Frank Fraser. Crofting agriculture. Its practice in the west highlands and islands. Edinburgh, Oliver & Boyd. 1945. 11, 163 p., plate.

*Darling, Frank Fraser. West highland survey: an essay in human ecology. London, Oxford University Press. 1955. 18, 438 p.

Davidson, Thomas. Animal treatment in eighteenth-century Scotland. Scottish Studies. 4 (1960): 134-149.

Davidson, Thomas Douglas. Rowan tree and red thread. A Scottish witchcraft miscellany of tales, legends and ballads; together with a description of the witches' rites and ceremonies. Edinburgh, Oliver & Boyd. 1949. 10, 286 p.

Dewar, John. The Dewar manuscripts; Scottish west highland folk tales; collected originally in Gaelic for George Douglas, 8th Duke of Argyll. Vol. 1. Glasgow, William MacLellan. 1964. 397 p.

Donaldson, James. General view of the agriculture of the county of Elgin or Moray, lying between the Spey and the Findhorn; including part of Strathspey, in the county of Inverness. London, London Board of Agriculture and Internal Improvement. 1794. 43 p.

Donaldson, James. General view of the agriculture of the county of Northampton . . . to which is added an appendix, containing a comparison between the English and Scotch system of husbandry. Edinburgh, London Board of Agriculture and Internal Improvement. 1794. 66 p. and 19 p. of appendix.

Donaldson, James. General view of the agriculture in the carse of Gowrie in the county of Perth. London, C. MacRae. 1794. 37 p.

Donaldson, James. General view of the agriculture of the county of Nairn, the eastern coast of Inverness-shire, and the parish of Dyke . . . London, B. Millan. 1794. 32 p.

Donaldson, Mary E. M. Wanderings in the western highlands and islands recounting highland and clan history, traditions . . . folk-lore. Paisley, Alex Gardner. 1920. 511 p.

Douglas, Rev. Robert. General view of the agriculture of the counties of Roxburgh and Selkirk. London, Board of Agriculture and Internal Improvement. 1798. 13, 378 p.

Drake-Carnell, F. J. It's an old Scottish custom. London, P. Davies. 1939. 14, 264 p.

Ducey, Paul Richard. Cultural continuity and population change on the island of Skye. Unpublished doctoral dissertation. New York, Columbia University, Department of Anthropology. 1956. 417 p.

Dunbar, J. G. Auchindrain: a mid-Argyll township. Folk Life. 3 (1965): 61-67.

Erskine, John Francis. General view of the agriculture of the county of Clackmannan; and some of the adjacent parishes, situated in the counties of Perth and Stirling. Edinburgh, London Board of Agriculture and Internal Improvement. 1795. 97 p., appendix, 8 tables, 2 tables.

Evan-Wentz, Walter Y. The fairy-faith in Celtic countries. London, Frowde. 1911: 84-116. (Reprinted. New Hyde Park, N.Y., University Books. 1966.)

Fenton, Alexander. Early and traditional cultivating implements in Scotland. Proceedings of the Society of Antiquaries of Scotland. 96 (1962-63): 264-317, 7 plates.

Fenton, Alexander. The Chilcarroch plough . . . Scottish Studies. 8 (1964): 80-84.

Ferguson, T., and J. Cunnison. In their early twenties: a study of Glasgow youth. London, Oxford University Press. 1956. 11, 110 p.

Findlater, Rev. Charles. General view of the agriculture of the County of Peebles. Edinburgh, London Board of Agriculture and Internal Improvement. 1802. 20, 413 p.

Flett, J. F., and T. M. Some Hebridean folk dances. Journal of the English Folk Dance and Song Society. 7 (1952-1955): 112-127, 182-184.

Flett, J. F., and T. M. Traditional dancing in Scotland. Nashville, Vanderbilt University Press. 1966. 11, 313 p.

Gaffney, Victor. Summer shealings. Scottish Historical Review. 38 (1959): 20-35.

Gailey, A. The role of sub-letting in the crofting community. Scottish Studies. 5 (1961): 57-76.

Gailey, R. Alan. The evolution of highland rural settlement: with particular reference to Argyllshire. Scottish Studies. 6 (1962): 155-177.

*Gaskell, Philip. Morvern transformed. A highland parish in the nineteenth century. Cambridge, The University Press. 1968. 20, 273 p., map.

Geddes, A. The changing landscape of the Lothians. Scottish Geographical Magazine. 54(1938): 129-142.

*Geddes, Arthur. The isle of Lewis and Harris. A study in British community. Edinburgh, Edinburgh University Press. 1955. 16, 340 p.

Gibb, Robert Shirra. A farmer's fifty years in Lauderdale. Edinburgh and London, Oliver and Boyd. 1927. 11, 286 p.

Gibson, W. J. The village in the outer isles of Scotland. Sociological Review. 38(1946): 247-269.

Girling, F. K. Joking relationships in a Scottish town. Man. 57(1957): 102.

Goldstein, K. S. Riddling traditions in northeastern Scotland. J.A.F.L. 76 (1963): 330-336.

Gomme, Lady Alice Bertha. The traditional games of England, Scotland and Ireland, with tunes, singing-rhymes, and methods of playing according to the variants extant and recorded in different parts of the kingdom. 2 vols. London, David Nutt. 1894-1898. (Reprinted. New York, Dover Publications. 1964.)

Goodrich-Freer, Adela M. Outer isles. Westminster, A. Constable. 1902. 15, 448 p.

Gordon, Seton. Highlands of Scotland. London, Hale. 1951. 328 p., illus.

Graham, Henry Grey. The social life of Scotland in the eighteenth century. 2 vols. London, A. and C. Black. 1899.

Graham, Patrick. General view of the agriculture of Stirlingshire. Edinburgh, London Board of Agriculture and Internal Improvement. 1812. 8, 415 p.

Graham, Patrick. A general view of the agriculture of the counties of Kinross and Clackmannan. Edinburgh, London Board of Agriculture and Internal Improvement. 1814. 2, 436 p., 8 plates.

*Grant, Isabel Frances. Everyday life on an old highland farm 1769-82. London, Longmans. 1924. 276 p.

Grant, Isabel Frances. The social and economic development of Scotland before 1603. Edinburgh, London, Oliver and Boyd. 1930. 12, 594 p.

*Grant, Isabel Frances. Everyday life in old Scotland. London, G. Allen & Unwin. 1931. 409 p., illus.

SCOTLAND

*Grant, Isabel Frances. Highland folk ways. London, Routledge & Kegan Paul. 1961. 13, 377 p.

Gray, Malcolm. The highland economy 1750-1850. Edinburgh, Oliver and Boyd. 1957. 8, 280 p., map.

Gray, Malcolm. Settlement in the highlands, 1750-1950: the documentary and written record. Scottish Studies. 6 (1962): 145-154.

*Great Britain. Commission of Inquiry into the Condition of Crofters and Cottars of Scotland. Report of Her Majesty's commissioners of inquiry into the conditions of the crofters and cottars in the highlands and islands of Scotland. 5 vols. Edinburgh, Printed by Neill. 1884.

Gregor, J. F., and Ruth Morey Crichton. From croft to factory. The evolution of an industrial community in the highlands. London, Thomas Nelson and Sons. 1946. 11, 148 p. (Village of Kinlochleven.)

Gregor, Walter. Notes on the folklore of the north-east of Scotland. London, The Folk-Lore Society. 1881. 12, 238 p.

Gregor, Walter. An echo of the olden time from the north of Scotland. Edinburgh and Glasgow, J. Menzies. 1874. 8, 167 p.

Gregory, Donald. The history of the western highlands and isles of Scotland. Glasgow, Thomas D. Morison; London, Hamilton, Adams. 1881. 39, 8, 453 p.

Greig, Gavin. Folk song in Buchan and folk song of the north east. Hatboro, Penn., Folklore Associates. 1963. 600 p.

Gunn, John. An historical inquiry respecting the performance of the harp in the highlands of Scotland, from the earliest times until it was discontinued, about the year 1734. To which is prefixed, an account of a very ancient Caledonian harp, and of the harp of Queen Mary. Edinburgh. 1807.

Guthrie, Ellen Emma. Old Scottish customs, local & general. London, Hamilton, Adams. 1885. 12, 234 p.

Guthrie, James Cargill. The vale of Strathmore: its scenes and legends. Edinburgh, W. Paterson. 1875. 15, 524 p.

Haldane, Archibald R. B. The drove roads of Scotland. London, New York, Nelson. 1952. 13, 266 p.

Hance, William C. Crofting settlements and housing in the Outer Hebrides. Annals of the Association of American Geographers. 41 (1951): 75-87.

Hance, William C. Crofting in the Outer Hebrides. Economic Geography. 28(1952): 37-50.

Hance, William C. The fishing industry of the Outer Hebrides. Economic Geography. 29(1953): 168-182.

*Handley, James Edmund. Scottish farming in the eighteenth century. London, Faber & Faber. 1953. 314 p.

Handley, James Edmund. The agricultural revolution in Scotland. Glasgow, John S. Burns and Sons. 1963. 317 p.

Headrick, Rev. James. View of the minerology, agriculture, manufactures and fisheries of the island of Arran . . . Edinburgh, London Board of Agriculture. 1807. 15, 396 p.

Headrick, Rev. James. General view of the agriculture of the county of Angus, or Forfarshire. Edinburgh, London Board of Agriculture and Internal Improvement. 1813. 21, 590 p. and 121 p. of appendix.

Henderson, Andrew. Scottish proverbs. Edinburgh, Oliver and Boyd. 1832. 254 p.

Henderson, George. The Norse influence on Celtic Scotland. Glasgow, J. MacLehose & Sons. 1910. 12, 371 p.

Henderson, Capt. John. General view of the agriculture of the county of Caithness. London, Board of Agriculture and Internal Improvement. 1812. 12, 371 p. and 222 p. of appendix.

Henderson, Capt. John. General view of the agriculture of the county of Sutherland. London, Board of Agriculture and Internal Improvement. 1812. 12, 238, 6 p.

Henderson, William. Notes on the folklore of the northern counties of England and the borders. London, Longmans, Green. 1866. 27, 344 p. (A new edition with many additional notes. London, The Folk-Lore Society. 1879. 17, 391 p.)

Heron, Robert. Observations made in a journey through the western counties of Scotland in the autumn of M, DCC, XCII relating to the scenery, antiquities, customs . . . political condition and literature of these parts . . . 2 vols. Perth, R. Morison. 1793.

Heron, Robert. General view of the circumstances of those isles, adjacent to the north-west of Scotland, which are distinguished by the common name of Hebudae or Hebrides. Edinburgh, J. Paterson. 1794. 99 p.

Highet, John. The churches in Scotland today; a survey of their principles, strength, work and statements. Glasgow, Jackson. 1950. 11, 257 p.

Highet, John. Scottish religious adherence. B.J.S. 4 (1953): 142-159.

Highet, John. The Scottish churches: a review of their state 400 years after the Reformation. London, Skeffington. 1960. 224 p.

Hunter, George McPherson. When I was a boy in Scotland. Boston, Lothrop, Lee & Shepard. 1920. 159 p.

Hunter, S. Leslie. The Scottish educational system. London, New York, Pergamon Press. 1968. 8, 269 p.

*Jaatinen, Stig T. H. The human geography of the Outer Hebrides, with special reference to the latest trends in land-use. Acta Geographica (Helsinki). 16, no. 2. 1957. 107 p.

Jirow, R. and I. Whitaker. The plough in Scotland. Scottish Studies. 1 (1957): 71-94.

Johnson, L. G. Laurence Williamson. Scottish Studies. 6 (1962): 49-59.

Johnston, James B. Place-names of Scotland. 3d ed. London, J. Murray. 1934. 16, 335 p.

Johnston, Thomas. General view of the agriculture of the county of Selkirk. London, Board of Agriculture and Internal Development. 1794. 50 p.

Johnston, Thomas. History of the working classes in Scotland. Glasgow, Forward Publishing Co. 1920. 408 p.

Keith, James. Fifty years of farming . . . London, Faber & Faber. 1954. 143 p.

Kerr, Robert. General view of the agriculture of the county of Berwick. London, Board of Agriculture and Internal Development. 1809. 32, 504, 73 p.

Kirk, Robert. The secret commonwealth of elves, fauns and fairies. Comment by Andrew Lang. 3d ed. Stirling, Eneas MacKay. 1933. 128 p. (Manuscript dated 1691.)

Kissling, Werner. House traditions in the Outer Hebrides, the black house and the beehive hut. Man. 44 (1944): 134-140.

Kissling, Werner. Tidal nets of the Solway. Scottish Studies. 2 (1958): 166-174. 8 plates.

Learmonth, A. T. A. The population of Skye. Scottish Geographical Magazine. 66 (1950): 77-103.

Leigh, Margaret M. Highland homespun. Reflections upon life on a highland farm. London, G. Bell & Sons, 1936. 7, 339 p.

Leslie, Rev. William. General view of the agriculture of the counties of Nairn and Moray. London, Board of Agriculture and Internal Improvement. 1813. 8, 536 p.

Lockhead, Marion. The Scots household in the 18th century: a century of Scottish domestic and social life. Edinburgh, Moray Press. 1948. 410 p.

Logan, James. The Scottish Gaël; or Celtic manners, as preserved among the highlanders: being an historical and descriptive account of the inhabitants, antiquities, and national peculiarities of Scotland. 2 vols. London, Smith, Elder. 1831.

Logan, James. The clans of the Scottish highlands. 2 vols. London, Ackermann. 1845-1847.

Lorimer, R. L. C. Studies in Pibroch. Scottish Studies. 6 (1962): 1-30; 8 (1964): 45-79.

Lowe, Alexander. General view of the agriculture of the county of Berwick . . London, B. Millan. 1794. 136 p., map.

MacAskill, Alexander J. Life in the highlands in the 17th and 18th centuries as seen through the eyes of the poets of that period. Transactions of the Gaelic Society of Inverness. 41 (1952): 157-177.

Macaulay, Kenneth. The history of St. Kilda. Containing a description of this remarkable island; the manners and customs of the inhabitants . . . London, T. Becket and P. A. de Hondt. 1764. 4, 1, 4, 5-278 p., map.

McCallum, Neil. It's an old Scottish custom. New York, Vanguard. 1952. 192 p.

McClintock, H. F. Old Irish and highland dress and that of the Isle of Man. 2d ed. Dundalk, Dundalgan Press. 1950. 141 p., 87 illus.

McDonald, Allan. Gaelic words and expressions from South Uist and Eriskay, collected by Rev. Fr. Allan McDonald, 1859-1905. Dublin, Dublin Institute for Advanced Studies. 1958. 301 p.

Macdonald, James. General view of the agriculture of the Hebrides, or western islands of Scotland. Edinburgh, London Board of Agriculture. 1811. 7, 824 p.

MacDougall, Rev. James. Folk tales and fairy tales in Gaelic and English. Edinburgh, John Grant. 1910. 15, 328 p.

McGibbon, John. The fisher folk of Buchan. A true story of Peterhead. London, Marshall Bros. 1922. 240 p.

MacGregor, Alasdair Alpin. Behold the Hebrides! or, wayfaring in the western isles. London, W. & R. Chambers. 1925. 16, 248 p., plate. (Rev. ed. Edinburgh and London, Ettrick Press. 1948. 16, 200 p., plate.)

MacGregor, Alasdair Alpin. Over the sea to Skye; or, ramblings in an elfin isle. London, Edinburgh, W. & R. Chambers. 1926. 24, 353 p.

MacGregor, Alasdair Alpin. Summer days among the western isles. Edinburgh and London, T. Nelson & Sons. 1929. 17, 342 p.

MacGregor, Alasdair Alpin. A last voyage to St. Kilda: being the observations and adventures . . . at the time of its evacuation. London, Cassella. 1931. 15, 316 p.

MacGregor, Alasdair Alpin. The haunted isles; or, life in the Hebrides! London, A. Maclehose. 1933. 14, 320 p.

MacGregor, Alasdair Alpin. The goat-wife; portrait of a village. London, Toronto, W. Heinemann. 1939. 13, 323 p.

MacGregor, Alasdair Alpin. Vanished waters; portrait of a highland childhood. London, Methuen. 1942. 13, 174 p.

Macgregor, D. R. The island of St. Kilda: a survey of its character and occupance. Scottish Studies. 4 (1960): 1-48.

McIver, David. An old-time fishing town: Eyemouth. Greenoch, James McKelvir. 1906. 356 p.

MacIver, Donald. Place-names of Lewis and Harris. Stornoway, printed at the "Gazette" office. 1934. 4, 1, 102 p., map.

Mackenzie, Alexander. The prophecies of the Brahan seer (Coinneach Odhar Fiosaiche). With an appendix on the superstitions of the highlanders. Inverness, A. & W. Mackenzie. 1882. 4, 156 p.

Mackenzie, Sir Compton. Whiskey Galore. London, Chatto and Windus. 1947. 264 p. (Fiction)

MacKenzie, Sir George Steuart, bart. A general view of the agriculture for the counties of Ross and Cromarty. London, Board of Agriculture. 1810. 11, 353 p.

Mackenzie, Osgood H. A hundred years in the highlands. London, E. Arnold. 1921. 15, 272 p., plate. (New ed. London, Geoffrey Bles. 1949. 221 p., plate.)

MacKenzie, W. C. The western isles: their history, traditions and place-names. Paisley, A. Gardner. 1932. 15, 351 p.

MacKenzie, William Leslie. Scottish mothers and children. Eastport, Dumferline, Carnegie United Kingdom Trust. 1917. 28, 632, 24 p.

MacKinlay, James Murray. Folklore of Scottish lochs and springs. Glasgow, W. Hodge. 1893. 12, 364 p.

MacLagan, R. C. The games and diversions of Argyllshire. London, The Folk-Lore Society. 1901. 7, 270 p.

MacLagan, R. C. Evil eye in the western highlands. London, David Nutt. 1902. 7, 332 p.

McLaren, Moray. The Scots. Harmondsworth, Penguin Books. 1951. 246 p.

McLaren, Moray. Understanding the Scots; a guide for south Britons and other foreigners. London, Mueller. 1956. 160 p.

McLaren, Moray. The wisdom of the Scots; a choice and comment. London, M. Joseph; New York, St. Martin's Press. 1961. 335 p.

MacLean, Calum I. Hebridean traditions. Gwerin. 1 (1956): 21-33.

MacLean, Calum I. Traditional beliefs in Scotland. Scottish Studies. 3(1959): 189-200.

MacLean, Calum I. The last sheaf. Scottish Studies. 8 (1964): 193-207.

Maclean, Magnus. The literature of the highlands. London, Blackie and Sons. 1904. 8, 236 p.

Maclellan, Angus. Stories from South Uist. (Translated from the Gaelic by John Lorne Campbell.) London, Routledge & Kegan Paul. 1961. 39, 254 p.

Maclellan, Angus. The furrow behind me: the autobiography of a Hebridean crofter. (Translated by John Lorne Campbell.) London, Routledge & Kegan Paul. 1962. 202 p.

McLennan, Malcolm. Peasant life; being sketches of the villagers and field-laborers in Glenaldir. Edinburgh, Edmonston and Douglas. 1869. 31, 329 p. (Fiction. There are many other editions.)

McNeill, Florence Marian. The Scots kitchen: its traditions and lore, with old-time recipes. London & Glasgow, Blackie and Son. 1929. 16, 259 p.

*McNeill, Florence Marian. The Scots kitchen. Its lore and recipes. 2d ed. London and Glasgow, Blackie and Son. 1963. 12, 282 p., plates.

McNeill, Florence Marian. The Scots cellar, its traditions and lore. Edinburgh, R. Paterson. 1956. 290 p. (Drinking customs.)

McNeill, Florence Marian. The silver bough. Vol. 1. Scottish folk-lore and folk belief. Glasgow, William MacLellan. 1957. 220 p.

McNeill, Florence Marian. The silver bough. Vol. 2. A calendar of Scottish national festivals. Candlemas to harvest home. Glasgow, William MacLellan. 1959. 163 p.

McNeill, Florence Marian. The silver bough. Vol. 3. A calendar of Scottish national festivals. Hallowe'en to Yule. Glasgow, William MacLellan. 1961. 180 p.

McPherson, Joseph McKenzie. Primitive beliefs in the north-east of Scotland. London, Longmans, Green. 1929. 12, 310 p.

Macrury, Rev. Ewen. A Hebridean parish. Inverness, Northern Chronicle Office. 1950. 12, 71 p.

Macsween, M., and A. Gailey. Some shielings in north Skye. Scottish Studies. 5 (1961): 77-84.

Martin, Martin. A late voyage to St. Kilda, the remotest of all the Hebrides, or western isles of Scotland. With a history of the islands, natural, moral, and topographical. Wherein is an account of their customs, religion, fish, fowl, etc. As also a relation of a late imposter there, pretending to be sent by St. John Baptist. London, printed for D. Brown, T. Goodwin. 1698. 158 p. (Many other later editions.)

Martin, Martin. A description of the western islands of Scotland. London. 1703.

*Martin, Martin. A description of the western islands . . . (p. 1-391) A late voyage to St. Kilda . . . (p. 394-476). Sir Donald Munro. A description of the western islands of Scotland called Hybrides . . . (p. 477-526). Edited with an introduction by D. J. Macleod. Stirling, Scotland, Eneas Mackay. 1934. 540 p.

Mathews, R. H., and P. J. Nuttgens. Two Scottish villages: a planning study. Scottish Studies. 3 (1959): 113-142.

Maxwell, Sir Herbert Eustace. Studies in the topography of Galloway, being a list of nearly 4,000 names of places, with remarks on their origin and meaning. Edinburgh, D. Douglas. 1887. 15, 340 p.

Maxwell, Sir Herbert Eustace. Scottish land-names; their origin and meaning. Edinburgh, Blackwood. 1894. 10, 219 p.

Maxwell, Sir Herbert Eustace. The story of the Tweed. London, J. Nisbet. 1905. 11, 270 p.

Maxwell, William Hamilton. Highlands & islands, being a sequel to "Wild sports of the west." 2 vols. London, G. Routledge. 1852.

Megan, J. V. S. Folklore and tradition on North Uist. Folk-Lore. 68 (1957): 483-489.

Megaw, B. R. S. Goat-keeping in the old highland economy. Scottish Studies. 7 (1963): 201-209; 8 (1964): 213-218.

Megaw, B. R. S. Evening in a Scots cottage. Scottish Studies. 9 (1965): 106-108.

Michie, G., and A. Fenton. Cheese-presses in Angus. Scottish Studies. 7 (1963): 47-56.

Miller, Hugh. Scenes and legends of the north of Scotland; or, the traditional history of Cromarty. 3d ed. Edinburgh, Johnstone and Hunter. 1853. 14, 482 p. (There are many other editions and reprints of this work.)

Miller, Hugh. Tales and sketches. Boston, Gould & Lincoln; New York, Sheldon. 1863. 16, 369 p.

Milligan, Jean C. The Scottish country dance. Glasgow and London, Paterson Sons. 1924. 16 p.

Milligan, Jean C., and D. G. MacLennan. Dances of Scotland. London, Parrish. 1950. 40 p., plate.

Mitchell, Arthur. Wattled houses in Scotland. Antiquity. 13 (1939): 342-344.

Moisley, H. A. Some Hebridean field systems. Gwerin. 3 (1960): 22-35.

Moisley, H. A. Harris tweed: a growing highland industry. Economic Geography. 37 (1961): 353-370.

*Moisley, H. A. Uig: a Hebridean parish. (4 parts in 2 vols.) Nottingham, Geographical Field Group, Geography Department, University of Nottingham. 1961-1962. 56 p., 25 figs.; 100 p., 21 figs.

Moisley, H. A. The deserted Hebrides. Scottish Studies. 10 (1966): 44-68.

Muir, Thomas S. Ecclesiological notes on some of the islands of Scotland. Edinburgh, D. Douglas. 1885. 12, 315 p.

Muir, Willa. Mrs. Grundy in Scotland. London, G. Routledge and Sons. 1936. 186 p.

Munro, R. W., ed. Munro's western isles of Scotland and genealogies of the clans 1594. Edinburgh, Oliver and Boyd. 1961. 172 p.

Murray, Joan E. L. The agriculture of Crail, 1550-1600. Scottish Studies. 8(1964): 85-95.

Naismith, John. General view of the agriculture of the county of Clydesdale . . . Brentford, P. Norbury. 1794. 82 p.

Napier, James. Folklore: or superstitious beliefs in the west of Scotland within this century. With an appendix, shewing the probable relation of the modern festivals of Christmas, May Day, St. John's Day, and Halloween, to ancient sun & fire worship. Paisley. 1879.

Nicholls, Sir George. A history of the Scotch poor law. London, John Murray. 1856. 10, 288 p. (Reprinted. New York, Augustus M. Kelley. 1967.)

Nicholson, Edward Williams Byron. Golspie: contributions to its folklore. By pupils of Golspie School. Collected and edited by D. Nutt. London, D. Nutt. 1897. 16, 352 p.

Payne, F. G. A Scottish ploughshare type. Gwerin. 1(1957): 184-186.

Peake, Frederick G. Change at St. Boswell's: the story of a border village. Galashiels, John MacQueen. 1961. 127 p.

Pennant, Thomas. A tour of Scotland, 1769. In John Pinkerton, ed. A general collection of . . . voyages and travels. Vol. 3. London. 1808-1814: 1-170.

Pennant, Thomas. A tour of Scotland, and voyage to the Hebrides in 1772. In John Pinkerton. A general collection of . . . voyages and travels. Vol. 3. London. 1808-1814: 171-569.

Pennell, Joseph. Our journey to the Hebrides. New York, Harper & Bros. 1889. 20, 225 p.

Plant, Marjorie. The domestic life of Scotland in the eighteenth century. Publications in History, Philosophy and Economics No. 2. Edinburgh, Edinburgh University Press. 1952. 319 p.

Polson, Alexander. Our highland folklore heritage. Inverness, Northern Chronicle; Dingwell, George Souter. 1926. 6, 167 p.

Polson, Alexander. Scottish witchcraft lore. Inverness, W. Alexander and Son. 1932. 8, 190 p.

Prebble, John. The highland clearances. London, Secker and Warburg. 1963. 352 p., plate, map.

Proceedings of the Society of Antiquaries of Scotland. Vol. 1- (1851-). Edinburgh. Index: vols. 1-24 (1851-1890), 25-48 (1890-1914).

Ramsay, Edward B. Reminiscences of Scottish life and character. London, George Routledge & Sons; New York, E. P. Dutton. 1907. 6, 310 p.

Rehfisch, F. Marriage and the elementary family among Scottish tinkers. Scottish Studies. 5 (1961): 121-148.

Rennie, James Alan. In the steps of the clansmen. London, Rich and Cowan. 1954. 240 p.

Rennie, James Alan. The Scottish people; their clans, families and origins. London, Hutchinson. 1960. 350 p.

Robertson, George. General view of the agriculture of the county of Midlothian . . . Edinburgh, Board of Agriculture and Internal Improvement. 1793. 90 p.

Robertson, George. General view of the agriculture of the county of Mid-Lothian. Edinburgh, London Board of Agriculture and Internal Improvement. 1795. 223 p., appendix 135, 4 p.

Robertson, George. A general view of the agriculture of Kincardeshire or, the Mearns. London, Board of Agriculture and Internal Improvement. 1813. 13, 477, 63 p.

Robertson, George. Rural recollections. Irvine, Cunningham Press, for the author. 1829. 8, 636 p.

Robertson, James. General view of the agriculture in the southern districts of the county of Perth. London, Board of Agriculture and Internal Improvement. 1794. 223, 135, 4 p.

Robertson, James. General view of the agriculture in the county of Perth. London, Board of Agriculture and Internal Improvement. 1799. 20, 575, 5 p.

Robertson, James. General view of the agriculture in the county of Inverness. London, Board of Agriculture and Internal Improvement. 1808. 66, 447, 4 p.

Robertson, Kenneth. Island weddings. Scotland's Magazine. 57 (Dec. 1961): 16-20. (Eriskay Island.)

Robertson, Robert Blackwood. Of sheep and men. New York, Knopf. 1957. 308 p.

Rock, Cyril H. Weaver's cottage, Kilbarchan. Edinburgh, The National Trust for Scotland. 1962. 16 p., 8 illus.

Rogers, Charles. Scotland; social and domestic. Memorials of life and manners in North Britain. London, printed for the Grampian Club. 1869. 380 p.

Rogers, Charles. Social life in Scotland. 3 vols. Edinburgh, W. Paterson. 1884-1886.

Ross, James. Bilingualism and folk life. Scottish Studies. 6 (1962): 60-70. (Skye.)

Roussell, Aage. Norse building customs in the Scottish isles. Copenhagen, Levin & Munksgaard. 1934. 113 p., 56 illus. (Also a London edition. Williams and Norgate. 1934.)

Sage, Rev. Donald. Memorabilia domestica; or, parish life in the north of Scotland. Edited by his son D. F. Sage. Wick, W. Rae. 1889. 14, 439 p. (Early nineteenth century.)

Sanderson, S. F. A packman's bivuy in Moidart. Scottish Studies. 1 (1957): 243-245.

Sands, J. Out of the world; or, life on St. Kilda. 2d ed. Edinburgh, Maclachlan & Stewart. 1878. 10, 142 p.

Scola, P. M., and A. M. MacKenzie. Types of farming in Scotland. Edinburgh, Department of Agriculture for Scotland. 1952. 102 p., maps.

*Scotland. Commission of Inquiry into Crofting Conditions. Report. Edinburgh, H. M. Stationery Office. 1954. 99 p.

Scotland. Crofters Commission. Report to the secretary for Scotland by the Crofters' Commission on the social condition of the people of Lewis in 1901, as compared with twenty years ago . . . Glasgow, Printed by J. Hederwick & Sons for H. M. Stationery Office. 1902. 104, 63 p.

Scottish Notes and Queries. Aberdeen, D. Wyllie. Vols. 1-12 (June 1887-June 1889), 2d series. Vols. 1-8 (July 1894-June 1907), 3d series. Vols. 1-13 (January 1923-December 1935).

Scottish Studies. Edinburgh, School of Scottish Studies, University of Edinburgh. 1957. Vol. 1-

Seton, George. St. Kilda; past and present. Edinburgh and London, W. Blackwood & Sons. 1878. 15, 346 p., 12 plates, maps.

Sharpe, Charles Kirkpatrick. A historical account of the belief in witchcraft in Scotland. London, Hamilton, Adams. 1884. 268 p.

Shaw, Margaret Fay. Folksongs & folklore of South Uist. London, Routledge & Kegan Paul. 1955. 14, 290 p., 32 plates.

Simpkins, John Ewart. Example of printed folk-lore concerning Fife with some notes on Clackmannan and Kinross-shire. County Folk-Lore. Vol. 7. London, The Folk-Lore Society. 1914. 35, 419 p.

Sinclair, Catherine. Scotland and the Scotch: or, the western circuit. New York, D. Appleton. 1840. 8, 346 p.

Sinclair, Colin. The thatched houses of the old highlands. Edinburgh, Oliver and Boyd. 1953. 78 p.

Sinclair, John. General view of the agriculture of the northern counties and islands of Scotland. London, Board of Agriculture and Internal Development. 1795. 21, 281 p.

Singer, Dr. General view of the agriculture, state of property, and improvements, in the county of Dumfries. Edinburgh, Board of Agriculture, and at the request of the landowners. 1812. 27, 696 p.

Smith, John. General view of the agriculture of the county of Argyll. Edinburgh, London Board of Agriculture and Internal Improvement. 1798. 7, 325, 10 p.

Smith, Rev. Samuel. General view of the agriculture of Galloway; comprehending two counties viz. the Stewarty of Kirkcudbright, and Wigtownshire. London, Board of Agriculture and Internal Improvement. 1813. 14, 388, 16 p.

Smith, William Anderson. Lewsiana, or life in the Outer Hebrides. 2d ed. London, Daldy, Isbister. 1875. 297 p.

Somerville, Robert. General view of the agriculture of East Lothian. London, Board of Agriculture and Internal Development. 1805. 326 p.

Souter, David. General view of the agriculture of the county of Banff. Edinburgh, London Board of Agriculture and Internal Development. 1812. 14, 339, 85 p.

Souter Johnie's cottage. Edinburgh, The National Trust for Scotland. 1963. 12 p., 6 illus.

*Steel, Tom. The life and death of St. Kilda. Edinburgh, The National Trust for Scotland. 1965. 136 p., 56 illus., map.

Stevens, Alex. The human geography of Lewis. Scottish Geographical Magazine. 41(1929): 75-88.

Stewart, Alexander. A highland parish: the history of Fortengal. Glasgow, A. Maclaren. 1928. 15, 4, 378 p.

Stewart, Major-General David. Sketches of the character, etc., of the highlanders of Scotland. 2 vols. Edinburgh, Constable. 1822.

Stewart, William Grant. The popular superstitions and festive amusements of the highlanders of Scotland. Edinburgh. 1823. (Many later editions exist.)

Stewart, William Grant. Lectures on the mountains; or, the highlands as they were and as they are . . . 2 vols. London, Saunders, Otley. 1860.

Storrie, Margaret C. Islay: a Hebridean exception. Geographical Journal. 56(1961): 87-108.

Storrie, Margaret C. Two early resettlement schemes in Barra. Scottish Studies. 6(1962): 71-84.

Svensson, Roland. Lonely isles. Being an account of several voyages to the Hebrides and Shetland. Translated by Albert Read. London, B. T. Batsford. 1955. 138 p.

Swire, Otto F. Skye: the island and its legends. 2d ed. Glasgow, Blackie. 1961. 244 p.

*Symon, J. A. Scottish farming, past and present. Edinburgh, Oliver and Boyd. 1959. 9, 475 p., illus.

Taylor, A. B. The Scandinavian settlements in the north and west of Scotland: documentary and place-name evidence. Scottish Studies. 6 (1962): 178-180.

Thomas, Frederick W. L. Notice of beehive houses in Harris and Lewis. Proceedings of the Society of Antiquaries of Scotland. 3(1857-1860): 127-144.

Thomas, Frederick W. L. On the primitive dwellings and "hypogea of the Outer Hebrides." Proceedings of the Society of Antiquaries of Scotland. 7(1866-1868): 153-195.

Thomson, John. General view of the agriculture of the county of Fife. Edinburgh, London Board of Agriculture and Internal Improvement. 1800. 8, 413 p.

Tivy, Joy. Four small Scottish burghs: an exercise in geographical field studies. Scottish Geographical Magazine. 77(1961): 148-164.

Tivy, Joy. Easter Ross: a residential crofting area. Scottish Studies. 9(1965): 64-84.

Trotter, James. General view of the agriculture of the county of West-Lothian. Edinburgh, London Board of Agriculture and Internal Improvement. 1811. 4, 340 p.

Tuckett, Angela. The Scottish carter. London, George Allen and Unwin. 1967. 448 p., plates.

Uhlig, Harald. Die ländliche Kulturlandschaft der Hebriden und der west-schottischen Hochlande. Erdkunde. 13(1959): 22-46.

Uhlig, Harald. Typen kleinbäuerlicher Siedlungen auf den Hebriden. Erdkunde. 13(1959): 98-124.

Ure, Rev. James. General view of the agriculture in the county of Dumbarton. London, Board of Agriculture and Internal Improvement. 1794. 106 p.

Vallee, F. G. Social structure and organisation in a Hebridean community. Unpublished Ph.D. dissertation. London, University of London. 1954. (Barra Island.)

*Vallee, F. G. Burial and mourning customs in a Hebridean community. J.R.A.I. 85(1955): 119-130.

Walker, John. An economical history of the Hebrides and highlands of Scotland. 2 vols. Edinburgh. 1808. (Another edition. 1812.)

Walton, J. Cruck-framed buildings in Scotland. Gwerin. 1, no. 3(1957): 109-122.

Walton, J. The Skye house. Antiquity. 31(1957): 155-162.

SCOTLAND

Walton, K. Population changes in north-east Scotland 1696-1951. Scottish Studies. 5 (1961): 149-180.

Wheeler, Philip T. The Sutherland crofting system. Scottish Studies. 8 (1964): 172-192.

Whitaker, Ian R. Two Hebridean corn-kilns. Gwerin. 1, no. 4 (Dec. 1957): 161-170.

Whitaker, Ian R. The harrow in Scotland. Scottish Studies. 2 (1958): 149-165.

Whitaker, Ian R. Some traditional techniques in modern Scottish farming. Scottish Studies. 3 (1959): 163-188.

Wilson, James. Farming in Aberdeenshire — ancient and modern. Transactions of the Highland and Agricultural Society of Scotland. 5th ser. 14 (1902): 76-102.

Cursiter, James W. List of books and pamphlets relating to Orkney and Shetland. Kirkwall, W. Peace & Son. 1894. 2, 1, 73 p.

---

*Banks, Mrs. M. Macleod. British calendar customs. Orkney and Shetland. London, The Folk-Lore Society. 1946. 12, 110 p.

Barclay, Robert S. The population of Orkney 1755-1961. A record of the parishes and islands. Kirkwall, W. R. MacKintosh, The Kirkwall Press. 1965. 28 p.

Barry, George. History of the Orkney Islands. Including a view of the manners and customs of their ancient and modern inhabitants . . . The present state of their agriculture; manufactures; fisheries; and commerce; and the means of their improvement. London, Longman, Hurst, Rees and Orme. 1805. 16, 512 p., map.

Black, G. F. Examples of printed folk-lore concerning the Orkney and Shetland Islands. London, The Folk-Lore Society. 1903. 277 p.

Brand, John. A brief description of Orkney, Zetland, Pightland-Firth & Caithness . . . Edinburgh, G. Mosman. 1701. 6, 50, 159 p.

Coleman, Stanley Jackson, comp. Lore of Orkney and Shetland. Douglas, Isle of Man, Folklore Academy. 1959. 13 p.

Coull, James R. Population trends and structure on the island of Westray, Orkney. Scottish Studies. 10 (1966): 69-77.

*Dennison, Walter Trail. Orkney folklore and tradition. Edited by Ernest W. Marwick. Kirkwall, The Herald Press. 1961. 16, 96 p. (A reprinting of a series of articles published over sixty years ago.)

Fea, James. Considerations on the fisheries in the Scotch islands: to which is prefixed a general account elucidating the history, soil, productions, curiosities, &c, of the same, the manners of the inhabitants &c. London, printed for the author. 1787. 7, 101, 88, 6 p., folding map.

Fenton, Alexander. Early and traditional cultivating implements in Scotland. Proceedings of the Society of Antiquaries of Scotland. 98 (1962-1963): 264-317. 7 plates, 21 figs.

Firth, John. Reminiscences of an Orkney parish. Stromness, W. R. Randall. 1920. 8, 158 p.

Garson, J. G. Exhibition of lamps from the Orkney Islands. J.A.I. 13 (1884): 275-276.

Gorrie, Daniel. Summers and winters in the Orkneys. London, Hodder and Stoughton. 1868. 7, 384 p.

Groundwater, Henrietta. Everyday food in 19th-century Orkney. Scottish Home and Country. 38 (1962): 105-106, 321.

Groundwater, Henrietta. Memories of an Orkney family. Kirkwall, The Kirkwall Press. 1967. 42 p.

Gunn, John. The Orkney book: readings for young Orcadians. London and New York, Nelson. 1909. 448 p.

Gunn, John. Orkney, the magnetic north. London, T. Nelson & Sons. 1932. 286 p.

Hossack, Buckham Hugh. Kirkwall in the Orkneys . . . with maps and illustrations. Kirkwall, W. Peace & Son. 1900. 18, 490 p.

*Leask, J. T. Smith. A peculiar people, and other Orkney tales. Kirkwall, W. R. Mackintosh. 1931. 280 p.

Low, George. A tour through the Islands of Orkney and Schetland containing hints relative to their ancient, modern and natural history . . . Kirkwall, W. Peace & Son. 1879. 24, 223 p.

Mackintosh, William R. Glimpses of Kirkwall and its people in olden time. Kirkwall, W. R. Mackintosh. 1887.

Mackintosh, William R. Around the Orkney peat fires: being sketches of notable Orcadians, smuggling, anecdotes . . . and other stories. 3d ed. Kirkwall, W. R. Mackintosh. 1914. 365 p. (Later editions also exist.)

Marwick, Hugh. Orkney. London, R. Hale. 1951. 8, 287 p., 48 illus., map.

Marwick, Hugh. Orkney farm names. Kirkwall, W. R. Mackintosh. 1952. 6, 267 p.

Mather, J. Y. Boats and boatmen of Orkney and Shetland. Scottish Studies. 8 (1964): 19-32.

Monteith, Robert, of Eglish and Gairsa. The description of the Isles of Orkney and Zetland . . . Edinburgh, published by S(ir) R.(obert) S.(ibbald). 1711. folio. (Reprinted in Edinburgh. 1845.)

Neill, Patrick. A tour through some of the islands of Orkney and Shetland . . . Edinburgh, A. Constable. 1806. 11, 239 p.

O'Dell, A. C. The geographical controls of agriculture in Orkney and Shetland. Economic Geography. 11(1935): 1-19.

Olcott, Charles S. The Orkneys and Shetlands: a mysterious group of islands. National Geographic Magazine. 39(1921): 197-228.

Orkney and Shetland Miscellany. Title changed, April 1909, to Old-Lore Miscellany of Orkney, Shetland, Caithness and Sutherland. 10 vols. London, Viking Society for Northern Research. 1907-1909, 1909-

Peterkin, Alexander. Notes on Orkney and Zetland; illustrative of the history, antiquities, scenery, and customs of those islands. Vol. 1. (No more were published.) Edinburgh, Macredie, Skelly. 1822.

Robertson, J. Uppies and doonies. Aberdeen, Aberdeen University Press. 1967. 239 p. (Folk football.)

Roussell, Aage. Norse building customs in the Scottish isles. Copenhagen, Levin & Munksgaard; London, Williams and Norgate. 1934. 113 p., 56 illus.

Shearer, John, ed. The new Orkney book. London, Nelson. 1966. 183 p., 17 plates, maps.

Shirreff, John. General view of the agriculture of the Orkney Islands. Edinburgh, London Board of Agriculture. 1814. 9, 195, 66, 12 p.

Simpson, E. J. Farm carts and waggons of the Orkney Islands: the introduction and development of wheeled vehicles in Orkney in the eighteenth and nineteenth centuries. Scottish Studies. 7 (1963): 154-169.

Smith, Charles Sprague. Orkneys and Shetland. Bulletin of the American Geographical Society. 23(1891): 131-155.

Sutherland, Douglas. Against the wind: an Orkney idyll. London, Heinemann. 1966. 210 p., 8 plates.

Tudor, John R. The Orkneys and Shetland: their past and present state . . . London, E. Stanford. 1883. 33, 703 p.

Cursiter, James W. List of books and pamphlets relating to Orkney and Shetland. Kirkwall, W. Peace & Son. 1894. 2, 1, 73 p.

Anon. Shetland marriages. Chambers Journal. 12(1859): 383-384.

*Banks, Mrs. M. Macleod. British calendar customs. Orkney and Shetland. London, The Folk-Lore Society. 1946. 12, 110 p.

Black, G. F. Examples of printed folk-lore concerning the Orkney and Shetland Islands. County Folk-Lore, Vol. 3. Printed Extracts No. 5. London, The Folk-Lore Society. 1903. 277 p.

Brand, John. A brief description of Orkney, Zetland, Pightland-Firth & Caithness . . . Edinburgh, G. Mosman. 1701. 6, 50, 159 p.

Cluness, Andrew T. The Shetland Isles. London, Hale. 1951. 12, 308 p., 49 plates, map.

Cluness, Andrew T., ed. The Shetland book. Lerwick, The Shetland Times. 1967. 9, 174 p., illus.

Coleman, Stanley J., comp. Lore of Orkney and Shetland. Douglas, Isle of Man, Folklore Academy. 1954. 13 p.

Cowie, Robert. Shetland: descriptive and historical; being a graduation thesis on the inhabitants of the Shetland Islands; and a topographical description of that country . . . Aberdeen, Lewis Smith. 1871. 16, 309 p.

Donaldson, G. Shetland life under Earl Patrick. Edinburgh, Oliver and Boyd. 1958. 8, 150 p., 19 plates, map.

Edmondston, Arthur. A view of the ancient and present state of the Zetland Islands; including their civil, political, and natural history; antiquities; and an account of their agriculture, fisheries, commerce, and the state of society and manners. 2 vols. Edinburgh, J. Ballyntine for Longman, Hurst, Rees, and Orme. 1809.

Edmondston, Biot, and Jessie M. E. Saxby. The home of a naturalist. London, Nisbet. 1888. 395 p.

Edmondston, Mrs. Eliza McBriar. Sketches and tales of the Shetland Islands. Edinburgh, Sutherland & Knox. 1856. 7, 256 p.

Eunson, J. The Fair Isle fishing-marks. Scottish Studies. 5(1961): 181-198.

Fea, James. Considerations on the fisheries in the Scotch islands: to which is prefixed a general account elucidating the history, soil, productions, curiosities &c. of the same, the manners of the inhabitants &c. London, printed for the author. 1787. 8, 101, 88, (6) p., folding map.

Fea, James. The present state of the Orkney Islands considered, and an account of the new method of fishing on the coasts of Shetland. Edinburgh, W. Brown. 1884. 1, 1, 6, 160 p. (The original edition was published in 1775.)

Fenton, Alexander. Early and traditional cultivating implements in Scotland. Proceedings of the Society of Antiquaries of Scotland. 96 (1962-1963): 264-317, 7 plates.

Fenton, Alexander, and J. J. Laurenson. Peat in Fetlar. Folk Life. 2 (1964): 3-26.

Fraser, Peter. Old time Shetland day wedding. Shetland Folk Book. 3 (1957): 57-62.

Goffman, Erving. Communication conduct in an island community. Unpublished Ph. D. dissertation in sociology. Chicago, University of Chicago. 1953.

Goffman, Erving. The presentation of self in everyday life. New York, Doubleday. 1959. 15, 255 p. (The author quotes many examples from his dissertation.)

Goudie, Gilbert. On the horizontal water mills of Shetland. Proceedings of the Society of Antiquaries of Scotland. N. S. 8 (1885): 257-297.

Grimshaw, T. H. Memories of the Shetland Islands: the delineation of an afterglow. New York, Exposition Press. 1955. 72 p.

*Halcrow, Adam. The sail fishermen of Shetland and their Norse and Dutch forerunners. Lerwick, T. & J. Manson. 1950. 15, 187 p.

Hibbert-Ware, Samuel. A description of the Shetland Islands, comprising an account of their geology, scenery, antiquities, and superstitions. Edinburgh, A. Constable. 1822. 18, 616 p.

Jakobsen, Jakob. The place-names of Shetland. (Translated by Anna Horsbøl.) London and Copenhagen, David Nutt. 1936. 12, 273 p., map.

Jamieson, Peter Andrew. Letters on Shetland. Edinburgh, Moray Press. 1949. 272 p.

SHETLAND ISLANDS

Livingston, William P. Shetland and the Shetlanders. London, Nelson. 1947.
10, 229 p., plates.

Low, George. A tour through the Islands of Orkney and Shetland containing
hints relative to their ancient, modern and natural history . . . Kirkwall,
W. Peace & Son. 1879. 24, 223 p.

Macgillivray, James. Agriculture in Shetland. Scottish Journal of Agriculture. 3 (1920): 414-428.

Maclean, Calum I., and Stewart F. Sanderson. A collection of riddles from
Shetland. Scottish Studies. 4 (1960): 150-186.

Mather, J. Y. Boats and boatmen of Orkney and Shetland. Scottish Studies.
8 (1964): 19-32.

Moffat, William. Shetland: the isles of nightless summer. London, Heath,
Cranton. 1934. 239 p., plates.

Monteith, Robert (of Eglisha and Gairsa). The description of the isles of
Orkney and Zetland . . . Edinburgh, published by S(ir) R(obert) S(ibbald).
1711. folio. (Another edition. Edinburgh. 1845.)

Murison, David D. Shetland speech today. [Annales Societatis Scientarum
Faeroensis]. Foeroya Frodskaparfelag, Annales 13 (1964): 122-129.

Neill, Patrick. A tour through some of the islands of Orkney and Shetland . . .
Edinburgh, A. Constable. 1806. 11, 239 p.

Nicholson, John. Some folk-tales & legends of Shetland. Edinburgh, Thomas
Allan & Sons. 1920. 93 p.

Nicholson, John. Shetland folk tales. Shetland Folk Book. 1 (1947): 1-16.

O'Dell, Andrew Charles. The geographical controls of agriculture in Orkney
and Shetland. Economic Geography. 11 (1935): 1-19.

O'Dell, Andrew Charles. A historical geography of the Shetland Isles.
Lerwick, T. & J. Manson. 1939. 19, 327 p.

Olcott, Charles S. The Orkneys and Shetlands: a mysterious group of islands.
National Geographic Magazine. 39 (1921): 197-228.

Orkney and Shetland Miscellany. Title changed, April 1909, to Old-Lore
Miscellany of Orkney, Shetland, Caithness and Sutherland. 10 vols.
London, Viking Society for Northern Research. 1907-1909, 1909-

Peterkin, Alexander. Notes on Orkney and Zetland; illustrative of the history, antiquities, scenery, and customs of those islands. Vol. 1. (No more were published.) Edinburgh, Macredie, Skelly. 1822.

Reid, John T. Art rambles in Shetland. Edinburgh, Edmonston and Douglas. 1869. 12, 62, [2] p., illus., map.

Robert, Ian McIntosh. Unst. Unpublished dissertation. Glasgow, University of Glasgow, Department of Geography. 1959.

Roussell, Aage. Norse building customs in the Scottish isles. Copenhagen, Levin & Munksgaard; London, Williams and Norgate. 1934. 113 p., 56 illus.

Saxby, Jessie M. E. Shetland traditional lore. Edinburgh, Grant & Murray. 1932. 208 p.

Seim, Einar. Shetland food in former times. Shetland Folk Book. 4 (1964): 13-16.

Shetland Folk Book. 4 volumes to date. Lerwick, The Shetland Times (for the Shetland Folk Society). 1947, 1951, 1957, 1964.

Shirreff, John. General view of the agriculture of the Shetland Islands. London, Board of Agriculture. 1814. 7, 135 p., 63 p. appendix, 8 p. index.

Sill, Ronnie. Counterspell: An eye-witness account of witchcraft at work. Shetland Folk Book. 4 (1964): 31-40.

Sinclair, Catherine. Shetland and Shetlanders. Edinburgh, W. Whyte; New York, R. Caiter. 1840. 4, 428 p.

Smith, Charles S. Orkneys and Shetland. Bulletin of the American Geographical Society. 23 (1891): 131-155.

Smith, Magnie. Shetland croft houses and their equipment. Shetland Folk Book. 4 (1964): 1-8.

Spence, J. Shetland folklore. Lerwick, Johnson & Greig. 1899. 256 p.

Stephen, Robert. Shetland fishing industry. A study in geographical controls. Unpublished dissertation. Aberdeen, University of Aberdeen, Department of Geography. 1962.

Svensson, Roland. Lonely isles. Being an account of several voyages to the Hebrides and Shetland. (Translated by Albert Read.) London, B. T. Batsford. 1955. 138 p.

Tait, E. S. Reid. A Shetland steading. Shetland Folk Book. 2 (1951): 77-82.

Tait, E. S. Reid. Some notes on the harvest and harvest customs of bygone days. Shetland Folk Book. 3 (1957): 17-20.

Train, Vera. An island in Shetland. Scotland's Magazine. 59 (1963): 14-20. (Fetlar Island.)

Tudor, John R. Orkneys and Shetland: Their past and present state . . . London, E. Stanford. 1883. 33, 703 p.

Venables, Ursula. Tempestuous Eden. London, The Museum Press. 1952. 238 p.

*Venables, Ursula. Life in Shetland, a world apart. Edinburgh, Oliver & Boyd. 1956. 175 p., illus.

Watterson, George. Fair Isle. Scottish Geographical Magazine. 62 (1946): 111-116.

*Wheeler, P. T. The island of Unst, Shetland. Nottingham, Geographical Field Group, University of Nottingham. 1964. 92 p., 49 p. of maps and diagrams, 34 tables.

Yarham, E. R. Shetland's Viking fire festival. American Scandinavian Review. 44 (1956): 319-324.

Arnot, Robert Page. South Wales miners. A history of the South Wales Miners Federation 1898-1914. London, George Allen and Unwin. 1967. 390 p., plates.

Ashby, Arthur W., and I. L. Evans. The agriculture of Wales. Cardiff, University of Wales Press. 1944. 300 p.

Baring-Gould, Sabine. A book of North Wales. London, Methuen. 1903. 10, 317 p.

Baring-Gould, Sabine. A book of South Wales. London, Methuen. 1905. 332 p.

Bagenal, H. The smaller house and its significance. Antiquity. 29(1955): 215-225. (Fifteenth-seventeenth centuries.)

Bingley, Rev. W. North Wales; including its scenery, antiquities, customs, and some sketches of its natural history. 2 vols. London, T. N. Longman and O. Rees. 1804. 20, 464; 12, 450 p.

Blake, Lois. Welsh folk dance and costume. Llangollen, North Wales, Gwynn. 1954. 24 p.

Borrow, George Henry. Wild Wales: its people, language, and scenery. 3 vols. London, J. Murray. 1862. (Many later reprints and editions of this volume. The most common reprint is: Wild Wales. New York, E. P. Dutton. 1928. 22, 617 p.)

*Brennan, Tom, et al. Social change in south-west Wales. London, Watts. 1954. 200 p.

Bowen, Emrys George. Wales: a study in geography and history. Cardiff, University of Wales Press. 1941. 16, 182 p.

Carter, Harold. The towns of Wales: a study in urban geography. Cardiff, University of Wales Press. 1965. 18, 360 p., 100 maps and diagrams, 15 plates.

Crooke, W. Betrothal customs in north Wales. Folk-Lore. 27 (1916): 432.

Davies, Elwyn. The Black Mountain; a study in rural life and economy. Carmarthenshire Antiquarian Society and Field Club. Transactions. 64 (1937): 53-64, maps.

*Davies, Elwyn, and Alwyn D. Rees. Welsh rural communities. Cardiff, University of Wales Press. 1960. 11, 254 p. (Reprinted 1965.)

Davies, Jonathan Cedrig. Folklore of west and mid-Wales. Aberystwyth, Printed at the "Welsh Gazette" offices. 1911. 10, 348 p.

Davies, Sir Leonard Twiston. Welsh life in the 18th century. London, Country Life. 1939. 12, 243 p.

Davies, Walter. General view of the agriculture and domestic economy of North Wales . . . London, Richard Phillips. 1810. 16, 510 p.

Davies, Walter. General view of the agriculture and domestic economy of South Wales . . . 2 vols. London, G. and W. Nicol. 1814.

Defoe, Daniel. A tour through England and Wales . . . 2 vols. London, J. M. Dent; New York, E. P. Dutton. 1935. (Many other editions of this work exist.)

Ellis, Thomas Peter. Welsh tribal law and custom in the Middle Ages. 2 vols. Oxford, The Clarendon Press. 1926.

Emmett, Isabel. Peacetime partisans in Wales. New Society. 1, no. 17 (Jan. 24, 1963): 16-17.

*Emmett, Isabel. A North Wales village; a social anthropological study. London, Routledge & Kegan Paul. 1964. 19, 154 p.

England, Edward. The mountain that moved. Grand Rapids, Mich., William B. Eerdmans. 1967. 126 p., plate (The Aberfan disaster and the children.)

Etheridge, Ken. Welsh costume. Ammanford, Wales, published by the author. 1958. 70 p.

*Evans, Eric Wyn. The miners of South Wales. Cardiff, University of Wales Press. 1961. 10, 274 p.

Evans, Hugh. The Gorse Glenn. Translated from the Welsh. Liverpool, Brython Press. 1948. 11, 211 p.

Evans-Wentz, Walter Y. The fairy-faith in Celtic countries. London, Frowde. 1911: 135-163. (Reprinted. New Hyde Park, N.Y. University Books. 1966.)

Fleure, Herbert John. The races of England and Wales; a survey of recent research. London, Benn Bros. 1923. 118 p.

Fleure, Herbert John. Wales and her people. Wexham, Hugh & Son. 1926. 20 p.

*Frankenberg, Ronald. Village on the border. A social study of religion, politics and football in a North Wales community. London, Cohen and West. 1957. 163 p.

Frankenberg, Ronald. Communities in Britain. Social life in town and country. Harmondsworth and Baltimore, Penguin Books. 1966. (Pages 45-65, 86-112.)

Giraldus Cambrensis. The itinerary of Archbishop Baldwin through Wales A.D. MCLXXXVIII. 2 vols. London, printed for W. Miller by W. Bulmer. 1806. (Twelfth century.)

Giraldus Cambrensis. The itinerary through Wales and the description of Wales. London and Toronto, J. M. Dent & Sons; New York, E. P. Dutton. 1935. 22, 210 p.

Glanffrwd, William Thomas. Llanwynno. Edited by Henry Lewis (in Welsh). Cardiff, University of Wales Press. 1949. 264 p. (Nineteenth-century folk life in a South Wales parish.)

Glynne-Jones, W. Legends of the Welsh hills. London, Mowbray. 1957. 9, 108 p.

Graves, Ralph H. A short visit to Wales . . . National Geographic Magazine. 44(1923): 635-675.

Griffith, Llewelyn Wyn. Spring of youth. New York, E. P. Dutton. 1935. 8, 134 p.

Griffith, Llewelyn Wyn. The Welsh. Harmondsworth, Penguin Books. 1950. 183 p.

Griffith, Llewelyn Wyn. The Welsh. 2d ed. Cardiff, University of Wales Press. 1964. 186 p.

Gwynn, Gwenith. "Besom wedding" in the Ceirog Valley. Folk-Lore. 39(1928): 149-166.

Harris, Christopher, and Colin Rosser. Family and social change. A study of family and kinship in a South Wales town. London, Routledge & Kegan Paul. 1965. 14, 337 p.

Howells, William. Cambrian superstitions, comprising ghosts, omens, witchcraft, traditions, etc. To which are added a concise view of the manners and customs of the principality, and some fugitive pieces. London, Longman. 1831. 194 p.

Hughes, Cledwyn. The northern marches. London, R. Hale. 1953. 218 p.

WALES

Hughes, Cledwyn. Poaching down the Dee. London, R. Hale. 1953. 224 p.

Hughes, Cledwyn. Royal Wales: the land and its people. London, Phoenix House. 1957. 204 p.

Hughes, Henry. Immortal sails: a story of a Welsh port & some of its ships. London, R. Ross. 1946. 240 p. (Portmodoc, Wales.)

Jenkins, Geraint. Agricultural transport in Wales. Cardiff, National Museum of Wales, Welsh Folk Museum. 1962. 107 p., 31 plates, fig.

Jennings, Hilda. Brynmawr: a study of a distressed area, based on the results of the social survey carried out by the Brynmawr Community Council. London, Allens. 1934. 11, 246 p.

John, Arthur Henry. The industrial revolution in South Wales, 1750-1850. Cardiff, University of Wales Press. 1950. 10, 201 p.

Jones, Daniel Parry. Welsh country upbringing. 2d ed. London, B. T. Batsford. 1949. 144 p.

Jones, Daniel Parry. Welsh country characters. London and New York, B. T. Batsford. 1952. 174 p.

Jones, Emrys. "Tregaron": a sociological study of a Welsh rural community. Unpublished doctoral dissertation in sociology. Cardiff, University of Wales. 1947.

Jones, Francis. The holy wells of Wales. Cardiff, University of Wales Press. 1954. 21, 226 p., 6 maps.

Jones, G. R. J. Some mediaeval rural settlements in North Wales. Institute of British Geographers, Transactions and Papers. 19 (1953): 51-72.

Kay, George. General view of the agriculture of North Wales (Anglesey, Caernarvonshire, Denbighshire, Flintshire, Merionethshire, Montgomery-shire) . . . 7 parts. Edinburgh, London Board of Agriculture and Internal Improvement. 1794.

Loudon, J. B. Kinship and crisis in South Wales. B.J.S. 12(1961): 333-350.

Loudon, J. B. Religious order and mental disorder: a study in a south Wales rural community. In Michael Banton, ed. The social anthropology of complex societies. London, Tavistock Publications. 1966: 69-96.

Martin, Violet Florence. Beggars on horseback; a riding tour in North Wales. Edinburgh and London, W. Blackwood & Sons. 1895. 6, 186 p.

Morgan, Thomas John. Peasant culture. Swansea, University College. 1962. 28 p.

Nicholas, Thomas. The history and antiquities of Glamorganshire and its families. London, Longmans, Green. 1847. 194 p.

Nicholas, Thomas. Annals and antiquities of the counties and county families of Wales: containing a record of all ranks of the gentry . . . with many ancient pedigrees and memorials of old and extinct families. 2 vols. London, Longmans, Green, Reader. 1872.

North, F. J. Sunken cities: some legends of the coast and lakes of Wales. Cardiff, University of Wales Press. 1957. 256 p.

*Owen, Trefor M. Welsh folk customs. Cardiff, National Museum of Wales, Welsh Folk Museum. 1959. 258 p.

Owen, Trefor M. A Breckonshire marriage custom. Folklore. 72 (1961): 372-384.

Owen, Trefor M. West Glamorgan customs. Folk Life. 3 (1965): 46-54.

Payne, F. G. Guide to the collection of samplers and embroideries. Cardiff, Welsh Folk Museum. 1939. 92 p., 20 plates.

Payne, F. G. Yr aradr gymreig. Cardiff, University of Wales Press. 1954. 205 p. (The Welsh plow.)

Payne, F. G. Welsh peasant costume. Folk Life. 2 (1964): 42-57.

Payne, F. G. Welsh peasant costume. Cardiff, Welsh Folk Museum. 1964. 16 p., 7 plates.

Peate, Iowerth Cyfeiliog. Guide to the collection of Welsh bygones. A descriptive account of old-fashioned life in Wales . . . together with a catalogue of the objects exhibited. Cardiff, National Museum of Wales. 1929. 21, 148 p.

Peate, Iowerth Cyfeiliog. Guide to the collection illustrating Welsh folk crafts and industries . . . 2d ed. Cardiff, National Museum of Wales. 1945. 13, 72 p., 16 plates.

Peate, Iowerth Cyfeiliog. The Welsh house. London, Honourable Society of Cymmrodorion. 1940. 18, 232 p., 86 plates. (2d ed. Liverpool, Brython Press. 1946. 18, 204 p.)

Peate, Iowerth Cyfeiliog. Clock and watch makers in Wales. Cardiff, National Museum of Wales. 1945. 6, 85 p., 7 plates. (2d ed. 1960. 6, 108 p., 7 plates.)

Peate, Iowerth Cyfeiliog. Welsh musical instruments. Man. 47(1947): 21-25, plate B.

Plowman, D. E. G. Local social status in England and Wales. Sociological Review. N.S. 10(1962): 161-202.

Rees, Alwyn D. Alternate generations in Wales. Man. 38(1938): 143-144.

*Rees, Alwyn D. Life in a Welsh countryside, a social study of Llanfihangel yng Ngwynfa. Cardiff, University of Wales Press. 1950. 188 p., 35 figs., 12 plates. (Reprinted. 1961.)

Rhys, John. Celtic folklore, Welsh and Manx. 2 vols. Oxford, The Clarendon Press. 1901.

Rosser, Colin, and C. C. Harris. Relationships through marriage in a Welsh urban area. Sociological Review. N.S. 9 (1961): 293-321.

*Rosser, Colin, and C. C. Harris. The family and social change: a study of family and kinship in a South Wales town. London, Routledge and Kegan Paul. 1965. 337 p.

Sayce, R. U. Welsh calendar customs. Committee on Welsh Calendar Customs. Montgomeryshire Collections. 50(1948): 92-119.

Seebohm, Frederic. The tribal system in Wales. London, New York, Longmans, Green. 1895. 14, 238 p.

*Sikes, Wirt. British Goblins: Welsh folk-lore, fairy mythology, legends and traditions. London, Sampson Low; Boston, J. R. Osgood. 1880. 16, 412 p. (Reprinted 1881.)

Sikes, Wirt. Rambles and studies in old South Wales. London, Sampson Low. 1881. 16, 304 p.

Stanyer, Jeffrey. County government in England and Wales. London, Routledge and Kegan Paul. 1967. 12, 116 p.

Thomas, Dylan. A child's Christmas in Wales. Norfolk, Conn., New Directions. 1954. 31 p.

Thomas, Maude Morgan. When I was a girl in Wales. New York, Lothrop, Lee & Shepard. 1936. 161 p.

Thurlow Craig, Charles William. The up-country book. London, Andre Deutsch. 1964. 208 p.

Trevelyan, Marie. Glimpses of Welsh life and character. London, J. Hogg. 1893. 6, 406 p.

Trevelyan, Marie. Folk-lore and folk-stories of Wales. London, Eliot Stock. 1909. 13, 350 p.

Vaughan, Herbert M. The South Wales squires. London, Methuen. 1926. 5, 216 p.

Welsh Folk Museum, St. Fagans. Handbook. Cardiff, Welsh Folk Museum. 1965. 32 p.

Williams, A. Bailey. Courtship and marriage in the late nineteenth century in Montgomeryshire. Montgomeryshire Collections. 51 (1950): 116-125.

Williams, A. Bailey. Customs and traditions connected with sickness, death and burial in Montgomeryshire in the late nineteenth century. Montgomeryshire Collections. 52 (1951-1952): 51-61.

Williams, C. R. The Welsh religious revival, 1904-5. B.J.S. 3 (1952): 242-259.

Williams, John David. The old Welsh farmhouse. London, Harrap. 1961. 238 p.

Cubbon, William. A bibliographical account of works relating to the Isle of Man . . . 2 vols. London, Oxford University Press, H. Milford. 1933, 1939. 1180 p.

---

*Birch, Jack William. The Isle of Man: a study in economic geography. Cambridge, published for the University of Bristol at the University Press. 1964. 15, 204 p.

Clague, John. Cooinaghtyn Manninagh. Manx Reminiscences. (In Manx and English.) Castletown, Isle of Man, M. J. Blackwell. 1911. 13, 265 p.

Clorett, J. Ancient aires of [the Isle of] Man. Countryman. 50 (1954): 85-87.

Cumming, Joseph G. The Isle of Man: its history, physical, ecclesiastical, civil and legendary. London, J. van Voorst. 1848. 36, 376 p.

Davies, Arthur S. The "mheillea" and its meaning. A note on the harvest in olden times in the Isle of Man and other Celtic countries. Iver Heath, A. Stanley Davies. 1949. 28 p.

Douglas, M. The Manx dirk dance as ritual. Journal of the International Folk Music Council. 9 (1957): 31-34.

Evans-Wentz, Walter Y. The fairy faith in Celtic countries. London, Frowde. 1911: 117-135. (Reprinted. New Hyde Park, N.Y. University Books. 1966.)

Farrant, Reginald D. Mann, its land tenure, constitution, lords rent and deemsters. London, Humphrey Milford. 1937. 83 p.

Feltham, John. A tour through the Isle of Mann in 1797 and 1798; comprising sketches of the ancient and modern history, constitution, laws, commerce, agriculture, fishing, &. Bath, R. Cruttwell. 1798. 7, 294 p.

Forrest, Katherine A. Manx recollections. London, J. Nisbet. 1894. 12, 341 p.

Gill, William Walter. A Manx scrapbook. London, Arrowsmith. 1929. 531 p.

Gill, William Walter. A second Manx scrapbook. London, Arrowsmith. 1932. 478 p.

Gill, William Walter. A third Manx scrapbook. London, Arrowsmith. 1963. 416 p.

Herbert, Agnes, and Donald Maxwell. The Isle of Man. London, The Bodley Head. 1909. (Reprinted 1926. 16, 270 p.)

Kinvig, R. H. A history of the Isle of Man. 3d ed. Liverpool, Liverpool University Press. 1966. 8, 200 p.

McClintock, H. F. Old Irish and highland dress and that of the Isle of Man. 2d ed. Dundalk, Dundalgan Press. 1950. 141 p., illus.

Manx Museum and National Trust. A guide to the Manx Museum. 2d ed. Douglas, Manx Museum and National Trust. 1963. 28 p.

Manx Museum and National Trust. A guide to the Manx Open-Air Folk Museum. Cregneash. Douglas, Manx Museum and National Trust. 1964. 24 p., illus.

Megaw, B. R. S. The "Manks spade." Journal of the Manx Museum. 4(1939): 165-170, plate 174.

Megaw, B., and E. Megaw. The development of the Manx fishing craft. Proceedings of the Isle of Man Natural History and Antiquarian Society. 5(1950-1952): 250-260.

Moore, Arthur William. Surnames & placenames of the Isle of Man. London, E. Stock. 1890. 14, 372 p.

Moore, Arthur William. The folklore of the Isle of Man . . . Douglas, Isle of Man, Brown & Son; London, D. Nutt. 1891. 192 p.

Moore, Arthur William. Manx ballads and music. Douglas, Isle of Man, G. & R. Johnson. 1896. 36, 265 p.

Müller, Harold. It's a fact. 400 illuminating facts relative to the Isle of Man. Douglas, Isle of Man, Examiner. 1949. 64 p.

*Paton, C. I., ed. Manx calendar customs. London, The Folk-Lore Society. 1943. 160 p.

Quayle, Basil. General view of the agriculture of the Isle of Man . . . London, Board of Agriculture. 1794. 40 p.

Rhys, Sir John. Celtic folklore, Welsh and Manx. 2 vols. London, Henry Frowde; Oxford, The Clarendon Press. 1901. 43, 718 p.

Roeder, Charles, ed. Manx notes and queries . . . Douglas, S. K. Broadbent, "Isle of Man Examiner" office. 1904. 155, 16 p.

Stenning, E. H. Isle of Man. London, Hale. 1950. 13, 448 p., plate.

Train, Joseph. An historical and statistical account of the Isle of Man, from the earliest times to the present date; with a view of the ancient laws, peculiar customs, and popular superstitions. 2 vols. Douglas, Isle of Man, M. A. Quiggin; London, Simpkin Marshall. 1845.

Waldron, George. Description of the Isle of Man: with some useful and entertaining reflections on the law, customs, and manners of the inhabitants. Douglas, printed for the Manx Society. 1865. 155 p.

Baring-Gould, Sabine. Cornish characters and strange events. London, New York, J. Lane. 1909. 774 p.

Baring-Gould, Sabine. Songs of the west: traditional ballads and songs of the west of England, with their traditional melodies. London, Methuen. 1913. 447 p.

Barton, Denys Bradford, ed. Historic Cornish mining scenes underground. Truro, D. Bradford Barton. 1967. 56 p., 50 plates. (Photographs taken in the late 1890s.)

Berry, Calude. Cornwell. London, Robert Hale. 1949. 14, 252 p., maps.

Borlase, William. The Islands of Scilly. Newcastle upon Tyne, Frank Graham. 1966. 48 p., map, 1 folding plate. (Reproduction of 1756 ed.)

Bottrell, William. Traditions and hearthside stories of West Cornwall. Penzance, printed for the author by W. Cornish. 1870. 287 p.

Bottrell, William. Traditions and hearthside stories of West Cornwall. 2d ser. Penzance, printed for the author by Beare and Son. 1873. 298 p.

Bottrell, William. Cornish drolls. Compiled from Bottrell [i.e. W. Bottrell's "Traditions and hearthside stories of West Cornwall"] by Sarah L. Enys. Plymouth, W. Brendon & Son. 1931. 288 p.

Burrow, J. C., and W. Thomas. 'Mongst mines and miners. Truro, D. Bradford Barton. 1965. 40 p., 24 plates.

Couch, Jonathan. The history of Polperro, a fishing town on the south coast of Cornwall; being a description of the place, its people, their manners, customs, modes of industry, &c . . . Truro and London, W. Lake. 1871. 6, 216 p.

Courtney, Margaret Ann. Cornish feasts and "festen" customs. Folk-Lore Journal. 4 (1886): 221-249.

Courtney, Margaret Ann. Cornish folk-lore. Folk-Lore Journal. 5 (1887): 14-61, 85-112, 177-220.

Courtney, Margaret Ann. Cornish feasts and folk-lore. Penzance, Beare and Son. 1890. 8, 208 p.

Devon and Cornwall Notes and Queries. Vol. 1 (1900):- Exeter. (There are 40 volumes so far.)

Devonshire, Elizabeth. Delabole—my village. Old Cornwall. 6 (1964): 270-276.

Dexter, Thomas F. G. Cornish names. An attempt to explore over 1,600 Cornish names. London, Longmans, Green. 1926. 90 p.

Edmonds, Richard. The Land's End district: its antiquities, natural history, natural phenomena and scenery. London, J. R. Smith. 1862. 269 p.

Evans-Wentz, Walter Y. The fairy-faith in Celtic countries. London, Frowde. 1911: 163-185. (Reprinted. New Hyde Park, N.Y., University Books. 1966.)

Exeter. University. Survey Committee. Devon and Cornwall: a preliminary survey. A report issued by the survey committee of the University of the South West. Exeter. Exeter, A. Wheaton. 1947. 318 p., 38 figs., 13 maps.

Fraser, Robert. General view of the agriculture in the county of Cornwall. London, London Board of Agriculture. 1794.

Gibson, Alexander G., and Herbert J. The Isles of Scilly. St. Mary's, Gibson & Sons. 1932. 10, 171 p. (Later editions.)

Heath, Robert. A natural and historical account of the Islands of Scilly, and . . . a general account of Cornwall. London, R. Manby and H. S. Cox. 1750. 16, 13, 456 p.

Heath, Robert. Account of the Isles of Scilly. Newcastle upon Tyne, Frank Graham. 1967. 96 p., map. (A reprint of the 1750 edition.)

Hudson, William Henry. The Land's End; a naturalist's impression in West Cornwall. New York, A. A. Knopf. 1927. 11, 299 p.

*Hunt, Robert. Popular romances of the west of England or the drolls, traditions, and superstitions of old Cornwall. London, Chatto and Windus. 1923. 480 p. (A reprint of the 3d ed. of 1881.)

*Jenkins, Alfred Kenneth H. The Cornish miner: an account of his life above and underground from early times. London, G. Allen and Unwin. 1927. 351 p.

*Jenkins, Alfred Kenneth H. Cornish seafarers; the smuggling, wrecking and fishing life of Cornwall. London and Toronto, J. M. Dent and Sons. 1932. 219 p.

*Jenkins, Alfred Kenneth H. Cornwall and the Cornish; the story, religion, and folklore of the "western land." London and Toronto, J. M. Dent and Sons. 1933. 308 p.

*Jenkins, Alfred Kenneth H. Cornish homes and customs. London and Toronto, J. M. Dent and Sons. 1934. 272 p.

Jenkins, Alfred Kenneth H. The story of Cornwall. London and New York, T. Nelson and Sons. 1935. 152 p.

Jenkins, Alfred Kenneth H. Cornwall and its people: Cornish seafarers, Cornwall and the Cornish, Cornish homes and customs. London, J. M. Dent and Sons. 1945. 487 p.

Johns, Rev. Charles Alexander. A week in the Lizard. London, Christian Knowledge Society. 1848. 8, 322 p.

Journal of the Royal Institution of Cornwall. Vol. 1 (1864)- Truro, Cornwall.

Martin, Edith. Cornish recipes, ancient and modern. Truro, Cornwall Federation of Women's Institutes. 1929. 63 p. (The 23d ed., with supplement, was published in 1967. 78 p.)

Martin, Ernest. A wanderer in the west country. London, Phoenix House. 1951. 223 p.

Nance, R. Morton. Helston furry day. Journal of the Royal Institution of Cornwall. N. S. 4 (1961): 36-48.

Nicholas, T. J. Cornwall and the "cousin Jack." 2d ed. Ilfracombe (England), A. H. Stockwell. 1947. 236 p. (In poetic form, but containing much useful information.)

Noall, Cyril. The Cornish midsummer eve bonfire celebration. St. Ives, Federation of Old Cornwall Societies. 1963. 11 p.

Norden, John. Description of Cornwall. Newcastle upon Tyne, Frank Graham. 1965. 68 p., 10 maps. (Originally written in 1728.)

Old Cornwall. Vol. 1 (1925):- Published by the Federation of Old Cornwall Societies.

Penny, G. Witchery of the west, some legends of Cornwall. Penzance, Cornish Library. 1950. 64 p.

Pentraeth, Dolly (pseud). In a Cornish township with old vogue folk. London, T. Fisher Unwin. 1893. 243 p.

Pool, P. A. S. Witchcraft at Penzance. Old Cornwall. 6 (1964): 320-322. (Text of a pamphlet published in 1686.)

Quiller-Couch, Mabel. Cornwall's wonderland. London and Toronto, J. M. Dent & Sons. 1914. 7, 243 p.

Quiller-Couch, Mabel, and L. Quiller-Couch. Ancient and holy wells of Cornwall. London, C. J. Clark. 1894. 31, 217 p.

Rowe, John. Cornwall in the age of the industrial revolution. Liverpool, Liverpool University Press. 1953. 367 p.

Rowse, Alfred Leslie. Tudor Cornwall; portrait of a society. London, J. Cape. 1941. 462 p.

Rowse, Alfred Leslie. Cornish childhood. London, J. Cape. 1942. 282 p.

Shaw, Thomas. A history of Cornish Methodism. Truro, D. Bradford Barton. 1967. 145 p., 29 plates.

Spooner, B. C. The giants of Cornwall. Folklore. 76 (1965): 16-32.

Staniforth, Thomas (edited by Jean Hext). The Staniforth diary: a visit to Cornwall in 1800. Truro, D. Bradford Barton. 1966. 68 p., 7 plates, maps.

Thomas, A. C. Some notes on the folk-lore of the Camborne District. Camborne (Cornwall), Camborne Printing Co. 1950. 16 p.

Thomas, A. C. The folk-lore of the Camborne district. Annual Report of the Royal Cornwall Polytechnic Society (Falmouth) for 1950. 1951: 26-27. (Printed by the Camborne Printing Co., Camborne, Cornwall.)

Thomas, Charles. Studies in Cornish folk-lore: No. 1, the taboo. Camborne, Camborne Printing Co. 1951. 40 p.

Thomas, Charles. Studies in Cornish folk-lore: No. 2, the sacrifice. Camborne, Camborne Printing Co. 1952. 60 p.

Tonkin, J. C., and R. W. Tonkin. Guide to the Isles of Scilly. 3d ed. Penzance, F. Rodda. 1893. 129 p.

Tregarthen, Enys (collected by Elizabeth Yates). Piskey folk: a book of Cornish legends. New York, The John Day Co. 1940. 203 p.

Tregellas, John Tabios. Cornish tales, in prose and verse. Truro, J. R. Netherton. 1865. 192 p.

Tregellas, John Tabios. Peeps into the haunts and homes of the rural population of Cornwall, being reminiscences of Cornish character and characteristics. Truro, J. R. Netherton. 1868. 16, 144 p.

Tregellas, Walter H. Cornish worthies: sketches of some eminent Cornish men and families. 2 vols. London, E. Stock. 1884.

Vulliamy, Colwyn Edward. Unknown Cornwall. London, John Lane. 1925. 12, 246 p.

*Vyvyan, Clara Coltman. The Scilly Isles. London, R. Hale. 1953. 8, 243 p., plate.

*Vyvyan, Clara Coltman. A Cornish Year. London, P. Owen. 1958. 181 p., illus.

Warren, Clarence Henry. West country (Somerset, Devon, and Cornwall). London, B. T. Batsford. 1938. 7, 120 p.

Whitcombe, Mrs. Henry Pennell. Bygone days in Devonshire and Cornwall, with notes of existing superstitions and customs. London, R. Bentley and Son. 1874. 15, 276 p.

Woodley, Rev. George. A view of the present state of the Scilly Islands: exhibiting their vast importance to the British Empire; the improvements of which they are susceptible; . . . London, F. C. and J. Rivington. 1822. 18, 344 p.

Worgan, G. B. General view of the agriculture of the county of Cornwall. London, Board of Agriculture. 1811. 16, 192 p.

Ahier, Philip. Stories of the Jersey seas, of Jersey's coast and of Jersey seamen. St. Helier, Jersey, published by the author. 1956. 302 p.

Balleine, G. R. The Bailiwick of Jersey. London, Hodder and Stoughton.
1951. 170 p., 115 illus.

Bisson, Sidney. Jersey, our island. London, Batchworth. 1950. 224 p.,
illus.

Carey, Edith F. The Channel Islands. National Geographic Magazine.
38(1920): 142-164.

*Carteret, Allan R. de. The story of Sark, the island where time stands still.
London, P. Owen. 1956. 185 p., illus.

Coleman, Stanley J. Lore of the Channel Islands. Douglas, Isle of Man,
Folklore Academy. 1954. 17 p.

*Dalido, Pierre. Jersey, île agricole anglo normande; étude de sociographie.
Vannes, A. Chaumeron. 1951. 6, 450 p., illus., maps.

Dicey, Thomas. An historical account of Guernsey—from its first settlement
before the Norman conquest to the present time . . . to which is added,
some proper remarks on Jersey, & the other islands belonging to the crown of
Great Britain on the French coast. London, printed for the author. 1751.
24, 220 p.

Dunlop, Andrew. A contribution to the ethnology of Jersey. J.A.I. 22(1893):
335-345.

Durand, Ralph. Guernsey: present and past. An island where feudalism
lingers. Guernsey, Guernsey Press. 1933. 124 p.

*Fleure, Herbert J. Guernsey: a social study. John Rylands Library, Man-
chester, Bulletin. 26(1942): 57-81.

Hathaway, Dame Sibyl. Dame of Sark. London, Heinemann. 1961. 211 p.,
18 illus.

Horton, P. W. I. A short history and guide to Alderney. Alderney. 1951.
56 p.

Huray, C. P. le. The Bailiwick of Guernsey. London, Hodder and Stoughton.
1952. 275 p., 124 illus.

*L'Amy, John H. Jersey folk lore. Jersey, J. T. Begwood. States Printer.
1927. 184 p.

Lane, Clarke Louisa. Recollections and legends of Sark. An account of its first settlement and early history and useful hints to visitors. Guernsey, J. Redstone. 1840. 187 p.

Lane, Clarke Louisa. The island of Alderney; its early history, antiquities, present state, scenery, customs, and trade . . . Guernsey, H. Brouard; London, Longman. 1851. 20, 120 p.

Lemasurier, Père René. Le droit de l'île de Jersey: la loi, le coutume et l'idéologie dans l'île de Jersey. Paris, A. Pedone. 1956. 348 p.

*MacCulloch, Sir Edgar. Guernsey folk lore. A collection of popular superstitions, legendary tales, peculiar customs, proverbs, weather sayings, etc. of the people of that island. Guernsey, F. Clarke; London, Elliot Stock. 1903. 616 p.

Mais, Stuart P. B. The Channel Islands. London, C. Johnson. 1953. 144 p., illus.

Maistre, Frank le. Dictionnaire Jersiais-Français. London and Colchester, Spottiswood Ballantyne. 1966. 652 p.

Marett, Thomas I., and Edith F. Carey. Channel Islands folklore items. Folk-Lore. 38(1927): 178-182.

Maugham, R. C. F. The Island of Jersey today. Rev. ed. London, W. H. Allen. 1950. 199 p., plate.

Plees, W. An account of the Islands of Jersey . . . London, Longmans; Southampton, I. Fletcher. 1817. 12, 358 p.

Toyne, Stanley M. Sark: a feudal survival. Eton, Windsor, Shakespeare Head Press. 1959. 41 p., illus.

Whitley, George. Memories of youth on a Jersey farm. London, Jersey Society in London. Occasional Publications No. 10. 1950 (?). 14 p.

Adams, G. B. The work and words of haymaking. Ulster Folklife. 12 (1966): 66-91.

Andrews, Elizabeth. Ulster folklore. London, E. Stock. 1913. 13, 121 p. (Another edition. New York, E. P. Dutton. 1919.)

Boyle, E. Embroidery and lacemaking in Ulster. Ulster Folklife. 10 (1964): 5-22.

Buchanan, Ronald H. Stapple thatch. Ulster Folk Life. 3 (1957): 19-28.

Buchanan, Ronald H. Thatch and thatching in North-east Ireland. Gwerin. 1, no. 3 (June 1957): 123-142.

Buchanan, Ronald H. The drift from the land. Ulster Folk Life. 6 (1960): 43-61.

Buchanan, Ronald H. Calendar customs. 1, New Year's day to Michaelmas. Ulster Folklife. 8 (1962): 15-34.

Buchanan, Ronald H. Calendar customs. 2. Harvest to Christmas. Ulster Folklife. 9 (1963): 61-79.

Buchanan, Ronald H. Tradition in Ulster. Folklore. 74 (1963): 565-574.

Buchanan, Ronald H. Tradition and change in rural Ulster. Folk Life. 3 (1965): 39-45.

Cox, J. M. Eshbralley scythe stones. Ulster Folklife. 11 (1965): 54-62.

Douglas, J. N. H. Emigration and Irish peasant life. Ulster Folklife. 9 (1963): 9-19.

*Evans, Emyr Estyn. Irish Heritage: the landscape, the people and their work. Dundalk, Dundalgan Press. 1942. 16, 190 p., 6 plates, 115 figs.

Evans, Emyr Estyn. Some archaic forms of agricultural transport in Ulster. In W. F. Grimes, ed. Aspects of archaeology in Britain and beyond. London, H. W. Edwards. 1951: 108-123.

*Evans, Emyr Estyn. Mourne Country: landscape and life in South Down. Dundalk, Dundalgan Press. 1951. 226 p.

Evans, Emyr Estyn. Field fences and gates. Ulster Folk Life. 2 (1956): 14-18.

*Evans, Emyr Estyn. Irish folk ways. London, Routledge and Kegan Paul; New York, Devin-Adair. 1957. 324 p.

Evans, Emyr Estyn. Ulster farmhouse: a comparative study. Ulster Folk Life. 3 (1957): 14-18.

Evans, Emyr Estyn. Folklife studies in Northern Ireland. Journal of the Folk-lore Institute. 2 (1965): 355-63.

Foster, Jeanne Cooper. Ulster Folklore. Belfast, H. R. Carter. 1951. 142 p.

Gailey, R. A. The use of mud in thatching. Ulster Folk Life. 6 (1960): 68-69.

Gailey, R. A. The cots of North Derry. Ulster Folklife. 9 (1963): 46-52.

Gailey, R. A. The disappearance of the horse from the Ulster farm. Folk Life. 4 (1966): 51-55, maps.

Gamble, John. Views of the society and manners in the north of Ireland, in a series of letters written in the year 1818. London, Longman, Hurst, Rees, Orme, and Brown. 1819. 6, 423 p.

Harris, Rosemary. The selection of leaders in Ballybeg, Northern Ireland. Sociological Review. N.S. 9 (1961): 137-149.

Hayward, Richard. In praise of Ulster. Belfast, W. Mullan. 1946. 8, 347 p.

Hayward, Richard. Belfast through the ages. Dundalk, Dundalgan Press. 1952. 74 p.

*Jones, Emrys. A social geography of Belfast. London, Oxford University Press. 1960. 14, 299 p.

Kennedy, G. Orchards in County Armagh. Ulster Folklife. 10 (1964): 86-87.

Logan, P. Folk medicine of the Cavan-Leitrim area. Ulster Folklife. 9 (1963): 89-92.

Logan, P. Folk medicine in the Cavan-Leitrim area, II. Ulster Folklife. 11 (1965): 51-53.

Lucas, A. T. Furze: a survey and history of its use in Ireland. Dublin, National Museum of Ireland. 1960. 204 p.

McCourt, Desmond. Weavers' houses round south-west Lough Neagh. Ulster Folklife. 8 (1962): 43-56.

McCourt, Desmond. Some cruck-framed buildings in Donegal and Derry. Ulster Folklife. 11 (1965): 39-50.

McCutcheon, A. Roads and bridges. Ulster Folklife. 10 (1964): 73-81.

Mackle, H. Fairies and leprechauns. Ulster Folklife. 10 (1964): 49-56.

McPolin, F. Fairy lore in the Hilltown District, County Down. Ulster Folk-life. 9 (1963): 80-88.

NORTHERN IRELAND

Mitchel, N. C. The Lower Bann fisheries. Ulster Folklife. 11 (1965): 1-32.

*Mogey, John M. Rural life in Northern Ireland. London, Geoffrey Cumber-
lege. 1947. 240 p.

Mogey, John M. The community in Northern Ireland. Man. 48 (1948): 85-
87.

Paterson, T. G. F. Housing and house types in County Armagh. Ulster Folk
Life. 6 (1960): 8-17.

Pollock, A. J. Hallowe'en customs in Lecade, County Down. Ulster Folk
Life. 6 (1960): 62-64.

Pollock, A. J. Notes on life in County Down during the late eighteenth century. Ulster Folklife. 8 (1962): 98-100.

Porter, S. T. A County Down school collection. Ulster Folklife. 10 (1964):
82-85.

Rhodes, Peter S. A guide to the Ballycopeland windmill. Belfast, Her Majesty's Stationery Office. 1962. 13 p., fold-out figure.

Symons, Leslie, ed. Land use in Northern Ireland. London, University of
London Press. 1964. 288 p.

Thompson, George B. Primitive land transport of Ulster. Belfast, Belfast
Museum and Art Gallery. 1958. 48 p. (Sleighs and sledges.)

Tnompson, George B. The blacksmith's craft. Ulster Folk Life. 4 (1958):
33-36.

Ulster Folklife. Vol. 1-6 published by the Committee on Ulster Folklife and
Traditions (Belfast) under the title Ulster Folk Life. Vol. 7- published by
the Ulster Folk Museum (Belfast) with the title Ulster Folklife. Vol. 1
(1955)-.

Aalen, F. H. A. A note on transhumance in the Wicklow mountains. Journal of the Royal Society of Antiquaries of Ireland. 93 (1963): 189-190.

Aalen, F. H. A. Clochans as transhumance dwellings in the Dingle peninsula, Co. Kerry. Journal of the Royal Society of Antiquaries of Ireland. 94 (1964): 39-45.

Aalen, F. H. A. Transhumance in the Wicklow mountains. Ulster Folklife. 10 (1964): 65-72.

Ainsworth, J. Sidelights on 18th century Irish estate management. Journal of the Royal Society of Antiquaries of Ireland. 93 (1963): 181-186.

*Arensberg, Conrad. The Irish countryman. New York, Macmillan. 1937. 11, 216 p. (Reprinted in 1958. New York, Peter Smith.)

*Arensberg, Conrad, and S. T. Kimball. Family and community in Ireland. Cambridge, Mass., Harvard University Press. 1940. 29, 322 p. (Reprinted in 1959, 1967.)

Atthill, Lombe. Recollections of an Irish doctor. London, R. T. S. 1911. 238 p.

Aughney, Eilis. Trends in Irish education. Eire-Ireland. 1, no. 4 (1966): 79-82.

Béaloideas: The Journal of the Folk-Lore of Ireland Society. Vol. 1- (1927)- Dublin.

Bicheno, James Ebenezer. Ireland and its economy; being the result of observations made in a tour through the country in the autumn of 1829. London, John Murray. 1830. 16, 308 p.

Binns, Jonathan. The miseries and beauties of Ireland. 2 vols. London, Longman, Orme, Brown. 1837.

Bonn, M. J. Modern Ireland and her agrarian problem. Translated from the German by T. W. Rolleston. Dublin, Hodges, Figgis. 1906. 168 p.

*Browne, Charles R. The ethnography of Inishbofin and Inishshark, County Galway. Proceedings of the Royal Irish Academy, 3d ser. 3 (1894): 317-370.

*Browne, Charles R. The ethnography of the Mullet, Inishkea Islands, and Portacloy, County Mayo. Proceedings of the Royal Irish Academy, 3d ser. 3 (1895): 587-649.

*Browne, Charles R. The ethnography of Balycroy. Proceedings of the Royal Irish Academy, 3d ser. 4 (1896-1898): 74-111.

*Browne, Charles R. The ethnography of Clare Island and Inishturk. Proceedings of the Royal Irish Academy, 3d ser. 5 (1898-1900): 40-72.

*Browne, Charles R. The ethnography of Garumna and Lettermullen. Proceedings of the Royal Irish Academy, 3d ser. 5 (1898-1900): 223-268.

*Browne, Charles R. The ethnography of Carna and Mweenish in the parish of Moyruss, Connemara. Proceedings of the Royal Irish Academy, 3d ser. 6 (1900-1902): 503-534.

*Browne, Charles R., and A. C. Haddon. The ethnography of the Aran Islands. Proceedings of the Royal Irish Academy, 3d ser. 2 (1891-1893): 768-830.

Buchanan, R. H. Thatch and thatching in north-east Ireland. Gwerin. 1 (1956-1957): 123-142.

Buchanan, R. H. Stapple thatch. Ulster Folk Life. 3 (1957): 19-28.

Buchanan, R. H. Rural change in an Irish townland 1890-1955. Advancement of Science. 14 (March 1958): 291-300.

Buck, A. M. When I was a boy in Ireland. New York, Lothrup, Lee & Shepard. 1936. 7, 173 p.

Bush, John. Hibernia curiosa. A letter from a gentleman in Dublin . . . giving a general view of the manners, customs, dispositions &c. of the inhabitants of Ireland. London, W. Flexney. 1769. 16, 143 p.

Campbell, Ake. Irish fields and houses. Béaloideas. 5 (1935): 57-74.

Campbell, Ake. Notes on the Irish house. Folk-Liv. 1 (1937): 205-234.

Campbell, Ake. Notes on the Irish house, II. Folk-Liv. 2 (1938): 173-196.

[Campbell, Thomas], published anonymously. A philosophical survey of the south of Ireland. Dublin, W. Whitestone. 1778. 16, 478 p.

Carleton, William. Traits and stories of the Irish peasantry. 2 vols. London, G. Routledge. 1852. (Fiction. There are many other editions of this work.)

Carney, J., and M. Carney. A collection of Irish charms. Saga och Sed. (1960): 144-152; (1961): 303-337.

The census of Ireland for the year 1851. Part V. Tables of Deaths. Vol. 1. Containing the report, tables of pestilences, and analyses of the tables of deaths. Presented to both Houses of Parliament by command of Her Majesty . . . Dublin, printed by Alexander Thom and Sons . . . . for Her Majesty's Stationery Office. 1856. (See especially pages 235-264, by Sir William Wilde.)

Chatterton, Lady Henrietta Georgiana L. Rambles in the south of Ireland during the year 1838. 2 vols. London, Saunders and Otley. 1839.

Coghlan, Daniel. The land of Ireland. Dublin, Veritas. 1931. 288 p.

Coghlan, Daniel. The ancient land tenures of Ireland. Dublin, Messrs. Browne & Nolan. 1933. 311 p.

Coleman, John Christopher. Journeys into Muskerry. Dundalk, Dundalgan Press. 1950. 105 p.

Colum, Padraic. The road round Ireland. New York, Macmillan. 1926. 5, 13, 492 p.

Colum, Padraic. Cross roads in Ireland. New York, Macmillan. 1930. 9, 375 p.

Connell, Kenneth Hugh. The population of Ireland, 1750-1845. New York, Oxford University Press. 1950. 11, 293 p.

Connell, Kenneth Hugh. Peasant marriages in Ireland after the great famine. Past and Present. 12 (Nov. 1957): 16-91.

Connell, Kenneth Hugh. Peasant marriage in Ireland: its structure and development since the famine. Economic History Review. 2d ser. 14 (1962): 502-523.

*Connell, Kenneth Hugh. Irish Peasant Society. London, Oxford University Press. 1968. 124 p. (Four historical essays: Illicit distillation, Illegitimacy before the famine, Ether drinking in Ulster, Catholicism and marriage in the century following the famine.)

Connery, Donald S. The Irish. New York, Simon and Schuster. 1968. 304 p. plates.

Coote, Sir Charles. Statistical survey of the county of Cavan . . . Dublin, Royal Dublin Society. 1802. 19, 304 p.

Coote, Sir Charles. Statistical survey of the county of Armagh, with observations on the means of improvement . . . Dublin, Craisberry and Campbell. 1804. 25, 395, 33 p.

Cornish, Vaughan. Historic thorn trees in the British Isles. London, Country Life. n.d. [1941]. 94 p.

Corry, Mrs. Patrick. Local government: organization and functions. Éire-Ireland. 1, no. 4 (1966): 74-79.

Coulter, Henry. The west of Ireland: its existing condition and prospects. Dublin and London, Hodges & Smith. 1862. 10, 372 p., plate, map, illus.

Cowell, Sidney Robertson. Songs of Aran. New York, Ethnic Folkways Library. 1957. (A 12 in. 33 1/3 RPM record, with an 11 p. booklet.)

Craig, John Duncan. Real picture of clerical life in Ireland. 2d ed. London, E. Stock. 1900. 8, 354 p.

*Cresswell, Robert. Une communauté rurale de l'Irlande. Paris, Université, Institut d'Ethnologie, Mémoires, no. 74. 1968. 571 p., 92 maps, 32 figs., 28 photos. (County Clare)

Croker, Thomas Crofton. Researches in the south of Ireland, illustrative of the scenery, architectural remains, and the manners and superstitions of the peasantry . . . London, J. Murray. 1824. 2, 393 p.

Croker, Thomas Crofton. Fairy legends and traditions of the south of Ireland. 3 vols. London, J. Murray. 1825-1828.

Croker, Thomas Crofton. The popular songs of Ireland. London, H. Colburn. 1839. 19, 340 p.

Croker, Thomas Crofton. The keen of the south of Ireland: as illustrative of Irish political and domestic history, manners, music, and superstitions. London, printed for the Percy Society by T. Richards. 1844. 59, 108 p.

Cross, Eric. The tailor and Ansty. London, Chapman & Hall. 1942 and 1964. 223 p.

Curtis, L. P., Jr. Anglo-Saxons and Celts. A study of anti-Irish prejudice in Victorian England. Bridgeport, Conn., University of Bridgeport Press. 1968. 11, 162 p.

Danaher, Kevin. Gentle places and simple things. Cork, Mercier Press. 1964. 125 p.

Danaher, Kevin. Irish country people. Cork, Mercier Press. 1966. 127 p.

Deeney, Daniel. Peasant-lore from Gaelic Ireland. London, D. Nutt. 1900. 12, 80 p.

Dubourdieu, John. Statistical survey of the county of Down . . . Dublin, Graisberry and Campbell. 1802. 16, 319 p., illus.

Dubourdieu, John. Statistical survey of the county of Antrim . . . 2 vols. Dublin, Dublin Society. 1812. 23, 630 p.; 112 p., plates and plans.

Duignan, M. Irish agriculture in early historic times. Journal of the Royal Society of Antiquaries of Ireland. 74, no. 3 (1944): 124-145.

Dutton, Hely. Statistical survey of the county of Clare. Dublin, Graisberry and Campbell. 1808. 24, 369 p.

*Edwards, R. Dudley, and T. Desmond Williams, eds. The great famine. Studies in Irish history, 1845-1852. New York, New York University Press. 1957. 20, 517 p.

Ettlinger, E. The Aran Isles, a folklorist's diary, July 1949. Lares. 17 (1951) 92-103.

Evans, Emyr Estan. Some survivals of the Irish open field system. Geography. 24 (1939): 24-36.

*Evans, Emyr Estan. Irish heritage: the landscape, the people and their work. Dundalk, W. Tempest, Dundalgan Press. 1942. 16, 190 p., 6 plates, 115 text figs.

*Evans, Emyr Estan. Irish folk ways. London, Routledge & Kegan Paul; New York, Devin-Adair. 1957. 324 p.

Evans, Emyr Estan. The peasant and the past. Advancement of Science. 16 (Nov. 1960): 293-302.

Evans-Wentz, Walter Yelling. The fairy-faith in Celtic countries. London, Frowde. 1911: 23-84. (Reprinted. New Hyde Park, N.Y., University Books. 1966.)

Fields, Mrs. Finian. Origins of local government in Ireland. Éire-Ireland. 1, no. 4 (1966): 69-74.

Flower, Robin. The western island, or the Great Blasket. New York, Oxford University Press. 1945. 6, 138 p.

*Fox, J. R(obin). The vanishing Gael. New Society. 1, no. 2 (1962): 17-19.

*Fox, J. R(obin). The structure of personal names on Tory Island. Man. 63 (1963): 153-155.

*Fox, J. R(obin). Kinship and land tenure on Tory Island. Ulster Folklife. 12 (1966): 1-17.

Fox, J. R(obin). Tory Island. In Burton Benedict, ed. Problems of smaller territories. London, Athlone Press. 1967: 113-133, map (p. 112).

Fox, J. R(obin). Multilingualism in two communities. Man. N.S. 3 (1968): 456-464.

Frankenberg, Ronald. Communities in Britain. Social life in town and country. Harmondsworth, Baltimore, Penguin Books. 1966: 25-44.

Freeman, Thomas Walter. Farming in Irish life. Geographical Journal. 110 (1948): 38-59.

Freeman, Thomas Walter. Ireland, its physical, historical, social and economic geography. London, Methuen; New York, Dutton. 1950. 15, 555 p.

Freeman, Thomas Walter. Pre-famine Ireland: a study in historical geography. Manchester, Manchester University Press. 1957. 8, 352 p.

Freeman, Thomas Walter. Inishbofin—an Atlantic island. Economic Geography. 34 (1958): 202-209.

Gamble, John. Views of the society and manners in the north of Ireland, in a series of letters written in the year 1818. London, Longman, Hurst, Rees, Orme, and Brown. 1819. 6, 423 p.

Giraldus Cambrensis. The first version of the topography of Ireland. Translated by J. J. O'Meara. Dundalk, Dundalgan Press. 1951. 128 p., 19 illus. (Life in twelfth-century Ireland.)

Gomme, Lady Alice Bertha. The traditional games of England, Scotland and Ireland, with tunes, singing-rhymes, and methods of playing according to the variants extant and recorded in different parts of the kingdom. 2 vols. London, David Nutt. 1894-1898. (Reprinted. New York, Dover Publications. 1964.)

Gorman, Michael, ed. Ireland by the Irish. London, Galley Press. 1963. 7, 162 p.

Graham, J. M. Transhumance in Ireland. Advancement of Science. 10 (1953): 74-97.

Gregory, Isabella A. Visions and beliefs in the west of Ireland. 2 vols. New York and London, G. P. Putnam's Sons. 1920.

Hall, James, of Walthstow. Tour through Ireland: particularly the interior & least known parts; containing an accurate view of the parties, politics, and improvements, in the different provinces. 2 vols. London, printed for R. P. Moore. 1813.

Handley, James E. The Irish in modern Scotland. Cork, Cork University Press. 1964. 337 p.

Haughey, Charles J. Rural sociology in Ireland. Éire-Ireland. 1, no. 4 (1966): 63-69.

Hayward, Richard. The story of the Irish harp. London, A. Guinness. 1954. 24 p.

Humphreys, Alexander J. Evolving Irishmen. Social Order. 4, no. 2 (Feb. 1954): 59-69.

Humphreys, Alexander J. The family in Ireland. In M. F. Nimkoff, ed. Comparative family systems. Boston, Houghton Mifflin. 1965: 232-258.

*Humphreys, Alexander J. New Dubliners. Urbanization and the Irish family. New York, Fordham University Press. 1966. 10, 295 p.

Hyde, Douglas. Beside the fire: Irish folk tales. London, David Nutt. 1890. 58, 203 p.

Inglis, Henry David. Ireland in 1834: a journey through Ireland during the spring, summer, and autumn of 1834. 2d ed. 2 vols. London, Whittaker. 1835. (First ed., 1834.)

Johnson, James H. Studies of Irish rural settlements. Geographical Review. 48(1958): 554-566.

Jones, William Bence. A life's work in Ireland of a landlord who tried to do his duty. London, Macmillan. 1880. 21, 338 p.

Joyce, Patrick Weston. English as we speak it in Ireland. 2d ed. London, Longmans, Green. 1910. 10, 1, 356 p.

Joyce, Patrick Weston. A social history of ancient Ireland, treating of the government, military system, and law; religion, learning, and art; trades, industries, and commerce; manners, customs, and domestic life of the ancient Irish people. 2d ed. 2 vols. Dublin, Gresham Publishing Co. 1913

Joyce, Patrick Weston. The origin and history of Irish names of places . . . 7th ed. 3 vols. Dublin, Talbot Press; London, Longmans. 1920.

Kaim-Caudle, P. Social policy in the Irish Republic. London, Routledge and Kegan Paul. 1967. 120 p.

Kimball, Solon T. The tradesman and his family in the economic structure of an Irish town. Unpublished doctoral dissertation. Cambridge, Mass., Harvard University. 1935.

Kinahan, G. H. Connemara folk-lore. Folk-Lore Journal. 2(1884): 257-266.

Klimm, Lester E. The relation between field patterns and jointing in the Aran Islands. Geographical Review. 25(1935): 618-624.

Lane, Ralph. Change and organization in rural Ireland. Human Organization. 14, no. 2(1955): 4-8.

deLatocnaye. A Frenchman's walk through Ireland 1796-1797. Translated by J. Stevenson. Dublin, Hodges, Figgis. 1917. 301 p. (Originally written in 1796.)

Le Fanu, William Richard. Seventy years of Irish life, being anecdotes and reminiscences. New York and London, Edward Arnold. 1893. 11, 306 p.

Lucas, A. T. Bogwood: a study in rural economy. Béaloideas. 23(1954): 71-134.

Lucas, A. T. Footwear in Ireland. County Louth Archaeological Journal. 13 (1956): 309-394.

Lucas, A. T. Wattle and straw mat doors in Ireland. Studia Ethnographica Upsaliensia. 11 (1956): 16-35.

Lucas, A. T. Furze: a survey and history of its uses in Ireland. Dublin, National Museum of Ireland. 1960. 204 p., 22 figs.

Lucas, A. T. Irish food before the potato. Gwerin. 3, no. 2 (Dec. 1960): 8-43.

Lynd, Robert. Home life in Ireland. London, Mills & Boon. 1909. 12, 317 p., 18 plates.

McCarthy, M. D. Some family facts in Ireland today. Christus Rex. 5, no. 1 (Jan. 1951): 46-64.

McCarthy, Michael. Priests and people in Ireland. Dublin, Hodges, Figgis. 1903. 15, 624 p.

McClintock, H. F. Old Irish and highland dress and that of the Isle of Man. 2d ed. Dundalk, Dundalgan Press. 1950. 141 p., illus.

McClintock, H. F. Handbook on the traditional old Irish dress. Dundalk, Dundalgan Press. 1958. 28 p.

McCourt, Desmond. The rundale system in Donegal: its distribution and decline. Donegal Annual. 3(1955): 47-60.

McCourt, Desmond. Infield and outfield in Ireland. Economic History Review. 2d ser. 7(1955): 369-376.

McCourt, Desmond. Some cruck-framed buildings in Donegal and Derry. Ulster Folklore. 11(1965): 39-50.

*McLysaght, Edward. Irish life in the seventeenth century: after Cromwell. London, Longmans, Green; Dublin and Cork, Talbot Press. 1939. 7, 463 p.

MacManus, Diarmuid A. Irish earth folk. New York, Devin-Adair. 1959 [i.e. 1960]. 192 p.

MacManus, Diarmuid A. The middle kingdom. The faerie world of Ireland. London, Max Parrish. 1959. 191 p.

MacNeil, Máire. The festival of Lughnasa. London and New York, Oxford University Press. 1962. 697 p.

McParlan, James. Statistical survey of the county of Donegal . . . Dublin, Graisberry and Campbell. 1802. 15, 127 p.

Mahaffy, J. P. On the introduction of the ass as a beast of burden into Ireland. Proceedings of the Royal Irish Academy. 33 (1916-1917): 530-538.

*Mason, Thomas H. The islands of Ireland: their scenery, people, life and antiquities. 3d ed. London, B. T. Batsford. 1950. 8, 135 p., plates. (Reprinted. Cork, Mercier Press. 1967. 141 p., no plates.)

Maxwell, C. E. Country and town in Ireland under the Georges. 2d ed. Dundalk, Dundalgan Press. 1949. 380 p.

Maxwell, William Hamilton. Wild sports of the west, with legendary tales and local sketches. 2 vols. New York, J. & J. Harper. 1833. (Many later editions.)

Messenger, John C. Anthropologist at play: the research implications of balladmongering. A. A. 66 (1964): 407-416.

Messenger, John C. Joe O'Donnell, seanchai of Aran. Journal of the Folklore Institute. 1 (1964): 197-213.

Messenger, John C. Literary vs. scientific interpretations of cultural reality in the Aran Islands of Eire. Ethnohistory. 11 (1964): 41-55.

Messenger, John C. Inis Beag. Isle of Ireland. New York, Holt, Rinehart and Winston. 1969. 96 p.

Miller, Hugh. An autobiography. My schools and schoolmasters; or the story of my education. Boston, Gould and Lincoln. 1854. 14, 537 p. (Many later editions.)

Morley, Henry, ed. Ireland under Elizabeth and James the First, described by Edmund Spenser, by Sir John Davies . . . and by Fynes Moryson. London, G. Routledge and Sons. 1890. 4, 445 p.

Moryson, Fynes. A description of Ireland . . . 1600-1603. In Henry Morley, ed. Ireland under Elizabeth and James the First . . . London, G. Routledge and Sons. 1890: 411-438.

Moryson, Fynes. The manners and customs of Ireland, and, A description of Ireland . . . In Caesar Falkiner, ed. Illustrations of Irish history and topography, mainly in the seventeenth century. London and New York, Longmans, Green. 1904: 211-325.

Mullen, Pat. Man of Aran. London, Faber and Faber. 1934. 286 p. (In part the story of the filming of Robert Flaherty's "Man of Aran.")

Mullen, Pat. Irish Tales. London, Faber and Faber. 1938. 336 p.

Murphy, Robert C. The timeless Arans. National Geographic Magazine. 59(1931): 747-775.

Murray, A. T. Farm tenancy in Ireland. Foreign Agriculture. 1 (1937): 557-582.

Nicholls, Sir George. A history of the Irish poor law. London, John Murray. 1856. 10, 424 p.

Norman, Sir Henry. Bodyke, a chapter in the history of Irish landlordism. New York, G. P. Putnam's Sons. 1887. 78 p.

*O'Brien, John Anthony, ed. The vanishing Irish. The enigma of the modern world. London, W. H. Allen; New York, McGraw-Hill. 1953. 240 p.

Ó Crohan, Tomás. The islandman. Translated from the Irish by Robin Flower. Oxford, The Clarendon Press; New York, C. Scribner's Sons. 1951. 245 p. (Blasket Islands.) (Another edition. New York, C. Scribner's Sons. 1935. 303 p.)

O'Curry, Eugene. On the manners and customs of the ancient Irish. Edited with an introduction, appendix, etc., by W. K. Sullivan. 3 vols. London, Williams and Norgate; New York, Scribner, Welford. 1873.

O'Danachair, Caoimhín. Hearth and chimney in the Irish house. Béaloideas. 16 (1946): 91-104.

O'Danachair, Caoimhín. Irish farmyard types. Studia Ethnographica Upsaliensia. 11 (1956): 6-15.

O'Danachair, Caoimhín. Materials and methods in Irish traditional building. Journal of the Royal Society of Antiquaries of Ireland. 87, no. 2 (1957): 61-74.

O'Doherty, E. F., and J. R. Morrison. Bilingualism. Advancement of Science. 14, no. 56 (1958): 282-290.

O'Donoghue, John. In a quiet land. New York, Coward-McCann. 1958. 208 p.

O'Donoghue, John. In Kerry long ago. London, B. T. Batsford; New York, Norton. 1960. 208 p.

O'Donovan, Michael. Leinster, Munster, and Connaught. London, Robert Hale. 1950. 296 p.

O'Flaherty, R. (James Hardiman, ed.). A chorographic description of the west or H-Iar Connaught. Dublin, Irish Archaeological Society. 1846.

O'Flaherty, Tom. Aranmen all. Dublin, At the Sign of the Three Candles; London, H. Hamilton. 1934. 192 p.

O'Flaherty, Tom. Cliffmen of the west. London, Sands. 1935. 286 p., plates. (Aran Islands.)

O'Rafferty, Peadar, and Gerald O'Rafferty. Dances of Ireland. London, M. Parrish. 1953. 40 p., plate.

Ó Sé, Michael. Old Irish cheeses and other milk products. Journal of the Cork Historical and Archaeological Society. 53 (1948): 82-87.

O'Shamus, S. (pseud.). The Irish guyed. London, Allen. 1956. 183 p.

Ó Siochain (Sheehan), Patrick A. Aran: islands of legend. New York, Devin-Adair. 1963. 192 p.

Ó Suilleabháin, Sean. Two death customs in Ireland. Studia Ethnographica Upsaliensia. 11 (1956): 208-215.

Ó Suilleabháin, Sean. A handbook of Irish folklore. Hatboro, Penn., Folklore Associates. 1963. 736 p. (Original edition, 1942.)

Ó Suilleabháin, Sean. Irish wake amusements. Cork, Mercier Press. 1967. 190 p.

O'Sullivan, Maurice. Twenty years a-growing. London, Chatto and Windus. 1933. 12, 322 p. (Blasket Islands.)

Ó Tuathail, Pádraig. Wicklow traditions of 1798. Béaloideas. 5 (1935): 154-188.

Otway, Caesar. Sketches in Ireland: descriptive of interesting, and hitherto unnoticed districts in the north and the south. Dublin, W. Curry. 1827. 4, 6, 411 p.

Otway, Caesar. A tour in Connaught: comprising sketches of Clonmacnoise, Joyce County, and Achill. Dublin, W. Curry. 1839. 11, 442 p.

Otway, Caesar. Sketches in Erris and Tyrawly, illustrative of the scenery, antiquities, architectural remains, and the manners and superstitions of the Irish peasantry. New ed. Dublin, T. Connolly. 1850. 15, 418 p. (Original edition 1841.)

de Paor, Risteard. Úll i mBarr an Ghéagáin. Dublin, Sáirséal agus Dill. 1959. 200 p. (Life on the Aran Islands.)

Petty, Sir William. The political anatomy of Ireland. London, D. Brown and W. Rogers. 1691. 142 p.

Robertson, Olivia. St. Malachy's court. New York, Odyssey Press. 1947. 170 p. (The Dublin poor.)

Robertson, Olivia. It's an old Irish custom. London, D. Dobson; New York, Vanguard Press. 1953. 140 p.

Rynne, Stephen. Green fields. A journal of Irish country life. London, Macmillan. 1938. 289 p. (Another edition. Dundalk, Dundalgan Press. 1946. 192 p.)

*Salaman, Redcliffe Nathan. The history and social influence of the potato. Cambridge, The University Press. 1949: 188-343.

Sampson, George Vaughan. Statistical survey of the county of Londonderry. Dublin, Graisberry and Campbell. 1802. 23, 509 p., 42 p. of illus.

Sampson, George Vaughan. Memoir: a memoir explanatory of the chart and survey of the county of London-Derry. London, G. and W. Nicol. 1814. 16, 359 p.

Sanderson, S. F. État des études de la vie traditionelle en Grande-Bretagne et en Irlande. Arts et Traditions Populaires. 12(1964): 247-254.

Schrier, Arnold. Ireland and the American emigration, 1850-1900. Minneapolis, University of Minnesota Press. 1958. 10, 210 p.

Scrope, George Julius D. P. Plan for a poor law for Ireland. London, J. Ridgeway. 1833. 8, 88 p.

Seymour, St. John Drelincourt. Irish witchcraft and demonology. Dublin, Hodges, Figgis. 1913. 8, 255 p.

Sigerson, G. History of land tenure and land classes in Ireland. London, Longmans, Green, Reader. 1871. 14, 333 p.

Spenser, Edmund. View of the present state of Ireland. London, Eric Partridge. 1934. 330 p. (Originally written in 1596.)

Stephens, James. The crock of gold. New York, Macmillan. 1956. 227 p. (Fiction.)

Synge, John Millington. The Aran Islands & other writings of John M. Synge. New York, Random House, Vintage Books. 1962. 23, 414 p. (There are many other editions of this excellent account of life on the Aran Islands at the beginning of this century.)

Szöverffy, Joseph. The well of the holy women: some St. Columba traditions in the west of Ireland. J.A.F.L. 68(1955): 111-122.

Thompson, Robert. Statistical survey of the county of Meath. Dublin, Royal Dublin Society. 1802.

Toner, Jerome. Rural Ireland, some of its problems. Dublin, Clonmore & Reynolds. 1955. 98 p.

Trench, William Stewart. Realities of Irish life. London, Longmans, Green. 1869. 14, 426 p.

Tuke, James H. Irish distress and its remedies. The land question. A visit to Donegal and Connaught in the spring of 1880. London, W. Ridgeway. 1880. 7, 120 p. (Many later editions.)

Ussher, Percy Arland. The face and mind of Ireland. London, V. Gollancz. 1940. 191 p.

Walker, Joseph Cooper. A historical essay on the dress of the ancient and modern Irish. Dublin, published for the author. 1818. 180 p. (Especially see: Appendix I. An account of the customs, manners and dress of the inhabitants of the Rosses, on the coast of the county of Donegal, in Ireland.)

Warren, Maude R. The Aran Islands. Harper's Monthly Magazine. 120(May 1910): 887-899.

Weld, Isaac. Statistical survey of the county of Roscommon. Dublin, R. Graisberry. 1832. 20, 710 p.

Went, A. E. J. The salmon fishery of Carrick-a-rede and Larry Bane, Co. Antrim. Journal of the Royal Society of Antiquaries of Ireland. 88 (1958): 57-65.

Went, A. E. J. The pursuit of salmon in Ireland. Proceedings of the Royal Irish Academy. Section C. 63(1964): 191-244.

*Westropp, Thomas J. A folk-lore survey of County Clare. Folk-Lore. 21 (1910): 180-199, 338-349, 476-487; 22(1911): 203-213, 332-341, 449-456.

*Westropp, Thomas J. A study of the folk-lore on the coast of Connacht, Ireland. Folk-Lore. 29(1918): 305-319.

Wibberley, Leonard P. O'C. The land that isn't there; an Irish adventure. New York, Washburn. 1960. 183 p.

Wilde, Lady Jane Francesca. Ancient legends, mystic charms, and superstitions of Ireland. 2 vols. Boston, Ticknor. 1887.

Wilde, Sir William R. W. Irish popular superstitions. Dublin, McGlashan. 1852. 140 p.

Wilson, Sloan. Ireland and the Irish (without the usual blarney). Fact. 3, no. 2 (March-April 1966): 28-37.

*Woodham-Smith, Cecil B. The great hunger: Ireland 1845-1849. New York, Harper and Row. 1962. 510 p.

Yeats, William Butler. The Celtic twilight. Men and women, dhouls and faeries. London, Lawrence and Bullen. 1893. 12, 212 p. (Many later editions.)

Yeats, William Butler, ed. Fairy and folk tales of the Irish peasantry. London, Walter Scott. 1888. 18, 326 p. (Many later editions.)

Young, Arthur. A tour in Ireland with general observations on the present state of that kingdom: made in the years 1776, 1777, and 1778 . . . 2 vols. Dublin, printed by G. Bonham for Whitestone, Sleater. 1780.

Centre d'Études Sociologiques. Bibliothèque. Sociologie et psychologie sociale en France 1945-1958. Bibliographie choisie et annotée. Paris, Centre d'Études Sociologiques. 1959. 93 p.

Gennep, Arnold van. Manuel de folklore français contemporain. 3 vols in 9 parts (vol. 1, parts 1-7; vols. 3 and 4; vol. 2 never published). Paris, Picard. 1937-1957. (See especially vol. 1, parts 3-6, and vols. 3 and 4.)

Girard, Joseph. Bibliographie vauclusienne. Avignon, Rullière. 1941. 68 p

Mendras, Henri, ed. Les sociétés rurales français. Elements de bibliographie réunis par le Group de Sociologie Rurale du Centre d'Études Sociologiques . Paris, Fondation Nationale des Sciences Politiques. 1962. 124 p.

Mendras, Henri, ed. Rural Sociology. French Bibliographical Digest No. 39, Series 2. New York, Cultural Services of the French Embassy. 1964. 156 (A translation of the preceding work.)

Séguin, Jean. Bibliographie critique de ouvrages se rapportant au folklore bas-normand. Avranches, n. p. 1944. 47 p.

Tenèze, M. L. Bibliographie der wichtigsten volkskundlichen Arbeiten Frankreichs seit 1945. Deutsches Jahrbuch für Volkskunde. 4 (1958): 479-516.

Accords, Michel des. Le mariage et la condition de la femme dans la famille paysanne. Informations Sociales. 12, no. 6 (1958): 66-81.

Agnew, Swanzie. Rural settlement in the coastal plain of Bas Languedoc. Geography. 31 (1946): 65-77.

Aitken, Robert. Some ploughs of Central France; notes on a journey made in 1938. In Homenaje a Don Luis de Hoyos Sáinz. Tomo 1. Madrid, Graficas Valera. 1949: 37-46.

Alford, Violet. Pyrenean festivals, calendar customs, music & magic, drama & dance. London, Chatto and Windus. 1937. 286 p.

Amardel, G. Le jetons de mariage et les médailles de Nîmes au pied de sanglier. Commission Archéologique le Narbonne, Bulletin. 7 (1902-1903): 421-483.

*Anderson, Robert T., and Barbara Anderson. Bus stop for Paris: the transformation of a French village. New York, Doubleday. 1965. 8, 303 p., 12 photos., 2 maps.

*Arbos, Philippe. La vie pastorale dans les alpes françaises, étude de géographie humaine . . . Paris, A. Colin. 1922. 716 p.

FRENCH

Ariès, Philippe. L'enfant et la vie familiale sous l'ancien régime. Paris, Librairie Plon. 1960. 502 p., plates.

Ariès, Philippe, et al. Les traditions sociales dans les pays de France. Paris, Éditions de la Nouvelle France. 1943. 198 p.

Arnaud, Camille. Une carte de restaurateur en MDXXXIII. Marseille, Typ. Barlatier-Feissat et Demonchy. 1856. 23 p.

Artisans et Paysans de France. Recueil d'études d'art populaire . . . 3 vols. Strasbourg, F. X. Le Roux. 1946, 1947, 1948. 247, 251, 226 p.

Arts et Traditions Populaires. Paris, Société d'Ethnographie Française. Vol. 1 (1953)--

Assier, Alexandre. Légendes, curiosités et traditions de Champagne et de la Brie. Paris, A. Aubrey. 1860.

Assier, Alexandre. Légendes, curiosités et traditions de la Bourgogne et de la Champagne. 2 vols. Paris, Rouveyre, Delahaye et de Libraires de la Bourgogne et Champagne. 1880-1881. 169; 159 p.

Babeau, Albert Arsène. L'école de village pendant la révolution. Paris, Didier. 1881. 11, 272 p.

Babeau, Albert Arsène. Le village sous l'ancien régime. Paris, Didier. 1882. 415 p.

Babeau, Albert Arsène. La vie rurale dans l'ancienne France. Paris, Didier. 1883. 8, 352 p.

Babeau, Albert Arsène. La ville sous l'ancien régime. 2 vols. Paris, Didier. 1884.

Babeau, Albert Arsène. Les artisans et les domestiques d'autrefois. Paris, Firmin Didot. 1886. 15, 362 p.

Babeau, Albert Arsène. L'évolution des institutions et des moeurs en Champagne. Réforme Sociale. 49 (1905): 44-57.

Bassere, M. Le Cantal. Économie agricole et pastorale. Aurillac. 1928. 225 p.

Bautier, R. H. Une institution sociologique du centre de la France: les reinages. Guéret, Impr. Lecante. 1945. 54 p.

Bavoux, F. Hantises et diableries dan la terre abbatiale de Luxeuil. D'un procés de l'inquisition (1529) à l'épidemie démoniaque de 1628-1630. Monaco, Éditions du Rocher. 1956. 7, 200 p.

Bayssat, Gabriel. Évolution du monde rurale de la Haute-Loire. Le Puy, Éd. de la Main de Bronze. 1955. 285 p., graphs, charts, etc.

Beech, G. T. Rural society in medieval France: the Gâtine of Poitou in the eleventh and twelfth centuries. Baltimore, Johns Hopkins Press. 1964. 141 p.

Bégouen, Comte H. La vallée de Bethmale. Maisons. Utensiles. Costume. Toulouse, Éd. du Muséum. 1942. 78 p.

Benoît, Fernand. Histoire de l'outillage rurale et artisanal. Paris, Didier. 1947. 168 p.

Benoît, Fernand. La Provence et le Comtat Venaissen. Paris, Gallimard. 1949. 409 p.

Bérenger-Féraud, L. B. J. Traditions et réminiscences populaires de la Provence; coutumes, légendes, superstitions, ... Paris, Leroux. 1886. 10, 406 p.

Bernadau, Alexis de. Sur les superstitions populaires du Bordelais. Bordeaux, Muséum d'Instruction Publique, Bulletin Polymathique. 1807: 75-88, 186-197.

Bernard, A., and C. Gagnon. Le Bourbonnais. Paris, Gallimard. 1954. 269 p

*Bernot, Lucien, and René Blancard. Nouville, un village français. Paris, Institut d'Ethnologie. 1953. 7, 447 p. (Travaux et Mémoires de l'Institut d'Ethnologie 57.)

Bettelheim, Charles, and Suzanne Frere. Une ville française moyenne: Auxerre en 1950. Étude de structure sociale et urbaine. Paris, A. Colin. 1950. 14, 270 p.

Beuret, G. When I was a girl in France. Boston, Lothrop, Lee & Shepard. 1925. 208 p.

*Beyer, Lotte. Der Waldbauer in den Landes der Gascogne. Haus, Arbeit und Familie. I. Wirtschaftsformen. Hamburger Studien zu Volkstum und Kultur der Romanen. Vol. 24. Hamburg, Paul Evert Verlag. 1937. 14, 84 p., 4 plates.

*Beyer, Lotte. Der Waldbauer in den Landes der Gascogne. Haus, Arbeit und Familie. II. Siedlung und Haus. Volkstum und Kultur der Romanen. 12 (1939): 186-277.

*Beyer, Lotte. Der Waldbauer in den Landes der Gascogne. Haus, Arbeit und Familie. III. Leben in der Familie. IV. Handwerk. Volkstum und Kultur der Romanen. 16 (1944): 1-69.

Bezard, Yvonne. La vie rurale dans le sud de la région parisienne de 1450 à 1560. Paris, Didot. 1929. 382 p., plates, map.

Bidault de l'Isle, Georges. Vieux dictons de nos campagnes. 2 vols. Paris, Nouvelles Éditions de la Toison d'Or. 1952. 608; 590 p. (A study of rural psychology.)

Billiard, Raymond. Vieilles coutumes, vieilles traditions, vieux couvenirs beaujolais. Villefranche-en-Beaujolais, Éd. du Cuvier (Jean Guilermont). 1941. 172 p.

Binet, Jacques. Un village de l'Île-de-France: les Ormes-sur-Voulzic, étude de folklore juridique. Paris, Université de Paris. 1943. 108 p. (Dissertation.)

Blanchard, Raphaël Anatole E. L'art populaire le Briançonnais. Le baeubert. Paris, E. Champion. 1914. 90 p.

Bloch, Marc Léopold B. Les caractères originaux de l'histoire rurale française. Nouv. éd. 2 vols. Paris, A. Colin. 1952-1956.

Bois, Paul. Paysans de l'ouest: le structures économiques et sociales aux options politiques depuis l'époque révolutionnaire dans la Sarthe. Paris-La Haye, Mouton. 1960. 19, 716 p.

Bollé, Louis. Histoire et folklore du Haut-Bugey. Oyonnax et ses environs. Bellegarde, Impr. Sadag. 1954. 191 p.

Bonnet, Baptiste. Un paysan du Midi. Tom. 1: Vie d'enfant. Tom. 2: Le valet de ferme. 2 vols. Paris. 1894, 1898. 36, 503; 11, 533 p.

Borias, G. A. Une famille de potiers de Saint-Quentin-la-Poterie: les Clop. Arts et Traditions Populaires. 9(1961): 321-333.

Bosquet, Amélie. Le Normandie romanesque et merveilleuse. Traditions, légendes et superstitions populaires de cette province. Paris, Rouen. 1845. 16, 519 p.

Boulanger, C. Monographie du village d'Allaines. Péronne, Loyson; Paris, Leroux. 1903. 198 p.

Bourgeois, J. Le mariage, coutume saisonnière. Contribution à une étude de la nuptialité en France. Population. 1(1946): 623-642.

Bouteiller, M. Oraisons populaires et conjurations. Arts et Traditions Populaires. 1(1953): 290-306.

Bouteiller, M. Le coutumier rural magique. Notes de folklore Berrichon. Ethnographie. N.S. 49(1954): 74-80.

Bouteiller, M. Sorciers et jetours de sorts. Paris, Plon. 1958. 18, 230 p.

Bouteiller, M. La médecine populaire en Anjou: résultats d'enquets (1961-1962). Bulletin de la Société d'Authropologie de Paris, sér. 11, 3 (1962): 523-539.

Bozon, Pierre. La vie rurale en Vivarais. Valence-sur-Rhône, Impr. Réunies. 1961. 641 p., figs., plates, maps.

Brownell, William C. French traits. New York, Charles Scribners' Sons. 1888. 411 p.

Brutails, Jean Auguste. Étude sur la condition rurales du Roussillon au moyen âge. Paris, Picard. 1891. 44, 314 p.

Bulletin Folklorique d'Île-de-France. Paris, Fedération Folklorique d'Île-de-France. Vol. 1 (1938)--

Burgess, Ernest W., ed. Aging in Western societies. Chicago, University of Chicago Press. 1960. 492 p.

Burns, Robert K. The ecological basis of French alpine peasant communities in the Dauphiné. Anthropological Quarterly. 34 (1961): 19-34.

Caillet, Armand. Puiselet-le-Marais, village de France. Largentiere (Ardeche), Impr. Humbert et Fils. 1951. 11, 256 p., figs., plates.

Caillot, Robert. L'usine de terre et la cité. L'example de Péage-du-Roussillon. Paris, Les Éditions Ouvrières. 1958. 214 p., figs., plates, maps.

Camp, W. D. Marriage and the family in France since the revolution; an essay in the history of population. New York, Bookman Associates. 1961. 203 p.

Canestrier, P. Les confréries actuelles de pénitents dans le Comté de Nice et dans la Principauté de Monaco. Nouvelle Revue des Traditions Populaires. 2 (1950): 291-304.

Carr, Philip. The French at home in town and country. London, Methuen. 1930. 8, 210 p.

Carrières, Marcel. Folklore et traditions du Midi de la France. Villefranche-de-Rouergue, Impr. Salingardes. 1954. 183 p.

Cavaillès, Henri. La transhumance pyrénéenne et la circulation des troupeaux dans les plaines de Gascogne. Paris, Colin. 1931. 134 p.

*Cavaillès, Henri. La vie pastorale et agricole dans les Pyrénées des Gaves, de l'Adour et des Nestes. Étude de géographie humaine. Paris, A. Colin. 1931. 413 p., plates.

Cavaillès, Henri. La route française, son histoire, sa fonction; étude de géographie humaine. Paris, A. Colin. 1946. 399 p.

Cecceldi, D. The family in France. Marriage and Family Living. 16 (1954): 326-330.

Chabot, Georges. Les villes; aperçu de géographie humaine. Paris, A. Colin. 1948. 224 p.

Chauvet, Horace. Traditions populaires du Roussillon. Perpignan, Impr. du Midi. 1947. 24, 242 p., illus.

Chevalier, Louis. Les paysans, étude d'histoire et d'economie rurale. Paris, Denoël. 1947. 231 p.

*Chevalier, Michel. La vie humaine dans les Pyrénées Ariègeoises. Paris, M. T. Génin. 1956. 1060 p., plates.

Child, Theodore. The praise of Paris. New York, Harper & Bros. 1893. 8, 299 p.

Chombart de Lauwe, Paul Henry. La vie quotidienne des familles ouvrières. Paris, C.N.R.S. 1956. 307 p., 77 tables, 75 graphs, plates.

Chombart de Lauwe, Paul Henry, et al. Paris et l'agglomération parisienne. 1. L'espace social dans une grande cité. 2. Méthodes de recherche pour l'étude d'une grande cité. 2 vols. Paris, Presses Universitaires de France. 1952. 260, 109 p.

Chrétien, L. J. Usages, préjugées, superstitions, proverbes et anciens mots de l'arrondissement d'Argentan. Alençon, Poulet-Malassis. 1835. 39 p.

Clément, Pierre, and Nelly Xydias. Vienne sur le Rhône. La vie et les habitants. Situations et attitudes. Sociologie d'une cité française. Paris, A. Colin. 1955. 279 p., figs., plates.

Coissac, G. Michel. Mon Limousin; moeurs, coutumes, légendes. Paris, Lahure. 1913. 438 p.

Cordier, Eugène. Le droit de famille aux Pyrénées: Barège, Lavedan, Béarn et pays basques. Paris, A. Durand. 1860. 119 p.

Cortet, Eugène. Essai sur les fêtes religieuses et les traditions populaires qui s'y rattachent. Paris, Thorin. 1867. 283 p.

Coulon, Henri. Érreurs et superstitions médicales dans la Cambrésis. Société d'Émulation de Cambrai, Mémoires. 65(1911): 1-51.

Cuzacq, Pierre. La naissance, le mariage et le décès; moeurs et coutumes, usages anciens, croyances et superstitions dans le sud-ouest de la France. Paris, Picard. 1902. 192 p.

Cuzacq, René. Nouvelle contribution à l'histoire du béret. Mont-de-Marsan, Éd. Jean-Lacoste. 1951. 32 p.

Dachler, Anton. Die bäuerliche Beziehung in Frankreich. M.A.G.W. 43(1913): 150-160.

Dardy, Abbé Léopold. Anthologie de l'Albret, sud-ouest de l'Argenais ou Gascogne landaise. Agen, Michel et Médan. 1891. 30, 366 p.

Daugé, Abbé C. Le mariage et la famille en Gascogne d'après les proverbes. 3 vols. Paris, Picard. 1916 (vol. 1) 8, 294 p.; Duhort-Bachon, Lande. 1930 (vols. 2 and 3) 1, 418; 1, 312 p.

Dauzat, Albert. Le argots; caractères, évolution, influence. Paris, Delagrave. 1929, 189 p.

Dauzat, Albert. Le village et le paysan de France. Paris, Gallimard. 1941. 219 p.

Deffontaines, Pierre. Les hommes et leurs travaux dans les pays de la moyenne Garonne (Agenais, Bas-Quercy). Lille, S.I.L.I.C., Facultés Catholiques. 1932. 33, 462 p., plates, map.

Delebecque, Édouard. Un village qui s'éteint. Avignon, Impr. Rullière Frères. 1951. 87 p.

Delisle, L. Études sur la condition de la classe agricole et l'état de l'agriculture en Normandie. Evreaux, Impr. de A. Herissey. 1851; Paris, H. Champion. 1903. 56, 758 p.

Demangeon, Albert. La Picardie et les régions voisines, Artois-Cambrésis-Beauvaisis. Paris, A. Colin. 1925. 496 p.

Demiashkievitch, Michael John. The national mind: English, French, German. New York, Cincinnati, American Book Co. 1938: 179-333.

Demongé, Gaston. Les terreux. Panoramas cauchois. Le patois normand, à travers poètes et conteurs. Gestes et visages. Fécamp, L. Durand. 1955. 242 p.

Desrousseaux, A. Moeurs populaires de la Flandre française. 2 vols. Lille, Quarré. 1889. 8, 312, 367 p.

Dion, Roger. Le val de Loire. Étude de géographie régionale. Tours, Arrault. 1934. 752 p., plates, maps.

Dion, Roger. Essai sur la formation du paysage rural français. Tours, Arrault. 1934. 162 p.

Dornheim, A. Die bäuerliche Sachkultur im Gebiet der oberen Ardèche. Volkstum und Kultur der Romanen. 9(1936): 202-388; 10(1937): 247-369.

Dubois, Ernest. L'industrie du tissage du lin dans les Flandres. Bruxelles, J. Lebègue. 1900. 225 p.

Duby, Georges. L'économie rurale et la vie des Campagnes dans l'Occident médieval. Paris, Aubier. 1962. 822 p.

Duffard, Paul. L'Armagnac noir ou Bas-Armagnac. 2d ed. Auch. 1902. 4, 348 p.

Dumont, Louis. La Tarasque. Essai de description d'un fait local du point de vue ethnographique. Paris, Gallimard. 1951. 252 p.

Dumont, René, Henri Mendras, et al. Les paysans. Esprit. 227 (June 1955): 897-1072.

Duplessis-le-Guelinel, Gérard. Les mariages en France. Paris, A. Colin. 1954. 12, 199 p.

Durand, Alfred. La vie rurale dans les massifs volcaniques des Dores, du Cézallier, du Cantal et de l'Aubrac. Aurillac, Impr. Moderne. 1946. 12, 530 p.

Edwards, Matilda Barbara B. France of today: a survey, comparative and retrospective. New York, Lovell, Coryell. 1892. 309 p.

Edwards, Matilda Barbara B. Home life in France. Chicago, A. C. McClurg. 1905. 12, 310 p., plates.

Ernle, Rowland Edmund P., Baron. The pleasant land of France. London, J. Murray; New York, E. P. Dutton. 1908. 7, 359 p.

Escholier, R. Gascogne, types et coutumes. Paris, A. Michel. 1933. 242 p.

Evans, Emyr Estyn. France, a geographical introduction. London, Christophers. 1937. 16, 183 p., maps.

Fahrhoz, Günther. Wohnen und Wirtschaft im Bergland der oberen Ariège. Hamburger Studien zu Volkstum und Kultur der Romanen. Vol. 9. Hamburg, Seminar für romanische Sprachen und Kultur. 1931. 164 p., 40 illus., 7 plates, map.

Farcy, Henri de. Paysans du Lyonnaise: la vie agricole dans la vallée de l'Yzeron. Lyon, Institut des Études Rhodaniennes. 1950. 170 p., figs., maps, table, plates.

Fel, André. Les hautes terres du Massif Central. Tradition paysanne et économie agricole. Paris, Presses Universitaires de France. 1963. 340 p., 48 illus.

Festy, Octave. L'agriculture pendant la révolution française. Les conditions de production et de récolte des céréales. Étude d'histoire économique, 1789-1795. Paris, Gallimard. 1947. 463 p., illus.

Festy, Octave. L'agriculture pendant la révolution française. L'utilisation de jachères 1789-1795. Étude d'histoire économique. Paris, Libr. Marcel Rivière. 1950. 156 p.

Festy, Octave. L'agriculture française sous le consulat. Paris, Éd. Académie Napoléon. 1952. 288 p.

Flagge, Ludwig. Provenzalisches Alpenleben in den Hochtälern des Verdon und der Bléone: ein Beitrag zur Volkskunde der Basses-Alpes. Firenze, L. S. Olschki. 1935. 190 p.

Fleure, Herbert J. French life and its problems. London, Hachette. 1943. 143 p.

Foix, V. Sorcières et loups-garous dans les landes. Auch, Impr. Centrale. 1904. 72 p.

Foley, Daniel J. Little saints of Christmas; the santons of Provence. Boston, Dresser, Chapman and Grimes. 1959. 150 p.

Le Folklore Vivant; Cahiers Internationaux d'Art et de Littérature Populaire. 1(1946)-- Paris, Éditions Elzevir.

Ford, Ford Madox. A mirror to France. New York, A. & C. Boni. 1926. 290 p.

Fournier, Gabriel. Le peuplement rural en Basse Auvergne durant le haut moyen age. Paris, Presses Universitaires de France. 1962. 678 p.

France. European conference on rural life. National monographs drawn up by governments. Series of League of Nations Publications. European Conference on Rural Life. 22. Geneva, League of Nations. 1939. 107 p., illus.

Fraysse, C. Le folk-lore du Baugeois, recueil de légendes, traditions, croyances et superstitions populaires. Baugé, Dangin. 1906. 196 p.

French Folklore Bulletin. Vol. 1 (1941)-- New York, French Folklore Society.

Friedman, G. Villes et campagnes. Civilisation urbaine et civilisation rurale en France. Paris, A. Colin. 1953. 480 p.

Gachon, Lucien. Les écoles du paysan. Paris, Presses Universitaires de France. 1942. 64 p.

Gachon, Lucien. L'Auvergne et le Velay. Paris, Gallimard. 1948. 351 p.

Gagnon, Camille. Le folklore bourbonnais. 1. La vie matérielle. Moulins, Crépin-Leblond. 1947. 156 p.

Gagnon, Camille. Le folklore bourbonnais. 2. Les croyances et les coutumes. Moulins, Crépin-Leblond. 1949. 399 p.

Ganiagé, J. Trois villages d'Île-de-France au XVIIIᵉ siècle; étude démographique. Paris, Presses Universitaires de France. 1963. 147 p.

Garavel, Joseph. Les paysans de Morette. Un siècle de vie rurale dans une commune du Dauphiné. Paris, A. Colin. 1948. 123 p., figs., map.

Gardette, P. Atlas linguistique et ethnographique du Lyonnais. 2 vols. Lyon, Institut de Linguistique Romane des Facultés Catholiques de Lyon. 1950, 1952.

Garneret, Jean. Un village comtois Lantenne; ses coutumes, son patois. Paris, Les Belles Lettres. 1959. 390 p., figs., plates, map.

Gauthier, Joseph Stany. Les maisons paysannes des vieilles provinces de France. New ed. Paris, C. Massin. 1951. 263 p., figs., plate.

Gennep, Arnold van. Le folklore: croyances et coutumes populaires françaises. Paris, Stock. 1924. 125 p.

*Gennep, Arnold van. Le folklore du Dauphiné (Isère): étude descriptive et comparée de psychologie populaire. 2 vols. Paris, G.-P. Maisonneuve. 1932. 792 p.

*Gennep, Arnold van. Le folklore de la Bourgogne (Côte d'Or) avec une discussion théorique su le prétendu culte des sources. Gap, Imprimerie Louis Jean. 1934. 204 p.

*Gennep, Arnold van. Le folklore de la Flandre et du Hainaut français (Département du Nord). 2 vols. Paris, G.-P. Maisonneuve. 1935-1936.

*Gennep, Arnold van. Manuel de folklore français contemporain. Tome 1, pts. 1 and 2. Du berceau à la tombe: mariage, funérailles. 2 vols. Paris, A. & J. Picard. 1946. 831 p., 10 maps.

*Gennep, Arnold van. Manuel de folklore français contemporain. Tome 1, pt. 3. Cérémonies périodiques et cycliques. 1. Carnaval-Carême-Pâques. Paris, A. & J. Picard. 1947. 15, 832-1416 p.

*Gennep, Arnold van. Manuel de folklore français contemporain. Tome 1, pt. 4. Les cérémonies périodiques, cycliques et saisonnières. 2. Cycle de mai, cycle de la St. Jean, et de la St. Pierre. Paris, A. & J. Picard. 1949. 19, 1417-2136 p.

*Gennep, Arnold van. Manuel de folklore français contemporain. Tome 1, pt. 5. Le cérémonies périodiques, cycliques et saisonnières. 3. Les cérémonies agricoles et pastorales de l'été. Paris, A. & J. Picard. 1951. 28, 2137-2544 p., maps.

*Gennep, Arnold van. Manuel de folklore français contemporain. Tome 1, pt. 6. Les cérémonies périodiques, cycliques et saisonnières. 4. Les cérémonies agricoles et pastorales de l'automne. Paris, A. & J. Picard. 1953. 24, 2545-2854 p., illus., maps.

*Gennep, Arnold van. Manuel de folklore français contemporain. Tome 1, pt. 7. Cycle des douze jours. Tournées et chansons de quête-Personnification du cycle feux, bûchers et brandons mobiles. La bûche et le tison de Noël. Paris, A. & J. Picard. 1957. 11, 2855-3166 p.

*Gennep, Arnold van. Manuel de folklore français contemporain. Tome 3. Questionnaires--Provinces et pays. Bibliographie méthodique. Paris, Picard. 1937. 552 p.

*Gennep, Arnold van. Manuel de folklore français contemporain. Tome 4. Bibliographie méthodique (fin). Index des noms d'auteurs. Index par provinces. Paris, Picard. 1938. p. 553-1078.

*Gennep, Arnold van. Le folklore des Hautes-Alpes. Étude descriptive et comparée de psychologie populaire. 2 vols. Paris, Maisonneuve. 1946, 1948. 434, 323 p.

*Gennep, Arnold van. Le folklore de l'Auvergne et du Velay. Paris, Maisonneuve. 1942. 371 p.

Gennep, Ketty van. Bibliographie des oeuvres d'Arnold van Gennep. Paris, A. & J. Picard. 1964. 91 p.

Giese, Wilhelm. Volkskundliches aus dem Hochalpen der Dauphiné. Hamburg Universität, Abhandlungen aus dem Gebiete der Auslandskunde, Bd. 37. Hamburg, W. de Gruyter. 1932. 10, 149 p.

Glath, Paul E. Un village lorrain, Bousseviller. Niederbronn, Impr. Commerciale. 1948. 319 p.

Goldstern, Eugenie. Hochgebirgsvolk in Savoyen und Graubünden. Ein Beitrag zur romanischen Volkskunde. Wien, Verlag des Vereins für Volkskunde. 1922. 4, 114 p., 28 plates.

Govin, Louis. Construction rurales. La ferme; ses constructions, son aménagement, son équipment. 2 vols. Paris, J. Baillière et fils. 1957. 1006 p.

Guillaumin, Émile. Notes paysannes et villageoises. Paris, Bibliothèque d'education. 1925. 192 p.

Guillaumin, Émile. Panorama de l'évolution paysanne. Colombes, Cahiers de la Quinzaine. 1935. 88 p.

Guillaumin, Émile. Paysans par eux-mêmes. Paris, Stock, Delamain et Boutelleau. 1935. 308 p.

Guillemaut, Lucien. Bresse louhannaise; les mois de l'années; usages, moeurs, fêtes, traditions populaires. Louhans, Romans. 1907. 239 p.

Guillemot, A. G. Essais de folklore marnais; contes, légendes, vieilles coutumes de la Marne. Châlons-sur-Marne. 1908. 316 p.

Hamerton, Philip Gilbert. Round my house. Notes of rural life in France in peace and war. Boston, Roberts Brothers. 1890. 12, 415 p.

Hamerton, Philip Gilbert. French and English. A comparison. Boston, Roberts Brothers. 1891. 22, 480 p.

Henrey, Mrs. Robert. A farm in Normandy & the return to the farm. London, Dent. 1952. 398 p.

Henrey, Mrs. Robert. The little Madeleine; the autobiography of a young girl in Montmartre. New York, Dutton. 1953. 350 p.

*Hoffmann, Stanley H., C. P. Kinderberger, L. Wylie, etc. In search of France. Cambridge, Mass., Harvard University Press. 1963. 14, 443 p.

Hunter, Neil. Peasantry and crisis in France. London, V. Gollancz. 1938. 287 p.

Jeanton, Gabriel. Le Mâconnais traditionaliste et populaire. 4 vols. 1. Le peuple, le costume, l'habitation. 2. Pélérinages et légendes sacrées. 3. Fêtes du terroir et coutumes du foyer. 4. Naissances, mariages, sépultures. Mâcon, Protat. 1920, 1921, 1922, 1923. 106, 104, 104, 100 p.

Jeanton, Gabriel. L'habitation rustique au pays mâconnais; étude de folklore, d'ethnographie et de géographie humaine. Tournus, Amis Arts et Science. 1932. 119 p., 45 figs., 32 plates.

Johnson, William Branch. Among French folk: a book for vagabonds. London, C. Palmer. 1922; Boston, Small, Maynard. 1923. 256 p.

Johnson, William Branch. Folk tales of Provence. London, Chapman and Hall. 1927. 224 p.

Johnson, William Branch. Folk tales of Normandy. London, Chapman and Hall. 1929. 13, 260 p.

Joisten, C. Contes et chansons folkloriques des Hautes-Alpes. Gap, Impr. Ribaud Frères. 1956. 95 p.

Jourdanne, Gaston. Contribution au folklore de l'Aude; usages, coutumes, littérature populaire, traditions légendaires. Paris, Maisonneuve; Carcassonne, Gabelle. 1899. 243 p.

Kayser, Bernard. Campagnes et villes de la Côte d'Azur. Essai sur les conséquences du développement urbain. Monaco, Éditions du Rocher. 1958. 595 p., graphs, maps.

Kesselman, Mark. The ambiguous consensus. A study of local government in France. New York, Alfred A. Knopf. 1967. 12, 201, 7 p.

Kohn, H. Making of the modern French mind. Toronto, New York, London, Van Nostrand. 1955. 191 p.

Krüger, Fritz. Sach- und Wortkundliches vom Wasser in Pyrenäen. Volkstum und Kultur der Romanen. 2(1929): 139-243.

*Krüger, Fritz. Die Hochpyrenäen, B. Hirtenkultur. Volkstum und Kultur der Romanen. 8(1935): 10-103, 8 plates.

*Krüger, Fritz. Die Hochpyrenäen. D. Hausindustrie, Tracht, Gewerbe. Volkstum und Kultur der Romanen. 8(1935): 210-328; 9(1936): 1-106.

*Krüger, Fritz. Die Hochpyrenäen, A. Landschaften, Haus und Hof. Bd. 1. Hamburg, Hansische Universität, Abhandlungen aus dem Gebiet der Auslandskunde. 44. Hamburg, de Gruyter. 1936. 18, 238 p., 44 plates, map.

*Krüger, Fritz. Die Hochpyrenäen. C. Ländliche Arbeit. Bd. 1. Transport und Transportgeräte. Butlletí de Dialectología Catalana. 23 (1936): 39-240. 14 figs., 89 photos.

*Krüger, Fritz. Die Hochpyrenäen. C. Ländliche Arbeit. Bd. 2. Getreide-Heuernte-Bienenwohnung-Wein-und Ölbereitung. Hamburger Studien zu Volkstum und Kultur der Romanen. 32. 1939. 10, 500 p., illus., 36 plates.

*Krüger, Fritz. Die Hochpyrenäen. A. Landschaften, Haus und Hof. Bd. 2. Hamburg, Hansische Universität, Abhandlungen aus dem Gebiet der Auslandskunde. 47. 1939. 18, 400 p., illus., 17 plates.

*Krüger, Fritz. Géographie des traditions populaires en France. Mendoza (Argentina), Universidad Nacional del Cuyo, Faculdad de Filosofía y Letras. 1950. 255 p.

Laborde, Camille. Essai sur les vieilles coutumes rustiques du pays marchois; le mariage, la naissance, le baptême, la mort. Guéret, Impr. Lecante. 1946. 79 p.

Labourasse, Henri. Anciens us, coutumes, légendes, superstitions, préjuges, etc. du dép. de la Meuse. Société des Lettres, Sciences et Arts de Bar-le-Duc, Mémoires. Sér. 4. 1 (1902): 1-225.

Lacroix, Paul. The XVIIIth century; its institutions, customs, and costumes. France 1700-1789. London, Chapman and Hall; New York, Scribner, Welford and Armstrong. 1876. 16, 489 p.

Lacroix, Paul. Directoire, consulat et empire. Moeurs et usages, lettres, sciences et arts. France 1795-1815. Paris, Didot. 1884. 564 p.

Lacroix, Paul. Curiosités infernales. Paris, Garnier Frères. 1886. 396 p.

Laisnel de la Salle, A. and C. Croyances et légendes du centre de la France. 2 vols. Paris, A. Chaix. 1875. 25, 748 p.

Laisnel de la Salle, Germaine. Souvenirs du vieux temps: Le Berry . . . 2 vols. Paris, J. Maisonneuve. 1900-1902.

Lallemont, Abbé Louis. Folklore argonnais. Almanach Matot-Braine. 56 (1914): 203-243.

Lambert, K. Chants et chansons populaires du Languedoc. 2 vols. Paris and Leipzig, H. Welter. 1906. 8, 375; 345 p.

Lancelin, Charles. La sorcellerie des campagnes. New ed. Paris, Durville. 1910. 493 p.

Landreau, Félix. Coutumes et légendes du pays d'Anjou. Angers, Impr. Centrale. 1949. 84 p., illus.

Lapaire, Hugues. Le folklore berrichon. Moulins, Crépin-Leblond. 1945. 127 p.

Laprade, Mme. Duguet de. French textiles. Survey of World Textiles. 9. Leigh-on-Sea, F. Lewis. 1955. 21 p., 92 plates.

Laroque, Pierre. Les institutions sociales de la France. Paris, La Documentation Française. 1963. 1022 p.

Lavergne, Leonée de. Économie rurale de la France depuis 1789. Paris, Guillaumin. 1860 (and later printings). 473 p.

Le Balle, Yves. L'ouvrier paysan en Lorraine mosellane. Étude sur l'alternance d'activités. Paris, Domat-Montchrestien. 1958. 116 p., maps.

*Lebeau, René. La vie rurale dans les montagnes du Jura méridional. Étude de géographie humaine. Trevoux, Impr. J. Petissier. 1955. 604 p., plates, maps.

Le Bras, G. Études de sociologie religieuse. Vol. 1. La pratique religieuse dans les campagnes françaises. Paris, Presses Universitaires de France, 1955. 394 p.

Ledieu, Alcius. Contributions au traditionnisme picard: baptêmes, mariage, enterrements. Conférence des Rosati Picards. Fasc. 18. Amiens, Ollivier. 1905. 41 p.

*Lefèbvre, Th. Les modes de vie dans les Pyrénées atlantiques orientales. Paris, A. Colin. 1933. 777 p., plates.

Leferrere, M. Lyon, ville industrielle. Essai d'une géographie urbaine des techniques et des enterprises. Paris, Presses Universitaires de France. 1960. 12, 548 p.

Lehucher, André. La vie agricole dans le Coutançais. Paris, de Boccard. 1927. 188 p., 2 plates. (Normandy)

*Le Play, Frédéric. Les ouvriers européens. 2d ed. 6 vols. Tours, Mame; Paris, Dentu, Larcher. 1877-1879. (Especially see vols. 4, 5, and 6.)

Leroy, Charles. Mariages en Basse-Normandie il y a cent ans. Bulletin de la Société d'Émulation Seine-Inférieure, exercice 1935: 303-338.

Leroy, Olivier. A dictionary of French slang. London, G. G. Harrap. 1935. 237 p.

Livet, R. Habitat rural et structures agraires en Basse-Provence. Gap, Ophrys. 1962. 465 p.

Llobet, Salvador. El medio y la vida en el Montseny, estudio geográfico. Barcelona, Consejo Superior de Investigaciones Científicas, Estación de Estudios Pirenaicos. 1947. 11, 518 p.

Locquin, J. Ethnographie de l'Auxois. Bulletin de la Société Scientifique, Historique et Naturelles de Semur. 1 (1865): 65-116.

Loew, Jacques. Les dockers de Marseille, analyse type d'un complexe. 2d ed. L'Arbresle, Éd. Économie et Humanisme. n.d. [1945?]. 10, 111 p.

Louis, M. L. A. La procession de la "sanch" à Perpignan. Folklore (Carcassonnei (Carcassonne). 23 (1960): 1-7.

Lugnier, Antoine. Cinq siècles de vie paysanne à Roche-en-Forez, Loire. (1440-1940). Saint-Étienne, Impr. Aumas. 1962. 414 p., map, plates.

Lynch, Hannah. French life in town and country. New York, London, G. P. Putnam's Sons. 1901. 7, 311 p., plates.

Madariaga, Salvador de. Englishmen, Frenchmen and Spaniards. London, Oxford University Press, H. Milford. 1931. 19, 256 p.

Maget, M. Remarques sur l'ethnographie française métropolitaine. Buts, méthodes, désignation. Bulletin de la Société Neuchâteloise de Géographie. 55 (1948): 39-58.

Maget, M. Ethnographie métropolitaine. Guide d'étude directe des comportements culturels. Paris, Civilisations du Sud. 1953. 260 p.

Maitre, J. Les fréquences des prénoms de baptême en France: rite de denommnation et linguistique statistique. Année Sociologique. Sér. 3. 14 (1964): 31-74, illus.

Martin, Eugéne. Folklore de Saint-Rémy, Vosges; croyances, coutumes, patois. Nancy, Éd. du Pays Lorrain et de la Revue Lorraine Illustrée. 1907. 27 p.

Mazaleyrat, Jean. La vie rurale sur le plateau de Millevaches. Essai d'ethnographie linguistique. Paris, Presses Universitaires de France. 1959. 297 p.

Mendras, Henri. Études de sociologie rurale: novis et virgin. Paris, A. Colin. 1953. 8, 156 p., figs., maps.

Mendras, Henri, and M. Jollivet. Les sociétés rurales françaises: inventaire typologique et étude de changements sociaux. Information, N. S. 4 (1965): 51-66.

Menon, P. L., and R. Lecotté. Au village de France: la vie traditionelle. 1.
De la chandleur à la Saint-Jean. 2. Des moissons à la Noël. 2 vols.
Paris, Bourrelier. 1954. 125, 128 p.

Mercier, A. L. Enquête sur les végétaux dans le folklore et l'ethnographie:
flore populaire. Ethnographie, N. S. 46 (1951): 125-139; 47 (1952): 86-
113; 48 (1953): 48-61; 49 (1954): 82-92.

*Métraux, Rhoda B. Themes in French culture; a preface to a study of French
community. Stanford, Stanford University Press. 1954. 11, 120 p.

Meyer, H. Bauerliches Hauswesen in Gebiete zwischen Toulouse und Cahors.
Volkstum und Kultur der Romanen. 5 (1932): 317-371; 6 (1933): 27-135.

Meyrac, Albert. Traditions, coutumes, légendes et contes des Ardennes
comparés avec les traditions, légendes, et contes de divers pays. Charleville, Impr. du Petit Ardennais. 1890. 589 p., plus 2 p. of corrections.

Meyrac, Albert. Villes et villages des Ardennes; histoire, légende des lieux-
dits et souvenirs de l'année terrible. Charleville, Impr. du Petit Ardennais.
1898. 602 p.

Michot, A. La Loire et ses mariniers. La Charité-sur-Loire, A. Delayance.
1955. 69 p., plate, maps. (A summary of an earlier work: R. Toscan.
1938.)

Mikes, G. Little cabbages. London, A. Wingate. 1955. 155 p.

Moiset, Charles. Les usages, croyances, traditions, superstitions, etc., ayant
existé autrefois ou existant encore dans les divers pays du départment de
l'Yonne. Bulletin de la Société des Sciences Historiques, et Naturelles de
l'Yonne. 42 (1888): 5-158.

Monin, Ernest. L'alcoolisme; étude médico-sociale. Paris, Doin. 1917.
274 p.

Monnier, Désiré, and Aimé Vingtrinier. Croyances et traditions populaires
recueillies dans la Franche-Comté, le Lyonnais, la Bresse et le Bugey. 2d
ed. Lyon, Georg. 1874. 2, 812 p.

Moreau, J. P. La vie rurale dans le sud-est du bassin parisien entre les
vallées de l'Armançon et de la Loire. Étude de géographie humaine. Paris,
Les Belles Lettres. 1958. 340 p., plate, maps.

Naudot, Carle. Ethnographie du pays d'Arles; contribution au folklore de
Camargue. Arles, the author. 194?. 45 p., illus.

Noblet, Gaston. De l'île d'Oleron à Mortagne-sur-Gironde; histoire de Royan et des ses environs, précédée de l'histoire générale de la Saintonge; moeurs, coutumes, etc. Fontenay-aux-Roses, Bellenand. 1905. 360 p.

Oddo, Henri. La Provence; usages, coutumes, idiomes depuis les origines; le félibrige, etc. Paris, Le Soudier. 1902. 320 p.

Orain, Adolphe. Folk-lore de l'Ille-et-Vilaine. De la vie à la mort. 2 vols. Paris, Maisonneuve. 1897-1898.

Padover, Saul K. French institutions: values and politics. Stanford, Stanford University Press. 1954. 6, 102 p.

Paret, Lotte. Das ländliche Leben einer Gemeinde de Hautes-Pyrénées, dargestellt auf Grund der mundartlichen Terminologie. Tübingen. 1932. 90 p. (Thesis.)

Pariset, F. Économie rurale, moeurs et usages du Lauraguais (Aude et Haute-Garonne). Paris, Bouchard-Huzard. 1867. 256 p., 2 plates.

Paul, Elliot Harold. Understanding the French. New York, Random House. 1955. 186 p.

Pauly, E. Folklore bourbonnais; les Brayauds de Combraille. Moulin, Crépin-Leblond. 1936. 160 p.

Peattie, Donald Culross. Vence: the story of a Provencal town through two thousand years. Nice, Imprimerie de l'Éclaireur de Nice. 1930. 167 p. (Reprinted: Chicago, University of Chicago Press. 1963. 21, 199 p., illus.)

Peattie, Roderick. The Conflent: a study in mountain geography. Geographical Review. 20(1930): 245-257. (Pyrenees)

Pérot, Francis. Folk-lore bourbonnais; ancien usages; sorciers et rebouteurs; meneurs de loups; vielles et musettes; jeux du temps passé; les fées; les noces; les sorts. Paris, Leroux. 1908. 248 p.

Perraudière, Xavier de la. Traditions locales et superstitions; notes prises au pays de Maine et d'Anjou. Mémoires de la Société Nationale d'Agriculture, Sciences et Arts d'Angers, 4th sér. 10(1896): 65-80.

Philippe, M.-P. La Normandie en 1834; moeurs, usages, antiquités, costumes et statistique des cinq départements composant cette ancienne province. Paris, Impr. Fain et Lithog. Mantoux. 1834. 76 p., 5 plates.

*Philipponneau, Michael. La vie rurale de la banlieue parisienne; étude de géographie humaine. Paris, A. Colin. 1956. 593 p., plates, maps.

Pilot de Throey, J. J. A. Usages, fêtes et coutumes existant ou ayant existé en Dauphiné. 2 vols. Grenoble, Drevet. 1882. 464 p.

*Pitt-Rivers, Julian. Social class in a French village. Anthropological Quarterly. 33(1960): 1-13.

*Pitts, Jesse R. Continuity and change in bourgeois France. In Stanley Hoffman et al. In Search of France. Cambridge, Harvard University Press. 1963: 235-304.

Pluquet, Frédéric. Contes populaires, préjugés, patois, proverbes, noms de lieux de l'arrondissement de Bayeux. 2d ed. Rouen, Frère. 1834. 13, 163 p. (1st ed. 1825.)

*Porak, René. Un village de France (Psycho-physiologie du paysan). Paris, G. Doin. 1943. 110 p.

Provence, Marcel. Calendrier des fêtes provençales. 2d ed. n.p., Bureau d'Études de l'École de Cadres du Coudou. 1942. 16, 150 p.

Quoist, Michel. La ville et l'homme. Rouen, étude sociologique d'un secteur prolétarien suivie de conclusions pour l'action. Paris, Éditions Ouvrières, Économie et Humanisme. 1952. 296 p., figs., graphs, maps.

Racoulet, Abbé Eugène (dit Alfred). Une famille de laboureurs: les Magnier de Loisy, essai d'histoire geneologique (Quatre cents ans de vie agricole en pays laonnais). Chauny, Impr. de A. Baticle. 1952. 295 p.

Rambaud, Placide. Economie et sociologie de la montagne. Albiez-le-Vieux en Maurienne. Paris, A. Colin. 1962. 292 p., maps, plates.

Rambaud, Placide, and Monique Vincienne. Les transformations d'une société rurale. La Maurienne (1561-1962). Paris, A. Colin. 1964. 280 p., tables, graphs, maps, plates.

Raynal, François Paul. Les artisans du village. Paris, Publications Techniques. 1943. 153 p., photos.

Revue des Traditions Populaires, recueil de mythologie, literature orale, ethnographie traditionnelle et art populaire. 32 vols. Paris, Société des Traditions Populaires, au Musée d'Ethnographie du Trocadéro. 1886-1918.

Revue Français de Sociologie. Paris, Centre d'Études Sociologiques. 1960. Vol. 1--

Richard fils, N. L. A. Traditions populaires, croyances superstitieuses, usages et coutumes de l'ancienne Lorraine. Remiremont, Mougin. 1848. 270 p.

FRENCH

Rivière, Cléry. La vallée de l'Aubetin. Un paysage de Brie. Paris, A. and
J. Picard. 1950. 390 p.

Rivière, G. H. Objects domestiques des provinces de France dans la vie
familiale et les arts ménagers. Paris, Éditions des Musées Nationaux. 1953.
62 p., illus.

Robert, Jean. La maison rurale permanente dans les Alpes françaises du nord.
Étude de géographie humaine. Tours, Allier. 1939. 8, 517 p., plus
album of 152 p. of plates.

Rocal, Abbé Georges. Les vieilles coutumes dévotieuses et magiques du
Périgord. Toulouse, Occitania, Marqueste. 1922. 220 p.

Rocal, Abbé Georges. Folklore: le vieux Périgord. Paris, Toulouse, and
Marseille, Occitania, Guitard. 1927. 256 p.

Root, Waverley. The food of France. New York, Vintage Books. 1966. 15,
450, 27 p., 10 maps. (Social history.)

Roquette-Buisson, Comte de. Les valées pyrénéennes, essai sur les coutumes
d'une région française. Tarbes, Impr. Pyrénéenne. 1921. 16, 352 p.

Rouchon, Ulysse. La vie paysanne dans la Haute-Loire; la terre, la race, la
maison, le costume, la nourriture, les moyens d'activité, les industries
rustiques de l'habitation, du vêtement, de l'alimentation et du travail.
Le Puy-en-Velay, Éd. Société Études Locales. 1933. 133 p., 9 plates.

Rouge, Jacques-Marie. Folklore de la Touraine: Tours, Chinon et Loches.
Tours, Impr. Tourangelle. 1923. 204 p.

Rouleaux, Claude. Essai de folklore de la Sologne bourbonnaise, il y a un
demi-siècle. Moulins, Crépin-Leblond. 1931. 181 p.

Royal Academy of Dancing and the Ling Physical Education Association.
Dances of France. 3 vols. 1. Brittany and Bourbonnais. 2. Provence and
Alsace. 3. Pyrenees. New York, Crown. 1950-1952. 40 p. plates; 40
p. plates; 40 p. plates.

Sadoun, Roland, Giorgio Lolli, and Milton Silverman. Drinking in French
culture. New Brunswick, Rutgers Center of Alcohol Studies. 1965. 151 p.

Sclafert, Thérèse. Cultures en Haute-Provence. Déboisemants et pasturages
au moyen âge. Paris, S. E. V. P. E. N. 1959. 264 p.

Sébillot, Paul. Le folk-lore de France. 4 vols. Paris, Librairie Orientale &
Américaine. 1904-1907.

Sébillot, Paul. Le paganisme contemporain chez les peuples celto-latins. Paris, O. Doin. 1908. 26, 378 p.

Seignolle, Claude. Le folklore du Languedoc (Gard, Hérault, Lozère). Cérémonies familiales, sorcellerie et médecine populaire, folklore de la nature. Paris, Besson et Chantemerle. 1960. 302 p.

Seignolle, Claude. Le folklore de la Provence. Paris, G.-P. Maisonneuve et Larose. 1963. 387 p.

Seignolle, Claude, and J. Seignolle. Le folklore du Hurepoix (Seine, S.-et-Oise, S.-et-Marne). Paris, G.-P. Maisonneuve. 1937. 333 p., 4 plates, 4 maps.

Siegfried, André. France: a study in nationality. London, Oxford University Press, H. Milford. 1930. 122 p.

Sion, Jules. Les paysans de la Normandie orientale: pays de Caux, Bray, Vexin normand, vallées de la Seine; étude géographique. Paris, Colin. 1909. 544 p., 14 figs., 8 plates.

Sion, Jules. La France méditerranéenne. Paris, A. Colin. 1934. 222 p.

Soboul, Albert, et al. Journées d'ethnographie française. Revue de Synthèse, sér. 3. 7(1957): 283-440.

Sorre, Max. Étude sur la transhumance dans la region montpellieraine. Bulletin de la Société Languedocienne de Géographie. 35(1912): 1-40.

Sorre, Max. Les Pyrénées. Paris, A. Colin. 1922.

Souché, B. Proverbes, traditions, diverses, conjurations (en Poitou). Société de Statistique, Sciences, et Arts du Département des Deux-Sèvres Bulletins. 4(1881): 483-540.

Sutter, J., and L. Tabah. Effets de la consanguinité et de l'endogamie. Une enquête en Morbihan et Loir-et-Cher. Population. 7(1952): 249-266.

Tabault, Roger. Mon village. Ses hommes. Ses routes. Son école. 1848-1914. L'Ascension d'un peuple. Paris, Delagrave. 1945. 252 p. (Deux-Sèvres region.)

Tardieux, S. Meubles régionaux datés. Paris, V. Fréal. 1950. 32 p.

Thompson, I. B., et al. The St. Malo region, Brittany. Regional Studies. 12. Nottingham, Geographical Field Group, Geography Department, University of Nottingham. 1967. 8, 98 p., illus., maps. (French-speaking region of Brittany.)

Thut, I. N., and Don Adams. Educational patterns in contemporary societies. New York, McGraw-Hill. 1964: 110-138. (Chapter on "French education: developing an intellectual elite.")

*Toscan, Raoul. L'épopée des mariniers de Loire. La Charité-sur-Loire, A. Delayance. 1938. 298 p.

Trenard, Gabrielle, and Louis Trenard. Les Bas-Bugey. La terre et les hommes. Belley, Société "Le Bugey." 1951. 418 p., 26 maps, photos.

Tricoire, Jean, and Raymonde Tricoire. Folklore du pays de Mantésegur (Ariège). Toulouse, Institut d'Études Occitanes; Paris, G.-P. Maisonneuve. 1947. 109 p.

Tulippe, Omer. L'habitat rural en Seine-et-Oise. Essai de géographie du peuplement. Liège, Wyckmans. 1934. 374 p., plates, maps, tables.

Vaultier, Roger. Les fêtes populaires à Paris. Paris, Éd. du Myrte. 1946. 267 p., 12 plates.

Veyret-Vernier, Germaine. L'industrie dans les Alpes françaises. Étude géographique. Grenoble and Paris, Arthaud. 1948. 373 p., figs., maps, plates.

Vidal de la Blache, Paul M. J. The personality of France. London, New York, A. A. Knopf. 1928. 9, 84 p.

Vingtrinier, Aimé. Études populaires sur la Bresse et le Bugey. Lyon, Storck. 1902. 349 p.

Vingtrinier, Emmanuel. La vie lyonnaise, autrefois-aujourdhui. Lyon, Bernoux & Cumin. 1898. 424 p.

Virtanen, Reino. French national character in the twentieth century. Annals of the American Academy of Political and Social Sciences. 370(March 1967): 82-92.

Waddington, Mme. Mary Alsop King. Chateau and country life in France. New York, Charles Scribner's Sons. 1908. 333 p.

Waddington, Mme. Mary Alsop King. My first years as a Frenchwoman. New York, Charles Scribner's Sons. 1914. 7, 278 p.

Wendell, Barrett. The France of today. New York, Charles Scribner's Sons. 1907. 379 p.

Wright, Gordon. Rural revolution in France; the peasantry in the twentieth century. Stanford, Stanford University Press. 1964. 11, 271 p.

Wylie, Laurence. Village in the Vaucluse. Cambridge, Harvard University Press. 1957. 345 p., plates.

Wylie, Laurence. Village en Vaucluse. (Translated and edited by Armand Bégué.) Cambridge, Riverside Press. 1961. 222 p.

*Wylie, Laurence. Village in the Vaucluse. 2d ed. Cambridge, Harvard University Press. 1964. 18, 377 p., 33 illus., 2 maps. (Reprinted: New York, Harper and Row-Colophon Books.)

*Wylie, Laurence. Social change at the grass roots. In Stanley Hoffmann et al. In Search of France. Cambridge, Harvard University Press. 1963: 159-234.

Wylie, Laurence. The life and death of a myth. In Melford E. Spiro, ed. Context and Meaning in Cultural Anthropology. New York, The Free Press of Glencoe. 1965: 164-185. (Southwestern Anjou.)

*Wylie, Laurence, et al. Chanzeaux. A village in Anjou. Cambridge, Harvard University Press. 1966. 22, 383 p.

Gennep, Arnold van. Manuel de folklore français contemporain. Paris, Picard. 1937-1957. (See various sections in tome 1: pts. 3-6, and in tomes 3 and 4.)

Sébillot, Paul. Bibliographie des traditions populaires de la Bretagne. 1. Haute-Bretagne; 2. Basse-Bretagne. Paris, Lechevalier. 1896. 42 p.

Anson, Peter F. Mariners of Brittany. London and Toronto, J. M. Dent and Sons; New York, E. P. Dutton. 1931. 13, 254 p.

Baring-Gould, Sabine. A book of Brittany. London, Methuen. 1901. 12, 299 p.

Boiboissel, Yves Marie Jacques G. de. Bretagne, ma mère bien-aimée. Paris, J. Peyronnet. 1955. 126 p.

Bourgeois, Alfred. Ballades et coutumes bretonnes: le carnaval de Tréguier. Société académique de Brest Bulletin. 2d sér. 11(1886): 112-118.

Buffet, Henri François. En Bretagne morbihannaise. Coutumes et traditions du Vannetais bretonnant au XIXe siècle. Paris, Grenoble, B. Arthaud. 1948. 286 p., 62 photos.

Buffet, Henri François. En haute Bretagne. Coutumes et traditions d'Ille-et-Vilaine, des Côtes-du-Nord, gallèses et du Morbihan gallo au XIXe siècle. Paris, Libraire Celtique. 1954. 380 p.

Chapron, J. Dictionnaire des coutumes, croyances et langage du pays de Châteaubriant. Châteaubriant. 1924. 2, 131 p.

Clark, Eleanor. The oysters of Locmariaquer. New York, Pantheon Books. 1964. 203 p.

Couffon de Kerdellec, Gabriel-Marie. Adages agricoles à l'usage Bosquilly, ou Trésor des laboureurs et adages à l'usage des fermiers du canton le Lamballe. Saint-Brieuc, Le Maout. 1841. 49 p.

Creston, René Y. Les costumes des populations bretonnes. I. Généralités. II. La Cornouaille. 2 vols. Rennes, Impr. Nouvelles de Bretagne. 1953-1954. 88, 174 p.

Croze, Austin de. La Bretagne païenne; le fétichisme et le clergé en Cornouaille. Paris. n.d. 31 p., 11 figs.

Decombe, Lucien. Le diable et la sorcellerie en Haute-Bretagne. Mélusine. 1(1877): cols. 61-64.

Diville, William, and André Guilcher. Bretagne et Normandie. Paris, Presses Universitaires de France. 1951. 231 p., plates, maps.

Droüart, Marie. Les saints guérisseurs, les saints protecteurs, et les saints qui regardent de travers en Haute-Bretagne. Vitré, Éd. Unvaniez Arvor; Rennes Impr. Presses de Bretagne. 1939. 56 p., illus.

Droüart, Marie. L'art populaire en Bretagne à travers les âges. 2 albums. Vitré, Éd. Unvaniez Arvor; Rennes, Impr. Centrale. 1940, 1947. 35 p., illus.; 36 p., illus.

Duine, François. Traditions, légendes et superstitions du pays de Dol, Ille-et-Vilaine. R.T.P. 8(1893): 369-375, 590-592; 15(1900): 505-507; 18(1903): 439-440, 523-524, 526-528, 531-532.

Dupouy, Auguste. Histoire de Bretagne. Paris, Boirin. 1932. 6, 424 p.

Esquieu, Louis. Le jeux populaires de l'enfance à Rennes. Rennes, Caillière. 1890. 75 p.

Evans-Wentz, Walter Y. The fairy-faith in Celtic countries. London, Frowde. 1911: 185-225. (Reprinted. New Hyde Park, N.Y., University Books. 1966.)

Favé, Abbé Antoine. Notes sur le vie rurale en Cornouailles pendant les deux derniers siècles. Société Archéologique de Finistère, Bulletin. 20(1893): 55-69.

*Frison-Morlec, Joseph. Les traditions de la Bretagne. Tome 1. Priziac (Morbihan), Impr. de l'Orphelinat Saint Michel. 1962. 296 p.

Gautier, Marcel. La Bretagne centrale. Étude géographique. Rennes, La-Roche-sur-Yon, A. Potier. 1947. 3, 453 p.

Gennep, Arnold van. Manuel de folklore français contemporain. Tomes 1 (pts. 1-7), 3, and 4. (Tome 2 never published.) Paris, A. & J. Picard. 1937-1957. (See sections on Brittany.)

Giese, Wilhelm. Beiträge zur volkstümlichen Siedlung und Wirtschaft in den Monts d'Arrée, Basse-Bretagne. Volkstum und Kultur der Romanen. 4(1931): 343-377.

*Guillotin de Corson, Abbé. Les pardons et pèlerinages de Basse-Bretagne; description des principaux sanctuares vénérés et des solennités qu'on y célèbre. Paris, Champion. 1898. 320 p.

Haberlandt, Arthur. Beiträge zur bretonischen Volkskunde; Erläuterungen zur bretonischen Sammlung des K.K. Museums für österreichische Volkskunde in Wien. Zeitschrift für Österreichische Volkskunde, 18, Ergänzungsheft 8. 1912. 40 p.

BRETONS

Herpin, Eugène. Noces et baptêmes en Bretagne. Rennes, Plihon et Hommay. 1904. 9, 168 p.

Jobbé-Duval, Émile. Les idées primitives dans la Bretagne contemporaine; essais de folklore juridique et d'histoire générale du droit . . . Paris, Libr. du Recueil Sirey. 1930. 96 p.

Johnson, William Branch. Folk tales of Brittany. London, Methuen. 1927. 11, 155 p.

Latour, A. Bretonische Trachten. Ciba-Rundschau. 105 (1952): 3832-3860.

La Villemarqué, Théodore C. H. Hersart, Vicomte de. Barzaz-Breiz. Chants populaires de la Bretagne. 2 vols. Paris, Charpentier (Vol. 1); Paris, A. Franck (vol. 2). 1839, 1846.

La Villemarqué, Théodore C. H. Hersart, Vicomte de. Ballads and songs of Brittany. London and Cambridge, Macmillan. 1865. 22, 239 p.

LeBihan, J. L'entraide paysanne en Bretagne intérieure. Paysans. 10 (1958): 55-64.

*Le Braz, Anatole. La légende de la mort en Basse-Bretagne; croyances populaires. Paris, H. Champion. 1893. 71, 495 p.

Le Braz, Anatole. Dealings with the dead; narratives from "La légende de la mort en Basse-Bretagne." London, G. Redway. 1898. 220 p.

Le Braz, Anatole. The night of fires and other Breton studies. New York, Longmans, Green. 1912. 272 p.

*Le Braz, Anatole. La légende de la mort chez les Bretons armoricains. 2 vols. Paris, Champion. 1923. 40, 448; 506 p.

*Le Braz, Anatole. The land of Pardons. New York, R. M. McBride. 1924. 222 p.

Le Braz, Anatole. Au pays des pardons. Paris, Calmann-Lévy. 1925. 369 p.

Le Braz, Anatole. La Bretagne . . . Paris, H. Laurens. 1928. 252 p.

Le Braz, Anatole. Iles bretonnes . . . Paris, Calmann-Lévy. 1935. 206 p.

Le Braz, Anatole. Les saints bretons d'après la tradition populaire en cornouaille. Paris, Calmann-Lévy. 1937. 8, 169 p.

Le Calvez, G. Rites et usages funéraires; la mort en Basse-Bretagne. R.T.P. 3 (1888): 45-51.

Le Doaré, Jos. Contribution à l'étude des costumes bretons: l'évolution des costumes bretons du pays de Chateaulin depuis 100 ans. Nouvelle Revue de Bretagne. 1950: 421-432; 1951: 35-40, 119-129.

Le Garguet, Henri. Étude ethnographique sur les Bigoudens. Société archaéologique de Finistère, Bulletin. 27(1900): 328-373.

Le Garguet, Henri. Pêcheurs du Raz-de-Sein. R.T.P. 14(1899): 610-613; 15(1900): 99-104.

Legonnidec. Notice sur les cérémonies des mariages dans la partie de la Bretagne connue sous le nom de Bas-Léon. Academie Celtique, Paris, Mémoires. 2(1808): 362-374.

*Le Lannou, Maurice. Géographie de la Bretagne. 2 vols. 1: Les conditions géographiques générales. 2: Économie et population. Rennes, Plihon. 1950 1952. 284, 464 p., illus., plates, maps.

Lelièvre, M. De l'exercise illégal de la médecine en Bretagne; guérisseurs, dormeuses et rebouteurs du pays breton. Paris, Jouve. 1907. 71 p. (Thesis.)

Le Men, R. F. Traditions et superstitions de la Basse-Bretagne. Revue Celtiqu 1(1870-71): 226-242, 414-435. (Reprinted: Paris, Franck. 1872. 36 p.)

Le Roux, M. Mariage, pratique religieuse et saisons en Bretagne. Nouvelle Revue de Bretagne. 2(1949): 116-124.

Le Rouzic, Zacharie. Carnac, légendes, traditions, coutumes et contes du pays. 2d ed. Nantes, Dugas. 1912. 218 p.

Lheur, Victor. Le costume breton de 1900 jusqu'à jpurs. Paris, Éd. au Moulir de-Fer. 1944. 99 plates, map.

Luzel, F. M. Veillées bretons: moeurs, chantes, contes et récits populaires des Bretons armoricains. Paris, Champion. 1879. 291 p.

Luzel, F. M. L'Île de Bréhat en 1873; traditions populaires, lutins, conjurés, revennants. Vannes, Lafolye. 1894. 23 p.

Millour, G. Les saints guérisseurs et protecteurs du bétail en Bretagne. Paris, Librairie Celtique. 194_? 126 p., 15 plates.

Moore, Robert W. The coasts of Normandy and Brittany. National Geographic Magazine. 80(1943): 205-232.

Musée National des Arts et Traditions Populaires. Paris. Exposition: Bretagne. Art populaire, ethnographie régionale. Paris, Éditions des Musées Nationaux 1951. 120 p., plates, illus.

Orain, Adolphe. Folklore de l'Ille-et-Vilaine; de la vie à la mort. 2 vols. Paris, Maisonneuve. 1897-1898.

*Pelras, Ch. Goulien, commune rurale du Cap Sizun (Finistère): étude d'ethnologie globale. Bulletins et Mémoires de la Société d'Anthropologie de Paris. 11 Série. 10 (1966): 141-587. 35 tables, 22 maps, 43 figs., 9 photos.

Pérennès, Chanoine H. Les hymnes de la fête des morts en Basse-Bretagne. Annales de Bretagne. 36 (1924-25): 31-69, 558-595.

Perrin, Olivier, and Alexandre Bouët. Galerie bretonne, ou moeurs et usages et costumes des bretons de l'Armorique. 3 vols. Paris, Perron. 1835-1838. (Reprinted: 3 vols. Paris, Dusillon. 1856. Also: 1 vol. Paris, Champion. 1918. 487 p.)

Pleven, René. Avenir de la Bretagne. Paris, Calmann-Lévy. 1961. 256 p.

Queffélée, Henri. La Bretagne des pardons. Paris, Librairie Hachette. 1962. 109 p.

Renwick, George. Sea-girt Brittany. London, Evans Bros. 1951. 160 p.

Rexroth, Franz von. Armoricana. Von Kult und Dichtung der Bretagne. Darmstadt, H. Luchterhand. 1961. 129 p.

*Robert-Muller, Charles. Pêches et pêcheurs de la Bretagne atlantique. Ouvrage terminé et mis au point par Maurice Le Lannou. Paris, A. Colin. 1944. 14, 616 p., 13 maps, figs., plates.

Salaun, Per. The midsummer bonfire in Brittany—Tantad Sant-Yann. Old Cornwall. 6 (1966): 442-444.

Sauvé, L. F. (Formules magiques et araisons.) Proverbes. Revue Celtique. 3 (1876-1878): 200-203.

Sauvé, L. F. Formulletes et traditions diverses de la Basse-Bretagne. Revue Celtique. 5 (1881-1883): 157-194.

Sauvé, L. F. Charms, oraisons et conjurations magiques de la Basse-Bretagne. Revue Celtique. 6 (1883-1885): 67-85.

Schroeder, W. Die Fischerboote von Finisterre. Volkstum und Kultur der Romanen. 10 (1937): 157-211.

*Sebillot, Paul. Traditions et superstitions de la Haute-Bretagne. 2 vols. Paris, Maisonneuve. 1882. 7, 368; 389 p.

*Sebillot, Paul. Coutumes populaires de la Haute-Bretagne. Paris, Maisonneuve. 1886. 376 p.

Sébillot, Paul. Littérature orale de la Haute-Bretagne. Paris, Maisonneuve. 1887. 400 p.

Sébillot, Paul. La Bretagne enchantée; poésies sur des thèmes populaires. Paris, Maisonneuve. 1899. 284 p.

Sébillot, Paul. Le folklore pêcheurs. Paris, Maisonneuve. 1901. 389 p.

Sébillot, Paul. Médecine superstitieuse en Haute-Bretagne. R. T. P. 18 (1903) 26-29.

Sébillot, Paul. Le paganisme contemporain chez les peuples celto-latins. Paris, O. Doin. 1908. 378 p.

See, Henri. Les classes rurales en Bretagne du XVIe à la Révolution. Paris, Giard et Brière. 1906. 21, 544 p.

Smith, Hugh M. Brittany: the land of the sardine. National Geographic Magazine. 20 (1909): 541-573.

Souvestre, Émile. Le foyer breton. Paris, Jean Vigneau. 1947. 288 p. (Originally published in 1845.)

Spence, Lewis. Legends and romances of Brittany. New York, Frederick A. Stokes. 1917. 423 p.

Strowski, Stéphane. Les Bretons. Essai de psychologie et de caractérologie provinciale. Rennes, Plihon. 1952. 474 p.

Vallaux, C. L'évolution de la vie rurale en Basse-Bretagne . . . Annales de Géographie. 14 (1905): 36-51.

Valloux, Camille. La Basse-Bretagne, étude de géographie humaine. Paris, Cornély. 1907. 320 p.

Vaugeois, Mme. Edmée. Usages et coutumes du pays nantais. R. T. P. 15 (1900): 177-189, 580-593; 23 (1908): 234; 24 (1909): 138-140.

Walter, Lavina Edna. The fascination of Brittany. London, A. & C. Black. 1911. 8, 119 p.

Wismes, Gaëtan de. Les fêtes religieuses en Bretagne: coutumes, légendes et superstitions. Société Académique de Nantes et du Département de la Loire Inférieure, Annales. 8e Série. 2 (1901): 109-242.

Wismes, Gaëtan de. Les fêtes religieuses en Bretagne: coutumes, légendes et superstitions. Nantes, Impr. C. Mellinet, Biroché & Dautais, successeurs. 1902. 144 p.

Wismes, Gaëtan de. La Toussaint et la commémoration des morts. Nantes. n.d. 12 p.

Gennep, Arnold van. Manuel de folklore français contemporain. Tomes 1
(pts. 1-7), 3, and 4. Paris, A. & J. Picard. 1937-1957. (Especially see
tomes 1 (pts. 3-6), 3, and 4.)

Allenges, H. Zwei elsässische Kinderspiele. Jahrbuch für Geschichte, Sprache
und Literatur Elsass-Lothringens. 16 (1900): 289-304.

Alsatia. Jahrbuch für elsaessische Geschichte, Sage, Altertumskunde, Sitte,
Sprache und Kunst. 1850-1861. 2d ser. 1861-1876. (Became Neue
Alsatia 1885-1895.)

Arnold, J. G. D. Der Pfingstmontag. Lustspiel in Strassburger Mundart in
fünf Aufzugen und in Versen nebst einem die eigenthümlichen einheimischen
Ausdrücke erklärenden Wörterbuch. Strasbourg, Treuttel et Wortz. 1816.
190 p. (Other editions: 1817, 1850, 1867. Revised ed. 1874.)

Beiträge zur Landes- und Volkskunde von Elsass-Lothringen. Vols. 1-9. 1888-
1890. Strasbourg.

*Bell, Timothy A. The Alsatian peasant and his land: a study in land tenure
change. Yearbook of the Association of Pacific Coast Geographers.
28 (1966): 75-95.

Bussière, Th. de. Culte et pélérinages de la Très Sainte-Vierge en Alsace.
Paris, Plon. 1862. 416 p.

Gennep, Arnold van. Manuel de folklore français contemporain. Tomes 1
(pts. 1-7), 3, and 4. Paris, A. & J. Picard. 1937-1957. (Tome 2 never
published.)

Hatt, Jacques. La vie strasbourgeoise il y a trois cent ans. Strasbourg, Éd. Les
Derniers Nouvelles de Strasbourg. 1947. 211 p., 46 plates.

*Juillard, Étienne. La vie rurale dans la plaine de Basse-Alsace. Essai de
géographie sociale. Paris, Les Belles Lettres. 1953. 582 p., maps.

Kolesch, H. Deutsches Volkstum im Elsass. Berlin, Wiss. Akademie Tübingen;
Tübingen, Mohr. 1941. 100 p.

Lamps, Aug. Ueber den Aberglauben im Elsass. Strasbourg, Heitz. 1880.
102 p.

Lefftz, Joseph. Elsässische Dorfbilder; ein Buch von ländlicher Art und Kunst.
Woerth, Sutter. 1958. 301 p.

Lefftz, Joseph, and A. Pfleger. Elsässische Weihnacht; ein Buch von unseres
Landes Art und Brauch. Guegwiller, Alsatia-Verlag. 1931. 239 p.

Lefftz, Joseph, and A. Pfleger. Elsässische Weihnacht. 2d ed. Colmar, Éd. Alsatia. 1941. 263 p., 18 plates.

Linkenheld, E. Quinze ans de folklore alsacien, 1918-1933. Revue Alsace. 82 (1936): 253-258, 418-490, 636-658. (Reprinted: Colmar, Hartman. 1936. 135 p.)

Lutz, Désiré. Das deutsche Volkstum im Elsass. Oberdeutsche Zeitschrift für Volkskunde. 3 (1929): 111-124.

Mayer, Adrian. Das Elsass. Oldenburg, Gerhard Stalling. 1919. 56 p.

Meiss, Honel. Traditions populaires alsaciennes (juives). Nice, Impr. du Palais. 1928. 234 p.

Pfleger, A. Die elsässischen Kräuterweihen. Archives für Elsässische Kirchengeschichte. 11 (1936): 205-258.

Polaczek, Ernst. Volkskunst im Elsass. München. n.d. [pre-1934] 48 p., 200 illus.

Richard, Leo. Coutumes, usages und modernes Recht in Lothringen. Gesellschaft für lothringische Geschichte und Altertumskunde, Jahrbuch. 21 (1909): 164-229.

*Rochefort, Michel. L'organisation urbaine de l'Alsace. Paris, Les Belles Lettres. 1960. 384 p., figs., maps.

Schaudel, Louis. Une coutume funéraire d'Alsace. Revue de Folklore Français et du Folklore Colonial. 3 (1932): 323-325.

Schneegans, Ludwig. Volkstümliche Gebräuche am Tage Sankt Johannis des Täufers, mit besonderer Rüksicht auf Strassburg und das Elsass. Alsatia. 1851: 181-201.

Spindler, Charles. Ceux d'Alsace; types et coutumes. Paris, Horizons de France. 1928. 136 p.

Spindler, François. L'économie agricole d'une petite region d'Alsace: le Sundgau. Colmar, Direction des Services Agricoles. 1958. 206 p., maps, graphs, plates.

Stöber, August. Volkstümliche gebräuche und abergläubische Meinungen im Elsass welche sich auf gewisse Tage und Feste beziehen . . . Alsatia. 1851: 92-180; 1852: 123-253.

Stöber, August. Elsässische Kinderspiele. Die deutschen Mundarten. 4 (1857): 7-10.

Variot, Jean. Contes populaires et traditions orales de l'Alsace. Paris, Firmin-Didot. 1936. 10, 310 p.

Weymann, Charles. Une ville d'Alsace au moyen-age: Thann. Légendes et histoire. Nancy, Berger-Levrault. 1926. 418 p.

Wolfram, Georg. Die völkische Eigenart Elsass-Lothringens. Basel, Finekh. 1918. 34 p.

Woltmann, Ludwig. Die Germanen in Frankreich. Leipzig, Justes Dörner. 1936. 152 p., plates.

CORSICA

Gennep, Arnold van. Manuel de folklore français contemporain. Tomes 1
(pts. 1-7), 3, and 4. Paris, A. & J. Picard. 1937-1957. (Especially see
tomes 1 (pts. 3-6), 3, and 4.)

Starace, Carmine. Bibliografia della Corsica; . . . Milano, Istituto per gli
Studi di Politica Internazionale. 1943. 16, 1033 p.

———————

Agostini, Jules. Coutumes, traditions, superstitions, etc., de la corse. R. T. P
12(1897): 513-527.

Archer, D. Corsica, the scented isle. London, Methuen. 1924. 266 p.

Bartoli, Abbé. Histoire de la Corse. Vol. 1. Moeurs, coutumes et langue de
la Corse. Paris, Fontaine. 1898. 375 p.

Bergerat, Émile. Wild sheep chase: notes of a little philosophic journey in
Corsica. London, Seeley. 1894. 315 p.

Biscottini, Umberto. L'anima della Corsica. 2 vols. Bologna, Zanichelli.
1928. 283, 386 p.

Blanken, Gerard Hendrik. Le Grecs de Cargèse (Corse): recherches sur leur
langue et sur leur histoire. Leiden, A. W. Sijthoff. 1951. (Maniote
Greeks in Corsica.)

Bonaparte, Prince Roland Napoléon. Une excursion en Corse. Paris, Impr.
pour l'Auteur. 1891. 273 p.

Boswell, James. The journal of a tour to Corsica; and memoirs of Pascal
Paoli. London, Williams and Norgate. 1951. 127 p.

Casanova, Antu. Primavera Corsa. Bastia, Impr. E. Cordier et Corsa. 1927.
237 p.

*Chiva, I. Social organisation, traditional economy, and customary law in
Corsica: outline of a plan of analysis. In Julian Pitt-Rivers, ed. Mediterranean Countrymen. Paris, Mouton. 1963: 97-112.

Chiva, I., and D. Ojalvo. La potérie corse à l'amiante. Arts et Traditions
Populaires. 7(1959): 203-227.

Coppolani, J. Cargèse, essai sur la géographie humaine d'un village corse.
Revue de Géographie Alpine. 37(1949): 71-108. (Maniote Greeks in
Corsica.)

Croze, Austin de. La chanson populaire de l'île de Corse. Paris, Libraire
Honoré Champion. 1911. 15, 188 p.

Dugmore, Arthur R. Corsica the beautiful. London, Hurst & Blackett. 1930.
288 p.

CORSICA

Feydel, Gabriel. Moeurs et coutumes des corses. Paris, Garnery. An 8 (1802). 3, 112 p.

Filippi, Julie. Légendes, croyances et superstitions de la corse. R.T.P. 9 (1894): 457-467.

Gennep, Arnold van. Manuel de folklore français contemporain. Tomes 1 (pts. 1-7), 3, 4. (Tome 2 never published.) Paris, A. & J. Picard. 1937-1957.

Giese, Wilhelm. Die volkstümliche Kultur des Niolo, Korsica. Wörter und Sachen. 14 (1932): 109-145.

Gregorovius, Ferdinand Adolf. Corsica, picturesque, historical, and social . . . Translated from the German by Edward Joy Morris. Philadelphia, Parry & M'Millan. 1855. 7, 522 p.

Hawthorne, Hildegarde. Corsica, the surprising island. New York, Duffield. 1926. 10, 235 p.

*Lear, Edward. Journal of a landscape painter in Corsica. London, R. J. Bush. 1870. 16, 272 p.

Méjean, Paul. Notes sur la maison corse. Revue de Géographie Alpine. 20 (1932): 655-676. 15 figs., 2 plates.

Mostratos, S. Kargkése. Athenai. 1957. 107 p. (Maniote Greeks in Corsica.)

Ortoli, Frédéric. Le mariage en corse. R.T.P. 1 (1886): 178-183.

Renwick, George. Romantic Corsica. London, T. F. Unwin. 1909. 333 p.

Sorvillo, Giulia. Moeurs et coutumes de la Corse dans l'oeuvre de Prosper Mérimée. Naples, l'Arte Tipografica. 1954. 123 p., illus.

*Viale, Salvatori. Studi critici di costumi còrsi. Firenze, Tip. Mariani. n.d. [1855?] 147 p. (Privately circulated—rare.)

Warren-Barry, M. A. Studies in Corsica, sylvan and social. London, Sampson-Low, Marston. 1893. 302 p.

Williams, Maynard Owen. The coasts of Corsica. National Geographic Magazine. 44 (1923): 221-312.

Young, Ernest. Corsica. London, A. & C. Black. 1909. 5, 87 p.

MONACO

Handley-Taylor, Geoffrey. Bibliography of Monaco. London, n.p. 1961. 35

Kayser, Bernard. Campagnes et villes de la Côte d'Azur. Essai sur les conséquences du developpement urbain. Monaco, Éditions du Rocher. 1958.
595 p., graphs, maps.

Ollivier, Gabriel. Les quatre villes de Monaco. Monaco, Impr. Nationale.
1956. 285 p., illus.

Pinon, Roger. Bibliographie der wichtigsten volkskundlichen Arbeiten Belgiens
seit 1955. Deutsches Jahrbuch für Volkskunde. 8 (1962): 413-449.

---

*Belgium. European conference on rural life, 1939. National monographs
drawn up by governments. Belgium. Series of League of Nations Publications. European Conference on Rural Life. 2. Geneva. 1939. 65 p.,
illus.

*Boulger, Demetrius Charles de K. Belgian life in town and country. New York,
G. P. Putnam's Sons. 1904. 10, 321 p.

Boulger, Demetrius Charles de K. Belgium of the Belgians. London, Sir I.
Pitman and Sons. 1911. 274 p.

Bourdon, T. Le Borinage, étude de géographie humaine. Hainaut Économique.
1956, pts. 3-4. 159 p., 18 plans, illus.

Bulletin des Enquêtes du Musée de la Vie Wallonne. 1 (1924)-- Liège.

Chalon, J. Les arbers fétiches de la Belgique. Anvers, Édit. Brusselman.
1912. 84 p.

Chalon, J. Idoles, fétiches et amulettes. 2 vols. Namur, the author. 1921-
1922. 652, 234 p.

Cornelissen, J. Nederlandsche volkshumor op stad en dorp, land en volk. 5
vols. Anvers, De Sikkel. 1929-1931.

Cremer, R. Les classes moyennes en Belgique. Bruxelles, F. Larcier. 1955.
118 p.

Delehaye, H. R. P. Les légendes hagiographiques. Bruxelles, Société des
Bollandistes. 1905. 264 p.

Denis, H. Recherches sur la matrimonialité en Belgique—de ses rapports avec
les prix du blé et de la houille. Société Royale Belge d'Anthropologie de
Bruxelles Bulletin. 1 (1882-1883): 35-53, tables.

Dufour, L. La météorologie populaire en Belgique. Bruxelles, Office de
Publicité. 1943. 125 p.

Evrard, René. Forges anciennes. Liège, Soléd. 1956. 226 p., 213 illus.

Le Folklore Brabançon. 1 (1921)-- Bruxelles, Service Provincial de Recherches
Historiques et Folkloriques.

Fostier, Walter. Folklore vivant. 2 vols. Bruxelles, L. de Meyer. 1960.

Guiette, Robert. Marionettes de tradition populaire. Bruxelles, Édit. Cercle d'Art. 1949. 184 p., 53 plates.

Hasse, Georges. Maneken-pis ou le petit Julien est-il un dieu du bonheur? Société Royale Belge d'Anthropologie de Bruxelles, Bulletin. 45(1930): 86-87.

Hermant, Paul, and Denis Boomans. La médecine populaire. Bruxelles, Éd. le Folklore Brabançon. 1929. 240 p., illus.

Heurck, Émile van. Les drapelets de pélérinage. Anvers, Éd. Buschmann. 1922. 532 p.

Keyser, P. de, ed. Ars folklorica Belgica. Monographieën over Vlaamse en Waalse volkskunst . . . 2 vols. Antwerpen, D. Sikke. 1949, 1956. 240 p., 155 illus.; 270 p., illus.

Lefèvre, M. A. L'habitat rural en Belgique. Liège, Impr. H. Vaillant-Carmanne. 1926. 6, 306 p.

Loder, D. The land and people of Belgium. Philadelphia, Lippincott. 1957. 115 p.

Louis, Andrée. Les hôtels de ville de Belgique. Bruxelles, Éd. du Cercle d'Art. 1945. 52 p., 32 plates.

*Marinus, Albert. Le folklore Belge. 3 vols. Bruxelles, Éditions Historiques. 1937-1951. 334, 323, 370 p., 1048 figs.

Moke, Henri Guillaume. Moeurs, usages, fêtes et solennités des Belges. 2 vols. Bruxelles. 1847-1849. (Also later editions.)

Neustadt, I. Some aspects of the social structure of Belgium. London, University of London. 1945. (Unpublished Ph.D. dissertation in economics.)

Ons Volksleven. Antwerpsch-Brabantsch Tijdschrift. 1 (1888)--

Le Pays Gaumais. 1 (1940)-- Virton, Musée Gaumais.

Peeters, Eugene. Le folklore en Belgique. I. La procession du Sant Sang à Bruges. La marches septennale de Fosses. Le jeu de Saint Evermare à Russon. Bruxelles, Charles Dessart. 1950. 64 p., 75 illus.

Pequet, Maurice. Toute la pêche (en Belgique). Bruxelles, Éditions du Jour. 1959. 300 p., illus.

Persyn, Julius. A glance at the soul of the low countries. London, R. & T. Washbourne. 1916. 138 p.

BELGIUM

Reisenberg-Dueringsfeld, Otto de. Calendrier belge; fêtes religieuses et
civiles, usages, croyance et pratique des belges anciens et modernes. 2
vols. Brussels, F. Claasen. 1861-1862.

Reisenberg-Dueringsfeld, Otto de. Traditions et légendes de la Belgique. 2
vols. Bruxelles, F. Claasen. 1870. 446, 372 p. (A reprint of the above,
under a different title.)

Schweisthal, Martin. Das belgische Bauernhaus in alter und neuer Zeit.
M.A.G.W. 38(1908): 295-311.

Smekens, F., and W. van Nespen. The folklore museum. A concise guide.
Antwerp, City of Antwerp Archaeological Museums. 1958. 32 p., 12
plates.

Staercke, Alphonse E. de. Notre-Dame des Belges; traditions et folklore du
culte marial en Belgique. Bruxelles. 1954. 188 p.

Tervarent, Guy de. L'origine des fontaines anthropomorphes. Bulletin de
l'Académie Royale Belge, Classe des Beaux-Arts. 38(1956): 122-129,
illus. (Manneken-Pis statue.)

Tock, Maurice, and Pierre Schroeder. Les processions et les pèlerinages.
Manifestations de notre folklore. Arlon, Éd. du Sorbier. 1955. 215 p.,
16 illus.

Vincennes, Jean de. Sous le ciel de furnes. La procession des pénitents.
Charleroi, P. Héraly. 1957. 86 p., 72 illus.

Volkskunde. 1 (1888)--

Wallonia. Liège. (1893-1914). Continued as La Vie Wallonne. 1920--
Liège.

Walter, Lavina Edna. The fascination of Belgium. London, A. & C. Black.
1915. 12, 122 p.

Zondervan, Richard. Modern Belgian handicrafts. 3d ed. New York, Belgian
Government Information Center. 1949. 55 p., illus.

FLEMINGS

Peeters, Karel Constant. Naar een bibliographie van de Vlaamsche folklore. Oostvlaamsche Zanten. 21(1946): 99-145.

Peeters, Karel Constant. Volkskundlige aantekeneningen nota's en bibliografie bij "Eigen aard. " Antwerp, de Vlijt. 1962. 287 p.

Baeyens, H. Het burgerhuis van de XVIIe en de XVIIIe eeuw in Brabant. Anvers, de Sikkel. 1950. 140 p., illus.

Boekenoogen, Gerrit Jacob, and Émile van Heurck. Histoire de l'imagerie populaire flamande. Bruxelles, van Oest. 1910. 730 p.

Bronne, C. Une affaire de sorcellerie en Flandre, en 1815. Synthèses. 12(1957): 228-240.

Cafmeyer, M. Van doop tot uitvaart. Een kijk op het volksleven in het noordoosten van Westvlaanderen. Brugge, Bond der Westvlaamse Folkloristen. 1958. 173 p., 36 illus.

Celis, Gab. Volkskundlige kalender voor het Vlaamse land. Gent, Heirnislaan. 1923. 336 p.

Cock, A. de. Spreekwoorden en zegwijzen over de vrouwen, de liefde en het huwelijk. Gand, Édit. A. Hoste. 1911. 320 p.

Cock, A. de. Volkssage, volksgeloof en volksgebruik. Anvers, Édit. Janssens. 1918. 224 p.

Cock, A. de. Spreekwoorden, gezegden en uitdrukkingen op volksgeloof. 2 vols. Anvers, de Sikkel. 1920. 242, 120 p.

Cock, A. de, and I. Teirlinck. Kinderspel en kinderlust in Zuid-Nederland. 8 vols. Gand, Édit. Siffer, Académie Royale Flamande. 1902-1908.

Cock, A. de, and I. Teirlinck. Brabantsch sagenboek. 3 vols. Gand, Académie Royale Flamande. 1909-1912.

Coppenolle, M. van. Westvlaamsche bedevaartvaantjes. Bruges, Édit. Walleyndruk. 1942. 76 p.

Cornelissen, J. Nederlandsche volkshumor op stad en dorp, land en volk. 5 vols. Anvers, de Sikkel. 1929-1931.

Cort, Aimé de. Vlaamsch kinderspel in West-Brussel. Bruxelles, L. J. Kryn. 1929. 200 p.

Cryns, Tilly M. Meisjesspelen uit onze streken. Brabantse Folklore 22(1950): 183-298.

Denys, Désiré. Het Roeselaerse volksleven. Roeselaer, the author. 1955. 262 p.

Flandria nostra; ons land en ons volk . . . 5 vols. Antwerpen, Standaard-Boekhandel. 1957-1960.

Ghesquiere, R. Kinderspelen uit Vlaamsch België. 2 vols. Gand, Académie Royale Flamande. 1905. 240, 485 p.

Gossenaerts, J. De taal van en om het landbouwbedrijf in het noordwesten van de kempen. Gent, Koninklijke Vlaamse Academie voor Taal- en Letter-kunde. Reihe 6, Nr. 76. 1956. 1094, 102 p., illus., maps.

Groodt, A., and Fr. de. De oude hoeven in het land van Waas. Antwerpen, N. V. Standaard-Boekhandel. 1955. 213 p., illus.

Hasse, Georges. La pêche dans le région d'Anvers de la période Robenhau-sienne an moyen âge. Société d'Anthropologie de Bruxelles. Bulletins et Mémoires. 27. Mémoires No. 5. 1908. 15 p., 10 illus., 12 plates.

Howes, H. W. Some Flemish customs and beliefs. Folk-Lore. 41 (1930): 99-103.

Jonckheere, Robert. When I was a boy in Belgium. Boston, Lothrop, Lee & Shepard. 1915. 153 p.

*Kruizinge, J. H. Levende folklore in Nederland en Vlaanderen. Assen, de Torenlaan. 1953. 285 p.

Lendval-Dircksen, Erna. Das germanische volksgesichte: Flandern. Bayreuth, Gauverlag Bayreuth. 1942.

Meyere, Victor de. L'Art populaire flamand. Bruxelles, Nouvelle Société d'Édition. 1934. 192 p., 322 plates.

Pauwels, Henri. De folklore van het Brabantsch boerenleven. Merchtem, Boekdrukkerij Sacré. 1948.

Peeters, Karel Constant. Het volksche kerstlied in Vlaanderen. Antwerpen, de Nederlandsche Boekhandel. 1942. 170 p.

Peeters, Karel Constant. Het Vlaamsche volkleven. Brugge, Wiek Op. 1943. 106 p.

Peeters, Karel Constant. Eigen aard—Grepen uit de Vlaamse folklore. Antwerpen, de Vlijt. 1946. 544 p. (2d ed. 1947. 542 p.)

Peeters, Karel Constant. Over volkskunst. Antwerpen, Standaard-Boekhandel. 1956. 39 p.

*Peeters, Karel Constant. Eigen aard; overzicht van het Vlaamse volksleven. 3d ed. Antwerpen, de Vlijt. 1958. 433 p., illus. (Reprinted 1963.)

Perckmans, Frans. Mechelsche volkskunde. Mechelen, Mechelsche Drukkerijen. 1946. 18 p.

Ronse, Alfred. Fermes-types en constructions rurales en West-Flandre. 2 vols. Bruges, C. Beyaert. 1918.

Sleeks, Ary. Bijgeloof en volksremedieën te Oostende. Oostende, the author. 1957. 62 p.

Slembrouck, B. Werken. Heemkundige studie over de gemeente Werken. Langenmark. 1955. 248 p., illus.

Stalpaert, Hervé. Oud-Vlaamse keuken en kookkunst. Heule, Uitgeverij voor Gemeenteadministratie. 1957. 62 p.

Stalpaert, Hervé. Magie et sorcellerie en Flandre maritime. Bruges, Gidsenbond. 1960. 79 p., illus.

Stalpaert, Hervé. Van vastenavond tot pasen. Oudvlaamse volksgebruiken. Historie en folklore. Heule, Uitgeverij voor Gemeenteadministratie. 1960. 56 p.

Sterkens-Cieters, Pauls. Volkskleederdrachten in Vlaanderen. Antwerpen, de Sikkel. 1935. 76 p., 34 illus.

Streuvels, Stijn. Land en leven in Vlaandern. Amsterdam. 1923. 359 p.

Teirlinck, Isidor. Folklore mythologique (Pays Flamand). Bruxelles, Rozez. 1895. 165 p.

Teirlinck, Isidor. Flora diabolica. Anvers, de Sikkel. 1922. 321 p.

Teirlinck, Isidor. Flora magica. Anvers, de Sikkel. 1930. 388 p.

Vincennes, Jean de. Veurne, spiegel van de westhoek. De boetprocessie. Charleroi, P. Héraly. 1957. 86 p., 72 illus.

Willems, J. Oud-vlaamsche liederen. Gand, Gijselinck. 1848. 548 p.

Lempereur, Émile. Essai de catalogue d'une bibliothèque de littérature et de folklore Wallons, 1890-1947. Bruxelles, Editions "Labor." 1949. 184 p.

Banneux, Louis. Légendaire ardennais. Bruxelles, Office de Publicité. 1929. 258 p.

Banneux, Louis. L'Ardenne mysterieuse. Bruxelles, Office de Publicité (Soc. Coop.). 1930. 269 p.

Banneux, Louis. L'Ardenne superstitieuse. Bruxelles, Libraire Vanderlinden. 1930. 207 p.

Barbiaux, G. Mon village. Nil St. Martin. Histoire. Géographie. (Folklore). Nil St. Vincent, Impr. Delsart. 1959. 106 p., map, notes.

Beddoe, J. Notes on the Wallons. J.A.I. 2(1872): 18-20.

Boxus, Robert. La flore médicale Wallonne. Huy, Impr. Degrace. 1939. 180 p.

Boxus, Robert. La météorologie et l'astronomie en Wallonie. Lessines, Postillon. 1954. 240 p.

Damas, H. Vieuxville: commune rurale de Wallonie. Centre d'Études et de Documentation Sociales de la Provence de Liège. 12, no. 7-8(1958): 168-194.

Harvengt, Raoul. Genly, mon village en Hainaut. Frameries, Impr. J. Godard. 1959. 247 p., illus., map.

Hock, A. Croyances et remèdes populaires au pays de Liège. Liège, Vaillant-Carmanne. 1888. 587 p.

Lange, Éd. J'étude ma région. Liège, Éditeur Desoer. n.d. 242 p. (Condroz region.)

Laport, George. Le folklore des paysages Wallonie. Folklore Fellows Communication No. 84. Helsinki, Suomalainen tiedeakatemia. 1929. 382 p.

Laport, George. Les contes populaires wallons. Folklore Fellows Communications No. 101. Helsinki, Suomalainen tiedeakatemia. 1932. 144 p.

Laport, George. Les gnomes en Wallonie. International Congress of Anthropology and Prehistoric Archaeology. 16th., Brussels . . . 1935 [Actes] 1936: 1024-1042.

Laport, George. Le folklore de Wallonie. Liège, Imprimerie Centrale. 1939. 55 p.

Poumon, Émile. Le Hainault; le livere des traditions. Vilvorde, Impr. A. Mees. 42 p.

Ravez, Walter. Le folklore de Tournai et du Tournaisis. Casterman-Tournai. 1949. 516 p.

Rousseau, Félix. Légendes et coutumes du pays de Namur. Bruxelles, Impr. Médicale et Scientifique. 1920. 143 p.

Rousseau, Félix. Le folklore et les folkloristes wallons. Bruxelles, G. Van Oest. 1921. 86 p.

*Turney-High, Harry Holbert. Château-Girard: the life and times of a Walloon town. Columbia, University of South Carolina Press. 1953. 297 p., illus., map.

Vereerstraeten-de Cock, Chr. Contribution à l'étude de l'influence des facteurs sémi-ruraux et non-ruraux au Petit-Brabant. Société Royale Belge de Géographie, Bulletin. 80 (1956): 102-134, maps, tables, figs.

Viane, Charles. Uccle au temps jadis. Recueil historique et folklorique illustre. 2d ed. Uccle, Centre d'Art. 1950. 310 p.

Warsage, Rod. de. Le calendrier populaire Wallon. Anvers, Éd. de Tavernier. 1920. 506 p.

Warsage, Rod. de. La sorcellerie et le culte populaire (en Wallonnie). Liège, Impr. Centrale. 1938. 136 p.

Yernaux, Edmond, and F. Fievet. Folklore wallon (de Montigny-sur-Sambre). Charleroi, Impr. de Charleroi. 1956. 398 p.

Hess, Joseph. Volkskundliche Bibliographie Luxemburgs von 1945-1955. Deutsches Jahrbuch für Volkskunde. 4 (1958): 210-216.

Arduenna. Zeitschrift für Sprach- und Volkskunde. 1-2. 1938-1939. Luxemburg, Ernest Platz.

Breisdorf, Nicolas. Hexenprozesse im Gebiete des Grossherzogtums Luxemburg. Publications de la Section Historique de l'Institut Grand-Ducal. 16. 1861. 52 p.

Edwards, Kenneth Charles. Luxemburg studies. London, The Le Play Society. 1933 [i.e. 1937]. 20 p.

Fontaine, Edmond de la. Die Luxemburger Kinderreime. Luxemburg, Buck. 1877. 62 p.

Fontaine, Edmond de la. Luxemburger Sitten und Bräuche. Luxemburg, Buck. 1883. 5, 168 p.

Fontaine, Edmond de la. Die Luxemburger Volkslieder älterer Zeit. Luxemburg, Worré-Mertens. 1904. 52 p.

Gredt, N., ed. Sagenschatz des Luxemburger Landes. Luxemburg, Buck. 1883. 17, 645 p.

Harpes, Jean. La peste au Duché de Luxembourg. Essai historique et médicale. Luxembourg, P. Linden. 1952. 108 p.

*Hess, Joseph. Luxemburger Volkskunde. Grevenmacher, Paul Faber. 1929. 16, 318 p.

Hess, Joseph. Hochzeits- und Ehegebräuche im Luxemburger Lande. Semaine Internationale d'Ethnologie Religieuse, 5th Session, Luxemburg, 1929, Compte rendu. Paris. 1931: 93-105.

Hess, Joseph. Luxemburger Volksleben in Vergangenheit und Gegenwart. Grevenmacher, Paul Faber. 1939. 175 p.

Hess, Joseph. Luxemburgisches Hausgerät. Uchtkalender. 1949: 65-71.

Hess, Joseph. Altluxemburger Denkwürdigkeit. Beiträge zur Luxemburgischen Sprach- und Volkskunde. 7. Luxemburg, Institut Grand-Ducal. 1960. 387 p.

Huss, Richard. Studien zum luxemburgischen Sprachatlas. Luxemburg, Linden & Hansen, for the Institut Grand-Ducal. 1927. 68 p., 3 maps.

Huss, Richard. Luxemburg und Siebenbürgen. Einwandergang der Deutschen nach Siebenbürgen . . . Luxemburg, Institut Grand-Ducal; Hermanstadt, Krafft & Dratleff. 1926. 86, 102 p., 2 maps.

Institut Grand-Ducal, Section de Linguistique, de Folklore et de Toponymie. Revue Trimestrielle; Vierteljahrblätter. Luxemburg, Institut Grand-Ducal. 1935-1950.

Institut Grand-Ducal, Section de Linguistique, de Folklore et de Toponymie. Bulletin Linguistique et Ethnologique. Luxembourg, Institut Grand-Ducal. 1 (1953):--

Keiffer, Jules. Jugenderinnerungen, Sitten und Gebräuche. Luxemburg, J. Keiffer. 1906. 115 p.

Künssberg, Eberhard Otto Georg Frh. von. Rechtliche Volkskunde. Halle and Saale, Max Niemeyer. 1936. 193 p.

Laport, George. Le folklore des paysages du grand-duché du Luxembourg. Helsinki, Suomalainen Tiedeakatemia. 1929. 66 p.

Laurent, Charles. Coutumes des pays Duché de Luxembourg et Comté de Chiny. 2d ed. Bruxelles, Gobbaerts. 1887. 485, 38 p.

Leclercq, Mathieu N. J. Coutumes des pays Duché de Luxemburg et Comté de Chiny. 2 vols. Bruxelles, F. Gobbaerts. 1867, 1869.

*Luxemburg. European conference on rural life. National monographs drawn up by governments. Luxemburg. Series of League of Nations Publications. European Conference on Rural Life. 24. Geneva. 1939. 36 p., illus.

Mersch, Carl. Luxemburger Kinderreime. Luxemburg, V. Buck. 1884. 10, 252 p.

Meyers, Joseph. Siedlung und Flur in Luxemburg. Cahiers Luxembourgeois. 20 (1948): 29-34.

Meyrac, Albert. Traditions, coutumes, légendes et contes des Ardennes . . . Charleville, Impr. du Petit Ardennais. 1890. 10, 589 p.

Pierret, Paul, François Bourgeois, et al. Art et folklore religieux du Luxembourg. Saint-Hubert, Albert Gofflot. 1958. 58 p., 14 illus., map.

Pletschette, Nicolas. Das Kind im Brauchtum. Uchtkalender. 1954: 169-173.

Ries, Nicolas. Essai d'une psychologie du peuple luxembourgeois. Diekirch, Schroell. 1911. 318 p.

Ries, Nicolas. Le peuple luxembourgeois; essai de psychologie. Diekirch, J. Schroell. 1920. 294 p. (Actually a second edition of the preceding work.)

*Schmithüsen, Josef. Das luxemburger Land: Landesnatur, Volkstum und bäuerliche Wirtschaft. Forschungen zur deutschen Landeskunde. 34. Leipzig, S. Hirzel. 1940. 431 p.

Schweisthal, Martin. Histoire de la maison rurale en Belgique et les contrées voisines. 2 parts. Bruxelles, Société d'Archéologie de Bruxelles. 1906.

Sibenaler, M. Coutumes phalliques dans le Luxembourg. Bulletin et Mémoires de la Société d'Anthropologie de Bruxelles. 31(1912): 113-117.

Société Luxembourgeoise d'Études Linguistiques et Dialectologiques. Annuaire. Luxembourg. 1925-1935. (Continued from 1935-1952 under the name of Institut Grand-Ducal.)

Spedener, Gregor. Die Bauernhochzeit in früheren Zeiten. Luxemburg, Schroell. 1933. 72 p.

Thill, Mathias. Singendes Volk. Volkslieder aus Luxemburg. Esch-Alzette, Kremer-Muller. 1937. 640 p.

Thill, Mathias, ed. Luxemburgische Volkslieder mit Bildern und Weisen. Landschaftliche Volkslieder. 29. Luxemburg, P. Linden. 1936. 78 p.

Tresch, Mathias. La chanson populaire luxembourgeoise. Luxembourg, Victor Buck. 1929. 10, 308 p.

Werveke, Nicolas van. Kulturgeschichte des Luxemburger Landes. 3 vols. Luxemburg, Soupert. 1923-1926.

Winandy, Adolf M. Eigenart und Fremdgut im luxemburgischen Bauerntum. Zur Wirtschaftsgeographie des Deutschen Bauerntum. 10. Berlin. 1943. 81 p.

Mollema, A. M. P. Bibliographia Neerlandica. The Hague, Martinus Nijhoff. 1962. 598 p.

Abma, E. Boer en coöperatie in Nederland. 2 vols. Wageningen, Afdeling Sociologie en Sociografie van de Landbouwhogeschool, Bulletins 4 and 12. Wageningen. 1956 and 1958. 64, 50 p.

Bicker, Caarten A. De molen in ons volksleven. Leiden, A. W. Sijthoff. 1958. 214 p.

Blecourt, A. S. de. Fivelgoër landleven. Assen, van Gorcum. 1942. 144 p.

Bork-Feltkamp, Adele Jeanette van. Anthropological research in the Netherlands. Historical survey. Verhandelingen der Koninklijke Nederlandsche Akademie van Wetenschappen, Afdeling Natuurkunde. 2^e sectie. 37, pt. 2. Amsterdam, Amsterdam Academy. 1938. 166 p.

Boulger, Demetrius C. de. K. Holland of the Dutch. New York, Charles Scribner's Sons. 1920. 268 p.

Braam, G. P. A. Bejaarden in Utrecht; repport naar aanleiding van een enquête onder bejaarden in de stad Utrecht, 1962. Utrecht, Social Instituut R.U. 1964. 6, 133 p. (The aged in Utrecht.)

Burgess, Ernest W., ed. Aging in western societies. Chicago, University of Chicago Press. 1960. 492 p.

Carr, Sir John. A tour through Holland, along the right and left banks of the Rhine, to the south of Germany, in the summer and autumn of 1806 . . . London, printed for R. Phillips by T. Gillet. 1807. 15, 468 p.

Cleerdin, Vincent. Het brabantsche dorp. Amsterdam, Allert de Lange. 1944. 114 p.

Cohen, Joseph. Nederlandse volksverhalen. Zutphen, W. J. Thieme. 1952. 12, 341 p.

Constandse, A. K. Het dorp in de Ijsselmeerpolders . . . Zwolle, W. E. J. Tjeenk Willink. 1960. 296 p., maps, tables, English summary.

De Groot, Cornelia. When I was a girl in Holland. Boston, Lothrop, Lee & Shepard. 1917. 208 p.

Dockum, H. C. van. Van nieuwjaarsmorgen tot oudejaarsavond in Drenthe. Assen, Uitg. "de Torenlaan." 1948. 182 p.

Doorn, J. A. A. van. The development of sociology and social research in the Netherlands. Mens en Maatschappij. 31(1956): 189-264.

Dutch textiles. Survey of World Textiles. 16. Leigh-on-Sea (England), F. Lewis. 1960. 20 p., plates.

Fischer, H. T. Het Nederlandse verwantschapsysteem. Mens en Maatschappij. 22 (1947): 104-117. (Dutch kinship system.)

*Frère, J. Limburghsche volkskunde. Hasselt, Limburghsche Drukkerij. 1926. 192 p. (2d ed. 1928. 286 p.)

*Gadourek, Ivan. A Dutch community; social and cultural structure and process in a bulb-growing region in the Netherlands. Leiden, Stenfert Kroese. 1956. 555 p. (2d ed. Groningen, J. B. Wolters. 1961. 16, 555 p.)

Gazenbeek, Jac. Dwalend tussen heuvels en valleien; natuur en folklore van de Veluwe. Wageningen, Gefr. Zomer & Keuning. 1958. 184 p.

*Goudsblom, Johan. Dutch society. New York, Random House. 1967. 12, 175 p.

Groenman, Sjoerd. Women's opinion about size of family in the Netherlands: attempts to measure desired size of family. Eugenics Quarterly. 2 (1955): 224-228.

Grünfeld, F., and J. Weima. Leven in een Rotterdamse randzone; verslag van een sociologisch onderzoek. Rotterdam, Gemeente Dienst voor Sociale Zaken. 1957. 8, 174 p. (Life in a Rotterdam suburb.)

Hendriks, G. Een stad en haar boeren. Kampen, J. H. Kok. 1953. 224 p.

Hermesdorf, B. H. D. De herberg in de Nederlanden; een blik in de beschavingsgeschiedenis. Assen, van Gorcum. 1957. 12, 296 p. (Dutch taverns.)

Heuvel, H. W. Oud-Achterhoeksch boerenleven. Het gehele jaar rond. 3d ed. Deventer, A. E. Kluwer. 1946. 439 p., illus.

Hofstee, E. W. Some remarks on selective migration. The Hague, Nijhoff. 1952. 28 p.

*Hofstee, E. W. Rural life and rural welfare in the Netherlands. The Hague, Government Printing and Publishing Office. 1957. 18, 364 p.

Hooft, P. J. 't. Dorpen in Zeeland. Amsterdam, Albert de Lange. 1944. 114 p.

*Hough, P. M. Dutch life in town and country. New York, G. P. Putnam and Sons. 1903. 291 p.

Huizenga-Onnerekes, E. J. Het menschelijk leven in 't Groninger land. Assen, van Gorcum. 1939. 118 p.

*Ishwaran, Karigoudar. Family life in the Netherlands. The Hague, van Keulen. 1959. 276 p.

Jones, Sydney Robert. Old houses in Holland. London, The Studio. 1913. 152 p., illus., plates.

Josselin de Jong, J. P. B. de. Cultural anthropology in the Netherlands. Higher Education Research in the Netherlands. 4(1960): 13-26.

*Keur, John Y., and Dorothy L. Keur. The deeply rooted. A study of a Drents community in the Netherlands. Monographs of the American Ethnological Society No. 25. New York, J. J. Augustin. 1955. 208 p., 4 plates, 2 folding maps.

Kruizinga, J. H. Levende folklore in Nederland en Vlandern. Assen, Torenlaan. 1953. 288 p.

Kunst, Jaap. Terschellinger volksleven. Uithuizen, H. H. Fongers. 1916. 172 p.

Kunst, Jaap. Terschellinger volksleven, gebruiken, feesten, liederen, dansen . . . Den Haag, H. P. Leopold. 1947. 208 p. (Reprinted: 1951. 272 p.)

Laan, Kornelis ter. Folklore in de Nederlandse overlederingen. Amsterdam, C. Hafkamp. 1949. 314 p.

Laan, Kornelis ter. Groninger volksleven. Groningen, P. Noordhoff. 1959.

Landheer, Barth. Dutch sociology. Social Forces. 12(1933): 191-198.

Laurijssen, C. De folklore van een Kempisch dorp (Hoogstraten). Nederlandsch Tijdschrift voor Volkskunde. 36(1931): 31-47, 121-148; 37(1932): 36-54, 128-147.

Meldrum, David Storrar. Holland and the Hollanders. New York, Dodd, Mead. 1898. 13, 405 p.

Meldrum, David Storrar. Home life in Holland. London, Methuen. 1911. 9, 370 p.

Mens en Maatschappij. 1 (1925)-- Groningen, Amsterdam.

Minneman, P. G., and Catherine L. Davis. Netherlands agriculture and the war. Foreign Agriculture. 4(1940): 459-492.

Molen, S. J. van der. Het friesshe boerenhuis in twintig eeuwen. Assen, van Gorcum. 1942. 151 p.

*Netherlands. European conference on rural life. National monographs drawn up by governments. The Netherlands. Series of League of Nations Publications. European Conference on Rural Life. 10. Geneva. 1939. 55 p., illus.

Het Nieuwe Brabant. Compiled by J. E. de Quay, et al. 3 vols. 's-Herto-
genbosch, Prov. Gen. Kunsten Wet. zuid-Nederlandsche Drukkerij. 1952-
1955.

Palm, C. H. M. Costumes of Staphorst; a village in the eastern Netherlands.
International Archives of Ethnography. 50 (1964): 43-59.

Persyn, Julius. A glance at the soul of the low countries. London, R. & T.
Washbourne. 1916. 138 p.

Peters-Nanninga, M. M. Family life in the Netherlands. Mens en Maatschappij. 37 (1962): 352-359.

Ponsioen, Johannes Antonius. Changing family life in the Netherlands. The
Hague, van Keulen. 1958. 16 p.

Post-Beuckens, Lipke, ed. Land en volk van gaast en klif; historie en
legenden, traditie, volkskarakter, volksleven, taal en folklore, dieren en
plantenwereld. Laren, A. G. Schoonderbeek. 1947. 156 p.

Rasch, J. Ons volk. Een Nederlandsche volkskunde. Lochem, de Tijdstroom.
1940. 179 p.

*Saal, C. D. Het boerengezin in Nederland; sociologische grondslagen van
gezin en bedrijf. Assen, van Gorcum. 1958. 307 p. (The family farm
and sociology of farming families.)

*Schrijnen, Josef. Nederlandsche volkskunde. 2 vols. Zutphen, W. J.
Thieme. 1933. 363, 399 p.

Simonse, J. Sociologische schets van de volksbuurt. De Schalm. 20 (1963):
1-127.

Sinninghe, J. R. W. Der Bauer in der niederländischen Volkserzählung. In
Gy. Ortutay and T. Bodrogy, eds. Europa et Hungaria. Budapest,
Akadémiai Kiadó. 1965: 243-255.

Sitwell, Sacheverell. The Netherlands; a study of some aspects of art,
costume and social life. 2d rev. ed. London, Batsford. 1952. 168 p.,
illus.

Slicher van Bath, B. H. Een samenleving onder spanning; geschiedenis van
het platteland van Overijssel. Assen, van Gorcum. 1957. 14, 768 p.

Smith, Hugh M. A North Holland cheese market. National Geographic
Magazine. 21 (1910): 1051-1066.

Stokhuyzen, F. The Dutch windmill. Bussum, C. A. J. van Dishoeck.
1962. 128 p., illus.

Teenstra, Anna, et al. Nederlandsche volkskunst. Amsterdam, U. M. Elsevier. 1941. 256 p., illus.

Tonckens, N. A., and E. Abma. Verdwijnende dorpen op het Groninger hoogeland. Wageningen, Afdeling Sociologie en Sociografie van de Landbouwhogeschool, Bulletin 8. 1957. 35 p.

Van de Ban, A. W. De landbouwkundige ontwikkeling van de Nederlandse boeren. Wageningen, Afdeling Sociologie en Sociografie van de Landbouwhogeschool, Bulletin 6. 1957. 84 p.

Van der Poel, J. M. G. De rijnsburgse ploeg. Volkskunde. 1 (1958): 1-10. Bruxelles.

Veen, Johan van. Dredge, drain, reclaim: the art of a nation. 5th ed. The Hague, Martinus Nijhoff. 1962. 200 p.

Ven, Dirk Jan van der. Neerlands-volksleven. Arnhem, Zalt Bommel. 1920. 10, 368 p.

Ven, Dirk Jan van der. Van vrijen en trouwen op 't boerenland. Amsterdam—Mechelen, de Spieghel. 1929. 187 p. (Marriage, courtship, etc.)

Ven, Dirk Jan van der. De herleving van het Nederlandsche volksspel. Naarden, A. Rutgers. 1944. 168 p.

Ven, Dirk Jan van der. Het carnavalsboek van Nederland. 2d ed. Heerlen, Winants. 1950. 246 p.

Ven-ten Bensel, Elsie van der. Dances of the Netherlands. New York, Chanticleer Press. 1949. 40 p., illus.

Volkskunde; driemandelijksch tijdschrift voor de studië van het volkleven. 1-25 (1888-1914). (Continued as Nederlandsch Tijdschrift voor Volkskunde. 26-42, 1915-1938.)

Weiland, A. Geloof en ongeloof in een Noord-Hollandse polder; een religiografie van de beemster. Groningen, Rijksuniversiteit. 1956. 145 p.

Weima, J. Authoritarianism, religious conservatism, and sociocentric attitudes in Roman Catholic groups (in the Netherlands). Human Relations. 18 (1965): 231-239.

Aarhus, Denmark. Statsbibliotek. Friserne; land og folk, sprog og literatur. Aarhus, Statsbibliotek i Aarhus. 1933. 48 p.

Aarhus, Denmark. Statsbibliotek. Friserne; land og folk, sprog og literatur. Katalog 2. Aarhus, Statsbibliotek i Aarhus. 1959. 70 p.

Kalma, J. J. Repertorium Frieslands verleden. Overzicht van tijdschrift-artikelen de Friese geschiedenis betreffende. Leeuwarden, Fries Genoot-schap. 1955. 416 p.

Akker, Klaas Jaspers van den. Van de mond der oude Middelzee; schetsen uit het oude leven op het land en uit het boerenbedrijf. Leeuwarden, De Friesche Madtschappi van Landbouw. 1948. 493 p., illus., map. (Agriculture, social life, and customs.)

Bischholz, E., and G. A. Reepmeyer. Das ostfriesche Bauernhaus in seiner Aupassung. Friesisches Jahrbuch. 1961: 144-162.

Bobzin, Ernst. Die Landschaften der Nordseeinseln Sylt. Forschungen zur deutschen Landes- und Volkskunde. 24, no. 3. Stuttgart, Englehorn. 1926. 31 p., 8 plates, figs.

Bröring, Jul. Das Saterland. Eine Darstellung von Land, Leben, Leuten. 2 vols. Oldenburg, Stallings Verlag. 1897-1901. 8, 149, 305 p.

Dekker, K. M. Generatiewisseling in de landbouw; een onderzock naar de bedrijfsovergang, oudedagsvoorziening en vererving in de provincie Friesland. 's-Gravenhage, Landbouw-Economisch Instituut afd. Streekonderzoek. 1964. 137 p.

Dircksen, Rolf. Amrum. Ein erd-, natur- und volkskundlicher Wegweiser. Bielefeld, Bethel. 1936. 110 p., 20 illus., 2 maps.

*Dykstra, Waling. Uit Frieslands Volkleven, van vroeger en later. 2 vols. Leeuwarden, H. Suringar. 1892-1896.

*Erickson, Vincent O. The evolution of an East Frisian marsch community as seen through social and cultural change. Seattle, University of Washington. 1968. (Unpublished Ph.D. dissertation in anthropology.)

Evers, E. D. Insel Föhr. Volksgliederung und soziale Ordnung. Volk und Gemeinschaft 4. Diss. Hamburg, Hänsischer Gildenverlag. 1939. 66 p.

Friesische Studien. Reihe A. Volks- und Stammeskunde. 1 (1948)-- Ham-burg, Hänsischer Gildenverlag.

Galiën, S. M. van der. Boerefolk, in forhael ut 'e Walden. Snits. Branden-burgh. 1948. 224 p.

Haas, H. Deutsche Nordseeküste, friesische Inseln und Helgoland. Land und Leute vol. 8. Bielefeld and Leipzig, Belhagen & Klasing. 1900. 176 p.

Hansen, C. P. Friesische Sagen und Erzählungen. Altona, Mendeborn. 1858. 11, 194 p.

Hansen, C. P. Der Badeort Westerland auf Sylt und dessen Bewohner. Altona, Lehmkuhl. 1868. 4, 236 p.

Heemskerck, Düker, et al. Friesland, Friezenland. 's Gravenhage, Hamer. 1942. 232 p.

Heslinga, Marcus Willem. Friese fabriekarbeiders; enige sociale aspecten van de industrialisatie in Friesland. Assen, van Gorcum. 1954. 129 p.

Jensen, Christian. Die nordfriesischen Inseln Sylt, Föhr, Amrum und die Halligen vormals und jetzt. Mit besonderer Berücksichtigung der Sitten und Gebräuch der Bewohner . . . Hamburg, Verlagsanstalt und Druckerei. 1891. 8, 392 p., maps, plates.

Jensen, Christian. Die nordfriesische Inselwelt. Braunschweig, Westermann. 1914. 6, 96 p.

*Jensen, Christian. Die nordfriesische Inseln Sylt, Föhr, . . . 2d ed. Lübeck, Ch. Coleman. 1927. 8, 468 p.

Junge, Karl. Das friesische Bauernhaus. Seine Verbreitung und Entwicklungsgeschichte. Oldenburg, Gerhard Stalling. 1936. 85 p., 156 illus.

Kalma, J. J. Dorpen willen leven: een studie over het Friese plattenland. 's Gravenhage, Boekencentrum. 1960. 132 p.

*Koehn, H. Die nordfriesischen Inseln. Die Entwicklung ihrer Landschaft und die Geschichte ihres Volkstums. Hamburg, Cram, de Gruyter. 1961. 20, 223 p., 167 photos.

Krause, August. Die Insel Amrum. Eine Landeskunde. Stuttgart, Strecker und Schröder. 1913. 3, 88 p.

Lübbers, Lübbert Eiken. Ostfrieslands Schiffahrt und Seefischerei. Tübingen, H. Laupp. 1903. 112 p.

Lübbing, Hermann. Friesische Sagen von Texel bis Sylt. Jena, Diedericks. 1928. 12, 283 p.

*Lüpkes, W. Ostfriesische Volkskunde. Emden, W. Schwalbe. 1908. 8, 260 p., 100 illus. (2d ed. 1925. 16, 397 p.)

Molen, S. J. van der. De friesche kalenderfeesten. 's Gravenhage, Hamer. 1941. 148 p.

Molen, S. J. van der. Het friesche boerenhuis in twintig eeuwen. 2d ed. Assen, van Gorcum. 1944. 160 p., illus.

Mulder, T., and S. J. van der Molen. The Frisians; the 20th century descendants of an ancient nation. Leeuwarden, Federation of Frisian Museums and Antique Rooms. 1952. 72 p.

Nyèssen, D. J. H. The passing of the Frisians. The Hague, M. Nijhoff. 1927. 295 p. (Primarily physical anthropology.)

Pessler, Willi. Hausgeographie der Wilster Marsch. Eine ethnogeographische Untersuchung. Stuttgart, J. Englehorns. 1913. 19 p., illus., 4 plates, map.

Peters, Franz C., ed. Nordfriesland. Heimatbuch für die Kreise Husum und Südtondern. Husum, C. F. Delff. 1929. 8, 726 p., plates (4 col. plates), map.

Peters, Lorenz Conrad. Zwischen West- und Nordgermanien. Beiträge zur Heimatkunde der nordfriesischen Uthlande und der benachbarten Geestharden. Husum, Bollmann. 1932. 71 p.

Philipp, Hans, and A. Kamphausen. Nordfriesland. Landschaft und Bauten von der Eider bis zur Wiedau. Heide (Holstein), Westholstein Verlag. 1958. 117 p.

Poppe, Fr. Zwischen Ems und Weser. Land und Leute in Oldenburg und Ostfriesland. 2d ed. Oldenburg and Leipzig, Schulze. 1902. 7, 472 p.

Rickers, J. Friesische Bauernhäuser im Kreise Rendsburg. Heimatkundliches Jahrbuch für den Kreis. 14 (1964): 95-125. (Rendsburg)

Schröder, Gerhard. Volksmedizin und Volkszahnheilkunde der Friesen. Deutsch-Nordische Gesellschaft für Geschichte der Medizin, der Zahnheilkunde und der Naturwissenschaften, Arbeiten. Bd. 6. Greifswald, L. Bamberg. 1929. 20 p.

*Siebs, Benno Eide. Die Helgoländer: eine Volkskunde der roten Klippe. Breslau, F. Hirt. 1928. 132 p.

*Siebs, Benno Eide. Die Norderneyer. Eine Volkskunde. Norden. 1930. 7, 206 p.

Siebs, Theodor. Das Saterland. Ein Beitrag zur deutschen Volkskunde. Z.d.V.f.V. 3 (1893): 239-278, 373-410. illus.

Siebs, Theodor. Westfriesische Studien. Berlin, G. Reimer. 1895. 61 p.

Siebs, Theodor. Zur friesische Volkskunde des Saterlandes. In Volkskundlich
Gaben, John Meier zum 70. Geburtstag Dargebracht. Berlin, Walter de
Gruyter. 1934: 199-222.

Sjaardema, Henryk. The individual society: a Frisian model. Kroeber
Anthropological Society. Papers. 23 (1960): 54-85.

Spahr van der Hoek, J. J. De heidedorpen in de noordelijke wouden;
historisch-sociologische studie. Drachten, Laverman. 1960. 154 p.

Strackerjan, Ludwig. Von Land und Leuten. Bilder und Geschichten aus dem
Herzogtum Oldenburg. Oldenburg, Schulze. 1881. 18, 171 p.

Sundermann, Fr. Sagen und sagenhafte Erzählungen aus Ostfriesland. Aurich,
Dunkmann. 1869. 5, 66 p.

Sundermann, Heinrich Friedrich. Friesische und niedersächsische Bestandteile
in den Ortsnamen Ostfrieslands. Ein Beitrag zur Siedlungsgeschichte der
Nordseeküste. Emden, 1901. 7, 48 p.

Thimme, Adolf. Volkskundliches aus Ostfriesland. Niederdeutsche Zeitschrift für Volkskunde. 7 (1929): 23-40.

Thomas, Hermann. Ostfriesland. Eine geographische Heimatkunde. Leer
(Ostfriesland), Rautenberg & Möckel. 1952. 176 p.

Vries, J. de, and Th. Focken. Ostfriesland. Land und Volk in Wort und Bild.
Emden, Haynel. 1881. 5, 469 p., illus.

SCANDINAVIA

Jansson, S. O. Bibliographie der wichtigsten Arbeiten auf dem Gebiete der dänischen, norwegischen und schwedischen Volkskunde 1945-1956. Deutsches Jahrbuch für Volkskunde. 7(1961): 229-266.

Sjödin, Åke. Nordisk antropologisk bibliografi 1926-1955. Ymer. 84, Supplement (1964): 1-90.

Dachler, Anton. Nordische Bauernhäuser. Z.f.Ö.V. 14(1908): 1-23.

Erixon, Sigurd E. Fångst, jakt och fiske. Stockholm, Bonnier. 1955. 145 p.

Erixon, Sigurd E. Landbrug og bebyggelse. Stockholm, Bonnier. 1956. 6, 314 p.

Eskeröd, Albert. Early Nordic-Arctic boats. Studia Ethnographica Upsaliensia. 11(1956): 57-87.

Glob, P. V. Ard og plov i Nordens oldtid. Aarhus, Universitets-forlaget. 1951. 183 p., illus.

Gutkind, Erwin Anton. Urban development in Central Europe and Scandinavia. New York, The Free Press of Glencoe. 1964. 17, 491 p.

Hendin, Herbert. Suicide in Scandinavia; a psychoanalytic study of culture and character. New York, Grune & Stratton. 1964. 153 p.

Holme, Charles, ed. Peasant art in Sweden, Lapland and Iceland. London, The Studio. 1910. 8, 48 p., plates.

Lagerkrantz, Sture. The Nordo-Baltic torsion traps. Studia Ethnographica Upsaliensia. 21(1964): 169-181.

Laid, Eerik. Uber den Ursprung der Nordosteuropäischen Riege. Folk-Liv. 16(1953): 28-35.

Magnus, Olaus. Historia de gentibus septentrionalibus. Antverpiae, ex officina C. Plantini. 1558. 8, 50, 192 p., illus. (Many other editions of this work.)

Puhvel, M. The seal in the folklore of northern Europe. Folklore. 74(1963): 326-333.

Steensberg, Axel. Med bragende flammer. Braendingskulturens metoder i fortid og nutid. Kuml. 1955: 65-130. (English summary: In crackling flames, pp. 125-127.)

Svalastoga, K. Prestige, class and mobility. Copenhagen, Gyldendal. 1959. 446 p.

Talve, Ilmar. Bastu och torkhus i Nordeuropa. Stockholm, Nordiska Museet. 1960. 12, 544 p. (Farm buildings, bathrooms, kilns.)

Thompson, Stith. Folklore trends in Scandinavia. In Richard M. Dorson, ed. Folklore Research around the World. Bloomington, Indiana University Pres 1961: 27-34.

United States. Bureau of the Census. Bibliography of social science periodicals and monograph series: Iceland, 1950-1962. Washington, Government Printing Office. 1962. 4, 10 p.

Anderson, Johann. Nachrichten von Island. Hamburg, G. C. Grund. 1746.

Anderson, Johann. Histoire naturelle de l'Islande, du Groenland, du détroit de Davis, et d'autres pays situés sous de nord, . . . 2 vols. Paris, S. Jorry. 1750.

Annandale, Nelson. The survival of primitive implements, materials and methods in the Faroes and South Iceland. J.A.I. 33(1903): 246-258, plates.

Annandale, Nelson. The Faroes and Iceland: studies in island life. Oxford, The Clarendon Press. 1905. 8, 238 p.

Árnadóttir, Hólmfrídur. When I was a girl in Iceland. Boston, Lothrop, Lee & Shepard. 1919. 6, 209 p.

Clark, Austin H. Iceland and Greenland. War Background Studies. No. 15. Washington, Smithsonian Institution. 1943: 1-46.

Clausen, Oscar. Aevikjör og aldarfar. Reykjavík, Iðunnarútgáfan. 1949. 203 p. (Traditions and stories.)

Fonblanque, Caroline Alicia de. Five weeks in Iceland. London, R. Bentley & Son. 1880. 6, 180 p.

Great Britain. Naval Intelligence Division. Iceland. Cambridge, prepared by the Cambridge Sub-Centre. 1942. 498 p.

Guðmundsson, Gils. Fráyztu nesjum. 5 vols. Reykjavík, Isafoldarprentsmiðja. 1942-1950. (Traditions from N. W. Iceland.)

Guðmundsson, Valtýr. Island am Beginn des 20. Jahrhunderts. Kattowitz in Schlesien, Gebrüder Böhm. 1904. 15, 223 p.

Henderson, Ebenezer. Iceland: or, the journal of a residence in that island during the years 1814 and 1815. Containing observations on the natural phenomena, history, literature, and antiquities of the island; and the religion, manners, and customs of its inhabitants. Edinburgh, Waugh & Innes. 1819. 14, 576 p.

Herrmann, Paul. Island, das Land und das Volk. Leipzig, Berlin, B. G. Teubner. 1914. 113 p.

Holme, Charles, ed. Peasant art in Sweden, Lapland and Iceland. London, The Studio. 1910. 8, 48 p., 88 plates.

Hooker, William Jackson. Journal of a tour in Iceland in the summer of 1809. Yarmouth, privately printed by J. Keymer. 1811. 62, 496 p.

Jaden, Hans, Freiherr von. Über den isländischen Bauernhof. M. A. G. W. 34 (1904): 102-103, illus.

Jaden, Hans, Freiherr von. Volkskundliches aus Island und aus Färöern. M. A. G. W. 47 (1917): 9-14.

Kneeland, Samuel. An American in Iceland. Boston, Lockwood, Brooks. 1876. 8, 326 p.

Mackenzie, George Steuart. Travels in the island of Iceland during the year MDCCCX. 2d ed. Edinburgh, A. Constable. 1811. 491 p.

Merrill, R. T. Notes on Icelandic kinship terminology. A. A. 66 (1964): 867-872.

Metcalfe, Frederick. The Oxonian in Iceland: or, notes of travel in that islaⁿ in the summer of 1860, with glances at Icelandic folk-lore and sagas. London, Longman, Green . . . 1861. 16, 424 p.

Miles, Pliny. Rambles in Iceland. New York, C. B. Norton. 1854. 15, 334

Nordal, Jóhannes. The recruitment of professions in Iceland. Transactions of the Second World Congress of Sociology. 2 (1955): 153-165.

Ólafsdóttir, Nanna. Þróun í húsaskipum Íslendinga að fornu. Nokkrar athuganir [Some observations on the development of the Icelandic farmhouse]. Saga. 1961: 300-320. (English summary.)

Olafsson, Eggert. Voyage en Islande, fait par ordre de S. M. danoise, contenant des observations sur les moeurs et les usages des habitants; une description des lacs, rivières, glaciers, sources chaudes et volcans; des diverses espèces de terres . . . 5 vols. Paris, Strassbourg, Frères Lerault. 1802.

Olafsson, Eggert, and Messrs. Povalsen. Travels in Iceland: performed by order of his Danish Majesty. London, R. Phillips. 1805. 162 p.

Stefánsson, Valtýr. Det islandske landbrug . . . København, A. F. Høst. 1920. 73 p. (Agriculture.)

Symington, Andrew James. Pen and pencil sketches of Faröe and Iceland. London, Longman, Green, Longman, and Roberts. 1862. 6, 315 p.

Thoroddsen, Th. Islandsk folketru. Kristiania, Aschenhoug. 1924. 47 p.

ICELAND

Troil, Uno von. Letters on Iceland . . . made during a voyage undertaken in the year 1772 by Joseph Banks, Esq., F.R.S. London, printed by and for W. Richardson. 1780. 26, 400 p.

Williams, Carl. Thraldom in ancient Iceland. Chicago, University of Chicago Press. 1937. 25, 168 p.

Annandale, Nelson. The survival of primitive implements, materials and methods in the Faroes and South Iceland. J.A.I. 33(1903): 246-258, plate.

Annandale, Nelson. The Faroes and Iceland: studies in island life. Oxford, The Clarendon Press. 1905. 8, 238 p.

*Blehr, Otto. Action groups in a society with bilateral kinship: a case study from the Faroe Islands. Ethnology. 2(1963): 269-275.

*Blehr, Otto. Ecological change and organizational continuity in the Faroe Islands. Folk. 6(1964): 29-34.

Bruun, Daniel. Fra de Färöiske bygder; samlede afhandlinger om gammeldags saed og skik. København, Gyldendal. 1929. 263 p.

Dahl, Sverri. Fortidsleven. Faerøerne. 1 (1958): 124-157.

Djurhuus, Hans Andreas. Livet paa Faerøerne i billeder og tekst. København, Dansk Kulturforlag. 1950. 564, 19 p., plates.

Elkaer-Hansen, N. The Faroe Islands today. American Scandinavian Review. 43(1955): 165-171.

Hamre, Håkon, ed. Ferøers beskrifvelser av Thomas Tarnovius (1669). København, Ejnar Munksgaard. 1950. 103 p., illus.

Hansen, Leo. Viking life in the storm-cursed Faeroes. National Geographic Magazine. 58(1930): 607-648. 50 illus., map.

Hansen, Maria Skylv. Gamlar Gøtur. Siðir-Sagnir-Søgur. Tórshavn, Felagið Varðin. 1950. 190 p. (General Faeroe culture.)

Hiort, E. Les îes Féroé, nature, culture, industrie-commerce. Copenhagen, Exposition à la Maison du Danemark à Paris. 1957. 16 p.

Huson, Gordon. The Faroes in pictures. London, G. Allen & Unwin. 1946. 82 p., plates.

Jacobsen, H. J. Landbruget paa Faerøerne. Turistf Aarb 1951: 59-70, fig. (Agriculture in the Faeroes.)

Jaden, Hans, Freiherr von. Volkskundliches aus Island und den Färöern. M.A.G.W. 47(1917): 9-14.

Jakobsen, Jakob, ed. Faerøske folkesagn og aeventyr udg. for Samfund til udgivelse af gammel nordisk litteratur. København, S. L. Møllers Bogtrykkeri. 1898-1901. 47, 648 p. (Folklore.)

Jeaffreson, Joseph Russell. The Farōe Islands. London, Sampson Low, Marston 1898. 16, 272 p.

Jirlow, Ragnar. Das Tragen mit dem Stirnband. Acta Ethnologica. 2 (1937): 137-148.

Joensen, Robert. Royvið. Teknað hevur oli egilstroð. Klaksvík, Dagprent. 1958. 104 p. (Sheepherding in the Faeroes.)

Kampp, Aage Hjalmer Hansen. Faerøerne, folk og ersherv. København, Folkeuniversitetsudvalget, i Kommission hos Munksgaard. 1949. 16 p.

Kielberg, Børge. Faerøfolk, i storm og sol paa fjeld og hav. København, Gyldendal. 1946. 154 p.

Krenn, Ernst. Das kleinste germanische Volk: das Brudervolk der Föroyinger. Volk und Rasse. 8 (1931): 105-115, 3 illus.

Krenn, Ernst. Föroyische Tanzlieder. Eine Heilige Kirche. 21, numéro spécial (1939): 168 p. (München.)

Krenn, Ernst. Föroyer--Faroe Isles, the smallest Germanic nation and land. Anthropos. 35-36 (1940-1941): 753-760.

Krenn, Ernst, and Franzi Krenn. Föroyer, die Insel des Friedens. Münster im Westfalen, Regensberg'sche Verlagsbuchhandlungen. 1943. 199 p., 64 plates.

Küchler, Carl. Land und Leute der Faeröer. Zeitschrift für Geographie. 17 (1911): 601-618.

*Landt, Jørgen. Description of the Feroe Islands, containing an account of their situation, climate and productions; together with the manners, and customs, of the inhabitants, their trade, etc. London, Longman, Hurst, Reese, and Orme. 1810. 14, 426 p.

Lockwood, W. B. The language and culture of the Faroe Islands. Saga-Book: Viking Society for Northern Research. 13 (1949-1950): 249-268.

Nicol, James. An historical and descriptive account of Iceland, Greenland, and the Faroe Islands. New York, Harper and Brothers. 1841. 12, 360 p.

Nyman, A. Hay harvesting methods on the Faeroe Islands. Folk-Liv. 21-22 (1957-1958): 101-106.

Olsson, Alfa. Färöiska kostvanor. Rig. 37 (1954): 79-91, including an English summary. (Food on the Faeroe Islands.)

Poulsen, Jóan Chr. Hestsøga. Tórshavn, Felagið Varðin. 1947. 191 p., illus. (Description of life on the island of Hest.)

Rasmussen, Holger. Faerøske kulturbilleder omkring aarhundredskiftet. København, Hassing. 1950. 44 p., 71 figs. (Faeroe culture in the twentieth century.)

Rasmussen, Holger. Koltur. En faerøsk bygd. Fra Nationalmuseets Arbejdsmark 1951: 5-14, 10 figs.

Rasmussen, Holger. Korntørring og -taerskning pa Faerøerne. Kuml. 1955: 131-157. (English summary: Corn drying and threshing in the Faeroe Islands, pp. 152-157.)

*Rasmussen, Holger. Der pfluglose Feldbau auf den Färöer. In Agrarethnographie. Berlin, Akademie der Wissenschaften zu Berlin. 1957: 68-81.

Rasmussen, Holger. Husbygning. Faerøerne. 1(1958): 296-314. (Architecture.)

Rasmussen, Holger. Carrying children "í kiltingi, " a Faroese christening custom. Folk. 1(1959): 133-140.

Rasmussen, R. K. Om drøbelen i den faerøske folkemedicin. English summary: The uvula in the popular medicine of the Faroe Islands. Budstikken. 1957: 31-40.

Rasmussen, R. K. Gomul føroysk heimarád. Foeroya Frodskapar felag, Annales, Supplementum (Annales Societatis Scientiarum Faeroensis, Supplementum). 3. Tórshavn. 1959. 151 p. (English summary: Folk medicine.

Rasmussen, Rasmus. Saer er siður á landi. Tórshavn, the author. 1950. 163 (Description of a farmer's life throughout the year in a small parish on the island of Vágar.)

Rasmussen, Rasmus. Føroysk plantunøvn. With a supplement, Uppískoyti til Føroysk plantunøvn. Tórshavn, by the author. 1951. 207, 45 p. (Faeroese plant names and popular beliefs and ideas about different plants.)

Rasmussen, Rasmus. Om spaede, faerøske børns påklaedning i gamle dage. Budstikken. 1954-1955: 54-60.

Stocklund, B. Faerøhuse til Frilandsmuseet. English summary: Faeroese houses for the Open-Air Museum in Sorgenfri. Budstikken. 1962: 31-52.

Stocklund, B. Den faerøske hjallur. English summary: The Faeroe Hjallur. Budstikken. 1963: 32-62.

Symington, Andrew James. Pen and pencil sketches of Farõe and Iceland. London, Longman, Green, Longman, and Roberts. 1862. 6, 315 p., illus.

Williamson, Kenneth. Horizontal water-mills of the Faeroe Islands. Antiquity. 20 (1946): 83-91, plates, plans, diagrams.

Williamson, Kenneth. The Atlantic islands. A study of the Faeroe life and scene. London, Collins. 1948. 360 p., illus.

Zachariasen, Louis. Føroyer sum raettarsamfelag 1535-1655. Foeroya Frodskaparfelag Annales (Annales Societatis Scientiarum Faeroensis). 4(1961): 289-423.

DENMARK

Bødker, L., B. Holbeck, and H. Rasmussen. Bibliografi over dansk folke-
kultur. Kopenhagen, Danmarks Folkeminder. 1961-1962. 60 p.

Jansson, S. O. Bibliographie der wichtigsten Arbeiten auf dem Gebiete der
dänischen, norwegischen und schwedischen Volkskunde 1945-1956.
Deutsches Jahrbuch für Volkskunde. 7(1961): 229-266.

United States. Bureau of the Census. Bibliography of social science periodicals and monograph series: Denmark 1945-1961. Washington, Government Printing Office. 1963. 115 p.

Abildtrup, Jens. Vestjydsk bondeliv i 1660' erne. Nørre Nissum, the author.
1953. 95 p. (Farm life in West Jutland around 1660.)

Andersen, Ellen Dorothea Johanna Brodersen. Sydfyns herregaarde. København.
J. Gjellerup. 1947. 94 p. (Domestic architecture of Fyen, Denmark.)

Andersen, Ellen Dorothea Johanna Brodersen. Danish folk costumes. Copenhagen, Gyldendal. 1948. 35 p., illus.

Andersen, Ellen Dorothea Johanna Brodersen. Folk costumes in Denmark;
pictures and descriptions of local dresses in the National Museum. Copenhagen, Hassing. 1952. 29 p., 30 plates.

Andersen, Ellen Dorothea Johanna Brodersen. Danske bønders klaededragt.
København, C. Andersen. 1960. 534 p., illus. (Danish peasant costumes.

Anderson, H. An analysis of 777 matrimonial ads in two Copenhagen news-
papers. Acta Sociologica. 3(1958): 173-183.

Anderson, Robert T., and Barbara Gallatin Anderson. Changing social stratification in a Danish village. Anthropological Quarterly. 33(1960): 98-105.

Anderson, Robert T., and Barbara Gallatin Anderson. Sexual behavior and
urbanization in a Danish village. S.W.J.A. 16(1960): 93-109.

*Anderson, Robert T., and Barbara Gallatin Anderson. The vanishing village.
A Danish maritime community. Seattle, University of Washington Press.
1964. 12, 148 p.

Birchenrod, J. Folketro og festskik, saerlig fra Fyn (1734). Danmarks Folkeminder 43. København. 1936. 131 p.

Bjerre, M., and H. P. Hansen. Bonde og Handelsmand. Danmarks Folkeminder 56. København. 1948. 162 p.

Boberg, Inger M. Dansk folketradition i tro og digting og deraf afhaengig skik.
Danmarks Folkeminder 72. København. 1962. 189 p.

DENMARK

Boers, Hedda. Folketro om taender, tandmilder og tandbehandling hos almuen i Danmark. Et studium i Dansk folkemedicin. København, Dansk Videnskabs Forlag. 1954. 184 p., 4 plates.

Boisgelinde Kerdu, Pierre Marie Louis de. Travels through Denmark and Sweden, a journal of a voyage down the Elbe from Dresden to Hamburgh. 2 vols. London, printed for Wilkie and Robinson. 1810.

Bondenkultur. København, Nationalmuseet. 1951. 76 p., 18 plates.

Borgland, Chr. Gennem storm og stille. København, Nationalmuseet. 1954. 183 p. (Childhood memoirs by the chairman of the Danish Seamans Union and life on Danish ships and trade unionism.)

Bröchner, Jessie. Danish life in town and country. New York, G. P. Putnam's Sons. 1903. 7, 266 p., plates. (Another edition: London, G. Newnes. 1903. 11, 241 p., plates.)

Budstikken. København, Nationalmuseet. 1 (1954):-- (Yearbook of the Danish National Museum.)

Bukh, Peder. Dansk Folkeliv. Odense. 1942. 192 p.

Butlin, F. M. Among the Danes. New York, J. Pott. 1909. 11, 278 p.

Christensen, Anders. Bondeliv i midten af forrige aarhundrede. Kolding, K. Jørgensens bogtr. 1955. 118 p., 1 plate. (Original published in 1918. A description of farm life in the last century.)

Christensen, Jens. Traek af Nordfynsk landsbyliv. Udvalg for Folkemaals Publicationer, ser. B., no. 4. København, J. H. Schultz. 1958. 124 p. (North Fynsk farm life.)

Christiansen, Tage. The village; pictures from Denmark's countryside. Copenhagen, Det Danske Selskab. 1954. 124 p., illus.

Clausen, V. E. Det folkelige danske traesnit i etbladstryk 1650-1870. Danmarks Folkeminder 71. København. 1961. 264 p., 9 plates.

Clemmensen, Mogens B. Bulhuse, studier over gammel dansk traebygnings-kunst. 2 vols. København, Levin & Munksgaard. 1937. 298, 282 p. (Bole houses in Denmark.)

Clemmensen, Tove. Danske interiørtegninger fra rococo til klunketid. København, no publisher. 1951. 78 p. (Upper-class house interiors.)

Curtis, William E. Denmark, Norway and Sweden. New York, The Solfield Publishing Co. 1903. 17, 24, 505 p., plates.

Dam, Ph. R. Folkeliv og indstiftelser (Einstiftung) paa Bornholm. Aakirkeby.
1933. 204 p.

Dania. Copenhagen. 1 (1890)--1903. Continued as Danske Studier.
1(1904):--

Danish peasant costume. Copenhagen, Dansk Folkemuseum. 1955. 92 p.,
illus.

Danmarks Folkeminder. København. No. 1(1908)--

Danmarks sociale lovgivning, 1891-1941. København, Udgivet af Socialt
Tidsskrift i Kommission hos G. E. C. Gads Boghandel. 1941. 12, 416 p.

*Den Danske bonde. Kulturbilleder. 2 vols. København, Nordisk Specialforlag.
1945-1946. 260, 228 p., illus., 8 col. plates.

*Denmark. European conference on rural life. National monographs drawn up
by governments. Denmark. Series of League of Nations Publications.
European Conference on Rural Life. 20. Geneva. 1939. 54 p., illus.

Ellekilde, H. Danske højtidsskikke. København, J. H. Schultz. 1943. 123 p.
(Folk festivals in Denmark.)

Ewald, Jasper. Danske folkeeventyr. København, Gyldendal. 1954. 233 p.

Faber, Harald. Cooperation in Danish agriculture. London, Longman, Green.
1918. 13, 176 p. (2d ed. 1931. 188 p.)

Feilberg, H. F. Dansk bondeliv, som det i vore oldeforaeldres tid førtes,
navnlig i Vestjylland. København, Gad. 1952. 516 p. (Danish farm
life in West Jutland, 1889-1899.)

Floud, Jean. Social stratification in Denmark (review article). B. J. S.
3(1952): 173-177. (Review of Theodor Geiger, Sociale Umschichtungen
in einer danischen Mittelstadt.)

Frifelt, Salomon J., and T. T. Kragelund. Nabo til kraen vesterfra smaas-
kaebner med en stor nabo. København, Gyldendal. 1948. 117 p., illus.

Frifelt, Salomon J., and T. T. Kragelund. Jyder vesterfra er mange slags.
København, Gyldendal. 1949. 124 p., illus.

Friis, Achton. De jyders land (Jutland). 2 vols. 2d ed. København. 1965,
1966. 511 p., illus., 37 plates; 335, 13 p., illus., 26 plates.

Frydendahl, H. C., comp. Fynske Folkeminder. Bd. 1, Krarup pr Espe.
Odense, Fynsk Hjemstavns Forlag. 1945. 240 p., illus.

DENMARK

*Geiger, Theodor.   Soziale Umschichtungen in einer danischen Mittelstadt.
Acta Jutlandica. 23, no. 1. Kopenhagen. 1951. 132 p.

Gravlund, Th.   Dansk folkekarakter. Sjaellaendere og jyder. Danmarks
Folkeminder 7. København. 1911. 123 p.

Gravlund, Th.   Dansk folkekarakter. Fynboer. Danmarks Folkeminder 14.
København. 1914. 127 p.

Griffin, Gilderoy Wells.   My Danish days. With a glance at the history, traditions and literature of the old northern country. Philadelphia, Claxton,
Remsen & Haffelfinger. 1875. 297 p.

Grüner, Nielsen H.   Laesøfolk i gamle dage. Danmarks Folkeminder 29.
København. 1924. 8, 255 p.

Gutkind, Erwin Anton.   Urban development in Alpine and Scandinavian countries. New York, The Free Press of Glencoe. 1965. 518 p.

Haggard, H.[enry] Rider.   Rural Denmark and its lessons. London, New York,
etc., Longmans, Green. 1917. 14, 335 p.

Hansen, G.   Saedelighedsforhold blandt landefolkningen i det 18 århundrede.
København, Det Dansk Forlag. 1957. 237 p. (Sexual morality among
18th-century Danish peasants.)

Hansen, Georg.   Praesten paa landet i Danmark i det 18. Aarh. København,
Det Danske Forlag. 1947. 256 p. (The rural minister in 18th-century
rural Denmark.)

Hansen, H. P.   Hyrdeliv paa Heden. København, Danmarks Folkeminder 49.
1941. 248 p. (Herding life in the moors.)

Hansen, H. P.   Kloge folk. Folkemedicin og overtro i vestjylland. 2 vols.
København. 1942-1943. 244; 242 p. (Folk medicine in West Jutland.)

Hansen, H. P.   Hedebønder i tre slaegtled. København, Rosenkilde og Bogger.
1958. 261 p. (Peasants in Jutland.)

Hansen, Severin.   Fra traeskoen til rigsdagen. København, Nationalmuseet.
1952. 255 p. (Zealand fishing life.)

Hendin, Herbert.   Suicide in Scandinavia; a psychoanalytic study of culture
and character. New York, Grune & Stratton. 1964. 153 p.

Højrup, Ole.   Landbokvinden: Rok og kaerne, grovbrød og vadmel. København, Nationalmuseet. 1966. 278 p., 309 figs., 5 maps, table. (Wom-
en's life, home life.)

Høyer, Bodil. Dagligt liv paa en nordsyaellandsk bondegaard i midten af forrige aarhundrede. Hillerød, Fredriksborg amts Historiske Samfund. 1955. 175 p. (Daily life on a farm on North Zealand in the last century.)

Jensen, Jens Peter. Sjaellandske bønder. Personskildringer fra den sjaellandske bondebevaegelse. København, Aschehoug. 1919. 192 p.

Jespersen, Svend. Studier i Danmarks bonderbygninger. København, Nationalmuseet. 1961. 149 p. (Farmhouses.)

Jones, Hugh. Modern Denmark: its social, economic and agricultural life. London, P. S. King & Son. 1927. 11, 83 p.

Junge, J. Den nordsjaellandske landalmues karakter, skikke, meninger og sprog (1798). Danmarks Folkeminder 13. København, 1915. 279 p.

Kammp, Aa. H. Some changes in the structure of Danish farming, particularly from 1940-1960. Geografisk Tijdskrift. 62 (1963): 80-101.

Kamp, Jens Nielsen. Dansk folktro, samlet af . . . Danmarks Folkeminder 51. København. 1943. 253 p.

Koblauch, H. I. Fra den gamle slagtergaard. Copenhagen, Nationalmuseet. 1954. 132 p. (Horse slaughterhouses.)

Kragelund, T. Tobiassen. Gamle vestjyder forteller om tegl- og kalkbraending. København, Nationalmuseet. 1953. 185 p., illus. (Brick and lime kilns on West Jutland.)

Kristensen, Evald Rejnholdt. Danmark og det danske folk. Omaha, Neb., A. H. Anderson. 1920. 371 p.

Kyrre, H. Dansk fiskerliv. Daglig dont, tro og taenkemaade. I: furboerne. Danmarks Folkeminder 9. København. 1912. 72 p.

Laing, Samuel. Observations on the social and political state of Denmark, and the duchies of Sleswick and Holstein, in 1851. London, Longman, Brown, Green & Longmans. 1852. 16, 446 p.

Langberg, Harald. Danmarks bygningskultur. 2 vols. København, Gyldendal. 1955. 318; 310 p.

Langeland, Marinus. Ad sandede Veje. En gammel hedebondes liv og minder. København, Det Danske Forlag. 1950. 260 p., illus.

Lorenzen, Poul. Vildt og vilddyr i dansk folketro. København, E. Munksgaard. 1948. 151 p. (Animal lore.)

Lorenzen, Poul, and Jeppe Jeppesen. Dances of Denmark. New York, Chanticleer Press. 1950. 40 p., 7 plates.

Marryat, Horace. A residence in Jutland, the Danish Isles, and Copenhagen. 2 vols. London, J. Murray. 1860.

Matthiesson, Hugo Albert. Gamle købmandsgaarde, provinshandelskammert 1901 - 7. August-1951. København, G. E. Gad. 1951. 85 p. (Architecture.)

Matthiesson, Hugo Albert. Gamle huse i Ribe. Copenhagen, Nationalmuseet. 1961. 2d rev. ed. 72 p. (Old houses in Ribe.)

Mejborg, Reinhold F. S. Das Bauernhaus im Herzogthum Schleswig und das Leben des schleswigischen Bauernstandes im 16., 17., und 18. Jahrhundert. Schleswig, J. Bergas. 1896. 7, 205 p., 56 p. of illus. (Translated from the Danish.)

Meyer, Paul. Danske Bylag. En fremstilling af det danske landesbystyre paa baggrund af retshistoriske studier over jordfaelleskabets hovedproblemer. København, Nyt Nordisk Forlag. 1949. 474 p.

Michelsen, Peter. Danish wheel ploughs, an illustrated catalogue. Copenhagen, National Museum. 1959. 16 p., 268 figs.

Minneman, P. G. Denmark's agriculture as affected by war. Foreign Agriculture. 4 (1940): 301-326.

Møller, J. S. Folkedragter i Nordvestsjaelland. Danmarks Folkeminder 34. København. 1926. 232 p., 155 illus., 12 col. plates. (Folk costumes in Northwest Zealand.)

Møller, J. S. Moder og barn i dansk folkeoverlevering. Fra svangerskab til daab og kirkegang. Danmarks Folkeminder 48. København. 1940. 603 p.

Mygdal, Elna. Amagerdragter. Vaevninger og syninger. Danmarks Folkeminder 37. København. 1930-1932. 8, 299 p., illus.

Nielsen, Enevold. Optegnelser og traek fra vive-ove-valsgaard sogne, Hinsted herred. Hobro, Haarsløv. 1954. 252 p., illus.

Ødegaard, Anne. Liv og leik i Valdres. Gjøvik, the author. 1945. 240 p.

Ovesen, Ove. Vandrebog for tømrer-svend. Efter håndvaerkets skik og brug. København, Nationalmuseet. 1953. 32 p. (Journal of a traveling salesman, describing the customs of the carpenter's trade, ca. 1902-1906.)

Pedersen, Anna. Fra bondestue og stegers. Danmarks Folkeminder 52. København. 1944. 152 p.

Pedersen, Peter Diderik. Et liv i arbejde. Erindringer fra 1870-1900. København, Nationalmuseet. 1954. 60 p. (Danish railroad workers.)

Raffaele, J. A. Labor leadership in Italy and Denmark. Madison, University of Wisconsin Press. 1962. 436 p.

Rasmussen, Holger. Das Fingerziehen (at traekke krog). Ethnologie in dänischen Rechtsquellen. Folk. 5 (1963): 283-286.

Rasmussen, Holger, ed. Dansk Folkemuseum & Frilandsmuseet. København, Nationalmuseet. 1966. 264 p., 123 figs. (History of the museum of Danish folk life.)

Rasmussen, Steen Eiler. Danish textiles. Leigh-on-Sea, England, F. Lewis. 1956. 24 p., 93 plates.

Redlich, Monica. Danish delight. London, Gerald Duckworth. 1939. 272 p

Reeps, Karl Aug. Grundzuge eine Landeskunde von Bornholm. Stuttgart, Strecker & Schröder. 1910. 111, 98 p.

Reimer, Christine. Nordfynsk bondeliv i mands minde. 3 vols. København, Gyldendal. 1910-1913.

Riis, Jacob August. The old town. New York, Macmillan. 1909. 14, 269 p (Ribe, Denmark.)

Schmidt, August F. Leksikon over landsbyens gilder. Festkikke og fester på landet. København, Rosenkilde & Bagger. 1950. 166 p.

Schmidt, August F. Aarhusegnens landsbyliv. Aarhus, Jdsk Centraltrykkeri. 1953. 144 p., illus. (Village life in Aarhus region.)

Schmidt, August F. Danmarks byremser. Danmarks Folkeminder 67. København. 1957. 232 p.

Schoubye, S. Folkekunsten på Tønderegnen. Tønder, Tønder Museet. 1955. 48 p., illus.

Seier, A. F. V. Bornholmske folkeminder. Rønne. 1934. 160 p.

Shanas, Ethel, Peter Townsend, et al. Old people in three industrial societies. New York, Atherton Press. 1968. 16, 478 p.

Skautrup, P. Bondesind. Aarhus, Universitets Forlaget. 1950. 72 p.

Smørum, Jens. Vejen jeg gik og mennesker jeg mødte. København, National museet. 1961. 151 p., illus. (Farm life on Zealand.)

Solheim, Svale. Arbeid og fester i eldre tider. Folketru og Folkeliv. 1944: 5-40.

Steensberg, Axel. Den danske bondegaard. Vi og vor Fortid. No. 8. København. 1942. 148 p. (Danish farmhouses.)

DENMARK

Steensberg, Axel. Den danske landsby; fra storfamilie til andelssamfund. København, J. H. Schultz. 1942. 107 p.

Steensberg, Axel. Gamle danske bøndergaarde. København. 1943. 192 p. (Old Danish farmhouses.)

Steensberg, Axel. Danske bondermøbler. København, Hassing. 1949. 53, 203 p., illus., 8 col. plates.

Steensberg, Axel. Bondehuse og vandmøller: farms and watermills in Denmark through two thousand years. Researches in Village Archaeology. 1. Copenhagen, National Museum. 1952. 325 p., illus., plates.

*Steensberg, Axel. Dagligliv i Danmark i det nittende og tyvende århundrede. 2 vols. København, Nyt Nordisk Forlag. 1963.

Steffensen, Steffen. Bag lave laenger. Fra en vestydsk landsby for 50 år siden. Ribe, Dansk Hjemstavns Forlag. 1955. 160 p.

Strange, Helene. I mødrenes spor. Nordfalsterske kninders arbejde gennem halvandet hundrede aar. Danmarks Folkeminder 54. København. 1945. 207 p.

Strunge, Mogens. Gamle amagerdragter. Deres historie. København, Hj. Joensen's Litogr. 1952. 38 p., 12 plates.

Svalastoga, K. Prestige, class and mobility. Copenhagen, Gyldendal. 1959. 446 p.

*Svalastoga, K. Where Europeans meet; a sociological investigation of a border-town. Copenhagen, the author. 1960. 144 p., (A town on the Danish-German border.)

Thomas, Margaret. Denmark, past and present. London, A. Treherne. 1902. 9, 302 p.

Thuberg, Karen. Det gamle harbøre. Optegnelser udg. af lt. ussing. Danmarks Folkeminder 36. København. 1928. 313 p.

Troels-Lund, Troels Frederik. Dagligt liv i norden i det 16de aarhundrede . . . 13 vols. Kjøbenhavn, C. A. Reitzel. 1880-1901.

Troels-Lund, Troels Frederik. Das täliche Leben in Skandinavien während des sechzehnten Jahrhunderts. Kopenhagen, Hoest & Sohn. 1882. 483 p. (Translated from books 2 and 3 of the Danish ed.)

Trolle-Steenstrup, H. When I was a boy in Denmark. Boston, Lothrop, Lee & Shepard. 1923. 214 p.

DENMARK

Ussing, H. Ingvor Ingvorsens fortaellinger om gammelt sjaelandsk bondeliv. Danmarks Folkeminder 20. København. 1918. 192 p.

Ussing, H. Aarets og livets højtider. Danmarks Folkeminder 32. København. 1925. 136 p.

Ussing, H. Mellem sydfynske sunde-hverday og højtid-paa grundlag af optegnelser fra Thorvald Hansen. Danmarks Folkeminder 41. København. 1934. 301 p.

Wendel, Carl. Skortensfejeren. København, Nationalmuseet. 1952. 2d ed. 1953. 28 p., illus. (Autobiography of a chimneysweep.)

Wiingaard, Georg. Dem fra Lolland. 2 vols. København, Hagerup. 1953-1954. 216, 146 p., illus. (People from Lolland Island.)

Yde-Andersen, D., ed. Smeden. København, Nationalmuseet. 1952. 341 p. (Twelve autobiographies of Danish smiths.)

Zangenberg, H. Danske bøndergaarde. Grundplaner og konstruktioner. Danmarks Folkeminder 31. København. 1925. 98 p.

NORWAY

Ås, Dagfin. Twelve years of social science research 1950-1962. Oslo, Norwegian Universities Press. 1962. 76 p.

Burchardt, Carl John B. Norwegian life and literature. English accounts, especially in the nineteenth century. London, Milford. 1921. 8, 230 p.

Grönland, Erling. Norway in English. Books on Norway and by Norwegians in English 1936-1959. Oslo, Norwegian Universities Press. 1961. 152 p.

Humaniora Norvegica; two years work in Norwegian humanities and social sciences. 6 vols. so far. Oslo, Akademisk Forlag, University of Oslo. 1956— (Each volume represents a two-year period from 1950 on.)

Jansson, S. O. Bibliographie der wichtigsten Arbeiten auf dem Gebiete der dänischen, norwegischen und schwedischen Volkskunde 1945-1956. Deutsches Jahrbuch für Volkskunde. 7(1961): 229-266.

United States. Bureau of the Census. Bibliography of social science periodicals and monograph series: Norway, 1945-1962. Washington, Government Printing Office. 1964. 4, 59 p.

Aars, Ferdinand. Norwegian arts and crafts, industrial design. Oslo, Dreyer. 1957. 77 p., illus.

Arneberg, Halfdan. Folkekunst fra Buskerud fylke. Drammen. 195_(?). 16 p., illus.

Arneberg, Halfdan. Norwegian peasant art. 2 vols. Oslo, Fabritius. 1949-1951.

Årviknes, Per. Folkeminne. Aamla, prenta og utg. Straumshamn, the author. 1952. 94 p., illus. (Volda, Sunmøre province.)

Aune, Hermann. Skikk og tru. Folkeminne frå Gauldal. Norsk Folkeminnelag. Skrifter. 42. 1939. 85 p.

*Barnes, J. A. Class and committees in a Norwegian island parish. Human Relations. 7(1954): 39-58.

*Barnes, J. A. Land rights and kinship in two Bremnes hamlets. J.R.A.I. 87 (1957): 31-56.

*Barth, Fredrik. The social organization of a pariah group in Norway. Norveg. 5(1955): 125-143. (Tinkers and tinsmiths.)

*Barth, Fredrik, ed. The role of the entrepreneur in social change in northern Norway. Bergen, Norway. Universitetet. Arbok. Humanitisk Serie. Acta. Series Humanorum Litterarum. 1963, No. 3. Bergen and Oslo, Norwegian Universities Press. 1963. 83 p.

Beito, Olav T. Norske saeternamn. Oslo, Instituttet for Sammenlignende
Kulturforskning. 1949. 340 p., 9 maps.

Berge, Rikard. Norsk bondesylv. Risör, E. Gunleikson. 1925. 592 p.,
200 figs.

Bjanes, Ole Taraldsen. Norwegian agriculture. Oslo, J. W. Cappelen. 1932.
134 p.

Bjerke, Gunnar. Landsbebyggelsen i Norge. 2 vols. Oslo, Dreyer. 1950-
1951. 358, 299 p., illus.

Bjerken, Martin. Grongs bygdebok for Grong, Harran, Nammskogen og
Röyrvik. Trondheim. 1950. 646 p., 37 figs. (Folk life in North
Tröndelag.)

Bjørndal, Martin. Segn og tru; folkeminne fra Møre. Norsk Folkeminnelag.
Skrifter 64. Oslo. 1949. 183 p.

Bø, Olav. Falcon catching in Norway. Studie Norvegica. Vol. 4, No. 11.
Oslo, Universitetsforlaget. 1962. 78 p.

Bondevik, Kjell. Jordbruket i Norsk folketru; ei jamførande gransking. Norsk
Folkeminnelag. Skrifter. 29, 66. Oslo. 1933, 1966.

Bosworth, A. L. Life in a Norway valley; an American girl is welcomed into
the homemaking and haying of happy Hallingdall. National Geographic
Magazine. 67(1935): 627-648, illus.

Brace, Charles Loring. The Norse-folk; or, a visit to the homes of Norway an
Sweden. New York, C. Scribner. 1857. 516 p.

Brown, John Croumbie. Forestry in Norway. Edinburgh, Oliver and Boyd. 188
7, 227 p.

Brox, Ottar. Natural conditions, inheritance and marriage in a North Norwegia
fjord. Folk. 6, No. 1 (1964): 35-45.

Bugge, Alexander. Vesterlandenes indflydelse paa nordboernes ydre kultur,
levesaet og samfundsforhold. Christiania. 1905.

Bull, Edvard. Arbeiderklassen i norsk historie. Oslo, Tiden. 1947. 374 p.,
illus. (The working class in Norwegian history.)

Burchardt, Carl John Birch. Norwegian life and literature. Oxford, London,
etc., Oxford University Press. 1920. 8, 230 p.

Castberg, Frede. The Norwegian way of life. Melbourne, Heinemann. 1954.
11, 110 p.

Christenson, Herbert. Fråkne. Bygd och folk i gangen tid. Ljungskile, the author. 1954. 475 p.

Christiansen, Reider Th. Norwegian folklore-research through 25 years. Folk. 1 (1937): 80-92. Leipzig.

Clough, Ethlyn T. Norwegian life; an account of past and contemporary conditions and progress in Norway and Sweden. Detroit, The Bay View Reading Club. 1909. 238 p.

*Daniels, H. K. Home life in Norway. New York, Macmillan. 1911. 11, 298 p.

Egan, Maurice Fr. Norway and the Norwegians. National Geographic Magazine. 45 (1924): 647-696.

Eggen, Eystein. Bardu bygdebok. I. Bardu. 1951. 492 p., 212 illus. (Folk life in Bardu, Norland.)

Eidnes, Hans. Tru og tradisjon. Gamalt frå Hålogaland. Trondheim, F. Brun. 1946. 176 p.

Eier, Sigfred L. Ströms historie. 2 vols. Oslo. 1951. 539 p., 318 figs., 12 maps; 224 p., 104 figs.

Eliot, Thomas Dawes, et al. Norway's families: trends, problems, progress. Philadelphia, University of Pennsylvania Press. 1960. 485 p.

Engelstad, Helen. Norwegian textiles. Leigh-on-Sea, England, F. Lewis. 1952. 16 p., 113 plates.

Falnes, Oscar Julius. National romanticism in Norway. New York, Columbia University Press. 1933. 399 p.

Fjellstad, Lars M. Till-till-tove; eventyr, segner, regler oganna; folkeminne frå Eidskog. Norsk Folkeminnelag. Skrifter. 68. Oslo. 1951. 128 p.

Flint, J. T. The secularization of Norwegian society. Comparative Studies of Society and History. 6 (1964): 325-344.

Grimstad, Edvard. Etter gamalt; folkeminne fa Gudbrandsdalen. 2 vols. Norsk Folkeminnelag. Skrifter. 58, 62. Oslo. 1945.

Grønoset, Dagfinn. Finnskog og trollskap. Oslo, Aschehoug. 1953. 121 p., 20 plates. (Magic among Finnish settlers in Norway.)

Gutkind, Erwin Anton. Urban development in alpine and Scandinavian countries. New York, The Free Press of Glencoe. 1965. 518 p.

Hall, John Oscar. When I was a boy in Norway. Boston, Lothrop, Lee & Shepard. 1921. 254 p., plates.

Hammer, Simon Christian. Things seen in Norway. London, Seeley, Service. 1927. 153 p.

Hammer, Simon Christian. Norway. London, A. & C. Black. 1928. 7, 196 p.

Hauglid, Roar, ed. The native arts of Norway. Oslo, Mittet. 1953. 174 p., illus.

Hauglid, Roar, ed. Norway; a thousand years of native arts and crafts. Oslo, Mittet. 1956. 123 p., illus.

Hendin, Herbert. Suicide in Scandinavia; a psychoanalytic study of culture and character. New York, Grune & Stratton. 1964. 153 p.

Henningsen, G. The art of perpendicular lying: concerning a commercial collection of Norwegian sailors' tall tales. Journal of the Folklore Institute. 2(1965): 180-219.

Hermundstad, Knut. Gamletidi taler. Gamal Valdreskultur 1. Norsk Folkeminnelag. Skrifter. 36. Oslo. 1936. 175 p.

Hermundstad, Knut. Bondeliv. Gamal Valdreskultur 2. Norsk Folkeminnelag. Skrifter. 45. Oslo. 1940. 145 p.

Hermundstad, Knut. I manns minne. Gamal Valdreskultur 3. Norsk Folkeminnelag. Skrifter. 55. Oslo. 1944. 222 p.

Hermundstad, Knut. Aettearv. Gamal Valdreskultur 4. Norsk Folkeminnelag. Skrifter. 65. Oslo. 1950. 208 p.

Hermundstad, Knut. Aettarminne. Gamal Valdreskultur 5. Norsk Folkeminnelag. Skrifter. 70. Oslo. 1952. 194 p.

Hermundstad, Knut. I kveldseta. Gamal Valdreskultur 6. Norsk Folkeminnelag. Skrifter. 75. Oslo. 1955. 247 p.

Hermundstad, Knut. Kvorvne tider. Gamal Valdreskultur 7. Norsk Folkeminnelag. Skrifter. 86. Oslo. 1961. 244 p.

Hoffmann, Marta. Bryllup pa Jaeren for hundre ar siden. By og Bygd. 1947: 33-55. (Marriage in Jaeren, in southwestern Norway, a hundred years ago.)

Hopp, Zinken. Norwegian folklore simplified. Chester Springs, Penn., Dufour Editions. 1961. 107 p.

Hoprekstad, Olav. Bygdabok for Vik i sogn. 1. Bergen. 1951. 526 p.,
119 illus. (Folk life in Vik.)

Hveding, Johan. Folketru og folkeliv pa Halogaland. 2 vols. Norsk Folkeminnelag. Skrifter. 32, 45. Oslo. 1935, 1944. 223, 104 p.

Jensen, Arne S. The rural schools of Norway. Boston, The Stratford Co.
1928. 280 p.

Jonassen, Christen T. The Protestant ethic and the spirit of capitalism in
Norway. American Sociological Review. 12(1947): 676-686.

Jungman, Mrs. Beatrix. Norway by Nico Jungman. London, A. & C. Black.
1905. 10, 199 p.

Kleiven, Ivar. Gamal bondekultur i Gudbrandsdalen. Østre og vestre Gausdal.
3 vols. Oslo, Ringebu. 1915-1926.

Laing, Samuel. Journal of a residence in Norway during the years 1835 and
1836 . . . New ed. London, Longman, Brown, Green, Longmans & Roberts.
1856. 306 p.

Landestad, M. B. Mystike sagn fra Telemarken. Norsk Folkeminnelag.
Skrifter. 13. Oslo. 1926. 161 p.

Landestad, M. B. Fra Telemarken. Skik og sagen. Norsk Folkeminnelag.
Skrifter. 15. Oslo. 1927. 96 p.

Langholm, M. Family and child welfare in Norway. Oslo, Norwegian Joint
Committee on International Social Policy. 1961. 150 p.

Latham, Robert Gordon. Norway and the Norwegians. 2 vols. London, R.
Bentley. 1840.

Martin, Anthony. Norwegian life and landscape. London, Elek Books. 1952.
167 p.

Medill, Robert (pseud. for McBride, Robert Medill). Norwegian towns and
people: vistas in the land of the midnight sun. New York, R. M. McBride.
1923. 85 p.

Metcalfe, Frederick. The Oxonian in Norway. 2 vols. London, Hurst &
Blackett. 1856.

Metcalfe, Frederick. The Oxonian in Thelemarken: or, notes of travel in
south-western Norway, in the summers of 1856 and 1857, with glances at
the legendary lore of that district. 2 vols. London, Hurst & Blackett. 1858.

Mørch, Andreas. Frå gamle dagar: folkeminne frå Sigdal og Eggedal.
Norsk Folkeminnelag. Skrifter. 27. Oslo. 1932. 131 p.

*Munch, Peter A. Gard: the Norwegian farm. Rural Sociology. 12 (1947): 356-363.

Munch, Peter A. Landhandelen i Norge. Oslo, Halvorsen & Larsen. 1948. 191 p. (Retail trade in Norway.)

Munch, Peter A. The peasant movement in Norway. B.J.S. 5(1954): 63-77.

Nordskog, John E. Social reform in Norway: a study of nationalism and social democracy. University of Southern California, Social Science Series. No. 12. Los Angeles. 1935. 7, 184 p.

Norveg. Folkelivsgransking. Oslo. Vol. 1 (1951):-- (annual). Journal of Norwegian Ethnology.

*Norway. European conference on rural life, National monographs drawn up by governments. Norway. Series of League of Nations Publications. European Conference on Rural Life. 25. Geneva. 1939. 66 p., illus.

Noss, Aagot. Høgtider og samkomer. Norsk Folkeminnelag. Skrifter. 90. Oslo. 1963. 106 p.

Olsen, Magnus Bernhard. Farms and fanes of ancient Norway. The place-names of a country discussed in their bearings upon social and religious history. Oslo, Instituttet for Sammenlignende Kulturforskning. 1928. 349 p.

Oxholm, Axel H. Country life in Norway . . . National Geographic Magazine. 75 (1939): 493-528, illus.

*Park, George Kerlin. An afterpiece to peasantry: a study of change in North Norway. Chicago, University of Chicago. 1958. Unpublished Ph. D. dissertation in anthropology.

Park, George Kerlin. Sons and lovers: characterological requisites of the roles in a peasant society. Ethnology. 1 (1962): 412-424.

*Park, George Kerlin, and Lee Soltow. Politics and social structure in a Norwegian village. American Journal of Sociology. 67 (1961): 152-164.

Reichborn-Kjennerud, I. Vår gamle trolldomsmedisin. Norske Videnskaps-Akademi, Oslo. Skrifter. II. Historisk-filosofisk Klasse. 1943, No. 2. 263 p.

*Reinton, Lars Sigurdson. Saeterbruket i Norge. 3 vols. — 2 published so far. Oslo, Instituttet for Sammenlignende Kulturforskning. 1955, 1957. 476 p., 126 illus., 3 maps; 20, 281 p., 93 illus. (Saeter farming in Norway.)

Roberts, Warren E. Folklore in Norway: addendum. In Richard M. Dorson, ed. Folklore research around the world. Bloomington, Indiana University Press. 1961: 35-38.

NORWAY

*Rodnick, David. The Norwegians; a study of national culture. Washington, Public Affairs Press. 1955. 165 p.

Rokkan, S., and H. Valen. Regional contrasts in Norwegian politics: a review of data from official statistics and from sample surveys. Transactions of the Westermarck Society. 10(1964): 162-238.

Rokkones, I. O. Sagn fortellingar fra Reenebu. Trøndheim, Brun. 1947. 197 p., illus. (Folklore from Rennebu, Sør-Trøndelag.)

Semb, Klara. Dances of Norway. London, M. Parrish. 1951. 40 p., plates.

Sidgwick, Charlotte S. The story of Norway. London, Rivingtons. 1885. 8, 220 p.

Skre, Brita G. Folk life research in Norway. Midwest Folklore. 2(1952): 221-228.

Solheim, Svale. Norsk saetertradisjon. Oslo, Instituttet for Sammenlignende Kulturforskning. 1952. 703 p., 90 illus.

Stewart, Janice S. The folk arts of Norway. Madison, University of Wisconsin Press. 1953. 17, 246 p., illus.

Svarre, Reider. Far etter fedrane, folkeminne innsamla i Vefsn. Mosjøen, Vefsn Historielag. 1950. 213 p.

Symes, D. G. Changes in the structure and role of farming in the economy of a West Norwegian island. Economic Geography. 39(1963): 319-331. (Radøy Island—40 miles from Bergen.)

*Symes, D. G. Vågsøy. A West Norwegian island. Geographical Field Group. Regional Studies 13. Nottingham, Geographical Field Group, Department of Geography, University of Nottingham. 1968. 10, 125 p., 78 p. of maps and diagrams.

Taraldlien, Bendik. Fyresdal. Oslo. 1949. 94 p., illus. (Folk life in Fyresdal, Telemark.)

Thomson, Claudia. Norwegian agriculture. Foreign Agriculture. 4(1940): 65-94.

Torgersen, U. The structure of urban parties in Norway during the first period of extended suffrage 1884-1898. Transactions of the Westermarck Society. 10(1964): 377-399.

Tromsø Museum. Norway north of 65. Head editor Ørnulv Vorren. Oslo, Oslo University Press; London, G. Allen & Unwin. 1961. 271 p.

Visted, Kristofer, and Hilmar Stigum. Vår gamle bondekultur. 2 vols. Oslo, J. W. Cappelen. 1951-1952. (First published in 1908.)

Vorren, Ørnulv. See Tromsø Museum.

Vreim, Halvor. Houses with gables looking on the valley; influence of the terrain on the placement of buildings. Folk-Liv. 2 (1939): 295-315.

Walter, Lavina Edna. Norway and the Lapps. London, A. & C. Black. 1917. 7, 88 p.

Weibust, Knut. The crew as a social system. Oslo, Norsk Sjofartsmuseum. 1958. 66 p. (Fishing boat crews.)

Wolfram, Richard. Totenklagen in Norwegen. Niederdeutsches Jahrbuch für Volkskunde. 22 (1947): 43-50.

SWEDEN

Essén, Matts. Sörmländsk bibliografi. Nykoping, Sörmlands Hembygdsförbund. 1954. 151 p.

Jansson, S. O. Bibliographie der wichtigsten Arbeiten auf dem Gebiete der dänischen, norwegischen und schwedischen Volkskunde 1945-1956. Deutsches Jahrbuch für Volkskunde. 7(1961): 229-266.

United States. Bureau of the Census. Bibliography of social science periodicals and monograph series--Sweden: 1950-1963. Washington, Government Printing Office. 1965. 87 p.

Acerbi, Joseph (Guiseppi). Travels through Sweden, Finland and Lapland to North Cape, 1798-1799. 2 vols. London, printed for J. Mowman. 1802.

Ahlbäck, Symnöve. Vägen ur bostad snöden. Helsingfors, Söderström. 1945. 52 p. (Housing in Sweden.)

Ahlberg, Birgitta. Göta kanal; en färd med kanalbåt Göteborg-Stockholm. Stockholm, Svenska Turistföreningens Förlag. 1952. 135 p.

Ahlberg, Gösta. Befolkningsutvecklingen och urbaniseringen: Sverige 1911-1950. Stockholm, K. L. Beckmans Boktr. 1953. 8, 420 p. (Internal migration.)

*Allwood, Martin S.,and Ingra-Britt Ranemart. Medelby. En sociologisk studie. Stockholm, Bonnier. 1943. 358 p.

Andrén, Erik. Simrishamn: bebyggelsens och stadsplanens historia. Stockholm, Fritzes Kungl. Hovbokhandel. 1942. 96 p.

Andrén, Erik. Möbelstilarna: en handbok i den svenska möbel- och inredningskonstens historia. Stockholm, Saxon & Lindström. 1950. 279 p.

Andrén, Erik. Swedish silver. Translated from the Swedish by Lillian Ollén. New York, Barrows. 1950. 160 p., illus.

Andrén, Folke J. B. Om delning av naturnytlighet; särskilt om alt "skipa skog." Stockholm, R. W. Statlanders Boktrykkeri. 1963. 165 p. (Land tenure.)

Arenander, Erik Oskar. Die altertümliche Milchwirtschaft in Norland (Nordschweden). Stockholm, I. Haeggströms Boktryckeri. 1911. 56 p.

Areskog, Carl. En bok om Öland. Lund, C. W. K. Gleerup. 1946. 268 p.

Arv. Stockholm and Uppsala. 1 (1945):-- (Formerly titled: Folkminnen och Folktanker. 1 (1914):--)

Baeckström, Arvid Fredrik Elimar. Rörstrand och dess tillverkningar, 1726-1926; en konst- och kulturhistorisk bakgrund. Stockholm, Nordiska Museets Förlag. 1930. 146 p. (Röstland pottery.)

Baeckström, Arvid Fredrik Elimar. Lofholmens theatersällskap 1828-1830. Stockholm, Nordiska Museet. 1954. 61 p. (A nineteenth-century theatrical company.)

Beckman, Lars. The frequency of regional intermarriage in North Sweden. Acta Genetica et Statistica Medica. 9(1959): 9-17, maps, tables.

Bellessort, André. La suède. Paris. 1911. 7, 412 p.

Bengtsson, Ludvig. En dalasocken berättar. Bjursås sockens historia skildrad. Bjursås, the author. 1950. 362 p., 94 figs., plates. (Social relations, economic life, beliefs, etc. in a Dalerna parish.)

Bengtsson, Ludvig. En dalabonde och hans krönikebok. Anteckningar av Rällsjo Anders Jansson 1917-1948. Skanes Fagerhult, the author. 1953. 205 p. (A Dalerna farmer's chronicle of events.)

Berg, Gösta. Sledges and wheeled vehicles. Ethnological studies from the viewpoint of Sweden. Stockholm, Nordiska Museet; Copenhagen, Levin & Munksgaard. 1935. 189 p., illus.

*Berg, Gösta, and S. Svensson. Svensk bondekultur. Stockholm, A. Bonnier. 1934. 291 p.

Bergman, Eva. Nationella dräkten. Stockholm, Nordiska Museet. 1938. 352 p. (Eighteenth-century upper-class costume.)

Bergsten, Karl. Östergötlands bergslag. Lund, Gleerupska Univ. Bokhandels. 1946. 254 p., 2 maps, illus. (Settlement and economy in a mountain district of Ostergotland.)

Björkquist, Lennart. Jämtlands folkliga kvinnodräkter. Uppsala, Applebergs Boktr. 1941. 255 p. (Jämtland—clothing.)

Boethius, Johannes, ed. Orsa. En sockenbeskrivning. Stockholm, Nordisk Rotogravyr. 1950. 618 p., 133 figs., 1 plate.

Boken om Ornö. Stockholm, Norstedts. 1945. 256 p., illus. (The island of Ornö.)

Böök, J., and C. E. Måwe. The incidence of cousin marriage in a West Swedish rural community. American Journal of Human Genetics. 7(1955): 426-429, map.

Brace, Charles Loring. The Norse-folk; or, a visit to the homes of Norway and Sweden. New York, C. Scribner. 1857. 516 p.

Bringéus, Nils Arvid. Kyrkans tjänare; Ökelljunga pastorat. Lund, Gleerup. 1950. 206 p.

Bringéus, Nils Arvid. Klockringningsseden i Sverige. Stockholm, Nordiska Museet. 1958. 351 p. (Bells in Sweden.)

Bringéus, Nils Arvid, ed. Sockenbeskrivningar från Hälsingland, 1790-1791, . . . Uppsala, Gustav Adolfs Akademie. 1961. 415 p. (Village communities — Hälsingland.)

Brodin, Linus. En bok om Västra Emtervik. Väster Emtervik, the author. 1948. 368 p., 97 figs. (Social life and customs in a Värmland parish.)

Burgess, Ernest W., ed. Aging in Western societies. Chicago, University of Chicago Press. 1960. 492 p.

Campbell, Åke. Skånske bygder under förra hälften av 1700- talet; etnografisk studie över den skånska allmogens äldre odlingar, hägnader och byggnader . . . Uppsala, A. B. Lundequistska. 1928. 1,1,5, 279 p.

Campbell, Åke. Det svenska brödet. En jämförande etnologisk-historisk undersökning. Stockholm, A. B. Bennel. 1950. 268 p., 97 illus., 1 plate. (English summary: Swedish bread.)

Carlberg, Gösta. Svensk landbygd som kulturmiljö. Stockholm, LT's. Förlag. 1949. 263 p.

Carlsson, Gösta. Swedish character in the twentieth century. Annals of the American Academy of Political and Social Sciences. 370 (1967): 93-98.

Cederblom, Gerda. Svenska allmogedräkter. Stockholm, Nordiska Museet. 1921. (Swedish peasant clothing.)

Celander, Hilding. Några danska och sevnska julvisor. Göteborg, Elanders Boktryckeri. 1946. 111 p. (Carols and songs.)

Celander, Hilding. Stjärngossarna, deras visor och julspel. Stockholm, Nordiska Museet. 1950. 500 p. (Christmas: stars, plays, etc.)

Celander, Hilding. Förkristen jul enligt norröna källor. Mit einer deutschen Zusammenfassung. Stockholm, Almqvist & Wiksell. 1955. 91 p.

Credner, Wilhelm. Landschaft und Wirtschaft in Schweden. Breslau, F. Hirt. 1926. 131 p., plates, map.

Dahlbäck, Sigurd. Gångstigslandet; nordskandinaviska studier, 1914, 1916-1932. Stockholm, Nordiska Museet. 1958. 341 p.

Dahlström, E., ed. Svensk samhällsstruktur i sociologisk belysning. Stockholm, Gyldendal. 1959. 474 p. (Structure of Swedish society.)

SWEDEN

Djurklou, Nils Gabriel. Lifvet i kinds härad i Västergötland i början af
sjuttonde århundradet. Stockholm, Nordiska Museet. 1885. 6, 88 p.

Djurklou, Nils Gabriel. Fairy tales from the Swedish. New York, F. A.
Stokes Co. 1901. 177 p.

Ek, Sven B. Väderkvarnar och vattenmöllor, en etnologisk studie i kvarnarnas
historie. Stockholm, Nordiska Museet. 1962. 9, 317 p. (Mills and mill
work.)

Ekenvall, Verner. De svenska ortnamnen på hester. Uppsala, Gustav Adolfs
Akademie. 1942. 21, 208 p. (Placenames.)

Erixon, Sigurd. Svenska gårds typer. Rig. 1919: 1-39. (House types.)

Erixon, Sigurd. Möbler och heminredning i svenska bygder. Stockholm,
Nordiska Museet. 1925. 5 p., illus., col. plates.

Erixon, Sigurd. Hur Norge och Sverige mötas. Studier rörande kulturgränser
och kultursamband på skandinaviska halvön. Bidrag til Bondesamfundets
Historie . . . 2. Stockholm. 1933.

Erixon, Sigurd. Die Frage der kartographischen Darstellung, vom Standpunkt
der nordischen Ethnologie in Schweden aus betrachtet. Folk. 1 (1937):
168-180. Leipzig.

*Erixon, Sigurd. Svenskt folkliv. Uppsala, J. A. Lindblads Förlag. 1938.
303 p.

Erixon, Sigurd. Folklig möbelkultur i svenska bygder. Stockholm, Nordisk
Rotogravyr. 1938. 147 p., illus.

Erixon, Sigurd. Den äldre folkliga bebyggelsen i Stockholmstrakten. Stockholm. 1941. 11, 327 p.

Erixon, Sigurd. Strövtåg i svenska bygder. Malmö, J. Kroon. 1941. 321 p.

Erixon, Sigurd. Kila, en östgotsk skogsby. Stockholm, Institutet för Folklivsforskning. 1946. 11, 226 p. (Kila, Sweden.)

Erixon, Sigurd. Svensk byggnadskultur, studier och skildringar belysandre den
svenska byggnadskulturens historia. Stockholm, Aktiebolaget Bokverk.
1947. 826 p. (Domestic architecture.)

Erixon, Sigurd. Stockholms hamnarbetare före fackföreningsrörelsens genom-
brott; en etnologisk studie. Stockholm, Nordisk Rotogravyr. 1949.
156 p. (Longshoremen.)

Erixon, Sigurd. Från trätill stål. Stockholm, Bonnier. 1953. 225 p. (Metal
work and mines.)

SWEDEN

Erixon, Sigurd. Byggnadskultur. Stockholm, Bonnier. 1953. 416 p.

Erixon, Sigurd. Lergods, ädelmetaller och vävnader. Stockholm, Bonnier. 1953. 122 p. (Pottery, goldsmithing, textiles.)

Erixon, Sigurd. Östgötska kulturbilder; en översikt med historiska aspekter på sentida miljöer och monument. På uppdrag av Ostgöta gille i Stockholm fram lagd vid firandet av dess 150-årsjubileum den 28. Stockholm, Institutet för Folklivsforskning. 1953. 31 p.

Erixon, Sigurd. Svenska byordningar. Folk-Liv. 17/18 (1953/54): 81-124. (Swedish village statutes.)

Erixon, Sigurd. Fångst, jakt och fiske. Stockholm, Bonnier. 1955. 145 p.

Erixon, Sigurd. Landbrug og bebyggelse. Stockholm, Bonnier. 1956. 6, 314 p. (Agriculture in Scandinavia.)

Erixon, Sigurd. Village and common lands in Sweden. Transactions of the Westermarck Society. 3 (1956): 121-134.

Erixon, Sigurd, ed. Atlas över svensk folkkultur [Atlas of Swedish folk culture]. Stockholm, Gustav Adolfs Akademie. Vol. 1 (1957)--

Erixon, Sigurd. Materiell och social kultur. Uddevale, Bokförlaget Niloé. 1957. 61 p.

Erixon, Sigurd. Technik und Gemeinschaftsbildungen im schwedischen Traditionsmilieu . . . Samfundet för Svensk Folklivsforskning, Skriftserie Liv och Folkkultur, serie A, vol. 8. Stockholm. 1957. 225 p.

Erixon, Sigurd. Svenska byar systematisk reglering; en jäförande historisk undersökning, . . . Stockholm, Nordiska Museet. 1960. 18, 266 p.

Erixon, Sigurd. Gammal mässing. Västerås, ICA Förlaget. 1964. 111 p. (Brass industry and trade.)

Erixon, Sigurd, and Åke Campbell. Svensk bygd och folkkultur i samling, forskning och vård. 4 vols. Stockholm, Bokförlaget Gothia. 1946-1948.

Erlandsson, T. Gotländskt i sägn och sed. Visby, Norrbys Bokhandel. 1946. 303 p. (Tradition and custom on the Island of Götland.)

Ernvik, Arvid. Glaskogen. Bygd, arbetsliv och Gillbergs härader under 1800-talet. Uppsala, Lundequistska Bokhandeln. 1951. 444 p. (Folk culture in West Värmland.)

*Eskeröd, Albert. Årets äring [The year's crop]. Etnologiska studier i skördens och julens tro och sed. Stockholm, Nordiska Museet. 1947. 381 p.

Eskeröd, Albert. Årets fester. Stockholm, LT's. Förlag. 1953. 254 p.

Eskeröd, Albert. Skånes kust. Stockholm, LT's. Förlag. 1960. 222 p.

Eskeröd, Albert. Gotländska stränder. Stockholm, LT's. Förlag. 1962. 302 p.

Eskeröd, Albert. Swedish folk art. Stockholm, Nordiska Museet. 1964. 67 p.

Essen-Möller, E., et al. Individual traits and morbidity in a Swedish rural population. Copenhagen, Ejnar Munksgaard. 1956. 160 p.

Folkkultur; meddelande från Lunds Universitets Folkminnesarkiv. 1.— årgången 1941. Lund, C. W. K. Gleerup.

Forner, Lars. De svenska spannmåtten. En ordhistorisk och dialektgeografisk undersökning. Uppsala, Almqvist & Wiksell. 1945. 238 p.

Frödin, John. Studier över skogsgränsernai norra delen av Lule Lappmark. Lund, C. W. K. Gleerup. 1916. 73 p.

Frödin, John. Siljansområdets fäbodbygd. Lund, C. W. K. Gleerup. 1925. 317 p. (Dairying.)

Frödin, John. Bygdestudier i norra Jämtland. Lund, C. W. K. Gleerup. 1927. 253 p. (Pastures.)

Frödin, John. Skogar och mytar i norra Sverige i deras funktioner som betesmark och slåtter. Oslo, Instituttet för Sammenlignende Kulturforskning. 1952. 210 p., illus. (Forest and moor life.)

Frödin, John. Uppländska betes—och slåttermarker i gamla tider, deras utnyttjander genom landskapets fäbodväser. Uppsala, Almqvist & Wiksell. 1954. 112 p.

Det glada Sverige. Våra fester och högtider genom tiderna. 3 vols. Stockholm, Natur und Kultur. 1947-1948. 2416 p., illus., plates.

Granberg, Gunnar. Die nordschwedische Riesengetreideharfe. Acta Ethnologica 2(1937): 83-104. (Agriculture.)

Granlund, Ingegerd. På den tiden. Stockholm, Wahlström & Widstrand. 1959. 216 p. (Stockholm—social life and customs.)

*Granlund, John. How fishermen became burghers. Studia Ethnographica Upsaliensia. 11(1956): 133-163.

Granlund, John Einar Ludvig. Träkärl i svepteknik. Stockholm, Nordiska Museet. 1940. 364 p., illus. (Wooden vessels made in chips.)

SWEDEN

Grundbo på sollerön. En byundersökning. Stockholm, Nordiska Museet. 1938.
583 p. (Research in a Dalerna village.)

Gustafsson, B. People's view of the minister and the lack of ministers in
Sweden. Archives of the Sociology of Religion. 22 (1966): 135-144.

Gustafsson, Berndt. Manligt, kvinnligt kyrligt i 1800-talets. Stockholm,
Diakonistyrelsen. 1956. 174 p., 2 plates. (Men and women in
eighteenth-century church folk life.)

Gutkind, Erwin Anton. Urban development in Alpine and Scandinavian countries. New York, The Free Press of Glencoe. 1965. 518 p.

Hallerdt, Björn. Leva i brukssamhälle. Stockholm, Nordiska Museet. 1957.
236 p. (Living conditions in an iron-manufacturing village, 1845-1920.)

Hammarstedt, Edvard. Såkaka och. såöl. Stockholm, Kungl. Boktryckeriet.
1905. 44 p.

*Hanssen, Börje. Österlen. En studie över social-antropologiska sammanhang
under 1600- och 1700-talen i sydöstra Skåne. Stockholm, LT (Seelig).
1952. 562 p., illus.

*Hanssen, Börje. Dimensions of primary group structure in Sweden. Recherches
sur la Famille. 1 (1956): 115-156.

Harbe, Daniel. Folkminnen från Edsbergs härad. 2 vols. Uppsala, Lundequistska Bokhandeln. 1950.

Hasslöf, Olof. Svenska västkustfiskarna. Studier i en yrkesgrupps näringsliv
och sociala kultur. Göteborg, Svenska Västkustfiskarnas Centralförbund.
1949. 570 p., illus.

Hazelius, Artur Immanuel. Inledning till Hávamál, eller Odens sång.
Uppsala, C. A. Leffler. 1860. 39 p.

Hazelius, Artur Immanuel. Ur de nordiska folkens lif. Stockholm, Nordiska
Museet. 1882.

Hazelius-Berg, Gunnel. Modedräkter från 1600-1900. Stockholm, Nordiska
Museet. 1952. 11 p.

Hedblom, Folke. De svenska ortnamnen på säter. En namngeografisk
undersökning. Lund, C. Bloms Boktryckeri. 1945. 19, 269 p.

Hedlund, Greta. Dräkt och kuinnlig slöjd i Ovansjö socken, 1750-1850.
Vasterberg, Storvik, Ovansjö Hembygdsförenings Förlag. 247 p.

Hedqvist, Ejnar, ed. Från Sommabygd till Vätterstrand. 4 vols. Tranås, Tranås Hembygdsgille. 1942-1950. 160 p., 250 figs.; 193 p., 255 figs.; 179 p., 241 figs.; 203 p., 214 figs., plates.

Heidenstam, Oscar Gustaf von. Swedish life in town and country. New York and London, G. P. Putnam's Sons. 1904. 286 p., plates.

Hellberg, Lars. Inbyggarnamn på -karlar i svenska ortnamn. Uppsala, Gustav Adolfs Akademie. 1950. 176 p.

Hendin, Herbert. Suicide in Scandinavia; a psychoanalytic study of culture and character. New York, Grune & Stratton. 1964. 153 p.

Henschen, I. Swedish textile art and its background. Ciba Review. 8 (1951): 3166-3191, illus.

Hertzman, A. When I was a girl in Sweden. Boston, Lothrop, Lee & Shepard. 1926. 158 p.

Hofrén, Manne. Herrgårder och boställen: en översikt över byggnadskultur och heminredning å Kalmar lans herrgårdar 1650-1850. Stockholm, P. A. Norstedt & Söne. 1937. 519 p. (Architecture.)

Hofrén, Manne. Pataholm; kulturhistoriska notiser kring Smålandskustens gamla köpingsväsende. Stockholm, Nordiska Museet. 1946. 129 p. (Life in a coastal town: Pataholm.)

Hofrén, Manne. Öländska byar och gårdar. Öland. 1 (1948): 399-475.

Hofrén, Manne. Nordsvenska studier och essayer. Kalmar, Tidningen Barometern. 1962. 231 p.

Hofsten, Nils von. Segerlöken, Allium victorialis, i folktro och folkmedicin. Uppsala, Lundequistska Bokhandeln. 1958. 91 p.

Hofsten, Nils von. Pors och andra humleersättningar och ölkryddor i äldre tider. Uppsala, Gustav Adolfs Akademie. 1960. 245 p. (Beer brewing.)

Holmbäck, Åke Ernst V. Dopen vid kullen; en gammal sjömanstradition i 1667 års sjölag och i Olaus Rudbeeks Atlantica. Uppsala, Lundequistska Bokhandeln. 1955. 28 p. (Seamen.)

Holme, Charles, ed. Peasant art in Sweden, Lapland and Iceland. London, The Studio. 1910. 8, 48 p., 88 plates.

Hvarfner, Harald. Kräftfångst i sjuhäradsbygden, en etnologisk undersökning. Stockholm, Nordiska Museet. 1952. 64 p. (Lobster fisheries.)

SWEDEN

Ingers, E. Bonden i Svensk historia. 3 vols. (Volume 3 by Sten Carlsson, with a contribution by Albert Eskeröd.) Stockholm, LT's. Förlag. 1943-1956. 355; 519; 544 p., illus.

Jirlow, R. Pflugloser Getreidebau in Schweden. Ethnographisch-Archäologische Forschungen. 4(1958): 28-44.

Johansson, Levi. Bebyggelse och folkliv i det gamla Frostviken. Uppsala, Lundequistska Bokhandeln. 1947. 360 p.

Jonsson, Oscar, and Brynolf Hellner. Smidda järnkors på Ekshärads kyrkogård. Stockholm, Nordiska Museet. 1932. 52 p., illus.

Karlsson, Georg. Adaptability and communication in marriage: a Swedish predictive study of marital satisfaction. 2d rev. ed. Uppsala, Almqvist & Wiksell. 1963. 89 p.

Kettunen, Lauri Einari. Vermlannin suomalaisten uskomuksia, taruja ja taikoja . . . Helsinki, Suomalaisen Kirkallisuuden Seura. 1935. 95 p.

Keyland, Nils. Folkliv i Värmlands finnmarker. Stockholm, Nordiska Museet. 1954. 81 p. (Folk life in the Finnish districts of Värmland.)

Laid, Eerik. Några sädesuppsättningar i nedre Sverige. Folk-Liv. 9(1946): 103-127. (Methods of putting up grain.)

Laid, Eerik. Säden torkar; Sädesuppsättningar i Sverige 1850-1900. En etnologisk undersökning. Lund, LT's.Förlag. 1952. 11, 344 p.

Laing, Samuel. A tour in Sweden in 1838; comprising observations on the moral, political, and economical state of the Swedish nation. London, Longman, Orme, Brown, Green and Longmans. 1839. 12, 431 p.

*Leighly, John Bargar. The towns of Mälaradalen in Sweden: a study in urban geography. University of California Publications in Geography. 3. Berkeley. 1928. 134 p., illus.

Lenhovda. En värendssocken berättar. Lenhovda, Hembygdsföreningen. 1948. 814 p. (Folk life in Lenhovda in Småland.)

Levander, Lars, and Ella Odstedt. Övre Dalarnes bondekultur. Uppsala, Gustav Adolfs Akademie. 1943.

Levander, Lars, and Ella Odstedt. Alvdalskt arbetsliv under årtiondena omkring 1800-talets mitt. Uppsala, Lundequistska Bokhandeln. 1953. 457 p., illus., map. (Working life in a Dalekarlien parish 100 years ago.)

Lidén, Oskar. Svältorna och livet i Svältbygden förr och Västergötland. Lund, Gleerup Univ. Bokhandeln. 1949. 223 p., illus.

SWEDEN

Lindberg, Ernst Folke, ed. Salaminnen. Stockholm, Nordiska Museet. 1954. 424 p. (Folk life in the town of Sala.)

Lindbom, Tage Leonard. Schweden Gestern und Heute. Hamburg, E. Tesslof. 1949. 116 p.

*Lindstrom, David E. The changing rural community in Sweden. Rural Sociology. 16(1951): 49-55.

Linnarsson, Linnar. Bygd, by och gard. Gammal bygd och folkkultur i Gäene, Laske och Skånings härader. 2 vols. Uppsala, Lundequistska Bokhandeln. 1948-1950. (Folk culture in Västergötland.)

Linné, Carl von. Carl Linnaei . . . Ölandska och Gothländska resa på riksens högloflige ständers befallning förrättad åhr 1741. Med anmårkningar uti oeconómien, naturhistorien, antiquiteter etc., med åtskillige figurer. Stockholm och Upsala, G. Kieswetter. 1745. 344 p.

Linné, Carl von. Wåstgöta-resa på riksens högloflige ständers befallning förrattåd år 1746. Med anmarkningar uti oeconomien, naturkunnogheten, antiquiteter, inwånårnes seder och lefnads-sått. Stockholm, Uplagd på L. Salvii Kostnad. 1747. 284 p.

Linné, Carl von. Carl Linaei . . . Skånska resa, på höga ofeverhetens befall ning förrättad år 1749. Stockholm, Uplagd på L. Salvii Kostnad. 1751. 14, 434 p.

Linné, Carl von. Reisen durch Oeland und Gothland, welche auf befehl der hochlöblichen reichsstände des Königreichs Schweden im Jahr 1741. angestellt worden. Halle, J. J. Curts. 1764. 364 p.

Linné, Carl von. Herrn Carl von Linné . . . Reisen durch Westgothland, welche auf befehl der hochlöbichen Stände des Königreichs Schweden im Jahr 1746. angestellt worden. Halle, J. J. Curts. 1765. 318 p.

Linné, Carl von. Linné om småland, några utdrag . . . Göteborg, W. Zackrissons. 1907. 88 p.

Liv och Folkkultur. Stockholm, Institutet för Folklivsforskning. 1 (1948):--

*Lloyd, Llewellyn. Peasant life in Sweden. London, Tinsley Brothers. 1870. 479 p.

Löfström, Frans. Här ostpå. Baskemölla, ostskånst fiskeläge under 1800-talets sista hälft. Lund, Gleerup. 1952. 279 p.

Lorénzen, Lilly. Of Swedish ways. Minneapolis, Gilbert Publishing Co. 1964. 276 p., illus.

Lundberg, Erik, et al. Folket i fest. Stockholm, LT's. Förlag. 1946. 212 p.

Marrayat, Horace. One year in Sweden; including a visit to the isle of Gotland. 2 vols. London, J. Murray. 1862.

Mattisson, Karl. Skörden genom tiderna. Lund, Gleerup. 1953. 212 p. (Harvesting grain.)

Mattisson, Karl. Det sydsvenska halmtaket. Lund, Gleerup. 1961. 179 p., 91 figs. (Thatched roofs in southern Sweden.)

Minneman, P. G. Sweden's agriculture and the war. Foreign Agriculture. 4 (1940): 577-616.

Modéer, Ivar. Smålandska skärgårdsnamn. En studie över holmnamnen i mönsterås. Uppsala, Gustav Adolfs Akademie. 1933. 263 p.

Modéer, Ivar. Skeppsnamn och skärgårdsnamn. Stockholm, Natur och Kultur. 1956. 164 p.

Nerén, John. Boka om Målsa. Boken om Stora Mellösa. 2 vols. Stockholm, Norstedt. 1944-1949. 533; 433 p., illus. (Närka Province.)

Nilson, Allan. Skolseder från Skara. Stockholm, Nordiska Museet. 1948. 91 p. (School customs from a Swedish town.)

Nilson, Allan. Studier i svenskt repslageri. Stockholm, Nordiska Museet. 1961. 245 p. (Rope handicrafts.)

Nilsson, Axel, and Nils Keyland. Guide to Skansen. I. The historical and ethnographic department of Skansen. 5th ed. Stockholm, The Northern Museum. 1923. 166 p., illus., map.

Nilsson, Ragnar, ed. Folktro och folksed på Värmlandsnäs folkminnen från Näs härad. 3 vols. Göteborg, Gumperts Förlag. 1952-1962.

Nilsson, Yngve. Bygd och näringsliv i norra Värmland. En kultur-geografisk studie. Meddelanden från Lunds Universitets Geografiska Institution. Avhandlingar 18. Lund, Gleerupska Univ. Bokhandeln. 1950. 6, 233 p. (A culture-geographical study of the settlement pattern and economic life in northern Värmland.)

Nordlander, Johan. Ångermanländska folkminnen från 1800-talets förra hälft. Stockholm, Björck und Börjesson. 1947. 154 p.

Nylen, Anna-Maja. Swedish peasant costumes. Stockholm, Nordiska Museet. 1949. 91 p., illus.

Nylen, Anna-Maja. Folkligt dräktskick i Västra Vingåker och Österåker. Stockholm, Nordiska Museet. 1949. 143 p., illus.

SWEDEN

Nylen, Anna-Maja. Folkdräkter. Stockholm, Nordiska Museet. 1949. 143 p illus.

Nylen, Anna-Maja. Broderier från herremans och borgarhem 1500-1850. Stockholm, Nordiska Museet. 1950. 87 p., illus. (Embroidery.)

Odstedt, Ella. Vurulven i svensk folktradition. Uppsala, Lundequistska Bokhandeln. 1943. 8, 243 p., German summary. (Werewolves.)

Olsson, Helmer. Folkliv och folkdikt i Vättle härad under 1800-talet. Uppsala, Almqvist & Wiksell. 1945. 300 p. (Folk life in Vättle, Sweden.)

Olsson, Ragnar. Bondeståndet under tidigare frihetstiden; val, organisation och arbetssätt. Lund, C. Bloms Boktryckeri. 1926. 16, 165 p.

Olsson, Reinhold. Norrländskt sågverksliv under ett sekel. Stockholm, Nordiska Museet. 1949. 175 p. (Working and living conditions at a northern Swedish sawmill in the nineteenth century.)

Osvald, Hugo, Lennart Gustafsson, et al. Swedish agriculture. Stockholm, Swedish Institute. 1952. 103 p., illus.

Petersens, Lennart. Vaxholm, skärgårdsstaden. Stockholm, Wahlström & Widstrand. 1963. 67 p.

Plath, Iona. The decorative arts of Sweden. New York, Scribner. 1948. 25, 247 p., illus.

Rääf, Leonhard Fredrik. Svenska skrock och signerier. Med inledning och anmark . . . K. R. V. Wikman. Stockholm, Almqvist & Wiksell. 1957. 445 p.

Ralf, E. The tradition of craftsmanship in Sweden. Geographical Magazine. 29(1956): 65-72.

Rank, Gustav. Die gemeinschaftliche Käsebereitung. Folk-Liv. 21-22 (1957 1958): 115-133.

Rank, Gustav. Från mjölk till ost. Stockholm. 1966. 207 p. (History of Swedish dairying.)

Reenstierna, Märta Helena. Arstadadagboken; journaler från åren 1793-1839, utg. genom Sigurd Erixon . . . 3 vols. Stockholm, Generalstabens Litografiska Anstalt. 1946-1953. 503; 554; 482 p., 3 col. plates, 2 maps. (Diary of a Stockholm burger's wife.)

Rehnberg, Mats Erik Adolf. Säckpipan i Sverige. Stockholm, Nordiska Museet. 1943. 76 p., illus. (English summary.)

Rehnberg, Mats Erik Adolf. Sverige i fest och glädje. Stockholm, Wahlström
& Widstrand. 1947. 253 p.

Rehnberg, Mats Erik Adolf. Rallarminnen. Stockholm, Nordiska Museet.
1949. 324 p. (Swedish railroad workers and railroads.)

Rehnberg, Mats Erik Adolf. Byggnadsarbetarminnen; snickare och timmermän
berättar. Stockholm, Nordiska Museet. 1950. 246 p. (Carpenters.)

Rehnberg, Mats Erik Adolf. Siljan. Stockholm, Wahlström & Widstrand.
1950. 135 p. (Folk life on Lake Siljan, southern Dalerna.)

Rehnberg, Mats Erik Adolf. Småländsk bystämma. Östraby och Västraby i
Lenhovda socken. Stockholm, Nordiska Museet. 1951. 197 p.

Rehnberg, Mats Erik Adolf. Verkstadsminnen. Stockholm, Nordiska Museet.
1953. 243 p. (Mechanics and their life in Sweden.)

Rehnberg, Mats Erik Adolf. Stora krogboken; bilder ur restauranglivets kultur-
historia. Stockholm, Wahlström & Widstrand. 1955. 214 p. (Restaurants,
lunch rooms, taverns, and hotels.)

Rehnberg, Mats Erik Adolf. Med bilen i Stockholmstrakten. Stockholm,
Wahlström & Widstrand. 1956. 219 p. (Automobiles.)

Rehnberg, Mats Erik Adolf. The Nordiska Museet and Skansen. An introduction to the history and activities of a famous Swedish museum. Stockholm,
Nordiska Museet. 1957. 194 p., photos.

Rehnberg, Mats Erik Adolf. Svensk jul; gamla och nya bilder med korta
kommentarer. Stockholm, Wahlström & Widstrand. 1957. 47 p.

Rehnberg, Mats Erik Adolf. Kommunalarbetarminnen. Stockholm, Nordiska
Museet. 1958. 263 p. (Municipal officials and employees.)

Rehnberg, Mats Erik Adolf. Seder och pynt. Sammanställd av. . . .
Västerås, ICA Förlaget. 1958. 75 p.

Rehnberg, Mats Erik Adolf. Gruvminnen. Stockholm, Nordiska Museet. 1960.
281 p. (Miners.)

Rehnberg, Mats Erik Adolf. Handelsminnen. Stockholm, Nordiska Museet.
1961. 240 p.

Rehnberg, Mats Erik Adolf. Snickarminnen. Stockholm, Nordiska Museet.
1961. 240 p.

Reuterskiöld, Edgar Hans C. Den folkliga vidskepelsen och den svenska
katekesen. Uppsala, Almqvist & Wiksell. 1921. 53 p.

SWEDEN

Rothman, Sven. Östgötska folkminnen. Uppsala, Gustav Adolfs Akademie.
1941. 8, 146 p.

Sahlgren, Jören. Svenska folkböcker. 8 vols. Stockholm, A. B. Bokverk.
1946-1956.

Salven, Erik. Dances of Sweden. New York, Chanticleer Press. 1949. 40 p
7 plates.

Sandklef, Albert. Om forkhus i Syd- och Västersverige. Göteborg, Elanders
Boktr. 1933. 90 p. (Farm buildings.)

Sandklef, Albert. Svensk biskötsel före 1850. Stockholm, LT's. Förlag.
1946. 55 p. (Beekeeping in Sweden before 1850.)

Sandklef, Albert. Hallandsgårdar; bebyggelse på gårdar och torp före 1900.
Stockholm, Nordiska Museet. 1953. 304 p. (Architecture.)

Schnell, Ivar. Sörmländskt jordbruk. Nyköping, Sörmlälanska Lantmännens
Centralförening. 1955. 170 p., illus. (Agriculture in Södermanland.)

Schoultz, Gösta Alexander B. von. Kistor. Stockholm, Nordiska Museet.
1949. 18 p. (Chests.)

Schoultz, Gösta Alexander B. von. Dalslandsgårdar. Stockholm, Nordiska
Museet. 1951. 184 p. (Houses and farms in central Sweden.)

*Schwedische Volkskunde: Quellen, Forschung, Ergebnisse. Festschrift für
Sigfrid Svensson zum sechzigsten Geburstag am 1. Juni 1961. Stockholm,
Almqvist & Wiksell. 1961. 511 p., illus.

Sidenbladh, Elis Theodor. Urmakare i Sverige under äldre tider. Stockholm,
Nordiska Museet. 1912. 2d ed. 1947. 256 p. (Clockmakers in Sweden
before 1850.)

Sjöstedt, L. G. Bärsebäcks fiskläge. En krönika från äldsta tid till våra dagar
Malmö, Framtiden. 1951. 342 p., illus. (Fishing village from old times
to today.)

Sjunneson, Oscar. Sydhalländskt allmogeliv i slutet av 1800-talet. Stockholm, LT's. Förlag. 1953. 278 p., illus. (Farm life in southern
Halland in the late nineteenth century.)

Statarminnen. Nysamling. (Edited by Mats Rehnberg.) Stockholm, Nordiska
Museet. 1949. 258 p. (Agricultural laborers.)

Steere, Lloyd V. Recent developments in Swedish agriculture. Foreign Agriculture. 2(1938): 213-234.

Stensland, Per Gustaf. Julita klosters godspolitik. Stockholm, Nordiska
Museet. 1945. 52 p. (The medieval farm policy of a monastery.)

Svahnström, Gunnar. Kattlunds. En sudgotländsk bondgårds historia. Visby,
Gotlands Fornsal. 1954. 152 p., 24 plates. (Farm houses in Gotland.)

Svärdström, Svante. Dalmålningar, samlade och kommenterade. Stockholm,
A. Bonnier. 1944. 231 p. (Folk art and decoration.)

Svärdström, Svante. Dalmålningarna och deras förlagor, en studie i folklig
bildgestaltning, 1770-1870. Stockholm, Nordiska Museet. 1949. 176 p.
(Mural paintings, folk art.)

Svärdström, Svante. Masters of Dala peasant paintings. Stockholm, A.
Bonnier. 1957. 51 p., illus.

Svensson, Sigfrid. Skånes folkdräkter. Stockholm, Nordiska Museet. 1935.
337 p., illus.

Svensson, Sigfrid. Die Malereien der Bauernstuben in der schwedischen
Forschung. Acta Ethnologica. 1 (1936): 53-59, 6 illus.

Svensson, Sigfrid. Bygd och yttervärld; studier över förhållandel mellan
nyheter och tradition. Stockholm, Nordiska Museet. 1942. 140 p. (The
countryside and the outer world—relationships.)

Svensson, Sigfrid. Allmogemöbler; folklig möbelkonst under sjuhundra år:
bilder från Nordiska Museet, . . . Stockholm, Nordiska Museet. 1949.
4 p., 44 plates. (Peasant furniture.)

*Sweden. European conference on rural life. National monographs drawn up by
governments. Sweden. Series of League of Nations Publications. European
Conference on Rural Life. 21. Geneva. 1939. 71 p., illus.

Swedish christmas. Göteborg, Tre Cryk Tryckare. 1954. 259 p., illus.

Thorsén, Edvin. Uppländskt torparliv. Stockholm, Nordiska Museet. 1949.
165 p. (Crofting in Uppland.)

Tillhagen, Carl Hermann. Folklig läkekonst. Stockholm, Nordiska Museet.
1958. 378 p. (Folk medicine, magic.)

Tillhagen, Carl Hermann. The conception of the nightmare in Sweden. In
Wayland D. Hand and G. O. Arlt, eds. Humaniora. New York, J. J.
Augustin. 1960: 317-329.

Tillhagen, Carl Hermann. Folklig spådomskonst. Stockholm, Bokförlaget Fabel.
1961. 225 p. (Divination, folklore.)

Trotzig, Dag. Slagan och andra tröskredskap. Stockholm, Nordiska Museet. 1943. 207 p. (The flail and other threshing tools.)

Veirulf, Olle, ed. Dalarna ett vida berömt landskap. Stockholm, A. B. Svensk Litteratur. 1951. 388 p., 27 figs., 115 plates.

Wagnér, Gottfried. Smålandska folkminnen. Alseda, the author. 1950. 158 p., 24 figs.

Walin, Stig. Die schwedische Hummel. Stockholm, Nordiska Museet. 1952. 158 p.

Wallensteen, J. P. Vidskepelser, vantro och huskurer i Danderyd och Lidingö i slutet af 1700-talet. Stockholm, Nordiska Museet. 1899. 22 p.

Walterstorff, Emelie von. Swedish textiles. Stockholm, Nordiska Museet. 1925. 89 p., 126 plates.

Walterstorff, Emelie von. Svenska vävnadstekniker och mönstertyper. Stockholm, Nordiska Museet. 1940. 205 p. (Swedish weaving techniques and types.)

Wikman, Karl Robert V. Die Magie des Webens und des Webstuhls im schwedischen Volksglauben. Åbo, Åbo Akademi. 1920. 21 p.

Wikman, Karl Robert V. Die Einleitung der Ehe, eine vergleichend ethnosoziologische Untersuchung über die Vorstufe der Ehe in den Sitten des schwedischen Volkstums. Åbo, Åbo Akademi. 1937. 44, 395 p.

Wikman, Karl Robert V. Livets högtider. Stockholm, A. Bonnier. 1944. 147 p.

Wilhelm, Prince of Sweden. Something of my country. London, W. Hodge. 1951. 244 p.

Wistrand, P. G. Svenska folkdräkter. Stockholm, Nordiska Museet. 1907. 159 p.

Wollin, Nils. Swedish textiles. Leigh-on-Sea, England, F. Lewis. 1952. 21 p., 77 plates.

Zink, Harald, Arne Wahlstrand, et al. Rural local government in Sweden, Italy and India. London, Stevens & Sons. 1957. 14, 142 p.

SWEDES IN FINLAND AND THE EAST BALTIC AREA

Ahlbäck, Ragna. Kökar. Näringslivet och dess organisation i en utskärssocken. Helsingfors, Svenska Litteratursällskapets i Finland Förlag. 1955. 377 p. (Kökar in the Åland Islands.)

Allardt, Anders. Sagor i urval. 2 vols. Helsingfors, Tidningsoch Tryckeri. 1917-1920.

Andersson, Otto Emanuel. Folkvisor. 1. Den äldre folkvisan. Finlands Svenska Folkdiktning 5. Helsingfors. 1934.

*Andersson, Otto Emanuel. Ur åländsk hävd och tradition. Stockholm, Saxon & Lindström. 1939. 165 p.

Andersson, Otto Emanuel. Folkdans. Äldre dansmelodier. Finlands Svenska Folkdiktning 6. Åbo. 1963.

Andersson, Sven. Åländskit skärgardsliv. Åbo, Bro. 1945. 331 p., illus.

Danell, Sven. Guldstrand: minnen från sju år i Estland. Stockholm, Svenska Kyrkans Diakonistyrelses Bokförlag. 1952. 299 p.

Forsblom, Valter W. Folktro och trolldom. 5. Magisk folkmedicin. Finlands Svenska Folkdiktning 7. 1927.

Franzén, Gösta. Runö ortnamm [The place-names of Runö]. Uppsala, Almqvist & Wiksell. 1959. 175 p.

Jaatinen, Stig. Regionala drag i befolkningsutrecklingen på Åland 1900-1950. Fennía. 76, no. 4 (1953): 1-88. (German summary.)

Jaatinen, Stig. De senaste decenniernas befolknings- och närings-geografiska utveckling på Åland. Terra. 66, no. 2 (1954): 37-51. (English summary.)

Jaatinen, Stig. Archipelagoes in comparison. The Outer Hebrides and the Åland Islands (Southwestern Finland). In Stig Jaatinen. The human geography of the Outer Hebrides. Acta Geographica. 16, no. 2. 1958: 97-104.

Laid, Eerik. Estlandssvenska samlingar i Nordiska Museet. Kustbon. 1960, no. 1 (1960): 4-8.

Landtman, Gunnar. Folktro och trolldom. 1. Övernaturliga väsen. Finlands Svenska Folkdiktning 7. Helsingfors. 1919.

Léouzon le Duc, Louis. Les îles d'Åland. Paris, Hachette. 1854. 6, 156 p.

Loit, Aleksander, and Nils Tiberg. Gammalsvenskbydokument. Estlandssvenskarnas folkliga kultur. Uppsala, Gustav Adolfs Akademie. 1958. 236 p.

SWEDES IN FINLAND AND THE EAST BALTIC AREA

*Mead, William R. Saltvik. Studies from an Åland Parish (Finland). Nottingham, Geographical Field Group, Geography Department, University of Nottingham. 1964. 63 p., 30 figs.

Nikander, Gabriel. Jul och nyår på Åland. Svenska Litteratur Sällskapets Folkloristika Samlingar i Helsingfors. 1911: 390-403.

Nikander, Gabriel. By och bonde i svenskkösterbotten. Folklivsstudier 5. Helsingfors, Svenska Litteratur-sällskapet i Finland. 1959. 244 p.

Nordenskiöld, Erland. Finland: the land and the people. Geographical Review. 7(1919): 361-376.

Den österbottniska byn. En samling minnesbilder. Helsinki, Hembygdsföreningen Svenska Österbottningar i Helsingfors. 1947. 610 p.

*Pipping, Knut. Changes in family structure in the Baltic Islands. Transaction of the Third World Congress of Sociology. 4(1956): 97-100.

*Russwurm, Karl Friedrich Wilhelm. Eibofolke, oder die Schweden an den Küsten Ehstlands und auf Runö. Eine historisch-ethnographische gegrönte. 2 vols. Revel, in Commission bei Fr. Fleischer in Leipzig. 1855.

Shaw, Earl B. The Aland Islands. Economic Geography. 15(1939): 27-42.

Söderbäck, Per. Rågöborna. Stockholm, Nordiska Museet. 1940. 379 p. (Swedish folk life at Rågöborna, Estonia.)

Tiberg, Nils. Runöbondens ägor. Uppsala, Gustav Adolfs Akademie. 1959. 89 p. (Farms and lands on Runö.)

Wessman, Vilhelm Eliel V. Finlands svenska folkdiktning. Sägner. 8 vols. Skrifter Utgivna av Svenska Litteratursällskapet i Finland. Nos. 174, 201, 226, 227, 327, 337, 349, 490. 1917-1962.

Wieselgren, Per. Från hammeren till hakkorset; Estland, 1939-1941. Stockholm, Idé och Form Förlag. 1942. 294 p.

Wieselgren, Per. Ortnamn och bebyggelse i Estlands forna och hittillsvarande svenskbygder. Ostharrien med Nargo. Uppsala, Gustav Adolfs Akademie. 1951. 382 p.

Wikman, K. Rob. V. Die Einleitung der Ehe; eine vergleichend ethnosoziologische Untersuchung über die Vorstufe der Ehe in den Sitten des schwedischen Volkstums. Acta Academiae Aboensis. Humaniora 11, 1. 1937. 44, 395 p., illus., maps.

FINLAND

Aaltonen, Hilkka. Books in English on Finland. Turku University Library, Publication 8. Turku. 1964.

Malliniemi, Aarno Henrik, and Ella Kivikoski. Suomen historiallinen bibliographia 1901-1925. 2 vols. in one. Helsinki, Suomen Historiallinen Seura. 1940. 527, 107 p.

Neuvonen, Eero K. A short bibliography on Finland. Turun Yliopiston Kirjaston Julkaisuja 7. Turku. 1955. 24 p.

United States. Bureau of the Census. Bibliography of social science periodicals and monograph series: Finland, 1950-1962. Washington, Foreign Demographic Analysis Division, Bureau of the Census. 1963. 4, 85 p.

Vallinkoski, Jorma, and Henrik Schauman. Suomen historiallinen bibliographia 1926-1950. 2 vols. Helsinki, Suomen Historiallinen Seura. 1955-1956.

Vallinkoski, Jorma, and Henrik Schauman. Suomen historiallinen bibliographia, 1544-1900. Helsinki, Suomen Historiallinen Seura. 1961. 571 p.

Acerbi, Joseph [Guiseppi] . Travels through Sweden, Finland and Lapland to North Cape, 1798-1799. 2 vols. London, printed for J. Bowman. 1802.

Allardt, E. Social sources of Finnish communism: traditional and emerging radicalism. International Journal of Comparative Sociology. 5 (1964): 49-72.

Allardt, E. Patterns of class conflict and working class consciousness in Finnish politics. Transactions of the Westermarck Society. 10 (1964): 97-131.

Bayley, Annie Margaret Clive. Vignettes of Finland. London, S. Low, Marston. 1895. 8, 301 p.

Brown, John Croumbie. Finland: its forests and forest management. Edinburgh, Oliver and Boyd; London, Simpkin, Marshall. 1883. 16, 290 p.

Brown, John Croumbie. People of Finland in archaic times. London, K. Paul, Trench, Trübner. 1892. 290 p.

Brummer, O. J. Über die Bannungsorte der finnischen Zauberlieder. Suomalais-ugrilaisen Seuran Tiomituksia. 38. Helsingfors, Société Finno-Ougrienne. 1909. 153 p.

Coxwell, C. Fillingham. Siberian and other folktales. London, C. W. Daniel Co. 1925: 641-660.

Desneiges, Georges. Finland. London, Vista Books; New York, Viking Press. 1964. 192 p., illus.

Englund, Eric. Peat-land farming in Finland. Foreign Agriculture. 14 (1950) 246-249.

Evers, W. Suomi-Finland. Land und Volk im hohen Norden. Stuttgart, Franckh'sche Verlagshandlung. 1950. 167 p.

Falk, Erik. Om säfsfinnarnas bygd i 1700-talets början [On the settlement of Finnish immigrants at Säfnäs in Dalerna at the beginning of the 18th century]. Stockholm, Jerkontoret. 1950. 87 p.

*Finland. European conference on rural life, 1939. National monographs drawn up by governments. Finland. Series of League of Nations Publications. European Conference on Rural Life. 1. Geneva. 1939. 59 p., illus.

Finland: its country and people, a short survey. Helsingfors, The Government Press. 1919. 89 p.

Finland, the country, its people and institutions. Helsinki, Otava Publishing Co. 1926. 598, 4 p.

Golitsyn, Emmanuil M. La Finlande: notes recuellies en 1848, pendant une excursion de Saint-Pétersbourg à Torneo. 2 vols. Paris, A. Bertrand; New York, R. Lockwood & Son. 1852.

Gothe, Richard. Hassela-finarna [The Hassela Finns]. Stockholm, the author. 1942. 214 p.

Haavio, Elsa [Enäjärvi]. The Finnish shrovetide. Folklore Fellows Communications. 146. Helsinki, Suomalainen Tiedakatemia. 1954. 75 p.

Haavio-Mannila, Elina. Kylätappelut; sosio loginen tutkimus Suomen kylätuppeluinstituutiosta. Porvoo, Söderström. 1958. 215 p. (Small groups in Finland.)

Haavio-Mannila, Elina. Local homogamy in Finland. Acta Sociologica. 8 (1964-1965): 155-162.

Halsten, Ilmi. La situation de la femme en Finlande. Helsingfors, Imprimeri du Gouvernment. 1924. 40 p., illus.

Hämäläinen, Albert. Keski-Suomen kansanrakennukset; asuntorhistoriallinen tutkimos. Helsinki, Suomalaisen Kirjallisunden Seuran Toimituksia. 1930. 366 p.

Hämäläinen, Albert. Bostads- och byggnadsskick hos skogs-finnarna i Mellan-Skandinavien [Houses and building arts of the Finns in central Scandinavia]. Stockholm, Nordiska Museet. 1945. 180 p.

Harva, Uno. Volkstümliche Zeitrechnung im eigentlichen Finnland. Folk-Liv. 1 (1937): 64-84.

FINLAND

Hautamäki, L. Development of settlement in some rural communes in western Finland since 1920. Fennia. 96, no. 2. 1967. 98 p.

Havukkala, Jaakko. Settlement and economic life in the district of the Lokka Reservoir in Finnish Lappland. Fennia. 90, no. 4. 1964. 46 p.

Heikel, Axel Olai. Die Volkstrachten in den Ostseeprovinzen und in Letukesien. Kansatieteellisiä Julkaisuja. Travaux Ethnographiques. 4. Helsinki. 1909. 114 p., illus.

Heikel, Yngvor Sigurd, and Anni Collan. Dances of Finland. New York, Chanticleer Press. 1948. 40 p., 7 plates.

*Heimonen, Henry Samuel. Finnish rural culture in South Ostrabothnia (Finland) and the Lake Superior Region (U.S.)—A comparative study. Madison, University of Wisconsin. 1941. 278 p., photos. (Unpublished Ph.D. dissertation in Geography.)

Helle, Reijo. Retailing in rural northern Finland: particularly by mobile shops. Fennia. 91, no. 3. 1964. 120 p.

Helle, Reijo. An investigation of reindeer husbandry in Finland. Fennia. 95, no. 4. 1966. 65 p., map.

Helms, Henrik. Finnland und die Finnländer. Leipzig, Fritsch. 1869. 4, 159 p.

Hjelt, Edvard, et al. Finnland, the country, its people, and institutions. Helsinki, Otava Publishing Co. 1926. 598, 4 p.

Honkala, Kauko. Social class and visiting patterns in two Finnish villages. Acta Sociologica. 5(1960-1961): 42-49.

Honko, Lauri. Krankheitsprojektile; Untersuchung über eine urtümliche Krankheitserklärung. Helsinki, Suomalainen Tiedeakatemia. 1959. 258 p.

Honko, Lauri. Geisterglaube in Ingermanland. Helsinki, Suomalainen Tiedeakatemia. 1962. 470 p.

Hovilainen, Erla. Roro till fiskeskär . . . Helsingfors, Söderström. 1945. 176 p., illus. (Fishing life on Tankar Island in the Gulf of Bothnia.)

Indiana. University. Graduate Program in Uralic and Asian Studies. Finland. By Eeva K. Minn. New Haven, printed by the Human Relations Area Files. 1955. 8, 391 p.

Jutikkala, Eino Kaarlo I., and Esko Aaltonen. Suomen talonpojan historia [History of the Finnish farmer]. Porvoo and Helsinki, Werner Söderström. 1942. 691 p.

Kuusi, P. Alcohol sales experiment in rural Finland. Helsinki, Finnish Foundation for Alcohol Studies. 1957. 11, 237 p.

McBride, Robert Medill. Finland and its people. New York, R. M. McBride. 1925. 10, 118 p.

MacDougall, Sylvia Borgström. By a Finnish lake. London, Methuen. 1903. 302 p.

Manninen, Ilmari. Die dämonistichen Krankheiten im finnischen Volksaberglauben; vergleichende volksmedizinische Untersuchung. Folklore Fellows Communications. 45. Helsinki, Suomalainen Tiedeakatemia. 1922. 253 p.

Maranda, Elli Köngäs. The cattle of the forest and the harvest of water: the cosmology of Finnish magic. In June Helm, ed. Essays on the verbal and visual arts. Proceedings of the 1966 annual spring meeting, American Ethnological Society. Seattle, University of Washington Press. 1967: 84-95.

Mead, William R. Agriculture in Finland. Economic Geography. 15(1939): 125-134, 217-234.

Mead, William R. The cold farm in Finland. Geographical Review. 41(1951) 529-543.

Mead, William R. Finnish Karelia: an international borderland. Geographical Journal. 118 (1952): 40-57.

*Mead, William R. Farming in Finland. London, University of London, Athlone Press. 1953. 14, 248 p.

Mead, William R. Land use in early 19th century Finland. Turku, Turun Ylopiston Maatieteelisen Laitoksen Julkaisuja. 26. 1953. 23 p.

Mechelin, L. H. S., ed. Finland in the nineteenth century; by Finnish author Helsingfors, F. Tilgmann. 1894. 367, 7 p.

Merritt-Hawkes, Onera Amelia. The fading monastery of Valamo. Geographical Magazine. 4(1936): 1-16.

Minneman, P. G. Finland's agriculture. Foreign Agriculture. 4(1940): 147-174.

Naponen, M., and P. Pesonen. The legislative career in Finland. Transactions of the Westermarck Society. 10 (1964): 441-463.

Nordenskiöld, Erland. Finland: the land and the people. Geographical Review. 7(1919): 361-376.

North, Ferdinand J. Finland in summer. Cambridge, Heffer. 1938. 233 p.

Olin, S. C. Finlandia: the racial composition, the language and a brief history of the Finnish people. Hancock, Michigan, The Book Concern. 1957. 21, 198 p.

Paulson, Ivar. Himmel und Erde in der Agrarreligion der finnischen Völker. Papers of the Estonian Theological Society in Exile, Scholarly Series. 13. 1963. 31 p.

Pelkonen, E. Uber volkstümliche Geburtshilfe in Finland. Acta Societas Medicorum Fennica "Duodecim." Ser. B. Tom. 16. Helsinki. 1931. 366 p.

Pettersson, Lars. Die kirchliche Holzbaukunst auf der Halbinsel Zaoneze in russische-Karelien; Herkunft und Werden. Helsinki, Suomen Muinais Muisstoyhdistyksen. 1950. 254 p.

Rantasalo, Aukusti Vilho. Der Ackerbau im Volksaberglauben der Finnen und Esten mit entsprechenden Gebräuchen der Germanen verglichen. 5 vols. Folklore Fellows Communications Nos. 30, 31, 32, 55, 62. Helsinki, Academia Scientiarum Fennica. 1919, 1919, 1920, 1924, 1925.

Rantasalo, Aukusti Vilho. Der Viehstall im Volksaberglauben der Finnen. Annales Academiae Scientarum Fennicae, ser. B, 38, no. 1. Helsinki. 1937. 253 p.

Rantasalo, Aukusti Vilho. Der Weidegang im Volksaberglauben der Finnen. 1. Die Vorbereitungen für das Viehaustreiben. Folklore Fellows Communications. 134. Helsinki, Suomalainen Tiedeakatemia. 1945. 129 p.

Rantasalo, Aukusti Vilho. Der Weidegang im Volksaberglauben der Finnen. 2. Die Hinausführung des Viehes auf die Weide. Folklore Fellows Communications. 135. Helsinki, Suomalainen Tiedeakatemia. 1947. 325 p.

Rantasalo, Aukusti Vilho. Der Weidegang im Volksaberglauben der Finnen. 3. Viehhüten und Weidegang. Folklore Fellows Communications. 143. Helsinki, Suomalainen Tiedeakatemia. 1953. 245 p.

Rantasalo, Aukusti Vilho. Einige Zaubersteine und Zauberpflanzen im Volksaberglauben der Finnen. Folklore Fellows Communications. 176. Helsinki, Suomalainen Tiedeakatemia. 1959. 79 p.

Reade, Arthur. Finland and the Finns. New York, Dodd, Mead. 1915. 11, 315 p.

Renwick, George. Finland today. London and Leipzig, T. F. Unwin. 1911. 12, 348 p.

Retzius, Magnus Gustav. Finnland. Schilderungen aus seiner Natur, seiner alten Kultur und seinem heutigen Volksleben. Berlin, G. Reimer. 1885. 8, 158 p.

Richmond, W. E. The study of folklore in Finland. In Richard M. Dorson, ed. Folklore research around the world. Bloomington, Indiana University Press. 1961: 39-49.

Rühs, Christian Friedrich. Finnland und seine Bewohner. Leipzig, Göschen. 1809.

Saarto, Martha. Finnish textiles. Leigh-on-Sea, England, F. Lewis. 1954. 20 p., 96 plates.

Sentzke, Geert. Die Kirche Finnlands. Göttingen, Vandenhoeck and Ruprecht 1935. 150 p.

Silberg, K. P. The athletic Finn. Some reasons why the Finns excel in athletics . . . Hancock, Michigan, Suomi Publishing Co. 1927: 15-76.

Sirelius, Uuno Taavi. The hand-woven rugs of Finland. Helsinki, Government Printing Office. 1925. 14 p.

Sirelius, Uuno Taavi. The genealogy of the Finns; the Finno-Ugrian peoples. Helsinki, Government Printing Office. 1925. 77 p.

Sirelius, Uuno Taavi. The ryijy rugs of Finland, a historical study. Helsinki, Otavo Publishing Co. 1926. 251 p., illus.

Sirelius, Uuno Taavi. Die Volkskultur Finnlands. Erster Band. Jagd und Fischerei in Finnland. Berlin und Leipzig, Walter de Gruyter. 1934. 9, 151 p., 67 plates.

*Sweetser, Dorrian A. Urbanization and patrilineal transmission of farms in Finland. Acta Sociologica. 7(1963-1964): 215-224.

Symposium on man's influence on nature in Finland. Fennia. 85. 1961. 128 p.

Talve, Ilmar. Kansanomaisen ruokatalouden alalta. Mit einer deutschen Zusammenfassung. Helsinki, Suomalaisen Kirjallisuuden Seura. 1961. 106 p. (Finnish food.)

Talve, Ilmar. Arbeit und Lebensverhältnisse der finnischen Bahnbauarbeiter und Eisenbahner. Scripta Ethnologica (Turku). 18 (1964). 40 p.

Three faces of Finland. Guidebooks for the three Finnish excursions at the XIX International Congress 1960 (Geography). 3 vols. Fennia. 84, nos. 1-3. 1960.

Tweedie, Mrs. Alec. Through Finland in carts. London, A. & C. Black. 1897. 9, 366 p.

Vallinheimo, Veers. Das Spinnen in Finnland; unter besonderer Berücksichtigung schwedischer Tradition. Suomen Muinaismuistoyhdistys, Helsingfors, Kansatieteellinen Arkisto. 11. Helsinki. 1956. 287 p., 116 illus., maps.

Valonen, N. Geflechte und andere Arbeiten aus Birkenrindenstreifen, unter besonderer Berücksichtigung finnischer Tradition. Suomen Muinaismuistoyhdistys, Helsingfors, Kansatieteellinen Arkisto. 9. Helsinki. 1952. 341 p.

Valonen, N. Zur Geschichte der finnischen Wohnstuben. Helsinki, Suomalais-Ugrilainen Seura. 1963. 600 p., illus.

Van Cleef, Eugene. Finland—The republic farthest north; the response of Finnish life to its geographic environment. Columbus, Ohio State University. 1929. 15, 210 p.

Varjo, Uuno. The Finnish farm seen from the viewpoint of geographical typology of agriculture. Fennia. 92, no. 1. 1965. 18 p.

Verkko, Veli. Homicides and suicides in Finland and their dependence on national character . . . Scandinavian Studies in Sociology. 3. København, G. E. C. Gads Forlag. 1951. 189 p., tables, diagrs.

Verkko, Veli. Supplementary notes to some chapters in my investigation "Homicides and suicides in Finland and their dependence on national character." Transactions of the Westermarck Society. 2(1953): 187-202.

Viherjuuri, H. J., ed. Finnische Sauna. Stuttgart, Hippokrates Verlag, Marquardt. 1943. 112 p.

Vilkuna, Kustaa. Zur Geschichte der finnischen Sicheln. Suomen Muinaismuis Toyhdistyksen. 40(1935): 223-235.

Vilkuna, Kustaa. Brödet och bakningens historia i Finland. Folk-Liv. 9(1945): 17-56. 6 plates.

Vilkuna, Kustaa. Tjo ja ilonpito, kansanomaisia työnjuhlia ja kestityksia. Helsinki, Kustannusosakeyhtio Otava. 1946. 236 p. (Occupational festivals.)

Vilkuna, Kustaa. Geographical areas of Finnish peasant culture. Fennia. 72 (1952): 309-314, map.

Vilkuna, Kustaa. Volkstümliche Arbeitsfeste in Finnland. Folklore Fellows Communications. 191. Helsinki, Suomalainen Tiedeakatemia. 1963. 287 p.

Vilppula, Hilkka. Das Dreschen in Finnland. Helsinki, Kansalieteellinen Arkisto. 10. 1955. 320 p., 131 figs.

Virrankoski, P. Suomen varhaiskantainen salaojitus. Suomen Museo. 66 (1959): 90-119. (Drainage in traditional agriculture in Finland.)

Voipio, Aarni. Sleeping preachers: a study in ecstatic religiosity. Annales Academiae Scientiarum Fennicae. B. 75, no. 1. 1951. 86 p.

Vuorela, Toivo. Etelä-pohjanmaan kansanrakennukset. Kansatieteellinen tutkimus. Kyrönmaa. Diss. Helsinki. 1949. 307 p. (Folk farm life in southern Ostra-Bothnia.)

*Vuorela, Toivo. The Finno-Ugric peoples. Uralic and Altaic Studies. 39. Bloomington, Indiana University Press; The Hague, Mouton. 1964: 16-46, 377-378.

Wainemann, Paul. A summer tour in Finland. London, Methuen. 1908. 16, 318 p.

Walter, Lavina-Edna. Finland and the tundra, the land of the bear and the walrus. London, A. & C. Black. 1917. 7, 88 p.

*Young, Ernest. Finland. The land of a thousand lakes. London, Chapman and Hall. 1912. 12, 313 p., plates.

Bergsland, K., and R. Th. Christiansen. Norwegian research on the language and folklore of the Lapps. J.R.A.I. 80 (1950): 79-95.

Gjessing, Gutorm. Norwegian contributions to Lapp ethnography. J.R.A.I. 78 (1947): 47-60.

Hultkrantz, Åke. Swedish research on the religion and folklore of the Lapps. J.R.A.I. 85 (1955): 81-100.

Manker, Ernst. Swedish contributions to Lapp ethnography. J.R.A.I. 82 (1952): 39-54.

Wickman, Bo. Swedish contributions to Lapp linguistics. J.R.A.I. 89 (1959): 149-154.

Acerbi, Joseph [Guiseppe]. Travels through Sweden, Finland and Lapland to North Cape, 1798-1799. 2 vols. London, printed for J. Mawman. 1802.

Acta Lapponica. 17 vols. so far. Stockholm, Almqvist & Wiksell for the Nordiska Museet. 1938--

Anderson, R. T. Lapp racial classifications as scientific myths. Anthropological Papers of the University of Alaska. 11 (1962): 102-121.

Beckman, Lars. On the anthropology of the Swedish Lapps. Studia Ethnographica Upsaliensia. 21 (1964): 35-44.

Bergsland, Knut. Some well-known mountain names and border questions in southern Lappland. Studia Ethnographica Upsaliensia. 21 (1964): 45-54.

*Bernatzik, Hugo A. Overland with the nomadic Lapps. New York, Robert M. McBride. 1938. 16, 136 p., 90 plates, map.

Birket-Smith, Kaj. Primitive man and his ways. New York, World Publishing Co. 1960: 103-140.

Bonaparte, Roland Napoléon, Prince. Note on the Lapps of Finmark. Paris, printed by G. Chamerot for private circulation. 1886. 11, 1 p.

Bosi, Roberto. The Lapps. London, Thames and Hudson; New York, Praeger. 1960. 220 p., illus. (Full of errors.)

*Collinder, Björn. The Lapps. Princeton, Princeton University Press. 1949. 12, 252 p., 26 plates (1 in color), 2 maps.

Coxwell, C. Fillingham. Siberian and other folktales. London, C. W. Daniel Co. 1925: 601-640.

Cramer, Tomas. Right of the Same to land and water. Studia Ethnographica Upsaliensia. 21 (1964): 55-62.

*Dikkanen, Siri Lavik. Sirma. Residence and work organization in a Lappish-speaking community. Samiske Samlinger. 8. Oslo, Norsk Folkemuseum. 1965. 46 p.

Eidheim, H. Lappish guest relationships under conditions of cultural change. A.A. 68(1966): 426-437.

Erixon, Sigurd. An innovation among the Lapps viewed in the light of northern Scandinavian practice. Studia Ethnographica Upsaliensia. 21(1964): 71-80. (Use of salt in coffee.)

Ficatier, Marc-Étienne, and Pierre Vassal. Les Lapons du Finnmark. Essai de géographie humaine et de psychologie des peuples. Le Havre, Ancienne Impr. Marcel Etiax. 1949. 23 p., map.

Fjellström, Phebe. Angelica archangelica in the diet of the Lapps and the Nordic people. Studia Ethnographica Upsaliensia. 21(1964): 99-115.

*Gjessing, Gutorm. Changing Lapps. London School of Economics. Monographs on Social Anthropology. 13. London, Athlone Press. 1954. 68 p.

Gjessing, Gutorm. Mountain-Saames (Mountain Lapps) fishing at the sea-coast in the 17th and the 18th centuries. Studia Ethnographica Upsaliensia. 11(1956): 198-202.

Gjessing, Gutorm. The disintegration of the village organization of the Sea-Saames (Sea-Lapps). An Hypothesis. Avhandlinger Utgitt av det Norske Videnskaps-Akademi i Oslo. Historisk-Filosofisk Klasse. 1960. No. 2. 1960. 25 p.

Gourlie, Norah. A winter with the Finnish Lapps. London, Blackie and Son. 1939. 12, 243 p., plates. (Finnish and Skolt Lapps.)

Graff, Ragnvald. Knots used by the Lapps. Studia Ethnographica Upsaliensia. 21(1964): 126-132.

Hasselbrink, Gustav. Volgsjö, a lake- and place-name in Swedish Lappland. Studia Ethnographica Upsaliensia. 21(1964): 133-158.

Helle, Reijo. An investigation of reindeer husbandry in Finland. Fennia. 95, no. 4. 1966. 65 p., map.

Hertzman, Mrs. Anna-Mia. Lapland legends; tales of an ancient race and its great gods. London, Oxford University Press, H. Milford; New Haven, Yale University Press. 1926. 10, 212 p.

Hill, Rowland G. P., ed. The Lapps today in Finland, Norway and Sweden. 1. Bibliothèque arctique et antarctique, publication du Centre d'Études Arctiques et Antarctiques. 1. Paris, Mouton. 1960. 230 p., 2 maps.

Holme, Charles, ed. Peasant art in Sweden, Lapland and Iceland. London, The Studio. 1910. 8, 48 p., 88 plates.

Indiana. University. Graduate Program in Uralic and Asian Studies. New Haven, Printed by the Human Relations Area Files. 1955. 12, 137 p., maps.

Itkonen, Toivo J. Lappalaisten ruokatalous. Suomalais-Ugrilaisen Seuran Tiomituksia 51. Helsinki, Société Finno-Ougrienne. 1921. 139 p. (Lapp cookery.)

Itkonen, Toivo J. Heidnische Religion und späterer Aberglaube bei den finnischen Lappen. Suomalais-Ugrilaisen Seuran Tiomituksia. 87. Helsinki, Société Finno-Ougrienne. 1946. 319 p.

*Itkonen, Toivo J. Suomen Lappalaiset vuoteen 1945 [The Lapps in Finland up to 1945]. 2 vols. Porvoo & Helsinki, Werner Söderström. 1948.

Itkonen, Toivo J. The Lapps of Finland. S.W.J.A. 7(1951): 32-68.

*Karsten, Raphael. The religion of the Samek. Leiden, E. J. Brill. 1955. 7, 136 p., 7 figs.

Keane, A. H. The Lapps: their origin, affinities, habits and customs. London, E. Stanford. 1885. 23 p.

Kolsrud, K. Finnefolket i Ofoten. En studie i Ofotens demografi og sjøfinnenes etnografi i eldre tid. Oslo. 1947. 223 p. (Ph.D. Dissertation, University of Oslo. Demography and ethnography of the Sea-Lapps in Ofoten in former times.

Krohn, Kaarle. Birth: Finns and Lapps. Hastings Encyclopedia of Religion and Ethics. 2(1910): 647-648.

Lagercrantz, Eliel. Lappische Volksdichtung. 6 vols. Suomalais-Ugrilaisen Seuran Tiomituksia. 112, 115, 117, 120, 124, 126. Helsinki, Société Finno-Ougrienne. 1957-1963.

Launis, Armas Emanuel. Lappische juoigomelodien. Suomalais-Ugrilaisen Seuran Tiomituksia. 26. Helsingfors, Druckerei der Finnischen Literatur-Gesellschaft. 1908. 209 p.

Leem, Knud. An account of the Lapplanders of Finnmark, their language, manners, and religion with the notes of Gunnar, Bishop of Trontheim; and a treatise by Jessen on the pagan religion of the Fins and Laplanders. In John Pinkerton, ed. A general collection of voyages. London, Longman, Hurst, Rees and Orme. 1804-1814. 1: 376-490.

Lid, Nils, ed. Liber saecularis in honorum J. Qvigstadii d. IV aprilis A.D. MCMLIII editus I-II. 2 vols. Oslo, Studia Septentrionala. 4-5. 1953. 163, 163 p.

Linne, Carl von. Lachesis lapponica; or, a tour in Lapland, now first published from the original manuscript journal of Linnaeus; . . . 2 vols. London, White & Cochrane. 1811.

Lowie, Robert H. A note on Lapp culture history. S. W. J. A. 1 (1945): 447-454.

Lundman, Bertil. Publications on the physical anthropology of the Lapps. Studia Ethnographica Upsaliensia. 11 (1956): 277-284.

Lundström, Karin. Swedish nomad-schools. Studia Ethnographica Upsaliensia. 21 (1964): 182-185.

Manker, Ernst. Die lappische Zaubertrommel: 1: Die Trommel als Denkmal materieller Kultur. Acta Lapponica. 1. Stockholm, Almqvist & Wiksell. 1938. 888 p., 869 figs.

Manker, Ernst. Die lappische Zaubertrommel. 2: Die Trommel als Urkunde geistigen Lebens. Acta Lapponica. 6. Stockholm, Almqvist & Wiksell. 1950. 447 p., 157 figs., col. plates.

Manker, Ernst. Lapland and the Lapps. Stockholm, LT's. Forlag. 1953. 112 p.

*Manker, Ernst. The nomadism of the Swedish mountain Lapps. The Siidas and their migratory routes in 1945. Acta Lapponica. 7. Stockholm, H. Geber and Almqvist and Wiksell. 1953. 261 p., maps, charts.

Manker, Ernst. Les Lapons des montagnes Suédoises. Paris, Gallimard. 1954. 289 p.

Manker, Ernst. The Lapps in northernmost Sweden. Stockholm, Svenska Turistföreningen. 1954. 46 p.

Manker, Ernst. Last of the reindeer Lapps. Natural History. 67 (Feb. 1957): 70-81.

Manker, Ernst. Lapparnas heliga ställen: kulplaster och offerkult i belysning av Nordiska Museets och Landsantikvariernas . . . Acta Lapponica. 13. Stockholm, Almqvist & Wiksell. 1957. 462 p. (Cults.)

Manker, Ernst. Fångstgropar och stalotomter: kulturlämningar från lapsk forntid. Acta Lapponica. 15. Stockholm, Almqvist & Wiksell. 1960. 406 p. (Reindeer, trapping, dwellings.)

Manker, Ernst. Lappmarksgravar; dödsförestallningar och gravskick i lappmarkerna. Acta Lapponica. 17. Stockholm, Almqvist & Wiksell. 1961. 325 p. (Funeral rites and ceremonies.)

Manker, Ernst. The Noaidde art. Folk. 5 (1963): 235-244.

Manker, Ernst. The bone age of the Lapps. Studia Ethnographica Upsaliensia. 21 (1964): 186-198.

*Manker, Ernst. People of eight seasons. New York, Viking. 1964. 214 p., illus.

Näkkäläjärvi, Oula. Preliminary report on investigation of wild reindeer trapping pits in Finland. Studia Ethnographica Upsaliensia. 21 (1964): 228-233.

Nesheim, Asbjörn. An ancient type of sledge in Ullsfjord, northern Norway. Studia Ethnographica Upsaliensia. 11 (1956): 46-56.

Nesheim, Asbjörn. Introducing the Lapps. Oslo, Norske Folkemuseum. 1963. 55 p.

Nesheim, Asbjörn. The Lapp fur and skin terminology and its historical background. Studia Ethnographica Upsaliensia. 21 (1964): 199-218.

Nesheim, Asbjörn, ed. (narrated by Anders Monsen). Traits from life in a Sea Lappish district. Nord-Norsk Samlinger Bd. 2, Heft 2, no. 3. pp. 139-168. Oslo, Universitets Etnografiske Museum. 1949.

Newhouse, Joan. Reindeer are wild too. London, J. Murray. 1952. 13, 174 p. (Kautokeino Lapps.)

*Nickul, Karl. The Skolt Lapp community Suenjelsijd during the year 1938. Acta Lapponica. 5. Stockholm, Almqvist & Wiksell. 1948. 90 p., plates.

Nickul, Karl. Changes in a Lappish community—a reflection of political events and state attitude. Studia Ethnographica Upsaliensia. 11 (1956): 88-95.

Nickul, Karl. Place names in Suenjel—a mirror of Skolt history. Studia Ethnographica Upsaliensia. 21 (1964): 219-227.

Nielson, Konrad. Lapp dictionary, based on the dialects of Polmak, Karasjok and Kautokeino. 4 vols. (Vol. 5 in preparation). Oslo, Instituttet for Sammenlignende Kulturforskning. 1932, 1934, 1938, 1956. 666, 718, 876, 560 p.

Nordström, Ester B. E. Tent folk of the far north. London, H. Jenkins. 1930. 255 p., plates.

*Paine, Robert. Coast Lapp society. 1: A study of neighborhood in Revsbotn Fjord. Tromsø Museums Skrifter 4: 1. Tromsø, Tromsø Museum. 1957. 18, 341 p., 18 tables, 9 figs., 16 maps.

*Paine, Robert. Coast Lapp society. 2. A study of economic development and social values. Tromsø Museums Skrifter. 4. 2. Tromsø, Tromsø Museum. 1965. 12, 194 p.

Paine, Robert. Herding and husbandry. Two basic distinctions in the analysis of reindeer management. Folk. 6, no. 1 (1964): 83-84.

*Paine, Robert. Lapp betrothal. Studia Ethnographica Upsaliensia. 21 (1964): 234-263.

Paine, Robert. The nature of ownership in pre-war Coast Lapp settlements. Ethnos. 29 (1964): 121-130.

*Paterson, Sten Sture. Anthropogeographical studies among the Jokkmokk mountain Lapps. Göteborgs Kungl. Vetenskaps- och Vitterhets-samhälles Handlingar. 6 Följd. Ser. A. Bd. 6, No. 2. Göteborg. 1956. 64 p. (Also issued nonserially: Göteborg, Elanders Boktr. 1956. 64 p.)

Paulson, Ivar. Waldgeister im Volksglauben der Lappen. Z.f.E. 86 (1961): 141-151.

Pehrson, Robert Neil. Culture contact without conflict in Lapland. Man. 50 (1950): 157-160, plates.

Pehrson, Robert Neil. Recent studies of the Lapps. Arctic. 3 (1951): 187-189.

Pehrson, Robert Neil. Naming among the Karesuando Lapps. Journal de la Société Finno-Ougrienne. 56, no. 5 (1952): 1-4.

*Pehrson, Robert Neil. Bilateral networks of social relations in Könkämä Lapp district. Indiana University Publications. Slavic and East European Series. 5. Bloomington. 1957. 10, 128 p., 12 charts, 3 tables. (Reprinted: Samiske Sammlinger. 7. Oslo. 1964.)

*Pelto, Pertti J. Individualism in Skolt Lapp society. Kansatieteellinen Arkisto. 16. Helsinki, Suomen Muinaismuistoyhdistys. 1962. 261 p., 57 photos., 10 tables, 14 maps.

Petterson, O. Jabmek and Jabmeaimo; a comparative study of the dead and the realm of the dead in Lappish religion. Lund, Gleerup. 1957. 253 p.

Porsanger, Samuli. The sense of solidarity among the Lapps. Studia Ethnographica Upsaliensia. 21 (1964): 264-266.

Qvigstad, Justus. Lappiske eventyr og sagn [Lapp tales and legends]. 4 vols. Oslo, Instituttet for Sammenlignende Kulturforskning. 1927-1929. 560, 736, 511, 566 p. (Lapp text and Norwegian translations.)

Qvigstad, Justus. Lappische Heilkunde. Oslo, Instituttet for Sammenlignende Kulturforskning. 1932. 270 p.

Rae, Edward. The land of the north wind, or travels among the Laplanders and the Samoyeds. London, J. Murray. 1875. 16, 352 p., plates.

Rånk, Gustav. Zum Problem des Sippenkultes bei den Lappen. Archiv für Völkerkunde. 9(1954): 79-90.

Rånk, Gustav. Lapp female deities of Madderakka group. Studia Septentrionalis. 6(1955): 7-79.

Ravila, Paavo. Reste lappischen Volksglaubens. Suomalais-Ugrilaisen Seuran Tiomituksia. 68. Helsinki, Suomalais-Ugrilainen Seura. 1934. 162 p.

Reuterskiöld, Edgar Hans Casimir. Källskrifter till Lapparnas mytologi. Stockholm, Nordiska Museet. 1910. 44, 120 p. (Original texts to Lapp mythology.)

Reuterskiöld, Edgar Hans Casimir. De nordiska Lapparnas religion. Stockholm, Cederquists Grafiske Aktiebolag. 1912. 149 p.

Rönn, Gunnar. The land of the Lapps. Stockholm, Saxon & Lindströms. 1961. 111 p.

Rosander, G. Njuoravuolle en odenmarksby. Svenska Landsmal. 277(1960): 183-211. (Njuoravolle, a Lapp community.)

Ruong, Israel. Types of settlement and types of husbandry among the Lapps in northern Sweden. Studia Ethnographica Upsaliensia. 11(1956): 105-132.

Sariola, Sakari. Drinking patterns in Finnish Lapland. Helsinki, Finnish Foundation for Alcohol Studies. 1956. 88 p.

*Scheffer, John. The history of Lapland: containing a geographical description, and a natural history of that country; with an account of the inhabitants, their original, religion, customs, habits, marriages, conjurations, employments &c. London, Tho. Newborough. 1704. 5, 416, 20 p., illus.

Schlachter, Wolfgang. Wörterbuch des Waldlappendialekts von Malå und Texte zur Ethnographie. Lexica Societatis Fenno-Ugricae. 14. Helsinki. 1958. 19, 294 p.

Schreiner, Kristian Emil. Zur Osteologie der Lappen. 3 vols. Oslo, Instituttet for Sammenlignende Kulturforskning. 1935, 1931, 1945. 294, 73, 46 p., illus., plates.

Shor, Frank, and Jean Shor. North with Finland's Lapps. National Geographic Magazine. 106 (1954): 249-280.

Sköld, Tryggve. The Scandinavian norðr and the Lappish system of orientation. Studia Ethnographica Upsaliensia. 21(1964): 267-283.

Skum, Nils Nilsson. Same sita-Lappbyn. Acta Lapponica. 2. Stockholm. Almqvist & Wiksell. 1938. 158 p., illus.

Skum, Nils Nilsson. Valla renar [Tending reindeer]. Acta Lapponica. 10. Stockholm, Almqvist & Wiksell. 1955. 102 p., illus.

Smith, P. L. Kautokeino og Kautokeinolappene. En historisk og ergologisk studie [Kautokeino and the Kautokeino Lapps. An historical and ergological study]. Oslo, Instituttet for Sammenlignende Kulturforskning. 1938. 602 p., 58 illus. (German summary.)

Solem, Erik. Lappiske rettsstudier [Studies in Lapp law]. Oslo, Instituttet for Sammenlignende Kulturforskning. 1933. 342 p.

Strömbäck, Dag. The realm of the dead on the Lappish magic drums. Studia Ethnographica Upsaliensia. 11 (1956): 216-220.

Svensson, T. G. Lapp research and applied anthropology. Ethnos. 31(1966): 111-118.

Thomasson, Lars. Om Lapparna i Jämtland och Härjedalen. Acta Lapponica. 12. Stockholm, Almqvist & Wiksell. 1956. 80 p. (Lapp population and its changes over 100 years in Jämtland and Härjedalen.)

Thomasson, Lars. Den Lapska bebygelsen i Offerdal. Svenska Landsmal. 277, no. 2(1960): 137-181. (Lapp population in Offerdal, Jämtland.)

Thomasson, Lars. The Lapp chapel at Handöl. Studia Ethnographica Upsaliensia. 21(1964): 284-294.

Tiren, Karl. Die lappische Volksmusik. Aufzeichnungen von Juoikos-Melodie. bei den schwedischen Lappen. Acta Lapponica. 3. Stockholm, Almqvist & Wiksell. 1944. 236 p.

*Turi, Johan. Turi's book of Lappland. New York, Harper and Bros. 1931. 295 p., 14 figs. (Reprinted: Gröningen, Anthropological Publications. 1966

Utsi, Mikel. The reindeer-breeding methods of the northern Lapps. Man. 48(1948): 97-101.

Valonen, Niilo. Ptarmigan trapping in the village of Nuorgam in Utsjoki. Studia Ethnographica Upsaliensia. 11 (1956): 164-174.

Vilkuna, Kustaa. The "Radno" of Lapland. Studia Ethnographica Upsaliensia. 11(1956): 41-45.

Virtanen, E. A. Hunting on another man's land. Transactions of the Wester-marck Society. 1 (1947): 94-112.

Vorren, Ørnulv. Samene i Norge: . . . [Lapps in Norway . . .] . Oslo, Norsk Riksringkasting. 1956. 48 p.

Vorren, Ørnulv. Finnmarksamenes nomadisme. 2 vols. Oslo, Universitets-forlaget. 1962. (Also issued as Tromsø Museum Skrifter. 9. Tromsø.)

Vorren, Ørnulv. Reindeer nomadism in the island region of Helgeland. An analysis of the ecology of the reindeer industry with special reference to the island area as winter pasture. Studia Ethnographica Upsaliensia. 21 (1964): 304-320.

Vorren, Ørnulv, ed. Norway north of 65. London, Faber and Faber; Oslo, Oslo University Press. 1960 (1961). 271 p., plates. (Also issued as Tromsø Museums Skrifter. 8. Tromsø.)

*Vorren, Ørnulv, and Ernst Manker. Samekulturen; en oversikt. Tromsø, Tromsø Museum. 1958. 215 p.

*Vorren, Ørnulv, and Ernst Manker. Lapp life and customs; a survey. London, New York, Oxford University Press. 1962. 183 p.

Vuorela, Toivo. The Finno-Ugric peoples. Uralic and Altaic Studies. 39. Bloomington, Indiana University Press; The Hague, Mouton. 1964: 47-91, 378-380.

Walter, Lavina Edna. Norway and the Lapps. London, A. & C. Black. 1917. 7, 88 p.

*Whitaker, Ian. Social relations in a nomadic Lappish community. Samiske Samlinger. 2. Oslo, Norsk Folkemuseum. 1955. 178 p., fig., 2 maps.

*Whitaker, Ian. Declining transhumance as an index of culture change. Studia Ethnographica Upsaliensia. 11 (1956): 96-104.

Wickman, Bo. A Lappish tale from Arjeplog. Studia Ethnographica Upsaliensia. 21 (1964): 321-330.

Widstrand, Carl Gösta. Lapp reindeer terminology. Studia Ethnographica Upsaliensia. 21 (1964): 331-357.

Wustmann, Erich. Klingende Wildnis; Erlebnisse in Lappland. Eisenbach, E. Röth. 1956. 141 p.

GERMANS

Bellmann, Herbert. Volkskundliches Schrifttum. In Adolf Spamer, ed. Die deutsche Volkskunde. Leipzig, Bibliographisches Institut. 1935. Vol. 2 (separate pagination): 2, 1-88.

Bömer, A., and H. Degering. Westfälische Bibliographie zur Geschichte, Landeskunde und Volkskunde. Veröffentlichungen der Historische Kommission des Provinzial-Instituts für Westfälische Landes- und Volkskunde. 24. Münster. 1961. 128 p.

Epstein, Fritz Theodor. German source materials in American libraries. Milwaukee, Marquette University Press. 1958. 14 p. (An address delivered before the Institute of German Affairs in the University Memorial Library, Marquette Univ., Nov. 14, 1957.)

Epstein, Fritz Theodor. East Germany, selected bibliography. Washington, Library of Congress. 1959. 7, 55 p.

Luther, Arthur. Land und Leute in deutscher Erzählung. Ein bibliographisches Literaturlexikon. Stuttgart, Hiersemann. 1954. 6, 555 p.

Rister, Herbert. Schlesische Bibliographie 1928-1934. T. A. Nr. 1-7966. (Allgemeiner Teil, Landeskunde, Bevölkerungswesen und Familienkunde.) Marburg/Lahn, Johann Gottfried Herder Institut. 1961. 18, 445 p.

United States. Bureau of the Census. Bibliography of social science periodicals and monograph series—Soviet zone of Germany: 1948-1963. Washington, Library of Congress. 1965. 194 p.

Weber-Kellermann, I. Eine Übersicht der gesamtdeutschen volkskundlichen Literatur von 1945 bis Mitte 1954. Deutsches Jahrbuch für Volkskunde. 1 (1955): 414-440.

Abel, Wilhelm. Geschichte der deutschen Landwirtschaft vom frühen Mittelalter bis zum 19. Jahrhundert. Deutsche Agrargeschichte 2. Stuttgart, Eugen Ulmer. 1962. 333 p.

Adrian, Walther. So wurde Brot aus Halm und Glut. Bielefeld, Ceres Verlag. 1951. 116 p., 59 illus.

Aichel, Otto. Der deutsche Mensch. Jena, Gustav Fischer. 1933. 8, 176 p.

*Andree, Richard. Braunschweiger Volkskunde. Braunschweig, F. Vieweg und Sohn. 1896. 14, 385 p. (Second ed. 1901. 18, 531 p.)

Andree, Richard. Votive und Weihegaben des katholischen Volks in Süddeutschland; ein Beitrag zur Volkskunde. Braunschweig, F. Vieweg und Sohn. 1904. 17, 191 p.

Andree-Eysn, Marie. Volkskundliches. Aus dem bayrisch-österreichischen Alpengebiet. Braunschweig, F. Vieweg und Sohn. 1910. 274 p., 225 illus.

Arensmier, A. Hüser on Hüsker. Altberg. Fachwerk als bodenständige Volkskunst. Wuppertal, Aussaat-Verlag. 1961. 187 p.

*Bach, Adolf. Deutsche Volkskunde. 3d ed. Heidelberg, Quelle und Meyer. 1960. 708 p.

Bächtold-Stäubli, Hanns. Deutscher Soldatenbrauch und Soldatenglaube. Strassburg, K. J. Trübner. 1917. 48 p.

Bächtold-Stäubli, Hanns. Handwörterbuch des deutschen Aberglauben . . . 9 vols. Berlin und Leipzig, W. de Gruyter. 1927.

Baring-Gould, Sabine. The book of the Rhine from Cleve to Mainz. New York, Macmillan. 1906. 12, 345 p.

Baring-Gould, Sabine. Germany present and past. New York, Henry Holt. 1882. 492 p.

Barthel, Helene. Der Emmentaler Bauer. Veröffentlichungen der Volkskundlichen Kommission des Provinzial-Instituts für westfälische Landes- und Volkskunde, 1 Reihe. Heft 3. Münster, Aschendorff'sche Verlagsbuchhandlung. 1931. 7, 147 p.

Bartsch, Karl. Sagen, Märchen und Gebräuche aus Mecklenburg. 2 vols. Wien, Braumüller. 1879, 1880. 524, 508 p.

Baumert, Gerhard. Jugend der Nachkriegszeit: Lebensverhältnisse und Reaktionsweisen. Darmstadt, E. Roether. 1952. 18, 266 p.

*Baumert, Gerhard. Deutsche Familie nach dem Krieg. Darmstadt, E. Roether. 1954. 20, 259 p.

Baumert, Gerhard. Some observations on current trends in the German family. Transactions of the Third World Congress of Sociology. 4(1956): 161-168.

Baumgarten, Karl. Zimmermannswerk in Mecklenburg; die Schenne. Berlin, Akademie-Verlag. 1961. 8, 198 p., illus.

Baumgarten, Karl. Das Bauernhaus in Mecklenburg. Veröffentlichungen des Institut für Deutsche Volkskunde. 34. Berlin, Akademie-Verlag. 1965. 100 p., 68 illus.

Beck, A. Das Ende der Mühlen und Speicher im Schwarzwald. Badische Heimat. 43(1963): 334-347.

Beck, Franziska. Vom Volksleben auf der Danziger Nehrung. Nach archivalischen Quellen von 1594-1814. Marburg/Lahn, Johann Gottfried Herder Institut. 1962. 9, 353 p.

*Becker, Albert. Pfälzer Volkskunde. Bonn und Leipzig, K. Schroeder. 1925. 15, 413 p., 153 figs., 5 maps.

Becker, Albert. Heidelberger Volkskunde. Badische Heimat. 6(1939): 313-361.

Becker, August. Die Pfalz und die Pfälzer. Leipzig, J. J. Weber. 1858. 16, 836 p.

Bednarski, Gerhard. Durchbruch zum deutschen Glauben. Ein Kampfruf an Deutschland: Gedanken eines Nationalsozialisten zum deutschen Glaubenskampf. Verden, F. Mahnke. 1942. 47 p.

Behrend, H. Die Aufhebung der Feldgemeinschaften. Neumünster, Wachholtz 1964. 149 p.

Beitl, Richard. Deutsche Volkskunde. Berlin, Deutsche Buch-Gemeinschaft. 1933. 542 p.

Beitl, Richard. Deutsches Volkstum der Gegenwart. Berlin, Volksverband der Bücherfreunde, Wegweiser-Verlag. 1933. 279 p.

Bell, Clair Hayden. Peasant life in old German epics: Meier Helmbrecht and Der arme Heinrich. New York, Columbia University Press. 1931. 184 p.

Benecke, Berthold A. Fische, Fischerei und Fischzucht in Ost- und Westpreussen. Königsberg, Hartungsche Verlagsdruckerei. 1880. 320 p.

Bentzien, U. Die mecklenburgischen Drescher und die Einführung des Maschinendreschens. Deutsches Jahrbuch für Volkskunde. 10(1964): 25-42.

Berger, Dieter. Zur Geschichte der Butterbereitung im Rheinland. In Agrarethnographie. Berlin, Akademie der Wissenschaft zu Berlin. 1957: 175-183.

Birlinger, Anton. Schwäbisch-augsburgisches Wörterbuch. München, in kommission bei G. Franz. 1864. 8, 490 p.

Birlinger, Anton. Schwäbische Volkslieder. Beitrag zur Sitte und Mundart des schwäbischen Volkes. Freiburg im Breisgau, Herder. 1864. 4, 172 p.

Birlinger, Anton. Aus Schwaben (Sagen, Legenden, Volksaberglauben, Sitten, Rechtsbräuche, Ortsneckereien, Lieder, Kinderreim). Neue Sammlung. 2 vols. Wiesbaden, Killinger. 1874. 512, 535 p.

Blätter für hessische Volkskunde. (Giessen, Vereinigung für hessische Volkskunde.) 1(1889)-- (After 1902, under the title of Hessische Blätter für
Volkskunde.)

Bohnenberger, K., et al. Volkstümliche Uberlieferungen in Württemberg.
Stuttgart, Silberburg Verlag. 1962. 33 p.

Bomann, Wilhelm. Bäuerliches Hauswesen und Tagewerk in alten
Niedersachsen. Weimar, Hermann Böhlaus. 1933. 282 p., 212 illus.
(Second ed., 1941.)

Boner, Charles. Chamois hunting in the mountains of Bavaria. London,
Chapman and Hall. 1853. 8, 410 p. (New ed. London, Chapman
and Hall. 1860. 13, 446 p.)

Brace, Charles Loring. Home-life in Germany. New York, Charles Scribner.
1853. 12, 443 p. (Also an 1860 edition.)

Brepohl, Wilhelm. Bäuerliche Heilkunde in einem Dorfe des Mindener Landes
um die Jahrhundertwende. Minden/Westfalen, Bruns. 1950. 34 p.

Brepohl, Wilhelm. Industrievolk im Wandel von der agraren zur industriellen
Daseinsform dargestellt am Ruhrgebiet. Tübingen, Mohr. 1957. 10, 400 p.

Brinkmann, Otto. Das Erzählen in einer Dorfgemeinschaft. Veröffentlichungen
der Volkskundlichen Kommission des Provinzial Instituts für Westfälische
Landes- und Volkskunde 1 Reihe, Heft 4. Münster im Westfalen, Aschendorff. 1933. 8, 72 p.

Brunner, Karl. Ostdeutsche Volkskunde. Leipzig, Quelle & Meyer. 1925.
11, 279 p., 69 figs., 32 plates.

Burgess, Ernest W., ed. Aging in western societies. Chicago, University of
Chicago Press. 1960. 492 p.

Burland, C. A. Modern Swabian folk beliefs about witches. Folk-Lore.
68(1957): 495-497.

*Buschan, Georg Herman T. Das deutsche Volk in Sitte und Brauch. (Vol. 4 of
Die Sitten der Völker.) Stuttgart, Union. 1922. 8, 462 p.

Buschan, Georg Herman T. Altgermanische überlieferung in Kult und Brauchtum
der Deutschen. München, J. F. Lehman. 1936. 257 p.

Carstens, Heinrich. Volksglauben und Volksmeinungen aus Schleswig-Holstein.
Z.d.V.f.V. 24(1914): 55-62.

Chandler, Douglas. Black-Forest carnival. Geographical Magazine. 6(1937-
1938): 313-320.

Clemen, Carl. Deutscher Volksaberglaube und Volksbrauch. Bielefeld und Leipzig, Velhagen und Klassing. 1921. 90 p.

Clemmer, Richard O. German pronomial address. In June Helm, ed. Essays on the problem of tribe. Proceedings of the 1967 Annual Meeting, American Ethnological Society. Seattle, University of Washington Press. 1968: 221-227.

Curtze, Ludwig Friedrich Christian. Volksüberlieferungen aus dem Fürstenthum Waldeck. Märchen, Sagen, Volksreime, Räthsel, Sprichwörter, Aberglaube Sitten und Gebräuche, . . . Arolsen, Speyer. 1860. 518 p.

Dawson, William Harbutt. Germany and the Germans. 2 vols. London, Chapman & Hall. 1894.

*Dawson, William Harbutt. German life in town and country. New York and London, G. P. Putnam's Sons. 1901. 8, 323 p., plates.

*Dawson, William Harbutt. The German workman; a study in national efficiency. London, P. S. King & Son; New York, C. Scribner's Sons. 1906. 7, 304 p.

Dawson, William Harbutt. Municipal life and government in Germany. London, Longmans, Green. 1914. 7, 16, 507 p.

Deecke, E., comp. Lübische Geschichten und Sagen. 7th ed. Lübeck, M. Schmidt-Romhild. 1956. 244 p.

Demiashkievitch, Michael John. The national mind: English, French, German. New York and Cincinnati, American Book Co. 1938: 335-498.

Deutsches Archiv für Landes- und Volksforschung. 8 vols. Leipzig. 1937-19

Deutsches Jahrbuch für Volkskunde. Berlin, Akademie-Verlag. 1 (1955)--

Didszun, Georg. Ostpreussisches Ahnenerbe; wie der ostpreussische Bauer einst lebte. Leer im Ostfriesland, Kommissionsverlag G. Rautenberg. 1956. 126 p.

Diener, Walter. Hunsrücker Volkskunde. Bonn und Leipzig, K. Schroeder. 1925. 15, 284 p., 83 figs., 2 maps. (Another ed.: Bonn, Rohrscheid. 1962. 259 p., illus.)

Dietze, Constantin von, et al. Lebensverhältnisse in kleinbäuerlichen Dörfern. Hamburg, P. Parey. 1953. 8, 186 p.

Drechsler, Paul. Schlesiens volkstümliche Überlieferungen. II. Sitte, Brauch und Volksglaube in Schlesien. In Sammlungen und Studien der schlesiens Gesellschaft für Volkskunde. 2 vols. Leipzig, B. G. Teubner. 1903-1906 Volume 2, pts. 1-2: 14, 340; 12, 348 p.

GERMANS

Durr, D. Ostschwäbische Handlerdörfer in Geschichte und Gegenwart. Volkskundliche Untersuchungen zu den Dörfern Matzenbach und Unterdeufstettin,
im Kreis Creibsheim. Tübingen. 1963. 84 p. (Dissertation.)

Eckert, Georg. Aus den Lebensberichten deutscher Fabrikarbeiter. Zusammengestellt. Braunschweig. 1953. 155 p.

Ehemann, Kurt. Das Bauernhaus in der Wetterau und im SW. Vogelsberg.
Forschungen zur deutschen Bundesanstalt für Landeskunde. 61. Remagen.
1953. 150 p.

Eitzen, Gerhard. Das Bauernhaus im Kreise Euskirchen. Euskirchen, Verein
der Geschichts- und Heimatfreunde des Kreises Euskirchen. 1960. 104 p.

Engelien, August, and W. Lahn. Der Volksmund in der Mark Brandenburg.
Sagen, Märchen, Spiele, Sprichwörter und Gebräuche. 1, pt. 1. (No
more published.) Berlin, W. Schultze. 1868. 8, 285 p.

Erich, Oswald Adolf, and Richard Beitl. Wörterbuch der deutschen Volkskunde.
Stuttgart, A. Kröner. 1955. 10, 919 p.

Esser, A. Das Dorf Blessem. Seine Geschichte und die Wandlung seiner
sozialen Struktur Beginn des 20. Jahrhundert. Enskirchen, Verein der
Geschichts- und Heimatfreunde des Kreises Enskirchen. 1963. 135 p.

Fehrle, Eugen. Deutsche Feste und Jahresbräuche. Leipzig und Berlin, B. G.
Teubner. 1916. 5, 116 p.

*Fehrle, Eugen. Badische Volkskunde. 1 Teil. Leipzig, Quelle & Meyer.
1924. 15, 199 p.

Fehrle, Eugen. Deutsche Hochzeitsbräuche. Jena, E. Diederichs. 1937. 75 p.

Fiedler, A. Zur Frage des privaten und kommunalen Backens in den Dörfern
Sachsens während des 18. und zu Beginn des 19. Jahrhunderts. Dresden,
Abhandlungen und Berichte aus dem staatlichen Museum für Volkerkunde.
22(1963): 181-202.

Findeisen, Hans. Sagen, Märchen und Schwänken von der Insel Hildensee.
Aus dem Volksmunde gesammelt, sowie mit einer Einleitung und Anmerkungen versehen. Stettin. 1925. 94 p.

Finder, Ernst. Die Elbinsel Finkenwerder. Ein Beitrag zur Geschichte, Landes-
und Volkskunde Niedersachsens. Hamburg, Christians Verlag. 1951. 348 p.,
87 figs., map.

Focke, Friedrich. Ritte und Reigen: Volkskundliches aus schwäbischer Gegenwart und nordischer Vergangenheit. Stuttgart und Berlin, W. Kohlhammer.
1941. 8, 113 p.

*Fox, Nikolaus. Saarländische Volkskunde. Bonn, F. Klopp. 1927. 498 p., 20 illus., plus 94 illus. and plates.

Franz, G. Bauernhausmuseen und landwirtschaftliche Gerätesammlungen in Deutschland. Z.f.A.A. 5(1957): 129-147.

Franz, G., ed. Deutsche Agrargeschichte. 3 vols. 1. Geschichte der deutschen Landwirtschaft vom frühen Mittelalter bis zum 19. Jahrhundert, by W. Abe. 2. Geschichte der deutschen Agrarverfassung vom frühen Mittelalter bis zum 19. Jahrhundert, by F. Lutge. 3. Die deutsche Landwirtschaft im technischen Zeitalter, by H. Haushofer. Stuttgart, Verlag Eugen Ulmer. 1962, 1963, 1963. 333, 269, 290 p.

Frenzel, Walter, Fritz Karg, and Adolf Spamer. Grundriss der sächsischen Volkskunde. 2 vols. Leipzig, Bibliographisches Institut. 1932-1933. 368, 142 p., 124 illus.

Freudenthal, Herbert. Die Wissenschaftstheorie der deutschen Volkskunde. Hannover, Niedersächsische Heimatkunde. 1955. 241 p.

Fyfe, Agnes. Dances of Germany. New York, Crown. 1951. 40 p., illus.

Gaerte, Wilhelm. Volksglaube und Brauchtum Ostpreussens. Beiträge zur vergleichenden Volkskunde. Würzburg, Holzner. 1956. 128 p.

Geiger, Theodor. Die soziale Schichtung des deutschen Volkes; soziographischer Versuch auf statistischer Grundlage. Stuttgart, F. Enke. 1932. 4, 142 p.

Geiger, W. Studien zum Totenbrauch im Odenwald. Heppenheim, Verlag der Südhessischen Post. 1960. 116 p.

Geiser, Karl Frederick. Peasant life in the Black Forest. National Geographic Magazine. 19 (1908): 635-649.

Gierlichs, Willy. Religious life in contemporary German villages. In Pitirim A. Sorokin, ed. Systematic source book in rural sociology. Minneapolis, University of Minnesota Press. 1931. Volume 2: 393-397.

Görlitz, W. Die Junker; Adel und Bauer im deutschen Osten, geschichtliche Bilanz von 7 Jahrhunderten. Glücksburg/Ostsee, C. A. Starke. 1956. 11, 462 p.

Grime, F. W. Das Sauerland und seine Bewohner. Iserlohn, Sauerland Verlag. 1928. 174 p.

Haas, Alfred Wilhelm M. G. Rügensche Sagen und Märchen. Griefswald, L. Bamberg. 1891. 12, 263 p.

Haas, Alfred Wilhelm M. G. Rügensche Skizzen. Griefswald, Abel. 1898.
140 p.

Haas, Alfred Wilhelm M. G. Rügensche Volkskunde. Stettin, A. Schuster.
1920. 63 p.

Hain, Mathilde. Sprichwörter und Volkssprache; eine volkskundlich-
soziologische Dorfuntersuchung. Giessen, Schmitz. 1951. 131 p.

Hanika, Josef. Volkskunde der Sudetendeutschen. Kitzingen am Main,
Holzner. 1951. 26 p., 4 figs., map.

Hanssen, Georg. Die Aufhebung der Leibeigenschaft und die Umgestaltung
des gutsherrlich-bauerlichen Verhältnisses überhaupt in den Herzogtümern
Schleswig-Holstein. St. Petersburg, Eggers. 1861. 195 p.

Hanssen, Georg. Agrarhistorische Abhandlungen. 2 vols. Leipzig, S. Hirzel.
1880-1884.

Harmjanz, Heinrich. Volk, Mensch und Ding: erkenntniskritische Untersuchungen zur volkskundlichen Begriffsbildung. Königsberg und Berlin,
Ost-Europa-Verlag. 1936. 187 p.

Harmjanz, Heinrich. Ostpreussische Bauern, Volkstum und Geschichte.
Königsberg, privately printed. 1938. 139 p., illus.

Harper, Mrs. Bertha. When I was a girl in Bavaria. Boston, Lothrop, Lee
& Shepard. 1932. 149 p.

Harvard University. The Soviet Zone of Germany. General editor: Carl J.
Friedrich. New Haven, printed by the Human Relations Area Files. 1956.
8, 646 p., illus.

Heckscher, Kurt. Die Volkskunde des Kreises Neustadt. Hamburg, M. Riegel.
1930. 23, 852 p., 32 illus.

Heckscher, Kurt. Heidmärker Volkskunde. Volkskunde der südlichen
Lüneburger Heide, nach Aufnahmen in den Landkreisen Celle und Falling-
bostel. Hannover, Niedersächsischer Heimatbund. 1938. 10, 294 p.

Hefte für Bayerische Volkskunde. München, Verein für Volkskunst und
Völkerkunde. 1914-1924.

Hellpach, Willy. Der deutsche Charakter. Bonn, Athaenäum. 1954. 245 p.

Hessische Blätter für Volkskunde. Leipzig, B. G. Teubner. 1902-to date.
(Formerly:—Blätter für Hessische Volkskunde. 1899-1901.)

*Hessler, Carl. Hessische Landes- und Volkskunde. Vol. 2. Hessische Volks-kunde. Marburg, N. G. Elwert. 1907. 662 p.

Hessling, Egon. Die schönsten Hausthüren und Thore Berlins und seiner Umgebung ausgeführt in Holz; ein Vorlagenwerk für Architekten und Bautischler. 2 vols. Berlin and New York, B. Hessling. 1902.

Hoerburger, F., and H. Segler, eds. Klare, klare Seide. Überlieferte Kindertänze aus dem deutschen Sprachraum. Kassel und Basel, Bärenrieter Verlag. 1962. 172 p.

Hoffmann, Wilhelm. Rheinhessische Volkskunde. Bonn und Köln, Röhrscheid. 1932. 287 p., 74 illus.

*Hoffmann-Krayer, Eduard, Hans Bächtold-Stäubli, et al. Handwörterbuch des deutschen Aberglaubens. 10 vols. Berlin und Leipzig, W. de Gruyter. 1927-1942.

Höfler, Max. Volksmedizin und Aberglaube in Oberbayern Gegenwart und Vergangenheit. München, O. Galler. 1893. 12, 243 p., illus.

Hornstein, F. von. Deutsche und altdeutsche Kultur in Ostpreussen. München Verlag Parcus. 1922. 111 p.

Hoppstädter, K. Hexenverfolgung im saarländischen Raum. Zeitschrift für die Geschichte der Saargegend. 9(1959): 210-267.

Hornberger, T. Der Schäfer. Landes- und volkskundliche Bedeutung eines Berufsstandes in Süddeutschland. Stuttgart, W. Kohlhammer. 1955. 246 p.

Howitt, William. Rural and domestic life of Germany: with illustrative sketches of its cities and scenery. London, Longman, Brown, Green & Longmans. 1842. 8, 520 p.

Howitt, William. German experiences: addressed to the English; both stayers at home and goers abroad. London, Longman, Brown, Green & Longmans. 1844. 16, 352 p.

*Howitt, William. Life in Germany; or, scenes, impressions, and everyday life of the Germans, including the popular songs, sports, and habits of the students of the universities. London, G. Routledge. 1849. 484 p.

Hübl, Karl. Bauerntum und Landbau der Sudetendeutschen. München, Sudetendeutsches Landvolk in der Ackermann-Gemeinde. 1963. 656 p., illus., map.

Hüsing, Georg. Die deutschen Hochzeiten. Wien, Eichendorf Haus. 1927. 16, 144 p.

Jacobeit, Wolfgang. Hirt und Schäfer. In Agrarethnographie. Berlin, Akademie der Wissenschaft zu Berlin. 1957: 184-197.

Jacobeit, Wolfgang. Zur Erforschung des bäuerlichen Arbeitsgeräte in Deutschland. Z.f.A.A. 5(1957): 154-156.

Jacobeit, Wolfgang. Schafhaltung und Schäfer in Zentraleuropa bis zum Beginn des 20. Jahrhunderts. Berlin, Akademie-Verlag. 1961. 15, 604 p., plates.

Jacobeit, Wolfgang. An inventory of farming implements in museums of the German Democratic Republic. Current Anthropology. 4(1963): 358-359.

Jacobeit, Wolfgang. Zur Geschichte der deutschen Völkerkunde 1890-1945. Acta Ethnographica. 15(1966): 75-91.

Jahn, Ulrich. Volkssagen aus Pommern und Rügen. Berlin, Mayer & Müller. 1889. 28, 566 p.

John, Alois. Sitte, Brauch und Volksglaube im deutschen Westböhmen. 2d ed. Reichenberg, Franz Kraus. 1924. 20, 420 p.

Julien, Rose. Die deutschen Volkstrachten zu Beginn des 20. Jahrhunderts. München, Bruckmann. 1912. 192 p., 250 illus.

Jungbauer, Gustav. Geschichte der deutschen Volkskunde. Prag, Calve. 1931. 199 p.

Jungbauer, Gustav. Deutsche Volksmedizin. Ein Grundriss. Berlin und Leipzig, W. de Gruyter. 1934. 6, 250 p.

Kaiser, Karl. Der Atlas der pommerschen Volkskunde. Baltische Studien, n.F. 37(1935): 262-273, 2 maps.

Kaiser, Karl. Beiträge zur Volkskunde Pommerns. Veröffentlichungen des volkskundlichen Archivs für Pommern. Bd. 8. Griefswald, Bamberg. 1939. 176 p.

Karger, Walter von. Das Dienstzeugnis. Berlin, H. Sack. 1928. 47 p.

Karlinger, Hans. Im Raum der obern Donau; Kunst, Landschaft und Volkstum. Salzburg und Leipzig, Anton Pustet. 1937. 321 p.

Karlinger, Hans. Deutsche Volkskunst. Berlin, Propyläen Verlag. 1938. 505 p., plates, illus.

Kauder, Viktor. Die deutsche Sprachinsel Bielitz-Biala. Deutsche Gaue in Polen, Heft 1. Plauen im Vogtland, Verlag das Junge Volk. 1923. 80 p.

Kehrein, Joseph. Volkssprache und Volkssitte in Herzogthum Nassau. Ein Beitrag zu deren Kenntniss. 2 vols. Weilburg, Lanz. 1860-1862. 12, 824 p.

Klapper, Joseph. Schlesische Volkskunde auf kulturgeschichtlicher Grundlage. Breslau, Ferdinand Hirt. 1925. 384 p., 61 illus.

Klenck, Wilhelm, and Walter Scheidt. Niedersächsische Bauern I. Geestbauern im Elb-Weser-Mündungsgebiet (Börde Lamstedt). Jena, Gustav Fischer. 1929. 112 p.

Klocke, Fritz. Harzer Schäfer und Hirten. Museumsbücherei Quedlinburg. Bd. 7. Quedlinburg. 1961. 32 p.

Knapp, Georg Friedrich. Die Bauernbefreiung und der Ursprung der Landarbeiter in den älteren Theilen Preussens. 2 vols. Leipzig und Altenburg, Duncker & Humblot. 1887. 352, 437 p. (Reprinted: München und Leipzig, Duncker & Humblot. 1927. 341, 352 p.)

Knapp, Georg Friedrich. Die Landarbeiter in Knechtschaft und Freiheit. Leipzig, Duncker & Humblot. 1891. 92 p.

Knoop, Otto. Volkssagen, Erzählungen, Aberglauben, Gebräuche und Märchen aus dem östlichen Hinterpommern. Posen, Jolowicz. 1885. 30, 240 p.

Knoop, Otto. Sagen der Provinz Posen, gesammelt und herausgegeben. Berlin-Friedenau, H. Eichblatt. 1913. 16, 183 p.

Köhler, Carl, ed. Volkslieder von der Mosel und Saar mit Bildern und Weisen. Herausgegeben mit Unterstützung des Deutschen Volksliedarchivs. Frankfurt am Main, M. Diesterweg. 1926. 110 p.

Köhler, Johann August E. Volksbrauch, Aberglauben, Sagen und andere alte Ueberlieferungen im Voigtlande. Leipzig, Fr. Fleischer. 1867. 7, 652 p.

König, Rene. Family and authority: the German father in 1955. Sociological Review. New series. 5(1957): 107-127.

Kötzschke, Rudolf. Ländliche Siedlung und Agrarwesen in Sachsen. Forschungen zur deutschen Bundesanstalt für Landeskunde. Bd. 77. Remagen, Verlag der Bundesanstalt für Landeskunde. 1953. 236 p.

Kramer, Karl Sigismund. Volksleben im Fürstentum Ansback und seinen Nachbargebieten (1500-1800). Würzburg, Schöningh. 1961. 358 p.

Krauss, Friedrich Salmo. Das Minnelied des deutschen Land- und Stadtvolkes. Leipzig, Ethnologischer Verlag. 1929. 316 p.

Krenzlin, Anneliese. Dorf, Feld und Wirtschaft im Gebiet der grossen Täler und Platten östlich der Elbe. Forschungen zur deutschen Landeskunde. Bd. 70. Remagen, Verlag des Amtes für Landeskunde. 1952. 144 p.

Krieg, Hans. Schleswig-Holsteinische Volkskunde aus dem Anfange des 19. Jahrhunderts in Auszügen aus den schleswig-holsteinischen Provinzial- berichten. I. Teil. Landschaftliche und wirstchaftliche Grundlagen. Lübeck. 1931. 127 p.

Kriss, Rudolf. Die religiöse Volkskunde Altbayerns. Baden bei Wien, Rudolf M. Rohrer. 1933. 190 p.

Kriss, Rudolf. Volkskundliches aus altbayrischen Gnadenstätten. Baden bei Wien, Rudolf M. Rohrer. 1933. 43 p.

*Kriss, Rudolf. Sitte und Brauch im Berchtesgadener Land. München-Pasing, Filser. 1947. 231 p.

Kriss, Rudolf. Die Volkskunde der altbayrischen Gnadenstätten. 3 vols. München-Pasing, Filser. 1953-1956.

*Kriss, Rudolf. Sitte und Brauch im Berchtesgadener Land, 2. Berchtesgaden, Berchtesgadener Anzeiger. 1963. 247 p.

Kriss-Rettenbeck, Lenz. Bilder und Zeichen religiösen Volksglaubens. München, Callwey. 1964. 186 p.

Kück, Eduard. Das alte Bauernleben der Lüneburger Heide. Studien zur niedersächsischen Volkskunde . . . Leipzig, Th. Thomas. 1906. 16, 279 p.

Kuhn, Adalbert. Sagen, Gebräuche und Märchen aus Westfalen. 2 pts. Leipzig, F. A. Brockhaus. 1859.

Kuhn, Adalbert, and W. Schwartz. Norddeutsche Sagen, Märchen und Gebräuche aus Mecklenburg, Pommern, der Mark, Sachsen, Thüringen, Braunschweig, Hannover, Oldenburg und Westfalen. Leipzig, F. A. Brockhaus. 1848. 42, 560 p.

Künssberg, Eberhard Otto Georg, Freiherr von. Rechtsbrauch und Kinderspiel; Untersuchungen zur deutschen Rechtsgeschichte und Volkskunde. Heidel- berg, C. Winter. 1920. 64 p.

Küppers, W. Mädchentagebücher der Nachkriegszeit; ein kritischer Beitragzum sogenannten Wandel der Jugend. Stuttgart, Klett Verlag. 1964. 334 p.

Laing, Samuel. Observations on the social and political state of Denmark, and the duchies of Sleswick and Holstein, in 1851; . . . London, Long- man, Brown, Green and Longmans. 1852. 16, 446 p.

*Lämmle, August. Schwäbische Volkskunde. 7 vols. Stuttgart, Verlag Silverberg. 1924-1931.

Lanz, J. Tow und Brotterkrippen in Sudetenland. Jahrbuch für ostdeutsche Volkskunde. 7(1963): 197-218.

Lauder, Mrs. Maria Elise T. Legends and tales of the Harz mountains. London, Hodder & Stoughton. 1881. 11, 259 p.

Lauffer, Otto. Über Geschichte und den heutigen volkstümlichen Gebrauch der Tätowierung in Deutschland. Wörter und Sachen. 6(1914): 1-14.

Lauffer, Otto. Der volkstümliche Gebrauch der Totenkronen in Deutschland. Z.d.V.f.V. 26(1916): 225-246. 7 illus.

Lauffer, Otto. Das deutsche Haus in Dorf und Stadt, ein Ausschnitt deutscher Altertumskunde. Leipzig, Quelle & Meyer. 1919. 126 p., illus.

Lauffer, Otto. Dorf und Stadt in Niederdeutschland. Berlin und Leipzig, W. de Gruyter. 1934. 234 p.

Lauffer, Otto. Land und Leute in Niederdeutschland. Berlin und Leipzig, W. de Gruyter. 1934. 10, 291 p.

Lauffer, Otto. Der Weinachtsbaum in Glauben und Brauch. Berlin und Leipzig, W. de Gruyter. 1934. 52 p.

Lauffer, Otto. Volkskundliche Erinnerungen aus Göttingen und dem oberen Leintal. Göttingen, Vandenhoeck & Ruprecht. 1949. 172 p.

Lechner, Maria-Lioba. Das Ei im deutschen Brauchtum. Beiträge zur Volkskunde. Freiburg/Schweiz. 1952. 6, 46 p. (Ph.D. dissertation. Printed in Zürich. 1953.)

Legrand, Robert. Die Eifel. Plaudereien über ihre Arbeit und ihr Brauchtum. Wittlich. 1941. 127 p., 71 illus.

Lehmann, Otto. Das Bauernhaus in Schleswig-Holstein. Altona, H. Ruhe. 1927. 8, 160 p., illus.

Lehmann, Otto. Deutsches Volkstum in Volkskunst und Volkstracht. Berlin, W. de Gruyter. 1938. 10, 125 p.

Leithäuser, Julius. Volks- und Heimatkunde des Wupperlandes. Elberfeld, A. Martini und Grüttefien. 1926. 248 p.

*Lemke, Elisabeth. Volksthümliches in Ostpreussen. 3 vols. Mohrungen (vols. 1 and 2), Allenstein (vol. 3). 1884, 1897, 1889. 16, 190; 16, 303; 15, 184 p.

Leschnitzer, Adolf. The magic background of modern anti-Semitism; an analysis of the German-Jewish relationship. New York, International Universities Press. 1956. 236 p.

GERMANS

Linné, Carl von. Linnaeus Auslandsreise, aus dem Schwedischen übersetzt . . .
Stockholm, Cederquists Grafiska Aktiebolag. 1919. 55 p.

Lowie, Robert Harry. The German people. New York, Farrar & Rinehart.
1945. 143 p.

*Lowie, Robert Harry. Toward understanding Germany. Chicago, University
of Chicago Press. 1954. 9, 396 p.

Mackensen, Lutz. Pommersche Volkskunde. Kitzingen am Main, Holzner.
1952. 32 p.

Martiny, Rudolf. Hof und Dorf in Altwestfalen: das westfälische Streusiedlungs-
problem. Forschungen zur deutschen Landes- und Volkskunde. Bd. 24,
Heft 5. Stuttgart, J. Engelhorns. 1926. 66 p.

Martiny, Rudolf. Die Grundrissgestaltung der deutschen Siedlungen. Gotha,
J. Perthes. 1928. 6, 75 p.

Marzell, Heinrich. Volksbotanik. Die Pflanze im deutschen Brauchtum.
Berlin, Enkelhaus. 1935. 195 p.

Mayhew, Henry. The upper Rhine: the scenery of its banks, and the manners
of its people. London, G. Routledge. 1858. 15, 448 p.

*Mayhew, Henry. German life and manners as seen in Saxony at the present
day: village life-town life-domestic life, etc. 2 vols. London, W. H.
Allen. 1864.

Meringer, Rudolf. Das deutsche Haus und sein Hausrat. Leipzig, Teubner.
1906. 8, 111 p.

Meyer, E. H. Wilhelm. Ein niedersächsisches Dorf am Ende des 19. Jahrhunderts. Sonderveröffentlichungen des Historischen Vereins für die
Grafschaft Ravensberg. Bd. 1. Bielefeld, Julius Opitz. 1927. 246 p.

Meyer, Elard Hugo. Deutsche Volkskunde. Strassburg, K. J. Trübner. 1898.
362 p.

Meyer, Elard Hugo. Badisches Volksleben im neunzehnten Jahrhundert.
Strassburg, K. J. Trübner. 1900. 12, 628 p.

Meyer, Hans, and Heinz Steiger. Einführung in das Recht der landwirtschaftlichen
Schuldenregelung. Berlin, F. Vahlen. 1936. 108 p.

*Meyer, Hans Bernhard. Das Danziger Volksleben. Würzburg, Holzner Verlag.
1956. 11, 223 p.

Meyer, Hans Heinrich Joseph. Das deutsche Volkstum. Leipzig und Wien,
Hans Zimmer. 1899. 679 p.

Meyer, Wilhelm. See Meyer, E. H. Wilhelm.

Mielke, Robert. Der deutsche Bauer und sein Dorf, in Vergangenheit und Gegenwart. Weimar, A. Duncker. 1936. 134 p.

Mitteilungen der Schlesischen Gesellschaft für Volkskunde. Breslau. Bd. 1(1894)--

Mitteilungen und Umfragen zur Bayerischen Volkskunde. Würzburg. 1895-1912. (Continued as: Blätter zur Bayerischen Volkskunde. 1912-1921; 1925--)

Mitteilungen des Vereins für Sächsische Volkskunde. 1897-1923. (Continued as: Mitteilungen des Landesvereins Sächsische Heimatschutz. 1924--)

Mitzka, Walter. Deutsche Bauern und Fischerboote. Heidelberg, Carl Winter 1933. 3, 116 p., 86 illus.

Moepert, Adolf. Die Anfänge der Rübezahlsage; Studien zum Wesen und Werden des schlesischen Berggeistes. Leipzig, H. Eichblatt. 1928. 136 p.

Moser, Hugo. Schwäbischer Volkshumor; die Necknamen der Städte und Dörfer in Württemberg und Hohenzollern, im bayerischen Schwaben und in Teilen Badens sowie bei Schwaben in der Fremde, mit einer Auswahl von Ortsneckreimen. Stuttgart, W. Kohlhammer. 1950. 466 p.

Müller, G. Zur Lage der Kleinbauern in Westdeutschland. Berlin, Verlag der Wirtschaft. 1956. 158 p.

Müller, Liselotte. Das Bauernhaus im Kreis Hofgeismar. Schriften der Volkskundliche Kommission im Provinzial-Institut für westfälische Landes- und Volkskunde. 4. Münster im Westfalen, Aschendorff. 1940. 52 p., 10 figs., 25 plates.

Müller-Freienfels, Richard. Psychologie des deutschen Menschen und seiner Kultur. 2d ed. München, Beck. 1929. 245 p.

Müller-Freienfels, Richard. The German, his psychology & culture; an inquiry into folk character. Los Angeles, New Symposium Press. 1936. 16, 243 p.

Mundigal, Joseph. Bayerische Volkskunde, Sitte und Brauchtum. München, H. Neuner. 1955. 144 p.

Myer-Heisig, E. Deutsche Bauerntöpferei: Geschichte und landschaftliche Gliederung. München, Prestel-Verlag. 1955. 159 p.

Myer-Heisig, E. Weberei, Nadelwerk, Zeildruck. Zur deutschen volkstümlichen Textilkunst. München, Picestel. 1956. 80 p., illus.

*Naroll, Raoul. German kinship terms. A.A. 60(1958): 750-755.

Naumann, Hans. Grundzüge der deutschen Volkskunde. Leipzig, Quelle & Meyer. 1929. 151 p.

Naumann, Walther. Zur Wohnungsfrage im Königreich Sachsen. Leipzig, Jäh & Schunke. 1902. 152 p.

Neppert-Boehland, Maria. German textiles. Leigh-on-Sea, England, F. Lewis. 1955. 21 p., 64 plates.

Niederdeutsche Zeitschrift für Volkskunde. Bremen. 1923-1947. (Continued as: Niederdeutsches Jahrbuch für Volkskunde. 1947--)

Nord, Rudolf. Volksmedizin in Waldeck. Waldeckisches Volkstum 2. Corbach, Wilhelm Bing. 1934. 100 p.

Oberdeutsche Zeitschrift für Volkskunde. Baden, A. G. Bühl. Bd. 1(1927)--

Obiditsch, F. Die ländliche Kulturlandschaft der Baar und ihr Wandel seit dem 18. Jahrhundert. Tübingen, Hopfer. 1961. 85 p.

Peesch, Reinhard. Agrarethnographische Themen im Atlas der deutschen Volkskunde. In Agrarethnographie. Berlin, Akademie der Wissenschaft zu Berlin. 1957: 166-174.

Peesch, Reinhard. Die Fischerkommunen auf Rügen und Hiddensee. Berlin, Akademie-Verlag. 1961. 8, 367 p.

Pelosse, J. L. Beitrag zum Studien der sozialen Verhältnisse zwischen den Fischern und Bauern der Elbinsel Alterwerder. Z.f.E. 80 (1955): 125-134.

Perlick, Alfons. Oberschlesische Berg- und Hüttenleute. Lebensbilder aus dem oberschlesischen Industrierevier. Kitzingen am Main, Holzner. 1953. 304 p.

Perlick, Alfons. Sitte und Brauch in Oberschlesien. Bonn, Landmannschaft der Oberschlesier. 1963. 55 p.

Pessler, Wilhelm. Das altsächsische Bauernhaus in seiner geographischen Verbreitung. Braunschweig, F. Vieweg und Sohn. 1906. 16, 260 p.

Pessler, Wilhelm. Niedersächsisches Trachtenbuch. Hannover, Th. Schulze. 1922. 100 p., illus.

Pessler, Wilhelm, et al. Handbuch der deutschen Volkskunde. 3 vols. Potsdam, Athenaion. 1938. 324, 487, 387 p.

Peter, Anton. Volksthümliches aus Osterreichisch-Schlesien. 2 vols. Troppau, Schüler. 1865. 15, 459; 16, 288 p.

Petersen, Carl Ernst J., and Otto Scheel, eds. Handwörterbuch des Grenz-
und Auslandsdeutschtums. 5 vols. Breslau, F. Hirt. 1933-1935.

Peuckert, Will Erich. Deutsches Volkstum in Märchen und Sage, Schwank
und Rätsel. Berlin, W. de Gruyter. 1938. 13, 215 p.

Peuckert, Will Erich. Schwarzer Adler unterm Silbermond; Biographie der
Landschaft Schlesien. Hamburg, H. Govert. 1940. 357 p.

Peuckert, Will Erich. Schlesische Volkskunde. Kitzingen am Main, Holzner.
1953. 36 p.

Pfister, Friedrich. Schwäbische Volksbräuche, Feste und Sagen. Augsburg,
Benno Filser. 1924. 111 p.

Pohlandt, Max. Lebuser Land, Leute und Leben. Eine Volkskunde. Frank-
furter Abhandlungen zur Geschichte. 7. Frankfurt am Oder, G. Harnecker
1929. 16, 196 p.

Radig, Werner. Das Bauernhaus in Brandenburg und im Mittelelbgebiet.
Veröffentlichungen des Instituts für deutsche Volkskunde. 38. Berlin,
Akademie-Verlag. 1966. 104 p., 61 illus.

Rehm, Hermann S. Deutsche Volksfeste und Volkssitten. Leipzig, Teubner.
1908. 4, 118 p., 11 illus.

Reichhardt, Rudolf. Geburt, Hochzeit und Tod im deutsche Volksbrauch und
Volksleben. Jena, H. Costenoble. 1913. 8, 176 p.

Reinsberg-Düringsfeld, Otto, Freiherr von. Das festliche Jahr. In Sitten,
Gebräuchen, Aberglauben und Festen der germanischen Völker. 2d ed.
Leipzig, H. Barsdorf. 1898. 7, 487 p.

Requate, H. Zur Geschichte der Haustiere Schleswig-Holsteins. Z.f.A.A.
4(1956): 2-19.

Retzlaff, Hans. Deutsche Bauerntrachten. Berlin, Atlantis Verlag. 1935.
223 p., illus.

Reuschel, Karl Theodor. Deutsche Volkskunde im Grundriss. 2 vols. Leipzig
und Berlin, B. G. Teubner. 1920-1924.

Rheinische Jahrbücher für Volkskunde. Bonn, F. Dümmler. Bd. 1 (1950)--

Rheinische Vierteljahrsblätter. Bonn, Bonn Universität für geschichtliche
Landeskunde der Rheinlande. Bd. 1 (1931)--

Rheinisch-Westfälische Zeitschrift für Volkskunde. Veröffentlichungen der Volkskundlichen Abteilungen des Instituts für Geschichtliche Landeskunde der Rheinland und der Universität Bonn, und der Volkskundlichen Kommission im Provinzialinstitut für Westfälische Landes und Volkskunde in Münster. Bd. 1(1954)--

Riehl, Wilhelm H. Die Pfälzer. Ein rheinisches Volksbild. Stuttgart, Gotta. 1857. 408 p.

Riehl, Wilhelm H. Die deutsche Arbeit. 2d ed. Stuttgart, Gotta. 1862. 330 p.

Riehl, Wilhelm H. The old German peasant household. In Pitirim A. Sorokin, ed. Systematic source book in rural sociology. Minneapolis, University of Minnesota Press. Vol. 2. 1931: 94-99.

Riemann, Erhard. Volkskunde des Preussenlands. Kitzingen am Main, Holzner. 1952. 36 p.

Riepenhausen, H. Die Bäuerliche Siedlung des Ravensberger Landes bis 1770. Arbeiten der geographischen Kommission, Provinzial Institut für Westfälische Landes- und Volkskunde. No. 1. Münster. 1938. 144 p.

Ringeling, Gerhard. Fischländer Volk. Geschichte und Schicksal einer mecklenburgischen Küstenlandschaft. Rostock, Hinstorff. 1947. 176 p., 7 illus.

Rodnick, David. Postwar Germans, an anthropologist's account. New Haven, Yale University Press. 1948. 12, 233 p.

Rörig, Maria. Haus und Wohnen in einem sauerländischen Dorfe. Schriften der Volkskundlichen Kommission im Provinzial-Institut für Westfälische Landes- und Volkskunde. 5. Münster im Westfalen, Aschendorff. 1940. 72 p., 7 maps, 31 plates.

Rosseck, Irmgard (née Röder). Das Brauchtum des Jahrkreises im Lommatzscher Land. Ein Beitrag zur sächsischen Volkstumsgeographie. 1942. 7, 371 p. Ph.D. dissertation, Universität Leipzig.

Rudolph, W. Die Schiffstypen der ländlichen Frachtschiffahrt in den Gewässern der Insel Rügen. Deutsches Jahrbuch für Volkskunde. 4(1958): 129-154.

Rudolph, W. Die Insel der Schiffer. Zeugnisse und Erinnerungen von rügischer Schiffahrt. Von Beginn der Entwicklung bis 1945. Rostock, Hinsdorf. 1962. 28, 246 p.

Rudwin, Maximilian J. The origin of the German carnival comedy. New York, Steckert. 1920. 10, 85 p.

Rumpf, Max. Religiöse Volkskunde. Schriften der Deutschen Akademie 15. Stuttgart, Kohlhammer. 1933. 15, 475 p., illus.

Rumpf, Max. Das gemeine Volk. Ein soziologisches und volkskundliches Lebens- und Kulturgemälde. 2 vols. Stuttgart, Kohlhammer. 1933, 1936

Rumpf, Max. Deutsches Bauernleben. Stuttgart, Kohlhammer. 1936. 20, 912 p.

Rumpf, Max. Deutsches Handwerkerleben und der Aufstieg der Stadt. Stuttgart, Kohlhammer. 1955. 242 p.

Sartori, Paul. Westfälische Volkskunde. Leipzig, Quelle & Meyer. 1922. 11, 209 p., 16 plates.

Sartori, Paul. Literatur der westfälischen Volkskunde, im Auftrage des westfälischen Heimatsbundes zusammengestellt. Münster, Aschendorff. 1932. 48 p.

Schädler, Karl. Die Lederhose in Bayern und Österreich. Ein Beitrag zur Kostüm-, Trachten-, und Zunftgeschichte. Innsbruck, Wagner. 1962. 204 p., illus.

Schaffner, Bertram. Fatherland: a study of authoritarianism in the German family. New York, Columbia University Press. 1948. 12, 203 p.

Scheele, G., and P. Autschbach. Ländliche Siedlung in Schleswig-Holstein. Köln-Braunsfeld, R. Müller. 1960. 111 p.

Scheidl, Josef. Das dachauer Bauernhaus. Eine Bau- und kulturgeschichtliche Untersuchung. München, Callwey. 1952. 144 p., 41 illus.

Schelsky, Helmut. Wandlungen der deutschen Familie in der Gegenwart. 3d Stuttgart, Ferdinand Enke. 1953. 357 p.

Schilli, Hermann. Das Schwarzwaldhaus. Stuttgart, Kohlhammer. 1953. 302 p., illus. (Another edition: 1964. 312 p., illus.)

Schlee, Ernst. Schleswig-Holstein. Deutsche Volkskunst. Weimar, Böhlau. 1940. 68 p., 222 illus.

Schmolitzky, Oskar. Thüringer Volkskunst. Jena und Weimar, Böhlau. 1950. 130 p., 20 p. of illus.

Schmolitzky, Oskar. Volkskunst in Thüringen vom 16. bis zum 19. Jahrhundert. Weimar, Böhlau. 1964. 118 p., illus.

Schneider, Karl. Heilmittel und Heilbräuche im Saargebiet. Unsere Saarheimat. fasc. 3. Saarbrucken. 1924. 54 p.

Scholz, Hugo. Die Dörfler. Menschen und Bräuche aus dem schlesischen Bergland. Breslau, Bergstadtverlag. 1926. 205 p.

Schremmer, Wilhelm. Schlesische Volkskunde. Breslau, Priebatsch's Buchhandlung. 1928. 189 p., illus., 9 plates.

Schröder, Albert. Bemalter Hausrat in Nieder- und Ostdeutschland. Leipzig, Schwartzhäupter. 1939. 152 p., 193 plates, 8 in color.

Schulenburg, Willibald von. Ein Bauernhaus im berchtesgadener Ländchen. M. A. G. W. 26(1896): 61-86, illus.

Schulte, Carl. Schulfeiern im Geiste der neuern Zeit. 5th ed. Langensalza, J. Beltz. 1940. 251 p.

Schultz, W. Volkstänze aus Pommern. Kassel, Basel, etc., Bärenreiter Verlag. 1962. 32 p.

Schwebe, J. Volksglaube und Volksbrauch im hannoverschen Wendland. Köln und Graz, Böhlau. 1960. 8, 272 p.

Schwindrazheim, Oskar. Deutsche Bauernkunst. Wien, M. Gerlach. 1904. 15, 168 p. (Another edition: Wien und Leipzig, Deutscher Verlag für Jugend und Volk. 1931. 8, 244 p., 12 col. plates, 202 illus.)

Shanas, Ethel, Peter Townsend, et al. Old people in three industrial societies. New York, Atherton Press. 1968. 16, 478 p.

*Sidgwick, Mrs. Alfred. Home life in Germany. 3d ed. New York, Macmillan. 1912. 6, 327 p.

Smith, Thomas F. A. The soul of Germany. A twelve years' study of the people from within. New York, George H. Doran Co. 1915. 15, 356 p.

Sohnrey, Heinrich. Die Sollinger. Volksbilder aus dem sollinger Wald. Berlin, Deutsche Landbuchhandlung. 1924. 392 p. (Lower Saxony.)

*Spamer, Adolf, et al. Die deutsche Volkskunde. 2 vols. Leipzig, Bibliographisches Institut. 1934-1935. 632; 410, 85 p., maps.

Spamer, Adolf, et al. Deutsche Fastnachtsbräuche. Jena, E. Diedrichs. 1936. 71 p.

Spamer, Adolf, et al. Weihnachten in alter und neuer Zeit. Jena, E. Diedrichs. 1937. 95 p.

Spamer, Adolf, et al. Hessische Volkskunst. Jena, E. Diedrichs. 1939. 122 p.

Steinbach, Fr. Das Bauernhaus der westdeutschen Grenzlande. Rheinische Vierteljahrsblätter. 1(1931): 26-47.

Stephan, Oskar. Beiträge zur askanischen Volkskunde. Aschersleben, Karl Kinzenbache. 1925. 11, 396 p.

Strackerjan, Ludwig [Peter Fredrich Ludwig]. Aberglaube und Sagen aus dem Herzogthum Oldenburg. 2d ed. 2 vols. Oldenburg, G. Stalling. 1909.

Taylor, Archer. Characteristics of German folklore studies. In Richard M. Dorson, ed. Folklore research around the world. Bloomington, Indiana University Press. 1961: 7-15.

Thies, W. Der hannoversche Bauer. Die Entwicklung des hannoversches Bauerntums von den Sachsenkämpfen bis zur Gegenwart. Hannover, C. V. Englehard. 1923. 187 p.

Thut, Isaak Noah, and Don Adams. Educational patterns in contemporary societies. New York, McGraw-Hill. 1964: 76-109. (Chapter on "German education: building a nation feeling.")

Tille, Alex. Die Geschichte der deutschen Weihnacht. Leipzig, E. Keil. 1893. 12, 355 p.

Tille, Alex. Yule and Christmas, their place in the Germanic year. London, D. Nutt. 1899. 218 p.

Treichel, A. Hochzeits-Gebräuche besonders aus Westpreussen . . . Z.f.E. 16 (1884): 105-133.

United States. Department of the Army. U.S. Army handbook for Germany. Department of the Army Pamphlet No. 550-29. Washington, Dept. of the Army, June 1960. 12, 955 p. (In particular, see pp. 1-474. Sociological background.)

Vagts, Alfred. The German army of the Second Reich as a cultural institution. In Caroline F. Ware, ed. The cultural approach to history. New York, Columbia University Press. 1940: 182-196.

Vogt, Friedrich Hermann T. Die schlesischen Weihnachtspiele. Leipzig, B.G. Teubner. 1901. 16, 500 p.

Wagner, E., and U. Planck. Jugend auf dem Land; Ergebnisse einer wissenschaftlichen Erhebung über die Lebenslage der westdeutschen Landjugend. München, Juvenate. 1957. 188 p.

Wähler, Martin. Thüringische Volkskunde. Jena, Diedrichs. 1940. 553 p.

Wähler, Martin, et al. Der deutsche Volkscharakter, eine Wesenskunde der deutschen Volksstämme und Volksschläge. Jena, Diedrichs. 1937. 559 p.

Walther, Paul. Schwäbische Volkskunde. Leipzig, Quelle & Meyer. 1929.
220 p., illus., 20 plates, map.

*Warren, Richard. Education in Rebhausen: a German village. New York,
Holt, Rinehart and Winston. 1967. 12, 114 p., plates.

Weber-Kellermann, I. Erntebrauch in der ländlichen Arbeitswelt des 19.
Jahrhunderts, auf Grund der Mannhardtbefragung in Deutschland von 1865.
Marburg, Elwert. 1965. 569 p.

Weismantel, Leo. Das alte Dorf. Die Geschichte seiner Jahres und der
Menschen, die in ihm gelebt haben. Berlin, Sebaldus. 1928. 453 p.

Wendt, R., ed. Bauernkultur in Mecklenburg. 1. Das Arbeitsgerät.
Schwerin, Statliches Museum, Volkskundliche Sammlungen. 1962. 107 p.,
illus.

Westfälische Forschungen. Mitteilungen des Provinzial-Instituts für Westfälische Landes- und Volkskunde in Münster im Westfälen. 1938--

Winter, H. Das Bürgerhaus zwischen Rhein, Main und Neckar. Tübingen,
Wasmuth. 1961. 306 p., illus.

Winterling, A. Die bäuerliche Lebens- und Sittengemeinschaft der hohen
Rhön. 1939. 199 p. Dissertation Köln.

Wirth, Alfred. Anhaltische Volkskunde. Dessau, Dünnhaupt. 1932. 8,
376 p.

Wossidlo, Richard. Mecklenburgische Volksüberlieferungen . . . 3 vols.
Wismar, Hinstorff's Verlag. 1897-1906. 34, 372; 13, 504; 9, 19, 453,
10 p.

Wossidlo, Richard. Aus dem Lande Fritz Reuters. Humor in Sprache und
Volkstum Mecklenburgs . . . Leipzig, O. Wigand. 1910. 211 p.

Wolf, Siegmund A. Wörterbuch des Rotwelschen; deutsche Gaunersprache.
Mannheim, Bibliographisches Institut. 1956. 432 p.

Wolf, Werner. Der Mond im deutschen Volksglauben. Bühl (Baden), Verlag
der Konkordia. 1929. 91 p.

*Wrede, Adam Joseph. Rheinische Volkskunde. Leipzig, Quelle & Meyer.
1919. 12, 237 p. (Second ed. Leipzig, Quelle & Meyer. 1922. 15, 363 p.)

*Wrede, Adam Joseph. Eifler Volkskunde. Bonn, Schroeder. 1922. 12, 294 p.

Wrede, Adam Joseph. Deutsche Volkskunde auf germanischer Grundlage. 2d ed.
Osterwieck Harz und Berlin, A. W. Zickfeldt. 1938. 228 p.

Wurzbacher, Gerhard. Das Dorf im Spannungsfeld industrieller Entwicklung. Untersuchung an den 45 Dörfern und Weilern einer westdeutschen ländlichen Gemeinde. Stuttgart, F. Enke. 1954. 12, 307 p.

Wüstenfeld, Karl. Eichsfelder Volkskunde. Volkskundliche Bilder vom Eichsfelde. Duderstadt, Mecke. 1919. 259 p.

Wüstenfeld, Karl. Eichsfelder Volksleben. Duderstadt, Mecke. 1921. 4, 259 p.

Wuttke, Robert. Sächsische Volkskunde. Dresden, F. Brandstetter. 1901. 578 p., 285 illus., 4 plates, map.

Wylie, I. A. R. The Germans. Indianapolis, Bobbs-Merrill. 1911. 361 p.

Zeitschrift des Vereins für rheinische und westfälische Volkskunde. 1904-- (Continued as: Westdeutsche Zeitschrift für Volkskunde. 1934-1936.)

Zeitschrift für Volkskunde. 1929-1940. (Issued from 1891-1928 as: Zeitschrift des Vereins für Volkskunde.)

Zender, Mathias. Volksmärchen und Schwänke aus der Westeifel. Bonn, Röhrscheid. 1935. 33, 171 p.

Zender, Mathias. Volkssagen der Westeifel. Bonn, Röhrscheid. 1935. 15, 372 p.

Zewe, Jakob. Sitte und Brauch im Saargebiet. Saarbrücken, Gebr. Hofer. 1924. 130 p.

Zimmermann, Walther. Badische Volksheilkunde. Karlsruhe, F. Müller. 1927. 110 p.

WENDS (SORBIANS)

Jarosch, Günther. Bibliographie zur sorbischen Volkskunde. Deutsches Jahrbuch für Volkskunde. 1 (1955): 376-403.

Jatzwauk, Jacob. Wendische (Sorbische) Bibliographie. Leipzig, in Kommission bei Market und Petters. 1929. 14, 353 p.

Młynk, Jurij. Sorbische Bibliographie, 1945-1957 (Serbska Bibliographie, 1945-1957). Deutsche Akademie der Wissenschaften zu Berlin, Schriftenreihe des Instituts für sorbische Volksforschung. 10. Budyšin, Domowina. 1959. 288 p.

Młynk, Jurij. Sorbische Bibliographie 1958-1965. Deutsche Akademie der Wissenschaften zu Berlin, Schriftenreihe des Instituts für Sorbische Volksforschung in Bautzen. 33. Budyšin, Domowina. 1968. 560 p.

Wajacsławk, Jacub (Jacub Jatzwauk). Serbska Bibliografija (Sorbische [Wendische] Bibliographie). Berichte über die Verhandlungen der Sächsischen Akademie der Wissenschaften zu Leipzig, Philologisch-historische Klasse. Band 98, heft 3. 2d improved ed. Berlin. 1952. 20, 500 p.

Andree, Richard. Wendische Wanderstudien. Stuttgart, J. Maier. 1874. 8, 191 p.

Boelcke, Willi. Bauer und Gutsherr in der Oberlausitz. Bautzen, Volkseigener Verlag Domowina. 1957. 315 p.

Brucher, H., et al. Die Sorben. Bautzen, Domowina. 1964. 235 p.

Charnock, R. S. The Wends of Bautzen. Anthropologia. 1 (1873-1875): 152-156. (London.)

Deutschmann, Eberhard. Lausitzer Holzbaukunst. Schriftenreihe des Instituts für sorbische Volksforschung. 11. Bautzen, Domowina. 1959. 184 p., illus.

Engerrand, George C. The so-called Wends of Germany and their colonies in Texas and Australia. University of Texas Bulletin No. 3417; Bureau of Research in the Social Sciences. Study No. 7. Austin. 1934. 179 p.

Gander, Karl. Volkskundliches aus dem Bereich der Viehzucht. Skizze aus dem Niederlausitzer Landleben. Globus. 72 (1897): 351-354.

Haupt, Leopold, and Jan Ernst Smoler (Schmaler). Pěsnički hornich a delnich Łužiskich Serbow—Volkslieder der Sorben in der Ober- und Niederlausitz. Anastatischer Neudruck der Ausgabe von 1841 und 1843. Deutsche Akademie der Wissenschaften zu Berlin. Veröffentlichungen der Kommission für Volkskunde. 3. 1953. 748 p., 6 illus.

WENDS (SORBIANS)

Institut za Serbski Ludospyt w Budyšinge. Lětopis, rjad C—Ludowěda. 1(1953)-- (Bautzen, Domowina.)

Krwc, Erich. Sorbische Volkstrachten. 3. Die Tracht der Sorben um Hoyerswerda. Bautzen, Domowina. 1959. 119 p., 70 illus.

Lücking, W. Die Lausitz sorbische Trachten. Berlin, Akademie-Verlag. 1956. 124 p., illus., 118 plates, 4 col. plates.

Meškank, Jan. Sorbische Volkstrachten. 2. Bautzen, Domowina. 1957. 129 p., 72 illus. (Catholic Sorbians.)

*Musiat, Siegmund. Zur Lebensweise des landwirtschaftlichen Gesindes in der Oberlausitz. Schriftenreihe des Instituts für sorbische Volksforschung, Band 22. Bautzen, Domowina. 1964. 180 p.

Nedo, Paul. Sorbische Volkstrachten. Bautzen, Domowina. 1954. 47 p., illus.

Nedo, Paul. Sorbische Volksmärchen. Systematische Quellenausgabe mit Einführung und Anmerkungen. Bautzen, Domowina. 1956. 9, 447 p.

Nowak-Njechornski, Měrćin. Sorbische Volkstrachten. 1. Bautzen, Domowina. 1954. 118 p., 65 illus. (Schleife district.)

Nowak-Njechornski, Měrćin. Der sorbische Volksmaler. Bautzen, Domowina. 1959. 148 p., illus.

Nowak-Njechornski, Měrćin. Die Tracht der Niederlausitzer Sorben. Bautzer Domowina. 1964. 64 p., illus.

Nowak-Njechornski, Měrćin. Sorbische Volkstrachten 4. Bautzen, Domowina 1965. 150 p., 86 illus. (Lower Lausitz.)

Páta, Josef. Aus dem kulturellen Leben der Lausitzer Serben nach dem Weltkriege. (Translated from the Czech.) Bautzen, Schmalers. 1930. 64 p.

Phalipau, M. de Vaux. Une Hollande slave. La vie dans les Blota de Lusace. L'Ethnographie. New series. 15-16(1927): 37-47.

Rauch, Walter J. Presse und Volkstum der Lausitzer Sorben. Marburger Ostforschungen. Bd. 9. Würzburg, Holzner Verlag. 1959. 11, 198 p.

Raupp, J. Sorbische Volksmusikanten und Musikinstrumente. Bautzen, Domowina. 1963. 247 p., illus.

Retzlaff, Hans. Osterbräuche in der wendischen Lausitz. Atlantis. 5(1933): 248-251.

WENDS (SORBIANS)

Schmidt, Otto Eduard. Les Wendes. Paris, A. Delpeuch. 1929. 191 p.,
   12 plates.

Schmidt-Kovar. Sorbische Ostereier. Bautzen, Domowina. 1965. 32 p.,
   illus.

*Schneeweis, Edmund. Feste und Volksbräuche der Lausitzer Wenden, . . .
   Veröffentlichungen des Slavischen Instituts an der Friedrich-Wilhelms-
   Universität Berlin, 4. Leipzig. 1931. 8, 251 p., 14 plates.

*Schneeweis, Edmund. Feste und Volksbräuche der Sorben. Deutsche Akademie
   der Wissenschaften zu Berlin. Veröffentlichungen des Instituts für Slawistik.
   Nr. 3. Berlin, Akademie-Verlag. 1953. 8, 186 p.

Schulenburg, W. von. Wendische Volkssagen und Gebräuche aus dem
   Spreewald. Leipzig, F. A. Brockhaus. 1880. 29, 312 p.

Simpich, F. The Wends of the Spreewald. National Geographic Magazine.
   43 (1923): 327-336.

*Tetzner, Franz. Die Slawen in Deutschland: . . . Braunschweig, F. Vieweg
   und Sohn. 1902: 282-344, illus.

Tetzner, Franz. Die Slowinzen und Lebakaschuben: Land und Leute, Haus
   and Hof, Sitten und Gebräuche . . . Berlin, E. Felber. 1899. 8, 272 p.

Vogel, Werner. Der Verblieb der wendischen Bevölkerung in der Mark
   Brandenburg. Berlin, Duncker und Humblot. 1960. 15 p.

Weinhold, R. Töpferhandwerk in der Oberlausitz. Berlin, Akademie-Verlag.
   1958. 200 p.

*Tetzner, Franz.   Die Slawen in Deutschland.   Braunschweig, F.   Vieweg und Sohn.   1902: 346-387.

Schwebe, J. Volksglaube und Volksbrauch um hannoverischen Wendland. Köln und Graz, Böhlau. 1960. 8, 272 p.

SWISS (FRENCH, GERMAN, AND ITALIAN)

Wildhaber, Robert. Bibliographie der wichtigsten volkskundlichen Arbeiten
der Schweiz aus den Jahren 1945-bis Mitte 1955. Deutsches Jahrbuch für
Volkskunde. 2(1956): 333-358.

Anastasi, Giovanni. Tessiner Leben. Zürich, Orel Füssli. 1915. 92 p.

Bächtold-Stäubli, Hanns. Die Gebräuche bei Verlobung und Hochzeit. Mit
besonderer Berücksichtigung der Schweiz. Basel, Schweizerische Gesellschaft für Volkskunde. 1914. 7, 328 p.

Balmer, Emil. Die Walser im Piemont. Vom Leben und von der Sprache der
deutschen Ansiedler hintern Monte Rosa. Bern, A. Francke. 1949. 239 p.,
plates.

Baud-Bovy, Daniel. Peasant art in Switzerland. London, The Studio. 1924.
24, 76 p., plates.

Baumberger, Georg. St. Galler Land, St. Galler Volk. Einsiedeln, Bensiger.
1903. 207 p., 19 figs., 14 plates.

Beretta-Piccoli, Maria. Die Bennung der weiblichen Kopftracht des Landvolks
der deutschen Schweiz. Basel, Schweizerische Gesellschaft für Volkskunde.
1936. 109 p.

Biermann, Charles. L'habitat rural en Suisse. Bulletin de la Société Neuchâteloise de Géographie. 41(1932): 5-40, map.

Biermann, Charles. La maison paysanne vaudoise. Lausanne, F. Rouge. 1946.
231 p., 12 maps, 17 plates, 29 illus.

Binder, Gottlieb. Aus dem Volksleben des Zürcher Unterlandes. S. A. f. V.
25(1925): 91-124, 197-228, 241-256; 26(1926): 30-46, 101-123, 188-201.

Binder, Gottlieb. Aus dem Volksleben des züricher Unterlandes. Basel,
Helbing und Lichtenhahn. 1925. 4, 2, 134 p.

Boettcher, P. Das Tessintal. Versuch einer länderkundlichen Darstellung.
Aarau, Graphische Werkstätten von H. P. Sauerländer. 1936. 8, 280 p.

Brandstetter, Renward. Renward Cysat (1545-1614). Der Begründer der
schweizerischen Volkskunde. Luzern, Haag. 1909. 110 p.

Braun, Rudolf. Industrialisierung und Volksleben. Bd. 1. Die Veränderungen
der Lebensformen in einem ländlichen Industriegebiet vor 1800 (Zürich-
Oberland). Erlenbach-Zürich, E. Rentsch. 1960. 287 p.

*Brockmann-Jerosch, Heinrich. Schweizer Volksleben. Sitten, Bräuche,
Wohnstätten. 2 vols. Zürich, E. Rentsch. 1929-1931. 4, 120 p.,
plates; 4, 144 p., plates.

*Brockmann-Jerosch, Heinrich. La terre helvétique, ses moeurs, ses coutumes, ses habitations; par le texte et par l'image. 2 vols. Neuchâtel, Éditions de la Baconnière. 1930-1931. (A translation of the preceding entry.)

Brockmann-Jerosch, Heinrich. Schweizer Bauernhaus. Bern, H. Huber. 1933. 8, 249 p.

Brooks, Robert Clarkson. Civic training in Switzerland. Chicago, University of Chicago Press. 1930. 21, 436 p.

Bruckner, Wilhelm. Schweizerische Ortsnamenkunde. Eine Einführung. Basel, Schweizerische Gesellschaft für Volkskunde. 1945. 232 p.

Buhler, Kristine. Swiss folk art. Basel, Amerbach Publishing Co. 1947. 16 p., 28 plates.

Burchardt, H. Zur Psychologie der Erlebnissage. Zürich, Juris Verlag. 1951. 110 p.

Burchardt, H. Schweizer Winterbräuche. Atlantis. 29(1957): 41-50.

Burckhardt, Titus. Tessin. Das Volkserbe der Schweiz. Bd. 1. Basel, Urs Graf Verlag. 1943. 123 p.

Burdet, Jacques. La danse populaire dans le pays de Vaud sous le régime bernois. Bâle, G. Krebs. 1957. 207 p.

Büren, Kurt von. Die Rovanatäler. Ein Beitrag zur wirtschaftsund Siedlungs- geographie des Tessins. Geographica Helvetica. 8 (1953): 69-186.

Caduff, Gian. Die Knabenschaften Graubündens. Chur, Sprecher, Eggerling. 1932. 4, 8, 256 p.

Chevallaz, Georges André. Aspects de l'agriculture vaudoise à la fin de l'ancien régime. Bibliothèque Historique Vaudois. 9. Lausanne, F. Rouge. 1949. 272 p., 7 maps.

Confrérie des Vignerons de Vevey. La louable Confrérie: les fêtes des vignerons de Vevey (1647-1955). Lausanne, Éditions Hermès. 1956. 372 p.

Cooper, James Fenimore. Excursions in Switzerland. 2 vols. London, R. Bentley. 1836.

Curti, Notker. Im Bündner Oberland; Land und Leute der Cadi. Luzern, Räber. 1940. 182 p. (Disentis, Switzerland.)

Curti, Notker. Volksbrauch und Volksfrömmigkeit im katholischen Kirchen- jahr. Basel, G. Krebs. 1947. 8, 151 p., 24 plates.

SWISS (FRENCH, GERMAN, AND ITALIAN)

Dawson, William Harbutt. Social Switzerland; studies of present-day social movements and legislation in the Swiss republic. London, Chapman & Hall. 1897. 10, 301 p.

Dorschner, Fritz. Das Brot und seine Herstellung in Graubünden und Tessin. Winterthur, Buchdruckerei Winterthur. 1936. 204 p.

Egli, Emil. Swiss life and landscape. London, Paul Elek. 1949. 160 p.

Erickson, Franklin Carl. Schächenthal: a regional study of a Swiss alpine valley. Clark University, Worcester, Mass. 1935. (Unpublished Ph.D. dissertation in Geography.)

Escher, Walter. Dorfgemeinschaft und Silvestersingen in St. Antönien. Basel, G. Krebs. 1947. 12, 138 p.

Escher, Walter. Das schweizerische Hirtenland. S.A.f.V. 60 (1964): 58-72.

Feierabend, M. A. Über Volksfeste und Volksspiele im Kanton Luzern. Abhandlungen vorgetragen . . . den 29. Juni 1843. Luzern Verhandlungen der Gesellschaft für Vaterländische Kultur im Kanton Luzern. 1843: 85-164.

Ferriere, Maud Trube. Swiss textiles. Leigh-on-Sea (England), F. Lewis. 1953. 20 p., 95 plates.

Fischer, Albin. Religiöse Bräuche des katholischen Aargauervolkes. In Erbe und Auftrag; Festgabe zum Aargauischen Katholikentag im Jubiläumsjahr 1953. Baden, Buchdruckerei Baden. 1953: 347-377, illus., 2 plates.

Fuller, G. J. Saignelegier and the Franches Montagnes district of the Bernese Jura. Nottingham, Geographical Field Group, University of Nottingham. 1957. 50 p., 23 figs.

Gabbud, Maurice. Les traditions valaisanners. Lausanne, A. Dupuis. 1917. 48 p.

Gargaty, T. J. The "Betruf" of the Swiss alps. J.A.F.L. 73(1960): 60-63.

Gassmann, Alfred Leon. Das Volkslied im Luzerner Wiggertal und Hinterland. Mit Melodien. Basel, Schweizerische Gesellschaft für Volkskunde. 1906. 10, 215 p.

Gassmann, Alfred Leon. Zur Tonpsychologie des schweizer Volkslieds. Zürich, Hug. 1936. 141 p.

Geiger, Paul, ed. Kleine Schriften zur Volkskunde von Eduard Hoffmann-Krayer. Basel, Buchdruckerei G. Krebs. 1946. 18, 249 p.

Geiger, Paul, and Richard Weiss. Atlas der schweizerischen Volkskunde. Atlas de folklore suisse. Basel, Schweizerische Gesellschaft für Volkskunde. 1950--

Giese, Wilhelm. Uber die Bewahrung volkstümlicher Eigenart in den rätoromanischen Tälern Graubündens. Basel, privately printed. 1953. 34 p., 3 illus.

Gillieron, R. Mein Dorf. Volkskunde von Pfeffingen. Aesch, Volksdruckerei. 1953. 69 p.

Goethe, Johann Wolfgang von. Letters from Switzerland; letters from Italy. Boston, F. A. Niccolls. 1902. 461 p.

Goldstern, E. Hochbirgsvolk in Savoyen und Graubünden. Ein Beitrag zur romanischen Volkskunde. Wien, Verlag des Vereins für Volkskunde. 1922. 114 p., 28 plates.

Greverus, I. M. Heimweh und Tradition. S. A. f. V. 61 (1965): 1-31.

Grolimund, Sigmund. Volkslieder aus dem Kanton Solothurn. Basel, Schweizerische Gesellschaft für Volkskunde. 1910. 6, 111 p.

Grolimund, Sigmund. Volkslieder aus dem Kanton Aargau. Basel, Schweizerische Gesellschaft für Volkskunde. 1911. 6, 279 p.

Gruber, Otto. Bauernhäuser am Bodensee. Koustany Lindau, Thorbecke. 1961. 137 p., illus.

Gschwend, Max. Das Val Verzasca (Tessin). Seine Bevölkerung, Wirtschaft und Siedlung. Aarau, Sauerländ. 1946. 8, 240 p.

Gschwend, Max. Ostschweizer Bauernhäuser. Schweizer Volkskunde. 45 (1955): 17-23.

Gschwend, Max. Schwyzer Bauernhäuser. Schweizer Heimatbucher, 81. Bern, Verlag Paul Haupt. 1957. 60 p., illus.

Gutkind, Erwin Anton. Urban development in Alpine and Scandinavian countries. New York, The Free Press of Glencoe. 1965. 491 p.

Gyr, Martin. Einsiedler Volksbräuche. Einsiedeln, Buchdruckerei "Neue Einsiedlerzeitung." 1935. 4, 2, 176 [118] p.

Gyr, Martin. La vie rurale et alpestre du Val d'Anniviers. Winterthur, Romanica Helvetica. 1942. 44, 52 p.

Gysling, Fr. Hochzeitsbräuche aus Rima (Piemont). S. A. f. V. 49 (1953): 16-33.

SWISS (FRENCH, GERMAN, AND ITALIAN)

Heierli, Julie. Die Volkstrachten der Schweiz. 5 vols. Erlenbach-Zürich,
E. Rentsch. 1922-1932. 688 p., 61 col. plates, 71 half-tone plates,
982 illus.

Heim, Walter. Briefe zum Himmel. Die Grabbriefe an Mutter M. Theresia
Scherer in Ingenbohl. Ein Beitrag zur religiösen Volkskunde der Gegenwart.
Basel, G. Krebs. 1961. 1414 p.

Herzog, Hans. Schweizersagen. Für Jung und Alt dargestellt. Aarau. 1882.
4, 239 p.

Herzog, Hans. Schweizersagen . . . Erste Sammlung. Aarau. 1887. 8,
224 p.

Herzog, Heinrich. Schweizerische Volksfeste, Sitten und Gebräuche. Aarau,
Sauerländer. 1884. 10, 326 p.

*Hoffman-Krayer, Eduard. Feste und Bräuche des Schweizervolkes. Zürich,
Atlantis-Verlag. 1940. 192 p.

Hoffman-Krayer, Eduard. Kleine Schriften zur Volkskunde. Mit einem
Lebensbild. Herausgegeben von Paul Geiger. Basel, Buchdruckerei G. Krebs.
1946. 18, 248 p.

Hösli, Jost. Glarner Land- und Alpwirtschaft in Vergangenheit und Gegenwart.
Glarus, Tschudi. 1948. 10, 358 p., 36 illus., tables, maps.

Howells, William Dean. A little Swiss sojourn. New York, Harper. 1892. 119 p.

Hugger, Paul. Amden. Eine volkskundliche Monographie. Basel, Schweizerische Gesellschaft für Volkskunde. 1961. 224 p.

Hugger, Paul. Werdenberg, Land im Umbruch; eine volkskundliche Monographie. Basel, G. Krebs for the Schweizerische Gesellschaft für Volkskunde.
1964. 193 p.

Hunziker, Jakob. Schweiz. Mit einer Sprachenkarte. München, J. F. Lehmann.
1898. 63 p.

Hunziker, Jakob. Das Schweizerhaus nach seinen landschaftlichen Formen und
seiner geschichtlichen Entwicklung. 8 vols. Aarau. 1900-1914.

Jacobeit, Wolfgang. Schafhaltung und Schäfer in Zentraleuropa bis zum Beginn
des 20. Jahrhunderts. Berlin, Akademie-Verlag. 1961. 15, 604 p., plates.

Jegerlehner, Johann. Sagen aus dem Unterwallis. Basel, Schweizerische
Gesellschaft für Volkskunde. 1909. 196 p.

Jegerlehner, Johann. Sagen und Märchen aus dem Oberwallis. Mit Register . . .
Basel, Schweizerische Gesellschaft für Volkskunde. 1913. 12, 348 p.

Jegerlehner, Johann. Günters Schweizerreise. Köln, H. Schaffstein. 1927. 211 p.

Jörger, Johann. Bei den Walsern des Valsertales. 2d ed. Basel, Buchdruckerei G. Krebs. 1947. 127 p., 29 illus.

Kern, Walter. Graubünden. 2 vols. 1. Die Täler des Rheins und ihre Umwelt. 2. Das Engadin, die Umwelt des Inn und der Süden. Basel, Urs Graf Verlag. 1944, 1946.

Knuchel, Eduard Fritz. Die Umwandlung in Kult, Magie und Rechtsbrauch. Basel, Schweizerische Gesellschaft für Volkskunde. 1919. 8, 116 p.

Könz, I. U. Das engadiner Haus. Bern, Paul Haupt. 1952. 32 p., 64 p. of illus. and plates.

Krebs, Werner. Alte Handwerksbräuche. Basel, Schweizerische Gesellschaft für Volkskunde. 1933. 8, 314 p.

Krömler, Hans. Der Kult der Eucharistie in Sprache und Volkstum der deutschen Schweiz. Basel, G. Krebs. 1949. 167 p.

Lauer, Ernst. Der schweizer Bauer, seine Heimat und sein Werk . . . Bern, Verbandsdruckerei. 1947. 16, 808 p.

Loessi, Henri. Der Sprichwortschatz des Engadins. Zürich, E. Lang. 1943. 24, 71 p.

Lorez, Christian. Bauernarbeit im Rheinwald, Landwirtschaftliche Methoden und Geräte und ihre Terminologie in der ältesten urkundlich belegeten Walserkolonie Bündens. Basel, Schweizerische Gesellschaft für Volkskunde. 1942. 11, 154 p.

Lovey-Troillet, Ernest. Le val Ferret. Neuchâtel and Paris, Victor Attinger. 1946. 191 p., 30 illus.

Maissen, Alfons. Werkzeuge und Arbeitsmethoden des Holzhandwerks in Romanischen-Bünden. Romanica Helvetica. 17. Geneva and Zürich. 1943. 58, 227 p.

Maissen, Alfons, Andrea Schorter, and Werner Wehrli. Die Lieder der Consolaziun dell'olma devoziusa. 2 parts. Basel, Schweizerische Gesellschaft für Volkskunde. 1945.

Manz, Werner. Volksbrauch und Volksglaube des Sarganserlandes. Basel, Schweizerische Gesellschaft für Volkskunde. 1916. 12, 162 p.

Masken der Schweiz und Europas. Basel, Schweizerische Gesellschaft für Volkskunde. 1960. 20 p., illus.

Medici, Mario. Le processioni della Settimana Santa a Mendrisio. Mendrisio, C. Stucchi. 1946. 52 p.

Messikommer, H. Aus alter Zeit. Sitten und Gebräuche im Züricher Oberlande. Ein Beitrag zur Volkskunde. Zürich: Orel Füssli. 1909-1911. 200 p.

Meuli, Karl. Schweizer Masken. Mit einer Einleitung über schweizerische Maskenbräuche und Maskenschnitzer. Zürich, Atlantis-Verlag. 1943. 163 p., 60 plates.

Meuli, Karl. Heimat und Humanität. Festschrift für Karl Meuli zum 60. Geburtstag. Basel, S.A.f.V. 47. 1951. 10, 291 p.

Mühll, Johanna von der. Basler Sitten. Herkommen und Brauch im häuslichen Leben einer städtischen Bürgerschaft. Basel, Helbing Lichtenhahn. 1944. 4, 212 p.

Müller, Iso. Die churrätische Wallfahrt im Mittelalter; ein Überblick. Basel, Schweizerische Gesellschaft für Volkskunde. 1964. 7, 112 p.

Niederer, Arnold. Gemeinwerk im Wallis. Bäuerliche Gemeinschaftsarbeit in Vergangenheit und Gegenwart. Basel, G. Krebs. 1956. 91 p.

Patterson, Mrs. Susanna Louise. When I was a girl in Switzerland. Boston, Lee & Shepard. 1921. 232 p.

Pellandini, Vittore. Usi e costumi de Bedano (Ticino): . . . S.A.f.V. 8(1904): 241-267.

Pellandini, Vittore. Tradizioni popolari Ticinesi. Lugano, Grassi. 1911. 16, 180 p.

Piguet, Edgar. L'évolution de la pastourelle du XIIe siècle à nos jours. Bâle, Société Suisse des Traditions Populaires. 1927. 207 p.

Rothenbach, Jakob Emil. Volkstümliches aus dem Kanton Bern. Zürich, Cäsar Schmidt. 1876. 82 p.

Rubattel, R. La petite propriété paysanne dans le canton de Vaud. Lausanne, Chambre vaudoise d'Agriculture. 1959. 129 p.

Rütimeyer, L. Beiträge zur schweizerischen Ethnographie. Ueber einige altertümliche Gebräuche bei der Verarbeitung der Cerealien und Kastanien zur menschlichen Nahrung im Kanton Tessin. Archives Suisses d'Anthropologie Générale. 2(1918): 229-249.

Scheuermeier, Paul. Bauernwerk in Italien, der italienischen und rätoromanischen Schweiz. 2 vols. Vol. 1. Erlenbach-Zürich, E. Rentsch. 1943. Vol. 2. Bern, Stämpfli. 1956. 4, 16, 319 p.; 16, 529 p.

Schmid, Heinrich. Die Oberengadiner Land- und Alpwirtschaft. Winterthur, P. G. Keller. 1955. 157 p., illus., maps, plates.

Schmolke-Mellwig, M. Das Wirtschaftsleben eines Hochgebirgsortes im romanischen Wallis (Evolène, Eringertal). Volkstum und Kultur der Romanen. 15(1942): 1-146.

Schriften der Schweizerischen Gesellschaft für Volkskunde. 1 (1902)--

Schweizer Volkskunde. Basel Schweizerische Gesellschaft für Volkskunde. 1 (1911)--

Schweizerische Archiv für Volkskunde. Zürich und Basel, Schweizerische Gesellschaft für Volkskunde. 1 (1897)--

Senn, Ulrich. Die Alpwirtschaft der Landschaft Davos. Geographica Helvetica. 7(1952): 265-350, illus., maps, tables.

Senn, Walter. Charakterbilder schweizerischen Landes, Lebens und Strebens. 2 vols. Glarus, Senn und Stricker. 1870-1871. 375 p. (Reprinted: St. Gallen, Schweizer Verlagsanstalt. 1883-1884. 275 p.)

Sooder, Melchior. Bienen und Bienenhalten in der Schweiz. Basel, G. Krebs. 1952. 341 p., 23 plates.

Sooder, Melchior. Habkern; Tal und Leute, Sagen, Überlieferungen und Brauchtum. Basel, G. Krebs. 1964. 158 p.

Stebler, F. G. Das Goms und die Gomser. Zürich, Schweizer Alpenclub Jahrbuch 38. 1903. 8, 112 p.

Stoffel, Johann Rudolf. Das Hochtal Avers, Graubünden. Die höchstgelegene Gemeinde Europas. 3d ed. Zofingen, Zofinger Tagblatt. 1948. 10, 263 p., 24 plates.

*Story, Alfred Thomas. Swiss life in town and country. New York and London, G. P. Putnam's Sons. 1902. 7, 282 p., plates.

Strübin, Eduard. Baselbieter Volksleben. Sitte und Brauch im Kulturwandel der Gegenwart. Basel, Schweizerische Gesellschaft für Volkskunde. 1952. 296 p., 19 plates, map.

Strübin, Eduard. Grundfragen des Volkslebens bei Jeremias Gotthelf. Basel, Schweizerische Gesellschaft für Volkskunde. 1959. 97 p.

Symonds, John Addington, and Margaret Symonds. Our life in the Swiss highlands. Edinburgh, A. & C. Black. 1892. 10, 366 p.

Thuriet, Charles. Traditions populaires de la Haute Saône et du Jura. Paris, Lechevalier. 1892. 10, 652 p.

SWISS (FRENCH, GERMAN, AND ITALIAN)

Thurnheer, E. Leben und Wirken der Bergbauern im Taminatal. 1948.
335 p. (Dissertation, Handelshochschule St. Gallen. Also published at
Zürich, Buchdruckerei Fluntern. 1948.)

Tobler, Alfred. Kühreihen oder Kühreigen, Jodel und Jodellied in Appenzell.
Leipzig, Gebrüder Hug. 1890. 82 p.

Tobler, Alfred. Das Volkslied im Appenzellerlande. Zürich, Schweizerische
Gesellschaft für Volkskunde. 1903. 147 p.

Tognina, R. Lingua e cultura della valle di Poschiavo. Basel, Schweizerische
Gesellschaft für Volkskunde. 1967. 407 p., 124 figs., 111 photos.

Tomamichel, Tobias. Bosco Gurin. Das Walserdorf im Tessin. Basel,
G. Krebs. 1953. 155 p.

Volkstum der Schweiz. Basel, Schweizerische Gesellschaft für Volkskunde.
Bd. 1/2 (1941)--

Wackernagel, Hans Georg. Altes Volkstum der Schweiz. Gesammelte
Schriften zur historischen Volkskunde. Basel, G. Krebs. 1956. 326 p.

Weiss, Richard. Teildruck umfassend das 1. Kapital über "Alpbewirtschaftung
und Alpzubehör," aus dem Buch "Das Alpwesen Graubündens." Chur,
Bischofberger. 1941. 160 p.

Weiss, Richard. Das Alpwesen Graubündens; Wirtschaft, Sachkultur, Recht,
Älplerarbeit und Alplerleben; . . . Erlenbach-Zürich, E. Rentsch. 1941.
385 p., 57 plates, illus.

*Weiss, Richard. Volkskunde der Schweiz, Grundriss. Erlenbach-Zürich, E.
Rentsch. 1946. 23, 435 p.

*Weiss, Richard. Häuser und Landschaften der Schweiz. Erlenbach-Zürich,
E. Rentsch. 1959. 368 p., plates, illus.

Weiss, Richard. Alpiner Mensch und alpines Leben in der Krise der Gegenwart.
S. A. f. V. 58 (1962): 232-254.

Weiss, Richard, Paul Geiger, et al. Atlas der schweizerischen Volkskunde.
Erlenbach-Zürich, E. Rentsch for the Schweizerische Gesellschaft für
Volkskunde. 1950--

Weiss, Richard, Paul Geiger, et al. Die Brünig-Napf-Reuss-Linie als Kultur-
grenze zwischen Ost- und Westschweiz auf volkskundlichen Karten. S. A. f. V.
58 (1962): 201-231.

Weiss, Richard, Paul Geiger, et al. Landschaft und Volksart (im Kanton
Zürich). S. A. f. V. 58 (1962): 255-268.

Weiss, Richard, Paul Geiger, et al. Drei Beiträge zur Volkskunde der Schweiz. Erlenbach-Zürich, E. Rentsch. 1963. 96 p.

Wilckens, Martin. Die Alpenwirthschaft der Schweiz, des Algäus und der westösterreichischen Alpenländer. Wien, Braunmüller. 1874. 8, 387 p.

Wildhaber, Robert. Schneckenzucht und Schneckenspeise. S. A. f. V. 46 (1950): 119-184.

Wiora, Walter. Zur Frühgeschichte der Musik in den Alpenländern. Basel, Schweizerische Gesellschaft für Volkskunde. 1949. 68 p.

Witzig, Louise. Dances of Switzerland. New York, Chanticleer Press. 1949. 40 p., 7 plates.

Witzig, Louise. Schweizer Trachtenbuch. Zürich, Schweizerische Trachtenverein. 1954. 279 p., plates, illus.

Zahler, Hans. Die Krankheit in Volksglauben des Simmenthals. Ein Beitrag zur Ethnographie des Berner Oberlands. Arbeiten aus dem Geographischen Institut der Universität Bern. 4. Bern, Hallersche Buchdruckerei. 1898. 140 p.

Zeugin, E. Pratteln. Beiträge zur Kulturgeschichte eines Bauerndorfs (1525-1900). Liestal, for the author. 1954. 214 p., illus.

Zoppi, Giuseppe. Mein Tessin. Zürich und Leipzig, Rascher. 1941. 235 p.

Züricher, Gertrud. Kinderlied und Kinderspiel im Kanton Bern. Zürich, Schweizerische Gesellschaft für Volkskunde. 1902. 168 p.

Züricher, Gertrud. Kinderlieder der deutschen Schweiz. Basel, Schweizerisch Gesellschaft für Volkskunde. 1926. 16, 599 p.

Alton, Johann. Beiträge zur Ethnologie von Ostladinien. Innsbruck, Wagner. 1880. 68 p.

Aronco, G. D. Il Friuli, aspetti etnografici. Udine. Camera di Commercio, Industria e Agricultura. 1965. 129 p.

Battisti, Carlo. Popoli e lingue nell'alto Adige; studi sulla latinità altoatesina. Firenze, R. Bemporad & Figlio. 1931. 11, 401 p.

Baumer, Iso. Rätoromanische Krankheitsnamen. Romanica Helvetica. 72. Bern, Francke Verlag. 1962. 202 p.

Brandstetter, Renward. Rätoromanische Forschungen. 1. Luzern, E. Haag. 1905. 85 p.

Brunialti, Attilio. L'Alto Adige, l'Ampezzano e il territorio di Sesto. Torino, Unione Tipografica Editrice Torinese. 1919. 188 p., 5 plates.

Dami, Aldo. Die Rätoromanen. Jahrbuch des Vorarlberger Landesmuseums-vereins. 1962. (1963): 37-50, map, 2 figs.

Decurtins, Caspar, ed. Rätoromanische Chrestomathie. 12 vols. Erlangen, F. Junge. 1896-1919.

Giese, Wilhelm. Über die Bewahrung volkstümlicher Eigenart in den räto-romanischen Tälern Graubündens. Basel, privately printed. 1953. 34 p., 3 illus.

Keller, Oscar. La boucherie à domicile dans la Suisse romande. S. A. f. V. 43 (1946): 561-587.

Kern, Walter. Graubünden. Bd. 1. Das Engadin, die Umwelt des Inn und der Süden. Basel, Urs Graf Verlag. 1944. 133 p.

Könz, I. U. Das Engadiner Haus. Bern, Paul Haupt. 1952. 32 p., 64 p. of illus.

Leonhardi, Georg. Rhätische Sitten und Bräuche. St. Gallen, Scheitlin & Zollikofer. 1844. 60 p.

Richter-Santifaller, Berta. Die Ortsnamen von Ladinien. Innsbruck, Wagner Verlag. 1937. 41, 291 p.

Scheuermeier, Paul. Bauernwerk in Italien, der italienischen und rätoroman-ischen Schweiz. 2 vols. Vol. 1. Erlenbach-Zürich, E. Rentsch. 1943. Vol. 2. Bern, Stämpfli. 1956. 4, 16, 319; 16, 529 p.

LIECHTENSTEIN

Dommer, Hermann. Die wirtschaftliche Entwicklung des Fürstentums
   Liechtenstein unter spezieller Berücksichtigung der gegenwärtigen Verhältnisse der Landwirtschaft. Vaduz. 1954. 96 p., folding map.

Heer, Jakob Christoph. Vorarlberg und Liechtenstein, Land und Leute. Feld-
   kirch (Vorarlberg), F. Unterberger. 1906. 4, 194 p., illus.

Krätzl, Franz. Liechtenstein. Brünn, C. Winkler. 1914. 8, 383 p.

Raton, Pierre. Les institutions de la principauté de Liechtenstein. Paris,
   Recueil Sirey. 1949. 254 p., map.

Rath, E. Die wichtigsten Neuerscheinungen zur Volkskunde Österreichs aus den Jahren 1945-1954. Deutsches Jahrbuch für Volkskunde. 1 (1955): 404-413.

Strassmayr, Eduard. Bibliographie zur oberösterreichischen Geschichte. 4 vols. Linz an der Donau, Winkler. 1929-1957.

Aitken, B. A country wedding in Austria, 1948. Folk-Lore. 62(1951): 458-463.

Andree-Eysin, Marie. Volkskundliches. Aus dem bayrisch-österreichischen Alpengebiet. Braunschweig, F. Vieweg & Sohn. 1910. 274 p., 225 illus.

Bein, Leopold. Beitrag zur Kenntnis des obersteirischen Haus- und Ackergerätes und zum Steirischen Wortschatz. M.A.G.W. 44(1914): 165-221.

Benyovsky, Karoly, ed. Die alten Pressburger Volksschauspiele "Christgeburtspiel." . . . Bratislawa-Pressburg, S. Steiner. 1934. 70 p.

Berger, H. Formen des Almwesens in den östlichen Karnischen Alpen. Mitteilungen der Geographischen Gesellschaft in Wien. 98(1956): 29-42.

Bertrand de Moleville, Antoine François. The costume of the hereditary states of the house of Austria, displayed in fifty colored engravings, with descriptions and an introduction. London, W. Bulmer. 1804. 3, 28(100) p., 50 col. plates.

Blum, Jerome. Noble landowners and agriculture in Austria, 1815-1848; a study of the origins of the peasant emancipation of 1848. Baltimore, Johns Hopkins Press. 1948. 295 p.

Brauner, Franz, ed. Steirisches Brauchtum im Jahrlauf. Graz, Leykam Pädagogischer Verlag. 1955. 136 p.

Breuer, Katherine. Dances of Austria. New York, Chanticleer Press. 1949. 30 p., 7 col. plates.

Brion, Marcel. Daily life in the Vienna at the time of Mozart and Schubert. New York, Macmillan. 1962. 288 p.

Buchinger, Josef. Bodenständige Naturkunde: unsere Bäume und Sträucher im Heimat- und Volksleben. Wien, Österreichischer Bundesverlag für Unterricht, Wissenschaft und Kunst. 1950. 196 p.

Buchinger, Josef. Der Bauer in der Kultur- und Wirtschaftsgeschichte Österreichs. Wien, Österreichischer Bundesverlag für Unterricht, Wissenschaft und Kunst. 1952. 471 p.

Bünker, J. R. Das Bauernhaus in der östlichen Mittelsteiermark und in benachbarten Gebieten. M. A. G. W. 27 (1897): 113-191, 55 illus., plans.

Bünker, J. R. Das Bauernhaus am Millstätter in Kärnten. M. A. G. W. 32 (1902): 12-103, 239-273, illus., plans.

Bünker, J. R. Windische Fluren und Bauernhäuser aus dem Gailtale in Kärnten. M. A. G. W. 35 (1905): 1-37, 39 illus.

Bünker, J. R. Dorffluren und Bauernhäuser im Lungau (Herzogtum Salzburg). M. A. G. W. 39 (1909): 66-86, 178-209, 37 illus.

Bünker, J. R. Das Bauernhaus der Gegend von Köflach in Steiermark. Wörter und Sachen. 3 (1911): 121-163, illus.

Burgstaller, Ernst. Met im oberösterreichischen Brauchtum. Oberösterreichische Heimatblätter. 10 (1956): 85-92.

Burgstaller, Ernst. Die bäuerlichen Burschenschaften in Oberösterreich. International Congress of Anthropological and Ethnological Sciences, 4th, Vienna, 1952. Actes. 3 (1956): pp. 101-111.

Burgstaller, Ernst. Gelegter Zauber. Carinthia Geschichte und Volkskundliche Beiträge zur Heimatkunde Kärntens. 147 (1957): 853-862.

Burgstaller, Ernst. Österreichisches Festtagsgebäck. Wien, Bundesinnung der Bäcker. 1958. 233 p., 35 plates, maps.

Byloff, Fritz. Das Verbrechen der Zauberei-Crimen magiae. Ein Beitrag zur Geschichte der Strafenpflege in Steiermark. Graz, Leuschner & Lubensky. 1902. 440 p.

Byloff, Fritz. Volkskundliches aus Strafprozessen der österreichischen Alpenländer, mit besonderer Berücksichtigung der Zauberei- und Hexenprozesse 1455 bis 1850. Quellen zur deutschen Volkskunde 3. Berlin und Leipzig, Walter de Gruyter. 1929. 68 p.

Byloff, Fritz. Hexenglaube und Hexenverfolgung in den österreichischen Alpenländern. Quellen zur deutschen Volkskunde 6. Berlin und Leipzig, Walter d Gruyter. 1934. 11, 194 p.

Christian, Victor. Volkskundliches aus dem Montafon (Vorarlberg). M. A. G. W. 52 (1922): 165-172.

Commenda, Hans. Volkskunde der Stadt Linz an der Donau. 2 vols. Linz, Kulturamt der Stadt. 1958-1959.

Czörnig von Czernhausen, Karl. Ethnographie der Österreichischen Monarchie. 3 vols. Wien, K. K. Hof- und Staatsdruckerei. 1855-1857.

Dachler, Anton, and Michael Haberlandt. Das Bauernhaus in Österreich-Ungarn und in seinem Grenzgebiet. Wien, Österreichischer Ingenieur- und Architektenverein. 1906. 17, 288 p., 67 illus., 6 plates, 75 folio plates, map.

Depiny, Adalbert. Oberösterreichisches Sagenbuch. Linz, Pirngruber. 1932. 10, 481 p.

Dopsch, Alfons. Die ältere Wirtschafts- und Sozialgeschichte der Bauern in den Alpenländern Österreichs. Oslo, Instituttet for Sammenlignende Kulturforskning. 1930. 181 p., 4 maps.

Dörrer, Anton. Tiroler Fasnacht, innerhalb der alpenländischen Winter- und Vorfrühlingsbräuche. Österreichischer Volkskultur. 5. Wien, Österreichischer Bundesverlag. 1951. 480 p., 77 illus.

Le Duc de Bar (Otto Habsburg). Coutumes et droits successoraux de la classe paysanne et l'indivision de la classe paysanne et l'indivision de propriétés rurales en Autriche. Louvain, Académie Lovaniensis-École des Sciences Politiques et Sociales. 1935. 358 p.

Engelhardt, Gottfried. Christliche Kunst und religiöses Brauchtum im Wachszieher- und Lebzelterladen. Amstetten, S. Ramharter. 1957. 35 p.

Fischer, Rosa. Österreichisches Bauernleben, mit einer Vorrede von Peter Rosegger. Wien, J. Deubler. 1903. 4, 280 p., illus.

Fossel, Victor. Volksmedizin und medizinischer Aberglaube in Steiermark. Ein Beitrag zur Landeskunde. Graz, Leuschner & Lubensky. 1886. 6, 172 p.

Fresacher, Walther. Der Bauer in Kärnten. 2 vols. 1. Die persönliche Stellung des Bauers in Kärnten. 2. Das Freistiftrecht. Archiv für vaterländische Geschichte und Topographie, 31 and 39. Klagenfurt, Verlag des Geschichtsvereins. 1950, 1952. 176, 173 p.

Fuchs, H. M. Der Ackerbau im Sulmtal (Steiermark). Z.f.V. 3(1932): 113-141, illus.

Gayda, Virginio. Modern Austria. Her racial and social problems, with a study of Italia irredenta. New York, Dodd, Mead. 1915. 350 p.

Geramb, Victor. Von Volkstum und Heimat. Graz, U. Moser. 1919. 148 p.

Geramb, Victor. Deutsches Brauchtum in Österreich, ein Buch zur Kenntnis und der Pflege guter Sitten. Graz, Alpenland Buchhandlung, Südmark. 1924 3, 159 p., illus.

Geramb, Victor. Um Österreichs Volkskultur. Salzburg, O. Müller. 1946. 161 p.

Geramb, Victor. Kinder- und Hausmärchen aus der Steiermark. Graz, Buchverlag vormals Leykam. 1946. 298 p.

*Geramb, Victor. Sitte und Brauch in Österreich. 3d ed. Graz, Alpenland-Buchhandlung. 1948. 312 p.

Geramb, Victor. Die Rauchstuben im Lande Salzburg. Ein Beitrag zur Hausforschung der Ostalpenländer. Veröffentlichungen des Instituts für Volkskunde, Salzburg. 4. Salzburg, Otto Müller. 1950. 50 p., 21 plates, 2 maps.

*Graber, Georg. Volksleben in Kärnten. Graz, Leykam Verlag. 1934. 16, 445 p., 105 plates. (Third ed., enlarged. 1949. 16, 443 p., plates.)

Graber, Georg. Sagen und Märchen aus Kärnten. Graz, Leykam Verlag. 1944. 16, 424 p.

*Grünn, Helene. Die Pecher. Volkskunde aus dem Lebensraum des Waldes. Wien, Maniutiuspresse. 1960. 156 p., illus., plates.

*Gugitz, Gustav. Das Jahr und seine Feste im Volksbrauch Österreichs. Studien zur Volkskunde. 2 vols. Wien, Brüder Hollinek. 1949-1950. 8, 368 p., 19 illus.; 391 p., 19 illus.

Gugitz, Gustav. Kärnter Wallfahrten im Volksglauben und Brauchtum; Versuc einer Bestandaufnahme. Klagenfurt, F. Kleinmayer. 1951. 70 p.

Gutkind, Erwin Anton. Urban development in alpine and Scandinavian countries. New York, The Free Press of Glencoe. 1965. 491 p.

Haberlandt, Michael, et al. Deutsch Österreich, sein Land und Volk und seine Kultur. Weimar, W. Stein. 1927. 158 p.

Hermann, E. Über Lieder und Bräuche bei Hochzeiten in Kärnten. Archiv für Anthropologie. 19 (1891): 157-172.

Hess-Haberlandt, Gertrud. Das liebe Brot; brauchtümliche Mehlspeisen aus dem bäuerlichen Festkalendar. Wien, Österreichischer Agrarverlag. 1960. 120 p., illus.

Hildenbrandt, Hans. Alpine villages of Austria. National Geographic Magazine. 66 (1929): 669-676, 15 col. plates.

Hoermann, Ludwig von. Haussprüche aus den Alpen. Leipzig, Liebeskind. 1890. 24, 201 p.

Holme, Charles. The art-revival in Austria. London, Paris, and New York, The Studio. 1906. 56 p.

Holme, Charles, ed. Peasant art in Austria and Hungary. London and New York, The Studio. 1911. 10, 54 p., plates.

*Honigmann, John J. Bauer and Arbeiter in a rural Austrian community. S.W.J.A. 19(1963): 40-53.

Honigmann, John J. Sociology of an Austrian village. American Philosophical Society. Yearbook. 1963: 418-421.

Ilwof, Franz. Zur Volkskunde der Steiermark. Z.f.Ö.V. 3(1897): 7-13, 42-54.

Jacobeit, Wolfgang. Schafhaltung und Schäfer in Zentraleuropa bis zum Beginn des 20. Jahrhunderts. Berlin, Akademie-Verlag. 1961. 15, 604 p.

Joham, Ludwig. Altes Volks- und Brauchtum im Lavanttal. Wolfsberg, Kärnten, E. Ploetz. 1958. 102 p.

Kastner, O. Die Krippe. Ihre Verflechtung mit der Antike, ihre Darstellung in der Kunst der letzten 16 Jahrhundert, ihre Entfaltung in Oberösterreich. Linz, Oberösterreichischer Landesverlag. 1964. 202 p., illus.

Klagenfurt, Austria. Landesmuseum für Kärnten. Aus Kärntens Volksüberlieferung. Klagenfurt, Landesmuseum für Kärnten. 1957. 176 p.

Koren, Hanns. Pflug und Arl: ein Beitrag zur Volkskunde der Ackergeräte. Veröffentlichungen des Instituts für Volkskunde, Salzburg. 3. Salzburg, O. Müller. 1950. 275 p., illus., map.

Koren, Hanns. Die Spende. Eine volkskundliche Studie über die Beziehung "arme Seelen, arme Leute." Graz, Verlag Styria. 1954. 171 p.

Krainz, Johann. Sitten, Bräuche und Meinungen des deutschen Volkes in Steiermark. Z.f.Ö.V. 1 (1895): 65-73, 243-252; 2(1896): 299-307.

Kretzenbacher, Leopold. Lebendiges Volksschauspiel in Steiermark. Wien, Österreichischer Bundesverlag. 1951. 10, 406 p.

Kretzenbacher, Leopold. Weihnachtskrippen in Steiermark. Veröffentlichungen des Österreichisches Museum für Volkskunde. 3. Wien. 1953. 64 p.

Kundegraber, M. Die bäuerlichen Museen und Sammlungen in Österreich. Z.f.A.A. 5(1957): 148-151.

Lex, Franz, et al. Landeskunde von Kärnten. Klagenfurt, W. Merkel. 1923. 240 p.

Link, Edith. The emancipation of the Austrian peasant, 1740-1798. New York, Columbia University Press. 1949. 204 p.

Lipp, Franz. Art und Brauch im Lande ob der Enns. Salzburg, O. Müller. 1952. 26 p., 10 col. plates.

Lipp, Franz. Volkskunst und Handwerk der Gegenwart in Österreich. Wien, Österreichischer Bundesverlag für Unterricht Wissenschaft und Kunst. 1957. 79 p., illus.

Loidl-Eckstein, I. Zur Situation der Bäuerin in Oberösterreich. In D. Assmann ed. Volkskundliche Studien. Innsbruck, Universitätsverlag Wagner. 1964: 201-211.

Mais, Adolf. Österreichische Volkskunde für Jedermann. Wien, Pro-Domo Verlag. 1952. 510 p., illus.

Mais, Adolf. Die Maisspeicher im Österreich. In Joseph Haekel et al., eds. Die Wiener Schule der Völkerkunde . . . Horn-Wien, Verlag Ferdinand Berger. 1956: 535-550.

Marschalek, Otto. Österreichische Forscher. Ein Beitrag zur Völker- und Landeskunde. Mödling bei Wien, Verlag St. Gabriel. 1949. 15, 172 p.

Marx, A. Aus dem Leben des steierischen Volkes im Mürzthal. Die Hochzeit. Z.f.Ö.V. 4(1898): 290-305.

Mautner, Konrad, and Victor Geramb. Steierisches Trachtenbuch. 2 vols. Graz, Leuschner & Lubensky. 1932, 1938. 8, 502; 619 p., 87 illus.

*Moro, Oswin. Volkskundliches aus dem Kärnter Nockgebiet; Volksmedizin, Volksglaube, Volksdichtung, Volkskunst, Hofwesen und Arbeitsleben. Klagenfurt, Verlag des Geschichtsvereins für Kärnten. 1952. 8, 303 p.

Moser, Oskar. Kärnter Bauernmöbel. Handwerksgeschichte und Frühformen von Truhe und Schrank. Klagenfurt, Verlag des Geschichtsvereins für Kärnten. 1949. 163 p., 29 illus.

Neweklowsky, Ernst. Die Schiffahrt und die Flösserei im Raume der oberen Donau. 2 vols. Linz, Oberösterreichischer Landesverlag. 1952-1954. (Reprinted in one volume. 1964. 658 p.)

Der österreichische Bauer. Sein Leben und Werk. Wien, Sator-Verlag. 1949. 300 p.

Die Österreichisch-Ungarische Monarchie in Wort und Bild. 24 vols. Wien, K. K. Hof- und Staatsdruckerei. 1886-1902. (For Austria proper see: Bd. 1. Wien und Niederösterreich. 1886; Bd. 4. Wien und Nieder-österreich. 1888; Bd. 6. Oberösterreich und Salzburg. 1889; Bd. 7. Steiermark. 1890; Bd. 8. Kärnten und Krain. 1891.)

AUSTRIA

Pailler, Wilhelm, comp. and ed. Weihnachtslieder und Krippenspiele aus
Oberösterreich und Tirol. 2 vols. Innsbruck, Wagner. 1881-1883.

Palmer, Francis H. E. Austro-Hungarian life in town and country. New York
and London, G. P. Putnam's Sons. 1903. 7, 301 p.

Peter, Ilka. Gasslbrauch und Gasslspruch in Österreich. Salzburg, O. Müller.
1953. 365 p.

Prasch, Helmut. Eine Volkskunde Oberkärntens . . . Spittal/Drau-Kärnten,
Bezirksheimatmuseum. 1965. 242 p.

*Rosegger, Peter. Das Volksleben in Steiermark in Charakter- und Sittenbildern.
2 vols. Graz, Verlag Leykam-Josefsthal. 1875. (Seventh ed. Leipzig,
L. Staackmann. 1899. 448 p.)

Salzburg-Atlas. Das Bundesland Salzburg in 66 Kartenblättern. 2 parts.
Salzburg, Otto Müller Verlag. 66 p., 138 maps; 136 p., diagrs., etc.

Schlossar, Anton. Deutsche Volkschauspiele in Steiermark. 2 vols. Innsbruck,
Wagner. 1881.

Schlosser, Paul. Bachern Sagen; Volksüberlieferungen aus der alten Unter-
steiermark. Wien, Verlag des Österreichischen Museums für Volkskunde.
1956. 96 p.

Schmidt, Leopold. Die Weihnachtspiele Niederösterreichs. Z.f.V. n.F.
7(1937): 269-307, plates.

Schmidt, Leopold. Wiener Volkskunde. Wien, Gerlach & Wiedling. 1940.
128 p.

Schmidt, Leopold. Volkslieder aus Niederdonau, mit Bildern und Weisen.
Kassel, Bärenreiter Verlag. 1943. 78 p.

Schmidt, Leopold. Wiener Schwänke und Witze der Biedermeierzeit. Wien,
Wiener Verlag. 1946. 81 p.

Schmidt, Leopold. Zwischen Bastei und Linienwall: Wiener Vorstädte und ihre
Gäste. Wien, Wiener Verlag. 1947. 282 p.

Schmidt, Leopold. Das Volkslied im alten Wien. Wien, Bellaria Verlag.
1947. 95 p.

Schmidt, Leopold. Geschichte der österreichischen Volkskunde. Wien,
Österreichischer Bundesverlag. 1951. 205 p.

Schmidt, Leopold. Die Linzer Stadtvolkskunde im Rahmen der Stadtvolkskunde Österreichs. Jahrbuch der Stadt Linz. 1953: 621-632.

Schmidt, Leopold. Burgenländische Beiträge zur Volkskunde. Die Vorträge der 6. österreichischen Volkskundetagung in Eisenstadt 1951. Veröffentlichungen des Österreichischen Museums für Volkskunde. 2. Wien, 1953. 113 p.

Schmidt, Leopold. Bauernwerk der alten Welt. Betrachtungen über den Stand der Erforschung des bäuerlichen Arbeitgerätes in Österreich. Archiv für Volkerkunde. 10 (1955): 254-274.

Schmidt, Leopold. Volkschauspiel der Bergleute. Wien, Montanverlag. 1957 74 p.

Schneiter, Fritz. Alpwirtschaft. Graz und Wien, Leykam. 1948. 458 p., 296 illus.

Schober, Karl. Die Deutschen in Nieder- und Ober-Oesterreich, Salzburg, Kärnthen und Krain. Wien und Teschen, Prochaska. 1881. 397 p.

Schultes, Anton. Die Nachbarschaft der Deutschen und Slawen an der March; kulturelle wirtschaftliche Wechselbeziehungen im nordöstlichen Niederösterreich. Wien, Verlag des Österreichischen Museums für Volkskunde. 1954. 161 p.

Schunko, F. Von den Weinhütern in Perchtoldsdorf. Eine Dokumentation aus dem Jahre 1962. Österreichische Zeitschrift für Volkskunde. 66 (1962): 154-167.

*Sinnhuber, K. A. The Eisenstadt area, Burgenland, Austria. Nottingham, Geographical Field Group, University of Nottingham. 1962. 81 p., 22 fig.

Stellwag-Carion, Fritz. Austrian textiles. Leigh-on-Sea (England), F. Lewis. 1960. 19 p., 56 plates.

Taves, Marvin J., and Hedwig Hönigschmied. Rural life in Austria. Rural Sociology. 27 (1962): 198-207.

Tremel, Ferdinand. Steiermark. Eine Landeskunde. Graz, Steierische Verlagsanstalt. 1949. 199 p., 53 plates.

Wallis, B. C. The peoples of Austria. Geographical Journal. 6 (1918): 52-65. 5 maps.

Wallner, J. Beiträge zur Geschichte des Fischereiwesens in der Steiermark. Archiv für Fischereigeschichte. 9 (1917): 1-53.

Wilckens, Martin. Die Alpenwirtschaft der Schweiz und des Algäus und der westösterreichischen Alpenländer. Wien, Braunmüller. 1874. 8, 387 p.

Wilthum, Erwin. Siedlungslandschaft im südwestlichen Kärnten. Carinthia. 140(1950): 941-1016.

Wolfram, Richard. Weiberbünde. Z.f.V. n.F. 4(1932): 137-148.

Wopfner, Hermann. Die Besiedlung unserer Hochgebirgstäler. Zeitschrift des deutsch-österreichischen Alpenvereins. 51(1920): 25-86.

Wutte, Martin. Hexenprozesse in Kärnten. Carinthia. 117(1927): 27-67.

Zeitschrift für österreichische Volkskunde. 1895-1918. (Became: Wiener Zeitschrift für Volkskunde. 1919-1946. Became: Österreichische Zeitschrift für Volkskunde. 1947--)

Rath, E. Die wichtigsten Neuerscheinungen zur Volkskunde Österreichs aus den Jahren 1945-1954. Deutsches Jahrbuch für Volkskunde. 1(1955): 404-413.

Baille-Grohman, William Adolphe. Tyrol and the Tyrolese: the people and the land in their social, sporting, and mountaineering aspects. 2d ed. London, Longmans, Green. 1877. 20, 278 p.

Beiträge zur Geschichte und Heimatkunde Tirols. Festschrift zu Ehren Hermann Wopfners. 1. Edited by Franz Huter. Innsbruck, Wagner. 1947. 340 p., map.

Beiträge zur Volkskunde Tirols. Festschrift zu Ehren Hermann Wopfners. 2. Edited by Karl Ilg. Innsbruck, Wagner. 1948. 328 p.

Boner, Charles. Chamois hunting in the mountains of Bavaria and in the Tyrol New ed. London, Chapman and Hall. 1860. 8, 410 p.

Brunialti, Attilio. L'Alto Adige, l'Ampezzano e il territorio di Sesto. Torino, Unione Tipografica Editrice Torinese. 1919. 188 p., 5 plates.

Bünker, J. R. Das Bauernhaus der Gegend von Stams im Oberinntale (Tirol). M. A. G. W. 36(1906): 187-238, 51 illus., plans, plates.

*Busk, Rachel Harriette. The valleys of Tirol; their traditions and customs, and how to visit them. London, Longmans, Green. 1874. 29, 453 p.

Dachler, Anton, and Michael Haberlandt. Das Bauernhaus in Österreich-Ungarn und in seinen Grenzgebiet. Wien, Österreichischer Ingenieur- und Architektenverein. 1906. 7, 288 p., 67 illus., 6 plates, 75 folio plates, map.

Dopsch, Alfons. Die ältere Wirtschafts- und Sozialgeschichte der Bauern in den Alpenländern Österreichs. Oslo, Instituttet for Sammenlignende Kulturforskning. 1930. 181 p., illus., 4 maps.

Dörrenhaus, Fritz. Das deutsche Land an der Etsch. Innsbruck, Verlagsanstalt Tyrolia. 1933. 183 p.

Dörrenhaus, Fritz. Wo der Norden dem Süden begegnet: Südtirol. Bozen, Verlagsanstalt Athesia. 1959. 256 p.

Dörrer, Anton. Die alten Tanzhäuser und Spieltennen in Tirol. Z.f.V. n.F. 3(1931): 50-56, 4 illus.

Dörrer, Anton. Thierseer Passionsspiele 1799-1935. Innsbruck, Mar. Vereins buchhandlung und Buchdruckerei. 1935. 154 p.

TYROLESE

Dörrer, Anton. Das Schemenlaufen in Tirol und verwandte alpenländische
Masken- und Fasnachtsbräuche. 2d ed. Innsbruck und Leipzig, Felizian
Rauch. 1938. 44 p., 4 plates.

Dörrer, Anton. Bozner Bürgerspiele, Alpendeutsche Prang- und Kranzfeste.
Leipzig, K. W. Hiersemann. 1941. 5 p., map, music facsims.

Dörrer, Anton. Hochreligion und Volksglaube. Der Tiroler Herz-Jesu-Bund
(1796 bis 1946). Volkskundliches Gesehen. In Volkskundliches aus Österreich und Südtirol. Hermann Wopfner zum 70. Geburstag dargebracht.
Österreichische Volkskultur, Forschungen zur Volkskunde. 1. Wien. 1947:
70-100.

Dörrer, Anton. Tiroler Fasnacht, innerhalb der alpenländischen Winter- und
Vorfrühlingsbräuche. Wien, Österreichischer Bundesverlag. 1951. 480 p.,
77 illus.

Dörrer, Anton. Passionen und Passionspiel in Tirol. Deutsches Jahrbuch für
Volkskunde. 2(1956): 319-324.

Dörrer, Anton. Tiroler Umgangsspiel, Ordnungen und Sprachtexte der Bozner
Fronleichnamsspiele und verwandte tiroler Figuralprozessionen. Innsbruck,
Wagner. 1957. 568 p.

Egger, Joseph Gebhard. Die Tiroler und Vorarlberger. Wien und Teschen,
K. Prochaska. 1882. 531 p.

Fink, Hans. Die Kirchenpatrozinien Tirols. Ein Beitrag zur tirolisch-deutschen
Kulturgeschichte. Passau, Verlag des Instituts für ostbairische Heimatforschung. 1928. 8, 246 p.

Fink, Hans, ed. Eisacktaler Sagen, Bräuche, und Ausdrücke. Innsbruck,
Wagner. 1957. 386 p.

Grabmayr, Karl von. Süd-Tirol. Land und Leute vom Brenner bis zur
Salurner Klause. Berlin, Ullstein. 1919. 255 p.

Grohman, W. A. Baillie. See Baillie-Grohman, William Adolphe.

Hahn, E. Zwei Erntegeräte aus Tirol. Z.f.E. 46(1914): 672-673.

Hensler, Emil. Die Landwirtschaft im Zillertal. Innsbruck, Wagner. 1953.
202 p., illus.

Heyl, Johann Adolph. Gestalten und Bilder aus Tirols Drang- und Sturm-
periode. Innsbruck, Wagner. 1890. 8, 203 p.

Heyl, Johann Adolph. Heimatglocken. Gedichte aus den Tiroler Bergen.
Innsbruck, Wagner. 1893. 172 p.

Hochenegg, H. Die tiroler Kupferstecher. Innsbruck, Wagner. 1963. 153 p.

Hoeniger, Karl Theodor. Südtiroler Volksleben in 170 Gemälden und Zeichnungen, von Albert Stolz (1875-1947). Innsbruck, Tyrolia Verlag. 1951. 103 p., illus.

Hoffmann, George W. South Tyrol: borderland rights and world politics. Journal of Central European Affairs. 7(1947): 285-308.

*Hörmann, Ludwig von. Tiroler Volksleben. Ein Beitrag zur deutschen Volks- und Sittenkunde. Stuttgart, A. Bonz. 1909. 14, 498 p.

Hupfauf, Erich. Sagen, Brauchtum und Mundart im Zillertal. Innsbruck, Wagner. 1956. 174 p.

Hupfauf, Erich. Zillertaler Volksmedizin. Innsbruck, Wagner. 1957. 38 p.

Hupfauf, Erich. Zillertaler Reimkunst und andere Beiträge zur Zillertaler Volkskunde. Innsbruck, Wagner. 1960. 166 p.

Ilg, K. Hauskundliches aus zwei Tiroler Nebentälern und ihrer Haupttalumgebung. Z.f.V. 54(1958): 61-93.

Kohl, Franz Friedrich. Die Tiroler Bauernhochzeit. Sitten, Bräuche, Sprüche, Lieder und Tänze mit Singweisen. Quellen und Forschungen der deutschen Volkskunde. 3. Wien, R. Ludwig. 1908. 281 p.

Koren, Hanns. Pflug und Arl; ein Beitrag zur Volkskunde. Veröffentlichungen des Instituts für Volkskunde, Salzburg. 3. Salzburg, O. Müller. 1950. 275 p., illus., map.

Lanser, Otto. Tiroler Volkstechnik. Innsbruck, Wagner. 1954. 118 p., illus.

Leidlmaier, Adolf. Bevölkerung und Wirtschaft in Südtirol. Tiroler Wirtschaftstudien. 6. Innsbruck, Universitätsverlag Wagner. 1958. 296 p.

Lüers, Friedrich. Volkskundliches aus Steinberg am Achensee in Tirol. Bayerische Hefte für Volkskunde. 6(1919): 106-130.

Mader, Ignaz. Ortsnamen und Siedlungsgeschichte von Mühlbach, Rodeneck (Südtirol). Innsbruck, Wagner. 1952. 167 p., maps.

Mang, Hermann. Unsere Weihnacht. Volksbrauch und Kunst in Tirol. Innsbruck, Verlagsanstalt Tyrolia. 1927. 158 p., 47 plates.

Mang, Hermann. Volksbrauch in Südtirol; eine volkskundliche Übersicht. Brixen, Weger. 1951. 71 p.

Menghin, Alois. Aus dem deutschen Südtirol. Mythen, Sagen, Legenden und Schwänke, Sitten und Gebräuche, Meinungen, Sprüche, Redensarten etc. des Volkes an der deutschen Sprachgrenze. Meran, Plant. 1884. 171 p.

Metzler, J. M. Gnadenwald; Volkstum und Geschichte einer Tiroler Berggemeinde. Innsbruck, Wagner. 1957. 98 p.

Moritz, Alois. Die Almwirtschaft im Stanzer Tal. Innsbruck, Wagner. 1956. 138 p.

Moser, Simon. Deutsche Bergbauern. Innsbruck, Deutscher Alpen-Verlag. 1940. 176 p., 153 illus.

*Naroll, Frada. Child training among Tyrolean peasants. Anthropological Quarterly. 33(1960): 106-114.

*Naroll, Raoul, and Frada Naroll. Social development of a Tyrolean village. Anthropological Quarterly. 35(1962): 103-120.

Ostern in Tirol. Nikolaus Grass, ed. Innsbruck, Wagner. 1957. 350 p.

Die Österreichisch-Ungarische Monarchie in Wort und Bild. 24 vols. Wien, K. K. Hof- und Staatsdruckerei. 1886-1902. (See: Bd. 13. Tirol und Vorarlberg. 1893.)

Osttiroler Heimatblätter. 1(1924)-- Lienz/Drau, Osttiroler Heimatmuseum.

Pailler, Wilhelm. Weinachtslieder und Krippenspiele aus Oberösterreich und Tirol. 2 vols. Innsbruck, Wagner. 1881-1883.

Palmer, Francis H. E. Austro-Hungarian life in town and country. New York and London, G. P. Putnam's Sons. 1903. 7, 301 p.

Reut-Nicolussi, Edouard. The Germans of South Tirol. Slavonic Review. 16(1938): 370-385.

Rudolph-Greiffenberg, Martin. Das Burggräflerhaus; Entwicklung und Erneuerung alpenländischer Baukultur an der Etsch. Innsbruck, Wagner. 1960. 94 p.

Rumpf, K. Geometrische Ornamentik an Südtiroler Stadeltoren. Rheinisches Jahrbuch für Volkskunde. 10 (1959): 222-231.

Schädler, Karl. Die Lederhose in Bayern und Österreich. Ein Beitrag zur Kostüm-, Trachten-, und Zunftgeschichte. Innsbruck, Wagner. 1962. 204 p., illus.

Schneller, C. Deutsche und Romanen in Süd-Tirol und Venetian. Petermann's Geographischer Mittheilungen. 10 (1877): 365-385, plate 17.

Schneller, C. Südtirolische Landschaften. Innsbruck, Wagner. 1900. 7, 448 p.

Schober, Karl. Die Deutschen in Nieder- und Oberösterreich, Salzburg, Kärnthen und Krain. Wien und Teschen, Prochaska. 1881. 397 p.

Schreiber, G. Alpine Bergwerkskultur. Bergleute zwischen Graubünden und Tirol in den letzten vier Jahrhunderten. Innsbruck, Wagner. 1956. 89 p.

Schreiber, Walter. Die Lage des bäuerlichen Besitzstandes in Südtirol und im Tretino. Tiroler Heimat. 12(1948): 93-112.

Sölch, Johann. Geographische Kräfte im Schicksal Tirols. Mitteilungen der Geographischen Gesellschaft in Wien. 66(1923): 13-45.

Sölch, Johann. The Brenner region. Sociological Review. 19(1927): 318-334.

Tappeiner, Franz. Beiträge zur Ethnologie und Anthropologie der Tiroler. Z.f.E. 12(1878): 47-58, 269-288.

Troger, Ernest. Bevölkerungsgeographie des Zillertals. Innsbruck, Wagner. 1954. 134 p., illus.

Warren, Clarence Henry. Tyrolean journal. London, Robert Hale. 1954. 190 p.

*Weigend, Guido Gustav. The cultural pattern of South Tyrol. Chicago, University of Chicago, Department of Geography. 1949. 8, 198 p.

Wilckens, Martin. Die Alpenwirtschaft der Schweiz und des Algäus und der westösterreichischen Alpenländer. Wien, Braunmüller. 1874. 8, 387 p.

Wolf, Eric R. Cultural dissonance in the Italian Alps. Comparative Studies in Society and History. 5(1962): 1-14.

Wopfner, Hermann. Das Almendregal des tiroler Landesfürsten. Innsbruck, Wagner. 1906. 14, 170 p.

Wopfner, Hermann. Die Lage Tirols zu Ausgang des Mittelalters und die Ursachen des Bauernkrieges. Berlin und Leipzig, W. Rothschild. 1908. 16, 232 p.

Wopfner, Hermann. Das tiroler Bauernhaus. Innsbruck, Verlagsanstalt Tyrolia. 1924. 29 p., 16 illus.

Wopfner, Hermann. Deutsche Siedlungsarbeit in Südtirol, eine volkskundliche Studie. Innsbruck, Wagner. 1926. 56 p.

Wopfner, Hermann. Über Beziehungen von Hausform und Volkstum. Untersucht an Formen bäuerlichen Hausbaues im westl. Tirol. Veröffentlichungen des Museum Ferdinandeum in Innsbruck. 8(1928): 287-334.

Wopfner, Hermann. Eine siedlungs- und volkskundliche Wanderung durch Villgraten. Zeitschrift des Deutschen und Österreichischen Alpenvereins. 62(1931): 246-276.

*Wopfner, Hermann. Bergbauernbuch, von Arbeit und Leben des Tiroler Bergbauern in Vergangenheit und Gegenwart. 3 parts. Innsbruck, Wien, und München, Tyrolia Verlag. 1951-1960. 731 p., 107 illus., map.

Zingerel, Ignaz von. Sitten, Bräuche und Meinungen des Tiroler Volkes. Innsbruck, Wagner. 1871. 23, 304 p.

Hauffen, Adolf. Bibliographie der deutschen Volkskunde in Böhmen. Reichen berg, Sudetendeutscher Verlag. 1931. 385 p.

Hobinka, Edgar. Bibliographie der deutschen Volkskunde in Mähren und Schlesien. Reichenberg, Sudetendeutscher Verlag Franz Kraus. 1928. 124

Kundegraber, M. Bibliographie zur Gottscheer Volkskunde. Jahrbuch für Ostdeutsche Volkskunde. 7(1963): 233-272.

Rez, Heinrich. Bibliographie der deutschen Volkskunde in den Karpathen-ländern. Reichenberg, Sudetendeutscher Verlag. 1934. 11, 155 p.

Rez, Heinrich. Bibliographie zur Volkskunde der Donauschwaben. München, Ernst Reinhardt. 1935. 158 p.

Aberle, Msgr. George P. From the steppes to the prairies. The story of the German settling in Russia on the Volga and Ukraine, also the German set-tling in the Banat and the Bohemians in Crimea. . . . Dickinson, North Dakota, the author. 1964. 213 p.

Bell, Karl. Banat, das Deutschtum im rumänischen Banat. Dresden, Deutsche Buch- und Kunstverlag. 1926. 175 p., map, 3 col. plates, 40 illus.

Bielz, Julius. Die Volkstracht der Siebenbürger Sachsen. Bukarest, Staats-verlag für Kunst und Literatur. 1956. 52 p., illus.

Bielz, Julius. The craft of the Saxon goldsmiths in Transylvania. Bucharest, Foreign Language Publishing House. 1957. 35 p., 52 plates, 8 in color.

Bielz, Julius. Die sächsische Goldschmiedekunst Siebenbürgens. Bukarest, Verlag für fremdsprachige Literatur. 1957. 38 p., 52 illus., 8 in color.

Boner, Charles. Transylvania; its products and people. London, Longmans, Green, Reader, and Dyer. 1865. 14, 642 p.

Bünker, J. R. Das siebenbürgisch-sächsische Bauernhaus. M.A.G.W. 29(1899): 191-231, illus. 48-99.

Cornish, Louis C. Transylvania—The land beyond the forest. Philadelphia, Dorrance. 1947. 258 p., 5 appendixes.

Cosma, Vasile. Cinci sate din Areal. Cluj, Tip. Nationalǎ. 1933. 199 p.

Deutsche Volkskunde im ausserdeutschen Osten. Vier Vorträge von G. Brandsch, G. Jungbauer, V. Schirmunski und E. von Schwartz. Berlin und Leipzig, Walter de Gruyter. 1930. 81 p.

Dimitz, August. Geschichte Krains von der ältesten Zeit bis auf das Jahr 1813.
Mit besonderer Rücksicht auf Culturentwicklung. 4 vols. Laibach,
Kleinmeyer & Bamberg. 1874-1876.

Diplich, Hans, and Hans Wolfram Hockl. Wir Donauschwaben. Salzburg,
Akademischer Gemeinschaftsverlag. 1950. 32, 405 p.

Ernyey, József, and Géza Kurzweil. Deutsche Volksschauspiele aus den
oberungarischen Bergstädten. 2 vols. Budapest, Ungarisches National-
museum. 1932, 1938.

Fischer, Emil. Die Kulturarbeit des Deutschtums in Rumänien. Ein Versuch
zur Grundlegung ihrer Geschichte. Hermannstadt, W. Krafft. 1911. 17,
398 p.

Fuchs, Karl. Dächer in Siebenbürgen. M.A.G.W. 36(1905-1906): 129-
131, illus.

Gauss, A. K., and J. Weidenheim. Die Donauschwaben. Bild eines Kolon-
istenvolkes. Freilassing, Pannonia Verlag. 1961. 108 p.

*Gerard, Emily. The land beyond the forest. Facts, figures and fancies from
Transylvania. New York, Harper and Brothers. 1888. 9, 403 p., map.
(Another edition: 2 vols. Edinburgh and London, W. Blackwood & Sons.
1888.)

Gräfe, Johannes. Zur Trachtenkunde in Ungarn und den Nachfolgestaaten.
Leipzig, Verlag der Werkgemeinschaft. 1935. 8, 88 p.

Greb, Julius. Zipser Volkskunde. Käsmark and Reichenberg, Verlag der
Anstalt für Sudetendeutsche Heimatforschung. 1932. 36, 342 p.

Grothe, Hugo. Die deutsche Sprachinsel Gottschee in Slowenien. Ein Beitrag
zur Deutschtumskunde des europäischen Südostens. Münster i. W.,
Aschendorff. 1931. 15, 264 p., 2 maps, 22 plates.

Gunda, Béla. Beiträge zur Volksheilkunde der Donauschwaben. Österreichische Zeitschrift für Volkskunde. 57(1954): 141-143.

Hall, Donald John. Romanian furrow. London, Methuen. 1933: 116-140.

*Haltrich, Josef. Zur Volkskunde der Siebenbürger Sachsen, kleinere Schriften
von J. Haltrich . . . Wien und Hermannstadt. 1885. 16, 535 p.

Hanika, Joseph. Sudetendeutsche Volkstrachten. Teil 1: Grundlagen der
weiblichen Tracht. Kopftracht und Artung. Reichenberg, Franz Kraus.
1937. 25, 290 p., illus.

Hauffen, Adolf. Die deutsche Sprachinsel Gottschee. Geschichte und Mundart
Lebensverhältnisse, Sitten und Gebräuche, Sagen, Märchen und Lieder.
Graz, 'Styria.' 1895. 16, 466 p., 4 illus.

Hermann, Albert. Die deutschen Bauern des Burgenlandes. Jena, G. Fischer.
1937. 136 p.

Hienz, H. Bücherkunde zur Volks- und Heimatforschung der Siebenbürger
Sachsen. München, R. Oldenburg. 1960. 20, 579 p.

Holme, Charles, ed. Peasant art in Austria and Hungary. London, The Studio
1911. 10, 54 p., plates, illus.

Jungbauer, Gustav. Die deutsche Volkskunde in der Tschechoslowakei. In
Deutsche Volkskunde im ausserdeutschen Osten. Berlin und Leipzig, W. de
Gruyter. 1930: 1-25.

Kaindl, Raimund Friedrich. Das Ansiedlungswesen in der Bukowina seit der
Besitzergreifung durch Österreich. Mit besonderer Berücksichtigung der
Ansiedlung der Deutschen. Innsbruck, Wagner. 1902. 16, 537 p.

Kaindl, Raimund Friedrich. Geschichte der Deutschen in den Karpathenländern
3 vols. Gotha, F. A. Perthes. 1907-1911.

Kaindl, Raimund Friedrich. Deutsche Volksbräuche in Galizien. Zeitschrift
des Vereins für Volkskunde. 21(1911): 251-255.

Kaindl, Raimund Friedrich. Deutsche Siedlung in Osten. Stuttgart und Berlin,
Deutsche Verlags-Anstalt. 1915. 40 p.

*Kaindl, Raimund Friedrich. Die Deutschen in Galizien und in der Bukowina.
Frankfurt, H. Keller. 1916. 6, 172 p.

Kaindl, Raimund Friedrich. Die Ansiedlung der Deutschen in den Karpathen-
ländern. Leipzig, A. Haase. 1917. 115 p.

Karasek-Langer, Alfred. Donauschwäbische Volkskunde. Kitzingen/Main,
Holzner Verlag. 1954. 35 p.

Kraushaar, Karl. Kurzgefasste Geschichte des Banates und der deutschen
Ansiedler. Wien, Buchhandlung der Verlagsanstalt "Herold." 1923. 280 p.

Kraushaar, Karl. Sitten und Bräuche der Deutschen in Ungarn, Rumänien und
Jugoslawien . . . Wien, Buchdruckerei Bruno Bartelt. 1932. 155 p.

Kriss, Rudolf. Die schwäbische Türkei. Beiträge zu ihrer Volkskunde, Zauber
und Segen, Sagen und Wallerbrauch. Düsseldorf, L. Schwann. 1937.
100 p., 12 illus., 6 plates.

Künzig, Johannes. Saderlach. Ein Alemannendorf im rumänischen Banat und seine Urheimat. Berlin-Dahlem, Ahnenerbe-Stiftung Verlag. 1943. 354 p., 47 plates.

Lane, Adolf. Deutsche Bauernkolonien in Russland; ein Beitrag zur Orientierung über ihren Zustand und über die Rückwandererbewegung. Berlin, W. Süssrott. 1910. 28 p.

Lehman, Emil. Sudetendeutsche Volkskunde. Leipzig, Quelle & Meyer. 1926. 11, 229 p., 38 figs., 24 plates.

Müller, Friedrich. Beiträge zur Geschichte des Hexenglaubens und des Hexenprocesses in Siebenbürgen. Braunschweig, Schwetschke. 1854. 77 p.

Müller, Friedrich. Siebenbürgische Sagen. Kronstadt, Schässburg. 1857. 31, 424 p.

Müller, Friedrich. Die Geschichte der Deutschen in Rumänien. Bilder aus Vergangenheit und Gegenwart. Hermannstadt, Krafft & Drotleff. 194_. 194 p.

Müller-Langenthal, Friedrich. Die Siebenbürger Sachsen und ihr Land. Dresden, Heimat und Welt Verlag. 1912. 164 p.

Otterstädt, Herbert. Gottschee, eine deutsche Volksinsel im Südosten. Eine Volkskunde in Bildern. Schriften des Südostdeutschen Instituts Graz. 6. Graz. 1941. 67 p., illus., map.

Paget, John. Hungary and Transylvania: with remarks on their condition, social, political, and economical. New ed. 2 vols. London, J. Murray. 1850. (American ed. Philadelphia, Lea & Blanchard. 1850.)

Piffl, Erna. Deutsche Bauern in Ungarn. Berlin, Verlag Grenze und Ausland. 1938. 64 p.

Radics, Peter von. Die altdeutsche Kolonie Gottschee in Krain. Österreichische Revue. 3(1964): 210-221; 4(1964): 220-231.

Retzlaff, Hans. Bildnis eines deutschen Bauernvolkes, die Siebenbürger Sachsen. Berlin, Verlag Grenze und Ausland. 1936. 24 p., 96 plates.

Schechtman, Josef B. The elimination of German minorities in southeastern Europe. Journal of Central European Affairs. 6(1946): 152-166.

Schullerus, Adolf. Siebenbürgische-sächsische Volkskunde im Umriss. Leipzig, Quelle & Meyer. 1926. 10, 179 p., illus., 16 plates.

Schullerus, Pauline. Pflanzen in Glaube und Brauch der Siebenbürger Sachsen. Archiv des Vereins für Siebenbürgische Landeskunde. 40(1916-1921): 78-188, 348-426.

Schuster, Friedrich Wilhelm. Siebenbürgisch-sächsische Volkslieder, Sprichwörter, Rätsel, Zauberformeln und Kinderdichtungen. Hermannstadt,
  Steinhausen's Buchhandlung. 1865. 26, 556 p.

Schwicker, Johann Heinrich. Die Deutschen in Ungarn und Siebenbürgen.
  Wien und Teschen, K. Prochaska. 1881. 509 p.

Teutsch, Friedrich. Die Siebenbürger Sachsen in Vergangenheit und Gegenwart. Leipzig, K. F. Koehler. 1916. 13, 350 p. (Second ed. Hermannstadt, W. Krafft. 1924. 367 p.)

Teutsch, Friedrich. Geschichte der Ev. Kirche in Siebenbürgen. 2 vols.
  Hermannstadt, W. Krafft. 1921-1922.

Teutsch, Friedrich. Kirche und Schule der Siebenbürger Sachsen in Vergangenheit und Gegenwart. Hermannstadt, W. Krafft. 1923. 328 p.

Thomae, Norbert. Deutsche Volkskunst in Siebenbürgen. München, Verlag
  Christ Unterwegs. 1954. 64 p., 26 plates, 108 figs.

Tschinkel, Wilhelm. Volksspiele in Gottschee. Z.f.O.V. 14(1908): 108-
  112, 169-177.

Tschinkel, Wilhelm. Zur Gottscheer Volkskunde. Z.f.O.V. 15(1909): 169-
  178.

Tschinkel, Wilhelm. Gottscheer Volkstum in Sitte, Brauch, Märchen, Sagen,
  Legenden und anderen volkstümlichen Überlieferungen. Kočevje. 1932.
  11, 256 p.

Wlislocki, Heinrich von. Siebenbürgische Kinderspiele. Ethnologische Mitteilungen aus Ungarn. 2(1890-1892): 213-218.

*Wlislocki, Heinrich von. Volksglaube und Volksbrauch der Siebenbürger
  Sachsen. Berlin, E. Felber. 1893. 212 p.

Wlislocki, Heinrich von. Neue Beiträge zur Volkskunde der Siebenbürger
  Sachsen. Ethnologische Mitteilungen aus Ungarn. 3(1894): 18-46.

Schiller, F. D. Literatur zur Geschichte und Volkskunde der deutschen
Kolonien in der Sowjetunion für das Jahre 1764-1926. Pokrowsk, Staats-
verlag. 1927. 67 p.

Aberle, Msgr. George P. From the steppes to the prairies. The story of the
German settling in Russia on the Volga and Ukraine, also the German set-
tling in the Banat and the Bohemians in Crimea. Their resettlement in the
Americas—North and South America and Canada. Dickinson, North Dakota,
the author. 1964. 213 p.

Anger, Helmut. Die Deutschen in Sibirien. Reise durch die deutschen Dörfer
Westsibiriens. Königsberg in Prussia, Ost-Europa Verlag. 1930. 103 p.,
44 illus., 4 maps.

Anonymous. Schools in the German Volga Republic. School and Society.
45(Feb. 20, 1937): 266-267.

Bartels, Bernhard. Die deutschen Bauern in Russland einst und jetzt. Moskau,
Central'noe Izdatel'stvo Narodov. 1928. 91 p.

Beratz, Gottlieb. Die deutschen Kolonien an der unteren Wolga in ihrer
Entstehung und ersten Entwicklung. Berlin, Verband der Wolgadeutschen
Bauern. 1923. 7, 306 p.

Bonwetsch, Gerhard. Geschichte der deutschen Kolonien an der Wolga. Stuttgart, Englehorn. 1919. 132 p.

Deutsche Post aus dem Osten. Berlin. 1936-1940.

Dinges, Georg. Beiträge zur Heimatkunde des deutschen Wolgagebietes.
Pokrowsk, Abteilung für Volksbildung des Gebietes der Wolgadeutschen.
1923. 88 p.

Eichhorn, Jakob. Die Anfänge des Weinbaues in den deutschen Wolgakolonien.
Wolgadeutsche Monatshefte. 1924: 105-107.

Harder, Hans. Das Dorf an der Wolga. Stuttgart, J. F. Steinkopf. n.d. 306 p.

Joachim, Rev. Salomon. Toward an understanding of the Russia Germans.
Concordia College Occasional Papers. 1. Moorehead, Minn., Concordia
College. 1939. 31 p.

Kagarov, E. G. Materialien zur Volkskunde der Wolga-Deutschen. Z.f.V.,
n.F. 3(1932): 241-251, plates.

Keller, Konrad. Die deutschen Kolonien in Südrussland. 2 vols. Odessa.
1905-1914.

Klaus, Aleksander Avgustovich. Unsere Kolonien. Studien und Materialien
zur Geschichte und Statistik der ausländischen Kolonisation in Russland.
Odessa, Verlag der "Odessaer Zeitung." 1887. 8, 386, 163 p.

Prechter, H. Deutsche Bauernhöfe in Russland. Bayerische Hefte für Volkskunde. 15(1942): 13-16.

Schirmunski, Viktor. Die deutschen Kolonien in der Ukraine. Geschichte,
Mundarten, Volkslied, Volkskunde. Moskau, Zentral-Völkerverlag der
Sowjet-Union. 1928. 162 p.

Schirmunski, Viktor. Volkskundliche Studienreise in den deutschen Siedlungen
der Sowjet-Union. Das Neue Russland. 8, nos. 4-5(1931): 26-29.

Schleuning, Johannes. Die deutschen Kolonien im Wolgagebiet, . . .
Schriften zum Selbstbestimmungsrecht der Deutschen ausserhalb des
Reiches. 9. Berlin. 1919. 43 p.

Schleuning, Johannes. In Kampf und Todesnot. Die Tragödie des Russland-
deutschtums. Berlin, Bernard & Graefe. 1930. 255 p.

Schorn, H. Bauernhäuser und Öfen in Russland. Bayerische Hefte für Volkskunde. 15(1942): 25-34.

Schwabenland, Emma D. German-Russians on the Volga and in the United
States. Boulder, Colorado, University of Colorado. 1929. (Unpublished
M.A. thesis.)

Toepfer, J. Verlobungs- und Hochzeitssitten im Wolgagebiet. Wolgadeutsche
Monatshefte. 3(1924): 84 ff., 110-112.

ITALIANS

Barbano, F., and M. Viterbi. Bibliografia della sociologia Italiana, 1948-
1958. Torino, Ramella. 1959. 168 p.

Crocioni, Giovanni. Bibliografia delle tradizioni popolari marchigiane.
Firenze, L. S. Olschki. 1953. 219 p.

Gabrieli, Giuseppe. Bibliografia del folklore pugliese. Bari, Soc. Ed.
Tipografica. 1931. 57 p.

Giannini, Giovanni. Bibliografia analitica del folklore luccese. Lucca, Tip.
Artigianelli. 1940. 96 p.

Pitrè, Giuseppe. Bibliografia delle tradizioni popolari d'Italia. Torino-
Palermo, Carlo Clausen. 1894. 20, 603 p.

Storai de Rocchi, Tina. Guida bibliografica allo studio dell'abitazione in
Italia. Ricerche sulle dimore rurali in Italia. 8. Firenze, Centro di
Studi per la Geografia Etnologica. 1950. 60 p.

Toschi, Paolo. Bibliografia delle tradizioni popolari d'Italia dal 1916 al 1940.
1. Firenze, Barbera. 32, 143 p. (The other volumes were never published.)

Acocella, Vito. Tradizioni popolari di Calitri. Napoli, P. Federico e G.
Ardia. 1936. 179 p. (Campania.)

Acquaviva, Cosimo. Taranto Tarantina. Contributo allo studio delle tradizioni popolari. Taranto, E. Mazzolino. 1931. 204 p.

Ahlman, Hans W. Études de géographie humaine sur l'Italie subtropicale.
Geografiska Annaler. 7(1925): 257-322; 8(1926): 74-124.

Alcini Tartaglini, C. La festa dei santi patroni nel territorio di civitella
dei Pazzi. Lares. 29(1963): 191-200.

Algranati, G. Basilicata e Calabria. Torino, Unione Tipografico Editrice
Torinese. 1929. 7, 358 p.

Alongi, Giuseppe. La mafia nei suoi fattori e nelle sue manifestazioni.
Roma-Torino, Fratelli Bocca Librai di S. M. il Re d'Italia. 1886. 163 p.

Alongi, Giuseppe. La Camora, studio di sociologia criminale. Torino,
Fratelli Bocca Editori-Librai di S. M. il Re d'Italia. 1890. 15, 237 p.

Aluisi, F. Variazioni strutturali della popolazioni attiva Italiana. Rivista di
Economia Agraria. 19, no. 4(1964): 117-128.

Ambrosi, Marietta. When I was a girl in Italy. Boston, Lothrop, Lee &
Shepard. 1906. 182 p.

*Anderson, Gallatin. A survey of Italian godparenthood. Kroeber Anthropological Society Papers. 15. Berkeley, Calif. 1956. 120 p.

*Anderson, Gallatin. Il comparaggio: the Italian grandparenthood complex. S. W.J. A. 13(1957): 32-53.

Anderton, Isabella M. Tuscan folk lore and sketches. London, Arnold Fairbairns. 1905. 271 p.

l'Archivio per lo Studio delle Tradizioni Popolari. 30 vols. Palermo. 1882-1906.

Aronco, Giafranco D. Vecchie usanze popolari di Ampezzo. Trieste, Tip. Giuliano. 1947. 11 p.

Ashby, Thomas. Festivals in the Abruzzi (1909). Anglo-Italian Review. December 1918: 308-319; January 1919: 45-51.

Ashby, Thomas. Some Italian scenes and festivals. London, Methuen. 1929. 15, 179 p.

Azzoni Storti, Maria. Alcune tradizioni cremonesi. Cremona, Stabilimento Tipografico Botti e Busini. 1925. 167 p.

Baldacci, Osvaldo. La Serra. Monografia antropogeografica di una regione calabrese. Memorie di Geografia Antropica 9. Roma, Centro di Studi per la Geografia Antropica. Presso l'Instituto di Geografia dell'Università di Roma. 1954. 253 p.

Baldacci, Osvaldo. Puglia. Torino, Unione Tipografico-Editrice Torinese. 1962. 10, 550 p., illus., plates, maps.

Balliano, Adolfo. Aria di leggende in Val d'Aosta. Bologna, Cappelli. 1951. 253 p.

Ballila Pratella, Francesco. Saggio di gridi, canzoni, cori e danze del popolo italiano, per una cultura della sensibilità musicale italiana. Bologna, F. Bongiovanni. 1919. 134 p.

Ballila Pratella, Francesco. Le arti e le tradizioni popolari d'Italia; etnofonia di Romagna. Udine, Istituto delle Edizioni Academiche. 1938. 205 p.

*Banfield, Edward C. The moral basis of a backward society. Glencoe, Ill., The Free Press. 1958. 204 p. (Potenza, in southern Italy.)

Barbero, G. Land reform in Italy: achievements and perspectives. Rome, Food and Agriculture Organization of the United Nations. 1961. 11, 199 map, diagrams, tables.

ITALIANS

Barbieri, Giuseppe. La casa rurale nel Trentino. Firenze, Leo S. Olschki. 1962. 216 p., illus.

Baretti, Giuseppe Marco A. An account of the manners and customs of Italy, with observations of the mistakes of some travellers. 2 vols. London, T. Davies. 1768.

Bark, L. G. Bee-hive dwellings in Apulia. Antiquity. 6(1932): 407-410. Plates.

*Barnes, F. B. The Alleghe area of the Italian Dolomites. Nottingham, Geographical Field Group, Geography Department, University of Nottingham. 1958. 72 p., 62 figs.

Barzini, Luigi. The Italians. A full-length portrait featuring their manners and morals. New York, Atheneum. 1964. 352 p.

Battaglia, Raffaello. Folklore delle lagune Venete. Rivista di Antropologia. 27(1926-1927): 19-42.

Bellucci, Giuseppe. Catalogue descriptif d'une collection d'amulettes italiennes envoyer à l'Exposition Universelle de Paris, 1889. Pérouse, Imprimerie Boncompagne. 1889. 81 p.

Bellucci, Giuseppe. Amuleti italiani contemporanei. Catalogo descrittivo dello collezione inviata all'Esposizione Nazionale di Torino. Perugia. 1898. 104 p.

Bellucci, Giuseppe. Il feticismo in Italia e le sue forme di adattamento. 2d ed. Perugia, Unione Typografica Cooperativa. 1919. 158 p.

Bellucci, Giuseppe. La placenta nelle tradizioni italiano e nell'etnografia. Archivio per l'Antropologia e la Etnologia. 40(1910): 316-352.

Bernardi, Amy A. Forme e colori di vita regionale Italiana. 3 vols. 1. Piemonte. 2. Liguria. 3. Venezia. Bologna, Nicola Zanichelli. 1927-1929.

Bernoni, D. G. Giuochi popolari veneziani. Venezia, Typografia M. Fontane. 1874. 94 p.

Bianchi, Giustino. La proprieta fondiaria e le classi rurali. Pisa, Tipografia Pisana. 1891.

Biasutti, Renato. La casa rurale nella Toscana. Bologna, Zanichelli. 1938. 211 p., 41 plates.

Bideri, G. E. Usi e costumi del popolo napoletano. 3d ed. Napoli, Libreria Editrice via Roma. 1880. 265 p.

Blunt, John James. Vestiges of ancient manners and customs, discoverable in modern Italy and Sicily. London, John Murray. 1823. 12, 293 p.

Boccardo, Gerolamo. Feste, giuochi o spettacoli. Genova, Tipografia del R. Istituto Sordo-muti. 1874. 425 p.

Bonaccorsi, A. Il folklore musicale in Toscana. Firenze, L. S. Olschki. 1956. 8, 153 p.

Bonasera, F., et al. La casa rurale nell'Umbria. Firenze, L. S. Olschki. 1955. 12, 219 p., illus.

Borrelli, Nicola. Vita domestica in Campania. Folklore Italiano. 4(1929): 194-209.

Borrelli, Nicola. Tradizioni Aurunche. Roma, Tip. Proja. 1937. 193 p.

Bottiglioni, Gino. Manuale dei dialetti italici; Osco, Umbro e dialetti minori. Grammatica, testi, glossario con note etimologiche. Bologna. 1954. 22, 455 p.

Bourcard, Francesco de, ed. Usi e costumi di Napoli. 2 vols. Napoli, Gaetano Nobile. 1853-1858. 19, 324; 340 p.

Bourcard, Francesco de. Usi e costumi di Napoli. Milano, Longanesi. 1955. 1091 p. (A reprint of the preceding title.)

Bower, Herbert Morris. The elevation and procession of the Ceri at Gubbio: an account of the ceremonies, together with some suggestions as to their origin, and an appendix consisting of the Inguvine lustration, in English. Folk-Lore, Extra Publications. 39. London, The Folk-Lore Society. 1897. 11, 146 p., 11 plates.

Branch, Daniel Paulk. Folk architecture of the east Mediterranean. New York, Columbia University Press. 1966. 14, 145 p., illus. (Especially see pp. 86-139.)

Bronzini, Giovanni. Tradizioni popolari in Lucania; ciclo della "vita umana Matera, Montemurro. 1953. 329 p.

Brown, Horatio F. Life in the lagoons. London, Rivingtons. 1900. 297 p. (Venice.)

Busk, Rachel Hariette. The folklore of Rome. Collected by word of mouth from the people. London, Longmans. 1874. 24, 439 p.

Busk, Rachel Hariette. The folk-songs of Italy. London, S. Sonnenschein, Lowrey. 1887. 290 p.

Calderini, Emma. Il costume popolare in Italia. Milano, Sperling & Kupfer. 1934. 166 p., 14 plates, 20 col. plates.

Campesi, Paul J. Ethnic family patterns: the Italian family in the United States. American Journal of Sociology. 53(1948): 443-449.

*Cancian, Frank. The southern Italian peasant: world view and political behavior. Anthropological Quarterly. 34(1961): 1-18.

Canziani, Estella. Costumes, traditions and songs of Savoy. London, Chatto and Windus. 1911. 13, 179 p., illus., plates.

Canziani, Estella, and Eleanour Rohde. Piedmont. London, Chatto and Windus. 1913. 203 p.; illus., plates.

Canziani, Estella. Abruzzese folklore. Folk-Lore. 39(1928): 209-247.

*Canziani, Estella. Through the Apennines and the lands of the Abruzzi; landscape and peasant life. Cambridge, W. Heffer & Sons. 1928. 14, 339 p., illus., plates.

Cappieri, Mario. Italy: an anthropological review for 1952-1954. In William L. Thomas, ed. Yearbook of Anthropology 1955. New York, Wenner-Gren Foundation for Anthropological Research. 1955: 481-500.

Carey, J. P., and A. G. Carey. The south of Italy: old despair and new hope. South Atlantic Quarterly. 54(1955): 29-43.

Carey, J. P., and A. G. Carey. South of Italy and the Cassa per il Mezzogiorno. Western Political Quarterly. 8(1955): 569-588.

Carlyle, Margaret. Modern Italy. London, Hutchinson's University Library. 1957. 159 p.

Carlyle, Margaret. The awakening of southern Italy. London and New York, Oxford University Press. 1962. 147 p.

Carr, Alice Vansittart. North Italian folk; sketches of town and country life. London, Chatto & Windus. 1878. 12, 282 p.

Cerni, Ferdinando. Credenze ed usi relativi al parto nella tradizioni popolare istriana. Lares. 13(1942): 155-156.

Chiara, Stanislao de. La mia Calabria. Milano, Quintieri. 1920. 157 p., 47 illus.

Cirese, A. M. Saggi sulla cultura meridionale. 1. Gli studi di tradizioni popolari nal Molise. Profilo storico e saggio di bibliografia. Roma, De Luca Editore. 1955. 170 p.

Clarke, Smith L. A survival of an ancient cult in the Abruzzi. Studi e Materiali di Storia delle Religioni. 1929: 106-119.

Cocchiara, Giuseppe. Il linguaggio del gesto. Torino, F. Ili Bocca. 1931. 131 p. (Language and psychology of gesture.)

Cocchiara, Giuseppe. Il linguaggio della poesia popolare. Palermo, Palumbo 1951. 265 p.

Colombo, Ruggero. Italian textiles. Leigh-on-Sea, England, F. Lewis. 1953 23 p., 65 plates.

Conti, Emilio. L'infanzia e la società. Lodi, Tipo-lit. C. dell'Avo. 1903. 343 p.

Cooper, John M. Preferential marriage in Italy. Primitive Man. 10 (1937): 10-11.

Coote, Colin R. Italian town and country life. New York, Brentano's; London, Methuen. 1925. 252 p.

Coro, F. Usi, costumi, tradizioni e feste nelle diverse regioni d'Italia con speciale reguardo all'Abruzzo. Lares. 25(1959): 390-406.

Corso, Raffaele. Das geschlechtleben in Sitten, Brauch, Glauben und Gewohnheitrecht des italienischen Volkes. Nicotera, the author. 1914. 238 p.

Corso, Raffaele. Folklore, storia, obbietto, metodo, bibliografia. Roma, Casa Editrice Leonardo da Vinci. 1923. 148 p.

Costa, Emilio. Country life in Italy. Cornhill Magazine. 44(1881): 604-618, 384-695.

*Covello, Leonard. The social background of the Italian-American school child. A study of the southern Italian family mores and their effect on the school situation in Italy and America. Leiden, E. J. Brill. 1967. 30, 488 p.

Craven, Keppel Richard. Excursions in the Abruzzi and northern provinces of Naples. 2 vols. London, R. Bentley. 1838. 7, 318; 8, 348 p.

*Crawford, Mabel Sharman. Life in Tuscany. London, Smith Elder; New York, Sheldon. 1859. 10, 327 p. (New York ed.: 11, 339 p.)

Crocioni, Giovanni. La gente marchigiana nelle sue tradizioni. Milano, Corticelli. 1951. 351 p.

Cucchetti, Gino. L'Alto Adige nostra. Bolzano, Casa Editrice Brennero. 1932. 311 p. (The Italian Tyrol.)

Cyriax, Tony. Among Italian peasants. London, W. Collins & Sons. 1919. 263 p.

Dean, Shirley. Rocks and olives; portrait of an Italian village. London, John Murray. 1954. 179 p. (Southern Italy.)

De Luca, Thomas. The cross-cousin relationship in Naples. Primitive Man. 10 (1937): 10.

Dickinson, Robert E. Land reform in southern Italy. Economic Geography. 30 (1954): 157-176.

Dickinson, Robert E. The population problem of southern Italy: an essay in social geography. Syracuse, Syracuse University Press. 1955. 11, 116 p.

Dorsa, Vincenzo. La tradizione Greco-Latina negli usi e nelle credenze popolari della Calabria citeriore. 2d ed. Cosenza, Tipografia Migliaccio. 1884. 67 p.

Douglas, George Norman. Old Calabria. 4th ed. London, Secker & Warburg. 1955. 16, 325 p. (Originally published: London, Martin Secker. 1915. 352 p.)

Duff-Gordon, Caroline Lucie (Mrs. Aubrey Waterfield). Home life in Italy: letters from the Apennines. London, Methuen. 1908. 14, 490 p.

Edelman, M. Causes of fluctuations in popular support for the Italian communist party since 1946. Journal of Commonwealth Political Studies. 20 (1958): 535-552.

Eustacchi-Nardi, Anna Maria. Contributo allo studio della tradizioni popolari marchigiane. Firenze, Leo S. Olschki. 1958. 14, 439 p.

Facco, Giannina. Tradizioni padovani. Padova, A. Draghi. 1958. 152 p.

Farinetti, Clotilde. Vita e pensiero del Piemonte. Milano, Trevisini. 1927. 218 p.

Ferrarotti, Franco. Sociology in Italy: problems and perspectives. In Howard Becker and Alvin Boskoff, eds. Modern sociological theory in continuity and change. New York, Dryden Press. 1957: 695-710.

Ferrarotti, Franco, E. Uccelli, and G. Giorgi-Rossi. La piccola città; dati per l'analisi sociologica di una comunità meridionale. Milano, Edizioni di Comunità. 1959. 183 p. (Social surveys in Castellamare di Stabia, Italy.)

Finamore, Gennaro. Credenze, usi e costumi Abruzzesi. Palermo, Libreria Internazionale L. Pedone Lauriel di Carlo Clausen. 1890. 8, 196 p.

Finamore, Gennaro. Tradizioni popolari Abruzzesi. Torino, no publisher.
1894. 241 p.

Finamore, Gennaro. Tradizione popolari Abruzzesi: natale. L'Abruzzo.
1 (1920): 3-22.

Fiorese, Sabino. Il contadino nelle terra di Bari. Considerazioni economiche
sociali a proposito di una inchiesta agraria. Bari, Tipografia Cannone.
1878. 120 p.

Folklore. 1-16(1925-1941). 1(1946)--. Vols. 1-10 (1925-1935) under the
title: Il Folklore Italiano. Vols. 11-16(1936-1941) under the title:
Archivio per la Raccolta e la Studio delle Tradizioni Popolari Italiani.
Vol. 1 (1946-) — under the title: Folklore: Rivista di Tradizioni Popolari.

Folklore nel Sannio: costumi, tradizioni, canti popolari, giochi, superstizioni,
feste, medicina popolare, "cunti, " legende; a cura di Francesco Romano
et al. Benvenuto, Ed. Secolo nuovo. 1958. 96 p.

Friedmann, Fredrick George. Osservazioni sul mondo contadino dell'Italia
meridionale. Quaderni di Sociologia. 1 (1952): 148-161.

*Friedmann, Fredrick George. The world of "La miseria. " Partisan Review.
20(1953): 218-231.

*Friedmann, Fredrick George. The hoe and the book: an Italian experiment in
community development. Ithaca, Cornell University Press. 1960. 179 p.

Fuller, G. J. The island of Elba. Nottingham, Geographical Field Group,
Geography Department, University of Nottingham. 1958. 111 p., 30
diagrams.

*Fuller, G. J. The Sele Plain: geographical studies in Campania, southern
Italy. Nottingham, Geographical Field Group, University of Nottingham.
1962. 84 p., 49 figs.

Galanti, Bianca M. Dances of Italy. London, Parrish. 1950. 40 p., illus.

Gambi, Lucio. La casa rurale nella Romagne. Firenze, Centro di Studi per
la Geografia Etnologica. 1950. 114 p., 67 figs., 20 tables.

Garigue, Philip, and Raymond Firth. Kinship organization of Italians in London. In Raymond Firth, ed. Two studies of kinship in London. London,
Athlone Press. 1956: 67-93.

Gaudio, Francesco Saveno de. La montagna calabrese. Milano, I.P.L. 1955
111 p., illus. (Economic conditions.)

Giannini, Giovanni. Canti popolari toscani. Firenze, G. Barbera. 1902. 493

Gini, Corrado, and Elio Caranti. The family in Italy. Marriage and Family Living. 16(1954): 354-361.

Ginobli, Giovanni. Costumanze Marchigiani. 3 pts. Macerata, Tipografia Maceratese. 1941, 1947, 1949. 64, 48, 85 p.

Ginobli, Giovanni. Bricciche di superstizioni e pregiudizi popolari marchigiani. Macerata, Tipografia Maceratese. 1959. 85 p.

Giordano, Ludovico. Antichi usi Liguri. Albenga, Soc. Storico-Archeologica Ingauna. 1933. 126 p., 6 plates.

Giovanni, Gaetano di. Usi, credenze e pregiudizi de Canavese. Palermo, Tipografia del Giornale di Sicilia. 1889. 12, 176 p.

Goethe, Johann W. Goethe's travels in Italy: together with his second residency in Rome and fragments on Italy. London, G. Bell and Sons. 1885. 589 p. (Note especially the chapter on the Roman carnival.)

Graham, Mary. Three months passed in the mountains east of Rome during the year 1819. London, Longman. 1820. 7, 305 p.

Grindrod, Muriel. The rebuilding of Italy: politics and economics 1945-1955. London, Royal Institute of International Affairs. 1955. 7, 269 p., maps, table.

Gubernatis, Angelo de. Storia comparata degli usi natalizi in Italia. Milano, Fratelli Treves. 1878. 223 p.

Gubernatis, Angelo de. Storia comparata degli usi nuziali in Italia. Milano, Fratelli Treves. 1878. 283 p.

Harris, Dottore. Le prostitute nel secolo XIX, i loro mezzain, la polizia. Saggio storico-critico-sociale. Milano, Cesare Cioffi Editrice. 1886. 202 p.

Hazen, N. William. Italian agriculture under Fascism and war. Foreign Agriculture. 4(1940): 627-702.

Hermann, Ferdinand. Beiträge zur italienische Volkskunde. Heidelberg, Carl Winter. 1938. 7, 79 p.

Hoare, Sir Richard Colt. A tour through the island of Elba. London, J. Murray. 1814. 4, 32 p.

Hoare, Sir Richard Colt. Classical tour through Italy and Sicily. London, J. Mawman. 1819. 12, 557 p.

Hobsbawm, Eric J. Primitive rebels: studies in archaic forms of social movement in the 19th and 20th centuries. Manchester, University of Manchester Press. 1959. 7, 208 p. (American edition entitled: Social bandits and primitive rebels: . . . Glencoe, Ill., The Free Press. 1959.)

Holme, Charles. Peasant art in Italy. London and New York, The Studio. 1913. 8, 39 p., 92 plates (12 in color).

Hutton, Edward. In unknown Tuscany. London, Methuen. 1909. 244 p.

Justman, Joseph. The Italian people and their schools. International Education Monographs. 1. Tiffin, Ohio, Kappa Delta Pi. 1958. 9, 65 p.

Laing, Gordon J. Survivals of Roman religion. New York, Longmans, Green. 1931. 13, 257 p.

Lancelloti, Arturo. Feste Tradizionale. 2 vols. Milano, Società Editrice Libraria. 1921. 16, 1096 p., 768 illus.

Lancelloti, Arturo. Il Lazio. Usi, costumi, tradizioni, canti dei popolo romano. Roma, Pinei. 1927. 8, 179 p.

Lares. Bollettino della Società di Etnografia Italiana. 1 (1912)—

Lasorsa, Giovanni. Aspetti demografici, economici, sociali e approvvigionamento idrico della Puglia. Bari, Collana di Studi. 1952.

Lasorsa, Giovanni. Demografia. 5th ed. Bari, F. Cacucci. 1952. 190 p. (Southern Italy.)

Lasorsa, Giovanni. Indagini sui bilanci della famiglie contadine di Puglia e Lucania. Bari, Adriatica Editrice. 1956. 166 p., illus.

Lear, Edward. Illustrated excursions in Italy. 2 vols. in one. London, T. M'Lean. 1846.

Lear, Edward. Journals of a landscape painter in southern Calabria. London, R. Bentley. 1852. 20, 284 p., plates.

Leland, Charles Godfrey. Etruscan remains in popular tradition. London, T. F. Unwin. 1892. 8, 385 p.

Lessa, William A. Disintegration and reintegration of the Italian community as the result of the war and military occupation. Chicago, University of Chicago. 1947. (Unpublished Ph.D. dissertation.)

Levi, Carlo. Christ stopped at Eboli. New York, Farrar, Straus. 1947. 268 p

Levine, Irving R. Main street, Italy. Garden City, N.Y., Doubleday. 196?. 10, 542 p.

Lolli, Giorgio. Alcohol in Italian culture; food and wine in relation to sobriety among Italians and Italian-Americans. Glencoe, Ill., The Free Press. 1959. 15, 140 p.

Lombardi Satriani, Raffaele. Credenze popolari calabresi. Biblioteca delle Tradizioni Popolari Calabresi. 7. Napoli. 1951. 239 p.

Lopreato, Joseph. Effects of emigration on the social structure of a Calabrian community. New Haven, Yale University. 1960. (Unpublished Ph. D. dissertation.)

Lopreato, Joseph. Social stratification and mobility in a South Italian town. American Sociological Review. 26(1961): 585-596.

Lopreato, Joseph. Interpersonal relations in peasant society: the peasant's view. Human Organization. 21(1962): 21-24.

Lopreato, Joseph. Economic development and cultural change: the role of emigration. Human Organization. 21(1962): 182-186.

*Lopreato, Joseph. How would you like to be a peasant (in Italy)? Human Organization. 24(1965): 298-307.

*Lopreato, Joseph. Peasants no more. Social class and social change in southern Italy. San Francisco, Chandler Publishing Co. 1967. 15, 281 p.

Lutz, Vera C. Italy: a study in economic development. London, Oxford University Press. 1962. 342 p., illus.

McBride, Robert Medill. Hilltop cities of Italy. New York, R. M. McBride. 1936. 173 p.

McDonald, J. S. Italy's rural social structure and emigration. Occidente. 12(1956): 437-456.

McDonald, J. S., and L. McDonald. Institutional economics and rural development: two Italian types. Human Organization. 23(1964): 113-118.

Macdonnell, Anne. In the Abruzzi. London, Chatto & Windus. 1908. 9, 309 p., 12 col. plates.

MacFarlane, Charles. Popular customs, sports and recollections of the south of Italy. London, Charles Knight. 1846. 224 p.

MacFarlane, Charles. A glance at revolutionary Italy: a visit to Messina, and a tour through the kingdom of Naples, the states of the church, Tuscany, Genoa, Piedmont . . . in the summer of 1848. 2 vols. London, Smith, Elder. 1849.

ITALIANS

McNee, Robert B. Rural development in the Italian south: a geographic case study. Annals of the Association of American Geographers. 45 (1955): 127-151.

Majoli Faccio, Virginia. L'insidia del meriggio; il Biellese nelle sue tradizioni. Bologna, Cappelli. 1953. 251, 6 p.

Manzini, G. M. Autori e temi della recente etnologia religiosa in Italia. Sociologia Religiosa. 3/4 (1959): 33-78.

Maragliano, Alessandro. Tradizioni popolari Vogheresi. Firenze, Le Monnier. 1962. 860 p.

Marcozzi, V. Osservazioni di psicologia antropologica nel nord e sud d'Italia. Difesa Sociale. 36 (1957): 7-43.

Marinelli, Olinto. The regions of mixed populations in northern Italy. Geographical Review. 7 (1919): 129-148, fold-out map.

Martellaro, Joseph A. Economic development in southern Italy, 1950-1960. Washington, Catholic University of America Press. 1965. 123 p.

Martino, Ernesto de. Sud e magia. Milano, Feltrinelli. 1959. 205 p. (Lucania.)

Martino, Ernesto de. La terra del rimorso. Milano, Il Saggiatore. 1961.

Martino, Ernesto de. Italie du sud et magie. (Translated from the Italian by Claude Poncet.) Paris, Gallimard. 1963. 256 p., 16 plates.

Martino, Ernesto de. La terre du remords. Paris, Gallimard. 1966. 440 p., 32 plates. (Southern Italy: Tarantulism as a sociopsychological phenomeno

Maturanzo, Salvatore. Tradizioni di Napoli. Napoli, G. Casella. 1956. 195 p.

Medici, Giuseppe. Italian agriculture and its problems. (Translated by Eric B. Shearer.) Champaign, Ill., Bartlett Foundation. 1945. 3, 1, 34 p.

Medici, Giuseppe. L'agricoltura e la riforma agraria. Milano, Rizzoli. 194(139 p., tables.

*Medici, Giuseppe. Land, property and land tenure in Italy. (Translated and abridged from the Italian.) Bologna, Edizioni Agricole. 1952. 246 p.

Messeri, Enrico. Analisi ecologica del suicidio in Italia. Archivio per l'Antropologia e la Etnologia. 86 (1957): 101-126, maps, tables.

Messeri, Enrico. Considerazioni geografiche su alcuni aspetti extra-economic della nostra emigrazione. Archivio per l'Antropologia e la Etnologia. 89 (1960): 193-226.

-302-

Metalli, E. Usi e costumi della campagna Romana. 2d ed. Roma. 1924.
12, 309 p.

Meyriat, Jean, et al. La Calabre: une région sous-développée de l'Europe
méditerranéenne. Paris, A. Colin. 1960. 24, 329 p.

Milone, Ferdinando. L'Italia nell'economia delle sue regione. 2d ed. 6 vols.
Torino, Edizioni Scientifiche Einaudi. 1958. 719 p., maps, diagrams.

*Moss, Leonard W., and Stephen C. Cappannari. Patterns of kinship, com-
paraggio and community in a south Italian village. Anthropological Quarterly. 33(1960): 24-32.

Moss, Leonard W., and Stephen C. Cappannari. Folklore and medicine in an
Italian village. J.A.F.L. 73(1960): 95-102.

*Moss, Leonard W., and Stephen C. Cappannari. Estate and class in a South
Italian hill village. A.A. 64(1962): 287-300.

*Moss, Leonard W., and Walter H. Thomson. The South Italian family: lit-
erature and observation. Human Organization. 18 (1959): 35-41.

Mosso, Angelo. Vita moderna degli Italiani. Milano, Fratelli Treves. 1906.
430 p.

Niceforo, Alfredo. Italiani del nord e Italiani del sud. Torino, Fratelli Bocca.
1901. 8, 619 p., tables.

Nino, Antonio de. Usi e costumi Abruzzesi. 6 vols. Firenze, Tipografia di
G. Barbera. 1879-1897.

Nitto, A. La cultura a Buccino. Nord e Sud. 3, no. 18 (May 1956): 37-45.
(Salerno region.)

Nobilio, E. Vita tradizionale dei contadini Abruzzesi nel territorio di Penne.
Biblioteca di Lares. 10. Firenze, L. S. Olschki. 1962. 252 p.

Notestein, Lucy Lilian. Hill towns of Italy. Boston, Little, Brown. 1963.
256 p.

Olbrich, R. Italienische Volkskultur in der Darstellung ausländischer Reisender
zwischen 1770 und 1850. Volkstum und Kultur der Romanen. 13(1940):
219-270; 14(1941): 49-103.

Ortolani, M. La casa rurale negli Abruzzi. Firenze, L. S. Olschki. 1961.
148 p., 67 figs., 28 plates.

Ostermann, Valentino. La vita in Friuli; usi, costumi, credenze popolari.
2d ed. 2 vols. Udine, Istituto delle Edizioni Accademiche. 1940.
558 p., plates.

Pagano, Giuseppe, and G. Daniel. Architettura rurale italiana. Milano, U. Hoepli. 1936. 140 p., illus.

Palazo, Agostino. Organizzazione sociale e vita di comunità; studio monografico su un villaggio etero-costituito. Bari, Edizioni del Levante. 1960. 124 p.

Pansa, Giovanni. Miti, leggende e superstizioni dell' Abruzzo. 2 vols. Sulmona, Ubaldo Caroselli. 1924, 1927. 8, 299; 7, 396 p.

Parsons, Anne. Family dynamics in South Italian schizophrenics. Archives of General Psychiatry. 3(1960): 507-518.

Parsons, Anne. A schizophrenic episode in a Neapolitan slum. Psychiatry. 24(1961): 109-121.

Parsons, Anne. Is the Oedipus complex universal? The Jones-Malinowski debate revisited and a South Italian "nuclear complex." In Warner Muensterberger and Sidney Axelrod, eds. The Psychoanalytic Study of Society. 3. New York, International Universities Press. 1964: 278-328.

Paulson, Belden, and Athos Ricci. The searchers. Conflict and communism in an Italian town. Chicago, Quadrangle Books. 1966. 16, 361 p.

Pazzini, Adalberto. La medicina popolare in Italia. Storia, tradizioni, leggende. Trieste. 1948. 358 p.

Pazzini, Adalberto. Storia, tradizioni e leggende nella medicina popolare. Correggio, Dr. Recordati. 1949 [1950]. 142 p., 37 illus.

Pazzini, Adalberto. Demoni, streghe a guaritori. Milano, V. Bompiani. 1951. 190 p.

Pellegrini, Angelo. The unprejudiced palate. New York, Macmillan. 1948. 235 p. (Mainly cookery—but here and there some very insightful notes and comments.)

Pellegrini, Angelo. Immigrant's return. New York, Macmillan. 1951. 269 p

Pellegrini, Luigi. Di alcuni paesi della montagna Lucchese. Lucca, Tipografia del Serchio. 1891. 88 p.

Penna, Renato. La Tarantella Napoletana. Naples, Rivista di Etnografia. 1963. 89 p., 24 plates.

Pennell, Joseph. An Italian pilgrimage. London, Seeley. 1887. 16, 228 p.

*Peruzzi, Duilio. Cortona: a valley-hill-mountain complex of modified Mediterranean agriculture in central Italy. Ann Arbor, University of Michigan. 1964. 242 p. (Unpublished Ph.D. dissertation, on Tuscany.)

Phieler, Willy. Volkskundliches aus den Marken. Eine Studie aus den italienischen Provinzen der "Marche." Hamburg Studien zu Volkstum und Kultur
der Romanen. 17. Hamburg, Hansischer Gildenverlag. 1934. 91 p., 6
plates.

Piantelli, Francesco. Folclore Cremasco. Crema, Vinci. 1951. 595 p.

Pigorini-Beri, C. Costumi e superstizioni dell' Apennino marchigiano. Città
di Castello. 1889. 16, 304 p.

Pilato, Sergio di. La Lucania. Potenza, Libreria Editrice Marchesiello. 1933.

*Pitkin, Donald S. Land tenure and family organization in an Italian village.
Cambridge, Harvard University. 1954. 8, 372 p. (Unpublished Ph. D.
dissertation in anthropology.)

*Pitkin, Donald S. A consideration of asymmetry in the peasant-city relation-
ship. Anthropological Quarterly. 32(1959): 161-167.

*Pitkin, Donald S. Marital property considerations among peasants: an Italian
example. Anthropological Quarterly. 33(1960): 33-39.

Price, Edward T. Viterbo: landscape of an Italian city. Annals of the Association of American Geographers. 54(1964): 242-275.

Priori, Domenico. Riti funerari abruzzesi. Folklore. 2(1947): 61-74.

Provenzal, Dino. Usanze e feste del popolo Italiano. Bologna. 1912. 15,
248 p.

Provenzal, Dino. I ragazzi e la loro educazione nei proberbii italiani. Catania,
F. Battiato. 1916. 124 p.

Raffaele, J. A. Labor leadership in Italy and Denmark. Madison, University of
Wisconsin Press. 1962. 436 p.

Ramponi, Carlo. Le tradizioni popolari di Borgo Lavezzaro. Novara, Stab.
Tipografia Cattaneo. 1939. 218 p.

Ranieri, Luigi. Basilicata. Torino, Unione Tipografico-Editrice Torinese.
1961. 10, 429 p., illus., maps.

Rasmussen, H. Kastaniekultur i Kalabrien. Kuml. 1961: 146-168.

Rennell, James Rennell Rodd. The Italian people. Proceedings of the British
Academy. 9(1924): 389-407.

Reynolds-Ball, E. A. Unknown Italy. Piedmont and the Piedmontese. London, A. & C. Black. 1927. 12, 254 p., illus., map.

Rita, Lidia de. I contadini en la televisione. Bologna, Società Editrice il Mulino. 1964. 307 p., diagr.

Riviello, Raffaele. Costumanze, vita e pregiudizi del popolo Potentino. Potenza, Garramone e Marchesiello. 1893. 229 p.

Rogers, Mrs. E. B. All-Fools day in Italy. J.A.F.L. 4(1891): 168-170.

Rosa, Gabrielle. Dialetti, costumi e tradizioni della provincia di Bergamo e Brescia. 3d ed. Brescia, Stab. Tip. Lit. di F. Fiori. 1870. 389 p.

Rosa, Gabrielle. Tradizioni e costumi Lombardi. Bergamo, Stab. Tipografi Fratelli Cattaneo successori Gaffuri e Gatti edit. 1891. 107 p.

Rose, Herbert J. The festival of San Zopito. Man. 23(1923): 107-108.

Rossi-Doria, Manlio. Riforma agraria e azione meridionalista. 2d ed. Bologn Edizioni Agricole. 1956. 10, 394 p. (Agricultural economics and land tenure in southern Italy.)

Rossi-Doria, Manlio. Dieci anni di politica agraria del Mezzogiorno. Bari, Laterza. 1958. 36, 412 p.

Rossi-Doria, Manlio. The land tenure system and class in southern Italy. American Historical Review. 64(1958): 46-53.

Roussel de Fontanes, M. Les costumes traditionnels calabrais (mission de juin 1962). Objets et Mondes. 3(1963): 71-80.

Rubić, Ivo. Talijani na primorju kraljevine Jugoslaviji. Split, Hravtska Štamparija Gradske Štedionice. 1930. 57 p. (Italians in Dalmatia.)

Saibene, C. La casa rurale nella pianura e nelle collina Lombarda. Firenze, L. S. Olschki. 1955. 6, 221 p., illus.

Salvadori, Massimo. Las ciencias sociales del siglo XX en Italia. Revista Mexicana de Sociología. 12(1950): 111-149.

Samuelli, Carlo. Progetti, particolari, norme tecniche e pratiche per la costruzione dei fabbricati colonici e opere rustiche annesse. Milano, Editoriale Italiana. 1945. 251 p.

Sandys, George. A relation of a journey begun An Dom 1610. Fovre bookes. Containing a description of the Turkish empire, of Aegypt, of the Holy Lan of the remote parts of Italy, and islands adioyning. London, printed for W. Barnett. 1615.

Satriani, Raffaele. Tradizioni popolari Calabresi. Reggio Calabria, Il Progresso. 1927.

Schachter, Gustav. The Italian south: economic development in Mediterranean Europe. New York, Random House. 1965. 244 p., maps.

Scheuermeier, Paul. Bauernwerk in Italien, der italienischen und rätoromanischen Schweiz. 2 vols. Vol. 1, Erlenbach-Zürich, Eugene Rentsch. Vol. 2, Bern, Stämpfli. 1943, 1956. 4, 16, 319; 16, 529 p., plates.

Scholz, H. Die Trulli Apuliens: Beiträge zur Siedlungsgeographie von Süditalien. Geographica Helvetica. 11 (1956): 236-241.

Scotellaro, Rocco. Contadini del sud. 3d ed. Bari, Laterza. 1955. 247 p.

Seronde, Anne-Marie, et al. La Calabre. Une région sous-dévelopée de l'Europe méditerranéenne . . . Paris, A. Colin. 1960. 24, 332 p., figs., maps.

Seymour, Fredrick H. Up hill and down dale in ancient Etruria. New York, D. Appleton. 1910. 320 p.

Sforza, Count Carlo. The real Italians, a study in European psychology. New York, Columbia University Press. 1942. 156 p.

Sforza, Count Carlo. Italy and Italians. New York, E. P. Dutton. 1949. London, Frederick Muller. 1948. 9, 165 p.

Silone, Ignazio. Bread and wine. New York and London, Harper and Brothers. 1937. 319 p. (Abruzzi: fiction but contains excellent material.)

*Silverman, Sydel F. Landlord and peasant in an Umbrian community. New York, Columbia University. 1963. 298 p. (Unpublished Ph.D. dissertation in anthropology.)

*Silverman, Sydel F. Patronage and community-nation relationships in central Italy. Ethnology. 4(1965): 172-189.

*Silverman, Sydel F. An ethnographic approach to social stratification: prestige in a central Italian community. A.A. 68 (1966): 899-921.

*Silverman, Sydel F. The life crisis as a clue to social functions. Anthropological Quarterly. 40(1967): 127-138.

*Silverman, Sydel F. Agricultural organization, social structure, and values in Italy: amoral familism reconsidered. A.A. 70(1968): 1-20.

Simeone, William E. Italian folklore scholars. In Richard M. Dorson, ed. Folklore research around the world. Bloomington, Indiana University Press. 1961: 58-67.

ITALIANS

Simoncini, Giorgio. Architettura contadina di Puglia. Genova, Vitali e
Ghianda. 1960. 139 p., illus.

Solinas, Giovanni. Credenze popolari sulle Verruche. Rivista di Etnografia.
6(1953): 26-36.

Sorrento, Luigi. Folklore e dialetti d'Italia. Aevum. 1 (1927): 635-797;
3(1929): 241-326.

Spranger, J. A. The festival of San Zopito and the ox at Loreto Aprutino.
J.R.A.I. 52(1922): 306-319.

Spurlin, P. Farmers in flight. Atlas. 9(1965): 138-141. (Southern Italy.)

Stancati, Filomena. Il mio paese. Tradizioni popolari nella famiglia, nella
vita, nell'arte. Nicastro, Stab. Arti Grafiche V. Nicotera. 1951. 273 p.

Sullam, Victor B. Fundamentals of Italian agriculture. Foreign Agriculture.
7(1943): 267-288.

Swinburne, Henry. Travels in the Two Sicilies . . . in the years 1777, 17
1779, and 1780. 2 vols. London, P. Elmsley. 1783, 1785. 31, 429;
85, 534 p. (Another edition: 4 vols. London, T. Cadell and P. Elmsley.
1790.)

Symonds, John Addington. Sketches & studies in southern Europe. 2 vols.
New York, Harper & Brothers. 1880.

Symonds, John Addington. Italian byways. New York, Henry Holt. 1883.
318 p.

*Tamassia, Giovanni. La famiglia italiana nei secoli decimoquinto e deci-
mosesto. Milano-Palermo-Napoli, Remo Sandron. 1911. 372 p.

Tarrow, Sidney G. Peasant communism in southern Italy. New Haven and
London, Yale University Press. 1967. 18, 389 p.

Tentori, Tullio. Le raccolte abruzzesi del Museo Nazionale delle Arte e
delle Tradizioni Popolari. Lares. 25(1959): 168-182.

Tentori, Tullio. L'antropologia culturale in Italia. Bollettino delle Ricerche
Sociali. 1 (1961): 477-500.

Tersenghi, Augusto. Costumanze antiche di Velletri. Velletri, Tipografia G
Zampetti. 1935. 138 p.

Toor, Frances. Festivals and folkways of Italy. New York, Crown Publishers
1953. 8, 312 p.

Toor, Frances. Made in Italy. New York, Knopf. 1957. 204 p. (Folk arts.

Toschi, Paolo. Guida allo studio delle tradizioni popolari. Roma, Edizioni Italiane. 1941. 255 p.

Toschi, Paolo. Il folklore. Roma, Universale Studium. 1951. 164 p.

Toschi, Paolo. Romagna tradizionale: usi e costumi, credenze e pregiudizi. Bologna, Cappelli. 1952. 38, 315 p., plates.

Toschi, Paolo. "Fabri" del folklore. Roma, A. Signorelli. 1958. 215 p.

Toschi, Paolo. Tradizioni popolari Italiane. Torino, Edizioni Radio Italiana. 1959. 193 p.

*Toschi, Paolo. Arte popolare Italiana. Roma, Carlo Bestetti Edizioni d'Arte. 1960. 450 p., illus., plates.

Toschi, Paolo. Buonsangue romagnola: racconti di animali, scherzi, aneddoti, facezie. Bologna, Cappelli. 1960. 282 p.

Toschi, Paolo. Saggi sull'arte popolare. Roma, Edizioni dell' Ateneo. 1960. 160 p.

Underhill, Ruth M. Child labor in Italy. Report of the Commission for Tuberculosis, issued by the American Red Cross in Italy. Roma, Tipografia Nazionale Bertero. 1919.

Unger, Leonard. Rural settlement in the Campania. Geographical Review. 43(1953): 506-524.

Valentini, Gianfranco. Folklore e leggende della Val di Fassa. Bologna, Cappelli. 1953. 274 p.

Verdone, M. Cacce e giostre taurine nelle città italiane. Lares. 29(1963): 171-190.

Vidossi, Giuseppe. Zur Geschichte der italienischen Volkskunde. Z.f.V. n.F. 48(1939): 7-17.

Villari, Luigi. Italian life in town and country. New York and London, G. P. Putnam's Sons. 1902. 9, 327 p., plates.

Villari, Rosario. L'evoluzione della proprietà fondiaria in un feudo meridionale nel settecento. Napoli, G. Macchiaroli. 1957. 87 p. (Lucania.)

Villari, Rosario. Mezzogiorno e contadini nell'età moderno. Bari, Editori Laterza. 1961. 288 p. (Land tenure and economic history.)

Villari, Rosario, ed. Il sud nella storia d'Italia. 2d ed. Bari, Editori Laterza. 1961. 8, 769 p.

Vincelli, G. Una comunità meridionale. Torino, Casa Editrice Taylor. 1958. 260 p.

Virone, L. E. Borgo a Mozzano: technical assistance in a rural community in Italy. Occasional Paper No. 4, World Land Use Survey. Bude, Cornwal Geographical Publications. 1963. 36 p., illus., folding map. (Tuscany.)

Volpi, L. Usi, costumi e tradizioni Bergamasche. Bergamo, Edizioni del "Giopi." 1937. 238 p. (Italian Tyrol.)

Waddington, Mrs. Mary Alsop King. Italian letters of a diplomat's wife, January-May 1880, February-April, 1904. New York, C. Scribner's Sons. 1905. 8, 324 p. (Rome.)

Walker, Donald S. A geography of Italy. New York, E. P. Dutton; London, Methuen. 1958. 256 p., illus., map.

Weigend, Guido Gustav. The cultural pattern of South Tyrol (Italy). University of Chicago, Department of Geography. Research Papers No. 3. Chicago, University of Chicago Press. 1949. 8, 198 p.

Wheeler, David L. Land reform and reclamation in the Po River delta. Ann Arbor, University of Michigan. 1962. 265 p. (Unpublished Ph. D. dissertation in Geography.)

Williams, Egerton R. Hill towns of Italy. Boston and New York, Houghton Mifflin. 1903. 14, 398 p.

Williams, Egerton R. Plain-towns of Italy; the cities of old Venetia. Boston and New York, Houghton Mifflin. 1911. 23, 603 p.

Williams, Egerton R. Lombard towns in Italy. New York, Dodd, Mead. 191 590 p.

*Williams, Phyllis. South Italian folkways in Europe and America. New Haven Yale University Press. 1938. 18, 216 p.

Wilstach, Paul. The stone beehive homes of the Italian heel. In Trulli-land the native builds his dwelling and makes his fields arable in the same operation. National Geographic Magazine. 57(1930): 228-260.

Zamboni, Armando. Vita sull'Appennino. Torino, Società Editrice Internazionale. 1951. 223 p.

Zanazzo, Luigi. Usi, costumi e pregiudizi del popolo di Roma. Torino, Società Tipografico-Editrice Nazionale. 1908. 499 p.

Zanetti, Zeno. La medicina delle nostre donne. Studio folk-lorico premiato la psicologia delle superstizione . . . Città di Castello, S. Lapi Tipograf: Editore. 1892. 19, 271 p.

Zimmerman, Carle C.   American roots in an Italian village.   Genus.
    11 (1955): 78-139.

Zink, Harold, Arne Wählstrand, et al.   Rural local government in Sweden,
    Italy and India.   London, Stevens & Sons.   1957.   14, 142 p.

SICILY

Cupertino, Enzo. Regione Siciliana. Bibliografia 1943-1953. Palermo,
V. Bellotti & Figlio. 1954. 282 p.

Evola, Niccolò Domenico. Bibliografia Siciliana, 1938-1953. Palermo,
S. Pezzino. 1954. 532 p.

Pitrè, Giuseppe. Bibliografia delle tradizioni popolari d'Italia. Torino-
Palermo, Carlo Clausen. 1894. 20, 603 p.

Toschi, Paolo. Bibliografia delle tradizioni popolari d'Italia dal 1916-al
1940. Tome 1. Firenze, Barbera. 32, 143 p. (No other volumes published.)

Agricoltura e credito agrario in Sicilia. Palermo, Banco di Sicilia. 1960.
73 p., plates, appendix.

Alongi, Giuseppe. La mafia nei suoi fattori e nelle sue manifestazioni.
Roma-Torino, Fratelli Bocca Librai di S. M. il Re d'Italia. 1886. 163 p.

Anfosi, Anna, Magda Talamo, and Francesco Indovena. Ragusa, comunità
in transizione; saggio sociologico. Torino, Taylor. 1959. 212 p.

Angas, George F. A ramble in Malta and Sicily, in the autumn of 1841.
London, Smith, Elder. 1842. 7, 168 p.

Anonymous. A curious custom in Sicily. J.A.I. 20(1891): 364-365.

Anonymous. Costume and habits of Sicilian peasantry. J.A.I. 21(1891):
68-72.

Barbero, G. Land reform in Italy: achievements and perspectives. Rome,
Food and Agriculture Organization of the United Nations. 1961. 11, 199
map, diagrams, tables.

Battaglia, Aristide. L'evoluzione sociale in rapporto alla proprietà fondiaria
in Sicilia. Palermo, Libreria Carlo Clausen. 1895. 420 p.

Baxter, Celana A. Sicilian family life. Family. 14(1933): 82-88.

Blok, A. Landhervorming in een westsiciliaans latifondodorp. Mens en
Maatschappij. 39(1964): 244-359.

Blok, A. Land reform in a West Sicilian latifondo village: the persistence of
a feudal structure. Anthropological Quarterly. 39(1966): 1-16.

Blunt, Rev. John James. Vestiges of ancient manners and customs, discoverable in modern Italy and Sicily. London, John Murray. 1823. 12, 293 p.

*Boissevain, Jeremy. The effects of emigration on the authority structure in Sicily. American Philosophical Society: Yearbook 1963. Philadelphia. 1964: 377-380.

*Boissevain, Jeremy. Patronage in Sicily. Man. New series. 1(1966): 18-33.

*Boissevain, Jeremy. Poverty and politics in a Sicilian agro-town: a preliminary report. International Archives of Ethnography. 50(1966): 198-236.

Buttita, A. La festa dei morti Sicilia. Annuario Museo Pitrè. 11/13(1960-1963.): 145-160.

Caico, Louise. Sicilian ways and days. New York, D. Appleton; London, J. Long. 1910. 18, 19-279 p.

Cocchiara, Giuseppe. Gli studi delle tradizioni popolari in Sicilia. Introduzioni alla storia del folklore italiano. Biblioteca Sandron di Scienze e Lettere 110. Palermo, Sandron. 1928. 176 p.

Cocchiara, Giuseppe. La vita e l'arte del popolo Siciliano nel Museo Pitrè. Palermo, F. Ciuni. 1938. 228 p., illus.

Cocchiara, Giuseppe. Il folklore Siciliano. 2 vols. Palermo, S. F. Flaccovio. 1957.

Cocchiara, Giuseppe, and Rubino Benedetto. Usi e costumi, novelle e poesie del popolo Siciliano. Palermo, Sandron. 1924. 192 p.

Coote, Henry Charles. Childrens' games in Sicily. Folk-Lore Journal. 2(1884): 82-88.

Coray, H. Bodenbestellung, ländliche Geräte, Ölbereitung, Weinbau und Fischerei auf den liparischen Inseln. Volkstum und Kultur der Romanen. 3(1930): 149-231, 305-391.

Corso, Raffaele. Reviviscenze. Studi di tradizioni popolari. Catania, Libreria Tirelli di F. Guitolini. 1927.

*Covello, Leonard. The social background of the Italo-American school child. A study of the southern Italian family mores and their effect on the school situation in Italy and America. Leiden, E. J. Brill. 1967. 30, 488 p.

Cumin, Gustavo. La Sicilia: profilo geografico-economico. Catania, Dott. G. Crisafulli-Editore. 1944. 232 p.

Dolci, Danilo. Report from Palermo. New York, Orion Press. 1959. 22, 310 p.

Dolci, Danilo. Outlaws. New York, Orion Press. 1961. 7, 296 p. (Social conditions and brigands.)

Dolci, Danilo. Waste: an eye-witness report on some aspects of waste in western Sicily. New York, Monthly Review Press. 1964; London, MacGibbon & Kee. 1963. 352 p., illus.

Dolci, Danilo. Poverty in Sicily: a study of the province of Palermo. Baltimore, Harmondsworth, Penguin Books. 1966. 317 p.

Franchetti, Leopoldo. Condizioni politiche e amministrative della Sicilia. (Vol. 1 of L. Franchetti and S. Sonnino. La Sicilia. 2 vols.) Firenze, Vallechi Editore Firenze. 1925. 63, 351 p.

Fuchs, H. Beiträge zur Anthropo-Geographie und Geschichte der Insel Linosa. Wiener Volkerkundliche Mitteilungen. 4(1956): 25-36.

Gower, Charlotte Day. The supernatural patron in Sicilian life. Chicago, University of Chicago. 1928. (Unpublished Ph.D. dissertation in anthropology.)

Grisanti, Cristoforo. Usi, credenze, proverbi e racconti popolari di Isuello, . Palermo. 1899. 250 p.

*Guercio, Francis Michael. Sicily, the garden of the Mediterranean; the country and its people. 2d ed. London, Faber and Faber. 1954. 310 p., plates, folding map.

Hoare, Sir Richard Colt. Classical tour through Italy and Sicily. London, J. Mawman. 1819. 12, 557 p.

Hobsbawm, Eric J. Primitive rebels: studies in archaic forms of social movement in the 19th and 20th centuries. Manchester, Manchester University Press. 1959. 7, 208 p. (The Mafia.)

Leadbetter, D. The Sicilian cart: origins of a western European folk art. In Marian W. Smith, ed. The artist in tribal society. London, The Royal Anthropological Institute. 1961: 36-47.

Levi, Carlo. Words are stones: impressions of Sicily. New York, Farrar, Straus & Cudahy. 1958. 212 p.

Ludwig Salvator, Archduke of Austria. Die liparischen Inseln. 8 vols. Prag, H. Mercy. 1893-1896.

Macfarlane, Charles. A glance at revolutionized Italy: a visit to Messina, and a tour through the Kingdom of Naples, the Abruzzi, the marches of Ancona, Rome, the states of the church, Tuscany, Genoa, Piedmont, etc. etc. in the summer of 1848. 2 vols. London, Smith, Elder. 1849.

Majorca, Antonio Pecoraro. La trasformazione del latifondo e la riforma agraria in Sicilia. Palermo, Flaccovio. 1948. 173 p.

Mangione, J. G. A passion for Sicilians: the world around Danilo Dolci. New York, Morrow. 1968. 369 p.

Martellaro, Joseph A. Economic development in southern Italy, 1950-1960. Washington, Catholic University of America Press. 1965. 123 p.

Maxwell, Gavin. The ten pains of death. New York, E. P. Dutton. 1960. 9, 272 p.

Milone, Ferdinando. Sicilia, la natura e l'uomo. Torino, P. Boringhieri. 1960. 462 p., illus.

Moss, Leonard W. Observations on "the day of the dead" in Catania, Sicily. J. A. F. L. 76 (1963): 134-135.

Pantaleone, Michele. The Mafia and politics. New York, Coward-McCann. 1966. 255 p., illus., maps.

Papa, Tommaso. Il culto dei morti in Sicilia. Alcamo, Edizioni Accademia di Studi Cielo d'Alcamo. 1958. 41 p.

Petrullo, Vincenzo M. A note on Sicilian cross-cousin marriage. Primitive Man. 10(1937): 8-9.

*Pitrè, Giuseppe. Biblioteca delle tradizioni popolari siciliane. 25 vols. Palermo, L. Pedone-Lauriel. 1872-1913.

Pitrè, Giuseppe. Popular marriage customs of Sicily. Lippincott's Magazine. 22(1878): 89-96.

Preconi, Hector G. Sizilianische Bauernwagen. Atlantis. 7(1935): 504-508.

*Prestianni, Nunzio. L'economia agraria della Sicilia. Palermo, Istituto Nazionale di Economia Agraria. 1947. 268, 12 p.

Renda, Francesco. Il movimento contradino nella società siciliana. Palermo, Edizione "Sicilia al Lavoro." 1956. 220 p.

Ruini, Carlo. Le vincende del latifondo siciliano. Firenze, G. C. Sansoni. 1940. 213 p.

Salomone-Marino, Salvatore. Leggende popolari siciliane in poesia. Palermo. 1880. 29, 435 p.

Salomone-Marino, Salvatore. Costumi e usanze dei contradini di Sicilia. Palermo. 1924. 330 p.

*Sardo, Joseph. A comparative study of selected aspects of rural social organization in Valle del Cauca, Colombia and Sicily, Italy. Gainesville, University of Florida. 1968: 28-117. (Unpublished Ph. D. dissertation in Sociology, based on field work in both Sicily and Colombia.)

Schachter, Gustav. The Italian south: economic development in Mediterranean Europe. New York, Random House. 1965. 244 p., maps.

Schenda, R., and S. Schenda. Eine sizilianische Strasse. Volkskundliche aus Monreale. Tübingen, Vereinigung für Volkskunde. 1965. 112 p.

Schifani, Carmelo. Il livello di vita delle famiglie agricole siciliane. Quaderni di Sociologia Rurale. Anno 2, no. 3(1963): 10-34.

Sciortino Gugino, Carola. Conscienza colletiva e giudizio individuale nella cultura contadina. Palermo, U. Manfredi Editore. 1960. 79 p.

*Sonnino, Sidney. I contadini in Sicilia. (Vol. 2 of L. Franchetti and S. Sonnino. La Sicilia.) Firenze, Vallecchi Editore. 1925. 365 p.

Sullam, Victor B. The agriculture of Sicily. Foreign Agriculture. 7(1943): 219-240.

Swinburne, Henry. Travels in the Two Sicilies. . . in the years 1777, 1778, 1779, and 1780. 2 vols. London, P. Elmsley. 1783-1785. 31, 429; 85, 534 p. (Another edition: 4 vols. London, T. Cadell and P. Elmsley. 1790.)

Tarrow, Sidney G. Peasant communism in southern Italy. New Haven and London, Yale University Press. 1967. 18, 389 p.

Thompson, W. H. Sicily and its inhabitants. Observations made during a residence in that country, in the years 1809 and 1810. London, printed for Henry Colburn. 1813. 8, 234 p.

Tiby, Octavio, ed. Corpus di musiche popolari Siciliane. 2 vols. Palermo, Accademia di Scienze, Lettre e Arti. 1957.

Titone, Virgilio. Storia, Mafia e costume in Sicilia. Milano, Edizioni del Milione. 1964. 308 p.

Vuillier, Gaston. La Sicilia. Milano, F. Treves. 1897. 459 p.

Wermert, Georg. Die Insel Sicilien in volkswirtschaftlicher, kultureller und sozialer Beziehung. Berlin, D. Reimer. 1905. 488 p.

Whyte, William Foote. Sicilian peasant society. A.A. New series. 46(1944): 65-74. (Data primarily from Pitrè and C. Gower.)

*Williams, Phyllis H. South Italian folkways in Europe and America. New Haven, Yale University Press. 1938. 18, 216 p.

Ciasca, Raffaele. Bibliografia Sarda. 5 vols. Roma, Collezione Meridionale Editrice. 1931-1934.

Alberoni, Francisco. I fattori culturali dello sviluppo economico in Sardegna. Milano, Società Editrice Vita e Pensiero. 1960. 171 p.

Alziator, D. Il folklore Sardo. Bologna, La Zattera. 1957. 14, 269 p.

Bottliglioni, Gino. Leggende e tradizioni di Sardegna. Genève, L. S. Olschki. 1922. 157 p.

Bottliglioni, Gino. Vita Sarda. Milano, Trevisini. 1925. 286 p.

Bresciani, Antonio. Dei costumi dell'isola di Sardegna . . . 2 vols. Napoli, all'Uffizio della Civiltà Cattolica. 1850. 71, 139; 298 p. (Reprinted: Napoli, Tipografia di Francesco Giannini. 1861. 464 p.)

Bresciani, Antonio. Dei costumi dell'isola di Sardegna comparati cogli antichissimi popoli orientali. 4 vols. Milano, Serafino Muggiani. 1872. 160, 144, 124, 179 p. (Reprinted: 1890.)

Cossu, Angelo. L'isola di Sardegna; saggio monografico di geografia fisica e di antropogeografia. Roma, Società Editrice Dante Alighieri. 1900. 202 p.

Cossu, Giuseppe. Descrizione geografica della Sardegna. Genova, Dalla Stamperia di A. Olzati. 1799. 112 p.

Cossu, Pietro Maria. Note ed appunti di folklore sardo. Bagnacavallo, Società Tipografica Editrice. 1925. 189 p.

Costa, Guido. The island of Sardinia and its people. National Geographic Magazine. 43(1923): 1-75.

Crespi, Pietro. Analisi sociologica e sottosviluppo economico; introduzione a uno studio d'ambiente in Sardegna. Milano, Giuffrè. 1963. 266 p., map.

Del Rio, C. La barbagia. Rivista Geografica Italiana. 48(1941): 262-271.

Dozier, Craig L. Establishing a framework for development in Sardinia: the campidano. Geographical Review. 47(1957): 490-506.

Eckert, Georg. Zum Votivwesen in Nordwest-Sardinien. Z.f.E. 82(1957): 261-266.

Edwardes, Charles. Sardinia and the Sardes. London, R. Bentley and Son. 1889. 12, 379 p.

Hayward, F., and J. Imbert. Sardaigne, terre de lumière. Paris, Nouv. Éd. Latines. 1956. 351 p.

SARDINIA

Heiderich, B. Das Banditenwesen im inneren Sardiniens. Zeitschrift für Vergleichende Rechwissenschaft. 67(1965): 189-202.

Lawrence, David H. Sea and Sardinia. New York, T. Seltzer. 1921. 355 p.

*Le Lannou, Maurice. Pâtres et paysans de la Sardaigne. Tours, Arrault. 1941. 364 p.

Levi, Doro. Sardinia: isle of antitheses. Geographical Review. 33(1943): 630-654.

Manca, Giuseppe. Saldigna. Cagliari, Fratelli Fossataro. 1960. 875 p., illus., folding map. (Guide book.)

Marotta, M. Società e uomo in Sardegna. Ricerca di sociologia positiva. Annali Economico-Sociali della Sardegna, ser. 1. 1. Cagliari. 1958. 21, 415 p.

Martino, Ernesto de, ed. Atti del convegno de studi religiosi Sardi. Padua, Antonio Milano. 1963. 8, 358 p.

Melichar, Herbert. Volkskundliche Streifzüge durch Sardinien. Wiener Völkerkundliche Mitteilungen. 1 (1953): 30-38.

Mossa, Vico. Architettura domestica in Sardegna. Cagliari, Edizioni della Zatera. 1957. 209 p., 173 plates, maps, plans.

Pampaloni, Enzo. L'economia agraria della Sardegna. Roma, Edizioni Italiane. 1937.

Papocchia, Raffaella Luisa. Note antropogeografiche sul Sàrrabus (Sardegna sud orientale). Bollettino della Reale Società Geografica Italiana, ser. 7. 1 (1936): 81-99.

Pigliaru, Antonia. Scuola a riforma agraria in Sardegna. Sassari, Scuola in Sardegna. 1956. 62 p. (Rural conditions and schools.)

Poggi, Francesco. Usi natalize e funebri della Sardegna. Mortara-Vigevana. 1897. 120 p.

Posse-Brazdova, Amelie. Sardinian sideshow. New York, E. P. Dutton. 1933. 261 p.

Prettenhofer, Emmerich. Sardienien und die Sarden. Mitteilungen der Geographischen Gesellschaft in Wien. 70(1927): 31-43.

Prettenhofer, Emmerich. Volkssitten in Sardinien. Der Erdball. 4(1929): 284-288.

Tucci, G. Old and new handicraft in Sardinia. Kultuurpatronen. 5/6(1963): 161-194.

Wagner, Max Leopold. Lautlehre der südsardischen Mundarten, mit besonderer berücksichtigung der um den Gennargentu gesprochenen Varietäten. Halle an der Saale, M. Niemeyer. 1907. 86 p.

Wagner, Max Leopold. Das ländliche Leben Sardiniens im Spiegel der Sprache. Heidelberg, C. Winter. 1921. 16, 206 p.

Wagner, Max Leopold. Die Binnenfischerei in Sardinien. Volkstum und Kultur der Romanen. 15(1942): 255-275, 359.

Walker, W. G., ed. Sardinian studies. London, Le Play Society. 1938. 60 p., 12 plates.

Weis Bentzon, Andreas Fridolin. Notes sur la vie musicale d'un village Sarde. Folk. 2(1960): 13-32.

Welte, Adolf. Ländliche Wirtschaftssysteme und mittelmeerische Kulturlandschaft in Sardinien. Zeitschrift der Gesellschaft für Erdkunde zu Berlin. 1933: 270-290.

Wright, Helen D. Little-known Sardinia. National Geographic Magazine. 30(1916): 97-120.

VATICAN CITY

Carnahan, Ann. The Vatican: behind the scenes in the holy city. New York,
Farrar, Straus. 1949. 190 p., illus., photos.

Neuveccelle, Jean. The Vatican: its organization, customs, and way of life.
(Translated from the French by George Libaire.) New York, Criterion.
1955. 250 p., illus.

Neville, Robert. The world of the Vatican. New York, Harper and Row.
1962. 256 p.

Pepper, Curtis G. The Pope's back yard. New York, Farrar, Straus.   1967.
184 p.

Toschi, Umberto. The Vatican City State: from the standpoint of political
geography. Geographical Review. 21(1931): 529-538.

SAN MARINO

Crocioni, Giovanni. Bibliografia delle tradizioni popolari di San Marino.
San Marino, Arti Graphiche Filippo della Balda. 1947. 95 p.

———————————

Brizi, Oreste. Quadro storico-statistico della serenissima repubblica di San
Marino. Firenze, Stabil. Artistico Fabris. 1842. 97 p.

Brizi, Oreste. Alcuni usi e costumi sammarinesi. Arezzo, Tip. di Antonio
Bellotti. 1856. 37 p.

Gozi, Manlio. Leggende e storia di San Marino. San Marino, Arti Grafiche.
1916. 64 p.

Crispi, Giuseppe. Memorie storiche di talune costumanze appartenenti alle colonie greco-albanesi di Sicilia. Palermo, Tipografia di Pietro Morvillo. 1853. 95 p.

Dorsa, Vincenzo. Su gli Albanesi. Ricerche e pensieri. Napoli, Tipografia Trani. 1847. 170 p.

Gaetano, F. de. Il matrimonio presso gli Albanesi. Folklore Calabrese. 3(1917): 7-12; 4(1918): 7-12; 5(1919): 1-6.

*Nasse, George N. The Italo-Albanian villages of southern Italy. Foreign Field Research Program Report. 25. Washington, National Academy of Sciences-National Research Council. 1964. 5, 81 p., plates.

Scura, A. Gli albanese in Italia. Saggi e Riviste. 5(1865): 117-158.

Skendi, Stavro. Albanian and South Slavic oral epic poetry. Memoirs of the American Folklore Society. 44. Philadelphia. 1954. 221 p.

Smilari, Alessandro. Gli Albanesi d'Italia, loro costumi e poesie popolari. Napoli, A. Bellisario & C-R. Tipografia de Angelis. 1891. 79 p.

MALTA

Simpson, Donald Herbert. Malta. Library Association, Special Subject List 15. London, Library Association. 1957. 6 p.

Angas, George F. A ramble in Malta and Sicily, in the autumn of 1841. London, Smith, Elder. 1842. 7, 168 p.

Aquilina, J. Maltese meteorological and agricultural proverbs. Malta, Malta University Press. 1961. 80 p.

Aquilina, J., et al. A new dialect survey of present-day spoken Maltese: preliminary notice. Journal of Maltese Studies. 3(1966): 42-46.

Ashbee, P., comp. A Maltese anthology. Oxford, Clarendon Press. 1960. 37, 280 p.

Beeley, Brian W. The farmer and rural society in Malta. Durham, Department of Geography, Durham Colleges in the University of Durham. 1959. 194 p. (Also contains an extensive bibliography.)

Bernardy, A. Il valore della tradizione a Malta. Lares. 7 (1935): 86.

Bezzina, J. Street niches at Rabat, Gozo. Maltese Folklore Review. 1(1963): 117-125.

Boissevain, Jeremy. Factions, parties, and politics in a Maltese village. A.A. 66(1964): 1275-1287.

*Boissevain, Jeremy. Saints and fireworks: religion and politics in rural Malta. London School of Economics. Monographs on Social Anthropology 30. London, Athlone Press. 1965. 12, 154 p.

*Boissevain, Jeremy. Hal-Farrug. A village in Malta. New York, Holt, Rinehart and Winston. 1969. 104 p., illus., map.

Bowen-Jones, Howard, et al. Agriculture in Malta. A survey of land use. Durham, Department of Geography, Durham Colleges in the University of Durham. 1955. 108 p., 50 figs.

*Bowen-Jones, Howard, et al. Malta, background for development. Research Paper No. 5. Durham, Department of Geography, Durham Colleges in the University of Durham. 1961. 356 p.

Brockman, Eric. Maltese memories; Tifkiriet. London, Rockliff. 1944. 134 p. (Mainly folklore.)

*Busuttil, Vincenzo. Holiday customs in Malta, and sports, usages, ceremonies, omens, and superstitions of the Maltese people. Malta, L. Busuttil. 1894. 165 p. (Also later editions.)

MALTA

Busuttil, Vincenzo. A tourist's guide to the Maltese Islands, including an historical summary. Malta, Malta Herald Printing Office. 1924. 148 p.

Buxton, L. H. Dudley. Personal and place names in Malta. Man. 21(1921): 146-147.

Buxton, L. H. The ethnology of Malta and Gozo. J.R.A.I. 52(1922): 164-211.

Buxton, L. H. Dudley. Malta: an anthropogeographical study. Geographical Review. 14(1924): 75-87.

Buxton, L. H. Dudley, and A. V. D. Hort. The modern pottery industry in Malta. Man. 21(1921): 130-131.

Cachia, P. An Arab's view of XIX C. Malta. 3, On Valetta, the capital of the island of Malta. Maltese Folklore Review. 1 (1963): 110-116.

Cassar, Paul. The corbelled stone huts of the Maltese Islands. Man. 61 (196 65-68.

Cassar, Paul. Medical votive offerings in the Maltese Islands. J.R.A.I. 94(1964): 23-29.

Cassar Pullicino, G. Canti sulla passione nella Isole Maltesi. Lares. 20(1954 138-158.

Cassar Pullicino, Joseph. Maltese customs and beliefs in 1575. Folk-Lore. 62(1951): 398-404.

Cassar Pullicino, Joseph. Social aspects of Maltese nicknames. Scientia (Valletta, Malta). 22(1956): 66-94.

Cassar Pullicino, Joseph. Nursery vocabulary of the Maltese archipelago. Orbis. 6(1957): 192-198.

Corso, R. Fondamentali carateri Italiani delle tradizioni Maltesi. Raza e Civiltà. 1 (1940): 309-317.

Cremona, A. Maltese funeral customs. Melitta (Valetta, Malta). 2(1922): 249-259.

Cremona, A. Maltese death, mourning, and funeral customs. Folk-Lore. 34(1923): 352-357.

Cremona, A. Weather and husbandry lore in the isles of Malta. Archivum Melitense. 6 (1923): 1-23.

Cremona, A. Folklore Maltese. Lingua, credence, costumi. Folklore (Naples). 9(1954): 16-39.

MALTA

Davy, John. Notes and observations on the Ionian Islands and Malta: with some remarks on Constantinople and Turkey . . . 2 vols. London, Smith, Elder. 1842.

Domeier, William. Observations on the climate, manners and amusements of Malta. London, J. Callow. 1810. 116 p.

Fleming, J. B. Notes on rural Malta. Scottish Geographical Magazine. 62(1946): 56-60.

Galea, J. The old flour mills of Malta and Gozo. Maltese Folklore Review. 1 (1963): 94-101.

Galea, L., and M. Murray. Maltese folk-tales. Malta, Empire Press. 1932. 58 p.

*Hornell, James. The fishing industry in Malta, with suggestions for its further improvement. Malta, Official Publications. 1931. 62 p.

Kininmonth, Christopher. Malta: a first impression. Geographical Magazine. 26(1953): 15-19.

Kininmonth, Christopher. The brass dolphins. A description of the Maltese archipelago. London, Secker and Warburg. 1957. 224 p.

Luke, Sir Harry. Malta; an account and an appreciation. 2d ed. London, Harrap. 1960. 260 p.

Malta Government: Office of Statistics. Census 1957; the Maltese Islands; report on economic activities. Valletta, Malta. 1959. 425 p.

Mitchell, P. K. Studies on the agrarian geography of Malta. 2 vols. Durham, Department of Geography, Durham Colleges in the University of Durham. 1960. 225 p.

*Price, C. A. Malta and the Maltese: a study in nineteenth century migration. London, Georgian House; Melbourne, Melbourne University Press. 1954. 19, 272 p.

Seers, D. A fertility survey of the Maltese Islands. Population Studies. 10(1957): 211-228.

Stumme, Hans. Maltesische Märchen, Gedichte und Rätsel. In deutscher Übersetzung. Leipzig, J. C. Hinrichs. 1904. 16, 102 p.

Underdown, H. W., and Margaret Eyre. Extracts from Signor V. Busuttil's Holiday Customs in Malta. Folk-Lore. 14(1903): 77-85.

Walter, Richard. Wanderers awheel in Malta. National Geographic Magazine. 78(1940): 253-272.

Weber, B. C. Some aspects of Maltese folklore. Southern Folklore Quarterly. 24(1960): 239-241.

Aitken, Mrs. B. F. M. Modern slab burials in northern Castile. Man.
35(1935): 50-52.

Aitken, Robert. El arado castellano: estudio preliminar. Anales del Museo
de Pueblo Español. 1 (1935): 109-138. Madrid.

Aitken, Robert. Routes of transhumance on the Spanish meseta. Geographical
Journal. 106(1945): 59-69.

Ajo G. Y. Sáinz de Zuniga, C. M. Historia milenaria de un pueblecito de
Castilla. Madrid, Imp., Ed. La Normal. 1956. 192 p.

Alford, Violet. Pyrenean festivals. Calendar customs, music & magic, drama
& dance. London, Chatto and Windus. 1937: 201-240.

Almela y Vives, Francisco. Menéndez Pelayo en Valencia y Valencia en
Menéndez Pelayo. Valencia, Excmo. Ayuntamiento. 1957. 180 p.

Almela y Vives, Francisco. El duc de Calabria i la seua cort. Valencia,
Sicania. 1958. 157 p.

Amades, Joan. Literatura carnestoltesca valenciana. Castelló de la Plana,
Societat Castellonenca de Cultura. 1957. 26 p. (Valencian carnival.)

Anderson, Ruth Matilda. Spanish costume: Extramadura. New York, Hispanic
Society of America. 1951. 7, 334 p., illus.

Anderson, Ruth Matilda. Costumes painted by Sorolla in his Provinces of Spain.
New York, Hispanic Society of America. 1957. 198 p., 109 illus., maps.

Aranzadi y Unamuno, Telesforo de. Etnografía, sus bases, sus metodos y
aplicaciones a España. Madrid, Biblioteca Corona. 1917. 239 p.

Arbelo, A. La mortalidad de la infancia en España. Madrid, Instituto
Balmes. 1962. 608 p.

Arco, Ricardo del. Antiguos gremios de Huesca: ordinaciones documentos;
transcripción y estudio preliminar. Zaragoza, Oficina Tipográfica de P.
Larra. 1911. 18, 269 p.

Arco, Ricardo del. Las calles de Huesca. Huesca, Talleres Tip. de la Viuda
de J. Martínez. 1922. 223 p.

Arco, Ricardo del. El traje popular altoaragonés. Huesca. 1924. 71 p.

Arco, Ricardo del. Costumbres y trajes en los Pirineos. Zaragoza, Artes
Gráficas E. Berdejo Casañal. 1930. 108 p.

Arco, Ricardo del. Aragón: geografía: historia: arte: apéndice bibliográfico.
Huesca, V. Campo. 1931. 11, 683 p.

Arco, Ricardo del. Notas de folk-lore altoaragonés. Madrid, Consejo Superior de Investigaciones Científicas, Instituto de Nebrija, Biblioteca de Tradiciones Populares. 1. 1943.

Arco, Ricardo del, and Luciano Labastida. El alto Aragón monumental y pintoresco. Huesca, J. Martínez. 1913. 7, 87 p.

Armstrong, Lucile. Dances of Spain. 2 vols. New York, Chanticleer Press. 1950-1951.

Aurousseau, Marcel. Beyond the Pyrenees. New York, A. H. King. 1931. 9, 402 p.

Barker, George C. Some aspects of penitential processions in Spain and the American Southwest. J. A. F. L. 70 (1957): 137-142.

Bensusan, Samuel Levy. Home life in Spain. New York, Macmillan. 1910. 11, 317 p.

Bierhenke, W. Das Dreschen in der Sierra de Gata (Spanien). Volkstum und Kultur der Romanen. 2 (1929): 20-82.

Borrow, George. The Bible in Spain. New edition with notes & glossary by U. R. Burke. 2 vols. London, John Murray. 1896. (There are many other editions of this work.)

Brenan, Gerald. The Spanish labyrinth, an account of the social and political background of the civil war. Cambridge, The University Press. 1943. 384 p. (2d ed. 1950.)

Brenan, Gerald. The face of Spain. New York, Farrar, Straus, and Cudahy. 1950. 310 p.

Brenan, Gerald. South from Granada. New York, Farrar, Straus, and Cudahy. 1957. 282 p.

Brugarola, P. M. Las fiestas de Nuestra Señora de la Balma. R. D. T. P. 12 (1956): 191-203.

Cabal, Constantino. La mitología asturiana. 3 vols. Madrid, Impr. de J. Pueyo. 1925-1928.

Cabal, Constantino. Las costumbres asturianas, su significación y sus orígenes. 2 vols. Vol. 1. El individuo. Oviedo, Ayuntamiento. 1926. 376 p. Vol. 2. La familia: la vivienda, los oficios primitivos. Madrid. 1931. 414 p.

Campo Urbano, S. del. La familia española en transición. Cuadernos de Investigación del Congreso de la Familia Española. 5. Madrid. 1960. 232 p.

Caro Baroja, Julio. Algunos mitos españoles; ensayos de mitología popular. Madrid, Editora Nacional. 1941. 186 p.

*Caro Baroja, Julio. Los pueblos del norte de la península ibérica. Madrid, Consejo Superior de Investigaciones Científicas, Instituto Bernardino de Sahagún. 1943. 241 p.

*Caro Baroja, Julio. La vida rural en Vera de Bidasoa (Navarra). Madrid, Consejo Superior de Investigaciones Científicas, Instituto Antonio de Nebrija. 1944. 246 p.

Caro Baroja, Julio. Contribución al estudio de los ritos clásicos conservados hasta el presente en la península ibérica. Madrid, Instituto 'Bernardino de Sahagún' de Antropología y Etnologia, Trabajos. 4(1946): 21-67.

*Caro Baroja, Julio. Los pueblos de España, ensayos de etnología. Barcelona, Barna. 1946. 495 p.

Caro Baroja, Julio. Análisis de la cultura; etnología, historia, folklore. Barcelona, Consejo Superior de Investigaciones Científicas. Centro de Estudios de Etnología. 1949. 254 p.

Caro Baroja, Julio. Los arados españoles. R. D. T. P. 5(1949): 3-96.

Caro Baroja, Julio. En la campiña de Córdoba. R. D. T. P. 12(1956): 270-299

Caro Baroja, Julio. Razas, pueblos y linajes. Madrid, Revista de Occidente. 1957. 358 p.

*Caro Baroja, Julio. Honour and shame: a historical account of several conflicts. In John G. Peristiany, ed. Honour and shame. The values of Mediterranean society. London, Weidenfeld and Nicolson. 1965: 79-137.

*Carreras y Candi, F., ed. Folklore y costumbres de España. 3 vols. Barcelon Casa Editorial Alberto Martin. 1931-1934. 608, 623, 705 p., illus. (Reprinted: 1943-1946 and again in 1960.)

Carrión, Pascual. Los latifundios en España. Madrid, Gráficas Reunidas. 1932 8, 439 p., plates, folding maps, tables.

Casas Gaspar, Enrique. Costumbres españolas de nacimiento, noviazgo, casamiento y muerte. Madrid, Editorial Escelier. 1947. 387 p.

Casas Gaspar, Enrique. Folklore campesino español. Madrid [no publisher given]. 1950. 310 p.

Casas Torres, Jose Manuel. La barraca de la Huerta de Valencia. Estudios Geográficos. 4(1943): 113-178.

Casas Torres, Jose Manuel. La vivienda y los núcleos de población rurales de la Huerta de Valencia. Madrid, Consejo Superior de Investigaciones Científicas, Instituto Juan Sebastian Elcano. 1944. 11, 328 p.

Casas Torres, Jose Manuel, and José V. Araus Axlor. Un mapa de los mercados de la provincia de Teruel. Estudios Geográficos. 6(1945): 525-555.

Castro, Américo. Ensayo de historiologia; analogías y diferencias entre Hispanos y Musulmanes. New York, F. C. Feger. 1950. 44 p.

Castro, Américo. The structure of Spanish history. Princeton, N.J., Princeton University Press. 1954. 689 p.

Cedilla, El Conde de. Las fiestas de Santa Agueda en Hoyuelos. Boletín de la Sociedad Española de Excursiones. 39(1931): 169-182.

Cela, Camilo José. Primer viaje andaluz. Notas de un vagabundaje. Barcelona, Noguer. 1959. 468 p.

Chantral, S. Andalusien. Atlantis. 34(1962): 289-299.

Clavien, Germain. Andalousie. Lausanne, Rencontre. 1962. 213 p.

Cortés y Vásquez, Luis L. Ganadería y pastoreo en Berrocal de Huebra (Salamanca). R.D.T.P. 8(1952): 425-465, 563-595.

Cortés y Vásquez, Luis L. Medicina popular riberana y dos conjuros de San Martin de Castañeda. R.D.T.P. 8(1952): 526-537.

Curtis, Freddie. The utility pottery industry of Bailén, southern Spain. A.A. 64(1962): 486-503.

Deane, Shirley. Tomorrow is mañana, in an Andalusian village. New York, Morrow; London, J. Murray. 1958. 198 p.

Decca Record Company. An anthology of cante flamenco. London, Decca Record Company. 1956. 32 p. (In Spanish and English.)

Dobby, E. H. G. Agrarian problems in Spain. Geographical Review. 26(1936): 177-189.

Ebeling, Walter. Die landwirtschaftlichen Geräte im Osten der Provinz Lugo (Spanien). Volkstum und Kultur der Romanen. 5(1932): 50-151.

Ellis, Havelock. The soul of Spain. Boston and New York, Houghton Mifflin. 1909. 9, 420 p.

Elorriaga, G. La familia en España. Madrid, Servicio Informativo Español. 1965. 94 p.

SPANISH

Fairhurst, H. Types of settlement in Spain. Scottish Geographical Magazine. 51(1935): 283-305.

Fernández de Castillejo, José Luis. Viaje de estudios por tierras Andaluzas: conferencia pronunciado en la Escuela Diplomatica el día 25 de Noviembre de 1954. Madrid. 1954. 25 p.

Fernández Pellitero, Manuel. Contribución al estudio de la personalidad en el muchacho Español. Antropología y Etnología. 13(1960): 43-118.

*Ford, Richard. A handbook for travellers in Spain and readers at home. 2 vols. London, John Murray. 1845. (Reprinted: Carbondale, Ill., Southern Illinois University Press. 1966.)

Ford, Richard. The Spaniards and their country. New York, G. P. Putnam. 1848. 8, 349 p. (Selected sections from the preceding work.)

Foster, George M. Report on an ethnological reconnaissance of Spain. A.A. 53(1951): 311-325.

Foster, George M. The fire walkers of San Pedro Manrique, Soria, Spain. J.A.F.L. 68(1955): 325-332.

*Foster, George M. Culture and conquest. America's Spanish heritage. Viking Fund Publications in Anthropology. 27. New York, Wenner-Gren Foundation for Anthropological Research. 1960. 10, 272 p.

*Freeman, Susan Tax. Dimensions of change in a Castilian village. Cambridge, Harvard University. 1965. (Unpublished Ph.D. dissertation in anthropology.)

Freeman, Susan Tax. Corporate village organization in the Sierra Ministra: an Iberian structural type. Man, New series. 3(1968): 477-484.

*Freeman, Susan Tax. Religious aspects of the social organization of a Castilian village . . . A.A. 70 (1968): 34-49.

Freyre, G. On the Iberian concept of time. American Scholar. 32(1963): 415-430.

Fribourg, André. La transhumance en Espagne. Annales de Géographie. 19(1910): 231-244.

Giese, Wilhelm. Volkskundliches aus Ost-Granada. Volkstum und Kultur der Romanen. 7(1934): 25-54.

*Giese, Wilhelm. Nordost-Cádiz. Ein kulturwissenschaftlicher Beitrag zur Erforschung Andalusiens. Beiheft zur Zeitschrift für Romanische Philologie. 89. Halle an der Saale, M. Niemeyer. 1937. 4, 254 p.

Giese, Wilhelm. Los tipos de casa de la península ibérica. R.D.T.P. 7(1951): 563-601.

Giese, Wilhelm. Telares de Astorga. R.D.T.P. 11 (1955): 3-14.

Gillmore, Frances. Folklore study in Spain. In Richard M. Dorson, ed. Folklore research around the world. Bloomington, Indiana University Press. 1961: 50-57.

Gómez-Tabenera, José M. Trajes populares y costumbres tradicionales. Madrid, Editorial Tesoro. 1950. 225 p., illus.

Gómez-Tabenera, José M. Ethnogenesis of the Spanish people. Madrid, Instituto Español de Antropología Aplicada. 1966. 58 p., 7 maps.

González Climent, Anselmo. Flamencología (toros, canto y baile). Madrid, no publisher. 1955. 404 p.

*Great Britain. Admiralty Office. Naval Intelligence Division. Spain and Portugal. 4 vols. London, Great Britain. Admiralty Office. Naval Intelligence Division. Geographical Handbook Series. 1941-1945. Vols. 1 and 3. 1941, 1944. 11, 264 p., plates, maps, illus.; 13, 680 p., illus., plates, maps.

Guichot y Sierra, Alejandro. Supersticiones populares andaluces. El Folk-Lore Andaluz. 1 (1882-1883): 21-27, 59-64, 199-203, 293-298, 337-341, 411-418.

Gutkind, Peter. Urban development in southern Europe: Spain and Portugal. New York, The Free Press of Glencoe. 1967. 544 p.

Heintz, P. Die Struktur der spanischen Personlichkeit. Eine kulturanthropologische Einfuhrung in das Werk Americo Castro. Kölner Zeitschrift für Soziologie. 7(1955): 101-118.

Henére, Enrique. Spanish textiles. Leigh-on-Sea, England, F. Lewis. 1955. 16 p., 57 plates.

Higgin, George. Commercial and industrial Spain. London, E. Wilson. 1886. 2, 114 p.

Higgin, L. Spanish life in town and country, with chapters on Portuguese life in town and country by Eugene E. Street. New York and London, G. P. Putnam's Sons. 1902. 10, 325 p. (Another edition: London, G. Newnes. 1902. 11, 289 p.)

*Hinderink, J. The Sierra de Gata. A geographical study of a rural mountain area in Spain. Groningen, J. B. Wolters. 1963. 10, 228 p., illus.

Houston, J. M. The western Mediterranean world: an introduction to its regional landscapes. London, Longmans, Green. 1964: 164-335.

Hoyos, Antonio de. Murcia, pueblos y paisajes. Murcia, Patronato de Cultura de la Excma. Deputación Provincial de Murcia. 1957. 347 p.

Hoyos Sáinz, Luis de. La densidad de población y el acrecentamiento en España. Madrid, Consejo Superior de Investigaciones Científicas, Instituto Juan Sebastian Elcano. 1953. 306 p.

Hoyos Sáinz, Luis de, and Nieves de Hoyos Sancho. Manual de folklore. La vida popular tradicional. Madrid, Rivista de Occidente. 1947. 15, 602 p.

Hoyos Sancho, Nieves de. La casa tradicional en España. Temas Españoles. 20. Madrid. 1952.

Hoyos Sancho, Nieves de. El traje regional en España. Temas Españoles. 123. Madrid. 1954.

Hoyos Sancho, Nieves de. El traje regional de Extramadura. R. D. T. P. 11(1955): 155-177, 353-385.

Iñigo Irigoyen, José. Folklore alavés. Vitoria, Impr. Provincial. 1949. 147

Jiménez de Gregorio, Fernando. La población en La Jara toledana. Estudios Geográficos. 11 (1950): 201-250; 12(1951): 527-581; 13(1952): 489-558; 15(1954): 209-245; 16 (1955): 585-635.

Kany, Charles Emil. Life and manners in Madrid, 1750-1800. Berkeley, University of California Press. 1932. 13, 483 p.

Kazantzakis, Nikos. Spain. New York, Simon and Schuster. 1963. 254 p.

Kehoe, Vincent J. Aficionado. A pictorial encyclopedia of the fiesta de toros of Spain. New York, Hastings House. 1960. 256 p., 478 illus.

*Kenny, Michael. Patterns of patronage in Spain. Anthropological Quarterly. 33(1960): 14-23.

*Kenny, Michael. A Spanish tapestry. Town and country in Castile. London, Cohen and West. 1961; Bloomington, Indiana University Press. 1962. 10, 243 p.

Kenny, Michael. Social values and health in Spain: some preliminary considerations. Human Organization. 21(1962-1963): 280-285.

Klein, Julius. The Mesta: a study in Spanish economic history. Harvard Economic Studies. 20. Cambridge, Harvard University Press. 1920. 18, 444 p.

Klemm, Gustav. Aus dem Leben des Landvolkes in Südspanien. Globus. 15(1869): 88-91, 113-115.

Krüger, Fritz. Die Gegenstandkultur Sanabrías und seiner Nachbargebiet. Hamburg, Hamburgische Universität, Abhandlungen aus dem Gebiet der Auslandskunde. Bd. 20. 1925. 10, 322 p., illus., plates.

Krüger, Fritz. Sach- und Wortkundliches vom Wasser in den Pyrenäen. Volkstum und Kultur der Romanen. 2(1929): 139-243.

*Krüger, Fritz. Die Hochpyrenäen. B. Hirtenkultur. Volkstum und Kultur der Romanen. 8(1935): 1-103, 8 plates.

*Krüger, Fritz. Die Hochpyrenäen. D. Hausindustrie, Tracht, Gewerbe. Volkstum und Kultur der Romanen. 8(1935): 210-328; 9 (1936): 1-106, illus., plates.

*Krüger, Fritz. Die Hochpyrenäen. A. Landschaften, Haus und Hof. Hamburg, Hänsische Universität, Abhandlungen aus dem Gebiet der Auslandskunde. 44, ser. B. 23. Hamburg, de Gruyter. 1936. 28, 238 p., 44 plates, map.

*Krüger, Fritz. Die Hochpyrenäen. C. Ländlichen Arbeit. Bd. 1. Transport und Transportgeräte. Butlletí de Dialectología Catalana. 23(1936): 39-240. 14 figs., 89 photos.

*Krüger, Fritz. Die Hochpyrenäen. C. Ländliche Arbeit. Bd. 2. Getreide-Heuernte- Bienenwohnung- Wein- und Olbereitung. Hamburger Studien zu Volkstum und Kultur der Romanen. 32. Hamburg, Hänsischer Gildenverlag. 1939. 10, 500 p., map, 19 pp. of illus., 36 plates.

*Krüger, Fritz. Die Hochpyrenäen. A. Landschaften, Haus und Hof. Bd. 2. Hamburg, Hänsische Universität, Abhandlungen aus dem Gebiet der Auslandskunde. 47. 1939. 28, 400 p., 17 plates.

Krüger, Fritz. Las Branas. Ein Beitrag zur Geschichte der Rundbauten im asturisch-galizische-portugiesischen Raum. Volkstum und Kultur der Romanen. 16 (1944): 158-203.

Linz, J. J. An authoritarian regime: Spain. Transactions of the Westermarck Society. 10 (1964): 291-341.

*Lison-Tolosana, Carmelo. Belmonte de los Caballeros. A sociological study of a Spanish town. Oxford, The Clarendon Press. 1966. 10, 369 p. (Aragon.)

Llano Rosa de Ampudia, Aurelio de. Del folklore asturiano: mitos, supersticiones, costumbres. Madrid, Talleres de Voluntad. 1922. 19, 277 p.

López Medel, J. La familia rural, la urbana y la industrial en España. Madrid, Ediciones del Congreso de la Familia Española. 1961. 125 p.

Lorenzo Fernández, Joaquín. Die Bremse am galizischen Wagen. Volkstum und Kultur der Romanen. 11 (1938): 282-289.

Lorenzo Fernández, Joaquín. Los silos de Villacañas (Toledo). R. D. T. P. 5(1949): 420-434.

Madariaga, Salvador de. Englishmen, Frenchmen and Spaniards; an essay in comparative psychology. London, Oxford University Press, H. Milford. 1949. 301 p.

Manfredi Cano, Domingo. Silueta folklórica de Andalucía. Madrid, Publicaciones Españolas. 1961. 158 p., illus.

Manuel, F. C. Two Spains. Antioch Review. 16 (1956): 3-22.

Marks, John. To the bullfight again. A spectator's guide. 2d ed. New York, Alfred A. Knopf. 1967. 160, 9 p., illus.

Martín Granizo, Leon. Paisaje, hombres y costumbres de la provincia de León. Boletín de la Real Sociedad Geográfica. 63(1922): 352-402.

Martín Granizo, Leon. La provincia de León. Paisajes, hombres, costumbres canciones. Madrid, J. Ortiz. 1929. 76 p.

May, Florence Lewis. Hispanic lace and lace making. New York, Hispanic Society of America. 1939. 417 p., 432 illus.

Mellor, F. H. A night in Seville. Geographical Magazine. 4(1936-1937): 407-414.

Mesonero y Romanos, Ramón de. Tipos, groupos y bocetos de cuadros de costumbres dibujados á la pluma por El curiosa parlante. Madrid, F. de P. Mellado. 1862. 308 p. (Madrid.)

Mesonero y Romanos, Ramón de. Escenas matritenses, por el curiosa parlante. Madrid, Oficinas de la Ilustración Española y Americana. 1881. 15, 396 p

Mesonero y Romanos, Ramón de. Panorama matritense. Madrid, Oficinas de la Ilustración Española y Americana. 1881. 15, 392 p.

Mikesell, Marvin K. Market centers of northeastern Spain: a review. Geographical Review. 50(1960): 247-251.

Monica, Sister. And then the storm. London, New York, Longmans, Green. 1937. 231 p.

Montoto, Luis. Costumbres populares andaluzas. Biblioteca de las Tradicione Populares Españolas. 1 (1883): 1-99; 4(1884): 281-314.

Newman, Bernard. Round about Andorra. London, G. Allen & Unwin. 1928. 300 p.

Olavarría y Huarte, Eugenio de. El folk-lore de Madrid. Biblioteca de las Tradiciones Populares Españolas. 2(1884): 5-100.

Paret, Lotte. Das ländliche Leben einer Gemeinde der Hautes-Pyrénées, dargestellt auf Grund der mundartlichen Terminologie. Tübingen Universität. 1932. 90 p. (Thesis.)

Parsons, James J. The acorn-hog economy of the oak woodlands of southwestern Spain. Geographical Review. 52(1962): 211-235.

Parsons, James J. The cork oak forests and the evolution of the cork industry in southern Spain and Portugal. Economic Geography. 38(1962): 195-214.

Partington, R. The annual feast of Santiago de Compostella. Folk-Lore. 68(1957): 358-364.

Paul, Elliot Harold. The life and death of a Spanish town. New York, Random House. 1937. 12, 427 p.

Peers, Edgar Allison, ed. Spain: a companion to Spanish studies. 5th ed. London, Methuen. 1956. 319 p., maps.

Peman, José María. Andalucía. Barcelona, Ediciones Destino. 1958. 570 p.

Peña Santiago, L. P., and J. San Martín. Estudio etnográfico del valle de Urraul Alto (Navarra). Munibe. 18(1966): 69-159.

Perez Moreno, L. El suelo agrícola de Alcañez. Teruel. 15-16 (1956): 259-326.

Perez Sánchez, Alfonso E. Murcia, Albacete y sus provincias. Barcelona, Editorial Aries. 1961. 199 p.

Pericot, L., S. Alcobé, and J. Caro Baroja. Spain and Portugal: an anthropological review for 1952-1954. In William L. Thomas, ed. Yearbook of anthropology 1955. New York, Wenner-Gren Foundation for Anthropological Research. 1955: 501-524.

*Pitt-Rivers, Julian A. The people of the Sierra. London, Weidenfeld and Nicolson; New York, Criterion Books. 1954. 232 p., illus.

*Pitt-Rivers, Julian A. Ritual kinship in Spain. Transactions of the New York Academy of Sciences, ser. 2. 20(1958): 424-431.

*Pitt-Rivers, Julian A. Honour and social status. In John G. Peristiany, ed. Honour and shame: the values of Mediterranean society. London, Weidenfeld and Nicolson. 1965: 19-77.

*Price, Richard, and Sally Price. Stratification and courtship in an Andalusian village. Man. New series. 1(1966): 526-533.

*Price, Richard, and Sally Price. Noviazgo in an Andalusian pueblo. S. W. J. A 22(1966): 302-332.

Pritchett, Victor S. The Spanish temper. London, Chatto & Windus. 1954. 218 p.; New York, Knopf. 1954. 269 p.

Revista de Dialectología y Tradiciones Populares. 1 (1944)-- Madrid, Consejo Superior de Investigaciones Científicas, Centro de Estudios de Etnología Peninsular.

Reyero, D. Historia, religión y costumbres de la montañas del Porma y Curneño (León). León, J. Lopez. 1926. 182 p.

Rhys, Udalap. An account of the most remarkable places and curiosities in Spain and Portugal. London, J. Osborn. 1749. 4, 332 p.

Rodríguez Santamaría, Benigno. Diccionario ilustrado, descriptivo, valorado, numérico y estadistico de los artes, aparejos, e instrumentos que usan para la pesca marítima en las costas del norte y noroeste de España. Madrid, Artes Gráficas "Mateu." 1911. 325 p.

Rodríguez Santamaría, Benigno. Diccionario de artes de pesca de España y sus posesiones. Madrid, Sucesores de Rivadeneyra. 1923. 32, 815 p., ma

Rose, Hugh James. Untrodden Spain, and her black country; being sketches of the life and character of the Spaniard of the interior. 2 vols. London, S. Tinsley. 1875.

Rose, Hugh James. Among the Spanish people. 2 vols. London, R. Bentley & Son. 1877.

Sanchez Perez, José Augusto. El culto mariana en España. Madrid, Consejo Superior de Investigaciones Científicas, Instituto Antonio de Nebrija. 1943. 482 p.

Sanchez Perez, José Augusto. Supersticiones españoles. Madrid, S. A. E. T. A. 1948. 302 p.

Stapley, Mildred. Popular weaving and embroidery in Spain. New York, W. Helburn. 1924. 12, 60 p., illus.

Subias Galter, Juan. El arte popular en España. Barcelona, Editorial Seix Barral. 1948. 628 p., illus.

Swinburne, Henry. Travels through Spain in the years 1775 & 1776. 2 vols. London, P. Elmsly. 1787.

SPANISH

Teijón Laso, Evelio. Los modos de vida en la dehesa Salamantina. Estudios
Geográficos. 9(1948): 421-441.

Teran, Manuel de, ed. Geografía de España y Portugal. 5 vols. Barcelona,
Montaner y Simón. 1952.

Thede, Max. Die Albufera von Valencia. Volkstum und Kultur der Romanen.
6(1933): 210-273, 317-383.

Thut, I. N., and Don Adams. Educational patterns in contemporary societies.
New York, McGraw-Hill. 1964: 48-75. (Chapter on "Spanish education:
imposing a foreign culture.")

Urabayen, Leoncio. La casa Navarra. Madrid, Espasa-Calpe. 1929. 240 p.,
illus.

Varey, J. E., and N. D. Shergold. La tarasca de Madrid. Claveleno. 4,
no. 20(1953): 19-26.

Very, F. G. The Spanish Corpus Christi procession: a literary and folkloric
study. Roig, Spanish Books. 1964. 12, 160 p.

*Violant y Simorra, Ramon. El Pirineo Español: vida, usos, costumbres,
creencias y tradiciones de una cultura milenaria que desaparece. Madrid,
Editorial Plus-Ultra. 1949. 675 p.

Violant y Simorra, Ramon. Sintesis etnografica del Pirineo español y problemas
que suscitan sus areas y elementos culturales. Zaragoza, Primer Congreso
Internacional de Pireneístas del Instituto de Estudios Pirenaicos. 1950. 50 p.

Violant y Simorra, Ramon. El arte popular español a través del Museo de Indus-
trias y Artes Populares. Barcelona, Aymá. 1953. 149 p., illus.

Voigt, Paul. Die Sierra Nevada. Haus- Hausrat- Häusliches und gewerbliches
Tagewerk. Hamburger Studien zu Volkstum und Kultur der Romanen. 23.
Hamburg, Hänsischer Gildenverlag. 1937. 76 p., 25 figs., map.

Whelpton, Eric. Southern Spain, with chapters on the Algarve. London, R.
Hale. 1964. 192 p., map.

CATALANS[1]

*Alford, Violet. Pyrenean festivals. Calendar customs, music & magic, drama & dance. London, Chatto and Windus. 1937: 11-100.

Almerich, Luis. Tradiciones, fiestas y costumbres de Barcelona. Barcelona, Millá. 1944. 93 p.

Amades, Joan. Les diades populars catalans. 4 vols. Barcelona, Editorial Barcino. 1932-1935, 1949.

Amades, Joan. Bruixes i bruixots. Barcelona. 1934. 104 p.

Amades, Joan. Les esposalles: costums i creences. Barcelona. 1934. 160 p.

Amades, Joan. El naixement: costums i creences. Barcelona. 1934. 112 p.

Amades, Joan. Les cent millors rondalles populars. 2 vols. Barcelona, Editorial Selecta. 1948-1949.

Amades, Joan. El Pirineu; tradicions i llegendes. Barcelona, Edicions "La Llumenera." 1949. 15, 167 p.

*Amades, Joan. Costumari català el curs de l'any. 5 vols. Barcelona, Salvat Editores. 1950-1956.

Amades, Joan. Guia de festes tradicionals de Catalunya. Barcelona, Editoria. Aedos. 1958. 158 p.

Amades, Joan. El pessebre. Barcelona, Editorial Aedos. 1959. 508 p. (Christmas.)

Amades, Joan. El testamento de animales en la tradición catalana. R.D.T.P. 18(1962): 339-394.

Amades, Joan, and José Tarin. Leyendas y tradiciones marineras. Barcelona, Sección de Prense de la Diputación Provincial de Barcelona. 1954. 75 p.

Arco, Ricardo del. Costumbres y trajes en los Pirineos. Zaragoza, Artes Graficas E. Berdejo Casañal. 1930. 108 p.

Biblioteca de Tradicions Populars. Barcelona. 1(1933)-- Joan Amades, ed. (Over 41 volumes to date.)

Caballé i Clos, Tomás. Costumbres y usos de Barcelona; narraciones populares. Barcelona, Seguí. 1947. 450 p.

Caballé i Clos, Tomás. Folklore catalán. Antiguas tradiciones, festividades populares y ferias. Barcelona, Freixinet. 1947. 277 p.

---

[1] Also see Balearic Islands

CATALANS

Caballé i Clos, Tomás. Tradicions de Catalunya. Barcelona, Freixinet. 1950. 234 p.

Capmany, Aureli. Calendari de llegendes, costums i festes tradicionals catalanes. Barcelona, Dolmau i Jover, Editors, Tallers Gràfics Rafel Salvá. 1951. 357 p., illus.

Darliat, A. Art Catalan. Paris, Arthaud. 1963. 417 p., illus.

Dobby, E. H. G. Catalonia: the geographical basis of its regionalism. Geographical Review. 28 (1938): 224-249.

Griera, A. Feines i costums que desapareixen. Butlletí de Dialectología Catalana. 16(1928): 1-40.

Krüger, Fritz. Sach- und Wortkundliches vom Wasser in den Pyrenäen. Volkstum und Kultur der Romanen. 2(1929): 139-243.

*Krüger, Fritz. Die Hochpyrenäen. B. Hirtenkultur. Volkstum und Kultur der Romanen. 8(1935): 1-103, 8 plates.

*Krüger, Fritz. Die Hochpyrenäen. D. Hausindustrie, Tracht, Gewerbe. Volkstum und Kultur der Romanen. 8(1935): 210-328; 9(1936): 1-106, illus., plates.

*Krüger, Fritz. Die Hochpyrenäen. A. Landschaften, Haus und Hof. Hamburg, Hänsische Universität, Abhandlungen aus dem Gebiet der Auslandskunde. 44, ser. B. 23. Hamburg, de Gruyter. 1936. 28, 238 p., 44 plates, map.

*Krüger, Fritz. Die Hochpyrenäen. C. Ländlichen Arbeit. Bd. 1. Transport und Transportgeräte. Butlletí de Dialectología Catalana. 23(1936): 39-240. 14 figs., 89 photos.

*Krüger, Fritz. Die Hochpyrenäen. C. Ländliche Arbeit. Bd. 2: Getreide-Heuernte- Bienenwohnung- Wein- und Ölbereitung. Hamburger Studien zu Volkstum und Kultur der Romanen. 32. Hamburg, Hänsischer Gildenverlag. 1939. 10, 500 p., map, 19 pp. of illus., 36 plates.

*Krüger, Fritz. Die Hochpyrenäen. A. Landschaften, Haus und Hof. Bd. 2. Hamburg, Hänsische Universität, Abhandlungen aus dem Gebiet der Auslandskunde. 47. 1939. 28, 400 p., 17 plates.

*Llobet, Salvador. El medio y la vida en el Montseny. Barcelona, Consejo Superior de Investigaciones Científicas, Estación de Estudios Pirenaicos. 1947. 11, 518 p.

Maspons i Labrós, F. Jocs d'infants. Barcelona. 1928. 108 p.

Paret, Lotte. Das ländliche Leben einer Gemeinde der Hautes-Pyrénées, dargestellt auf Grund der mundartlichen Terminologie. Tübingen, Tübingen Universität. 1932. 90 p. (Thesis.)

Plá, Jose. Guia de la Costa Brava. Barcelona, Ediciones Destino. 1945. 388 p.

Plá, Jose. Llagosta i pollastre, sobre la cuina catalana. Barcelona, Editorial Selecta. 1952. 248 p.

Plá, Jose. Cataluña. Barcelona, Ediciones Destino. 1961. 630 p.

Stancliffe, Merton. Cultural and ecological aspects of marriages, succession, and migration in a peasant community in the Catalan Pyrenees. New York, Columbia University. 1966. (Unpublished Ph.D. dissertation in anthropology.)

Trueta, J. The spirit of Catalonia. London, Oxford University Press. 1946. 198 p.

Valldaura, Anna de. Tradicions religioses de Catalunya. Barcelona, Milla. 1948. 76 p.

Violant y Simorra, Ramón. Elaboració del cánem i de la llana al pallars. Barcelona. 1934. 58 p. (Textiles.)

Violant y Simorra, Ramón. Art popular decoratiu a Catalunya. Barcelona, Les Belles Ediciones. 1948. 248 p., illus.

Violant y Simorra, Ramón. Características tradicionales, antiguas y evolucionadas, del hogar doméstico popular en Cataluña. R.D.T.P. 6(1950): 430-495.

Violant y Simorra, Ramón. Instrumentos músicos de construcción infantil y pastoril en Cataluña. R.D.T.P. 10 (1954): 331-399, 548-590.

Ziesemer, Wilhelm. Katalanisches Volkstum. Atlantis. 10 (1938): 309-315

Amades, Joan. Cançons funeráries. Trabalhos de Antropologia e Etnologia. 17(1959): 271-292.

Baker, Roy W. The Balearics, island sisters of the Mediterranean. National Geographic Magazine. 54(1928): 177-206.

Candel-Vila, Joaquina. L'île de Minorque: essai de géographie humaine. Bulletin de la Société Languedocienne de Géographie, 2 sér. 21(1950): 132-169.

*Chamberlin, Frederick. The Balearics and their people. London, John Lane, The Bodley Head; New York, Dodd, Mead. 1927. 261 p.

Colom, Antonio. Economía balear. Palma, no publisher. 1953. 16 p., illus.

Dallimore, W. Agriculture and horticulture in Majorca. Kew Bulletin of Miscellaneous Information. 9(1927): 369-374.

Déon, Michel. Iles Baléares. Paris, Hachette. 1958. 126 p., plates, map. (Guide book—but good.)

Foster, George M. The feixes of Ibiza. Geographical Review. 42(1952): 227-237.

Galmés Riera, Antonio. Mallorca, Menorca, Ibiza, folklore, danzas, costumbres, canciones. Palma. 1950. 171 p.

Galmés Riera, Antonio. Bailes populares mallorquines. Palma. 1952. 16 p.

Gilbert, E. W. The human geography of Mallorca. Scottish Geographical Magazine. 50(1934): 129-147.

Graves, Robert, and Paul Hogarth. Majorca observed. London, Cassell. 1965. 150 p.

Ludwig Salvator, Archduke of Austria. Märchen aus Mallorca. Würzburg und Leipzig, L. Woerl. 1895. 24, 275 p.

Maplesden, M. Social studies in Majorca. Sociological Review. 21(1929): 150-155.

Morey, Lorenzo. Danzas típicas de Mallorca; danses typiques de Majorque. Mallorca. 1951. 10, 30 p.

Mulet, Antonio. El traje en Mallorca. Aportación a su conocimiento. Palma de Mallorca. 1955. 79 p. (Costume.)

Plá, Jose. Guia de Mallorca, Menorca e Ibiza. Barcelona, Ediciones Destino. 1950. 581 p.

Ribas de Pina, Miguel. El habitat rural in la isla de Mallorca a fines del siglo XVIII y en la actualidad. Boletín de la Sociedad Geográfica Nacional. 72(1932): 259-288.

Rosselló Verger, Vicente. La huerta de levante en Palma de Mallorca. Estudios Geográficos. 20, 77(1960): 523-578.

Santaner Marí, Juan. Geografía de la Baleares. Palma, Atlante. 1958. 297 p., illus.

Sheppard, Lady Margaret Kinloch Forbes. Cottage in Majorca. London, Skeffington & Sons. 1936. 287 p.

Shor, Jean, and Frank Shor. The Balearics are booming. National Geographic Magazine. 111 (1957): 621-660.

Solberg, Thorwald. Some notes on the Balearic Islands, with special reference to their bibliography. Papers of the Bibliographical Society of America. 22(1928): 67-146.

Vila Valentín, J. Formentera: estudio de geografía humana. Estudios Geográficos. 11 (1950): 389-442.

Vila Valentín, J. Ibiza y Formentera, islas de la sal. Estudios Geográficos. 14(1953): 3-48.

Whelpton, Eric. The Balearics: Majorca, Minorca, Ibiza. London, Robert Hale. 1952. 276 p., illus.

Gennep, Arnold van. Manuel de folklore français contemporain. Vol. 1, pts. 1-7, Vol. 3, Vol. 4. (Vol. 2 never published.) Paris, Picard. 1937-1957. (See especially Vol. 1, pts. 3-6; Vol. 3, and Vol. 4.)

Alford, Violet. The Basque masquerade. Folk-Lore. 39(1928): 68-90.

*Alford, Violet. Pyrenean festivals. Calendar customs, music & magic, drama & dance. London, Chatto and Windus. 1937: 135-200.

Apraiz, A. de. Baskische Volkskunst. Z.f.E. 55(1923): 89-90.

Aranzadi y Unamuno, Telesforo de. El pueblo Euskalduna. Estudio de antropología. San Sebastián. 1899. 15, 46 p.

Aranzadi y Unamuno, Telesforo de. De cosas y palabras vascas. Anthropos. 7 (1912): 407-428.

Arin Dorronsoro, Juan de. Pueblo de Atuán. Anuario de Eusko-Folklore. 6(1926): 17-69.

Baeschlin, Alfredo. La arquitectura del caserío vasca . . . Barcelona, Editorial Canosa. 1930. 222 p.

Barandiarán, José Miguel de. Creencias y ritos funerarios. Anuario de Eusko-Folklore. 3(1923): 1-138.

Barandiarán, José Miguel de. Nacimiento y expansión de los fenómenos sociales. Anuario de Eusko-Folklore. 4 (1924): 151-229.

Barandiarán, José Miguel de. Establecimientos humanos y casa rural. Anuario de Eusko-Folklore. 5(1925): 1-150; 6(1926): 1-146; 7(1927): 1-136; 8(1928): 1-54; 9 (1929): 1-46.

Barandiarán, José Miguel de. Vida pastoril vasca; albergues veraniegos. Transhumancia intrapirenaica. Anales del Museo del Pueblo Español. 1(1935): 88-97. (Madrid.)

Barandiarán, José Miguel de. Materiales para un estudio etnográfico del pueblo vasco: en Liginaga. Eusko-Jakintza (Revue d'Études Basques). 3(1949): 433-449.

Barandiarán, José Miguel de. Bosquejo etnográfico de Sara. 3. Los establecimientos humanos y la casa rural. Anuario de Eusko-Folklore. 19(1962): 47-123.

Barandiarán, José Miguel de, et al. El mundo en la mente popular vasca. Creencias, cuentos y leyendas. Colección Auñamendi. 18. San Sebastián, Editorial Auñamendi. 1961. 166 p.

Barandiarán, S. de. Basque ceremonial dances. Journal of the International Folk Music Council. 9(1957): 43-45.

Baroja y Nessi, Pio. El pais vasco. 1st ed. Barcelona, Ediciones Destino. 1953. 519 p. (2d ed. 1961. 560 p., folding col. map.)

Barriola, J. M. Medicina popular en el país vasco. Archivos Iberoamericano de Historia de la Medicina. 4(1952): 239-294.

Bernoville, Gaëtan. Le pays des basques; types et coutumes; . . . Paris, Éditions des Horizons de France. 1930. 12, 294 p., illus.

Blazy, E. La pelote basque. Bayonne, Lodes. 1929. 98 p., illus.

Buen, Fernando de. La navegación y la pesca. Primero Congreso de Estudios Vascos. Oñate. 1918: 198-218.

Burgaña, José Maria de. Aspectos de la vida del pescador. Ikuska. 1947, núm. 2: 59-68; núm. 3: 89-100.

Calbéton, F. Proyecto de organación de los pescadores libres. Primero Congreso de Estudios Vascos. Oñate. 1918: 144-163.

Caro Baroja, Julio. Datos para el estudio de la mentalidad del campesino vasco. San Sebastián. 1946. 39 p.

*Caro Baroja, Julio. Los Vascos, etnología. San Sebastián, Biblioteca Vascon gada de los Amigos del País. 1949. 559 p. (2d ed. Madrid, Ediciones Minotauro. 1958. 540 p.)

Caro Baroja, Julio. Dos notas descriptivas: la agricultura en Vera de Bidasoa y caza de palomas en Echalar. Eusko-Jakintza (Revue d'Études Basques). 5(1951): 107-119.

Caro Baroja, Julio. Vasconiana; de historia y etnología. Madrid, Ediciones Minotauro. 1957. 177 p.

Caro Baroja, Julio. El ritual de la danza en el pais Vasco. R.D.T.P. 20(1964): 40-76.

Chalbaud, Louis. La familia como forma típica y trascendental de la consti- tución social vasca. Primero Congreso de Estudios Vascos. Oñate. 1918: 43-64.

Ciriquiain-Gaiztarro, M. Los vascos en la pesca de la ballena. San Sebastiá Biblioteca Vascongada de los Amigos del País. 1961. 360 p., illus.

BASQUES

Colas, Louis. La tombe basque. Recueil d'inscriptions funéraires et domes-
tiques du pays basque français. Études, notes et références diverses.
Bayonne, Société des Sciences, Lettres, Arts et Études Régionales de
Bayonne. 1923 [1924]. 93 p., illus.

Colas, Louis. La tombe basque, recueil d'inscriptions funéraires et domestiques du pays basque français . . . . Paris, H. Champion. 1923. 402 p.,
illus.

Colas, Louis. La mobilier basque (ensemble & détails). Paris, C. Massin.
1924. 9 p., 40 plates.

Cordier, Eugène. La droit de famille aux Pyrénées: Barège, Lavedan, Béarn
et pays Basques. Paris, S. Durand. 1860. 119 p.

Cordier, Eugène. De l'organisation de la famille chez les Basques. Revue
Historique de Droit Français et Étranger. 14(1868): 332-366, 576-605;
15(1869): 208-254.

Cordier, Eugène. Usages basques relatifs aux naissances, aux mariages et aux
enterrements. Explorations Pyrénéennes (Bulletin de la Société Ramond,
Bagnères-de-Bigorre). 4(1869): 50-74.

Cuzacq, René. Dans le folklore basque. Processions de la Fête-Dieu et
chapelles, chasse à la palombe, sur la maison basque, et varia. Mont-de-
Marsan, J. Lacoste. 1953. 110 p.

*Douglass, William A. Opportunity, choice-making, and rural depopulation in
two Spanish Basque villages. Chicago, University of Chicago. 1967. (Unpublished Ph. D. dissertation in anthropology.)

Echegaray, B. d'. Significación jurídica de algunos ritos funerarios del país
vasco. Revista Internacional de Estudios Vascos. 16(1925): 94-118, 184-
222.

Echegaray, B. d'. La vecindad. Revista Internacional de Estudios Vascos.
33(1932): 4-26, 376-405, 546-564.

Elbée, Jean d'. Le pays basque français. Bordeaux, R. Picquot. 1942. 104 p.

Elsner, E. The romance of the Basque country and the Pyrenees. London,
Herbert Jenkins. 1927. 319 p.

Esla, Constantino del. Estampas vascas. Buenos Aires, Editorial Vasca Ekins.
1945. 171 p.

Estornes Lasa, Bernardo. Origenes de los vascos; civilizaciones primitivas,
albores historicos. 2 vols. Zaruz, Editorial Icharopena, Serie Aralar.
1959, 1961.

Fedden, R., and K. Fedden. The Basque country. London, A. and C. Black. 1921. 189 p.

*Gallop, Rodney. A book of the Basques. London, Macmillan. 1930. 12, 294 p.

Gallop, Rodney. Pelote: game of the Basques. Geographical Magazine. 21(1948): 81-88, illus.

Gallop, Rodney, and Philippe Veyrin. Pays Basques de France et d'Espagne. Paris, Arthaud. 1951. 32 p.

Gandía, Enrique de. Los navegantes del Cantábrico. Revista Geográfica Americana. 27(1947): 64-66.

Gárate, J. Los estudios de medicina popular en el país vasco. Revista Internacional de Estudios Vascos. 20(1929): 378-396.

Garo, B. M. Ensayo sobre la propiedad comunal en la toponima vasca. Boletin de la Real Sociedad Vascongada de Amigos del País. 13(1957): 200-219.

Gennep, Arnold van. Manuel de folklore français contemporain. Vol. 1, pts. 1-7, Vol. 3, Vol. 4 (Vol. 2 never published.) Paris, Picard. 1937-1957.

Giese, Wilhelm. Notas sobre abejas y apicultura en el país vasco. Eusko-Jakintza (Revue d'Études Basques). 3(1949): 373-378.

Guilbert, Robert. La Toussaint au pays basque. Bulletin de la Société Normande de Géographie. 28(1906): 237-253.

Hérelle, Georges. Les charivaris nocturnes dans le pays basque français. Revista Internacional de Estudios Vascos. 15(1924): 505-522.

Karutz, Richard. Aus dem Lande der Basken. Lübeck. 1900. 280 p., illus.

Krüger, Fritz. Sach- und Wortkundliches vom Wasser in den Pyrenäen. Volkstum und Kultur der Romanen. 2(1929): 139-243.

*Krüger, Fritz. Die Hochpyräen. B. Hirtenkultur. Volkstum und Kultur der Romanen. 8(1935): 1-103, 8 plates.

*Krüger, Fritz. Die Hochpyrenäen. D. Hausindustrie, Tracht, gewerbe. Volkstum und Kultur der Romanen. 8(1935): 211-328; 9(1936): 1-106, illus., plates.

*Krüger, Fritz. Die Hochpyrenäen. A. Landschaften, Haus und Hof. Hamburg, Hänsische Universität, Abhandlungen aus dem Gebiet der Auslandskunde. 44, ser. B. 23. Hamburg, de Gruyter. 1936. 28, 238 p., 44 plates, map.

*Krüger, Fritz. Die Hochpyrenäen. C. Ländlichen Arbeit. Bd. 1. Transport und Transportgeräte. Butlletí de Dialectología Catalana. 23(1936): 39-240. 14 figs., 89 photos.

*Krüger, Fritz. Die Hochpyrenäen. C. Ländliche Arbeit. Bd. 2: Getreide-Heuernte- Bienenwohnung- Wein- und Ölbereitung. Hamburger Studien zu Volkstum und Kultur der Romanen. 32. Hamburg, Hänsischer Gildenverlag. 1939. 10, 500 p., map, 19 pp. of illus., 36 plates.

*Krüger, Fritz. Die Hochpyrenäen. A. Landschaften, Haus und Hof. Bd. 2. Hamburg, Hänsische Universität, Abhandlungen aus dem Gebeit der Auslandskunde. 47. 1939. 28, 400 p., 17 plates.

La raza vasca. 2 vols. Zarauz, Editorial Icharopena. 1959-1962.

Lefèbvre, Th. Les modes de vie dans les Pyrénées atlantiques orientales. Paris, A. Colin. 1933. 775 p., 36 plates.

Lekuona, M. de. Pueblo de Oyartzun. Barrios de Elizalde. Anuario de Eusko-Folklore. 5(1925): 99-130.

Levine, Morton H. Basque isolation: fact or problem? In Ernestine Friedl, ed. Symposium on community studies in anthropology. Proceedings of the 1963 annual spring meeting of the American Ethnological Society. Seattle, University of Washington Press. 1964: 20-31.

Levine, Morton H. The Basques. Natural History. 76, no. 4(1967): 44-51.

McBride, Harry A. The land of the Basques. National Geographic Magazine. 41(1922): 63-87.

Michel, F. X. Le pays basque, sa population, sa langue, ses moeurs, sa littérature et sa musique. Paris, Didot. 1857. 547 p.

Monteiro, Mariana. Legends and popular tales of the Basque people. London, Unwin. 1887. 274 p.

Nolan, John E. Life in the land of the Basques; a proud people of an unknown origin clings to its unique language and traditional way of life in the western Pyrenees. National Geographic Magazine. 105(1954): 147-186.

Olphe-Gaillard, G. Le paysan basque du Labourd. Paris, Science Sociale. 1905. 193 p.

Ormond, P. S. The Basques and their country. London, Butler & Tanner. 1925. 143 p., map.

O'Shea, Henri. La tombe basque; étude des monuments et usages funéraires des Euskarians. Pau. 1889. 77 p., 12 plates.

BASQUES

O'Shea, Henri. La maison basque. Bayonne, Lamaignère. 1897. 87 p., illus.

Oyarzun et al. La religiosidad del pueblo. Anuario de Eusko-Folklore. 4(1924): 1-149.

Paret, Lotte. Das ländliche Leben einer Gemeinde der Hautes-Pyrénées, dargestellt auf Grund der mundartlichen Terminologie. Tübingen, Tübinger Universität. 1932. 90 p. (Thesis.)

Reicher, Gil. La vie d'un village basque. Bordeaux, Féret. 1936. 75 p.

Revista Internacional de Estudios Vascos [Revue International des Études Basques. Paris, Société des Études Basques "Eusko-Ikazkuntza. 1 (1907)--1936?

Rowe, Vivian. The Basque country. London, Putnam. 1955. 247 p.

Saint-Léger, A. de, and E. Delbert. Pêcheur-cotier de Saint Sebastien (Pays Basque). Revista Internacional de Estudios Vascos. 18 (1927): 665-698; 19 (1928): 49-57.

Staffe, Adolf. Beiträge zur Monographie des Baskenrindes. Revista Internacion al de Estudios Vascos. 17(1926): 34-93.

Thalamas Labandíbar, Juan. Estudio etnográfico del pueblo vasco continental. Anuario de Eusko-Folklore. 11 (1931): 1-120.

Veyrin, Ph. Systématisation des motifs usités dans la décoration populaire basque. Quinto Congreso de Estudios Vascos. Vergara. 1930: 48-78.

*Veyrin, Ph. Les Basques de Labourd, Soule et Basse-Navarre. Paris, Arthaud. 1955. 350 p., plates, illus.

Vincent, Marvin R. In the shadow of the Pyrenees from Basque-land to Carcassonne. New York, Charles Scribner's Sons. 1883. 276 p.

Vinson, Julien. Les Basques et le pays basque; moeurs, langue et histoire. Paris, Cerf. 1882. 149 p., illus.

Vinson, Julien. La tradition au pays basque. Ethnographie, folklore, art populaire, historie, hagiographie. Paris, Gougy. 1899. 598 p.

Webster, Wentworth. Basque legends collected chiefly in the Labourd; with an essay on the Basque language. London, Griffith and Farran. 1877. 233 p.

Yrizar, Joaquín. Las casas vascas. San Sebastián, Librería Internacional. 1929. 115 p., 108 plates.

Alford, Violet. The feast of Santiago in Galicia. Folk-Lore. 68(1957): 489-495.

Anderson, Ruth Matilda. Gallegan provinces of Spain: Pontevedra and La Coruña. New York, Hispanic Society of America. 1939. 17, 496 p.

Dobby, E. H. G. Galicia: a little known corner of Spain. Geographical Review. 26(1936): 555-580.

Elías de Tejada, Francisco. La tradición gallega. Madrid. 1944. 173 p.

Herbert, Henry John George, 3d Earl of Carnarvon. Portugal and Galicia: with a review of the social and political state of the Basque. 3d ed. London, J. Murray. 1848. 11, 376 p.

*Krüger, Fritz. Die nordwestiberische Volkskultur. Wörter und Sachen. 10(1927): 45-137.

Krüger, Fritz. Las Brañas. Ein Beitrag zur Geschichte der Rundbauten im asterisch-galizisch-portugiesischen Raum. Volkstum und Kultur der Romanen. 16(1944): 158-203.

Krüger, Fritz. El léxico rural der noroeste ibérico. Madrid, Consejo Superior de Investigaciones Científicas, Instituto Antonio de Nebrija. 1947. 142 p., plates. (A translation of Krüger, 1927.)

Lis Quiben, Victor. Datos de medicina popular en Galicia. Archivos Iberoamericanos de Historia de la Medicina. 5(1953): 248-265.

Lorenzo Fernandez, Joaquin. Die Bremse am galizischen Wagen. Volkstum und Kultur der Romanen. 11 (1938): 282-289.

Martínez-Barbeito, Carlos. Galicia. Barcelona, Ediciones Destino. 1957. 524 p.

Otero Pedrayo, Ramón. Paisajes y problemas geográficos de Galicia. Madrid, Compañía Ibero-Americana de Publicaciones. 1928. 214 p.

*Rodriguez Lopez, Jesus. Supersticiones de Galicia y preocupaciones vulgares. Buenos Aires, Editorial Nova. 1895. 203 p. (Many later reprints of this work.)

Taboada, Jesus. La medicina popular en el Valle de Monterrey (Orense). R.D.T.P. 3(1947): 31-57.

Taboada, Jesus. La noche de San Juan en Galicia. R.D.T.P. 8 (1952): 600-632.

GALICIA

Taboada, Jesus. Moros y cristianos en tierras de Laza (Orense). R. D. T. P. 11 (1955): 334-352.

Yglesias, José. The goodbye land. New York, Pantheon Books. 1967. 218 p.

CANARY ISLANDS

Cuzcoy, L. Diego. Tradiciones populares. Folklore infantil. La Laguna de Tenerife, Instituto de Estudios Canarios. 1944. 252 p.

Edwardes, Charles. Rides and studies in the Canary Islands. London, T. F. Unwin. 1888. 20, 365 p.

Great Britain. Admiralty Office. Naval Intelligence Division. Canaries. In Spain and Portugal. 4 vols. London, Great Britain. Admiralty Office. Naval Intelligence Division. Vol. 4, 1945: 115-220.

Hooton, Ernest Albert. The ancient inhabitants of the Canary Islands. Harvard African Studies. 7. Cambridge, Peabody Museum of Harvard University. 1925. 25, 401 p.

Jensen, Sören. Agricultural methods in the Canaries—Fuerteventura and Lanzarote. Economic Geography. 10(1934): 99-108.

Jiménez Sanchez, Sebastián. Del folklore canario. El mes de San Juan y sus fiestas populares. R.D.T.P. 10 (1954): 176-189.

Krämer, Augustin. Ein Besuch von Gran Canaria. Globus. 78(1900): 362-370.

Pérez Vidal, José. Contribución al estudio de la medicina popular Canaria. Tagoro. Anuario del Instituto de Estudios Canarios. 1944: 29-88. (Printed in 1945.)

Pérez Vidal, José. La fiesta de San Juan en Canarias. La Laguna de Tenerife, Instituto de Estudios Canarios. 1945. 99 p.

GIBRALTAR

Howes, Henry William. The story of Gibraltar; first outpost of empire. Fulham, London, Philip & Tacey. 1946. 95 p.

Howes, Henry William. The Gibraltarian. The origin and development of the population of Gibraltar from 1704. Colombo, City Press. 1950. 8, 224 p.

Pla, Jose. Gibraltar. London, Hollis & Carter. 1955. 157 p.

ANDORRA

Alford, Violet. Pyrenean festivals. Calendar customs, music & magic, drama & dance. London, Chatto and Windus. 1937: 61-65.

Aurousseau, Marcel. Highway into Spain. New York, Alfred H. King. 1931. 294 p.

Deane, Shirley. The road to Andorra. New York, William Morrow. 1961. 186 p.

Krüger, Fritz. Sach- und Wortkundliches vom Wasser in den Pyrenäen. Volkstum und Kultur der Romanen. 2(1929): 139-243.

*Krüger, Fritz. Die Hochpyrenäen. B. Hirtenkultur. Volkstum und Kultur der Romanen. 8(1935): 1-103, 8 plates.

*Krüger, Fritz. Die Hochpyrenäen. D. Hausindustrie, Tracht, Gewerbe. Volkstum und Kultur der Romanen. 8(1935): 210-328; 9(1936): 1-106, illus., plates.

*Krüger, Fritz. Die Hochpyrenäen. A. Landschaften, Haus und Hof. Hamburg, Hänsische Universität, Abhandlungen aus dem Gebiet der Auslandskunde. 44, ser. B. 23. Hamburg, de Gruyter. 1936. 28, 238 p., 44 plates, map.

*Krüger, Fritz. Die Hochpyrenäen. C. Ländlichen Arbeit. Bd. 1. Transport und Transportgeräte. Butlletí de Dialectología Catalana. 23(1936): 39-240. 14 figs., 89 photos.

*Krüger, Fritz. Die Hochpyrenäen. C. Ländliche Arbeit. Bd. 2. Getreide-Heuernte- Bienenwohnung- Wein- und Ölbereitung. Hamburger Studien zu Volkstum und Kultur der Romanen. 32. Hamburg, Hänsischer Gildenverlag. 1939. 10, 500 p., map, 19 pp. of illus., 36 plates.

*Krüger, Fritz. Die Hochpyrenäen. A. Landschaften, Haus und Hof. Bd. 2. Hamburg, Hänsische Universität, Abhandlungen aus dem Gebiet der Auslandskunde. 47. 1939. 28, 400 p., 17 plates.

*Llobet, Salvador. El medio y la vida en Andorra, estudio geográfico. Barcelona, Instituto Elcano, Estación de Estudios Pirenaicos. 1947. 347 p.

Llobet Reverter, S. La casa en Andorra "Ilerda." Lérida. Año 2(1944): 357-376.

Newman, Bernard. Round about Andorra. Boston and New York, Houghton Mifflin Co. 1928. 300 p.

O'Connor, Vincent Clarence S. Travels in the Pyrenees. London, John Long. 1913. 348 p.

ANDORRA

Paret, Lotte. Das ländliche Leben einer Gemeinde der Hautes- Pyrénées, dargestellt auf Grund der mundartlichen Terminologie. Tübingen, Tübinger Universität. 1932. 90 p. (Thesis.)

Peattie, Roderick. Andorra: a study in mountain geography. Geographical Review. 19(1929): 218-233.

Solé Sabaris, L. Los Pirineos. El medio y el hombre. Barcelona, Ed. Albert Martin. 1951. 625 p.

Pereira, Benjamim Enes. Bibliografia analítica de etnografia portuguesa. Lisboa, Centro de Estudos de Etnologia Peninsular. 1965. 15, 672 p.

Abelho, Azinhal. Memória sobre os barros de Estremoz. Lisboa, Edições Panorama. 1964. 71 p.

Armstrong, Lucile. Dances of Portugal. New York, Chanticleer Press. 1948. 40 p., illus.

Baldaque da Silva, Antonio A. Estado actual das pescas em Portugal. Lisboa, Imprensa Nacional. 1892. 519 p., 390 figs.

Basto, Cláudio. Traje a vianesa. Vila Nova de Gaia, Ediçoes Apolino. 1930. 56 p., 19 figs.

Basto, E. A. Lima, and Henrique de Barros. Inquérito a habitação rural. 1. Lisboa. 1943. 445 p., 261 figs. (The northern provinces.)

Bastos, Carlos. Industria e arte têxtil. Porto. 1960. 323 p. plus 50 p., 286 figs.

Braga, Alberto Vieira. See Vieira Braga, Alberto.

Braga, Theophilo. O povo Português nos seus costumes, crenças e tradições. 2 vols. Lisboa, Livraria Ferreira. 1885. 416, 546 p.

Brito, J. Maria Soeiro de. Astronomia, meteorologia e chronologia populares. Espozende. 1890. 42 p.

Buescu, Maria Leonor Carvalhão. Monsanto: etnografia e linguagem. Lisboa, Centro de Estudos Filologicos. 1961. 400 p., 18 figs.

Cabral, Manoel Medeiros. These Portuguese. Rev. ed. Philadelphia, Kemi-color Publishing Co. 1955. 98 p., maps.

Caldas da Rainha, Portugal. Museu Provincial José Malhoa. Exposição de cerâmica e olaria das Caldas da Rainha: Maria dos Cacos a Costa Mota. Lisboa, Impresso na Oficina Gráfica do S.N.I. 1963. 58 p.

Cancio, Francisco. Ribatejo, casos e tradições. 1. Lisboa. 1948. 525 p., 246 figs.

Carneiro, A. Lima. A alimentação da criança na primeira infância. A amamentação. Congresso do Mundo Português. 2, 18 (1940): 126-140.

Carvalho, José Gonçalo C. Herculano de. Coisas e palavras—alguns problemas etnográficos e linguísticos relacionados com os primitivos sistemas de debulha na península ibérica. Coimbra. 1953. 413 p. (Includes data on threshing.)

Carvalho, José Luís Brandão de. Portas ornamentados. Lisboa, Edições Panorama. 1960. 28 p., 17 plates, 4 fold-out pages.

Castro, José de. Estudos etnográficos. 2 vols. Lisboa, Instituto para a Alta Cultura. 1943-1945.

Castro, Manuel Chaves. Aspectos etnográficos na literatura portuguesa. Coimbra, Livraria Almedina. 1956. 44 p., illus.

Castro Pires de Lima, Fernando de. Cantares do Minho. Barcelos, Impresão Companhia Editora do Minho. 1937. 154 p.

Castro Pires de Lima, Fernando de. O simbolismo cristão na cantiga popular; com a cola boração arística do prof. Cláudio Carneiro. Pôrto, Portucalense Editora, S.A.R.L. 1941. 88 p.

Chaves, Luís. Ex-votos do Museu Etnologico Português. Miscelânea de Etnolo gia e Arqueologia. 1915: 3-50. (Lisboa.)

Chaves, Luís. O amor Português. Lisboa. 1922. 166 p. (Love and courtship

Chaves, Luís. Portugal além--notas etnográficas. Gaia, Edições Pátria. 1932. 168 p.

Chaves, Luís. Páginas folclóricas. Porto. 1942. 199 p.

Chaves, Luís. Folclore religiosa. Porto. 1945. 189 p.

Chaves, Luís. Do barro se faz a louça: na louça se come o trigo. Lisboa, Federação Nacional dos Produtores de Trigo. 1953. 87 p.

Chaves, Luís. Os transportes populares em Portugal--carros e barcos (tipos e decorações). Lisboa. 1958. 57 p., 28 figs.

Cordeiro, Adelino. Etnografia da Beira: religião e crendices, lendas e costumes de Penamacôr. Viana, Tip. com. "Aurora do Lima." 1937. 111 p.

Correia, Vergílio. Etnografia artística portuguesa. Porto. 1916. 149 p., 109 figs. (Reprinted: Barcelos, Companhia Editora do Minho. 1937. 184 p., 109 illus.)

Correia, Vergílio. O carro rural portugues. A Terra Portuguesa. 3(1917): 193-208; 4(1918): 90-193.

Correia, Vergílio. A arte em Coimbra e arredores. Coimbra. 1949. 109 p.

Costa, Maria de Lurdes de Oliveira Monteiro dos Santos. Porto Santo—mono- grafia linguística, etnográfica e folclórica. Revista Portuguesa de Filologia. (Coimbra) 1, 2, 3. (1947-1949): 1-182.

PORTUGAL

Costa, Maria Lila Dias. Uma povoação do concelho de Loures—Etnografia, linguagem, folclore. Lisboa. 1961. 338 p., 69 figs.

Costigan, Arthur William. Sketches of society and manners in Portugal. 2 vols. London, T. Vernor. 1787.

Cunha, Fernanda de Matos. Notas etnográficas sobre Barcelos. Porto. 1932. 114 p., 47 figs.

Cunha, José Germano da. Apontamentos para a historia do concelho do Fundão. Lisboa, Typographia Minerva Central. 1892. 267 p.

*Descamps, Paul. Le Portugal: la vie sociale actuelle. Paris, Firmin-Didot. 1935. 18, 507 p.

Descamps, Paul. Histoire sociale du Portugal. Paris, Firmin-Didot. 1959. 538 p.

Dias, Antonio Jorge. Os arados portugueses e as suas prováveis origens; estudo etnográfico. Porto, Instituto para a Alta Cultura. 1948 [1950]. 169 p., 61 figs. (Also printed in: Revista da Universidade de Coimbra. 16(1949): 245-388.)

*Dias, Antonio Jorge. Vilarinho da Furna, uma aldeia comunitária. Porto, Instituto para a Alta Cultura. 1948. 15, 274 p., 59 figs.

Dias, Antonio Jorge. Cultura popular e cultura superior. Santiago de Compostela. 1949. 20 p.

Dias, Antonio Jorge. Minho, Trás-os-Montes et Haut-Douro. Lisboa. 1949. 130 p.

Dias, Antonio Jorge. Sacrifícios simbólicos associados às malhas. Lisboa, Livraria Ferin. 1951. 15 p. (Folklore of agriculture and threshing.)

*Dias, Antonio Jorge. Rio de Onor: comunitarismo agro-pastoril. Porto, Instituto de Alta Cultura, Centro de Estudos de Etnologia Peninsular. 1953. 610 p.

Dias, Antonio Jorge. Os elementos fundamentais da cultura Portuguesa. Actas do Coloquio Internacional de Estudos Luso-Brasileiros, Washington 1950. Nashville, Tenn. 1953: 51-65. (Reprinted: Coimbra, Tipografia da Atlantida. 1955. 30 p.)

Dias, Antonio Jorge. Ensaios etnológicos. Lisboa, Junta de Investigações do Ultramar. 1961. 9, 198 p.

Dias, Antonio Jorge. Portuguese contribution to cultural anthropology. Johannesburg, Witwatersrand University Press. 1961. 112 p., map.

Dias, Antonio Jorge, and Herculano de Carvalho. O falar de Rio de Onor.
Biblos. 30(1954): 191-240.

Dias, Antonio Jorge, and Margot Dias. Contribuição ao estudo do "culto dos
mortos. " Associação Portuguesa para o Progresso das Ciencias. 23 Congresso Luso-Espanhol, Coimbra. 1956: 483-501.

Dias, Antonio Jorge, and Fernando Galhano. Aparelhos de elevar a água de
rega. Porto, Junta de Província do Douro-Litoral. 1953. 261 p., 154
figs. (Traditional irrigation systems.)

Dias, Antonio Jorge, Ernesto Veiga de Oliveira, and Fernando Galhano.
Sistemas primitivos de moagem em Portugal. Moinhos, azenhas de água e
atafonas. 2 vols. Vol. 1. Moinhos de água e azenhas. Vol. 2. Moinhos
de vento. Porto, Instituto de Alta Cultura. 1959. 102 p., 78 figs.;
95 p., 88 figs.

Dias, Antonio Jorge, Ernesto Veiga de Oliveira, and Fernando Galhano.
Sistemas primitivos de secagem e armazenagem de productos agricolas: os
espiqueiros Portugueses. Porto, Instituto de Alta Cultura. 1961 [1963 on
cover] . 291 p., illus.

Dias, Jaime Lopes. See Lopes Dias, Jaime.

Dias, Margot, and Antonio Jorge Dias. A encomendação das almas. Porto.
1953. 76 p., 21 musical notations. (Cult of the dead.)

Duro, Antonio Rodovalho. História do toureio em Portugal. Lisboa. 1907.
304 p.

Felgueiras, Guilherme. Monografia de Matsosinhos. Lisboa. 1958. 909 p.,
133 figs.

Ferro, Antonio, et al. Vida e arte do povo portugues. Lisboa, Secretariado de
Propagande Nacional. 1940. 263 p., illus., col. plates.

Ferro, Gaetano. Ricerche di geografia urbana nell'Algarve (Portogallo): Faro
el Vila Real de Santo Antonio. Annali di Ricerche e Studi de Geografia.
10(1954): 41-70.

Ferro, Gaetano. La pesca nel mare dell'Algarve. Annali di Ricerche e Studi
de Geografia. 10(1954): 125-176.

Fiedler, H. Portugals Landwirtschaft in volkskundlicher Sicht. In Hans Flasch
ed. Aufsätze zur portugiesischen Kulturgeschichte. Münster in Westfallen,
Aschendorff. 1961: 154-203.

Fiedler, H. Volkstrachten in Portugal. In Hans Flasche, ed. Aufsätze zur portugiesischen Kulturgeschichte. Münster in Westfallen, Aschendorff. 1961: 221-236.

Flowers, Nancy. Majestic workboats of a Portuguese lagoon. Natural History. 74, no. 2(1965): 20-25.

Flowers, Nancy. Pottery of Barcelos. Natural History. 75, no. 6(1966): 44-51.

*Gallop, Rodney Alexander. Portugal, a book of folkways. Cambridge, The University Press. 1936. 15, 281 p.

Gallop, Rodney Alexander. Cantares do povo Português; estudo critico, recolha e comentario. Lisboa, Edição do Instituto para a Alta Cultura; despositaria, Livraria Ferin. 1937. 149 p.

Gascon, José Antonio Guerreiro. Subsídios para a monografia de Monchique. Portimão, Portucalense Editora. 1955. 403 p., illus.

Giese, Wilhelm. Portugiesische Hochzeitssitten in Rahmen romanischen Brauchtums. Congresso do Mundo Português. 2, 18 (1940): 150-186.

Giese, Wilhelm. Zur bäuerlichen Kultur der Tierra de Miranda (NO-Portugal). Z.f.E. 82(1957): 250-256.

Gonçalves, Flávio. Procissões de mordomos. Douro Litoral. Quinta série. 1-2(1952): 80-88.

Gourou, P. Habitations au Portugal. l'Homme. 4(1964): 90-92.

Graça, A. O poveiro. Póvoa de Varzim. 1932. 238 p., 30 figs.

*Great Britain. Admiralty Office. Naval Intelligence Division. Spain and Portugal. 4 vols. London, Great Britain. Admiralty Office. Naval Intelligence Division. Geographical Handbook Series. 1941-1945. Vol. 2. Portugal. 1942. 16, 450 p., figs., plates.

Guerriro, M. V. Contos populares portugueses. Lisboa, Fundacão Nacional para a Alegria no Trabalho. 1955. 404 p.

Guimarães, Alfredo. Mobiliário artistico português (elementos para a sua história). 2. Guimarães. Vila Nova de Gaia. 1935. 184 p., 132 figs.

Guimarães, Alfredo, and Albano Sardoeira. Mobiliário artistico português (elementos para a sua história). 1. Lamego. Porto, M. Abreu. 1924. 108 p., 96 figs.

Gutkind, Peter. Urban development in southern Europe: Spain and Portugal. New York, The Free Press of Glencoe. 1967. 544 p.

Hayes, R. A peasant economy in North-west Portugal. Geographical Journal. 122 (1956): 54-70.

Higgin, L. Spanish life in town and country with chapters on Portuguese life in town and country by Eugene E. Street. London, G. Newnes. 1902. 11, 289 p. (Another edition: New York, London, G. P. Putnam's Sons. 1902. 10, 325 p.)

Koebel, William Henry. Portugal. Its land and people. New York, Dodd, Mead. 1909. 17, 405 p.

Krüger, Fritz. Notas etnográfico-linguísticas da Póvoa de Varzim. Boletim de Filologia (Lisboa). 4 (1936): 109-182.

Krüger, Fritz. Der Beitrag Portugal zur europäisches Volkskunde. Congresso do Mundo Português. 2, 18 (1940): 296-351.

Krüger, Fritz. Las Brañas (Ein Beitrag zur Geschichte der Rundbauten im asturisch-galicisch-portugiesischen Raum). Congresso do Mundo Português. 2, 18 (1940): 239-295, 23 figs.

Landolt, Cândido. Subsidios para o estudo do folk-lore infantil portuguez. Espozende. 1892. 14 p.

Landolt, Cândido. Folk-lore Varzino — costumes e tradições populares do século XIX. Póvoa de Varzim. 1915. 230 p., 27 figs.

Lapa, João Ignácio Ferreira. Artes chimicas, agricolas e florestais ou technologia rural. 1. Lisboa. 1865. 382 p., 107 figs.

Leão, Armando. Notas de medicina popular minhota. Arquivo de Medicina Popular. 1 (1944): 11-44.

Leite de Vasconcellos, José. Religiões da Lusitania. 3 vols. Lisboa, Imprensa Nacional. 1897, 1905, 1913. 441 p., 112 figs.; 372 p., 8 figs.; 636 p., 339 figs.

Leite de Vasconcellos, José. Etnografía Portuguesa. 4 vols. Lisboa, Imprensa Nacional de Lisboa. 1933-1958. (Many reprints of individual volumes in this series.)

Lima, Américo Pires de. See Pires de Lima, Américo.

Lopes Dias, Jaime. Etnografia da Beira—lendas, costumes, tradições, crenças e superstições. 3. Lisboa. 1929. 176 p.

Lopes Dias, Jaime. Etnografia da Beira. 5. Lisboa. 1937. 232 p., 17 figs.

Lopes Dias, Jaime. Etnografia da Beira. 6. Lisboa, Tôrres, Livraria Ferin. 1942. 314 p.

Lopes Dias, Jaime. Etnografia da Beira. 1. Lisboa, Emprêsa Nacional da Publicidade. 1944. 215 p.

Lopes Dias, Jaime. Etnografia da Beira. 7. Lisboa. 1948. 280 p., 18 figs.

Lopes Dias, Jaime. Etnografia da Beira. 8. Lisboa, 1953. 269 p., 58 figs.

Lucena, Armando de. Arte popular. Usos e costumes. 2d ed. 3 vols. Lisboa, Emprêsa Nacional de Publicidade. 1944-1945. 206, 210, 198 p., illus.

Machado, C. H. de M. Subsidios para a história do Mogadouro; o culte das almas, usos e crencas. Porto, Douro Litoral. 1956. 21 p.

Marques, Pinheiro. Terras de Algodres (Concelho de Fornos). Lisboa, 1938. 331 p.

Martins, Firmino A. Folklore do concelho de Vinhais. 1. Coimbra, Imprensa da Universidade. 1928. 356 p., 12 figs.

Martins, Firmino A. Folklore do concelho Vinhais. 2. Lisboa. 1939. 575 p.

Matos Cunha, Fernanda de. Aspects de la vie des paysans de Barcelos. L'Ethnographie. New series. No. 25(1932): 117-121.

Mattos, Armando de. A arte dos jogos e cangas do Douro-Litoral. Porto. 1942. 238 p., 202 figs. (Yokes and harnesses.)

*Messerschmidt, H. Haus und Wirtschaft in der Serra da Estrêla (Portugal). Volkstum und Kultur der Romanen. 4(1931): 72-163, 246-305.

Moreira, Vasco. Terras da Beira — Cernancelhe e seu alfoz. Porto. 1929. 354 p., 39 figs.

Museu de Arte Popular. Lisboa, Museu de Arte Popular. n.d. [195_]. No pagination, illus. (A guide book. Reprinted: 1963. No pagination.)

Oliveira, Carlos de. Apontamentos para a monografia da Guarda. Guarda. 1949. 360 p.

Oliveira, Ernesto Veiga de. Aspectos de compadrio em Portugal. Actas do Colóquio Internacional de Estudos Luso-Brasileiros. 3, 1(1957-1959): 154-169.

Oliveira, Ernesto Veiga de, and Fernando Galhano. A arquitectura popular em Portugal. A Arte Popular em Portugal. 1(n.d.): 15-137, 82 figs. (Lisboa.)

O'Malley, Mary Dolling Saunders, and Susan Lowndes. The selective traveler in Portugal. London, Evans Bros. 1949. 10, 293 p.

Pan, Ismael del. Aspectos etnologo-geograficos de Portugal (Folklore Hispano-Portugues). Sociedad Española de Antropología, Etnología y Prehistoria, Actas y Memorias. 18(1943): 5-216.

Peixoto, Rocha. Indústrias populares. As olarias do Prado. Portugália. 1 (190? 227-270, 94 figs.

Peixoto, Rocha. Etnografia portuguesa—iluminação popular. Portugália. 2 (1908): 35-48, 36 figs.

Pereira, Nuno Teotónio, et al. Arquitectura popular em Portugal. 2. Lisboa. 1961. 374 p., 769 figs.

Pessanha, Sebastião. Doçaria popular portuguesa (estudo etnográfico). Lisboa. 1957. 67 p., 58 figs.

Pessanha, Sebastião. Mascarados e máscaras populares de Trás-os-Montes. Lisboa. 1960. 66 p., 65 figs.

Picão, José da Silva. See Silva Picão, José da.

Pina, Luís de. Bruxes e medicina. Trabalhos de Antropologia e Etnologia. 4, no. 3(1929): 117-150.

Pires de Lima, Américo. Curandeiros e curandeirismo. Porto. 1912. 12 p.

Pires de Lima, Américo. Tradições populares de Santo Tirso. Revista Lusitana (Instituto Cultural de Ponta Delgada). 17(1914): 17-54, 282-337; 18 (191? 183-204; 19 (1916): 233-257.

Pires de Lima, Américo. Jogos e canções infantis. Porto. 1943. 167 p.

Pires de Lima, Américo. S. João na lma do povo. Porto. 1944. 96 p.

Queiroz, José. Cerâmica portuguesa. Lisboa, Typ. do Annuario Commercial. 1907. 449 p., 195 figs. (Historical study.)

Resende, João Vieira. Monografia da Gafanha. 2d ed. Coimbra. 1944. 364 ? 26 figs.

Ribeiro, António Lopes. Monografia da freguesia de Reguengo Grande (Concelh? da Lourinhã). Anais do Instituto Superior de Agronomia. 11 (1940): 49-215, 30 figs.

Ribeiro, Orlando. Contribuição para o estudo do pastoreio na Serra da Estrela. Revista du Faculdade de Letras da Universidade de Lisboa. 7(1940-1941): 213-303.

*Riegelhaupt, Joyce F. In the shadow of the city: integration of a Portuguese village. New York, Columbia University. 1964. 279 p. (Unpublished Ph. D. dissertation in anthropology.)

Riegelhaupt, Joyce F. Prognosticative calendar systems II. A.A. 69(1967): 82-83.

*Riegelhaupt, Joyce F. Saloio women: an analysis of informal and formal political and economic roles of Portuguese peasant women. Anthropological Quarterly. 40(1967): 109-126.

Rocha da Silva Guimarães, Bertino Daciano. Cinfães. Subsídios para uma monografia do concelho. Porto. 1954. 268 p., 38 figs.

Siegel, Bernard J. Social structure and the medical practitioner in rural Brazil and Portugal. Sociologia (São Paulo). 20(1958): 463-476.

*Siegel, Bernard J. Conflict, parochialism and social differentiation in Portuguese society. Journal of Conflict Resolution. 5(1961): 35-42.

Silva, Cristóvão, and Manuel Mendes de Morais. Jogos tradicionais portugueses. Lisboa. 1928. 170 p.

Silva Picão, Jose da. Através dos campos. Usos e costumes agrícola-alentejanos (Concelho de Elvas). 2d ed. Lisboa. 1947. 21, 370 p.

Smith, T. L. The social relationships of man to the land in Portugal. Sociologia (São Paulo). 25(1963): 319-343.

Sousa, Alberto. O traje popular em Portugal nos séculos XVIII e XIX. Lisboa. 1924. 252 p.

Sousa, Tude Martins de. Gerez (Notas etnografícas, arqueológicas e historicas). Coimbra. 1927. 272 p., 34 figs.

Southey, Robert. Journals of a residence in Portugal, 1800-1801, and a visit to France. Oxford, The Clarendon Press. 1960. 23, 285 p.

*Stanislawski, Dan. The individuality of Portugal. Austin, University of Texas Press. 1959. 14, 248 p., illus.

Stanislawski, Dan. The livelihood of the ordinary people of the Portuguese Algarve. In Stanley Diamond, ed. Culture in history; essays in honor of Paul Radin. New York, Columbia University Press. 1960: 253-280.

*Stanislawski, Dan. Portugal's other kingdom: the Algarve. Austin, University of Texas Press. 1963. 273 p., illus.

Távora, Fernando, et al. Arquitectura popular em Portugal. 1. Lisboa. 1961. 351 p., 964 figs.

PORTUGAL

Teran, Manuel de, ed. Geografia de España y Portugal. 5 vols. Barcelona, Montaner y Simón. 1952.

Tinelli, I. W. A arte de cultivar a sêda. Porto, Typographia Commercial Portuense. 1843. 88 p.

Urtel, Hermann. Beiträge zur portugiesischen Volkskunde. Hamburg Universität. Abhandlungen aus dem Gebiet der Auslandskunde. 27. 1928. 8, 88 p., 4 plates.

Veiga de Oliveira, E., and F. Galhano. Casas de pescadores da Póvoa de Varzim. Trabalhos de Antropologia e Etnologia. 15(1955-1957): 219-264

Veiga de Oliveira, E., and F. Galhano. A aphano do sargaço no norte de Portugal. Porto, Universidade do Porto, Instituto de Antropologia. 1958. 114 p.

Viana, A. Para o cancioneiro popular algarvio. Lisboa, Alvaro Pinto. 1956. 321 p.

Vieira Braga, Alberto. De Guimarães, tradições e usanças populares. Esposende. 1924. 473 p.

Vieira Braga, Alberto. Curiosidades de Guimarães—mortórios. Revista de Guimarães. 52(1942): 155-226; 53(1943): 14-97.

Vitorino, Pedro. Ceramica Portuense. Gaia, Edições Apolino. 1930. 75 p., illus.

Vitorino Ribeiro, Emmanuel P. La vertu de l'osier et du genêt (dessins de Alice d'Azevedo) version, selon l'original portugais inédit. Coimbra, Imprensa da Universidade. 1930. 87 p.

Weibust, Knut. The crew as a social system. Oslo, Norsk Sjofartsmuseum. 1958. 66 p.

Willems, Emilio. Die Familie in Portugal und Brasilien: ein strukturvergleichender Versuch. Kölner Zeitschrift für Soziologie. 7(1955): 24-42.

Willems, Emilio. A familia Portuguêsa contemporânea. Sociologia (São Paulo). 17 (1955): 3-55.

*Willems, Emilio. On Portuguese family structure. International Journal of Comparative Sociology. 3(1962): 65-79.

Wood, Ruth Kedzie. The tourists' Spain and Portugal. New York, Dodd, Mead. 1913. 16, 357 p.

Ribeiro, Luís Silva. Os estudos etnográficos nos Açores. Portucale. 11(1938): 155-160.

Costa, Francisco Carreiro da. As festas do Espírito Santo nos Açores. Revista Insulana. 13(1957): 5-54.

Figueiredo, Jaime de. Império Marienses Folclore Açoriano. Lisboa. 1957. 160 p., 23 figs.

Gomes, Maria Luísa Ataíde da Costa, and Lygia Maria da Camara da Almeida Mattos. Trajos regionais e danças populares da ilha S. Miguel. Ponta Delgada. 1955. 60 p.

Great Britain. Admiralty Office. Naval Intelligence Division. Azores. In Spain and Portugal. 4 vols. London, Great Britain. Admiralty Office. Naval Intelligence Division. Geographical Handbook Series. 1941-1945. Vol. 3. 1944: 267-338.

Krüger, Fritz. El Hogar y el mobiliário popular de ilha Terceira. Boletim do Instituto Histórico da Ilha Terceira. 14(1956): 90-148. 45 figs.

Leite de Vasconcellos, J. Mes de sonho—Conspecto de etnografia açórica. Lisboa. 1926. 318 p., 33 figs.

Meireles, C. Panorama folklorico dos Açores especialmente da Ilha de S. Miguel. Ponta Delgada. 1955. 116 p. (Also published in: Revista Insulana. 11(1955): 1-112.)

Ribeiro, Luís Silva. Notas de etnografia da Ilha Terceira. Revista Lusitana. 32(1934): 250-274.

Ribeiro, Luís Silva. As festas e tradições populares de São João na Ilha Terceira. Revista Açoriana. 4(1947): 127-148.

Ribeiro, Luís Silva. As touradas da Ilha Terceira (Açores). Revista Açoriana. 4(1949): 295-301.

Brüdt, Kate. Madeira—Estudo linguístico-etnográfico. Boletim de Filologia
(Lisboa). 5(1939): 59-91, 289-349.

Dias, Antonio Jorge. Nótulas de etnografia madeirense. Contribuição para o
estudo das origens étnico-culturais população da ilha da Madeira. Biblos.
28(1952): 179-201.

Cruz, Visconde do Porto da. Folclore madeirense. Funchal. 1955. 290 p.

Ferreira, Manuel Juvenal Pita. O natal na Madeira. Estudo folclórico.
Funchal. 1956. 400 p.

Great Britain. Admiralty Office. Naval Intelligence Division. Madeira. In
Spain and Portugal. 4 vols. London, Great Britain. Admiralty Office.
Naval Intelligence Division. Geographical Handbook Series. 1941-1945.
Vol. 4. 1945: 221-266.

Koebel, William Henry. Madeira: old and new. London, F. Griffiths. 1909.
16, 216 p., 3 plates.

Martins, Mário Resende, Jose F. de s. Texeira, and Manuel D. da Silva. Mono
grafia da vila de S. João da Madeira. Porto. 1944. 140 p.

Pereira, Eduardo C. N. Ilhas de Zardo. 2d ed. 2 vols. Funchal. 1956-1957
609 p., 207 figs.; 784 p., 370 figs.

Ribeiro, Orlando. L'île de Madère. Étude géographique. Lisbon, Union Géographique Internationale. 1949. 175 p.

Santos, Vitorino José dos. Indústrias madeirenses. Bordados e artefactos de
verga embutidos. Boletim do Trabalho Industrial. 5(1907): 32 p.

Sarmento, Alberto Artur. Fasquias e ripas da Madeira. Funchal. 1951. 253 p

CAPE VERDE ISLANDS

Cardoso, P. Folclore caboverdeano. Porto, Ed. Maranus. 1933. 120 p.

Parsons, Elsie Clews. Folk-lore from the Cape Verde Islands. 2 vols.
Memoirs of the American Folklore Society. 15. New York, G. E. Steckert.
1923. 640 p.

Bibliographie Balkanique. 8 vols. Paris, La Revue des Balkans. 1931-1939. (Covers period 1920-1938.)

Kerner, R. J. Social sciences in the Balkans and in Turkey. A survey of resources for study and research in these fields of knowledge. Berkeley, University of California Press. 1930. 137 p.

Krallert-Sattler, Gertrud. Südosteuropa-Bibliographie. 3 vols. Bd. 1. 1945-1950. Bd. 2. 1951-1955. Bd. 3. 1956-1960. München, R. Oldenbourg. 1956--

Arbatsky, Yury. Beating the tupan in the central Balkans. Chicago, Newberry Library. 1953. 7, 64 p.

Belović, Jesna. Die Sitten der Südslawen. Dresden, Paul Aretz Verlag. 1927. 318 p., 120 illus.

Carrier, Elsé H. Water and grass. A study in the pastoral economy of southern Europe. London, Christophers. 1932. 11, 434 p.

Craven, Lady Elizabeth Berkeley, Baroness Craven. A journey through the Crimea to Constantinople. London, G. G. J. & J. Robinson. 1789. 4, 327 p. (Vienna, R. Sammer. 1800. 468 p.)

*Cvijić, Jovan. La péninsule balkanique, géographie humaine. Paris, A. Col. 1918. 8, 528 p., illus., maps.

Diefenbach, Lorenz. Völkerkunde Osteuropas, insbesondere der Haemoshalbins und der unteren Donaugebiete. 2 vols. Darmstadt, L. Brill. 1880.

Durham, Mary Edith. Through the lands of the Serb. London, E. Arnold. 1904. 11, 345 p.

Durham, Mary Edith. The burden of the Balkans. London, E. Arnold. 1905. 12, 331 p.

Durham, Mary Edith. Extract from a letter from Miss M. E. Durham. Balkan —head hunting. Man. 12(1912): 178-179.

Durham, Mary Edith. Some tribal origins, laws and customs of the Balkans. London, G. Allen & Unwin. 1928. 318 p., illus.

Durham, Mary Edith. My Balkan note book. 3 albums. n.d. Containing photos and drawings. Vol. 1: Primitive implements, boats, hearths, buildings in various Balkan districts; Serbian costumes, buildings, etc. Vol. 2: Sun and moon designs, taboos, graves in Bosnia and Albania, Montenegro. Vol. 3: Albania: tribes, buildings, etc. Deposited in the Royal Anthropological Institute Library in London. n.d.

Evliya, Efendi. Narrative of travels in Europe, Asia, and Africa, in the seventeenth century. 2 vols. in 3. London, printed for the Oriental Translation Fund of Great Britain and Ireland; sold by Parbury, Allen. 1834-1850.

Frolec, Václav. La communauté culturelle en architecture populaire dans la région limitrophe bulgaro-serbe. Národopisný Vestník Československý. 2, no. 35(1967): 65-102.

*Garnett, Lucy Mary Jane. Balkan home life. London, Methuen. 1917. 309 p.

Gopčević, Spiridion. Makedonien und alt-Serbien. Wien, L. W. Seidel und Sohn. 1889. 7, 511 p.

Gunda, Béla. Ethnographica Carpathica. Budapest, Akadémiai Kiadó. 1966. 418 p. (In Hungarian.)

Gunda, Béla. Fish poisoning in the Carpathian area and in the Balkan Peninsula. In William G. Lockwood, ed. Essays in Balkan ethnology. Kroeber Anthropological Society, Special Publications No. 1. 1967: 1-34.

Haberlandt, Arthur. Kulturwissenschaftliche Beiträge zur Volkskunde von Montenegro, Albanien und Serbien. Wien, Verein für Österreichische Volkskunde. 1917. 8, 187 p.

Haberlandt, Arthur. Volkskunst der Balkanländer in ihren Grundlagen. Wien, A. Schroll. 1919. 78 p., illus.

Hahn, Johann Georg von. Reise von Belgrad nach Salonik. Wien, Königlich Akademie der Wissenschaften, Philosophisch-historische Klasse, Denkschriften. Bd. 11, Abt. 2. 1861. 245 p.

*Hammel, Eugene A. Alternative social structures and ritual relations in the Balkans. Englewood Cliffs, N. J., Prentice-Hall. 1968. 128 p.

Helle von Samo, A., Ritter zur. Die Völker des osmanlischen Reiches. Wien, G. Gerold's Sohn. 1877. 130 p.

Karcz, Jerzy, ed. Proceedings of the Conference on Soviet and East European agriculture. Berkeley, University of California Press. 1967. 25, 445 p.

Kostrowicki, Jerzy. An attempt to determine the geographical types of agriculture in East-central Europe on the basis of the case studies on land utilization. In Jerzy Kostrowicki, ed. Land utilization in East-central Europe. Geographia Polonia. 5. Warszawa, Institute of Geography, Polish Academy of Sciences. 1965: 453-498.

Kostrowicki, Jerzy, ed. Land utilization in East-central Europe. Geographia Polonia. 5. Warszawa, Institute of Geography, Polish Academy of Sciences. 1965. 498 p., illus., plates, maps, charts.

Krauss, Friedrich Salomon. Sagen und Märchen der Südslaven. 2 vols. Leipzig, W. Friedrich. 1883-1884.

*Krauss, Friedrich Salomon. Sitte und Brauch der Südslaven. Wien, A. Hölder 1885. 26, 681 p.

Krauss, Friedrich Salomon. Das Bauopfer bei den Südslaven. M.A.G.W. 17(1887): 16-24.

Krauss, Friedrich Salomon. Volksglaube und religiöser Brauch der Südslaven. Münster in Westfalen, Aschendorff. 1890. 16, 176 p.

Krauss, Friedrich Salomon. Slavische Volksforschungen: Abhandlungen über Glauben, Gewohnheitsrechte, Sitten, Bräuche, und die Guslarenlieder der Südslaven. Leipzig, W. Heims. 1908. 431 p.

Küppers-Sonnentag, G. A. Ornamente und Symbole südslawischer Bauern-lauten (Guslen). Z.f.E. 84(1959): 88-109.

Küppers-Sonnentag, G. A. Balkanisches Festtagsbackwerk (Gebildebrot) Ornamentik, Symbolik, Stellung im Festbrauch. Z.f.E. 87(1962): 93-114

Lefèvre, M. A. La zadruga. Annales de Géographie. 39(1930): 316-320.

Lejean, Guillaume. Les populations de la péninsule des Balkans. Revue d'Anthropologie. 2 sér., 5(1882): 201-259, 628-675.

Meibohm, Anatole de. Démons, derviches et saints . . . Paris, Plon. 1956. 278 p.

Mosely, Philip E. The distribution of the zadruga within Southeast Europe. Jewish Social Studies, Publication No. 5(1953): 219-230.

*Mosely, Philip E. The peasant family: the zadruga, or communal joint-family in the Balkans, and its recent evolution. In Caroline F. Ware, ed. The cultural approach to history. New York, Columbia University Press. 1940: 95-108.

Newbigin, Marion Isabel. Geographical aspects of Balkan problems in their relation to the great European war. New York, G. P. Putnam's Sons. 1915. 9, 243 p.

Ogilvie, A. G. Physiography and settlements in southern Macedonia. Geographical Review. 11 (1921): 172-197.

Oxford University. Pitt-Rivers Museum. An exhibition of Balkan peasant work presented by Miss M. E. Durham. Oxford, Oxford University Press. 1940. 7, 1 p.

Pittard, Eugène. Les peuples des Balkans; recherches anthropologiques dans la péninsule des Balkans. Genève, Lyon, Georg; Paris, Leroux. 1920. 634 p.

Rosen, Georg. Die Balkan-Haiduken. Leipzig, F. A. Brockhaus. 1878. 10, 336 p.

*Sicard, Émile. La zadruga sud-slave dans l'évolution du groupe domestique. Paris, Éditions Ophrys. 1943. 10, 705 p.

Sicard, Émile. Problèmes familiaux chez les Slaves du sud. Paris, Éditions Familiales de France. 1947. 205 p.

Silvio, Dragomir. The ethnical minorities in Transylvania. Genève, Sonor Printing Co. 1927. 129 p.

Start, Laura. The Durham collection of garments and embroideries from Albania and Yugoslavia. Bankfield Museum Notes, 3d ser. No. 4. Halifax, England, Bankfield Museum. 1939. 76 p., illus., 2 plates.

Stoianovich, Traian. The conquering Balkan orthodox merchant. Journal of Economic History. 20(1960): 234-313.

Stoianovich, Traian. The social foundations of Balkan politics, 1750-1941. In Charles and Barbara Jelavich, eds. Balkans in transition. Berkeley, University of California Press. 1963: 297-345.

Stoianovich, Traian. A study in Balkan civilization. New York, Alfred A. Knopf. 1968. 12, 215, 6 p.

Stotz, Alfred. The ethnographical map of Transylvania. [n.p., 1928?]. 10 p., map.

Thurnher, Majda. A survey of Balkan houses and farm buildings. Kroeber Anthropological Society, Paper No. 14(1956): 19-92.

Tomasić, Dinko. The structure of Balkan society. American Journal of Sociology. 52(1946): 132-140.

*Tomasić, Dinko. Personality and culture in eastern European politics. New York, George W. Stewart. 1952. 249 p. (Reprinted: Cambridge, Mass., M.I.T. Press. 1964. 249 p.)

Ubicini, Jean Henri A. Letters on Turkey; an account of the religious, political, social, and commercial conditions of the Ottoman Empire . . . Translated from the French . . . by Lady Easthope. 2 vols. London, J. Murray. 1856.

Vinski, Zdenko. Die südslavische Grossfamilie in ihrer Beziehung zum asiatischen Grossraum . . . Zagreb, Tiskara K. Rožmanić. 1938. 98 p.

Warriner, Doreen, ed. Contrasts in emerging societies. Readings in the social and economic history of south-eastern Europe in the nineteenth century. Bloomington, Indiana University Press. 1965. 19, 402 p.

*Wilkinson, Henry Robert. Maps and politics: a review of the ethnographic cartography of Macedonia. Liverpool, Liverpool University Press. 1951. 16, 366 p., maps.

Wolfram, Richard. Der Volkstanz als kulturelle Ausdrucksform der süosteuropäischen Völker. Südosteuropa-Jahrbuch. 6(1962): 63-84.

Wünsch, Walter. Die Geigentechnik der südslawischen Guslaren. Veröffentlichungen des Musikwissenschaftlichen Institutes der Deutschen Universität in Prag. 5. Brünn, Prag, Leipzig, Rudolf M. Rohrer. 1934. 60 p.

YUGOSLAVIA

Krallert-Sattler, Gertrud. Südosteuropa-Bibliographie. 3 vols. to date. Bd. 1: 1945-1950. Bd. 2: 1951-1955. Bd. 3: 1956-1960. München, R. Oldenbourg. 1956--

Lopac, Matija. Bibliografski podaci etnografsko-folklorrih radova o Bosni i Hercegovini [Bibliography of ethnographic and folkloric work on Bosnia and Hercegovina]. Glasnik Zemaljskskog Muzeja u Sarajevu. New series. 6(1951): 339-409.

United States. Bureau of the Census. Bibliography of social science periodicals and monograph series: Yugoslavia: 1945-1963. Washington, U.S. Government Printing Office. 1965. 156 p.

United States. Library of Congress. Geography of Yugoslavia. A selected bibliography. Washington, Library of Congress. Reference Department. Slavic and Central European Division Publications. 1955. 79 p.

Asboth, Janos. An official tour through Bosnia and Herzegovina, with an account of the history, antiquities, agrarian conditions, religion, ethnology, folk-lore and social life. London, S. Sonnenschein. 1890. 20, 496 p.

Balen, M. Family relations and their changes in the village of Jalžabet. Sociologija. 4(1962): 254-283.

*Barić, Lorraine. Levels of change in Yugoslav kinship. In Maurice Freedman, ed. Social organization. Essays presented to Raymond Firth. Chicago, Aldine Publishing Co. 1967: 1-24.

*Barić, Lorraine. Traditional groups and new economic opportunities in rural Yugoslavia. In Raymond Firth, ed. Themes in economic anthropology. London, Tavistock Publications. 1967: 253-281.

Bartók, Béla. Serbo-Croatian folk songs. New York, Columbia University Press. 1951. 17, 431 p.

Baumberger, Georg. Blaues Meer und schwarze Berge. Volks- und Landschaftsbilder aus Krain, Istrien, Dalmatien, Montenegro. Einsiedeln, Verlagsanstalt Benziger. 1902. 336 p., illus.

Bicanić, R. Occupational heterogeneity of peasant families in the period of accelerated industrialization. Third World Congress of Sociology. 4(1956): 80-96.

Bjelskositche, L. G. Animal folklore from the Herzegovina. Man. 4(1904): 132-136.

Bogišić, Baltazar. Pravni običaji u slovena. Zagreb, U Štampariji D. Albrechta. 1867. 8, 196 p. (Customary law.)

Bogišić, Baltazar. Gragja u odgovorima iz različnih krajeva slovenskoga juga, osnovao skupio uredio V. Bogišić. Zagreb, U Knjižarnici F. Župana. 187- 74, 714 p. (Southern Slavic customary law.)

Bordeaux, Albert François Joseph. La Bosnie populaire. Paysages. Moeurs et coutumes. Legends. Chants populaires. Mines. Paris, Plon. 1904. 307 p.

Boreli, R., and L. Žunić. Nasa narodne svatanja o vatri [Our popular beliefs about fire]. Beograd, Savez Drustava za Materijala. 1960. 138 p.

Bratanić, Branimir. Bericht über die Erforschung der Geräte zur Bodenbearbeitung in Jugoslawien. In Agrarethnographie. Berlin, Akademie der Wissenschaften zu Berlin. 1957: 1-10.

Bresloff, Leon M. Economic adaptation and development of family types in a Bosnian town. In William G. Lockwood, ed. Essays in Balkan ethnology. Berkeley, Kroeber Anthropological Society, Special Publications No. 1. 1967: 35-54.

Brewster, P. G. A group of Jugoslav games. Southern Folklore Quarterly. 20(1956): 183-191.

Bukurov, B. R. Nikolić, and M. Filipović. Hera villages in Yugoslavia. Rad Vojvodjanskih Muzefa. 7(1958): 38-50.

Cornish, V. Bosnia, the borderland of Serb and Croat. Geography. 20(1935 260-270.

Ćurčić, Vejsil. Die volkstümliche Fischerei in Bosnien und der Herzegowina mit besonderer Berücksichtigung der Savefischerei bei Dônja Dolina. Wissenschaftliche Mitteilungen aus Bosnien und der Herzegowina. 12(1912): 490-589.

Ćurčić, Vejsil. Rezente Pfahlbauten von Donja Dolina in Bosnien. Z.f.Ö.V. Erg. Bd. 9. Wien. 1913. 78 p., 22 text figs., 87 figs., 13 plates.

Ćurčija-Prodanović, N. Yugoslav folk-tales. London, Oxford University Pres 1957. 210 p.

Dachler, Anton, and Michael Haberlandt. Das Bauernhaus in Österreich-Unga und in seinen Grenzgebiete. Wien, Ingenieur- und Architektenverein. 190 17, 288 p., 67 illus., 6 plates, 75 folio plates, map.

Djordjević, Tikhomir R. Naš narodni život . . . 10 vols. Beograd, Izdava Knižarnidza G. Kona. 1930-1934. (A collection of materials on ethnolog customs, beliefs, etc.)

Drobnjaković, B. Etnologija naroda jugoslavije. Prvi deo [Ethnography of the peoples of Yugoslavia. Part 1]. Beograd, Naučna Knjiga. 1960. 260 p.

Durham, Mary Edith. Review of "Peasant life in Jugoslavia" by Olive Lodge. Man. 42(1942): 140-141.

Edwards, Lovett Fielding. Profane pilgrimage: wanderings through Yugoslavia. London, Duckworth. 1938. 292 p.

Edwards, Lovett Fielding. A wayfarer in Yugoslavia. New York, R. M. McBride. 1939. 272 p.

Erlich, Vera St. The southern Slav patriarchal family. Sociological Review. 32(1940): 224-241.

Erlich, Vera St. The pre-industrial phase of development; some southern Slav examples. Sociologus. Neue Folge. 2(1952): 117-131.

*Erlich, Vera St. Family in transition. A study of 300 Yugoslav villages. Princeton, Princeton University Press. 1966. 656 p., plates.

Filipović, M. S. Ethnic pluralism in the Yugoslav province of Vojvodina. Etnoloski Pregled 4(1962): 7-10. (In Serbo-Croatian, with an English summary.)

Fortis, Alberto. Travels into Dalmatia. London, printed for J. Robson. 1778. 584 p.

Franck, Otto. Studien zur serbokroatischen Ortsnamenkunde. Leipzig, Verlag Gustav Fock. 1933. 239 p. (Thesis, University of Berlin.)

Gavazzi, Milovan. The dug-out coffin in Central Bosnia. Man. 53(1953): 129-130.

Great Britain. Admiralty Office. Naval Intelligence Division. Jugoslavia. 3 vols. London, Great Britain. Admiralty Office. Naval Intelligence Division. Geographical Handbook Series. 1944-1945. 14, 337 p., plates, illus.; 12, 403 p., plates, illus.; 14, 566 p., plates, illus.

*Halpern, Joel M. Yugoslav peasant society in transition — stability in change. Anthropological Quarterly. 36(1963): 156-182.

Halpern, Joel M. Peasant culture and urbanization in Yugoslavia. Human Organization. 24(1965): 162-174.

*Halpern, Joel M. Farming as a way of life: Yugoslav peasant attitudes. In Jerzy Karcz, ed. Proceedings of the Conference on Soviet and East European agriculture. Berkeley, University of California Press. 1967: 356-384.

Halpern, Joel M. The process of modernization as reflected in Yugoslav peasant biographies. In William G. Lockwood, ed. Essays in Balkan ethnology. Kroeber Anthropological Society, Special Publications No. 1. 1967: 109-126.

*Hammel, Eugene A. Serbo-Croatian kinship terminology. Kroeber Anthropological Society Papers. 16(1957): 45-75.

*Hammel, Eugene A. Alternative social structures and ritual relations in the Balkans. Englewood Cliffs, N.J., Prentice-Hall. 1968. 128 p.

Hoffman, G. W. Yugoslavia: changing character of rural life and rural economy. American Slavic and East European Review. 18(1959): 554-578.

Holme, Charles, ed. Peasant art in Austria and Hungary. London, The Studio 1911. 10, 54 p., plates.

Janković, Ljubica S., and D. S. Lubitsa. Dances of Yugoslavia. New York, Crown. 1952. 40 p., 7 plates.

*Kemp, Phyllis. Healing ritual — studies in the technique and tradition of the southern Slavs. London, Faber & Faber. 1935. 16, 335 p., plates.

Kostić, C. Changement de structure des villages yougoslaves. Cahiers Internationaux de Sociologie. 23(1957): 141-156.

Krauss, Friedrich Salomon. Sagen und Märchen der Südslaven. 2 vols. Leipzig, W. Friedrich. 1883-1884.

Krauss, Friedrich Salomon. Volksglaube und religiöser Brauch der Südslaven. Münster in Westfalen,Aschendorff. 1890. 176 p.

Krauss, Friedrich Salomon. Slavische Volksforschungen. Abhandlungen über Glauben, Gewohnheitsrechte, Sitten, Bräuche, und die Guslarenlieder der Südslaven. Leipzig, W. Heims. 1908. 431 p.

Lear, Edward. Journals of a landscape painter in Albania and Illyria. London, R. Bentley. 1851. 428 p.

Lesic, D. Vodenica i valjavice u Istoku [Water mills and fulling mills at Istok] Glasnik Etnografskog Muzeja u Beogradu. 17(1954): 186-200.

Lilek, E. Familien- und Volksleben in Bosnien und der Herzegowina. Z.f.Ö.V 6(1900): 23-30, 53-71, 164-172, 202-225.

Lodge, Olive C. Some studies in vital statistics among primitive village communities in Jugoslavia. International Congress of Anthropology and Prehistoric Archaeology. 15th. 2d Part. Paris. 1931. Paris (1933): 608-615.

Lodge, Olive C. Villages and houses in Yugoslavia. Geography. 21(1936): 94-106.

*Lodge, Olive C. Peasant life in Jugoslavia. London, Seeley, Service. 1942. 332 p.

Lodge, Olive C. Folk festivals in Yugoslavia. Folk-Lore. 55(1944): 59-68.

Lopashich, A. A negro community in Yugoslavia. Man. 58(1958): 169-173.

Lord, Albert Bates. The singer of tales. Cambridge, Harvard University Press. 1960. 15, 309 p. (New York, Atheneum. 1965. 15, 309 p.)

Mais, Adolf J. Die serbokroatischen Ziehbauern . . . Wien. 1947. 130 p. (Thesis. Universität Wien.)

Meringer, Rudolf. Die Stellung des bosnischen Hauses und Etymologien zum Hausrath. Kaiserliche Akademie der Wissenschaften. Sitzungsberichte. Philosophe-historische Klasse. Bd. 144. Wien. 1902. 118 p. (Also published as book: Wien, C. Gerold's Sohn. 1902. 118 p.)

Mladenović, Tanasije. The soil and the peasant. Jugoslavija. 15(1958): 134-141.

Die Österreichisch-Ungarische Monarchie in Wort und Bild. 24 vols. K. K. Hof- und Staatsdruckerei. 1886-1902. (See: Bd. 10. Das Küstenland [Görz, Gradiska, Triest und Istrien]. 1891; Bd. 11. Dalmatien. 1892; Bd. 22. Bosnien und Herzegovina. 1901; Bd. 24. Croatien und Slavonien. 1902.)

Parry, M. Serbocroatian heroic songs. 2 vols. Vol. 1. Novi Pazar: English translations. Vol. 2. Novi Pazar: Serbocroatian texts. Cambridge, Harvard University Press. 1953-1954.

Pusić, E. The family in the process of social change in Yugoslavia. Sociological Review. 5(1957): 207-224.

Rayner, Louisa. Women in a village; an Englishwoman's experience and impressions of life in Yugoslavia under German occupation. London, William Heinemann. 1957. 247 p.

Reed, Harry E. The hog industry in Yugoslavia. Foreign Agriculture. 1(1937): 503-524.

Roller, N. Huxley. Notes on some south Slav beliefs and festivals. Folk-Lore. 37(1926): 35-75.

Schneeweiss, Edmund. Volksnahrung im Plivatal (Bosnien). Z.f.Ö.V. 24(1918): 81-97.

Schneeweiss, Edmund. Die Weihnachtsbräuche der Serbocroaten. Wien, Verlag des Vereines für Volkskunde. 1925. 8, 232 p.

Schneeweiss, Edmund. Grundriss des Volksglaubens und Volksbrauchs der Serbocroaten. Cilli, Družba Sv. Mohorja Celju. 1935. 267 p.

*Schneeweiss, Edmund. Serbokroatische Volkskunde. Erster Teil. Volksglaube und Volksbrauch. Berlin, Walter de Gruyter. 1961. 218 p.

Sicard, Émile. La zadruga sud-slave dans l'évolution du groupe domestique. Paris, Éditions Ophrys. 1943. 10, 705 p.

Skendi, Stavro. Albanian and South Slavic oral epic poetry. Memoirs of the American Folklore Society. 44. Philadelphia. 1954. 221 p.

Somerville, R. M. The family in Yugoslavia. Journal of Marriage and the Family. 27(1965): 350-362.

Start, Laura. The Durham collection of garments and embroideries from Albania and Yugoslavia. Bankfield Museum Notes. 3d ser. No. 4. Halifax, England, Bankfield Museum. 1939. 76 p., 2 plates.

Stevenson, Beatrice L. The gusle singer and his songs. A. A. New series. 17 (1915): 58-68.

Stoinovich, Traian. A study in Balkan civilization. New York, Alfred A. Knopf. 1968. 12, 215, 6 p.

Strangford, Emily Anne Beufort Smythe, Viscountess. Eastern shores of the Adriatic in 1863. With a visit to Montenegro. London, R. Bentley. 1864. 4, 386 p., plates.

Sugar, Peter F. Industrialization of Bosnia-Hercegovina 1878-1919. Seattle, University of Washington Press. 1963 [1964]. 11, 275 p.

Szana, Alexander. Länder- und Völkerkunde Jugoslawiens. Heidelberg, Julius Gross Verlag. 1921. 174 p.

Thurnher, Majda. A survey of Balkan houses and farm buildings. Kroeber Anthropological Society Papers. 14(1956): 19-92. (See pp. 20-66.)

Titelbach, Vladislav. Das heilige Feuer bei den Balkanslaven. International Archiv für Ethnographie. 13 (1900): 1-4. 4 plates.

*Tomasević, Jozo. Peasants, politics, and economic change in Yugoslavia. Stanford, Stanford University Press; London, Oxford University Press. 1955. 12, 743 p.

Tomašić, Dinko. Sociology in Yugoslavia. American Journal of Sociology. 44(1941): 53-69.

*Trouton, Ruth. Peasant renaissance in Yugoslavia, 1900-1950; a study of the development of Yugoslav peasant society as affected by education. London, Routledge & Kegan Paul. 1952. 13, 344 p.

Vinski, Zdenko. Die südslavische Grossfamilie in ihrer Beziehung zum asiatischen Grossraum: ein ethnologischer Beitrag zur Untersuchung des vaterrechtlichgrossfamilialen Kulturkreises. Zagreb, Tiskara K. Rožmanić. 1938. 100 p.

Vucinich, Alexander S. Yugoslav society: the tribal period. East Lansing, Michigan State University. 1950. 306 p. (Unpublished Ph. D. dissertation.)

*Warriner, Doreen. Contrasts in emerging societies. Readings in the social and economic history of south-eastern Europe in the nineteenth century. Bloomington, Indiana University Press. 1965: 283-387.

Waterston, A. Planning in Yugoslavia. Baltimore, Johns Hopkins Press. 1962. 109 p.

West, Rebecca [pseudonym]. Black lamb and grey falcon; a journey through Yugoslavia. 2 vols. New York, Viking Press. 1941. 1181 p.

Wilkinson, Sir G. [Sir John Gardner]. Dalmatia and Montenegro: with a journey to Mostar in Herzegovina, and remarks on the Slavonic nations; the history of Dalmatia and Ragusa; . . . 2 vols. London, J. Murray. 1848.

Wilkinson, Henry R. Maps and politics: a review of the ethnographic cartography of Macedonia. Liverpool, Liverpool University Press. 1951. 16, 366 p., maps.

Yugoslavia. European conference on rural life. National monographs drawn up by governments. Yugoslavia. Series of League of Nations Publications. European Conference on Rural Life. 23. Geneva. 1939. 83 p., illus.

Zganec, V. Folklore elements in the Yugoslav Orthodox and Roman Catholic liturgical chant. Journal of the International Folk Music Council. 8(1956): 19-22.

SLOVENES

Breznika, Antona, et al., eds. Narodopisje Slovencev. 2 vols. Ljubljana, Klas. 1944-1952.

Copeland, F. S. Slovene folklore. Folk-Lore. 42(1931): 405-446.

Dachler, Anton, and Michael Haberlandt. Das Bauernhaus in Österreich-Ungarn und in seinen Grenzgebiete. Wien, Ingenieur- und Architektenverein. 1906. 17, 288 p., 67 illus., 6 plates, 75 folio plates, map.

*Jeršič, M., J. Lojk, L. Olas, and M. Vojvoda. The village of Seboborci on the Slovenian fringes of the Great Pannonian Plain. In Jerzy Kostrowicki, ed. Land utilization in East-central Europe. Geographia Polonia. 5. Warszawa, Institute of Geography, Polish Academy of Sciences. 1965: 215-234.

*Klemenčič, V. The village of Podgorje in the Slovenian sub-alpine region. In Jerzy Kostrowicki, ed. Land utilization in East-central Europe. Geographia Polonia. 5. Warszawa, Institute of Geography, Polish Academy of Sciences. 1965: 195-214.

Krek, Ivan. Les Slovènes. Paris, Félix Alcan. 1917. 85 p.

Lončar, Dragnotin. The Slovenes. Cleveland, Jugoslav American Printing and Publishing Co. 1939. 8, 77 p. (Social history.)

Möderndorfer, Vinko. Verovanja, uvere in običaji Slovencev. 2 vols. Celje, Druzba sv. Mohorja. 1946-1948. (Folk beliefs, customs, and folk life.)

Novak, Vilko. Vprašanje nabiralništva pri Slovencih [The problem of gathering among the Slovenes]. Slovenski Etnograf. 10(1957): 19-28.

*Novak, Vilko. Übersicht über Viehhaltungsformen und Alpwesen in Slowenien. In László Földes, ed. Viehzucht und Hirtenleben in Ostmitteleuropa. Budapest, Akadémiai Kiadó. 1961: 647-662.

Stamp, Laurence Dudley, ed. Slovene studies. London, LePlay Society. 1933 72 p., map.

Šuman, Josef. Die Slowenen. Wien und Teschen, K. Prochaska. 1881. 183

Thurnher, Majda. A survey of Balkan houses and farm buildings. Kroeber Anthropological Society Papers. 14(1956): 19-92. (See pp. 20-27.)

Velter, Theodor. Slowenische Volksgruppen in Kärnten. Wien, Deutscher Verlag für Jugend und Volk. 1936. 186 p.

Vilfan, S. Kobdelavi polja v slovenski Istri [Field tillage in Slovenian Istria]. Slovenski Etnograf. 10 (1957): 61-70.

SLOVENES

Warriner, Doreen. Contrasts in emerging societies. Bloomington, Indiana
University Press. 1965: 349-363.

*Winner, Irene P. Zerovnica, a village in Slovanie. Chapel Hill, N.C. 1967.
443 p. (Unpublished Ph. D. dissertation in Anthropology. University of
North Carolina.)

Zablatnik, Paul. Die geistige Volkskultur der Kärnten Slowenen. Graz. 1950.
609 p. (Ph. D. dissertation, Karl-Franzens Universität.)

Balch, Emily Greene. Our Slavic fellow citizens. New York, Charities Publication Committee. 1910: 156-190.

Bartók, Béla. Serbo-Croatian folk songs. New York, Columbia University Press. 1951. 17, 431 p.

Bihalji-Merin, Oto, ed. Adriatic islands, Yugoslavia. Beograd, Jugoslavija. 1961. 144 p., plates.

Bihalji-Merin, Oto, ed. Croatia, Yugoslavia. Beograd, Jugoslavija. 1961. 138 p., illus.

*Blanc, André. La Croatie occidentale; étude de géographie humaine. Paris, Institut d'Études Slaves de l'Université de Paris. 1957. 15, 498 p., illus., maps.

Bogišić, Valtagar. De la forme dite "inokosna" de la famille rurale chez des Serbes et les Croates. Paris. 1884. 49 p.

Brlić-Mažuranić, Ivana. Croatian tales of long ago. London, G. Allen & Unwin. 1924. 258 p.

Brown, Horatio Robert Forbes. Dalmatia. London, A. & C. Black. 1925. 11, 187 p.

Dachler, Anton, and Michael Haberlandt. Das Bauernhaus in Österreich-Ungarn und in seinen Grenzgebiete. Wien, Ingenieur- und Architektenverein. 1906. 17, 288 p., 67 illus., 6 plates, 75 folio plates, map.

*Erlich, Vera St. Family in transition. A study of 300 Yugoslav villages. Princeton, Princeton University Press. 1966. 656 p., plates.

Eterovich, Francis H., and Christopher Spalatin, eds. Croatia: land, people, culture. Vol. 1. Toronto, University of Toronto Press. 1964. 408 p. (Somewhat propagandistic.)

Faber, G. L. The fisheries of the Adriatic and the fish thereof. A report on the Austro-Hungarian sea-fisheries . . . London, Bernard Quaritch. 1883. 26, 292 p., illus., engravings.

Filipović, Milenko S. Vicarious paternity among Serbs and Croats. S. W. J. A. 14(1958): 156-167.

Fortis, Alberto. Travels in Dalmatia. London, printed for J. Robson. 1778. 584 p.

Fuller, G. J. Coast and karst in Istria Rossa. Nottingham, Geographical Field Group, Geography Department, University of Nottingham. 1960. 63 p., 58 figs.

Gavazzi, Milovan. Der Aufbau der kroatischen Volkskultur. Baessler-Archiv. 20(1937): 138-167, 22 illus.

Goetz, Leopold. Koseworte, Scherz- und Schimpfworte für die Liebenden der Kroaten und Serben. Z.f.V., n.F. 3(1932): 213-241.

Goetz, Leopold. Volkslied und Volksleben der Kroaten und Serben. 2 vols. Heidelberg, Carl Winter. 1936-1937. 12, 226; 4, 243 p.

Gönczi, Franz. Die Kroaten in Muraköz. Ethnologische Mitteilungen aus Ungarn. 4(1895): cols. 163-175, 201-209, plates.

Hacquet, Belsazar. L'Illyrie et la Dalmatie, ou moeurs, usages et costumes de leurs habitans . . . 2 vols. Paris, Nepveu. 1815. (Translated from the German edition of 1801.)

Horvat, V. The Croatian village community in Yugoslavia. Ithaca, N. Y. 1929. (Thesis, Cornell University.)

Horvat, V. Forms of the family among the Croatians and the southern Slavs. In Pitirim Sorokin, ed. Source book in rural sociology. Vol. 2. Minneapolis, University of Minnesota Press. 1931: 57-70.

Ivančan, I. Istarski narodni plesovi [Istrian folk dance]. Zagreb, Institut za Narodnu Umjetnost. 1963. 320 p.

Jelić, D., M. Jeršić, J. Lojk, and M. Vojvoda. The Cadastrian commune of Trebijovi in the karstland of Hercegovina. In Jerzy Kostrowicki, ed. Land utilization in East-central Europe. Geographia Polonia. 5. Warszawa, Institute of Geography, Polish Academy of Sciences. 1965: 267-284.

Johnston, W. B., and I. Crkvenčić. Examples of changing peasant agriculture in Croatia, Yugoslavia. Economic Geography. 33(1957): 50-71.

Koch, Feliz J. In quaint, curious Croatia. National Geographic Magazine. 19 (1908): 809-832.

Kus-Nikolajev, Mirko. Der zeitlose Charakter der kroatischen Bauernkunst. Z.f.E. 83(1958): 274-280, illus.

Levetus, A. S. Croatia and Slavonia. In Charles Holme, ed. Peasant art in Austria and Hungary. London, The Studio. 1911: 51-54, plates.

*Lodge, Olive. Peasant life in Jugoslavia. London, Seeley, Service. 1942. 332 p., plates.

Malina, J. R. Menschen im Karst; Eindrücke aus Kroatien. Atlantis. 1 (1929): 324-333.

CROATIANS

Markotic, Vladimir. The Croats in Albania. Journal of Croatian Studies.
1 (1960): 25-31.

Markovac, Marijan. Şelo i seljaci u slavonskoj Posavini [The village and the
farmers in Slavonic Sava territory]. Zagreb. 1940. 128 p., illus.

Marković, Tomo. Božični običaji Hrvata u Bosni i Hercegovini [Christmas cus
toms among Croats in Bosnia and Hercegovina]. Etnografska Istraživanja i
Graota. 2(1940): 5-86.

Mihanovich, Clement S. Religious folklore of the Poljica region of Dalmatia.
J.A.F.L. 61 (1948): 261-282.

Orr, Dorothea. Portrait of a people. Croatia today. New York and London,
Funk & Wagnalls. 1936. 9, 246 p.

Ostric, Ante. La structure et les moeurs de la société croate. Genève, Impr.
du Château Thonon. 1950. 304 p., map. (Thèse de l'Université de
Genève.)

Palčok, Z. Narodna umjetnost [Folk art]. Zagreb, Institut za Narodnu
Umjetnost. 1963. 16, 160 p., illus.

Pusić, Eugen, and Annamarie Hauck Walsh. Urban government for Zagreb,
Yugoslavia. New York, Praeger, 1968. 14, 151 p.

Reinsberg-Düringsfeld, Ida von. Aus Dalmatien. 3 vols. Prag, C. Bellmann.
1857.

Sindik, Ilija. Dubrovnik i okolina [Ragusa and its region]. Srpski Etnografiski
Zbornik. 38(1925): 1-249.

Thurnher, Majda. A survey of Balkan houses and farm buildings. Kroeber
Anthropological Society Papers. 14(1956): 19-92. (See pp. 27-42.)

Varga, Mathilda. Die Hochzeitsbräuche der Kroaten des österreichischen
Burgenlandes. Wien. 1951. 8, 143 p. (Dissertation, Universität Wien.)

Warriner, Doreen. Contrasts in emerging societies. Bloomington, Indiana
University Press. 1965: 319-348.

Andrić, Ivo. The bridge on the Drina. London, George Allen and Unwin;
New York, Macmillan. 1959. 314 p. (A novel, with excellent material
on Bosnia.)

Arsenović, Nikola. National costumes of Serbia in the Ethnographic Museum in
Belgrade 1823-1885 . . . Beograd, Jugoslavija. 1954. 16 p., illus.

Bartók, Béla. Serbo-Croatian folk songs. New York, Columbia University
Press. 1951. 17, 431 p.

Bihalji-Merin, Oto, ed. Serbia, Yugoslavia. Beograd, Jugoslavija. 1961.
119 p., illus.

Bogišić, Valtagar. De la forme dite "inokosna" de la famille rurale chez les
Serbes et les Croates. Paris, E. Thorin. 1884. 49 p.

Braun, Maximilian. The problem of "moral concepts" in Serbian traditional
epic poetry. Journal of the Folklore Institute. 1 (1964): 82-91.

Brkić, Jovan. Moral concepts in traditional Serbian epic poetry. 's Gravenhage,
Mouton. 1961. 177 p.

Brown, Catherine. A Whitsunday festival at Salakovac in N. E. Serbia. Man.
47 (1947): 20.

Castellan, Yvonne. La culture serbe au seuil de l'independance (1800-1840).
Publications de la Faculté des Lettres et Sciences Humaines de Poitiers 4.
Paris, Presses Universitaires de France. 1967. 166 p., maps.

Dachler, Anton, and Michael Haberlandt. Das Bauernhaus in Österreich-Ungarn
und in seinen Grenzgebiete. Wien, Ingenieur- und Architektenverein. 1906.
17, 288 p., 67 illus., 6 plates, 75 folio plates, map.

Davies, Ellen Chivers. A farmer in Serbia. London, Methuen. 1916. 248 p.

Davies, Ellen Chivers. When I was a boy in Serbia. London, G. G. Harrap.
1920. 159 p.

Denton, Rev. William. Servia and the Servians. London, Bell & Daldy. 1862.
294 p.

Djordjević, M. Život i običaji narodni u Leskovačkoja Moravi [Life and customs of the people of Leskovacka Morava]. Beograd, Srpska Akademija
Nauka. 1958. 724 p.

Durham, Mary Edith. Through the lands of the Serb. London, E. Arnold.
1904. 11, 345 p.

Erdeljanović, Jovan. Etnološka gradja Šumadincima [Ethnographic materials
on Sumadija]. Beograd, Srpska Akademija Nauka. 1951. 203 p.

*Erlich, Vera St. Family in transition. A study of 300 Yugoslav villages. Princeton, Princeton University Press. 1966. 656 p., plates.

Filipović, Milenko. Galipoljski Srbi [Serbs of Galipoli]. Beograd, Srpska Akademija Nauka. 1946. 124.p.

Filipović, Milenko. Zivot i običaji narodni u Visočkoj Nihiji [Life and folk customs in the district of Visoko]. Beograd, Srpska Akademija Nauka. 1949. 336 p. (Bosnia.)

Filipović, Milenko. Folk religion among the Orthodox population in eastern Yugoslavia. Harvard Slavic Studies. 2(1954): 359-374.

Filipović, Milenko. Vicarious paternity among Serbs and Croats. S.W.J.A. 14(1958): 156-167.

Filipović, Milenko. Symbolic adoption among the Serbs. Ethnology. 4(1965): 66-71.

*French, Reginald M. Serbian church life. London, S.P.C.K. 1942. 7, 64 p., plates.

Goetz, Leopold Karl. Koseworte, Scherz- und Schimpfworte für die Liebenden in Volkslied der Kroaten und Serben. Z.f.V., n.F. 3(1932): 213-241.

Goetz, Leopold Karl. Volkslied und Volksleben der Kroaten und Serben. 2 vols. Heidelberg, C. Winter. 1936-1937. 12, 226; 4, 244 p.

Gopčević, Spiridion. Serbien und die Serben. Leipzig, B. Elischer Nachfolger (B. Winckler). 1888. 7, 492 p.

Halpern, Joel. Social and cultural change in a Serbian village. New Haven, Human Relations Area Files. 1956. 26, 619 p., illus., maps.

*Halpern, Joel. A Serbian village. New York, Columbia University Press. 1958. 24, 325 p. (Another edition: New York, Harper and Row. 1967. 27, 359 p.

Halpern, Joel. The economies of Lao and Serb peasants. S.W.J.A. 17(1961): 165-177.

*Hammel, Eugene A. Serbo-Croatian kinship terminology. Kroeber Anthropological Society Papers. 16(1957): 45-75.

Hammel, Eugene A. The Jewish mother in Serbia or les structures alimentaires de la parenté. In William G. Lockwood, ed. Essays in Balkan ethnology. Kroeber Anthropological Society. Special Publications No. 1. 1967: 55-62.

*Hammel, Eugene A. Alternative social structures and ritual relations in the Balkans. Englewood Cliffs, N.J., Prentice-Hall. 1968. 128 p.

Kanitz, Felix Philipp. Serbien. Historisch-ethnographische Reisestudien aus den Jahren 1859-1868. Leipzig, H. Fries. 1868. 24, 744 p.

Karadzhić, Vuk Stefanović. Volksmärchen der Serben. Berlin, G. Reimer. 1854. 345 p.

Karadzhić, Vuk Stefanović. Zivot i običaj naroda Srpskoga. Beograd, Srpska Knjizevna Zadruga. 1957. (Peasant life and customs.)

*Kemp, Phyllis. Healing ritual: studies in the techniques and traditions of the southern Slavs. London, Faber & Faber. 1935. 16, 335 p., 25 plates.

Konstantinović, Zoran. Deutsche Reisebeschreibungen über Serbien und Montenegro. München, Oldenbourg. 1960. 240 p.

Kuppers, G. Rosalienfest und Trancetänze in Duboka: Pfingstbräuche im ostserbischen Bergland. Z.f.E. 79(1954): 212-224, illus.

Lazarovich-Hrenlianovich, Prince and Princess. The Servian people; their past glory and their destiny. 2 vols. London, Laurie. 1910.

*Lodge, Olive. Peasant life in Jugoslavia. London, Seeley, Service. 1942. 332 p.

Lutovac, M. The village of Ritopek on the Danube in the suburban zone of Belgrade. In Jerzy Kostrowicki, ed. Land utilization in East-central Europe. Geographia Polonia. 5. Warszawa, Institute of Geography, Polish Academy of Sciences. 1965: 235-266.

Matić, T. Totenkult bei den Serben. Diss. Leipzig. Bleicherode, Nieft. 1940. 90 p.

Maxwell, Grant. Slava (Servian national custom). Folk-Lore. 2(1891): 65-72.

Mijatović, Chedomil. Servia and the Servians. Boston, L. D. Page. 1908. 10, 296 p.

Mijatović, Chedomil. Servia of the Servians. London, Sir Isaac Pitman & Sons. 1911. 9, 234 p.

Petrovich, Vojislav M. Serbia, her history and customs. New York, Frederick Stokes. 1915. 280 p.

Pupin, Michael I. Serbian Orthodox Church. London, J. Murray. 1918. 64 p.

Pupin, Michael I. From immigrant to inventor. New York, London, C. Scribner's Sons. 1923. 396 p.

Ranke, Leopold von. The history of Servia and the Servian revolution with a sketch of the insurrection in Bosnia. London, Henry G. Bohn. 1853. 15, 520 p. (Especially see pp. 35-55, "Condition, character and poetry of the Servians. ")

Sebright, Georgina Mary Muir Mackenzie, and A. P. Irby. Travels in the Slavonic provinces of Turkey-in-Europe. 2 vols. 5th ed. London, Dalby, Isbister. 1877.

Serbian Orthodox Church. Its Past and Present. Belgrade, Srpska Patrijaršija. 1(1965):--

Servia and Montenegro. National Geographic Magazine. 19(1908): 774-789.

Showalter, William Joseph. The kingdom of Serbia. National Geographic Magazine. 27(1915): 417-432.

Skendi, Stavro. Albanian and South Slavic oral epic poetry. Memoirs of the American Folklore Society. 44. Philadelphia. 1954. 221 p.

Srpski Etnografski Zbornik [Serbian Ethnographic Journal]. Beograd, Srpska Kraljevska Akademija. 1 (1894):--

Stanković, Borislav. Sophka. (Translated by Alec Brown.) London, Jonathan Cape. 1929. 301 p. (Fiction, but excellent on family life.)

Stead, Alfred. Servia by the Servians. London, William Heinemann. 1905. 12, 377 p.

Stefanović Vilovsky, Theodor. Die Serben im südlichen Ungarn, in Dalmatien, Bosnien und in der Herzegovina. Wien und Teschen, K. Prochaska. 1884. 403 p.

Stewart, Cecil. Serbian legacy. London, G. Allen & Unwin. 1959. 135 p., illus., plates. (Mainly church art and architecture.)

Thallóczy, Lajos. Beiträge zum Vampyr-Glauben der Serben. Ethnologische Mitteilungen aus Ungarn. 1 (1888): cols. 162-164.

Thurnher, Majda. A survey of Balkan houses and farm buildings. Kroeber Anthropological Society Papers. 14(1956): 19-92. (See pp. 48-64.)

Trajković, Ljubica D. Serbia tourist guide. Beograd, Putnik's Publicity and Publishing Dept. 1953. 367 p., 2 end maps.

Troyanović, Sima. Alterthümliche Speisen- und Getränkebereitung bei den Serben. Archiv für Anthropologie 28(1902): 239-264, 8 illus.

Vékovitch, Divna. Vie et coutumes du peuple serbe. L'Ethnographie, New series. 17/18(1928): 9-29.

Vékovitch, Divna. Costume national de la Tzarna Gora de Skoplyé. L'Ethnographie, New series. 32 (1936): 1-20, plate.

Velimirovic, N. Bishop. Serbia in light and darkness. London, Longmans. 1916. 147 p.

Velimirovich, Nikolaj. The life of St. Sava. Libertyville, Illinois, Serbian Orthodox Monastery of St. Sava. 1951. 233 p.

Vlahović, M., and P. Milosavljević. Monuments funéraires paysans de Serbie. Beograd, Revue Yugoslavija. 1956. 31 p., illus.

Vukanović, T. P. Monogamic wives of Orthodox priests. Folk-Lore. 70 (1959): 394-397.

Warriner, Doreen. Contrasts in emerging societies. Readings in the social and economic history of south-eastern Europe in the nineteenth century. Bloomington, Indiana University Press. 1965: 294-313.

Zbornik Etnografskog Muzeja u Beograda. Beograd. 1 (1901):--

Chotch, Pierre G. Bibliografia del Montenegro. Napoli, R. Ricciardi, for the Istituto per l'Europa Orientale in Roma. 1924. 84 p.

Bihalji-Merin, Oto, ed. Montenegro, Yugoslavia. Beograd, Jugoslavija. 1961. 92 p., illus.

*Boehm, Christopher. Montenegrin social organization and values. Cambridge, Department of Social Relations, Harvard University. 1962. 139 p. (Mimeographed.)

Boulongne, Alfred. Le Monténégro, le pays et ses habitants. Paris, V. Rozier. 1867. 111 p.

Cubrilović, V. Terminologija plemenkog drustva u crnoj gori [Terminology of the tribal society of Montenegro]. Srpska Akademija Nauka, Etnografskog Institut, Posebna Izdanja. 9. 1959. 59 p.

Denton, William. Montenegro, its people and their history. London, Dalby, Isbister. 1877. 10, 292 p.

Ðonović, Nikola. Rad i karakter crnogoraca [The life and character of the Montenegrins]. Beograd. 1935. 7, 238 p.

Durham, Mary Edith. Through the lands of the Serb. London, E. Arnold. 1904. 11, 345 p.

Durham, Mary Edith. Some Balkan taboos. Man. 23(1923): 83-85.

Durham, Mary Edith. Preservation of pedigrees and commemoration of ancestors in Montenegro. Man. 31(1931): 154-155.

Durham, Mary Edith. The making of a saint. Man. 33(1933): 146-147.

*Erlich, Vera St. Family in transition. A study of 300 Yugoslav villages. Princeton, Princeton University Press. 1966. 656 p., plates.

Führer, L. von. Skizzen aus Montenegro. Z.f.Ö.V. 23(1917): 69-81.

Führer, L. von. Die Montenegriner als Jäger und Fischer. Z.f.Ö.V. 24(1918): 48.

Führer, L. von. Die Bevölkerung Montenegros. Z.f.Ö.V. 25(1919): 44-46.

Gesemann, Gerhard. Heroische Lebensform. Berlin, Viking Verlag. 1943. 371 p.

Gopčević, Spiridion. Montenegro und die Montenegriner. Leipzig, H. Fries. 1877. 194 p.

Grothe, Hugo. Durch Albanien und Montenegro; zeitgemässe Betrachtungen zur Völkerkunde, Politik und Wirtschaftswelt der westlichen Balkanhalbinsel. München, M. Märike. 1913. 224 p.

Karadžić, Vuk Stefanović. Montenegro und die Montenegriner. Ein Beitrag zur Kenntniss der europäischen Türkei und des serbischen Volkes. Stuttgart, Widenmann und Hauff. 1837. 114 p.

Konstantinović, Zoran. Deutsche Reisebeschreibungen über Serbien und Montenegro. München, Oldenbourg. 1960. 240 p.

Kostrowicki, Jerzy, and D. Kowalczyk. Barsko Polje — on the Adriatic sea coast of Montenegro. In Jerzy Kostrowicki, ed. Land utilization in East-central Europe. Geographia Polonia. 5. Warszawa, Institute of Geography, Polish Academy of Sciences. 1965: 285-344.

Kühnelt, R. Das Weib in Montenegro. Z.f.Ö.V. 23 (1917): 108-112.

*Lodge, Olive. Peasant life in Jugoslavia. London, Seeley, Service. 1942. 332 p., illus.

Nenadović, Ljubomir. O crnogorcima, pisma sa cetinja 1877 godine [About Montenegrin letters from the year 1878]. Belgrade, Srpska Književna Zadruga. 1929. 6, 229 p.

Neweklowsky, E. Das westmontenegrinische Bauernhaus. Z.f.Ö.V. 23(1917): 6-16.

Neweklowsky, E. Volkskundliches aus Westmontenegro. Z.f.Ö.V. 23(1917): 59-69.

Neweklowsky, E. Die Montenegriner als Jäger und Fischer. Z.f.Ö.V. 25(1919): 49.

Petar II, Prince Bishop of Montenegro [Nyegosh, Petar Petrovitch]. The mountain wreath. 2d ed. London, G. Allen & Unwin. 1930. 250 p.

*Simić, Andrei. The blood feud in Montenegro. In William G. Lockwood, ed. Essays in Balkan ethnology. Kroeber Anthropological Society. Special Publication No. 1. 1967: 83-94.

Start, Laura. The Durham collection of garments and embroideries from Albania and Yugoslavia. Bankfield Museum Notes. 3d ser., no. 4. Halifax, England, Bankfield Museum. 1939. 76 p., 2 plates, illus.

Trevor, Roy. Montenegro, a land of warriors . . . London, A. and C. Black. 1913. 8, 87 p.

Vialla de Sommières, L. C. Travels in Montenegro; containing a topograph-
cal, picturesque, and statistical account of that hitherto undescribed count
London, printed for Sir Richard Phillips. 1820. 4, 108 p.

Vialla de Sommières, L. C. Voyage historique et politique au Monténégro,
contenant l'origine des Monténégrins, peuple autocthone ou aborigène, et
très peu connu. 2 vols. Paris, A. Eymery. 1820.

Warriner, Doreen. Contrasts in emerging societies. Bloomington, Indiana
University Press. 1965: 367-371.

Weiser, M. E. Die Feiertage der Brüder aus den Schwarzen Bergen. M.A.G.
7(1878): 159-161.

Wyon, Reginald. The land of the Black Mountain, the adventures of two Englishmen in Montenegro. London, Methuen. 1903. 18, 300 p.

Balikci, Asen. Quarrels in a Balkan village. A.A. 67(1965): 1456-1469.

Bihalji-Merin, Oto, ed. Macedonia, Yugoslavia. Belgrade, Jugoslavija. 1957. 94 p., illus.

Brailsford, H. N. Macedonia: its races and their future. London, Methuen. 1906. 20, 340 p.

Cvijíc, Jovan. Remarques sur l'ethnographie de la Macedonie. Paris, G. Roustan. 1907. 56 p.

Doflein, Franz. Mazedonien. Jena, Gustav Fischer. 1921. 592 p., 4, 12 tables, 279 figs.

Eliot, Sir Charles N. Turkey in Europe. London, Edward Arnold. 1908. 475 p., 2 folding maps.

*Erlich, Vera St. Family in transition. A study of 300 Yugoslav villages. Princeton, Princeton University Press. 1966. 656 p., plates.

Filipović, Milenko S. Obicaji i verovanja u Skopskoj kotlini—Gradia [Customs and beliefs in the Skopje area—the data]. Srpski Etnografski Zbornik. 54 (1939): 279-566, 8 tables.

Geiges, Leif. Hochzeit in Galicnik; ein Bildbericht aus den Bergen Mazedoniens. Atlantis. 11(1939): 421-426.

Georgevitch, T. R. Macedonia. London, Allen and Unwin. 1920. 283 p.

Hoffmann, Otto. Die Makedonier, ihre Sprache und ihr Volkstum. Göttingen, Vandenhoeck und Ruprecht. 1906. 5, 284 p.

Klickova, Véra. Les coutumes de pâcques dans la région de Poretch, Macédonie. Glasnik 1, no. 11. Skopje, Etnoloski Muzej. 1957. 62 p., 25 illus.

Lebon, J. H. G. The Jezera, a mountain community in southwest Yugoslavia. Geography. 20(1935): 271-282.

Lodge, Olive. Dzamutra, or the bridegroom; some marriage customs in the villages around Tetovo in Serbian Macedonia or southern Serbia. Folk-Lore. 46(1935): 244-267, 306-330.

*Lodge, Olive. Peasant life in Jugoslavia. London, Seeley, Service. 1942. 332 p.

Phillips, Bernard S. The urban personality and rural personality in Skopje, Yugoslavia. Milwaukee, University of Wisconsin, Department of Sociology, Clearinghouse for Sociological Literature. 1965.

Schultz, L. Makedonien. Jena, Gustav Fischer. 1927. 250 p., 86 tables, 3 maps.

Thurnher, Majda. A survey of Balkan houses and farm buildings. Kroeber Anthropological Society Papers. 14(1956): 19-92. (See pp. 64-66.)

Walker, Mrs. Mary Adelaide. Through Macedonia to the Albanian lakes. London, Chapman & Hall. 1864. 11, 274 p.

Wilkinson, Henry Robert. Maps and politics: a review of the ethnographic cartography of Macedonia. Liverpool, Liverpool University Press. 1951. 16, 366 p., maps.

*Erlich, Vera St. Family in transition. A study of 300 Yugoslav villages. Princeton, Princeton University Press. 1966. 656 p., plates.

Filipović, Milenko S. Kristeni Muslimani. Baptised Moslems. Iz Zbornika Radova Ethnografsk. Instituta Srpske Akademije Nauka Kn. 2(1951): 119-128. (Also published separately. Beograd. 1951. 10 p.)

Filipović, Milenko S. Die serbokroatischen Mohammedaner. Tribus, n. F. 9(1960): 55-60.

*Hangi, Antun. Die Moslims in Bosnien-Hercegovina. Ihre Lebensweise, Sitten und Gebräuche. Translated by Herman Tausk. Sarajevo, D. A. Kajon. 1907. 6, 267 p., illus.

Mitrović, Bora. Naši Muslimani [Our Muslims]. Beograd. 1926. 172 p.

Statuto della comunità religiosa Islamica nella Repubblica Federativa Popolare Jugoslava. Oriente Moderno (Roma). 43(1963): 662-674.

Allodiatoris, Irma. A Kárpát-medence antropológiai bibliográfiája [Bibliography on the anthropology of the Carpathian Mountain range]. Budapest, Akadémiai Kiadó. 1958. 183 p.

Chiţima, I. C. Bibliographie zur rumänischen Volkskunde seit 1944. Deutsc Jahrbuch für Volkskunde. 4(1958): 517-538.

Fischer-Galati, Stephen A. Rumania: a bibliographic guide. Washington, Library of Congress. 1963. 8, 75 p.

Herseni, Paula. Publicaţiile şcoalei sociologice de la Bucureşti; bibliografie. Bucureşti. 1939. 36 p.

Institutul de Ştiinţe Sociale al României, 25 ani de publicaţii, 1919-1944. Biblioteca de Sociologie, Etică şi politică. Note şi Comunicări 4. Bucureşti, Institutul de Ştiinţe Sociale al României. 1944. 139 p.

Juga, Caius. Contribuţiuni la bibliografia satului rominesc. Fogarasch. 1946. 94 p. (Village life.)

Krallert-Sattler, Gertrud. Südosteuropa-Bibliographie. 3 vols. to date. Bd. 1: 1945-1950. Bd. 2: 1951-1955. Bd. 3: 1956-1960. München, R. Oldenbourg. 1956–

Romanian Scientific Abstracts. Social Science. Bucharest, Academy of the Socialist Republic of Romania. Scientific Documentation Centre. 1 (1964)

United States. Bureau of the Census. Bibliography of social science periodica and monograph series: Rumania, 1947-1960. Washington, Government Printing Office. 1961. 31 p.

Alexandri, Vasile. Ballades et chants populaires de la roumanies. Paris, E. Dentu. 1855.

Alexandri, Vasile. Rumänische volkspoesie. Berlin, R. Decker, 1857. 16, 178 p.

Alexandru, Tiberiu. Instrumentele muzicale ale poporului roman. Bucureşti, Editura de Stat Pentru Literatură şi Artă. 1956. 386 p.

Anuarul Arhivei de Folklor. Cluj. 1(1932)-(1948).

Apolzan, Lucia. Cercetări etnografice in Munţii Apuseni. Apulum. 1(1942): 257-284. (French summary, pp. 316-317.)

Apolzan, Lucia. Portul şi industria casnică textilă în Munţii Apuseni. Biblioteca de Sociologie, Etică şi politică. Sociologia României 5. Bucureşti, Institutul de Ştiinţe Sociale al României. 1944. 255 p., illus., maps.

Apolzan, Lucia. Sate, oraşe şi reguini cercetate de Institutul Social Romîn 1925-1945. Bucureşti. 1945. 151 p.

Avramescu, Elena, and Florea Bobu-Florescu. Broderiile la romîni. Bucureşti, Editura de Stat Pentru Imprimate şi Publicaţii. 1959. 49 p., 78 plates.

Banateanu, Tancred. Le plugusor, une coutume agrare roumaine. Rivista di Etnografia (Napoli). 2(1948): 15-26, map, table.

Banateanu, Tancred. Portul popular din Tara Oasului. Bucureşti, Editura de Stat Pentru Literatură. 1956. 20 p., illus.

Banateanu, Tancred. Georghe Foçsa and Emilia Ionescu. Folk costumes, woven textiles and embroideries of Rumania. Bucharest, State Publishing House for Literature and the Arts. 1958. 422 p., 433 illus., 56 col. plates.

Banateanu, Tancred, and M. Foçsa. The ornament in the Rumanian folk art. Bucharest, Meridiane. 1963. 50 p., plates.

Bărbat, Al. Drăguş. Un sat din Ţara Oltului (Făgăraş). Bucureşti, Institut de Sciences Sociales de Roumanie. 1944. 9, 188 p., 25 illus.

Bartók, Béla. Cântece poporale româneşti din comitatul Bihor (Ungaria). Chansons populaires roumaines du département Bihar (Hongrie) . . . Bucureşti, Socec, şi C. Sfetea. 1913. 22, 360 p.

*Bartók, Béla. Volksmusik der Rumänen von Maramures. München, Drei Masken Verlag. 1923. 37, 226 p.

Bartók, Béla. Melodien der rumänischen colinde (Weihnachtslieder); 484 Melodien, mit einem einleitenden Aufsatz. Wien, Universal, 1935. 14, 106 p.

Bellessort, André. La Roumanie contemporaine. Paris, Perrin. 1905. 304 p.

*Benedict, Ruth. Rumanian culture and behavior. New York, Institute for Intercultural Studies. 1943. 63 p. (Printed for private use.)

Bergner, Rudolf [Karl Heinrich Rudolf]. Rumänien. Eine Darstellung des Landes und der Leute. Breslau, J. U. Kern's Verlag. 1887. 11, 412 p.

Beza, Marcu. Paganism in Roumanian folklore. London, J. M. Dent; New York, E. P. Dutton. 1928. 10, 161 p.

Bielz, Julius. Portul popular al sasilor din Transilvania. Bucureşti, Editura de Stat Pentru Literatură şi Artă. n.d. [1959-1961?]. 51 p., 4 col. plates, 34 illus.

Bogza, Geo. Land of stone; the land of the Motzi. (Translated from the Rumanian.) Bucharest, Book Publishing House. 1954. 141 p.

*Boner, Charles. Transylvania; its products and people. London, Longmans, Green, Reader, and Dyer. 1865. 14, 642 p.

Borza, Horatiu D. Chants de mort roumains du district de Turda. Strasbourg Fides Romana. 1953. 35 p.

Buhociu, Octavian. Folklore and ethnography in Rumania. Current Anthropology. 7(1966): 295-314.

Butura, V. Die siebenbürgischen Turbinenmühlen. Ethnographica. 1 (1959) 19-26.

Calverley, Amice. Notes on the Calusari dancers of Roumania. Recorded by cine-camera in remote villages in the wheat- and maize-growing plains of Walachia. Man. 46(1946): 85-88.

Camilar, Ensehiu. The Bistrita Valley. Bucharest, Foreign Languages Publishing House. 1957. 15 p., 92 plates.

Camilar, Ensehiu. La vallée de la Bistrita. Bucarest, Editions en Langues Étrangéres. 1957. 17 p.

Candrea, I. Aurel. Folclorul medical romîn comparat. Bucureşti. 1944. 30, 478 p.

Cantemir, Dimitrie. Descrierea Moldovei. Bucureşti, Edit Tineretului. 196 264 p.

Christian, V. Über einen siebenbürgisch-rumänischen Brauch zur Abwehr der Pest (Cholera). M.A.G.W. 46(1916): 25-29. 5 illus.

Conea, Ion. Clopotiva, om şi natură în Ţara Haţegului. Bucureşti, M.O. Impr. Centrală. 1939. 18 p., 5 tables.

Conea, Ion. Clopotiva un sat din Haţeg, monografie sociologică întocmită de echipa regala studenţească 19/935 sub conducerea lui Ion Conea. 2 vols. Biblioteca de Sociologie, Etică şi Politică. Sociologia României 3. Bucureşti, Institutul de Ştiinţe Sociale al României. 1940.

Constante, C., and Anton Golopentia, eds. Românii din Timoc, culegere de izvoare. 3 vols. in 2. Bucureşti, Tip. Bucovina, I.E. Torouţiu. 1943-1944. (Volume 3 was published in 1943.)

Creanga, Ion. Contes populaires de Roumanie (Povesti). Paris, Maisonneuve. 1931. 17, 247 p.

Creanga, Ion. Folk tales from Roumania. London, Routledge and Kegan Paul; New York, Roy Publishers. 1952. 170 p.

Cristescu-Golopenţia, Stefania. Gospodăria în credinţele şi riturile magice ale femeilor din Drăguş (Făgăraş). Bucureşti, M.O. Imprimerie Naţională. 1940. 116 p., 8 tables.

Dachler, Anton, and Michael Haberlandt. Das Bauernhaus in Österreich-Ungarn und in seinen Grenzgebiete. Wien, Ingenieur- und Architektenverein. 1906. 17, 288 p., 67 illus., 6 plates, 75 folio plates, map.

Densuşianu, Ovid. Vieţa păstorească în poezia noastră populară. 2 vols. Bucureşti. 1923.

Dima, Al. Drăguş. Un sat Ţara Oltului (Făgăraş). Impodibirea porţilor, interioarelor caselor; opinii despre frumos. Bucureşti, Institut de Sciences Sociales de Roumanie. 1945. 43 p.

Dokić, Jovan. Kroz naselja s. i. Srbije, Banata i Susednih Krajeva. Istoriska etnografiska opažanja. Beograd, Stamparija Skerlić. 1934. 402 p., illus. (Rumanians in Yugoslavia.)

Dragomir, Silviu. The ethnical minorities of Transylvania. Geneva, Sonor. 1927. 129 p.

Dragomir, Silviu. La Transylvanie roumaine et ses minorités ethniques. Bucarest, Imprimerie Nationale. 1934. 281 p.

Dunăre, Nicholae. Die Verzierung der Ostereier bei den Rumänen. Z.f.E. 84(1959): 70-80.

Dunăre, Nicholae. Arta populara din Valea Jiului. (Regiunea Hunedoară.) Bucureşti, Editura Academiai Republicii Popularae Romîne. 1963. 588 p., plates.

Dunăre, Nicholae. Recherches ethnographiques roumaines sur l'agriculture et la vie pastorale. Acta Ethnographica. 12(1963): 179-183.

Filipescu, Teodor. Coloniile române din Bosnia. Studiu etnografie şi antropogeografic. Bucureşti, Inst. de Arte Grafica Carol Göbl. 1906. 310 p., illus., plans.

Firu, Nicolae. Monografia comunei Chişoda (j. Timiş). Revista Institutului Social Banat-Crişana. 13(1944): 127-144, 309-324.

Fischer, Emil. Über den Ursprung der rumanischen Bojarenfamilien. Z.f.E. 40(1908): 343-361.

Fischer, Emil. Die Küche des rumänischen Bauern. Archiv für Anthropologie. 36(1909): 246-248.

*Fleure, Herbert J., and E. E. Evans, eds. South Carpathian studies: Roumani
London, Le Play Society. 1939. 58 p.

*Fleure, Herbert J., and R. A. Pelham, eds. Eastern Carpathian studies:
Roumania. London, Le Play Society. 1936. 79 p.

Florescu, Florea Babu. Opincile la Romîni. Bucureşti, Academia Republicii
Populare Romîne. 1957. 169 p.

Focşa, Gheorghe. Le village roumain pendant les fêtes religieuses d'hiver.
Zalmoxis, Revue d'Histoire des Religions. 1940-1942: 61-102.

Focşa, Gheorghe. The Village Museum in Bucharest. Bucharest, Foreign
Languages Publishing House. 1959. 211 p., plates, illus., map.

Focşa, Gheorghe. The Village Museum in Bucharest. Bucharest, Meridiane.
1962. 62 p., plates, map.

Focşa, Gheorghe. Muzeul Satului. Muzeu Etnografic in Aer Liber. Bucureşti,
Fondul Plastic-Agenţia de Publicitate "Artis." 1966. 34 p., plates.

Focşa, Gheorghe. Muzeul Satului Anuar. 1966. Bucureşti, Fondul Plastic-
Agenţia de Publicitate "Artis." 1966. 326 p., plates, illus.

Folk dances in Romania. Viltis. 17 (Jan.-Feb. 1958): 14-16.

Frâncu, Teofil, and George Candrea. Românii din Munţii Apuseni (Moţii),
scriere etnografică. Bucureşti, Academia Română. 1888. 2, 2, 303 p.

Fuchs, Karl. Die Törzburger Hausburgen. M.A.G.W. 32(1902): 20-24, illus

Gaster, Moses. Rumanian popular legends of the Lady Mary. Folk-Lore. 34
(1923): 43-85.

*Gerard, Emily. The land beyond the forest. Facts, figures and fancies from
Transylvania. New York, Harper and Brothers. 1888. 9, 403 p., map.
(2 vols. Edinburgh and London, W. Blackwood & Son. 1888.)

Golopenţia, Anton, and D. C. Georgescu. 60 [i.e. şasezeci de] sate
româneşti cercetate de echipele studenţesti în vara 1938. Anchetă sociologică condusă de Anton Golopenţia şi D. C. Georgescu. 5 vols. Bucureşti,
Institutul de Ştiinţe Sociale al Romănici. 1941-1943.

Gore, James Howard. Roumania, the pivotal state. National Geographic Maga
zine. 28(1915): 360-390.

Grindea, Miron, and Carole Grindea. Dances of Rumania. London, Parrish.
1952. 40 p., illus.

RUMANIANS

Grothe, Hugo. Zur Landeskunde von Rumänien: Kulturgeschichtliches und Wirtschaftliches. Halle an der Salle, Gebauer-Schuretschke Druckerei. 1907. 15, 126 p.

Gunda, Béla. Zusammenhänge zwischen Hofanlage und Viehzucht in Siebenbürgen. In László Földes, ed. Viehzucht und Hirtenleben in Ostmitteleuropa. Budapest, Akadémiai Kiadó. 1961: 243-282.

Gunda, Béla. Ethnographica Carpathica. Budapest, Akadémiai Kiadó. 1966. 418 p. (In Hungarian.)

Gunda, Béla. Fish poisoning in the Carpathian area and in the Balkan peninsula. In William G. Lockwood, ed. Essays in Balkan Ethnology. Kroeber Anthropological Society. Special Publications No. 1. 1967: 1-34.

*Gusti, D., et al. La vie rurale en Roumanie. Congrès International de Sociologie. 14th. Bucharest. 1939. (Projected, not held.) Bucharest. 1940. 297 p.

Hall, Donald John. Romanian furrow. London, Methuen. 1933. 10, 224 p. (New ed. London, Harrap. 12, 224 p.)

Herseni, Traian. Sociologia românească: încereare istorică. Bucureşti. 1940. 168 p.

Herseni, Traian. Drăguş. Un sat din Ţara Oltului (Făgăraş). Unităţi sociale. Bucureşti, Institutul de Ştiinţe Sociale al României. 1944. 8, 158 p., 10 plates.

Hielscher, Kurt. Rumänien. Landschaft, Bauten, Volksleben. Leipzig, F. A. Brockhaus. 1933. 32, 304 p.

Ila, B. Die walachische Bevölkerung der Herrschaften Murány, Scetnek und Kraszhahorka. Studia Slavica. 3(1957): 113-148.

Ionescu, Emilia. Rumanian folk art. Antiquity and Survival. 1 (1955): 155-168, photos.

Ionica, Ion. Draguş, un sat din Ţara Oltului (Făgăraş). Manifestări spirituali. Reprezentarea cerului. Bucureşti, Institut de Sciences Sociales de Roumanie. 1944. 7, 83 p.

Irimie, C. Das Hirtenwesen bei den Rumänen. Mitteilungen der Südosteuropa-Gesellschaft. 1 (1964): 1-60.

Jännecke, W. Das rumänische Bauern- und Boyarenhaus. Bucharest, König Carol-Verlag. 1918. 72 p., 199 illus.

Kirke, Dorothea. Domestic life in Rumania. London, John Lane. 1916. 200 p. (Travelogue — thin data.)

LaGorce, John Oliver. Roumania and its Rubicon. National Geographic Magazine. 30(1916): 185-202.

Loughborough, Margaret R. Roumanian pilgrimage. London, S.P.C.K. 1939 5, 143 p. (Thin material on the Rumanian church.)

Lucasi, Larisa. About the Calusarii. Viltis. 17 (Jan.-Feb. 1958): 8-9.

Lucasi, Larisa. The Romanian wedding. Viltis. 17(Jan.-Feb. 1958): 10-12.

Lutz, Francisca. Contribuţiuni la cunoaşterea medicinei populare din comuna Şanţ, Jud. Năsăud. Teză in medicină. Cluj, Tip. Universala. 1939. 36

Manuila, Sabin. Étude ethnographique sur la population de la Roumanie. Ethnographical survey of the population of Rumania. Bucureşti, Impr. Statulu 1938. 39 p., illus., maps. (English and French texts in parallel columns.

Manuila, Sabin. Studiu etnografic asupra populaţiei României. Bucureşti, Editura Institutului Central de Statistică. 1940. 107 p., maps, diagr.

Manuila, Sabin. Atlas etnografic al României, 1930. Bucureşti, Impr. Naţională. 1943— Maps (Scale 1: 300,000).

Marianu, Simion Florea. Nunta la Români. Bucureşti, Académia Română. 1890. 6, 856 p. (Rumanian wedding customs.)

Marianu, Simion Florea. Inmormîntarea la Români. Bucureşti, Académia Română. 1892. 593 p. (Rumanian funeral customs.)

Marianu, Simion Florea. Naşcerea la Români. Bucureşti, Académia Română. 1892. 441 p. (Rumanian birth customs.)

Marriner, J. Theodore. Transylvania and its seven castles; a motor circuit through Rumania's new province. National Geographic Magazine. 49(1926) 319-352.

Mehedinţi, Simeon. Rumania and her people, an essay in physical and human geography. Rumanian Studies. 1. Bucharest, Rumanian Academy. 1939. 111 p., illus., maps, plates.

Millant, M. Sur les scop-itz (skoptzy) de Roumanie. L'Anthropologie, Supplement. 8(1913): 153-164.

Mitrany, David. Greater Rumania: a study in national ideals. London, New York, Hodder & Stoughton. 1917. 20 p.

RUMANIANS

*Mitrany, David. The land and the peasant in Rumania: the war and agrarian reform (1917-1921). London, Oxford University Press, H. Milford; New Haven, Yale University Press. 1930. 34, 627 p., map, diagr.

Murgoci, Agnes. Roumanian Easter eggs. Folk-Lore. 20(1909): 295-303, 4 col. plates.

Murgoci, Agnes. Customs connected with death and burial among the Roumanians. Folk-Lore. 30(1919): 89-102.

Murgoci, Agnes. The evil eye in Roumania, and its antidotes. Folk-Lore. 34(1923): 357-362.

Murgoci, Agnes. The vampire in Roumania. Folk-Lore. 37(1926): 320-349.

Murgoci, Agnes. The devil in Roumanian folklore. Folk-Lore. 40(1929): 134-167.

Murgoci, Agnes. Roumanian salt signs and other identification marks. Folk-Lore. 42(1931): 265-290.

Muşlea, Ion. Cercetări folklorice în Oaşului. Anuarul Archivei de Folklor. 1 (1933): 117-237. (Oaş region.)

Niculescu-Varone, G. T. Costumele naţionale din România întregită. Bucareşti, Editura Ziarului Universul. 1940. 96 p., illus.

Niculescu-Varone, G. T. Monografia satului Săuleşti plasa Deva, judeţul Hunedoara. Cu o sehiţă topografică, un plan şi 9 fotografii. Bucureşti. 1945. 136 p.

Noe, Constantin, and Marin Popescu-Spineni. Die Rumänen in Bulgarien. Craiova, Verlag Ramuri. 1939. 97 p., plates, maps.

Novacoviciu, Emilian. Folklor bănăţeon. Partea 3. A dunat de . . . Oraviţa, Tip. Isoif Kaden. 1933. 64 p.

Oancea, D. I. Contribuţii la studiul monografic al oraşului Roman. Probleme di Geographie. 6(1959): 129-145.

Obedenaru, Gheorghe Mihail. La Roumanie économique d'après les données les plus recentes . . . Géographie, état économique, anthropologie, avec une carte de la Roumanie. Paris, E. Leroux. 1876. 11, 435 p.

*Oprescu, George. Peasant art in Roumania. London, The Studio. 1929. 17, 182 p., plates, illus.

*Paget, John. Hungary and Transylvania: with remarks on their condition, social, political, and economic. New ed. 2 vols. London, J. Murray; Philadelphia, Lea & Blanchard. 1850.

Papahagi, Tache. Griaul şi folklorul Maramureşului. Bucureşti, Cultura Naţională. 1925. 83, 240 p., 49 figs., 22 plates, map.

Papahagi, Tache. Images d'ethnographie roumaine. 2 vols. Bucureşti, Cultura Naţională. 1928-1930. 173, 227 p.

Papahagi, Tache. Images d'ethnographie roumaine. Tome troisième: Banat-Olténie. Bucureşti, Impremerie Socec. 1934. 294 p., 561 photos.

Parkinson, Maude R. Twenty years in Roumania. London, G. Allen & Unwin. 1921. 255 p.

Patmore, Derek. Invitation to Roumania. London, Macmillan. 1939. 12, 157 p.

Patterson, Arthur John. The Magyars: their country and institutions. 2 vols. London, Smith, Elder. 1869.

Pavelescu, Gheorghe. Cercetări asupra magiei la Românii din Munţii Apuseni. Biblioteca de Sociologie, Etică şi politică. Sociologia României 6. Bucureşti, Institutul Social Român. 1945. 197 p.

Pavelescu, Gheorghe. Cercetări folclorice în sudul judeţului Bihor. Hermannstadt. 1945. 122 p., map, 2 plates.

Petrescu, P. Casa cu foisor tărăncască la romîni. Studii si Cercertări de Istoria Artei. 5(1958): 27-52.

Petrescu, Paul, and Nicholas Rodna. Romanian textiles. Leigh-on-Sea, England, F. Lewis. 1966. 23 p., 48 plates.

Petrovici, Emil. Folklor dela Moţii din Scarişoara. Anuarul Archivei de Folklor. 5(1939): 111-175.

Pittard, Eugène. La Roumanie: Valachie, Moldavie, Doubroudja. Paris, Bossard. 1917. 327 p.

Podea, Titus. Transylvania. Bucarest, Oltenia. 1936. 8, 174 p.

Pop, Mihai. Nunta din satul Sălişte. Revista de Folclor. 3, no. 2(1958): 47-78.

Popinceann, I. Religion, Glaube und Aberglaube in rumänischen Sprache. Nürnberg, Carl. 1964. 11, 312 p.

Proca-Ciortea, V. Rumänische Volkstanze. Leipzig, Zentralhaus für Kulturarbeit. 1963. 39 p.

Rădulescu-Codin, Codru. Legende, tradiţii şi amintiri istorice, adunate din Oltenia. Bucureşti, Libraria Socec & Comp. 1910. 15, 133 p.

Rădulescu-Codin, Codru. Ingerul Romậnului; povești și legende din popor. București, Socec. 1913. 31, 384 p.

Rădulescu-Codin, Codru. Literatura, traditi și obiceuri din Corbii-Musçelului . . . București, Cultura Nationalặ. 1929. 126 p.

Rădulescu-Codin, Codru, and D. Mihalache. Sặrbặtorile poporului, cu obiceiurile, credintele și unele traditii legate de ele, culegere din pặntile. București, Tipografia "Cooperativa." 1909. 122 p.

Revista de Folclor. București. 1(1956):-- Later title changed to Revista de Etnografie și Folclor. 1 (1964):--

Romstorfer, K. A. Typen der Landwirtschaft Bauten im Herzogtume Bukowina . . . M. A. G. W. 22(1892): 193-215.

Rosen, Georg. Die Balkan-Haiduken. Leipzig, F. A. Brockhaus. 1878. 10, 336 p.

Die rumậnische Volkswirtschaft; ein Handbuch hrsg. im Auftrage der Militặrverwaltung in Rumặnien. Berlin, Druck der Germania. 1917. 120 p., map.

Sadoveanu, Mihail. Evening tales. Bucharest, Foreign Languages Publishing House. 1958. 443 p. (Fiction, but good on peasantry.)

Schuck, A. Über die Istro-Rumanen. Anthropologische Studien. M. A. G. W. 43(1913): 210-234.

Sevastos, Elena. Nunta la Romậnĭ. Studiŭ istorico-etnograficŭ comparativŭ. București, Académia Romận̆ă. 1889. 8, 406 p.

Sitwell, Sacheverell. Rumanian wedding. Geographical Magazine. 6(1937/ 38): 427-440, illus., map.

Slavici, Ioan. Die Rumận̆en in Ungarn, Siebenbürgen und der Bukowina. Wien und Teschen, K. Prochaska. 1881. 236 p.

*Stahl, Henry H., ed. Nerej, un village d'une région archaïque; monographie sociologique. 3 vols. Bibliothèque de Sociologie, Éthique et Politique. Sociologie de la Roumanie, 1. Bucharest. 1939.

Stahl, Henry H., ed. Sociologia satului devặlmas romận̆ese. Biblioteca de Sociologie, Eticặ și Politiçặ. Sociologia Romận̆iei, 7. Bucureşti. n. p.

Stahl, Henry H., ed. Contribuții la studiul satelor devặlmașe romînesti. 2 vols. Bibl. Istorica. 6, 7. București, Editura Academiei R. P. R. 1959. 367 p.

Stotz, Alfred. The ethnographical map of Transylvania. Bucharest. 1928. 10 p., map.

*Stratilesco, Tereza. From Carpathian to Pindus: pictures of Roumanian country life. London, T. F. Unwin. 1906. 12, 379 p.

Studii şi Cercetări de Istorie Literară şi Folclor. Bucureşti. 1 (1952):--

Teutsch, Julius. Einiges vom Aberglauben der Rumänen. M. A. G. W. 37(1907): 11-16.

Thurnher, Majda. A survey of Balkan houses and farm buildings. Kroeber Anthropological Society Papers. 14(1956): 19-92. (See pp. 74-79.)

Topa, Leon. La sociologia in Rumania. Genus. 3(1938): 137-158.

Turczynski, Emanuel. Elemente der rumänischen Volkskunst. Südosteuropa-Jahrbuch. 6(1962): 116-124.

Văcărescu, Elena. The bard of Dimbovitza, Roumanian folk-songs. Collected from the peasants. First and second series. 2 pts. London, Osgood, McIlvaine. 1897. 130, 146 p. (Reprinted: London, Harper & Brothers. 1902. 12, 274 p.)

Văcărescu, Elena. Songs of the valiant voivode and other strange folk-lore for the first time collected from Roumanian peasants and set forth in English. London and New York, Harper and Brothers. 1905. 12, 238 p.

Van Teslaar, James Samuel. When I was a boy in Roumania. Boston, Lothrop Lee & Shepard. 1917. 179 p.

Veress, Andreas. Die Baba Dokia-Sage und die mit ihr zusammenhängenden Volksgebräuche in Rumänien. Ethnologische Mitteilungen aus Ungarn. 2(1892): columns 56-58.

Vlăduţiu, Ion. Almwirtschaftliche Viehhaltung und Transhumance in Brangeb (Südkarpaten, Rumänien). In Lászlo Földes, ed. Viehzucht und Hirtenleb in Ostmitteleuropa. Budapest, Akadémiai Kiadó. 1961: 197-242.

Vuia, R. Flechterei mit Stäbchen bei den Rumänen. Z. f. E. 46(1914): 824-828.

Vuia, R. Tara Haţegului şi gegiunca Pădurenilor. Studiu antropogeografic şi etnografic. Extras din Lucrările Institutului de Geografie al Universitătii di Cluj. 2. Cluj, Institutul de Arte Grafice "Ardealul." 1926. 135 p.

Vuia, R. The Roumanian hobby-horse, the căluşari. Journal of the English Folk Dance and Song Society. 2(1935): 97-111.

RUMANIANS

Vulpesco, Michael [Mihai]. Coutumes roumaines. Revue d'Ethnographie. 6(1925): 136-171; 7(1926): 53-68, 125-161; 8(1927): 62-99, 255-282; 9(1928): 111-128.

*Vulpesco, Michael [Mihai]. Les coutumes roumaines périodiques. Études descriptives et comparées . . . Paris, Librarie Émile Larose. 1927. 303 p.

Walker, Mary Adelaide. Untrodden paths in Roumania. London, Chapman & Hall. 1888. 16, 355 p.

Wallis, B. C. The Rumanians in Hungary. Geographical Review. 6 (1918): 166-171, 3 illus., 2 plates.

*Warriner, Doreen. Contrasts in emerging societies. Readings in the social and economic history of south-eastern Europe in the nineteenth century. Bloomington, Indiana University Press. 1965: 117-203.

Weslowski, E. Osterbräuche bei den Rumänen in den Karpathen der Bukowina (mit Abbildungen). Z.f.Ö.V. 11 (1905): 125-128.

Wolfram, Richard. Alterklassen und Männerbünde in Rumänien. M.A.G.W. 64(1934): 112-128, 2 illus.

Zderciuc, Boris. The hand-woven rugs of Maramures, Rumania. Bucharest, Meridiane. 1963. 27 p., illus.

Zderciuc, Boris, Paul Petrescu, and Tancred Banateanu. Folk art in Rumania. Bucharest, Meridiane. 1964. 176 p., illus., plates.

VLACHS OR AROMUNES

(Also known as Aromans, Cincars, or Tsintsars.)

Capidan, Theodor. Românii nomazi, studiu din viaţa Românilor din sudul peninsulei Balkanice. Dacoromania. 4(1926): 183-352.

Capidan, Theodor. Les Macédo-Roumains. Esquisse historique et descriptive des populations roumains de la péninsule balcanique. Connaissaince de la Terre et de la Pensée Roumaine. 5. Bucarest. 1937. 76 p., plates.

Capidan, Theodor. Die Mazedo-Rumänen. Bukarest, Die Dacia-Bücher. 1941. 151 p.

*Capidan, Theodor. Les Macédo-Roumains. Ethnographie, histoire, langue. Bucureşti. 1943. 286 p.

Eckert, Georg, and Cuschan Araia. Das Schulterblattorakel bei den Aromunen Volkskundliche Miszellen aus Mazedonien. 4. Thessaloniki, for the author 1944. 28 p., illus.

Eliot, Sir Charles N. Turkey in Europe. London, Edward Arnold. 1908. 475 p., 2 maps.

Filipović, Milenko S. Cincari u Bosni [Tsintsars in Bosnia]. Srpske Akademi Nauka. Etnografski Institut Beograd. Zbornik Rodova. 2(1951): 53-108.

Fürer-Haimendorf, Christoph von. A wedding in the Bulgarian mountains. Ge graphical Magazine. 4(1937): 203-214.

Garnett, Lucy Mary Jane. The women of Turkey and their folk-lore. Vol. 1. The Christian women. London, David Nutt. 1890: 1-29.

Gunda, Béla. Ethnological researches among the Moravian Valachs. Man. 57(1957): 129-131, plate K.

Hâciu, Anastase N. Aromânii. Focşani. 1936. 616 p.

Keramopoullos, Antonios D. Ti einai oi Koutsovlachoi [Who are the Koutso-vlachs?]. Athens. 1939. 152 p.

Lazar, Victor. Die Südrumänen der Türkei und der angrenzenden Länder. Beitrag zur Ethnographie der Balkanhalbinsel . . . Bukarest [no publisher given]. 1910.

Löpelmann, Martin. Aus der Volksdichtung der Mazedonischen Rumaenen. Leipzig, Armanen Verlag. 1934. 133 p.

Murvar, Vatro. The Balkan Vlachs; a typological study. Madison, Wisconsin 1956. 212 p. (Unpublished Ph.D. dissertation in anthropology. Madison, University of Wisconsin.)

Nenitescu, Ioan. De la Romănii din Turcia europeana: studiu etnic şi statistic asupra Armănilor, cu aproape una sută de gravuri şi cu o hartă etnografica. Bucureşti, C. Göbl. 1895. 641 p.

Papahagi, Nicolas. Les Roumains de Turquie. Bucarest. 1905. 184 p.

Papahagi, Pericle. Sammlung aromunischer Sprichwörter und Rätsel. Leipsic, Institut für Rumänische Sprache. 1894.

Papahagi, Pericle. Basme aromane şi de Per. Papahagi . . . Bucureşti, Inst. de Arte Grafice "C. Göbl." 1905. 27, 748 p.

Papahagi, Tache. Images d'ethnographie roumaine (Daco-roumaine et Aroumaine). Photographies, avec texte francais et roumain. 3 vols. Bucureşti, Societatea Cultural-Nationala Apostol Margarit. 1928-1934.

Petera, J. Wedrówki pasterzy Aromunow w Albanii [Migrations of Aromani shepherds in Albania]. Etnografia Polska. 6(1962): 192-201.

Petrovic, P. Ž. Stari Vlach. Beograd, Etnografski Muzej, Bulletin. 24(1961): 25-46.

Picot, É. Le Roumains de la Macédonie. Revue d'Anthropologie. Sér. 1. 4(1875): 385-427.

Popović, Dušan J. O cincarima; prilozi pitanju postanka našeg gradjanskog društva. 2d ed. Beograd, G. Kon. 1937. 520 p., illus., maps.

Sanders, Irwin T. The nomadic peoples of northern Greece: ethnic puzzle and cultural survival. Social Forces. 33(1954): 122-129.

Stuart, Robert. The Vlakhs of Mount Pindus. Transactions of the Ethnological Society of London. 6(1868): 311-327.

Trifunoski, J. F. Cincari u Ovcenoljskoj Kotlini [The Vlachs in the Ovcepolia Basin]. Etnoloski Pregled. 1(1959): 35-50.

Vikas, V. T. Ethima para Vlahofonois [Customs of the Vlach-speaking people]. Laographia. 6(1917): 169-188.

Vukanovic, T. P. Les Valaques: habitants autochtones des pays balkaniques. Ethnographie, New series. 56(1962): 11-41.

*Wace, Alan John B. The nomads of the Balkans, an account of life and customs among the Vlachs of northern Pindus. London, Methuen. 1914. 332 p., plates.

Weigand, Gustav Ludwig. Die Aromunen; ethnographische-philologische-historische Untersuchungen über das Volk der sogenannten Makedo-Romanen oder Zinzaren. 2 vols. Leipzig, J. A. Barth. 1894-1895.

Bulgaria. The Turkish minority in the Peoples' Republic of Bulgaria. Sofia. 1951. 70 p.

Byhan, A. Beitrag zur Volkskunde der Gagausen. Mémoires de la Société Finno-Ougrienne. 67(1933): 51-64.

Coxwell, C. Fillingham. Siberian and other folktales. London, C. W. Danie 1925: 399-437.

Hoppe, F. M. Die Gagauzen. International Archives of Ethnography. 48(195 119-129. (Bulgarian Gagauzi)

Hoppe, F. M. Die türkischen Gagauzen-Christen. Ein Beitrag zu ihrer Kenntnis. Oriens Christianus. 41(1957): 125-137.

Kostanick, Huey L. Turkish resettlement of Bulgarian Turks, 1950-1953. University of California Publications in Geography. 8, No. 2. Berkeley, University of California Press. 1957: 65-163.

Krohn, Else. Dorf, Haus und Hof der Gagausen in Bulgarien. Ethnologischer Anzeiger. 3, pt. 2(1935): 318-326, 9 illus., plans.

*Marinov, Vasil Aleksandrov. Prinos kŭm izuchavaneto na bita i kulturata na tursite i gagauzite v severoiztochna Bulgariia [Contribution to research on the life and culture of the Turks and Gagauzi of northeastern Bulgaria]. Sofia, Bulgarska Akademiiă na Naukite. 1956. 360 p.

Krallert-Sattler, Gertrud. Südosteuropa-Bibliographie. 3 vols. to date. Bd. 1: 1945-1950. Bd. 2: 1951-1955. Bd. 3: 1956-1960. München, R. Oldenbourg. 1956—

Pundeff, Marin V. Bulgaria; a bibliographic guide. Washington, Library of Congress, Reference Department. Slavic and East European Division. 1965. 9, 99 p.

United States. Bureau of the Census. Bibliography of social science periodicals and monograph series: Bulgaria, 1944-1960. Washington, Government Printing Office. 1961. 40 p.

Vakarelski, Christo. Bibliographie der bulgarischen Volkskunde . . . Zeitschrift für Slavische Philologie. 6(1929): 417-448; 7(1930): 183-209; 17(1941): 383-420; 18(1942): 163-193, 434-452; 19 (1944): 189-214. (For the years 1929-1944.) Continued in: Bulgarska Akademiia na Naukite, Sofia, Izvestiia na Etnografskiia Institut s Muzei. 2(1955): 451-500. (For the years 1944-1952.)

———

Arnaudov, Mikhail. Die bulgarischen Festbräuche. Leipzig, Parlapanoff. 1917. 7, 82 p.

Arnaudov, Mikhail. Kukeri i rusalii. Vgradena nevěsta. Studii vărhu bălgarskitě obredi i legendi, čast' 3 i 4. Sbornik za Narodni Umotvorenija i Narodopis. Kniga 34. Sofia. 1920. 528 p. (Kukeri and other festivals.)

Arnaudov, Mikhail. Očerki po bălgarskija folklor [Outline of Bulgarian folklore]. Sofia, Staatsdruckerei. 1934. 7, 695 p.

Arnaudov, Mikhail. Bŭlgarski narodni prazdnits. Sofia, Hemis. 1943. 162 p.

Barbar, Leo. Baumkult der Bulgaren. Anthropos. 30(1935): 797-802.

Barkley, Henry C. Between the Danube and the Black Sea; or five years in Bulgaria. London, J. Murray. 1876. 18, 313 p.

Barkley, Henry C. Bulgaria before the war during seven years' experience of European Turkey and its inhabitants. London, J. Murray. 1877. 24, 344 p.

Bernard, Henry. The shade of the Balkans: being a collection of Bulgarian folksongs and proverbs (in English). With an essay on Bulgarian popular poetry, & another on the origin of the Bulgars. London, D. Nutt. 1904. 327 p.

Bourchier, James D. The rise of Bulgaria. National Geographic Magazine. 23(1912): 1105-1118.

*Bulgaria. European conference on rural life. National monographs drawn up by governments. Bulgaria. Series of League of Nations Publications. European Conference on Rural Life. 28. Geneva. 1940. 59 p., illus.

Bulgaria, the peasant state. National Geographic Magazine. 19(1908): 760-773.

Bulgarska Akademiia na Naukite, Sofia. Etnografski Institut. Costumes nationaux Bulgares. 2 vols. so far. Sofia, Bulgarska Akademiia na Naukite. 1961--

Choukanova, Rossita. Bulgarian national embroidery: western regions. Sofia, Bulgarski Houdozhnik Publ. House. 1957. 9 p., 135 col. plates.

Corman, Mathieu. Drougar; vie intime d'une république populaire. Bruxelles, Éditions Tribord. 1955. 310 p.

Dellin, L. A. D., ed. Bulgaria. New York, F. A. Praeger. 1957. 17, 457

Dicey, Edward. The peasant state. London, John Murray. 1894. 4, 332 p.

Djoudjeff, Stoyan. Rythme et mesure dans la musique populaire Bulgare. Paris, Libraire Honoré Champion. 1931. 364 p.

Dozon, Auguste. Chansons populaires bulgares inédites. Paris, Maisonneuve. 1875. 47, 427 p.

Eliot, Sir Charles N. Turkey in Europe. London, Edward Arnold. 1908. 475, 2 folding maps.

Etnografskiya Institut i Muzey (Sofia). Etnografski materiali i nablyudeniya v bita i kulturata na rodopskite bãlgari [Ethnographic materials and investigations of the way of life and culture of the Bulgarians of the Rodope Mountain region]. Sofia, Etnografskiya Institut i Muzey. 1968. 340 p.

Fligier, Cornelius. Ethnologische Entdeckungen im Rhodope-Gebirge. M. A. G. 9(1880): 165-198.

Frolec, Václav. Die Volksarchitektur in Westbulgarien im 19. und zu Beginn des 20. Jahrhunderts. Brno, Universita J. E. Purkyně 1966. 164 p., 43 plates, 83 text figs.

*Frolec, Václav. The joint family and its dwelling in western Bulgaria. (Translated from the Russian.) In William G. Lockwood, ed. Essays in Balkan Ethnology. Kroeber Anthropological Society. Special Publication No. 1. 1967, 63-82.

Fürst, C. M. Volkmedizin und Gebräuche in Bulgarien. Z. f. E. 50(1918): 70-73.

Garnett, Lucy Mary Jane. The women of Turkey and their folk-lore. Vol. 1. The Christian women. London, David Nutt. 1890: 297-365.

Geliazkova, Nevena. Bulgarian textiles. Leigh-on-Sea, England, F. Lewis. 1958. 21 p., plates.

Gellert, J. F. Ostbulgarische Bauernhaustypen. Z.f.E. 66(1934): 1-15, illus., plans.

Geshov, I. E. Zadrugata v zapadna Bălgariya [The zadruga in western Bulgaria]. Periodichesko Spisinie. 5th Year. Vols. 21/22(1887): 426-449.

Girard, André. Les minorités nationales ethniques et religieuses en Bulgarie. Paris, Marcel Giard. 1933. 206 p.

Grothe, Hugo. Bulgarien: ein Beitrag zur Landeskunde. Wien, L. W. Seidel & Sohn. 1921. 7, 155 p.

Handjieff, W. Zur Soziologie des bulgarischen Dorfes. Leipzig, Verlag G. Fock. 1931. 100 p.

Hirstov, D. Tehniceskijat stroež na bălgarskata narodna muziaka; metrika tonalni i harmonični osbenosti [The technical structure of Bulgarian folk music; tempo, rhythm, tonal and harmonic peculiarities]. Sofia, Nauka i Izkustvo. 1956. 56 p.

Hoffman, George W. Transformation of rural settlement in Bulgaria. Geographical Review. 54(1964): 45-64.

IÁnchev, Naum I. La Bulgarie et l'étranger: la nationalité bulgare, étude comparative entre la loi bulgare et les lois de la Turquie de la Grèce, de la Serbie. Paris, É. Duchemin. 1892. 118 p.

Ishirkov, Anastasy. Bulgarien: Land und Leute. 2 pts. Leipzig, I. Parlapanoff. 1916-1917.

Ishirkov, Anastasy. Les Bulgares en Dobroudja; aperçu historique et ethnographique. Berne, Impr. Pochon-Jent & Bühler. 1919. 189 p.

Jenkins, Hester Donaldson. Bulgaria and its women. National Geographic Magazine. 27(1915): 377-400.

Jireček, Constantin. Das Fürstenthum Bulgarien. Seine Bodengestaltung, Natur, Bevölkerung, wirtschaftliche Zustände, geistige Kultur, Staatsverfassung, Staatsverwaltung und neueste Geschichte. Wien, F. Tempsky. 1891. 16, 573 p.

Johnson, Stowers. Gay Bulgaria. London, Robert Hale. 1964. 207 p.

Kaculer, I. Cvirkaistvots v selo Sipka [The making of musical instruments in the village of Shipka]. Isvestija na Instituta za Muzika. 2-3(1957): 215-248.

Kanitz, Felix Philipp. Reisen in Süd-Serbien und Nord-Bulgarien. Wien, Gerold. 1864. 66 p.

Kanitz, Felix Philipp. Donau-Bulgarien und der Balkan. Historisch-geograph. ethnographische Reisestudien aus den Jahren 1860-1879. 2d ed. 3 vols. Leipzig, Renger'sche Buchhandlung. 1882.

Katsarova, Raina. Dances of Bulgaria. New York, Crown Press. 1951. 40 p., plates.

Kaufman, N. Part-singing in Bulgarian folk music. Journal of the International Folk Music Council. 15(1963): 48-49.

Kostrowicki, Jerzy, S. Hauzer, I. Velchev, and Z. Borisov. The collective farm of Petârch in the suburban zone of Sofia. In Jerzy Kostrowicki, ed. Land utilization in East-central Europe. Geographia Polonia. 5. Warszawa, Institute of Geography, Polish Academy of Sciences. 1965: 345-372.

Kostrowicki, Jerzy, W. Stola, I. Velchev, and Z. Borisov. The collectivized village of Dermantsi in the northern foothills of the Balkan Range. In Jerzy Kostrowicki, ed. Land utilization in East-central Europe. Geographia Polonia. 5. Warszawa, Institute of Geography, Polish Academy of Sciences 1965: 373-406.

Kowatscheff, J. D. Bulgarischer Volksglaube aus dem Gebiet der Himmelskun. Z.f.E. 63(1931): 322-346.

Kremenliev, Boris A. Bulgarian-Macedonian folk music. Berkeley, University of California Press. 1952. 165 p.

Kremenliev, Boris A. Some social aspects of Bulgarian folksongs. J.A.F.L. 69(1956): 178-182.

Leslie, Henrietta [Gladys H. Schütze]. Where east is west: life in Bulgaria. Boston, Houghton Mifflin. 1933. 320 p.

*Lodge, Olive. Infant and maternal mortality in Bulgarian villages, with a background of general conditions. Population. 4(1937): 6-80.

Lodge, Olive. Babin Den: midwives' day in Bulgaria. Man. 47(1947): 83-85.

Logio, George Clenton. Bulgaria, past & present. Manchester, Sherratt & Hughes. 1936. 8, 480 p.

Marinow, Wasil. Traditionelle und moderne alpine Schafzucht im mittleren Stara Planina (Balkan). In Gyula Ortutay and T. Bodrogi, eds. Europa et Hungaria. Budapest, Akadémiai Kiadó. 1965: 417-430.

Markham, Reuben H. Meet Bulgaria. Sofia, the author. 1931. 390 p.

Mazon, André. Contes slaves de la Macédoine sud-occidentale. Paris, Champion. 1923. 236 p.

Monroe, Will Seymour. Bulgaria and her people, with an account of the Balkan Wars, Macedonia, and the Macedonian Bulgars. Boston, Page. 1914. 20, 410 p.

Newman, Bernard. Bulgarian background. London, Robert Hale. 1961. 206 p.

Panov, T. Psikhologiia na bulgarskiia narod [Psychology of the Bulgarian people]. Sofia. 1914. 306 p.

Petroff, Louis. Peasant primary groups in Bulgaria. Sociology and Social Research. 13(1929): 557-565.

Petroff, Louis. Magical beliefs and practices in old Bulgaria. Midwest Folklore. 7(1957): 214-220.

Pohl, Irmgard. Beiträge zur Landes- und Volkskunde des Jantregebietes in Bulgarien. Horn (Nieder-Österreich), F. Berger. 1932. 145 p.

Primovski, A. Bit i kultura na Rodopskite Bălgari [Way of life and culture of the Bulgarians from the Rhodope Mountain region]. Sofia, Etnografskiya Institut i Muzey. 1968. 660 p.

Romanska, Cvetana. Die Haiducken in der bulgarischen Volksdichtung. Südosteuropa-Jahrbuch. 6(1962): 34-41.

St. Clair, S. G. B., and Charles A. Brophy. A residence in Bulgaria; or, notes on the resources and administration of Turkey: the condition and character, manners, customs and language of the Christian and Muslim populations, . . . London, John Murray. 1869. 15, 426 p.

Sanders, Irwin T. The social contacts of a Bulgarian village. Rural Sociology. 4(1939): 315-327.

Sanders, Irwin T. The rural cooperative in Bulgaria. Foreign Agriculture. 8(1944): 21-24.

*Sanders, Irwin T. Balkan village. Lexington, University of Kentucky Press. 1950. 5, 174 p., plates.

BULGARIANS

Sebright, Georgina Mary Muir Mackenzie, and A. P. Kirby. Travels in the Slavonic provinces of Turkey-in-Europe. 2 vols. 5th ed. London, Dalby, Isbister. 1877.

Shishmanov, Dimitri. A survey of Bulgarian literature. Williamsport, Bayard Press. 1932. 40 p.

Shishmanova, Lidiya M. Légendes religieuses Bulgares traduites. Paris, Lerou: 1896. 5, 300 p.

Shopov, V. I. Marriage customs in Bulgaria. Archives of the International Folklore Association. 1. The International Folklore Congress of the World': Columbia Exposition. Chicago. 1898: 417-423.

Sineonoff, Stefan. Die Zadruga und Ehegüterrechtsverhältnisse Bulgariens. Thesis, University of Hamburg. Leipzig, Verlag G. Fock. 1931. 61 p.

Stoin, V. Bălgarskata narodna muzika [Bulgarian national music]. Sofia, Nauka i Izk. 1956. 100 p.

Stoin, V. Narodni pesni ot zapadnite pokrajnini [Folksongs from the southern frontier territories]. Sofia, Bulgarska Akademiia na Naukite. 1959. 360 p

*Strausz, Adolf. Die Bulgaren. Ethnographische Studien. Leipzig, Th. Grieben's Verlag. 1898. 477 p.

Thurnher, Majda. A survey of Balkan houses and farm buildings. Kroeber Anthropological Society Papers. 14(1956): 19-92. (See pp. 70-74.)

Vakarelski, Christo. Lovni sposobi i uredi u bălgarite [Hunting methods and implements among the Bulgarians]. Lud Słowanski (Krakow). 2(1931): 149-164.

Vakarelski, Christo. Brunnen und Wasserleitungen in Bulgarien. Folk-Liv. 3(1939): 5-43.

Vakarelski, Christo. Die bulgarischen wandernden Hirtenhütten. Acta Ethnographica. 5(1956): 2-82; 6(1957): 1-40.

Vakarelski, Christo. Überreste des pfluglosen Feldbaues bei den Bulgaren. In Agrarethnographie. Berlin, Akademie der Wissenschaften zu Berlin. 1957: 100-111.

Vakarelski, Christo. Charakteristische Merkmale der bäuerlichen Volkskultur in Bulgarien. Südosteuropa-Jahrbuch. 6(1962): 125-133.

Vakarelski, Christo. Etnografia Bułgarii. Prace Etnologiczne 7. Wrocław, Polski Towarzystwo Ludoznawcze. 1965. 16, 392 p., 153 figs., 22 tables, 4 plates. (Summary in French.)

BULGARIANS

*Vakarelski, Christo. Bulgarische Volkskunde. Grundriss der Slavischen Philologie und Kulturgeschichte. Bd. 15. 1968. 390 p., 52 plates.

Velev, Dimitŭr D. Bulgarski kilimi do kraya na XIX bl [Bulgarian carpets of the nineteenth century]. Sofia, Bulgarska Akademiia na Naukite. 1960. 299 p., illus.

Veleva, Mariia G. Bŭlgarskata dvuprestilchena nosiia. Sofia, Bulgarska Akadmiia na Naukite. 1963. 162 p. (Folk costume.)

Veleva, Mariia G., and E. I. Lepavtsova. Bulgarian folk costumes of North Bulgaria in the 19th and early 20th centuries. Bulgarian Folk Costumes, Vol. 1. Sofia, Bulgarian Academy of Sciences. Ethnographic Institute and Museum. 1961. 324 p., 120 plates, 35 plates in color.

Vovk, Fedir K. Svadebnye obriady v Bulgarii [Wedding customs in Bulgaria]. Etnograficheskoe Obozrienie (Moscow). 7, no. 4(1895): 1-58.

*Warriner, Doreen. Contrasts in emerging societies. Readings in the social and economic history of south-eastern Europe in the nineteenth century. Bloomington, Indiana University Press. 1965: 207-280.

Weis-Bartenstein, W. K. Bulgariens Volkswirtschaft . . . Berlin, Carl Heymanns Verlag. 1918. 36, 490 p., maps.

Wilhelmy, Herbert. Hochbulgarien. I. Die ländlichen Siedlungen und die bäuerliche Wirtschaft. Kiel, Geographisches Institut der Universität Kiel. 1935. 12, 316 p., 32 text figs., 23 plates.

Wilhelmy, Herbert. Hochbulgarien. II. Sofia, Wandlungen einer Grossstadt zwischen Orient und Okzident. Kiel, Geographisches Institut der Universität Kiel. 1936. 11, 220 p.

Wilkinson, Henry R. Maps and politics: a review of the ethnographic cartography of Macedonia. Liverpool, Liverpool University Press. 1951. 16, 366 p., maps.

Zaharieff, Malomir. Les minorités bulgares en Roumanie (Conditions d'une entente bulgaro-roumaine). Paris, Domat-Montchrestien. 1940. 99 p.

Zdansky, Rossina. Die Feuertreter in Thrazien. In Josef Haekel et al. Die Wiener Schule der Völkerkunde. Horn-Wien, F. Berger. 1956: 551-563.

Zorn, E. R. Eine Hochzeit in Bulgarien. Völkerkunde (Wien). 4(1928): 83-88.

POMAKS

Hazai, G. Textes turcs der Rhodope. Acta Orientalia (Budapest). 10(1960): 185-229.

Kanitz, F. I. Die moslimisch-bulgarischen Pomaci und Zigeuner im nördlichen Balkangebiete. M.A.G.W. 6(1876): 75-79.

Khristov, Khristo, and V. Khadzhinikolov. Iz minaloto na bulgarite-mokhamedani v Rodopite. Sofia, Bulgarska Akademiia na Naukite. 1958. 171 p.

St. Clair, S. G. B., and Charles A. Brophy. A residence in Bulgaria; or, notes on the resources and administration of Turkey: the conditions and character, manners and customs and language of the Christian and Muslim populations, . . . London, John Murray. 1869. 15, 426 p.

Sanders, Irwin T. The Moslem minority of Bulgaria. Moslem World. 24(1934) 356-369.

Shishkov, Stoio N. Bulgaro-Mokhamedanite (pomatsi); istoricheskozemepisen i narodouchen pregled s obrazi. Plovdiv, Librairie Khristo G. Danov. 1936. 118 p., illus.

Vasilev, Kiril. Rodopskite bulgari-mokhamedani; istoricheski ocherk. Plovdiv Danov. 1961. 288 p.

Vranchev, Nikolai. Bulgari mokhamedani; pomatsi. Sofia. 1948. 61 p.

YÜRÜKS

*Eckert, Georg. Die Jürüken in Zentral-Mazedonien. Buletinul Institutului Român din Sofia. Anûl 1(1941): 561-566. (Printed in Bucharest. 1942)

Garnett, Lucy Mary Jane. The women of Turkey and their folk-lore. Vol. 2. The Jewish and Moslem women. London, David Nutt. 1891: 207-213.

Hoppe, Ernst Max. Die Jürüken. International Archives of Ethnographie. 32(1934): 185-187.

Traeger, P. Die Jürüken und Konjaren in Makedonien. Z.f.E. 37(1905): 198-206.

Argenti, Philip. Bibliography of Chios. Oxford, The Clarendon Press. 1940. 30, 836 p.

Kyparissiotis, Niove, ed. The Modern Greek collection in the Library of the University of Cincinnati: a catalogue. Athens, Greece, Hestia Press for the University of Cincinnati Library. 1960. 16, 387 p.

Kyriakidis, S. P. Le folklore en Grèce de 1919 à 1930. Byzantion. 6(1931): 737-770.

Spenser, Floyd A. War and postwar Greece. An analysis based on Greek writi Washington, Library of Congress, European Affairs Division. 1952. 16, 17

Swanson, Donald C. Modern Greek studies in the West. A critical bibliograp of studies of modern Greek linguistics, philology, and folklore, in language other than Greek. New York, New York Public Library. 1960. 93 p.

United States Bureau of the Census. Bibliography of social science periodicals and monograph series: Greece, 1960-1961. Washington, Bureau of the Census. 1962. 19 p.

Vlachos, Evan. An annotated bibliography on Greek migration. Athens, Social Science Centre. 1966. 127 p.

Vlachos, Evan. Modern Greek society: continuity and change. An annotated classification of selected sources. Special Monograph Series. 1. Fort Collins, Colorado, Department of Sociology and Anthropology, Colorado State University. 1969. 177 p.

Weber, Shirley Howard. Voyages and travels in the Near East during the XIX century; . . . Princeton, American School of Classical Studies at Athens. 1952. 10, 252 p.

Weber, Shirley Howard. Voyages and travels in Greece, the Near East and adjacent regions, made previous to the year 1801 . . . Princeton, American School of Classical Studies at Athens. 1953. 7, 208 p.

_____

Abbot, George Frederick. Songs of modern Greece. Cambridge, The University Press. 1900. 307 p.

*Abbot, George Frederick. Macedonian folklore. Cambridge, The University Press. 1903. 372 p.

Abbot, George Frederick. The tale of a tour in Macedonia. London, E. Arnol 1903. 11, 343 p.

About, Edmund. Greece and the Greeks of the present day. New York, Dix, Edwards. 1857. 16, 360 p.

GREEKS

About, Edmund. The Greek brigand; or, the king of the mountain. London, J. and R. Maxwell. 1881. 15, 252 p. (Fiction, but useful.)

Adams, Phoebe-Lou. A rough map of Greece. Boston, Little, Brown. 1962. 177 p.

Adossides, Andreas. Fishermen of the Aegean. Geographical Magazine. 14(1941): 86-91.

Adossides, Andreas. The shepherds of Greece. Geographical Magazine. 16(1943): 217-225.

Aghnides, T. What ancient Greece means to the modern Greek. John Rylands Library Bulletin (Manchester, England). 27(1943): 260-270.

Alexander, Alec. Greek industrialists: an economic and social analysis. Athens, Centre of Planning and Economic Research. 1965. 182 p.

*Allbaugh, Leland G. Crete; a case study of an underdeveloped area. Princeton, Princeton University Press. 1953. 20, 572 p., plates.

Allen, Harold B. Come over into Macedonia; the story of a ten-year adventure in uplifting a war-torn people. New Brunswick, N.J., Rutgers University Press. 1943. 18, 313 p.

Andrews, Mary Evans. Messenger by night. New York, Longmans, Green. 1953. 206 p. (Juvenile literature, but excellent on the village of Apollona on Rhodos.)

*Andromedas, John. Greek kinship terms in everyday use. A.A. 59(1957): 1086-1088.

*Andromedas, John. The inner Maniat community type: a study of the local community's changing articulation with society. New York, N.Y. 1962. (Unpublished Ph.D. dissertation. Columbia University, Anthropology Department.)

Anthony, Anne. Meet the Greeks. Athens, Icaros Publishing Co. 1950. 141 p.

Anthony, Anne. Greek Holiday. Athens, Icaros Publishing Co. 1957. 427 p. (Reprinted: 1960. 429 p., plates.)

*Antonakaki, Kalliniki (Dendrinou). Greek education: reorganization of the administrative structure. New York, Bureau of Publications, Teachers College, Columbia University. 1955. 13, 274 p.

Antoniades, Anne Gault. The Anastenaria. Thracian firewalking festival. Thracian Archives, Society of Thracian Studies. Publication 36. Athens. 1954. 22 p., 12 plates.

Argenti, Philip Pandely. The costumes of Chios, their development from the XVth to the XXth century. London, Batsford. 1953. 13, 338 p., col. plates.

*Argenti, Philip Pandely, and H. J. Rose. The folk-lore of Chios. 2 vols. Cambridge, The University Press. 1949. 14, 1-594; 12, 595-1199 p., illus.

Armstrong, Isabel J. Two roving Englishwomen in Greece. London, S. Low, Marston. 1893. 11, 300 p.

Association' for International Research. Greek social characteristics. Cambridge, Mass., Association for International Research. 1956. [172 p.]

Athas, Daphne. Greece by prejudice. Philadelphia, Lippincott. 1962. 284 p

*Baird, Henry Martyn. Modern Greece: a narrative of a residence and travels in that country, with observations on its antiquities, literature, language, politics and religion. New York, Harper & Brothers. 1856. 12, 380 p.

Bardis, Panos. The changing family in modern Greece. Sociology and Social Research. 40(1955): 19-23.

Bardis, Panos. Main features of the Greek family during the early twentieth century. Alpha Kappa Deltan. 26(1956): 17-21.

Bardis, Panos. Influences on the modern Greek family. Social Science. 32(1957): 155-158.

Bardis, Panos. Ivan and Artemis. New York, Pageant Press. 1957. 197 p.

Bardis, Panos. A comparative study of familism. Rural Sociology. 24(1959): 362-371.

Barrows, Samuel J. The isles and shrines of Greece. Boston, Roberts Brothers. 1898. 12, 390 p.

Baud-Bovy, Daniel. In Greece; journeys by mountain and valley. Genève, Éditions d'Art F. Boissonnas. 1920. 132 p.

Baud-Bovy, Samuel. La chanson populaire grecque du Dodécanèse. Paris, Société d'éditions "Les Belles Lettres." 1936.

Baud-Bovy, Samuel. Chansons du Dodécanèse. 2 vols. Athènes, J. N. Sidéris. 1935-1938.

Baud-Bovy, Samuel. Études sur la chanson cleftique, avec 17 chansons cleftiques de Roumélie . . . Athènes, J. N. Sidéris. 1958. 123 p.

Beer, Ethel. Marvelous Greece; an appreciation of the country and its people. New York, Walker. 1967. 272 p.

Benaki Museum. Hellenic national costumes. 2 vols. Athens, Benaki Museum. 1948, 1954. 24, 86 p., 104 col. plates.

Bent, James Theodore. Aegean islands. The Cyclades, or life among the insular Greeks. London, Longmans, Green. 1885. 20, 501 p. (Reprinted: Chicago, Argonaut. 1966. 74, 592 p.)

Bent, James Theodore. Greek peasant life. Fortnightly Review. August 1886: 214-224.

Bent, James Theodore. On insular Greek customs. J.A.I. 15(1886): 391-401.

*Bernard, H. Russell. Kalymnian sponge diving. Human Biology. 39(1967): 103-130.

*Bernard, H. Russell. Kalymnos: Economic and cultural change on a Greek sponge fishing island. Urbana, Ill. 1968. 288 p. (Unpublished Ph.D. dissertation in anthropology. University of Illinois.)

*Bialor, Perry A. What's in a name? Aspects of the social organization of a Greek farming community related to naming customs. In William G. Lockwood, ed. Essays in Balkan ethnology. Kroeber Anthropological Society. Special Publications. 1(1967): 95-108.

Bikelas, Demetrios. Loukis Laras; reminiscences of a Chiote merchant during the War of Independence. London, Macmillan. 1881. 273 p.

*Blum, Richard, and Eva Blum. Health and healing in rural Greece. A study of three communities. Stanford, Stanford University Press. 1965. 269 p., plates.

Boehm, Fritz. Die neugriechische Totenklage. Berlin, Minerva-Verlag. 1947. 98 p.

Bonser, K. J. Easter in Greece. Folklore. 75(1964): 269-271.

Booth, C. D., and Isabelle B. Booth. Italy's Aegean possessions. London, Arrowsmith. 1928. 324 p.

Boyazoglou, Alexander J. Contribution à l'étude de l'économie rurale de la Grèce d'après guerre. Paris, Berger-Levrault. 1931. 6, 268 p.

Bramsen, Jens A. Travels in Egypt, Cyprus and Greece . . . 2 vols. London, H. Colburn. 1820.

*Branch, Daniel Paulk. Folk architecture of the East Mediterranean. New York, Columbia University Press. 1966: 18-85.

Burgel, Guy. Pobia. Étude géographique d'un village crétois. Athens, Centr des Sciences Sociales d'Athènes. 1965. 14, 141 p.

Carroll, Michael. Gates of the wind. London, John Murray. 1965. 205 p. (Northern Sporades.)

Chaconas, Stephen G. Adamantios Korais: a study in Greek nationalism. Studies in History, Economics and Public Law by the Faculty of Political Science of Columbia University. 490. New York, Columbia University Press. 1942. 181 p.

Chassiotis, Georges. L'instruction publique chez les Grecs. Paris, Ernest Leroux. 1881. 16, 550 p.

Cheston, Charles. Greece in 1887. London, Effingham House. 1887. 137 p.

Cicelis, Kay. Greek village wedding. Geographical Magazine. 28(1955): 83-85.

Clift, Charmian. Mermaid singing. Indianapolis, New York, Bobbs-Merrill. 1956. 320 p. (Kalymnos Island)

Codellas, P. S. Modern Greek folklore: the smerdaki. J.A.F.L. 58(1945): 236-244.

Colton, Rev. Walter. Land and lee in the Bosphorus and Aegean; or views of Constantinople and Athens. New York, A. S. Barnes. 1851. 366 p.

Crosfield, Domini Elliadi, Lady. Dances of Greece. New York, Chanticleer Press. 1948. (Reprinted: 1950. 40 p., 4 col. plates.)

*Cummings, D., trans. and ed. The rudder (pedalion). Metaphorical ship of state of the One Holy Catholic and Apostolic Church of the Orthodox Christians or all the sacred and divine canons . . . Chicago, Orthodox Christian Educational Society. 1957. 1034 p. (Excellent source on marriage law, etc.)

Davy, John. Notes and observations on the Ionian Islands and Malta: with some remarks on Constantinople and Turkey, . . . 2 vols. London, Smith, Elder. 1842.

Dawkins, Richard M. The modern carnival in Thrace and the cult of Dionysus Journal of Hellenic Studies. 26(1906): 191-206.

Dawkins, Richard M. Folk-memory in Crete. Folk-Lore. 41(1930): 11-42.

Dawkins, Richard M. Folklore in stories from the Dodecanese. Folk-Lore. 53(1942): 5-26.

Dawkins, Richard M. Soul and body in the folklore of modern Greece. Folk-Lore. 53(1942): 131-147.

Dawkins, Richard M. The art of story-telling in the Dodecanese. Byzantion. 15(1942-1943): 357-380.

*Dawkins, Richard M., ed. and trans. Forty-five stories from the Dodecanese. Cambridge, The University Press. 1950. 11, 559 p.

*Dawkins, Richard M., ed. Modern Greek folktales. Oxford, The Clarendon Press. 1953. 38, 491 p.

*Dawkins, Richard M., ed. More Greek folktales. Oxford, The Clarendon Press. 1955. 178 p.

Dayton, Daryle. Education in modern Greece. Claremont Quarterly. 8, no. 3(Spring 1961): 5-21.

Demetrios, George. When I was a boy in Greece. Boston, Lothrop, Lee & Shepard. 1913. 168 p. (Macedonian area.)

Douglas, Frederick Sylvester North. An essay on certain points of resemblance between the ancient and modern Greeks. London, J. Murray. 1813. 6, 198 p.

Doxiades, K., et al. Dodekanesos: to oikistiko kai plastiko provlema [The Dodecanese: the problem of housing from the point of design]. Athens, Ministry of Reconstruction, Series no. 12. 1950. 122 p., 46 pages of illus.

Durham, Mary Edith. Old beliefs and modern politics. Man. 21(1921): 73-74. (The curse of excommunication against King Alexander and Venizelos by the Greek clergy in Athens.)

Durrell, Lawrence. Prospero's cell: a guide to the landscape and manners of the island of Corcyra. London, Faber and Faber. 1945. 142 p., plates. (Many later reprintings.)

Durrell, Lawrence. Reflections on a marine Venus: a companion to the land-scape of Rhodes. London, Faber and Faber. 1953. 198 p., plates.

Dyer, L. On the breaking of vessels as a funeral rite in modern Greece. J.A.I. 23(1893): 28-41.

Eckels, Richard P. Greek wolf-lore. Philadelphia. 1937. 88 p. (Ph.D. dissertation. University of Pennsylvania.)

Eckert, Georg. Siedlungsgeographische Beobachtungen aus der Chalkidike. Volkskundliche Miszellen aus Mazedonien. 1. Thessaloniki, the author. 1943. 36 p.

Eckert, Georg. Die Wanderbienenzucht in der Chalkidike. Volkskundliche Miszellen aus Mazedonien. 2. Thessaloniki, the author. 1943. 7 p.

Eckert, Georg. Schädelamulette in Griechisch-Mazedonien. In Georg Eckert and Udo Oberem, eds. Hermann Trimborn zum 60. Geburtstag. Braunschweig, Albert Limbach Verlag. 1961: 23-28, 11 photos.

*Eckert, Georg, and P. E. Formozis. Beiträge zur mazedonischen Volksmagie. Volkskundliche Beobachtungen und Materialien aus Zentralmazedonien und der Chalkidike. 1. Thessaloniki, the authors. 1942. 107 p., 7 plates.

*Eckert, Georg, and P. E. Formozis. Mazedonischer Volksglaube, Magie, Aberglaube und religiöse Vorstellungen in Saloniki und der West-Chalkidike Volkskundliche Beobachtungen und Materialien aus Zentralmazedonien und der Chalkidike. 2. Thessaloniki, the authors. 1943. 107 p.

*Eckert, Georg, and P. E. Formozis. Regenzauber in Mazedonien. Volkskundliche Beobachtungen und Materialien aus Zentralmazedonien und der Chalkidike. 3. Thessaloniki, the authors. 1943. 97 p.

Eckert, Georg, and P. E. Formozis. Das Hirtenleben in der Chalkidike. Volkkundliche Miszellen aus Mazedonien. 7. Thessaloniki, the authors. 1944

Eddy, Charles B. Greece and the Greek refugees. London, G. Allen & Unwin 1931. 280 p.

Edmonds, E. M. Notes on Greek folklore. Folk-Lore Journal. 2(1884): 168-172.

Edwardes, Charles. Letters from Crete. Letters written during the spring of 1886. London, R. Bentley and Son. 1887. 14, 394 p.

Eliot, Sir Charles N. Turkey in Europe. London, Edward Arnold. 1908. 475 p., 2 folding maps.

Ephtaliotis, Argyris. (Translated by W. H. D. Rouse.) Tales from the isles of Greece. Being sketches of modern Greek peasant life. London, J. M. Dent 1897. 16, 231 p. (Reprinted under the title: Modern tales of the Greek islands. London, Thomas Nelson and Sons. 1942. 238 p.)

Etteldorf, Raymond. The soul of Greece. Westminster, Md., Newman Press. 1963. 235 p.

Fairchild, Henry Pratt. Greek immigration to the United States. New Haven, Yale University Press. 1911: 1-70.

*Fermor, Patrick Leigh. Mani; travels in the southern Peloponnese. London, John Murray. 1958. 320 p., plates.

Fermor, Patrick Leigh. Roumeli; travels in northern Greece. London, John Murray. 1966. 8, 248 p., 22 plates.

*Ferriman, Z. Duckett. Home life in Hellas, Greece and the Greeks. London, Mills & Boon. 1910. 338 p.

*Ferriman, Z. Duckett. Greece and the Greeks. New York, J. Potts. 1911. 338 p. (Actually the same as the above title.)

Ferriman, Z. Duckett. East and west of the Hellespont, memories of fifty years. London, J. Cape. 1926. 320 p.

*Fielding, Xan. The stronghold, an account of the four seasons in the White Mountains of Crete. London, Secker & Warburg. 1953. 17, 316 p.

Formozis, Pandelis. Grèce. Contribution à l'étude de la chanson et de la musique populaire grecque. Thessaloniki, the author. 1938. 107 p., 6 illus.

Forte, John, ed. Corfu; Venus of the isles. Essex, East Essex Gazette. 1963.

Friedl, Ernestine. Hospital care in provincial Greece. Human Organization. 16, no. 4(1958): 24-27.

*Friedl, Ernestine. Dowry and inheritance in modern Greece. Transactions of the New York Academy of Sciences. Ser. 2. 22(1959): 49-54.

*Friedl, Ernestine. The role of kinship in the transmission of national culture to rural villages in mainland Greece. A.A. 61 (1959): 30-38.

*Friedl, Ernestine. Some aspects of dowry and inheritance in Boeotia. In Julian Pitt-Rivers, ed. Mediterranean Countrymen. Paris, La Haye, Mouton. 1963: 113-135.

*Friedl, Ernestine. Vasilika. A village in modern Greece. New York, Holt, Rinehart and Winston. 1963. 14, 110 p.

*Friedl, Ernestine. Lagging emulation in post-peasant society. A.A. 66(1964): 569-586.

Friedl, Ernestine. The position of women: appearance and reality. Anthropological Quarterly. 40(1967): 97-108.

Galt, John. Letters from the Levant; containing views of the state of society, manners, opinions, and commerce, in Greece, and several of the principal islands of the archipelago . . . London, T. Cadell and W. Davies. 1813. 8, 386 p.

Gardner, Ernest A. Greece and the Aegean. London, Harrap. 1938. 260 p.

Garnett, Lucy Mary Jane. Greek brigand and village superstitions. Gentleman's Magazine. 256 (March 1884): 283-287.

*Garnett, Lucy Mary Jane. The women of Turkey and their folk-lore. Vol. 1. The Christian women. London, David Nutt. 1890: 30-193.

Garnett, Lucy Mary Jane. New folklore researches. Greek folk poesy: annotated translations, from the whole cycle of Romaic folk-verse and folk-prose [Edited, with essays on the science of folklore, Greek folkspeech, and the survival of paganism]. 2 vols. Guildford, Billing & Sons. 1896.

Garnett, Lucy Mary Jane. Greek wonder tales. London, A. & C. Black. 1913. 12, 231 p.

Garnett, Lucy Mary Jane. Greece of the Hellenes. New York, C. Scribner's Sons. 1914. 7, 246 p.

Garnett, Lucy Mary Jane. Balkan home life. London, Methuen. 1917. 309 p.

Geil, William Edgar. The isle that is called Patmos. London, Marshall Bros. ; Philadelphia, A. J. Rowland. 1904. 12, 195 p.

Golding, Louis. Goodbye to Ithaca. London, Hutchinson. 1955. 254 p.

Gorer, Geoffrey, and Dorothy Demetrocopolou. The Greek community and the Greek child from the viewpoint of relief and rehabilitation. [New York, Institute for Intercultural Studies, Columbia University. 194_. 33 p.]

Gray, Peter S. The people of Poros. A portrait of a Greek island village. New York and London, Whittlesey House, McGraw-Hill. 1942. 325 p.

Great Britain. Admiralty Office. Naval Intelligence Division. Greece. 3 vols. London, Great Britain. Admiralty Office. Naval Intelligence Division. Geographical Handbook Series. 1944-1945.

Gubbins, J. K. Some observations on the evil-eye in modern Greece. Folk-Lore. 57 (1946-1947): 195-198.

Hadjimichali, Haghimichali, and Hagihihali. See: Hadzimihali, Angelikis.

Hadzi-Manov, V. Instruments folkloristiques en Macedonie—"Kavalis." Journal of the International Folk Music Council. 12 (1960): 21-22.

Hadzimihali, Angelikis. Elliniki laiki techni. Skyros, P. G. Makris. 1925. 199 p.

Hadzimihali, Angelikis. L'art populaire grec—l'île d'Icarie. Byzantin-Neugriechische Jahrbuch. 6 (1927): 32-51.

Hadzimihali, Angelikis. L'art populaire grec. Athènes, Pyrsos. 1937. 52 p., 108 plates.

Hadzimihali, Angelikis. La maison grecque. L'Hellénisme Contemporain. 1949: 169-190, 250-265.

Hadzimihali, Angelikis. La maison grecque. Collection de l'Hellénisme Contemporain. 1. Athens. 1949. 44 p., 36 illus. (A reprint of the above.)

Hadzimihali, Angelikis. National Greek costumes. Greek Heritage. 2, no. 5(1965): 47-56.

*Hamilton, Mary. Greek saints and their festivals. Edinburgh and London. W. Blackwood & Sons. 1910. 8, 211 p.

*Hammond, Peter. The waters of Marah. The present state of the Greek church. London, Rockliff. 1956. 9, 186 p., 7 plates.

Handlin, Oscar. The returned immigrants. In Oscar Handlin. Race and nationality in American life. Garden City, Doubleday Anchor Books. 1957: 201-217.

Hasluck, Margaret M. The evil eye in some Greek villages of the upper Haliakmon valley in West Macedonia. J.R.A.I. 53(1923): 160-172.

Hasluck, Margaret M. The significance of Greek personal names. Folk-Lore. 34(1923): 249-251.

Hasluck, Margaret M. The Basil-cake of the Greek New Year. Folk-Lore. 38(1927): 143-177.

Hauttecoeur, Henri. Le folklore de l'île de Kythnos. Bruxelles, Havermans. 1898. 40 p.

Hege, Walter. Griechische Schattenspiele. Atlantis. 2(1930): 566-572. 15 illus.

Hesseling, D. C. Charos. Ein Beitrag zur Kenntniss des neugriechischen Volksglaubens. Leipzig, Harrassowitz; Leiden, van Doesburgh. 1897. 86 p.

Heuzey, Léon A. Le mont Olympe et l'Acarnanie; exploraton de ces deux régions, avec l'étude de leurs antiquités, de leurs populations anciennes et modernes, de leur géographie . . . Paris, Didot. 1860. 2, 494 p.

Hope, John. Lindos, Isle of Rhodes. Ekistics. 23(1967): 246-251.

Horton, George. Home of nymphs and vampires. Indianapolis, Bobbs-Merrill. 1929. 319 p. (The Aegean Islands.)

Howe, Robin. Greek cooking. London, Andre Deutsch. 1960. 282 p.

Iliadis, Konst. I Halki tis Dodekanisou. Tom. 1 (Only volume ever published.) Athenai, the author. 1950. 560 p., plates, illus. (Folklore, history, geography, and folk life on Halki Island.)

*Jenkins, Romilly. The Dilessi murders. London, Longmans. 1961. 16, 190 p. (In particular, see Chapter 1: "Greek brigandage" and Chapter 2: "Truth and ethnic truth.")

Jensen, Hans. Vulgärgriechische Schattenspieltexte. 1. Berlin, Deutscher Verlag der Wissenschaft. 1954. 92 p., illus.

Johnson, Clarence R. Courtship and marriage customs of the Turks and Greeks. Journal of Applied Sociology. 10 (1925): 54-62.

*Johnstone, Pauline. Greek island embroidery. London, Alec Tiranti. 1961. 4, 58 p., 84 photos.

Kakouri, Katerina J. Dionysiaka: aspects of popular Thracian religion of to-day. Athens, G. C. Eleftheroudakis. 1965. 19, 174 p.

*Kasperson, Roger E. The Dodecanese: diversity and unity in island politics. Department of Geography Research Paper. 108. Chicago, University of Chicago, Geography Department. 1966. 14, 184 p., illus., photos.

Kayser, Bernard. Géographie humaine de la Grèce. Paris, Presses Universitaires de France; Athènes, Centre de Sciences Sociales d'Athènes. 1964. 16, 150 p.

Kayser, Bernard, et al. Margariti. Village d'Épire. Athènes, Centre des Sciences Sociales d'Athènes. 1964. 39 p., plates.

Kazantzakis, Nikos. Journey to the Morea. New York, Simon and Schuster. 1965. 190 p.

Kazantzakis, Nikos. Report to Greco. New York, Simon and Schuster. 1965. 512 p.

Kazavis, Georgiou N. Nisyrou laografika. Nea Yorki, D. C. Divry. 1940. 211 p., illus. (Nisyros Island: folklore.)

Kazavis, Iakovou N. Oi Dodekanisioi. Nea Yorki, Cosmos Greek American Printing Co. 1950. 94 p.

Kendrick, T. C. The Ionian Islands; manners and customs, sketches of the ancient history; . . . London, James Haldane. 1822. 12, 287 p.

Kephala, Euphrosyne. Sketches of eastern church life. London, Faith Press. 1920. 76 p.

Kephala, Euphrosyne. The church of the Greek people past and present. London, Williams & Norgate. 1930. 128 p.

Kephala, Euphrosyne. A Greek church and its furnishings. London, S.P.C.K. 1936. 16 p.

Kimbrough, Emily. Forever old, forever new. New York, Harper & Row. 1964. 241 p.

Kininmonth, Christopher. The children of Thetis. A study of islands and islanders in the Aegean. London, John Lehmann. 1949. 224 p., plates.

Kitto, Humphrey D. F. In the mountains of Greece. London, Methuen. 1933. 9, 150 p.

Kosmetatos-Phokas, K. P. Kephalliniaka. Ai Phoresies. Athenai. 1953. 50 p., 8 plates. (Folk costumes on Kephalonia Island.)

Koty, John. Greece. In Arnold Rose, ed. The institutions of advanced societies. Minneapolis, University of Minnesota Press. 1958: 330-383.

Kyriakidou-Nestoros, Alke. Folk art in Greek Macedonia. Balkan Studies. 4(1963): 15-36, 11 plates.

Lacey, Thomas James. A study of social heredity as illustrated in the Greek people. New York, Edwin S. Gorham. 1916. 76 p.

Ladas, Stephen P. The exchange of minorities: Bulgaria, Greece and Turkey. New York, Macmillan. 1932. 11, 849 p.

Lambiri, Ioanna. The impact of industrial employment on the position of women in a Greek country town. British Journal of Sociology. 14(1963): 240-247.

Lambiri, Ioanna. Social change in a Greek country town: the impact of factory work on the position of women. Research Monograph. 13. Athens, Centre of Planning and Economic Research. 1965. 163 p.

*Lawson, John Cuthbert. Modern Greek folklore and ancient Greek religion: a study in survivals. Cambridge, The University Press. 1910. 12, 620 p.

*League of Nations. Greek refugee settlement. (Translation.) Geneva, Publications of the League of Nations. II. Economic and Financial, 1926. II. 32. Geneva. 1926. 16, 216 p., plates, maps.

Leake, William Martin. The topography of Athens, with some remarks on its antiquities. London, J. Murray. 1821. 3, 114, 435 p., 9 plates.

Leake, William Martin. Travels in the Morea. 3 vols. London, J. Murray. 1830.

Leake, William Martin. Travels in northern Greece. 4 vols. London, J. Rodwell. 1835.

Leake, William Martin. Peloponnesiaca: a supplement to travels in the Morea London, J. Rodwell. 1846. 15, 432 p.

Lee, Clarence P. Athenian adventure, with alarums & excursions. New York, Knopf. 1957. 274 p.

Lee, Dorothy D. Greek accounts of the vrykolakas. J.A.F.L. 55(1942): 126-132.

*Lee, Dorothy D. Greece. In Margaret Mead, ed. Cultural patterns and techni cal change. Paris, New York, UNESCO. 1953: 77-114.

Legrand, Émile Louis J. Recueil de contes populaires grecs. Paris, E. Leroux. 1881. 19, 274 p.

Levy, Harry L. Property distribution by lot in present day Greece. Transaction of the American Philological Association. 87(1956): 42-46.

Lewis, Mrs. Agnes Smith. Glimpses of Greek life and scenery. London, Hurst and Blackett. 1884. 10, 352 p.

Liddell, Robert. Aegean Greece. London, Jonathan Cape. 1954. 284 p., plates.

Liddell, Robert. The Morea. London, Jonathan Cape. 1958. 255 p., plates.

Liddell, Robert. Mainland Greece. London, Longmans. 1965. 225 p.

Loucatos, D. Religion populaire à Céphalonie. Collection de l'Institut Français. 46. Athènes, Institut Français. 1951. 221 p., map.

Loukópoulos, Dimitrios. Aitolikai oikesseis, skeve kai trophai [Aetolian housing, tools and food]. Athens, P. D. Sakellariou. 1926. 145 p.

Ludwig Salvator, Archduke of Austria. Paxos und Antipaxos. Würzburg und Wien, L. Woerl. 1889. 15, 480 p.

*McNeill, William Hardy. Greece: American aid in action. New York, Twentieth Century Fund. 1957. 240 p., plates.

Maloney, George A. The Orthodox Church in Greece today. America. 116, no. 10 (March 1967): 340-345.

Manus, Willard. Kalymnos and its sponge divers. Greek Heritage. 1 (1964): 52-63.

Marangoni, M. Alcune tradizioni popolari vigenti nella Grecia del XXe secole. Sociologica Religiosa. 5-6 (1960): 65-75.

Marketos, Babes I. A proverb for it: 1510 Greek sayings. New York, New World Publishers. 1945. 191 p.

*Marshall, Grace E. Eternal Greece. Rochester, N. Y., Du Bois Press. 1938. 9, 214 p. (Peloponnesos.)

Mattenberger, Heidi, and Paul Schnellmann. Die zwei Gesichter Griechenlands. Zürich, Flamberg Verlag. 1959. 140 p., plates.

Maurer, Georg Ludvig von. Das griechische Volk in öffentlicher, kirchlicher und privatrechtlicher Beziehung vor und nach dem Freiheitskampfe bis zum Juli 1834. 3 vols. Heidelberg, Mohr. 1835.

Mavrogordato, John. Modern Greek folksongs of the dead. Journal of Hellenic Studies. 75(1955): 42-53.

Mavrogordato, John, ed. Digenes Akrites. Oxford, The Clarendon Press. 1956. 273 p.

Mayne, Peter. The private sea. London, J. Murray. 1958. 251 p.

Mears, Eliot G. Greece today; the aftermath of the refugee impact. Stanford, Stanford University Press. 1929. 22, 336 p.

*Megas, George A. The Greek house: its evolution and its relation to the houses of the other Balkan peoples. Series of Publications of the Ministry of Reconstruction. 37. Athens. 1951. 134 p.

Megas, George A. Der Bartlose im neugriechischen Märchen. Folklore Fellows Communications. 157. Helsinki, Suomalainen Tiedeakatemia. 1955. 16 p.

*Megas, George A. Greek calendar customs. Athens, Press and Information Department, Prime Minister's Office. 1958. 159 p. (Other later reprintings.)

Mendras, Henri, et al. Six villages d'Épire. Problèmes de développement socio-économique. Paris, UNESCO. 1961. 92 p., map.

Merrick, Gordon. Hydra. The story its houses tell. Greek Heritage. 2, no. 5(1965): 57-69.

*Michaelides, Constantine E. Hydra: a Greek island town, its growth and form. Chicago, University of Chicago Press. 1967. 93 p., plates, plans.

Michelis, P. A. To elliniko laiko spiti [The Greek secular house]. Athenai, E. M. Polytechneicu. 1960. 350 p., illus.

Miller, Helen Day Hill. Greece. New York, Charles Scribner's Sons. 1965. 190 p.

Miller, Henry. The colossus of Maroussi. New York, New Directions. 1958. 244 p. (Other editions.)

*Miller, William. Greek life in town and country. London, G. Newnes. 1905 10, 310 p., plates.

Miller, William. Greece. London, E. Benn. 1928. 8, 351 p.

Mills, A. Raymond. Peasant remedies from the Greek islands. Bulletin of the History of Medicine. 22(1948): 441-450.

*Moustaka, Calliope. The internal migrant. A comparative study in urbanization. Athens, Social Sciences Centre. 1964. 18, 105 p.

*Moustaka, Calliope. Attitudes, sociometric status and ability in Greek schools Paris, The Hague, Mouton. 1967. 11, 151 p.

National Organization of Hellenic Handicrafts. The handwoven fabrics of Thessaly. Athens, National Organization of Hellenic Handicrafts. 1961. (One volume, mainly of colored illustrations.)

Nicol, Donald P. Meteora. The rock monasteries of Thessaly. London, Chapman & Hall. 1963. 210 p., plates.

Notopoulos, James A. Homeric and Cretan heroic poetry. American Journal of Philology. 73(1952): 225-250.

Notopoulos, James A. The warrior as an oral poet. Classical Weekly. 46(195 17-19.

Notopoulos, James A. Folk music of Greece. Notes by Spyros Peristeres. Folkways Record FE4454. New York, Folkways Records. 1955. (A 12" LP, with a 21-page booklet.)

Notopoulos, James A. Folk dances of Greece. Notes by Spyros Peristeres. Ethnic Folkways Library FE4467. New York, Folkways Records. 1956, 1962. (A 12" LP record, with a 12-page booklet.)

Notopoulos, James A. Modern Greek heroic oral poetry. Ethnic Folkways Library Album FE4468. New York, Folkways Records. 1959. (A 12" LP record, with a 34-page booklet.)

O'Connor, Vincent Clarence S. Isles of the Aegean. London, Hutchinson & Son. 1929. 384 p.

Ogilvie, Alan G. Physiography and settlements in southern Macedonia. Geographical Review. 11 (1921): 172-197.

Orkney, George William F. Four years in the Ionian Islands. Their political and social condition. With a history of the British protectorate. 2 vols. London, Chapman and Hall. 1864.

Orlandos, A. La maison paysanne dans l'île de Rhodes. L'Hellénisme Contemporaine. 2 sér. 1(1947): 223-231.

Paleologas, Emmaline. I married a Greek. Where an English village girl made an international marriage in U.S.A. with a Greek laborer, became the mother of five children summering, sweltering, smiling and suffering through the mountains and lowlands of ancient Greece. Mansfield, Ohio, Stirling Press. 1941. 9, 225 p., plates. (Contains some excellent comments on Greek family life.)

Papas, Constantin Christo. L'urbanisme et l'architecture populaire dans les Cyclades. Paris, Dunod Éditeur. 1957. 12, 155 p., illus., col. plates.

Pappageotes, George C., and James Macris. The language question in modern Greece. Word. Special Publication 5. Supplement to vol. 20, no. 3(Dec. 1964): 53-59.

Pashley, Robert. Travels in Crete. 2 vols. London, J. Murray. 1837.

Passow, Arnold Thomas G. Popularia carmina Graeciae recentioris. Leipzig, Teubner. 1860. 11, 650 p.

Paton, W. R. Sacrifices to the dead. Folk-Lore. 5(1894): 164-166.

Paton, W. R. Folk-medicine, nursery-lore, etc., from the Aegean Islands. Folk-Lore. 18(1907): 329-331. (Mainly from Cos.)

Paton, W. R., and W. R. Halliday. Modern Greek carols in honour of St. Basil. Annual of the British School at Athens. 20(1913-1914): 32-58.

Pentzopoulos, Dimitri. The Balkan exchange of minorities and its impact upon Greece. Paris, Mouton. 1962. 293 p.

Pepelasis, A. A. The image of the past and economic backwardness. Human Organization. 17, no. 4(1958-1959): 19-27.

Perdicaris, G. A. The Greece of the Greeks. 2 vols. New York, Paine and Burgess. 1845.

Perrot, Georges. L'Île de Crète. Paris, L. Hachette. 1867. 31, 278 p.

Perspective of Greece. An Atlantic supplement. Atlantic. 195, no. 6(1955): 97-168.

Petrides, Theodore, and Elfleida Petrides. Folk dances of the Greeks. New York, Exposition Press. 1961. 78 p.

Petropoulos, D. A. Ethima synergasias kai allelovoetheias tou hellenikou laou [Customs of collaboration and mutual-aid of the Greek people] . Epeteris Laographikou Archeiou. 1943-1944: 59-85.

Petropoulos, Demetrios. The study of ethnography in Greece. Midwest Folklore. 2(1952): 15-20.

Philippson, Alfred. Zur Ethnographie des Peloponnes. Petermann's Geographische Mitteilungen. 36(1890): 1-11, 33-41, map.

Philippson, Alfred. Der Peloponnes. Versuch einer Landeskunde auf geologischer Grundlage. Nach Ergebnissen eigner Reisen. Berlin, R. Friedländer und Sohn. 1892. 7, 4, 642 p.

Philippson, Alfred. Thessalien und Epirus. Reisen und Forschungen im nördlichen Griechenland. Berlin, W. H. Kühl. 1897. 11, 422 p., 8 maps.

Photiadis, John Democritos. The coffee house and its role in the village of Stavroupolis, Greece. Ithaca, N. Y. 1957. 7, 187 p. (Unpublished M. S. thesis. Cornell University.)

Photiadis, John Democritos. The position of the coffee house in the social structure of the Greek village. Sociologia Ruralis. 5(1965): 45-56.

Politis, N. G. Croyances populaires sur le rétablissement de la nation hellénique. Revue de Grèce. 1 (1919): 151-170.

Pollard, John. Journey to the Styx. London, Christopher Johnson. 1955. 216 p., illus.

*Pollis, Adamantia. Political implications of the modern Greek concept of self. British Journal of Sociology. 16 (1965): 29-47.

Polyzos, Nicos J. Essai sur l'émigration grecque; étude démographique, économique et sociale. Paris, Recueil Sirey. 1947. 247 p.

Pouqueville, François C. H. L. Voyage en Morée, à Constantinople, en Albanie, et dans plusieurs autres parties de l'Empire Othoman, pendant les années 1798, 1799, 1800 et 1801. 3 vols. Paris, Gabon. 1805.

Pouqueville, François C. H. L. Travels through the Morea, Albania, and several other parts of the Ottoman Empire. London, H. Colburn. 1813. 12, 482 p.

Pouqueville, François C. H. L. Voyage dans la Grèce. 5 vols. Paris, Firmin Didot. 1820.

Pouqueville, François C. H. L. Travels in southern Epirus, Acarnania, Aetolia, Attica and Peloponesus, or the Morea, &c. &c. in the years 1814-1816. London, Sir R. Phillips. 1822. 128 p.

Psychoundakis, George. The Cretan runner: his story of the German occupation. London, J. Murray. 1955. 11, 242 p.

Rennell, James Rennell Rodd, Baron. The customs and lore of modern Greece. London, D. Stott. 1892. 16, 294 p.

Rhodokanakes, Konstantinos. Athens and the Greek miracle. London, Routledge & Kegan Paul. 1948. 11, 194 p. (Reprinted: Boston, Beacon Press. 1951. 11, 194 p.)

Rinvolucri, Mario. Anatomy of a church. Greek orthodoxy today. London, Burns & Oates. 1966. 192 p.

Robertson, D. S. A Greek carnival. Journal of Hellenic Studies. 39(1919): 110-115.

Rohlfs, G. La Grecia Italica. Anthropos. 23(1928): 1021-1028. 15 illus., 1 plate. (Greeks in southern Italy.)

Roland, Betty. Lesbos, the pagan island. London, Angus and Robertson; Melbourne, F. W. Cheshire. 1963. 164 p., 23 illus.

Romaios, C. Cultes populaires de la Thrace. Collection de l'Institut Français. 18. Athens, Institut Français. 1949. 15, 213 p., 5 illus., map.

Roussel, Louis. Karagheuz, ou un théâtre d'ombres à Athènes. 2 vols. Athènes, Imprimerie de A. Raftanis. 1921. 52, 60; 116 p.

Ruheman, Barbara. Ghost marriages. Man. 48(1948): 60.

Safilios-Rothschild, Constantina. Morality, courtship, and love in Greek folklore. Southern Folklore Quarterly. 29(1965): 297-308.

Safilios-Rothschild, Constantina. Some aspects of fertility in urban Greece. Proceedings of the World Population Conference, 1965. 2(1967): 228-231. New York, United Nations Department of Economic and Social Affairs.

Safilios-Rothschild, Constantina. Class position and success stereotypes in Greek and American cultures. Social Forces. 45(1967): 374-383.

Safilios-Rothschild, Constantina. Comparison of power structure and marital satisfaction in urban Greek and French families. Journal of Marriage and the Family. 29(1967): 345-352.

Safilios-Rothschild, Constantina. "Good" and "bad" girls in modern Greek movies. Journal of Marriage and the Family. 30(1968): 527-531.

*Safilios-Rothschild, Constantina. Socio-psychological factors affecting fertility in urban Greece: a preliminary report. Journal of Marriage and the Family. (In press 1968.)

Safilios-Rothschild, Constantina. "Honor" crimes in contemporary Greece. British Journal of Sociology. 20(1969): 205-218.

*Saloutos, Theodore. They remember America: the story of the repatriated Greek-Americans. Berkeley, University of California Press. 1956. 18, 152 p.

Sanders, Daniel Hendel. Das Volksleben der Neugriechen dargestellt und erklärt aus Liedern, Sprichwörtern . . . Mannheim, Vassermann. 1844.

Sanders, Irwin T. Village social organization in Greece. Rural Sociology. 18(1953): 366-375.

*Sanders, Irwin T. Rainbow in the rock: the people of rural Greece. Cambridge, Harvard University Press. 1962. 363 p., plates.

Sandys, George. Sandys travailes: containing a history of the originall and present state of the Turkish empire . . . the Mahometan religion and ceremonies. A description of Canstantinople . . . also, of Greece . . . of Egypt . . . 5th ed. London, J. Svveeting. 1652. 2, 240 p. (Original edition: 1615.)

Schmidt, B. Totenbräuche und Gräberkultus im heutigen Griechenland. Archiv für Religionswissenschaft. 24(1926/27): 281-318; 25(1927/28): 52-82.

*Schmidt, Bernard. Das Volksleben der Neugriechen und das hellenische Altertum. Leipzig, Teubner. 1871. 252 p. (Emphasis on the Ionian Islands.)

Schmidt, Bernard. Die Insel Zakynthos. Erlebtes und Erforschtes. Freiburg im Breisgau, Friedrich Ernst Fehenfeld. 1899. 11, 177 p.

Scott, Charles Rochfort. Rambles in Egypt and Candia; with details of the military power and resources of those countries, and observations on the government, policy and commercial system of Mohammed Ali. 2 vols. London, H. Colburn. 1837.

Sebright, Georgina Mary Muir Mackenzie, and A. P. Irby. Travels in the Slavonic provinces of Turkey-in-Europe. 2 vols. 5th ed. London, Dalby, Isbister. 1877.

Sieber, Franz Wilhelm. Reise nach der Insel Kreta im griechischen Archipelagus im Jahre 1817. 2 vols. Leipzig und Sorau, Fleischer. 1822.

Simpson, Evan John. Time after earthquake: an adventure among Greek islands in August 1953. London, Heinemann. 1954. 140 p.

Skinner, John Edwin Hilary. Roughing it in Crete in 1867. London, R. Bentley. 1868. 32, 272 p., folding map.

Skouvaras, Vangelis. Meteora the sacred rocks of Thessaly. Greek Heritage. 1, no. 4(1964): 50-62.

Smith, Agnes [later Mrs. Agnes Lewis]. Glimpses of Greek life and scenery. London, Hurst & Blackett. 1884. 10, 352 p.

Smith, Arnold C., and Philip Argenti, eds. The architecture of Chios (1450-1900); subsidiary buildings, implements and crafts. London, A. Tiranti. 1962. 8, 171 p., illus., plates.

Smith, Michael Llewellyn. The great island; a study of Crete. London, Longmans. 1965. 182 p.

Smithsonian Institution. Greek costumes and embroideries from the Benaki Museum, Athens. Washington, Smithsonian Institution. 1959. 39 p., plates.

Smothers, Frank, et al. Report on the Greeks . . . New York, Twentieth Century Fund. 1948. 16, 226 p., illus.

Smyth, H. W. The dialects of northern Greece. American Journal of Philology. 7 (1886): 421-445.

Smyth, H. W. The sounds and inflections of the Greek dialects. Oxford, The Clarendon Press. 1894. 27, 668 p.

Sophocles, S. M. The religion of modern Greece. Thessaloniki, Institute for Balkan Studies. 1961. 74 p. (Mainly history.)

Spanos, Dem. Gr. Psariani laographia [Psarian folklore]. Athens. 1962. 152 p.

Stadi, Demetrio. Les fondaments psychologiques du devenir néo-grec. Mercure de France. 218 (May 1, 1930): 513-553.

Stephanides, Charalambos. A sociological sketch of the village of Megali Vrisi, Greece. Ithaca, N. Y. 1941. 108 p. (Unpublished M. A. thesis. Cornell University.)

Stephanopoli, Dimo, and Nicolo Stephanopoli. Voyage de Dimo et Nicolo Stephanopoli en Grèce pendant les années V et VI (1797 et 1798 v. st) . . . 2 vols. Paris, Guilleminet. An VIII. (1800) 16, 303; 319 p. (A careful description of the manners and customs of the people of Maina.)

GREEKS

Stroup, Herbert. Social change in Greece. Sociology and Social Research. 39(1955): 387-393.

Stycos, J. M. Patterns of communication in a rural Greek village. Public Opinion Quarterly. 16(1952): 59-70.

Summers, Montague. The vampire in Europe. New York, E. P. Dutton. 1929: 217-281.

Swanson, Donald C. Vocabulary of modern spoken Greek. Minneapolis, University of Minnesota Press. 1959: 1-63.

Tarsouli, Athena N. Ellinikes foresies. Costumes grecs. Athenai, V. Papachrysanthou. 1941. 12 p., 65 plates.

*Tarsouli, Athena N. Dodekanesa. 3 vols. 1: Rodos, Karpathos, Kasos, Chalk 2: Patmos, Leros, Kalymnos, Astypalia. 3: Kos, Nisyros, Tilos, Symi, Kasteloriso. Athens, Alpha Press. 1947, 1948, 1950. 331 p., illus; 357 p., illus.; 430 p., illus. (One of the finest works on folklore and folk life for any region of Greece.)

Tarsouli, Athena N. Embroideries and costumes of the Dodecanese. Athens. 1951. 14 p., 68 col. plates.

Tarsouli, Georgia. Christmas in Greece. Midwest Folklore. 3(1953): 231-235.

Theotokos, George. Some questions of the psychology of the modern Greeks. The Link: A Review of Mediaeval and Modern Greek. 1 (June 1938): 66-70.

*Thompson, Kenneth. Farm fragmentation in Greece: the problem and its setting, with 11 village case studies. Research Monograph Series No. 5. Athens, Center of Economic Research. 1963. 23, 263 p.

Thumb, A. Zur neugriechischen Volkskunde, 1-3. Z.d.V.f.V. 2(1892): 123-134, 285-293, 392-406.

Thumb, A. Die Maniaten. Ein Beitrag zur Volkskunde des heutigen Griechenlands. Deutsche Revue. 24(1898): 110-127.

Tozer, Henry F. Researches in the highlands of Turkey . . . Notes on the ballads, tales and classical superstitions of the modern Greeks. 2 vols. London, John Murray. 1869.

Tozer, Henry F. The islands of the Aegean. London, Oxford, The Clarendon Press. 1890. 12, 362 p.

Trant, Capt. T. Abercromby. Narrative of a journey through Greece in 1830. London, Henry Colburn and Richard Bentley. 1830. 11, 435 p., illus.

Trevor-Battye, Aubyn Bernard R. Camping in Crete: with notes on the animal and plant life of the island. London, Witherby. 1913. 21, 308 p.

Triandis, Harry C., Vasso Vassiliou, and Erich K. Thomanek. Social status as a determinant of respect and friendship acceptance. Sociometry. 29(1966): 396-405.

*Tuckerman, Charles K. The Greeks of today. New York, G. P. Putnam & Sons. 1872. 366 p.

Tuckerman, Charles K. Political characteristics of modern Greeks. Harper's Magazine. 45(1872): 538-546.

Valassis, Vlassios T. The living past and technical change. College Park, Md. 1956. (Unpublished M.A. thesis. University of Maryland.)

Varvaressos, A. Land ownership in Greece. Foreign Agriculture. 14(1950): 180-183.

Vonderlage, Bernard. Das griechische Osterfest; ein Einblick in die Oster-liturgie der Ostkirche, sieben Osternovellen moderner griechischer Autoren. Hamburg, de Gruyter. 1952. 127 p.

Vooys, A. C. de. Western Thessaly in transition. Tijdschrift van het Konink-lijk Nederlandsch Aardrijkskundig Genootschap. 2 reeks. 76(1959): 31-54.

Wace, A. J. B., and R. M. Dawkins. Greek embroideries. Burlington Maga-zine. 26(Nov. 1914): 49-50; (Dec. 1914): 99-107. 5 figs., 2 plates.

Walker, Mary Adelaide. Through Macedonia to the Albanian lakes. London, Chapman & Hall. 1864. 11, 274 p.

Walker, Mary Adelaide. Some Greek folklore. Folk-Lore Journal. 1(1883): 217-220.

Walker, Mary Adelaide. Eastern life and scenery, with excursions in Asia Minor, Mytilene, Crete, and Roumania. 2 vols. London, Chapman & Hall. 1886.

Walpole, Rev. Robert, ed. Memoirs relating to European and Asiatic Turkey . . . London, Longman, Hurst, Rees, Orme, and Brown. 1818. 22, 615 p.

Walpole, Rev. Robert, ed. Travels in the various countries of the east; being a continuation of Memoirs relating to European and Asiatic Turkey . . . London, Longman, Hurst, Rees, Orme, and Brown. 1820. 21, 603, 8 p.

Whipple, Clayton E. The agriculture of Crete. Foreign Agriculture. 7(1943) 212-216.

Whipple, Clayton E. The agriculture of Greece. Foreign Agriculture. 8(1944): 75-96.

Wilcox, George M. Education in modern Greece. New York, 1933. (Unpublished Ph. D. dissertation. Columbia University.)

Wilkinson, Henry R. Maps and politics: a review of the ethnographic cartography of Macedonia. Liverpool, University of Liverpool Press. 1951. 16, 366 p., maps.

*Zarraphtes, Iakobos E. (Richard M. Dawkins, ed.) Forty-five stories from the Dodecanese. Cambridge, The University Press. 1950. 11, 559 p.

Brewster, R. The six thousand beards of Athos. New York, Appleton. 1936. 219 p.

Byron, Robert. The Station Athos: treasures and men. London, Duckworth. 1928. 292 p. (Reprinted: New York, Knopf. 1949. 263 p.)

Cavarnos, Constantine. Anchored in God. Life, art, and thought on the holy mountain of Athos. Athens, Astir Publishing Co. 1959. 230 p., illus.

*Choukas, Michael. Black angels of Athos. Brattleboro, Vt., Stephen Daye Press. 1934. 23, 327 p., plates.

Curzon, Robert. Visits to the monasteries in the Levant. London, John Murray. 1849. 23, 390 p. (See pp. 282-390 for Athos and pp. 204-281 for Meteora. Reprinted: Ithaca, N.Y., Cornell University Press. 1956. 351 p., illus.)

Dawkins, Richard McGillivray. The monks of Athos. London, G. Allen & Unwin. 1936. 408 p.

Dawkins, Richard McGillivray. Notes on life in the monasteries of Mount Athos. Harvard Theological Review. 46(1953): 217-231.

Décarreaux, Jean. Une république de moines. Paris, Fayard. 1956. 156 p.

Dölger, Franz. Mönchsland Athos. München, F. Bruckmann. 1943. 303 p., 188 illus.

Eller, K. Der heilige Berg Athos, Landschaft, Kloster, Mensch, Kunst. München-Planegg, O. W. Barth. 1954. 239 p., plates.

Fallmerayer, Jacob Philipp. Hagion-Oros oder der heilige Berg Athos. Wien, Thomas Morus Presse. 1949. 162 p.

Georgirenes, Joseph, Archbishop of Samos. Description of the present state of Samos, Nicaria, Patmos and Mount Athos. London, W. G. for M. Pitt. 1678. 112 p.

Hasluck, Frederick William. Athos and its monasteries. London, Kegan Paul, Trench, Trubner; New York, E. P. Dutton. 1924. 12, 213 p.

Kästner, Erhart. Die Stundentrommel vom heiligen Berg Athos. Wiesbaden, Insel Verlag. 1956. 254 p.

Kästner, Erhart. Mount Athos, the call from sleep. London, Faber & Faber. 1961. 192 p.

Leake, William M. Travels in northern Greece. London, J. Rodwell. 1835. (See vol. 3, Chapter 25.)

*Loch, Sidney. Athos, the holy mountain. London, Lutterworth Press. 1957. 264 p.

Nicol, Donald M. Meteora. The rock monasteries of Thessaly. London, Chapman & Hall. 1963. 210 p.

Perilla, Francesco. Le Mont Athos. Salonique, l'auteur; Paris, J. Danguin. 1927. 3, 15, 188 p., plates.

Perkins, Elizabeth. With the monks at Meteora: the monasteries of Thessaly. National Geographic Magazine. 20(1909): 799-807.

Rand, Christopher. Christmas in Bethlehem, and Holy Week at Mount Athos. New York, Oxford University Press. 1963. 168 p.

Riley, Athelstan. Athos; or the mountain of the monks. London, Longmans, Green. 1887. 14, 409 p.

Rinvolucri, Mario. Anatomy of a church. Greek Orthodoxy today. London, Burns & Oates. 1966: 61-80.

*Sherrard, Philip. Athos, the mountain of silence. London, New York, Oxford University Press. 1960. 8, 110 p., plates.

Sofronii, Archimandrite. The undistorted image: Staretz Siluan, 1866-1938. (Translated from the Russian by Rosemary Edmonds.) London, Faith Press. 1958. 207 p.

Stewart, Cecil. Byzantine legacy. London, Allen & Unwin. 1949. 202 p., plates, illus.

Valentin, Jacques. Monks of Mount Athos. London, Andre Deutsch. 1960. 191 p.

Campbell, John K. The kindred in a Greek mountain community. In Julian Pitt-Rivers, ed. Mediterranean countrymen. Paris, Mouton. 1963: 73-96.

*Campbell, John K. Honour, family and patronage. A study of institutions and moral values in a Greek mountain community. Oxford, The Clarendon Press. 1964. 11, 393 p., 5 plates, map.

Campbell, John K. Honour and the devil. In J. G. Peristiany, ed. Honour and shame. The values of Mediterranean society. London, Weidenfeld and Nicolson. 1965: 139-170.

Fermor, Patrick Leigh. The black departers. An adventure in Greece. Atlantic. 209, no. 6 (June 1962): 73-88.

Fermor, Patrick Leigh. Roumeli. Travels in northern Greece. London, John Murray. 1966: 3-63, 235-236.

Georgacas, D. J. Peri tes kataloges ton Sarakatsanaion kai tou onomatos auton [Concerning the origin of the Sarakatsans and their name]. Archeion Thrakikou Glossikou. 14 (1948-1949): 193-270.

*Hatzimihali, Angeliki. I Sarakatsanoi. 2 vols. Athens, the author. 1957.

Höeg, Carsten. Les Saracatsans, une tribu Nomadique grecque. 2 vols. Paris, É. Champion; Copenhagen, V. Pio P. Branner.

*Kavadias, Georges B. Pasteurs-nomades méditerranéens. Les Saracatsans de Grèce. Paris, Gauthier-Villars. 1965. 11, 444 p., 109 figs.

*Marinow, Wasil. Die Schafzucht der nomadisierenden Karakatschanen in Bulgarien. In László Földes, ed. Viehzucht und Hirtenleben in Ostmitteleuropa. Budapest, Akadémiai Kiadó. 1961: 147-196.

Peters, H. B. Karakatschani: Nomaden mitten in Europa. Atlantis. 8 (1936): 286-288.

Dephner, Michail. Deigmata Tzakionikis. Laographia. 10(1921): 159-180. (General ethnographic notes.)

Deville, Gustave. Étude du dialecte Tzakonien. Paris, Impr. de A. Laine et J. Havard. 1866. 140 p.

Hatzimihali, Angeliki. I tsakoniki phoresia tou prastou. Peloponnisiaki Protochronia. 6(1962): 123-129. (Tzakonian costumes.)

*Thumb, Albert. Die ethnographische Stellung der Zakonen. Indogermanische Forschung. 4(1894): 195-213.

Kyparissiotis, Nove, ed. The modern Greek collection in the library of the University of Cincinnati. A Catalogue. Athens, Greece, Hestia Press for the University of Cincinnati Library. 1960. 16, 380 p.

Swanson, Donald C. Modern Greek studies in the West; a critical bibliography of studies on modern Greek philology and folklore, in languages other than Greek. New York, New York Public Library. 1960. 93 p.

Akoglou, X. Apo ti zoi tou Pontou. Laografia Kotyoron. Athens. 1939. 532 p. (Folk life in the Pontos.)

Dawkins, Richard McGillivray. Modern Greek in Asia Minor; a study of the dialects of Sílli, Cappadocia and Phárasa, with grammar, texts, translations and glossary; with a chapter on the subject-matter of the folk-tales. Cambridge, The University Press. 1916. 12, 695 p.

Eckert, Georg, and P. E. Formozis. Geister- und Dämonenglaube im Pontus. Nach Mitteilungen von Charilaos Serassis. Volkskundliche Miszellen aus Mazedonien. 3. Thessaloniki. 1943. 45 p.

Finger, Sep. Märchen aus Laristan. M. A. G. W. 69 (1939): 174-224.

*Garnett, Lucy Mary Jane. The women of Turkey and their folk-lore. Vol. 1. The Christian women. London, David Nutt. 1890: 30-193.

Halliday, W. R. A Greek marriage in Cappadocia. Folk-Lore. 23(1912): 81-88, 4 plates.

Ladas, Stephen P. The exchange of minorities; Bulgaria, Greece and Turkey. New York, Macmillan. 1932. 11, 849 p.

Leake, William Martin. Journal of a tour in Asia Minor, with comparative remarks on the ancient and modern geography of that country. London, J. Murray. 1824. 27, 362 p.

Mengous, Petros. Narrative of a Greek soldier: containing anecdotes and occurrences illustrating the character and manners of the Greeks and Turks in Asia Minor, and detailing events of the late war in Greece, in which the author was actively engaged by land and sea, . . . New York, Elliot and Palmer. 1830. 256 p.

Vaka, Demetra [Mrs. Kenneth Brown]. A child of the orient. Boston, Houghton Mifflin. 1914. 297 p. (Sea of Marmara area.)

United States. Bureau of the Census. Bibliography of social science periodicals and monograph series: Turkey, 1950-1962. Washington, Government Printing Office. 1964. 4, 88 p.

Afetinan, A. The emancipation of the Turkish woman. Paris, UNESCO. 1962. 63 p.

Andreades, K. G. The Moslem minority in western Thrace. Publication No. 12. Thessaloniki, Institute for Balkan Studies. 1956. 96 p., 12 figs. (Mainly political problems, somewhat propagandistic.)

Baker, James. Turkey in Europe. London, Paris, and New York, Cassell, Petter & Galpin. 1877. 15, 560 p., 2 maps.

Bayri, Halit. Istanbul folkloru. Istanbul, Turkiye Yayinevi. 1947. 236 p.

Boué, Ami. La Turkuie d'Europe; ou, observations sur la géographie, la géologie, l'histoire naturelle, la statistique, les moeurs, les coutumes, l'archéologie, l'agriculture, l'industrie, le commerce, les gouvernements divers, le clergé, l'histoire et l'état politique de cet empire. 4 vols. Paris, A. Bertrand. 1840.

Boué, Ami. Die europäische Türkei. (Translated from the French.) 2 vols. Wien, F. Tempsky. 1889.

Colton, Rev. Walter. Land and lee in the Bosphorus and Aegean; or views of Constantinople and Athens. New York, A. S. Barnes. 1851. 366 p.

Eliot, Sir Charles N. E. Turkey in Europe. London, Edward Arnold. 1908. 475 p., maps.

Evliyā, Efendi. Turkish instruments of music in the 17th century, as described in the Siyāhat nāma of Ewliyā Chelebī. Glasgow, Civic Press. 1937. 6, 45 p.

Ferriman, Z. Duckett. Turkey and the Turks. London, Mills & Boon. 1911. 9, 334 p.

*Garnett, Lucy Mary Jane. The women of Turkey and their folk-lore. Vol. 2. The Jewish and Moslem women. London, David Nutt. 1891: 382-546.

*Garnett, Lucy Mary Jane. Turkish life in town and country. New York and London, G. P. Putnam's Sons. 1904. 8, 336 p., plates.

Garnett, Lucy Mary Jane. The Turkish people, their social life, religious beliefs and institutions, and domestic life. London, Methuen. 1909. 16, 296 p.

Garnett, Lucy Mary Jane. Home life in Turkey. New York, Macmillan. 1909. 16, 296 p.

Garnett, Lucy Mary Jane. Turkey of the Ottomans. London, Sir I. Pitman & Sons. 1911. 304 p.

Garnett, Lucy Mary Jane. Mysticism and magic in Turkey, an account of the religious doctrines, monastic organisation, and ecstatic powers of the Dervish orders. London, Sir I. Pitman & Sons; New York, C. Scribner's Sons. 1912. 10, 202 p., plates.

*Johnson, Clarence Richard. Constantinople to-day or the Pathfinder survey of Constantinople. A study in Oriental social life. New York, Macmillan. 1922. 418 p.

Lejean, Guillaume. Ethnographie de la Turquie d'Europe. Gotha, J. Perthes. 1861. 38 p.

Németh, Gyula. Die Türken von Vidin. Sprache, Folklore, Religion. Budapest, Akadémiai Kiadó. 1965. 419 p.

Pardoe, Julia. The city of the sultan, and domestic manners of the Turks in 1836. 2 vols. London, Henry Colburn. 1837.

Patrick, Mary Mills. The emancipation of Mohammedan women. National Geographic Magazine. 20(1909): 42-66.

Porter, Sir James. Observations on the religion, law, government, and manners of the Turks. London, J. Nourse. 1768. 2d ed. 1771. 36,464 p.

Suzuki, Peter. Encounters with Istanbul: urban peasants and village peasants. International Journal of Comparative Sociology. 5(1964): 208-215.

Vaka, Demetra [Mrs. Kenneth Brown]. Haremlik. Some pages from the life of Turkish women. Boston and New York, Houghton Mifflin. 1909. 275 p.

White, Charles. Three years in Constantinople, or, domestic manners of the Turks in 1844. 2d ed. 3 vols. London, Henry Colburn. 1846.

ALBANIANS

Kersopoulos, Jean G. Albanie. Bibliographie des ouvrages et articles de revues parus de 1555 à 1934. Athènes, Flamna. 1934. 114 p.

Krallert-Sattler, Gertrud. Südosteuropa Bibliographie. 3 vols. to date. Bd. 1: 1945-1950. Bd. 2: 1951-1955. Bd. 3: 1956-1960. München, R. Oldenbourg. 1956--

Legrand, Émile Louis Jean. Bibliographie albanaise; description raisonnée des ouvrages pub. en albanais ou relatifs à l'Albanie du quinzième siècle à l'année 1900. Paris, H. Walter. 1912. 8, 228 p.

Manek, F., et al. Albanische Bibliographie. Wien, Gerold. 1909. 12, 147 p.

Mann, Stuart Edward. Albanian literature; an outline of prose, poetry and drama. London, B. Quaritch. 1955. 5, 121 p.

Stockmann, E. Völkerkundliche Bibliographie Albaniens von 1945-1956. Deutsches Jahrbuch für Volkskunde. 2(1958): 203-209.

United States. Bureau of the Census. Bibliography of social science periodicals and monograph series: Albania, 1944-1961. Washington, Government Printing Office. 1962. 16 p.

Adhami, S. Les musées albanais [Museums in Albania]. Museum. 13 (1960): 67-73.

Almagià, Roberto. Modern Albania: a review. Geographical Review. 22 (1932): 464-473.

Andrasfalvy, B. Formen der albanischen Weinbaues. Acta Ethnographica. 11 (1962): 293-373.

Archetti, Sandro. Sula pescosità delle acque interne e sull' industria peschereccia in Albania. Accademia Scientifica Veneto-Trentino-Istriana, Padova Atti. Ser. 3. 22(1931): 119-127.

Archiv za arbanasku starina, jezik i etnologiju [Archives for Albanian antiquity, language and ethnology]. Belgrade. 1923-1926. (Vols. 1-3 only.)

Arti në Republikën të Shqipërisë. Berlin, V.E.B. Deutscher Zentral-verlag. 1953. 72 p., plates. (Albanian folk art.)

Baldacci, Antonio. Itinerari Albanesi (1892-1902) con uno squardo generale all'Albania e alle sue comunicazioni stradali. Roma, Reale Società Geografica Italiana. 1917. 23, 541 p.

Balota, Anton B. Albania și Albanezii [Albania and the Albanians] . Al-
   banica. 1. București, Tip. Leopolod Geller. 1936. 434 p.

Barbarich, Eugenio Giovanni G. Albania (Monografia antropogeografica).
   Roma, E. Voghera. 1905. 20, 344 p.

Bernatzik, Hugo Adolf. Albanien. Das Land der Skipetaren. Wien, L. W.
   Seidel. 1931. 96 p., plates.

Best, James John. Excursions in Albania; comprising a description of the wild
   boar, deer, and woodcock shooting in that country, and a journey from
   thence to Thessalonica & Constantinople, and up the Danube to Pest. London, W. H. Allen. 1842. 12, 359 p.

Blanc, A. Recherches sur les communautés patriarchales et les structures
   agraires en Albanie du nord. Bulletin de l'Association de Géographes
   Français. 292/293 (1960): 117-128.

Bonasera, F. Il'Bazar nei centri Albanesi. Lares. 20 (1954): 129-134.

Bourcart, Jacques. L'Albanie et les Albanais. Paris, Éditions Bossard. 1921.
   264 p.

Brailsford, Henry Noel. Macedonia: its races and their future. London,
   Methuen. 1906. 20, 340 p.

Broughton, John Cam Hobhouse. A journey through Albania, and other provinces of Turkey in Europe and Asia, to Constantinople, during the years
   1809 and 1810. London, J. Cawthorn. 1813. 19, 1152 p., 17 col. plates,
   6 folding maps, 2 folding maps.

Brown, H. A. A winter in Albania. London, Griffith, Farrow, Okeden &
   Welsh. 1888. 8, 295 p.

Çabej, E. Sitten und Gebräuche der Albaner. Revue Internationale des Études
   Balkaniques. 1 (1934): 556-572.

Chater, Melville. Europe's newest kingdom. National Geographic Magazine.
   59 (1931): 131-182.

Chekrezi, Constantin Anastasi. Albania past and present. New York, Macmillan. 1919. 15, 255 p., maps.

*Coon, Carleton. The mountains of giants: a racial and cultural study of the
   North Albanian mountain Ghegs. Papers of the Peabody Museum of American Archaeology and Ethnology, Harvard University. 23, no. 3. 1950.
   8, 105 p.

Cooper, Paul Fenimore. Tricks of the women & other Albanian tales. New York, W. Morrow. 1928. 16, 204 p.

Cozzi, Ernesto. Malattie, morte, funerali nelle montagne Albanesi. Anthropos. 4(1909): 903-918.

Cozzi, Ernesto. Lo stato agricalo in Albania, con speciale riguardo alle montagne di Scutari. Revue d'Ethnographie et de Sociologie. 1 (1910): 33-49.

Cozzi, Ernesto. La vendetta del sangue. Anthropos. 5(1910): 654-687.

Cozzi, Ernesto. La donna Albanese. Anthropos. 7(1912): 309-335, 617-626.

Cozzi, Ernesto. Credenze e superstizioni nelle montagne dell'Albania. Anthropos. 9(1914): 449-476.

Dako, Christo A. Albania, the master key to the Near East. Boston, E. L. Grimes. 1919. 12, 290 p., maps. (Only Chapter 1 is of any value: primarily a political polemic.)

Damon, Theron J. The Albanians. National Geographic Magazine. 23(1912): 1090-1103.

Degrand, Jules Alexandre T. Souvenirs de la haute-Albanie. Paris, H. Welter. 1901. 333 p.

Dibra, J., and P. Vako. La population de l'Albanie d'après des recensements de 1955 à 1960. Population. 20(1965): 253-264.

Dozon, Auguste. Contes albanais. Paris, E. Leroux. 1881. 27, 264 p.

Durham, Mary Edith. The burden of the Balkans. London, E. Arnold. 1906. 12, 331 p.

*Durham, Mary Edith. High Albania. London, E. Arnold, 1909. 12, 352 p.

Durham, Mary Edith. High Albania and its customs in 1908. J.R.A.I. 40(1910): 453-472.

Durham, Mary Edith. Head-hunting in the Balkans. Man. 23(1923): 19-21.

Durham, Mary Edith. A bird tradition in the Balkans. Man. 23(1923): 55-61.

Durham, Mary Edith. Some Balkan embroidery patterns. Man. 23(1923): 69-72.

Durham, Mary Edith. Some Balkan taboos. Man. 23 (1923): 83-85.

Durham, Mary Edith. The seclusion of maidens from the light of the sun, and a further note on the bird tradition in the Balkans. Man. 23(1923): 102-103.

Durham, Mary Edith. Some Balkan remedies for disease. Man. 23(1923): 131-135.

*Durham, Mary Edith. Some tribal origins, laws and customs of the Balkans. London, G. Allen & Unwin. 1928. 318 p., illus., plates.

Eckert, Georg. Eine Kula bei Saloniki. Z.f.E. 75(1950): 105-107.

Edmonds, Paul. To the land of the eagle; travels in Montenegro and Albania. London, G. Routledge & Sons. 1927. 15, 288 p.

Eliot, Sir Charles N. Turkey in Europe. London, Edward Arnold. 1908. 475 p., 2 folding maps.

*Erlich, Vera St. Family in transition. A study of 300 Yugoslav villages. Princeton, Princeton University Press. 1966. 656 p. (Some data on Albanians in Yugoslavia.)

Federal Writers' Project. Massachusetts. The Albanian struggle in the old world and new. Boston, The Writer. 1939. 9, 168 p.

Frashëri, Stavre Th. Some Albanian games. Folk-Lore. 40(1929): 369-374.

Galanti, Arturo. L'Albania. Notizie geografiche, etnografiche e storiche. Biblioteca Italo-Albanese. 1. Roma. 1901. 261 p.

Garnett, Lucy Mary Jane. The women of Turkey and their folk-lore. Vol. 2. The Jewish and Moslem women. London, David Nutt. 1891: 214-345.

Garnett, Lucy Mary Jane. Turkish life in town and country. London, George Newnes. 1904: 147-158.

Gjecov, Stetano Constantino. Codice di Lek Dukagjini, ossia diritto cosuetudinario delle montagne d'Albania. Tradotto del P. Paolo Dodaj. Publications, No. 2. Roma, Centro Studi per l'Albania. 1941. 337 p.

Gopčevitch, Spiridion. Oberalbanien und seine Liga. Ethnographisch-politisch-historisch. Leipzig, Duncker & Humblot. 1881. 20, 586 p.

Gopčevitch, Spiridion. Das Fürstentum Albanien, seine Vergangenheit, ethnographischen Verhältnisse, politische Lage und Aussichten für die Zukunft. Berlin, H. Paetel. 1914. 4, 364 p.

*Great Britain. Naval Intelligence Division. Albania. Oxford, prepared by the Oxford Sub-Centre. 1945. 416 p., illus., maps.

Grothe, Hugo. Durch Albanien und Montenegro. München, M. Mörike. 1913. 224 p.

Haberlandt, Arthur. Kulturwissenschaftliche Beiträge zur Volkskunde von Montenegro, Albanien und Serbien. Z.f.Ö.V. Ergänzungsband. 12. Wien, Verein für Österreichische Volkskunde. 1917. 8, 187 p.

*Hahn, Johann Georg von. Albanesische Studien . . . nebst einer Karte und andern artistischen Beilagen. 3 vols. Jena, Mauke. 1854. 13, 347; 6, 169; 8, 244 p.

Hahn, Johann Georg von. Reise durch die Gebiete des Drin und Wardar im Auftrage der Kaiserl. Akademie der Wissenschaften, . . . im Jahre 1863. Kaiserliche Akademie der Wissenschaften, Wien. Philosophisch-historische Classe. Denkschriften. 15-16. Wien. 1867-1869. 188 p. 177 p.

Hahn, Johann Georg von. Griechische und albanesische Märchen. 2 vols. München und Berlin, G. Müller. 1918.

Hasluck, Frederick William. Letters on religion and folklore. London, Luzac. 1926. 256 p.

Hasluck, Margaret. The non-conformist Moslems of Albania. Contemporary Review. 127(May 1925): 599-606.

Hasluck, Margaret. Physiological paternity and belated birth in Albania. Man. 32(1932): 53-54.

Hasluck, Margaret. Bride-price in Albania. A Homeric parallel. Man. 33(1933): 191-195.

Hasluck, Margaret. Couvade in Albania. Man. 39(1939): 18-20.

Hasluck, Margaret. The bust of Berat. Man. 46(1946): 36-38.

Hasluck, Margaret. Oedipus Rex in Albania. Folk-Lore. 60(1949): 340-348.

*Hasluck, Margaret. The unwritten law in Albania. (Edited by J. H. Hutton.) Cambridge, The University Press. 1954. 15, 285 p.

Hecquard, Louis Hyacinthe. Histoire et description de la haute-Albanie ou Ghégarie. Paris, A. Bertrand. 1858. 17, 516 p. (There is also an 1863 printing.)

Heseltine, Nigel. Scarred background; a journey through Albania. London, L. Dickson. 1938. 234 p.

Jaray, Gabriel Louis. L'Albanie inconnue: ouvrage illustré de 60 gravures tirées hors texte et d'une carte en noir. Paris, Hachette. 1913. 23, 238 p.

Jovićević, A. Malesija. Srpski Etnografiski Zbornik. 27(1923): 1-149. (Albanian folklife in Yugoslavian Malesija.)

Kastrati, Qazim. Some sources on the unwritten law in Albania. Man. 55(1955): 124-127.

Knight, Edward Frederick. Albania: a narrative of a recent travel. London, Sampson Low, Marston, Searle & Rivington. 1880. 8, 278 p.

Lambertz, Maximilian. Die Volkspoesie der Albaner, eine einführende Studie. Sarajevo, im Kommissionsverlag von J. Studnička. 1917. 80 p.

Lambertz, Maximilian. Albanische Märchen- und andere Texte zur albanischen Volkskunde. Akademie der Wissenschaften, Wien. Balkankommisschen. Schriften . . . Linguistische Abteilung. 12. Wien, A. Hölder. 1922. 7, 255 p.

Lane, Rose W. Peaks of Shala. New York, Harper & Bros. 1923. 10, 349 p., 14 plates.

Lear, Edward. Journals of a landscape painter in Albania and Illyria. London, R. Bentley. 1851. 428 p., illus.

Lloyd, A. L. Folk music of Albania. London, Topic Records. n.d. [1967?]. (A 12" L.P. record, with an 8-page booklet containing notes on Albanian music and musical instruments.)

Louis, Herbert. Albanien. Eine Landeskunde vornehmlich auf Grund eigener Reisen. Stuttgart, J. Engelhorns. 1927. 8, 164 p., 16 plates, map, 8 tables.

Miller, Elizabeth Cleveland. Children of the mountain eagle. Garden City, N.Y., Doubleday, Doran. 1927. 328 p. (Juvenile literature, but done through Albanian-American informants. Excellent data.)

Miller, Elizabeth Cleveland. Pran of Albania. New York, Doubleday, Doran. 1929. 257 p. (Same comments as above.)

Mladenov, Stefan. Bemerkungen über die Albaner und das Albanische in Nordmakedonien und Altserbien. Balkan-Archiv. 1 (1925): 43-70.

Mustafa, Ikbal. Albanian popular motives: textiles and needlework. Tirana, Ikbal Mustafa. 1959. 6 p., 161 col. illus.

Nopcsa, Ferencz. Aus Šala und Klementi, albanische Wanderungen. Sarajevo, D. A. Kajon. 1910. 115 p.

*Nopcsa, Ferencz. Haus und Hausrat im katholischen Nordalbanien. Zur Kunde der Balkanhalbinsel. 1. Reisen und Beobachten. 16. Sarajevo, Institut für Balkanforschung. 1912. 90 p., illus.

*Nopcsa, Ferencz. Albanien; Bauten, Trachten und Geräte Nordalbaniens. Berlin und Leipzig, W. de Gruyter. 1925. 8, 257 p., illus.

ALBANIANS

Nowack, Ernest. A contribution to the geography of Albania. Geographical Review. 11 (1921): 503-540.

Pedersen, Holgar. Zur albanesischen Volkskunde. Kopenhagen, S. Michaelsen. 1898. 125 p. .(Mainly texts.)

Pisko, J. E. Volksmedicin in Nordalbanien. M.A.G.W., Sitzungsberichte. 25(1895): [63] -[64] .

Pisko, J. E. Gebräuche bei der Geburt und Behandlung der Neugeborenen bei den Albanesen. M.A.G.W. 26(1896): 141-146.

Redlich, Marcellus D. Albania yesterday and today. Worcester, Mass., Albanian Messenger. 1936. 269 p.

Rivista d'Albania. Vols. 1-4. Milano. 1940-1944.

Roucek, Joseph S. Economic conditions in Albania. Economic Geography. 9(1933): 256-264.

Ruches, P. J. Albanian historical folksongs 1716-1943. A survey of oral epic poetry from southern Albania . . . Chicago, Argonaut. 1967. 10, 126 p. (Propagandistic.)

Schwanke, Robert. Volksmusik und Volkslied in Albanien. Neue Forschungen und Ergebnisse. Südosteuropa-Jahrbuch. 6(1962): 85-95.

Scriven, George P. Recent observations in Albania. National Geographic Magazine. 34(1918): 90-113.

Sebright, Georgina Mary Muir Mackenzie, and A. P. Irby. Travels in the Slavonic provinces of Turkey-in-Europe. 5th ed. 2 vols. London, Dalby, Isbister. 1877. 19, 313; 3, 342 p.

Siebertz, Paul. Albanien und die Albanesen. Landschaft und Charakterbilder. Wien, Manz. 1910. 274 p.

Skendi, Stavro. Albanian and South Slavic oral epic poetry. Memoirs of the American Folklore Society. 44. Philadelphia. 1954. 221 p.

Skendi, Stavro. Albania. New York, Praeger. 1956. 389 p.

Stadtmüller, Georg. Altheidnischer Volksglaube und Christianisierung in Albanien. Orientalia Christiana Periodica (Rome). 20(1954): 211-246.

Start, Laura E. The Durham collection of garments and embroideries from Albania and Yugoslavia. With notes by M. Edith Durham. Bankfield Museum Notes, Third Series, No. 4. Halifax, England, Bankfield Museum. 1939. 76 p., illus., plates.

Stockmann, Doris, Wilfrid Fiedler, and Erich Stockmann. Albanische Volksmusik. 1. Gesange der Çamen. Berlin, Akademie-Verlag. 1965. 6, 302 p., map.

Stockmann, Erich. Volksmusiksammlung in Albanien 1957. Deutsches Jahrbuch für Volkskunde. 4(1958): 185-186.

Stockmann, Erich. Klarinettentypen in Albanien. Journal of the International Folk Music Council. 12(1960): 17-20.

Thurnher, Majda. A survey of Balkan houses and farm buildings. Kroeber Anthropological Society Papers. 14(1956): 19-92. (See pp. 66-70.)

Tozer, Henry Fanshawe. Researches in the highlands of Turkey: including visits to Mounts Ida, Athos, Olympos, . . the Mirdite Albanians, and other remote tribes . . . 2 vols. London, J. Murray. 1869.

Traeger, Paul. Zur Forschung über alte Schiffstypen. C. Schiffsfahrzeuge in Albanien und Mazedonien. Deutsche Gesellschaft für Anthropologie, Ethnologie und Urgeschichte, Correspondenz-Blatt. 35(1904): 25-38.

Treimer, K. Tabu im Albanischen. Lingua. 4(1954): 42-62.

Urban, Martin. Die Siedlungen Südalbaniens. Öbringen, Verlag der Hohenlohe'schen Buchhandlung F. Rau. 1938. 200 p., illus., maps.

*Valentini, Giuseppe. La famiglia nel diritto tradizionale albanese. Annali Lateranensi. 9. 1945. 204 p.

Walker, Mary Adelaide. Through Macedonia to the Albanian lakes. London, Chapman & Hall. 1864. 11, 274 p., 11 col. plates.

*Whitaker, Ian. Tribal structure and national politics in Albania, 1910-1950. In Ioan M. Lewis, ed. History and social anthropology. London, Tavistock Publications. 1968: 253-293.

Wilkinson, Henry R. Maps and politics: a review of the ethnographic cartography of Macedonia. Liverpool, Liverpool University Press. 1951. 16, 366 p., maps.

Wyatt, Colin. The Christian peasants of Albania. Blackfriars. 1949: 472-476.

Zaimi, Nexhmie. Daughter of the eagle; the autobiography of an Albanian girl. New York, I. Washburn. 1937. 271 p. (South Albanians.)

Balogh, István. Die Typen der Viehaltung in den zentralen Gebieten des Karpatenbeckens im 19. Jahrhundert. In Gyula Ortutay and T. Bodrogy, eds. Europa et Hungaria. Budapest, Akadémiai Kiadó. 1965: 409-416.

Benesch, Ladislaus Edler von. Old lamps of Central Europe and other lighting devices. (Translated by Leroy Thwing.) Rutland, Vt., Charles E. Tuttle. 1963. 108 p., 60 illus.

Földes, László, ed. Viehzucht und Hirtenleben in Ostmitteleuropa. Budapest, Akadémiai Kiadó. 1961. 8, 699 p., plates, illus.

Frødin, John. Zentraleuropas Alpwirtschaft. 2 vols. Oslo, Instituttet for Sammenlignende Kulturforskning. 1940-1941. 411 p., 79 illus.; 583 p., 141 illus.

Gunda, Béla. Ethnographica Carpathica. Budapest, Akadémiai Kiadó. 1966. 418 p. (In Hungarian.)

Gunda, Béla. Fish poisoning in the Carpathian area and in the Balkan peninsula In William G. Lockwood, ed. Essays in Balkan ethnology. Kroeber Anthropological Society. Special Publications 1. 1967: 1-34.

Gutkind, Erwin Anton. Urban development in Central Europe. New York, The Free Press of Glencoe. 1964. 17, 491 p.

Jacobeit, Wolfgang. Schafhaltung und Schäfer in Zentraleuropa bis zum Beginn des 20. Jahrhunderts. Berlin, Akademie-Verlag. 1961. 604 p., illus., plates.

Jacobeit, Wolfgang. Sheep-keeping and the shepherd in central Europe up to the beginning of the 20th century. Current Anthropology. 2(1961): 269-270.

Jettmar, Karl. Jägertum als Problem der mitteleuropäischen Ethnologie. Paideuma. 8, no. 2(1962): 65-69.

Kostrowicki, Jerzy. An attempt to determine the geographical types of agriculture in East-central Europe on the basis of the case studies on land utilization. In Jerzy Kostrowicki, ed. Land utilization in East-central Europe. Geographia Polonia. 5. Warszawa, Institute of Geography, Polish Academy of Sciences. 1965: 453-498.

Kostrowicki, Jerzy, ed. Land utilization in East-central Europe. Geographia Polonia. 5. Warszawa, Institute of Geography, Polish Academy of Sciences. 1965. 498 p., illus., maps, charts.

Machatschek, Fritz. Landeskunde der Westkarpathenländer. Stuttgart, J. Engelhorns. 1927. 11, 444p., 17 plates, 42 figs.

Morant, Geoffrey M. The races of Central Europe: a footnote to history. London, G. Allen & Unwin. 1939. 163 p.

Pfeifer, Gottfried. The quality of peasant living in Central Europe. In William L. Thomas, Jr., ed. Man's role in changing the face of the earth. Chicago, University of Chicago Press. 1956. 240-277.

CZECHOSLOVAKIA

Allodiatoris, Irma. A Kárpát-medence antropológiai bibliográfiája [A bibliography on the anthropology of the Carpathian mountain basin]. Budapest, Akadémiai Kiadó. 1958. 183 p.

Čapek, Thomas, and Anna V. Čapek. Bohemian (Čech) bibliography: a finding list of writings in English relating to Bohemia and the Čechs. New York Revell. 1918. 256 p.

Krallert-Sattler, Gertrud, ed. Südosteuropa-Bibliographie. 3 vols. to date. Bd. 1. 1945-1950. Bd. 2. 1951-1955. Bd. 3. 1956-1960. München, R. Oldenbourg. 1956--. (Sections on Slovakia.)

Kunz, Ludvík. Eine Übersicht bedeutender Arbeiten auf dem Gebiet der tschechischen und slowakischen Volkskunde von 1945 bis 1955. Deutsches Jahrbuch für Volkskunde. 2(1956): 359-378.

Maas, W. Kritische Bibliographie zum Almwesen in den Karpathen. Karpathenland. 4(1931): 40-46, 94-95.

United States. Bureau of the Census. Bibliography of social science periodicals and monograph series: Czechoslovakia, 1948-1963. Washington, Government Printing Office. 1965. 134 p.

Ankert, Heinrich. Amtszeichen, Ladungszeichen und aehnliches im nördlichen Theil Böhmens. Z.f.Ö.V. 7(1901): 105-116.

*Balch, Emily Greene. Our Slavic fellow citizens. New York, Charities Publication Committee. 1910. 20, 536 p., plates. (Especially see Chapters 3 and 4 on Bohemian village life.)

*Bednárik, Rudolf. Slowakische Volkskultur. Bratislava-Pressburg, Verlag die Slowakische Rundschau. 1943. 243 p., illus.

Bednárik, Rudolf. L'udové náhrobníky na Slovensku. Turčiansky sv. Martin, Matica Slovenská. 1949. 113 p. (Folk grave markers.)

Bednárik, Rudolf. Pastierske rezbárske umenie [Wood carving art of shepherds] Bratislava, Slovenské Vydavatel'stvo Krásnej Literatúry. 1956. 219 p.

Bednárik, Rudolf. Slovenské úle [Slovak bee hives]. Bratislava, Slovenské Vydavatel'stvo Krásnej Literatúry. 1957. 145 p.

Bednárik, Rudolf. Slováci v Juhoslávii [Slovaks in Yugoslavia]. Bratislava, Vydavatel'stvo Slovenskey Akadémie vied. 1964. 272 p.

Benyovsky, Karoly, ed. Die alten Pressburger Volksschauspiele "Christgeburtspiel" . . . Bratislawa-Pressburg, S. Steiner. 1934. 70 p.

Bláha, Arnošt. Contemporary sociology in Czechoslovakia. Social Forces. 9 (1931): 167-179.

Blau, Josef. Böhmerwälder Hirtenleben. Z.f.Ö.V. 17(1911): 48-67.

Blau, Josef. Landes- und Volkskunde der Tschechoslowakischen Republik. Reichenberg, Paul Sollves Nachfolger. 1927. 381 p.

Brewster, P. G. Some games from Czechoslovakia. Southern Folklore Quarterly. 21(1957): 165-174.

Chasteigner, Marie Anne. A village in lower-Slovakia. Living Age. 17(1921): 40-52.

Chicago. University. Division of the Social Sciences. A study of contemporary Czechoslovakia. Jan Hajda, ed. New Haven, printed for the Human Relations Area Files. 1955. 6, 637 p., illus., maps.

Čižmář, Josef. Lidové lékařství v Československu. 2 vols. Brno, Melantrich. 1946. 311, 282 p. (Folk medicine.)

Dachler, Anton, and Michael Haberlandt. Das Bauernhaus in Österreich-Ungarn und in seinen Grenzgebieten. Wien, Ingenieur- und Architektenverein. 1906. 17, 288 p., 67 illus., 6 plates, 75 folio plates, map.

Deffontaines, Pierre. La vie forestière en Slovaquie. Travaux publiés par l'Institut d'Études Slaves 13. Paris, Librairie Ancienne Honoré Champion. 1932. 94 p., plates, maps.

Dunăre, N. Trepanácia oviecjako l'udova liečebná praktika v Karpatskom pastierstve [Trepanation of sheep as a medical folk practice among Carpathian shepherds] . Slovenský Národopis. 9(1961): 579-609.

Foltyn, Ladislav. Volksbaukunst in der Slowakei. Praha, Artia. 1960. 233 p., 224 plates.

Frolec, Vaclav. On the question of the origin of the irregular nucleated village. Národopisný Věstník Československý. 1(1966): 64-77.

Frolec, Vaclav, Dušan Holý, and Josef Tomeš, eds. Strážnice 1946-1965. Národopisné Studie. Brno, Nakladopisné Blok. 1966. 416 p., 134 plates.

Giles, Dorothy. The road through Czechoslovakia. Philadelphia, Penn Publishing Company. 1930. 420 p.

Gunda, Béla. Fish poisoning in the Carpathian area and in the Balkan peninsula. In William G. Lockwood, ed. Essays in Balkan Ethnology. Special Publications No. 1. Kroeber Anthropological Society. Berkeley, Calif. 1967: 1-34.

Holme, Charles, ed. Peasant art in Austria and Hungary. London, The Studio 1911. 54 p., plates.

Hrdlička, Aleš. Bohemia and the Czechs. National Geographic Magazine. 31(1917): 163-192.

*Jirásek, Alois. Some aspects of Czech culture. New Haven, Human Relations Area Files. 1953. 54 p., illus.

Jurkovič, D. , S. Hurban, et al. Slovak peasant art and melodies. London, Constable. 1911. 5, 40 p.

Kalesný, František. Ľudové umenie na Slovensku [Folk art in Slovakia]. Osveta, Martin. 1956. 274 p., illus.

Kovač, Edward. Slovenské zvyky. Scranton, Penn., Obrana Press. 1953. 164 p. (Slovakian customs.)

Ksír, J. Lidové stavitelstvi na Haná. Stodoly [Folk architecture in Hana. Barns]. Ceskoslovenska Etnografie. 9(1961): 135-176, 222-256.

*Kunz, Ludvik. Bäuerliche Viehzucht und Weidenwirtschaft im Flachland Mittelmährens im 19. Jahrhundert. In László Földes, ed. Viehzucht und Hirtenleben in Ostmitteleuropa. Budapest, Akadémiai Kiadó. 1961: 439-464.

Lewis, Frank. Czechoslovak textiles. Leigh-on-Sea, England, F. Lewis. 1962 23 p., plates.

Lubinova, Mila. Dances of Czechoslovakia. New York, Chanticleer Press. 1949. 40 p., 3 plates.

Lukas, Jan. Das Buch vom Wein. The book of wine. De la vigne au vin. Praha, Artia. 1964. 80 p., 70 plates.

Machatschek, Fritz. Landeskunde der Westkarpathenländer. Stuttgart, J. Engelhorns. 1927. 11, 444 p., 17 plates, 42 figs.

Markov, J. The Slovak national dress through the centuries. Prague, Artia. 1956. 37, 3, 4 p., plates.

Marková, Ema. Slovenské čipky [Slovak lace work]. Bratislava, Slovenské Vydavateľstvo Krásnej Literatúry. 1962. 276 p.

Matiegka, J. The origin and beginnings of the Czechoslovak people. Smithsonian Report for 1919. Washington. 1921: 471-486. 4 plates.

Mjartan, Jan. Agrarethnographische Forschungen in der Slowakei. In Agrarethnographie. Berlin, Akademie der Wissenschaften zu Berlin. 1957: 23-27.

Mrlian, Rudolf, ed. Slovak folk art: architecture, costumes and embroideries, ceramics and pottery. Prague, Artia. 1953. 15, 15 (47) p., 265 plates.

Mrlian, Rudolf, ed. Slowakische Volkskunst. 2 vols. Bratislava, Tatran. 1953-1954.

Národopisný Sborník. Bratislava. Vols. 1-11. 1939-1952. Became Slovenský Národopis. 1 (1953)--

Nižnanský, J. R. Prípava a osev úhorového a poúhorového pola v Brestovanoch [Preparation and seeding of a fallow and after-fallow field at Brestovany]. Slovenský Národopis. 8(1960): 122-152.

Obrdlik, Antonin. Social attitudes of the Czechoslovakian peasant towards the other occupational groups. Rural Sociology. 1(1936): 296-305.

Die Österreichisch-Ungarische Monarchie in Wort und Bild. Bds. 14, 15, 17. Bd. 14. Böhmen. Bd. 15. Böhmen. Bd. 17. Mähren und Schlesien. Wien, K. K. Hof- und Staatsdruckerei. 1894, 1896, 1897.

Patkova, Jarmila. Ľudový odev v okolí Trnevy [Folk costumes in the Trnava region]. Bratislava, Slovenské Vydavateľstvo Krásnej Literatúry. 1957. 297 p., illus.

Piprek, Johannes. Slawische Brautwerbungs- und Hochzeitgebräuche. Stuttgart, Strecker und Schröder. 1914. 193 p.

Plicka, Karel, and František Wolf. Český rok v pohádkách, písních, hrách a tancích, říkadlech a pohádkách. 2 vols. Praha, Družstevní Práce. 1950. 369, 416 p. (The yearly cycle in Czech folk customs.)

Podolák, J. Klčovanie a žiarové hospodárenie na Slovensku [Grubbing swidden cultivation in Slovakia]. Národopisny Věstník Československý. 1 (1966): 15-48. (English summary.)

Pospíšil, Fr. Die volkskundliche Abteilung des Mährischen Landesmuseum in Brünn. Brünn. 1928. 12 p., illus.

Prazak, Vilem. Zur Frage der Entstehung der Stube und des Hausflurs im Tschechoslovakischen Haus und ihre Beziehungen zum altslawischen und altfränkischen Haus. Národpisny Věstník Československý. 1 (1966): 49-63.

Přikryl, Franz. Die Bevölkerung am Záhoři in Mähren. Z.f.Ö.V. 1(1895): 193-204, 234-243.

Rank, Josef. Aus dem Böhmerwalde und volkskundliche Beiträge aus Ranks übrigen Werken. Prag, J. G. Calve. 1917.

Rechcigl, Miloslav, Jr., ed. The Czechoslovak contribution to world culture. The Hague, Paris, Mouton. 1964. 682 p., 7 figs., 1 plate, 2 tables.

Reinsberg-Dueringsfeld, Otto von. Fest-Kalender aus Böhmen. Ein Beitrag zur Kenntniss des Volkslebens und Volksglaubens in Böhmen. Prag. 1862.

Sasinek, Franko V. Die Slovaken; eine ethnographische Skizze. 2d rev. ed. Prague. 1875. 50 p.

Sawicki, L. von. Almenwirtschaft und Hirtenleben in der mährischen Walache Z.f.Ö.V. 21(1915): 1-18, 37-52, 69-85.

Sborník Slovenskej Muzeálnej Spoločnosti. 44 vols. Brno, Mjartan. 1896-19

Sborník Slovenského Národného Múzea. Brno, Mjartan. 1952--

Schier, Bruno. Aufbau der slowakischen Volkskultur. Eine volkskundliche Skizze. Deutsches Archiv für Landes- und Volksforschung. 7(1943): 227-260.

Schier, Bruno. Räume und Schichten der slowakischen Volkskultur. Südosteuropa Jahrbuch. 6(1962): 58-62, plates 1-8.

Seckar, Alvena V. Slovak wedding customs. New York Folklore Quarterly. 3(1947): 189-205.

Selecká, Zuzka. Ľudové tkaniny z okolia Zvolena [Folk fabrics from the Zvol region]. Bratislava, Osveta. 1963. 211 p., plates. (English summary.)

Slovenské ludové unemie [Slovak folk art]. 2 vols. Bratislava, Tatran. 1953 1954. 20 p., 265 illus.; 265 illus.

Šolková, B. Volkstrachten in der Tschechoslowakei. Praha, Artia. 1956. 76 p., plates.

Šourek, K. Volkskunst in Bildern. Praha, Artia. 1957. 347 p., plates.

Summers, Montague. The vampire in Europe. New Hyde Park, N.Y., University Books. 1961: 132-216.

Švecová, Soňa. Die Beziehungen zwischen Architektur und Familienorganisation in der Slowakei. In Gy. Ortutay and T. Bodrogy, eds. Europa et Hungaria. Budapest, Akadémiai Kiadó. 1965: 431-442.

Tetzner, Franz Oskar. Die Slaven in Deutschland. Braunschweig, F. Vieweg. 1902. 20, 520 p.

Václavík, A., and J. Orel. Textile folk art. London, Spring Books. 1958. 58 p., illus.

CZECHOSLOVAKIA

Vydra, Jozef. Ľudová architektúra na Slovensku [Folk architecture in Slovakia].
Bratislava, S.A.V. 1958. 337 p., illus.

Wiskmann, Elizabeth. Czechs and Germans; a study of the struggles in the
historic provinces of Bohemia and Moravia. Oxford, London, and New York,
Oxford University Press. 1938. 8, 299 p.

HUNGARIANS (MAGYARS)

Allodiatoris, Irma. A Kárpát-medence antropológiai bibliográfiája [Bibliography of the anthropology of the Carpathian mountain range]. Budapest, Akadémiai Kiadó. 1958. 183 p.

Index ethnographicus. Budapest, Magyar Nemzeti Museum. Neprajzi Muzeumanak Konyvtari Tajekoztatoja. 1(1956)-- (Annual bibliography of Hungarian ethnography.)

Krallert-Sattler, Gertrud. Südosteuropa-Bibliographie. 3 vols. to date. Bd. 1. 1945-1950. Bd. 2. 1951-1955. Bd. 3. 1956-1960. München, R. Oldenbourg. 1956--.

Sándor, István, ed. A Magyar néprajztudomány bibliográfiája 1945-1954. Budapest, Akadémiai Kiadó. 1965. 463 p.

Szolnoky, L. Überblick über die bedeutende ethnographische Literatur Ungarns im Laufe der letzten zehn Jahre 1945-1954. Deutsches Jahrbuch für Volkskunde. 2(1956): 379-400.

United States. Bureau of the Census. Bibliography of social science periodical and monograph series. 13. Hungary, 1947-1962. Washington, Government Printing Office. 1964. 4, 137 p.

Andrásfalvy, Bertalan. Viehhaltung in einem überschwemmungsgebiet der Donau im 18.-19. Jahrhundert (Sárköz, Ungarn). In László Földes, ed. Viehzucht und Hirtenleben in Ostmitteleuropa. Budapest, Akadémiai Kiadó 1961: 581-608.

L'art populaire hongrois. Budapest, Impr. de l'Université Royale Hongroise. 1928. 20, 12, 230 p., illus.

Bakó, Ferenc. Bäuerliches Kalkbrennen in Ungarn. Acta Ethnographica. 3(1953): 339-420.

Bakó, Ferenc. Formen der Arbeitsorganisation bei den Kalkbrennern im Bükkgebirge. Acta Ethnographica. 13(1964): 187-211.

Balassa, Ivan. Der Maisbau in Ungarn. Acta Ethnographica. 5(1956): 103-181.

Balassa, Ivan. Die ungarischen Geräte der Bodenbestellung und ihre Beziehung. In Gyula Ortutay and Tibor Bodrogi, eds. Europa et Hungaria. Budapest, Akadémiai Kiadó. 1965: 59-69.

Balassa, Ivan. Die Sagen eines Dorfes (Karcsa, Ungarn). Acta Ethnographica. 15(1966): 233-291.

Balint, S. A szegedi paprika termesztése [The cultivation of paprika in Szeged]. Ethnographia. 70 (1959): 130-170.

Balint, S. A szegedi paprika [Paprika of Szeged] . Budapest, Akadémiai Kiadó. 1962. 138 p.

Balogh, István. Das Einbringen des Getreides ins Karpatenbecken im 16.-19. Jahrhundert. Acta Ethnographica. 13(1964): 369-401.

Balogh, István. Formen der extensiven Viehhaltung auf der Pussten von Debrecen. In László Földes, ed. Viehzucht und Hirtenleben in Ostmitteleuropa. Budapest, Akadémiai Kiadó. 1965: 465-504.

*Bartha, Károly, et al. A magyarság néprajza. 4 vols. Budapest, Királyi Magyar Egyetemi Nyomda. 1933-1937. (An encyclopedic coverage of Hungarian folklore and folk-life.)

Bartók, Béla. Das ungarische Volkslied, . . . Berlin und Leipzig, W. de Gruyter. 1925. 2, 236 p., illus.

Bartók, Béla. Cigányzene? Magyar zene? [Gypsy music? Magyar music?]. Ethnographia-Népélet. 42(1931): 48-62.

*Bartók, Béla. Hungarian folk music. London, Oxford University Press. 1931. 218 p.

Bátky, Sigmund [Zsigmond] . Das ungarische Bauernhaus. Ungarische Jahrbücher. 18 (1938): 247-262.

Belényesy, Márta. Kultura és tánc a bukovinai székelyeknél [Culture and dance among the Bukovinan Szekely] . Budapest, Akadémiai Kiadó. 1958. 175 p.

Belényesy, Márta. Über den Brandfeldbau in Ungarn. Ethnographisch-Archäologische Forschungen. 4(1958): 9-21.

Belényesy, Márta. Viehzucht und Hirtenleben in Ungarn im 14. und 15. Jahrhundert. In László Földes, ed. Viehzucht und Hirtenleben in Ostmitteleuropa. Budapest, Akadémiai Kiadó. 1961: 13-82.

Bene, Zsuzsana. Die Schafzucht und die Verarbeitung der Schafmilch auf dem Gebiet des Cserehát (Nordostungarn). In László Földes, ed. Viehzucht und Hirtenleben in Ostmitteleuropa. Budapest, Akadémiai Kiadó. 1961: 559-580.

Béres, András. Treiber und Treibgeräte der Hirten auf den Pussten in der Umgebung von Debrecen. In László Földes, ed. Viehzucht und Hirtenleben in Ostmitteleuropa. Budapest, Akadémiai Kiadó. 1961: 505-528.

Beynon, Erdman D. Migrations of Hungarian peasants. Geographical Review. 27(1937): 214-228.

Beynon, Erdman D. The eastern outposts of the Magyars. Geographical Review 31(1941): 63-78.

Bing, M. The crafts of the Puszta herdsmen. Ciba Review. 4(1943): 1626-1649.

*Bodrogi, Tibor. Some problems regarding investigations into Hungarian kinship terminology. Acta Ethnographica. 11(1962): 273-291.

*Boner, Charles. Transylvania: its products and people. London, Longmans, Green, Reader, and Dyer. 1865. 14, 642 p.

Bowring, Sir John. Poetry of the Magyars, preceded by a sketch of the language and literature of Hungary and Transylvania. London, printed for the author and sold by R. Heward. 1830. 16, 83, 312 p.

Bright, Richard. Travels from Vienna through Lower Hungary . . . Edinburgh, A. Constable. 1818. 18, 642 p.

Buday, Gyorgy. Dances of Hungary. New York, Chanticleer Press. 1950. 40 p., illus.

Bünker, J. R. Das Bauernhaus in der Heanzerei (West-Ungarn). M. A. G. W. 25(1895): 89-154, illus. 141-240, plans.

Busk, Rachel H. The lakes of western Hungary and the dwellers on their banks. In H. W. Bates, ed. Illustrated travels. London. 2(1870): 138-141.

Csilléry, Klára K. Historische Schichten in der Wohnkultur der ungarischen Bauern. In Gyula Ortutay and T. Bodrogi, eds. Europa et Hungaria. Budapest, Akadémiai Kiadó. 1965: 111-136.

Dachler, Anton, and Michael Haberlandt. Das Bauernhaus in Österreich-Ungarn und in seinen Grenzgebieten. Wien, Ingenieur- und Architekten-verein. 1906. 17, 288 p., 67 illus., 6 plates, 75 folio plates, map.

Dégh, Linda. Some questions of the social function of story-telling. Acta Ethnographica. 6(1957): 91-147.

Dégh, Linda, ed. Folktales of Hungary. Chicago, University of Chicago Press; London, Routledge & Kegan Paul. 1965. 46, 381 p.

Dioszegi, Vilmos. Sámánok nyomában Szibéria földjén; egy néprajzi kutatóút története. Budapest, Magvető Könyvkiadó. 1960. 251 p. (Survivals of shamanism in Hungary.)

Dobos, I. Egy somogy parasztcsalád meséi [Tales of a peasant family in Somogy]. Budapest, Akadémiai Kiadó. 1962. 546 p.

Dömötör, S. Aratószerszámok nyugatmagyarországon [Harvesting implements from western Hungary]. Néprajzi Közlémenyek. 3(1958): 129-151.

Dömötör, Tekla. Principal problems of the investigation on the ethnography of the industrial working class in Hungary. Acta Ethnographica. 5(1956): 331-349.

Dömötör, Tekla. Ethnographische Forschung in Ungarn 1950-1962. Hessische Blätter für Volkskunde. 54(1963): 665-674.

Dömötör, Tekla. Ungarischer Volksglauben und ungarische Volksbräuche zwischen Ost und West. In Gyula Ortutay and T. Bodrogi. Europa et Hungaria. Budapest, Akadémiai Kiadó. 1965: 311-323.

Ecsedi, István. A Hortobágy puszta élete. Debrecen. 1914. 6, 295 p. (Life on the Hortobagy steppe.)

Enyedi, I. The "Kossuth" Collective Farm of Békéscsaba in the southern part of the Great Hungarian Plain. In Jerzy Kostrowicki, ed. Land utilization in East-central Europe. Geographia Polonia. 5. Warszawa, Institute of Geography, Polish Academy of Sciences. 1965: 407-420.

Erdei, Ferenc. Futóhomok [Drift sand]. Budapest, Athenaeum. 1937. 242 p., 35 photos. (Topographic and ethnographic description of the region between the Danube and the Tisza.)

Erdei, Ferenc. Magyar falu [Rustic Hungary]. Budapest, Athenaeum. 1940. 236 p. (Rural society of Hungary.)

Erdésc, Sandor. The world conception of Lajos Ámi, storyteller. Acta Ethnographica. 10(1961): 372-444.

Erdésc, Sandor. The cosmological conceptions of Lajos Ámi, storyteller. Acta Ethnographica. 12(1963): 57-64.

Erdey-Grúz, Tibor, et al., eds. Science in Hungary. Budapest, Corvina Press. 1965. 316 p.

Falls, De Witt Clinton. Saint Stephan's fete in Budapest. National Geographic Magazine. 18(1907): 548-558.

Fél, Edit. Women's clothing in the Sárköz. Folia Ethnographica. 2(1950): 19-54.

*Fél, Edit. Some data concerning kinship institutions among the Szeklers of Bukovina. Acta Ethnographica. 8(1959): 85-97.

Fél, Edit. Hungarian peasant embroidery. London, B. T. Batsford. 1961. 138 p., illus.

*Fél, Edit, and Tamás Hofer. Proper peasants. Viking Fund Publications in Anthropology 46. New York, Wenner-Gren Foundation for Anthropological Research; Chicago, Aldine Publishing Co. 1968. 384 p., plates, figs., tables.

*Fél, Edit, Tamás Hofer, and Klára K. Csillery. Hungarian peasant art. Budapest, Corvina. 1958. 82 p., 241 p. of plates.

Földes, László. Esztena und Esztena-Genossenschaft bei den Szeklern. In László Földes, ed. Viehzucht und Hirtenleben in Ostmitteleuropa. Budapest Akadémiai Kiadó. 1961: 283-328.

Fuchs, Karl. Über das Székler Haus. M. A. G. W. 31(1902): 334-339, illus. 156-167.

Gábor, Magda. Hungarian textiles. Leigh-on-Sea, England, F. Lewis. 1961. 18 p., 52 plates.

Garay, Ákos. Szlavóniai régi magyar faluk [Old Hungarian villages in Slavonia]. Ertesitö. 12(1911): 221-248.

*Gerard, Emily. The land beyond the forest. Facts, figures, and fancies from Transylvania. 2 vols. Edinburgh and London, W. Blackwood & Sons. 1888. (Reprinted: New York, Harper and Brothers. 1888. 9, 403 p., map.)

Gombás, A. Juhtartás Szentmihályon [Sheep-breeding at Szentmihály]. Nyíregyházi Jósa András Múzeum Évkönyve. 3(1960): 223-248.

Gower, Sir Robert. Hungarian minorities in the succession states. London, G. Richards. 1937. 122 p.

Gunda, Béla. Asiatische Maulkorbformen in der ungarischen Hirtenkultur. Ethnos. 3(1938): 8-17.

*Gunda, Béla. The anthropogeography of pasturing on the Great Hungarian Plain International Review of the Hungarian Geographical Society. 68(1940): 28-49.

Gunda, Béla. Work and cult among Hungarian peasants. S. W. J. A. 3(1947): 147-163.

Gunda, Béla. Wandering healers, medicine hawkers in Slovakia and Transylvania. S. W. J. A. 5(1949): 147-150.

Gunda, Béla. Plant gathering in the economic life of Eurasia. S. W. J. A. 5(1949): 369-378.

Gunda, Béla. Research into Hungarian folk-culture; an ethnological and folkloristic survey. J. A. F. L. 63(1950): 72-84.

Gunda, Béla. Néprajzi gyüjtöuton. Debrecen, Alföldi Magvetö. 1956. 171 p.

Gunda, Béla. Zusammenhänge zwischen Hofanlage und Viehzucht in Sieben-
bergen. In László Földes, ed. Viehzucht und Hirtenleben in Ostmitteleuropa.
Budapest, Akadémiai Kiadó. 1961: 243-282.

Gunda, Béla. Die regionalen und strukturellen Belange der ungarischen Volkskultur. In Gyula Ortutay and Tibor Bodrogi, eds. Europa et Hungaria.
Budapest, Akadémiai Kiadó. 1965: 13-26.

Gunda, Béla. Ethnographica Carpathia. Budapest, Akadémiai Kiadó. 1966.
418 p. (In Hungarian.)

Gunda, Béla. Fish poisoning in the Carpathian area and in the Balkan peninsula. In William G. Lockwood, ed. Essays in Balkan ethnology. Kroeber
Anthropological Society. Special Publications No. 1. 1967: 1-34.

Györffy, I. Matyó nepviselet [Matyá folk costumes]. Budapest, Képző-
müvéséti Alap. 1956. 207 p., illus.

Hegedus, Adam de. Hungarian background. London, Hamish Hamilton. 1937.
302 p.

Herbert, János. Egy alföldi község társadalomrajza. Társadalomtudomány.
7(1927): 403-438. (Social anthropology of an Alföld township.)

Hofer, Tamás. Eine eigenartige ungarische Siedlungsform und ihre europäischen
Beziehungen. In Gyula Ortutay and Tibor Bodrogi, eds. Europa et Hungaria.
Budapest, Akadémiai Kiadó. 1965: 95-110.

Hoffmann, Tamás. Egy paloc falu foldmüvelö technikájának nehány jelleg-
zetessége a századffordulo tájékan [Some characteristic traits of agrarian
life of a Paloc village]. Ethnographia. 67(1956): 536-561.

Hoffmann, Tamás. A gabonanemüek nyomtatása a magyar parasztok gazdál-
kodásábon [Threshing grain in Hungarian peasant farming]. Budapest,
Akadémiai Kiadó. 1963. 374 p.

Hoffmann, Tamás. Einige Merkmale der Agrotechnik in einem Palozendorf um
die Jahrhundertwende. Acta Ethnographica. 13(1964): 349-368.

Hollander, A. N. S. de. The Great Hungarian Plain: a European frontier area.
Comparative Studies in Society and History. 3(1960): 74-88.

Holme, Charles, ed. Peasant art in Austria and Hungary. London, The Studio.
1911. 54 p., plates.

Honti, John Th. [János]. Hungarian popular balladry. Journal of the English
Folk Dance and Song Society. 1(1932): 166-172.

HUNGARIANS (MAGYARS)

Horváth, Pál. A középkori falusi földközösség jogtörténeti vonatkozásai. Budapest, Akadémiai Kiadó. 1960. 283 p. (Village communities.)

Hunfalvy, János. Pesth und Ofen. Pest, Lauffer. 1859. 4, 306 p. (Excellent cultural geography.)

Hunfalvy, Pál. Ethnographie von Ungarn. Budapest, Franklin-Verein. 1877. 446 p.

Hunfalvy, Pál. Die Ungarn oder Magyaren. Wien und Teschen, K. Prochaska. 1881. 254 p.

Hunfalvy, Pál. Ueber die ungarische Fischerei. Ethnologische Mitteilungen aus Ungarn. 1 (1888): cols. 153-160.

*Hungary. European conference on rural life. National monographs drawn up by governments. Hungary. Series of League of Nations Publications. European Conference on Rural Life. 27. Geneva. 1940. 80 p., illus.

*Illyés, Gyula. People of the Puszta. Budapest, Corvina Press. 1967. 308 p. (The Hungarian edition was printed in 1936.)

*Indiana. University. Graduate Program in Uralic and Asian Studies. The Hungarians. By Victor E. Manzeli. New Haven, printed by the Human Relations Area Files. 1955. 13, 267 p., illus., maps. (Also contains critical bibliographic notes.)

Jacobi, Elizabeth P. When I was a girl in Hungary. Boston, Lothrop, Lee & Shepard. 1930. 142 p.

Jancsó, Benedek. The Székelys, a historical and ethnographical essay. Budapest, V. Hornyánszky. 1921. 46 p.

Jankó, János. Torda, Aranyosszék, Torockó magyar (székely) népe [The Hungarian (Szekler) people of Komitate Torda, Aranyosszék and Torockó]. Budapest. Magyar Földrajzi Társág. 1893. 7, 296 p.

Jankó, János. Haus und Hof am Balatan. Ethnologische Mitteilungen aus Ungarn. 6, heft 8-10. (1904): 3-76, 57 illus.

Jones, W. H., and J. L. Kropt. Magyar folk-lore. Folk-Lore Journal. 1(1883) 354-368.

Jones, W. H., and J. L. Kropt. Szekely folk-medicine. Folk-Lore Journal. 2(1884): 97-105.

Kálmány, Ludwig. Der Mond im ungarischen Volksglauben. Ethnologische Mitteilungen aus Ungarn. 1(1887): cols. 23-27.

Karbos, L. Etnograficheskie voprosy sofsialisticheskogo razvitiiā vengerskoĭ derevni [Ethnographic problems of socialist development of the Hungarian village]. Acta Ethnographica. 5(1956): 247-280.

Károlyi, Alexander F. Hungarian pageant; life, customs and art of the Hungarian peasantry. Budapest, G. Vajna. 1939. 113 p., illus.

Károlyi, Alexander, I. Perényi, et al. A magyar felu épitészete [Hungarian village architecture]. Budapest, Muszaki Konyokiadó. 1955. 202 p., illus.

Kerék, Mihály. A magyar föld. Budapest, Magyar Élet. 1941. 128 p. (Peasant land tenure.)

Kerék, Mihály. A földreform útja. Budapest, Magyar Élet. 1942. 158 p. (Land tenure.)

Kinner, A. B. A békési Vásár [The market in the parish of Békés]. Gyula, Erkel Ferenc Múzeum. 1964. 140 p.

Kiss, L. Vásárheliji kistükör. Budapest, Magverö. 1964. 422 p. (Ethnography of the village of Vásárhelyr.)

Klein, Valesca. Der ungarische Hexenglaube. Z.f.E. 66(1935): 374-402.

Kódaly, Zoltán. Die ungarische Volksmusik. Budapest, Corvina. 1956. 181 p.

Kódaly, Zoltán. Folk music of Hungary. New York, Macmillan. 1960. 166 p.

Kodolányi, J. Ormánság. Budapest, Gondolat. 1960. 135 p. (In southeastern Transdanubia.)

Köhler, Heinrich. Von der Landwirtschaft in Süd-Ungarn, mit besonderer Berücksichtigung des ungarländisch-deutschen Bauerntums. Stuttgart, Ausland und Heimat Verlags-Aktiengesellschaft. 1930. 100 p.

Kovács, L. K. Beiträge zur Frage der Esztena-Genossenschaften (Melkgenossenschaften) in der Siebenbürger Heide. In László Földes, ed. Viehzucht und Hirtenleben in Ostmitteleuropa. Budapest, Akadémiai Kiadó. 1961: 329-362.

Kovács, László. Ackergeräte in Ungarn. Ungarisches Jahrbuch. 18(1938): 263-301.

Kovács, László. Die ungarischen Dreschflegel und Dreschmethoden. Acta Ethnographica. 1(1950): 41-95.

Kresz, M. Ungarische Bauerntrachten (1820-1867). 2 vols. Berlin, Budapest, Verlag der Ungarischen Akademie der Wissenschaften and Henschel Verlag Kunst und Gesellschaft. 1957. 164, 254 p., illus., plates.

Lederer, Mrs. Charlotte. Made in Hungary. Budapest, Vajna. 1933. 96 p., illus., plates.

Lükő, Gábor. A hortobágyi pásztorműveszet [The art of the Hortobágy herdsmen]. A Déri Múzeum Néprajzi Ostályának Közleményei. No. 13. Debrecen. 1940. 32 p.

Maenner, E. K. Hochzeit in Merzőkövesd. Atlantis. 8(1936): 283-285.

Manga, J. Hungarian bagpipers. Acta Ethnographica. 14(1965): 1-97.

Márkus, Mihály. A bokortanyak népe [The people of the Borkotany]. Budapest, K. M. Pázmány P. Tudományegytem Magyarságtudományi Intézete. 1943. 293 p.

Marót, Károly. Szent Iván Napja [Saint John's Day]. Ethnographia-Népélet. 50(1939): 254-296.

Martin, György. East-European relations of Hungarian dance types. In Gyula Ortutay and Tibor Bodrogi, eds. Europa et Hungaria. Budapest, Akadémiai Kiadó. 1965: 469-515.

Martin, György, and Ernó Pesovár. A structural analysis of the Hungarian folk dance: a methodological sketch. Acta Ethnographica. 10(1961): 1-40.

Moór, E. Slawischer Einfluss auf das Fischerei- und Jagdwesen der Ungarn im Mittelalter im Lichte des sprachlichen Materialen. Acta Ethnographica. 12(1963): 1-56.

Morvay, Judit. The joint family in Hungary. In Gyula Ortutay and Tibor Bodrogi, eds. Europa et Hungaria. Budapest, Akadémiai Kiadó. 1965: 231-242.

Nagy, G. Speicherung von Körnerfürchten (Getreide) in Oroshaza (Ungarn). Acta Ethnographica. 13(1964): 281-312.

Nagy, Zoltan. Les régimes légaux des coopératives en Transylvanie. Dijon, Imprimerie du Palais, M. Pornon. 1934. 276 p.

Nagy-Czirok, László. Pásztorélet a Kiskúnságon [Herdsmen's life on Kiskunsag]. Budapest, Gondolat. 1959. 383 p.

Nyary, Albert. Die Hochzeit bei den Paloczen. Anzeiger der Ethnographischen Abteilung des Ungarischen National-Museum. 5(1910): 117-125.

Oláh, J. Föld- és szőlőművélés a sárospataki regéci uradalmakban a XIX.
század első felében [Agriculture and viticulture on the estates of Sárospatak
and Regéc in the first half of the 19th century]. Agrártorténti Szemle. 6
(1964): 189-222.

Ortutay, Gyula. The science of folklore in Hungary between the two world-wars
and during the period subsequent to the liberation. Acta Ethnographica.
4(1955): 5-89.

Ortutay, Gyula. Principles of oral transmission in folk culture (variations,
affinity). Acta Ethnographica. 8(1959): 175-221.

Ortutay, Gyula. Hungarian folk tales. Budapest, Corvina. 1962. 544 p.

*Ortutay, Gyula. Kleine ungarische Volkskunde. Budapest, Corvina. 1963.
230 p.

Die Österreichisch-Ungarische Monarchie in Wort und Bild. 24 vols. For
Hungary, see vols.: 5(1888), 9(1891), 12(1893), 16(1896), 18(1898),
21(1900), 23(1902). Wien, K. K. Hof- und Staatsdruckerei. 1886-1902.

*Paget, John. Hungary and Transylvania: with remarks on their condition, so-
cial, political, and economical. New ed. 2 vols. London, J. Murray;
Philadelphia, Lea & Blanchard. 1850.

Paládi-Kovaks, Attila. A keleti Palócok pásztorkodása [Herding in the eastern
Palóc]. Debrecen, Kossuth Lajos Tudományegyetem. 1965. 214 p., 83
figs., map. (French summary.)

*Palmer, Francis H. E. Austro-Hungarian life in town and country. New York,
London, G. P. Putnam's Sons. 1903. 7, 301 p.

Pálóczi Horvath, György. In darkest Hungary. London, Victor Gollancz. 1944.
158 p. (A Hungarian peasant's view, by a Social Democrat.)

Palotay, Gertrud von. Hungarian folk costumes. Budapest, Officina. 1938.

Palotay, Gertrud von. Ungarische Volkskunst in Siebenbürgen. Budapest, O. J.
Officina Druck- und Verlag s-G. m.b.H. n.d. [1939 or 1940?] 40 p., 32
plates.

Papai, Karl. Der Holzbau der Palovzen. Ethnologische Mitteilungen aus Ungarn.
3(1893-1894): cols. 141-147.

Papy, Karl. Zur Volkskunde der Csepel-Insel. Ethnologische Mitteilungen aus
Ungarn. 1(1888-1889): cols. 160-162, 270-273.

*Pardoe, Julia. The city of the Magyar, or Hungary and her institutions in 1839-
1840. 3 vols. London, G. Virtue. 1840.

HUNGARIANS (MAGYARS)

Paton, Andrew A. Researches on the Danube and the Adriatic. 2 vols. Leipzig. 1861.

Patterson, Arthur J. The Magyars; their country and institutions. 2 vols. London, Smith, Elder. 1869.

Peter, K. Szabad és dézsmás szölök Zemplén megyében a XVII. sz. végén [Zemplén county at the end of the 17th century]. Agrártörténti Szemle. 6(1964): 170-188.

Prinz, Gyula. Die Siedlungsformen Ungarns. Ungarische Jahrbücher. 4(1924): 127-142, 335-352.

Prónay, Gábor. Esquisses de la vie populaire en Hongrie. Pest, H. Geibel. 1855. 9, 136 p., col. plates.

Prónay, Gábor. Skizzen aus dem Volksleben in Ungarn. Pest, Leipzig, H. Geibel. 1855. 7, 100 p.

Pulszky, Ferencz A., and Teréz Pulszky. Tales and traditions of Hungary. 3 vols. London, H. Colburn. 1851.

Pulszky, Károly. Ornements de l'industrie domestique de la Hongrie. Budapest, Impr. de l'Université royale hongroise. 1878. 7 p., 40 plates, 35 col. plates.

Pulszky, Terézia Walder. Tales and traditions of Hungary. New York, Redfield. 1852. 345 p.

Rae, Margery. A Sunday in Mezőköesd. National Geographic Magazine. 67(1935): 489-504.

Roheim, Géza. Hungarian calendar customs. J.R.A.I. 56(1926): 361-384, plates 47, 48.

Roheim, Géza. Magyar néphit es népszokások [Hungarian folk beliefs and folk customs]. Budapest. 1928. 324 p.

Sárfalvi, B. The village of Csepreg in western Hungary. In Jerzy Kostrowicki, ed. Land utilization in East-central Europe. Geographia Polonia. 5. Warszawa, Institute of Geography, Polish Academy of Sciences. 1965: 437-452.

Sebestyén, Karl [Károly]. Ungarische Bauernmöbel. Ungarische Jahrbücher. 18(1938): 234-246.

Simon, L. Nyiradony—The village in north east of the Great Hungarian Plain. In Jerzy Kostrowicki, ed. Land utilization in East-central Europe. Geographia Polonia. 5. Warszawa, Institute of Geography, Polish Academy of Sciences. 1965: 421-436.

Solymos, E. Fischertypen des ungarländischen Donaugebietes [Fishermen types of the Hungarian Danubian area]. Acta Ethnographica. 13(1964): 133-157.

Summers, Montague. The vampire in Europe. New Hyde Park, N.Y., University Books. 1961: 132-216.

Szabó, F. Adatok a söprücirok népráyzahoz Orashaza kornyekenol [Data on the ethnography of broomcorn in the vicinity of Oroshaza]. Szeged, József Attila Tudomonyegyetem. 1963. 15 p.

Szabó, F. A délalföldi betyárvilág [World of Betyars in the southern plains]. Gyula, Erkel Ferenc Muzeum. 1964. 171 p.

Szekely, Betty Blanche. Hungarian national and peasant costumes. Viltis. 8(March-April 1950): 3-5.

Szendrey, Ákos. Népi buntetószokások [Punitory folk customs]. Ethnographia-Népélet. 47(1936): 65-72.

Szendrey, Ákos. A nepi társadalom tagozódásak [The divisions of rural society]. Ethnographia-Népélet. 48(1937): 187-198.

Szendrey, Ákos. A társadalom érintkezés formál [The formalities of social communication]. Ethnographia-Népélet. 48(1937): 372-385.

Szendrey, Ákos. A népi élet tasasösszejövetelei [Social gatherings of the peasants]. Ethnographia-Népélet. 49(1938): 124-138.

Szendrey, Ákos. A magyar lélekhit [Hungarian beliefs about the soul]. Ethnographia-Népélet. 52(1943): 44-53.

Szendrey, Ákos. Hexe-Hexendruck. Acta Ethnographica. 4(1955): 129-169.

Szücs, S. Pusztai Szabadok [The free men of the Puszta]. Budapest, Magveto Konyvkiado. 1958. 304 p.

Takács, L. A. Dohánytermerztés magyarorszagon [Tobacco plantations in Hungary]. Budapest, Akadémiai Kiadó. 1964. 463 p.

Takács, Lajos. Zur Zwiespältigkeit der ungarischen Landwirtschaft. In Gyula Ortutay and Tibor Bodrogi, eds. Europa et Hungaria. Budapest, Akadémiai Kiadó. 1965: 71-77.

Tálasi, István. Research into Hungarian peasant farming, poaching and fishing. Folia Ethnographica. 1 (1949): 44-71.

Tálasi, István. Die materielle Kultur des ungarischen Volkes in Europa. In Gyula Ortutay and Tibor Bodrogi, eds. Europa et Hungaria. Budapest, Akadémiai Kiadó. 1965: 27-57.

Temesváry, Rudolf. Volksbräuche und Aberglauben in der Geburtshilfe und der Pflege des Neugeborenen in Ungarn. Leipzig, T. Grieben. 1900. 8, 146 p.

Timaffy, László. Das Hirtenwesen auf den Donauinseln (Szigetköz, Westungarn. In László Földes, ed. Viehzucht und Hirtenleben in Ostmitteleuropa. Budapest, Akadémiai Kiadó. 1961: 609-646.

Tomori, Viola. Zur Psychologie der ungarischen Volksbräuche. Ungarische Jahrbücher. 17(1937): 293-316.

Townson, Robert. Travels in Hungary with a short account of Vienna in the year 1793. London, G. and J. Robinson. 1797. 18, 506 p.

Transylvanus (pseud.). Ethnical minorities of Transylvania. London, Eyre and Spottiswoode. 1934. 55 p.

Ujavary, Z. Primitive Methoden der Feuerbereitung aus Nordungarn. Acta Ethnographica. 10 (1961): 389-394.

Vajkai, Aurél. A bakony néprajza [The ethnography of the Bakony mountains]. Budapest, Gondolat. 1959. 176 p.

Vajkai, Aurél. Szentgál egy bakonyi falu néprojza [Szentgál, ethnography of a Bakony village]. Budapest, Akadémiai Kiadó. 1959. 398 p.

Vajkai, Aurél. Balatonmellék [The Lake Balaton region]. Budapest, Gondolat 1964. 243 p.

Varga, Gyula. Hauptformen der bäuerlichen Rinderhaltung in der Berettyóniederung (Südostungarn). In László Földes, ed. Viehzucht und Hirtenleben in Ostmitteleuropa. Budapest, Akadémiai Kiadó. 1961: 529-558.

Vegh, J. A hagyomanyos paraszti gazdálkodás ismeretanyaga és szókncse. 1. Szántésvetés [The knowledge and vocabulary of the traditional peasant household. 1. Tillage]. Budapest, Néprajzi Muzeum. 1962. 60 p.

Virágh, F. A Békés megyei szegényparasztság és a munkásság helyzete 1919-1933 [The situation of the poor peasants and workers in the department of Békés 1919-1933]. Békéscsaba, Megyei Tanacs. 1964. 248 p.

Viski, Karl. Forschungsbericht über die Entwicklung der ungarischen Volkskunde seit 1919. Südost-Forschungen. 11 (1946-1952): 211-272.

Visky, Károly. Hungarian peasant customs. Budapest, G. Vajna. 1932. 194 p. illus. (2d ed. Budapest, G. Vajna. 1937. 187 p., illus.)

Visky, Károly. Hungarian dances. Budapest, G. Vajna; London, Simpkin Marshall. 1937. 192 p.

Visky, Károly. Etnikai csoportok vidékek [Ethnic groups and regions]. A Magyar Nyelvtudomány Kézikönyve. 1, no. 8. 1938. 25 p. Budapest, Magyar Tudományos Akadémia.

Vuorela, Toivo. The Finno-Ugric peoples. Bloomington, Indiana University Press; The Hague, Mouton. 1964: 342-370, bibliog.: 391-392.

Wallis, B. G. Distribution of nationalities in Hungary. Geographical Journal. 47(1916): 177-188, maps.

Wallis, B. G. The Slavs of northern Hungary. Geographical Review. 6(1918): 268-281, maps.

Wallis, B. G. The Slavs of southern Hungary. Geographical Review. 6(1918): 341-353, plates 14, 16; maps.

Wallis, B. G. Central Hungary: Magyars and Germans. Geographical Review. 6(1918): 421-435, 3 maps, 10 tables.

Warriner, Doreen. Contrasts in emerging societies. Readings in the social and economic history of southeastern Europe in the nineteenth century. Bloomington, Indiana University Press. 1965: 29-113.

Weiner, P. Carved honeycake moulds. Budapest, Corvina. 1964. 50 p., illus.

Weinstock, S. A. Motivation and social structure in the study of acculturation: a Hungarian case. Human Organization. 23(1964): 50-52.

Wlislocki, Heinrich von. Die Szekler und Ungarn in Siebenbürgen. Hamburg, Verlagsanstalt und Druckerei. 1891. 8, 188 p.

Wlislocki, Heinrich von. Volksglaube und religiöser Brauch der Magyaren. Münster in Westfalen, Aschendorff. 1893. 13, 171 p.

Allodiatoris, Irma. A Kárpát-medence antropológiai bibliográfiája. Budapest, Akadémiai Kiadó. 1958. 183 p. (Bibliography of the Carpathian Mountain range.)

Bittner-Szewczykowa, Halina. Materialy do bibliografii etnografii Polskiej za 1945-1954 r. Lud. 43. Supplement. Wroclaw, Polskie Towarzystwo Ludoznawcze. 1958. 355 p.

Bystron, Jan S. Bibliografja etnografii Polskiej. 1. Biblioteka "Luda Slowianskiego." 1. Krakow, Gebethner i Wolff. 1929. 6, 160 p.

Maas, W. Kritische Bibliographie zum Almwesen in den Karpaten. Karpathenland. 4(1931): 40-46, 94-95.

United States. Bureau of the Census. Bibliography of social science periodicals and monograph series: Poland, 1945-1962. Washington, Government Printing Office. 1964. 316 p.

Beliajus, Vytautas F. St. John's Day in Poland. Viltis. 6, no. 7(1948): 3.

Beliajus, Vytautas F. Polish costumes (Krakow, Sącz, Goral). Viltis. 6, no. 7(1948): 6-7.

Benda, Wladyslaw T. Life in a Polish village. Century. 72(1908): 323-332.

*Benet, Sula. Song, dance and customs of peasant Poland. London, D. Dobson; New York, Roy. 1951. 247 p.

Benet, Sula. Patterns of thought and behavior in the culture of Poland. A study of a national culture. New York, Columbia University, Research in Contemporary Cultures. 1952. 137 p.

Bergmann, Eugen von. Zur Geschichte der Entwicklung deutscher, polnischer und jüdischer Bevölkerung in der Provinz Posen seit 1829. Tübingen, H. Laupp. 1883. 8, 365 p.

Bergmann, Felix. La Pologne et la protection des minorités. Paris, Librairie L. Rodstein. 1935. 200 p.

Bernaut, Elsa. Polish peasant autobiographies. New York. 1950. 342 p. (Unpublished Ph.D. dissertation. Columbia University.)

Biegajło, W. Borysówka, Grodzisko and Hruskie villages in the north-eastern undeveloped corner of Poland. In Jerzy Kostrowicki, ed. Land utilization in East-central Europe. Geographia Polonia. 5. Warszawa, Institute of Geography, Polish Academy of Sciences. 1965: 29-60.

Biegeleisen, Henryk. Wesele. Lwów, Instytut Stauropigjanski. 1928. 3, 512 p., 26 plates. (Marriage customs.)

Biernacka, Maria. Potakówska—wieś powiatu jasielskiegs. 1890-1960 . . . [Potakówska—a village in the Jasto district during the years 1890-1960 . . .]. Warszawa, 1962. 233 p., maps, table.

Bohdanowicz, L. The Polish Tatars. Man. 44(1944): 116-121.

Boyd, Louise A. The marshes of Pinsk. Geographical Review. 26(1936): 376-395.

Boyd, Louise A. Polish countryside. New York, American Geographical Society. 1937. 10, 369 p., illus., plates.

Brandes, Georg Morris Cohen. Polen. München, A. Langen. 1898. 7, 390 p., illus.

Brandes, Georg Morris Cohen. Poland; a study of the land, people, and literature. London, W. Heinemann. 1903. 8, 310 p.

Braun, Hermann Adalbert. Alte und neue Bilder von Masuren. Angerburg, Lyck. 1886-1888 (published in 8 parts). 3, 192 p.

Brewater, Paul G. Bierki and other Polish games of chance and skill. Z.f.E. 83(1958): 83-85.

Brown, John Croumbie. Forests and forestry in Poland, Lithuania, the Ukraine, and the Baltic provinces of Russia. Edinburgh, Oliver and Boyd. 1885. 8, 276 p.

Bugiel, V. La demonologie du peuple polonais. Revue de l'Histoire des Religions. 1902: 158-170.

Bugiel, V. Les chants funéraires de la Pologne. Étude comparative. Société d'Anthropologie de Paris, Bulletins et Mémoires. Sér. 7. 6(1925): 122-147; 7(1926): 57-73; 10 (1929): 7-36.

Bugiel, V. Les fêtes annuelles de la Pologne. L'Ethnographie, New series. no. 15/16(1927): 68-74.

Bystrón, Jan Stanisław. Nazwiska Polskie [Polish names]. Lwow, Lwowska Bibljoteka Slawistyczna. 4. 1927. 8, 243 p.

Bystrón, Jan Stanisław. Dzieje obyczajów w dawnej Polsce, wiek XVI-XVIII. 2 vols. Warszawa, Nakl. Trzaski, Everta i Michalskiego. 1933-1934.

Bystrón, Jan Stanisław. Megalomanja Narodowa. Warszawa, Towarzystwo Wyodawnicze "Roj." 1935. 268 p.

Bystrón, Jan Stanisław. Ksiegaimion w Polsce uzywanych. Warszawa, Towarzystwo Wyodawnicze "Roj." 1938. 376 p. (Personal names.)

Bystroń, Jan Stanisław. Etnografia polska. Warszawa, W. Poznaniu Czytelnik. 1947. 232 p.

Chicago. University. Division of the Social Sciences. Contemporary Poland. Editor: Alicja Iwańska. New Haven, Printed by the Human Relations Area Files. 1955. 6, 578 p.

Coleman, M. M. Saints, spirits and soil. Polish Folklore. 6(1961): 1-5.

Conrad, Hally H. Farm aid in Poland. Foreign Agriculture. 2(1938): 409-432.

Czaplicka, Marie A. The Polish peasant through American eyes. [Book review of Thomas, W., & Fl. Znaniecki, The Polish peasant.] Folk-Lore 29(1918): 248-251.

Czaplicka, Marie A. Poland. Geographical Journal. 53(1919): 361-381.

*Czarnecka, Irena. Folk art in Poland. Warsaw, Polonia. 1957. 234 p., illus., plates. (Also German, Polish, and French editions.)

Dachler, Anton, and Michael Haberlandt. Das Bauernhaus in Österreich-Ungarn und in seinen Grenzegebieten. Wien, Ingenieur- und Architektenverein. 1906. 17, 288 p., 67 illus., 6 plates, 75 folio plates, map.

Davies, Arthur, ed. Polish studies. London, Le Play Society. 1934. 66 p.

*Dobrowolski, Kazimierz. Die Haupttypen der Hirtenwanderungen in den Nord-karpaten vom 14. bis zum 20. Jahrhundert. In László Földes, ed. Viehzucht und Hirtenleben in Ostmitteleuropa. Budapest, Akadémiai Kiadó. 1961: 113-146.

Fischer, Adam. Lud polski. Podręcznik etnografji Polski [The Polish people. Handbook of Polish ethnography]. Lwow, Wydawn Zakładu narod im. Osselinskich. 1926. 4, 240 p.

Fischer, Adam. Etnografja Słowianska. Zeszyt 3. Polacy [Slavic folk-lore. Vol. 3. The Poles]. Lwow, Warszawa, Ksiaznica-Atlas. 1934. 7, 121, and 256 p., map.

Fournier, Eva. Poland. London, Vista Books. 1964. 191 p.

Francastel, Pierre. Les origines des villes polonaises. Paris, Mouton. 1960. 244 p.

Gajek, Józef. Die Erforschung der Ackerbaugeräte im Zusammenhang mit dem polnischen Ethnographischen Atlas. In Agrarethnographie. Berlin, Akademie der Wissenschaften zu Berlin. 1957: 11-22.

Gajek, Józef, ed. Polski atlas etnograficzny. Polish ethnographic atlas. Warszawa, Panstwowe Wydawnictwo Naukowa. No. 1(1964):--

Galęski, Boguslaw. Chlopi izawód rolnika; studia z socjologii wsi. Warszawa, Panstwowe Wydawn Naukowe. 1963. 162 p. (Peasantry and rural conditions.)

Ginet-Pilsudzki, B. Almen-Viehzucht im Tatra-Gebirge in Polen. S.A.f.V. 20(1916): 236-258.

Gini, Corrado. I Caraimi di Polonia e Lituania. Genus. 2(1936): 1-56, plates, table.

Grabowski, J. Wycinanska ludowa. Warszawa, Wydanionictwo "Sztuka." 1955. 184 p., illus. (Folk art.)

Grisebach, H. Das polnische Bauernhaus. Berlin, Gea-Verlag. 1917. 106 p., illus.

*Gross, Feliks. The Polish worker, a study of a social stratum; translated in part by Norbert Guterman. New York, Roy Publishers. 1945. 274 p.

Hensel, Anton. Masuren. Ein Wegweiser. Königsberg. 1896. 97 p. (Reprinted in 1923.)

Hervet, E. Ethnographie Polens. Bericht über die Arbeiten der Frau Severine Duchinska, gelesen in der Ethnographischen Gesellschaft zu Paris in der Sitzg. vom 15 März 1869. Wien, Gerold's Sohn. 1871. 12, 52 p.

Jarecka, Louise L. Popular art in Poland. Geographical Magazine. 8(1939): 345-362.

Jarecka, Louise L. Made in Poland; living traditions of the land. New York, Knopf. 1949. 289 p., illus.

Kennedy, H. E. Polish peasant courtship and wedding customs and folk-song. Folk-Lore. 36(1925): 48-68.

Knoop, D. Aberglaube und Brauch aus der Provinz Posen: 1. Liebe, Brautstand, Hochzeit, Ehe. 2. Mutter und Kind. Mitteilungen der Schlesischen Gesellschaft für Volkskunde. 7(1905): 43-57.

Knoop, D. Aberglaube und Brauch aus der Provinz Posen: 3. Krankheiten, Tod und Begräbnis; das Leben nach dem Tode. Mitteilungen der Schlesischen Gesellschaft für Volkskunde. 7(1905): 70-77.

Knoop, D. Beiträge zur Volkskunde der Provinz Posen . . . Rogasener Familienblatt. 9(1905): no. 1: 1-4; no. 3: 9-12; no. 4: 13-16; no. 5: 17-20.

Knoop, D. Polnische Dämonen. Hessische Blätter für Volkskunde. 4(1905): 24-32.

Knoop, D. Polnische Dämonen. Hessische Blätter für Volkskunde. 17(1918): 26-37.

Kohl, Johann Georg. Reisen im Inneren von Russland und Polen. 3 vols. Dresden und Leipzig, Arnold. 1841.

*Kopczynska-Jaworska, Bronislawa. Das Hirtenwesen in den polnischen Karpater In László Földes, ed. Viehzucht und Hirtenleben in Ostmitteleuropa. Budapest, Akadémiai Kiadó. 1961: 389-438.

Kossak-Szczucka, Z. Rok Polski: obyczaj i wiara [The Polish year: customs and beliefs]. London, Veritas. 1955. 238 p.

Kukier, R. Etnograficke oblasti a etnicke skupiny na polskem uzemi. In Vacla Frolec, ed. Straznice 1946-1965. Brno, Nakladatelstvi Blok. 1966: 293-314. (English summary. Ethnographic regions and ethnic groups in Polish territory.)

Kyrle, Georg. Siedlungs- und Volkskundliches aus den wolhynischen Poljesje. M.A.G.W. 48-49(1918-1919): 118-145, 39 illus.

Laskowski, Maria. Some Polish Christmas traditions. Lore (Milwaukee). 4(1953): 2-5, 29.

Little, Frances Delanoy. Sketches in Poland. London, A. Melrose. 1914. 7, 344 p.

Lösch, Karl Ch. von. Der polnische Volkscharakter. Berlin, Schriften für Politik und Auslandskunde. 1940. 100 p.

Machatschek, Fritz. Landeskunde der Westkarpathenländer. Stuttgart, J. Engelhorns. 1927. 11, 444 p., 17 plates, 42 text figs.

Markowska, D. Rodzina w środowiskim; studium wsi pedkrakowskiej [The family in peasant environments, study of a village near Krakow]. Wrocław, Zakład Narodowy im. Ossolińskich. 1964. 214 p. (English summary.)

Moszyński, Kazimierz. Polesie wschodnie. Materjały etnograficzne z wschodniej części b. powiatu mozyrskiego oraz z powiatu rzeczyckiego [East Poland, ethnographic materials from the regions of Mozyr and Rzeczyca]. Warszawa, Wydawnictwo Kasy im. Mianowskiego. 1928. 15, 328 p., 14 plates.

Ostafin, Peter A. The Polish peasant in transition: a study of group integration as a function of symbiosis and common definitions. Ann Arbor. 1948 [i.e., 1949]. 6, 394, 1 p. (Unpublished Ph.D. dissertation in sociology. University of Michigan.)

Die Österreichisch-Ungarische Monarchie in Wort und Bild. 24 vols. Wien, K. K. Hof- und Staatsdruckerei. 1886-1902. (See Bd. 17. Mähren und Schlesien. 1897 and Bd. 19. Galizien. 1898.)

Pawłowski, S. Recherches sur l'habitat rural en Pologne. Comptes Rendus Congrès International de Géographie. Paris. 1931. 1934: 244-249.

Piskorz-Skocka, H. The commune of Miłogoszcz on the Pomeranian coast. In Jerzy Kostrowicki, ed. Land utilization in East-central Europe. Geographia Polonia. 5. Warszawa, Institute of Geography, Polish Academy of Sciences. 1965: 157-194.

*Poland. European conference on rural life. National monographs drawn up by governments. Poland. Series of League of Nations Publications. European Conference on Rural Life. 29. Geneva. 1940. 49 p., illus.

Polish folklore. 7 vols. Cambridge, Penn., Alliance College. 1956-1962.

Reymont, Wladyslaw [Ladislas] S. The peasants. 4 vols. New York, Alfred A. Knopf. 1924-1925. (Fiction, but an excellent portrayal of pre-World War I peasant life.)

Reynolds, Rothay. My Slav friends. London, Mills & Boon. 1916. 7, 311 p.

Rogowski, J. Mazurzy pruscy [Prussian Mazuria]. Lwów, Nakł. Nakładu Narod. im. Ossolinskich. 1926. 6, 35, 3 p.

Rutkowski, Jan. Histoire économique de la Pologne avant les partages. Paris, Champion. 1927. 12, 268 p. (Economics and land tenure.)

Sapieha, Virgilia Peterson. Polish profile. Garden City, N. Y., Garden City Publishing Co. 1942. 319 p.

Schultz, Arved. Ethnographischer Bilderatlas von Polen. 5 vols. Veröffentlichungen der Landeskundliche deutsch Generalgouvernement Warschau. Reihe B. Berlin. 1917.

Slomka, Jan. From serfdom to self-government; memoirs of a Polish village mayor 1842-1927. Toronto, Macmillan; London, Minerva Publishing Co. 1941. 11, 274 p. (Dzikow, Poland.)

Stola, W. The commune of Czersk in the Warsaw suburban zone. In Jerzy Kostrowicki, ed. Land utilization in East-central Europe. Geographia Polonia. 5. Warszawa, Institute of Geography, Polish Academy of Sciences. 1965: 87-124.

Sukertowa, E. Mazury w Prusach wschodnich [The Mazurians of East Prussia]. Bibl. geogr. "Orbis." Ser. 3. Bd. 10. Krakow, 1927. 199 p.

Super, Paul. Elements of Polish culture as seen by a resident foreigner. London, J. S. Bergson; Toruń, Baltic Institute. 1934. 74 p.

Super, Paul. The Polish tradition. London, G. Allen and Unwin. 1939. 15, 215 p. (Reprinted in 1944.)

Szczęny, R. The Carpathian commune of Cergowa. In Jerzy Kostrowicki, ed. Land utilization in East-central Europe. Geographia Polonia. 5. Warszawa Institute of Geography, Polish Academy of Sciences. 1965: 61-86.

Szujski, Józef. Die Polen und Rutenen in Galizien. Wien und Teschen, K. Prochaska. 1882. 282 p.

Tende, Gaspar de. An account of Poland. Containing a geographical description of the country, the manners of the inhabitants, and the wars they have been engaged in. London, T. Goodwin, etc. 1698.

Tetzner, Franz Oskar. Die Slaven in Deutschland . . . Braunschweig, F. Vieweg. 1902: 181-211 (Mazurians); 469-499 (Poles).

*Thomas, William Isaac, and Florian Znaniecki. The Polish peasant in Europe and America. 5 vols. Chicago, University of Chicago Press. 1918-1921. (2d ed. 2 vols. New York, Alfred A. Knopf.)

Toeppen, Max P. Aberglauben aus Masuren, mit einem Anhange, enthaltend: Masurische Sagen und Märchen . . . Danzig, Bertling. 1867. 168 p.

Tyszkiewicz, W. The commune of Kruszwica on the Cuiavian Plain in central Poland. In Jerzy Kostrowicki, ed. Land utilization in East-central Europe. Geographia Polonia. 5. Warszawa, Institute of Geography, Polish Academy of Sciences. 1965: 125-156.

Vincenz, Stanislaw. On the high uplands. Sagas, songs, tales and legends of the Carpathians. (Translated by H. C. Stevens.) New York, Roy Publishers. 1955. 344 p.

Wierzbicki, Z. T. Poł wieku przemian na wsi Malopolskiej [A half century of change in the rural area of Malpolska]. Kultura i społeczenstwo. 2, no. 3(1958): 74-94.

Wolska, Helen. Dances of Poland. New York, Chanticleer Press. 1952. 38 p. 7 plates.

Zienkowicz, Leon. Les costumes du peuple polonais, suivis d'une description exacte de ses moeurs, de ses usages et de ses habitudes. Paris. 1841. 125 p., plates, musical notes, etc.

Znamierowska-Prüffer, Maria. Thrusting implements for fishing in Poland and neighboring countries. Translated from the Polish. Published for the U. S. Department of Interior and the National Science Foundation, Washington, D.C., by Scientific Publications Foreign Cooperative Center of the Central Institute for Scientific, Technical and Economic Information. Warsaw, Poland. [Available from the U. S. Department of Commerce, Clearinghouse for Federal Scientific and Technical Information, Springfield, Virginia.] 536 p., plates, tables.

KASHUBIANS (CASSUBIANS)

Bukowski, Andrzej. Regionalizm kaszubski, ruch naukowy, literacki i
kultuuralny. Zarys monografi historycznej. Poznań, Instytut Zachodni.
1950. 8, 399 p.

Gulgowski, Izydor. Kaszubi. Kraków, Ksiegarnia "Orbis." 1924. 128 p.

Lorentz, Friedrich. Geschichte der Kaschuben. Berlin, R. Hobbing. 1926.
172 p., map.

Lorentz, Friedrich. Zarys etnografji kaszubskiej. Toruń, Wyd. Instutut
Bałtycki. 1934. 5, 139 p.

*Lorentz, Friedrich, Adam Fischer, et al. The Cassubian civilization. London,
Faber and Faber. 1935. 26, 407 p., illus.

Seefried-Gulgowski, Ernst. Von einem unbekannten Volke in Deutschland. Ein
Beitrag zur Volks- und Landeskunde der Kaschubei. Berlin, Deutsche Landesbuchhandlung. 1911. 228 p., 88 illus.

Seefried-Gulgowski, Ernst. Kaschubische Hausindustrie. Berlin, Deutsche
Landesbuchhandlung. 1911. 4, 36 p., 32 illus.

Seefried-Gulgowski, Ernst. Ländlicher Hausfliess in der Kaschubei. Berlin,
Deutsche Landesbuchhandlung. 1914. 36 p., 25 illus.

Tetzner, Franz Oskar. Die Slowinzen und Lebakaschuben: Land und Leute,
Haus und Hof, Sitten und Gebräuche, Sprache und Literatur im östlichen
Hinter-Pommern . . . Berlin, E. Felber. 1899. 8, 272 p.

Tetzner, Franz Oskar. Die Slawen in Deutschland. Braunschweig, F. Vieweg
und Sohn. 1902: 388-468.

Wienkowski, G. von. Die pommerischen Kaschuben. M. A. G. W. 15 (1885):
537-555.

Hollander, Bernhard. Bibliographie der baltischen Heimatkunde. Ein Wegweis für den heimatkundlichen Unterricht in Lettland und Estland. Riga, Gesellschaft für Geschichte und Altertumskunde der Russischen Ostsee-Provinzen . 1924. 104 p.

Mackensen, Lutz, ed. Bibliographie zur deutsch-baltischen Volkskunde. Veröffentlichungen der Volkskundlichen Forschungsstelle am Herderinstitut zu Riga. 4. Riga, Verlag der "Ernst Plates." 1936. 74 p.

Thomson, Erik. Baltische Bibliographie, 1945-1956. Würzburg, Holzner Verlag. 1957. 218 p.

Braun, Gustav. Das Ostseegebiet. Leipzig, Teubner. 1912. 3, 108 p.

Hagar, Helmut. Zur Geschichte des baltischen Hakenpfluges. Apophoreta Tartensia (Stockholm). 1949: 119-128.

Hagar, Helmut. Der osteuropäische Arbeitsschlitten bei den Ostseefinnen. Finnische-Ugrische Forschungen. 33 (1958): 182-284.

Kohl, Johann Georg. Die deutsch-russischen Ostsee Provinzen; oder Natur und Völkerleben in Kur-, Liv- und Esthland. 2 vols. Dresden und Leipzig, Arnold. 1841.

Kupffer, K. R. Baltische Landeskunde. Riga, G. Löffler. 1911. 16, 557 p., plus atlas.

Léouzon Le Duc, Louis A. La Baltique. Paris, L. Hachette. 1855. 6, 548 p.

Paris. Musée National d'Histoire Naturelle. Musée de l'Homme. Guide de l'exposition d'art populaire baltique; Estonie, Lettonie, Lithuanie. Paris, Musée. 1935. 60 p., plates.

Ränk, Gustav. Eldstadsformer i de Östbaltiska förstuköken [Hearth types in the East-Baltic hall kitchen] . Folk-Liv. 9 (1945): 140-160.

*Ränk, Gustav. The Baltic culture area. Baltic Review. 1 (1946): 161-170.

Ränk, Gustav. Baltic farm-house types, their regional distribution and historical stratification. Laos. 1 (1951): 139-153.

Ränk, Gustav. Om äldre mjölkushållning i Balticum [Ancient dairy farming in the Baltic area] . Svio-Estonica. 13 (1956): 165-200.

Ränk, Gustav. Das baltische Herrenhaus als Gegenstand der volkskundlichen Forschung. Zeitschrift für Ostforschung. 1957: 524-530.

Ränk, Gustav. Volkskunde der Deutschbalten. Baltische Heft. 4 (1958): 158-174

*Tetzner, Franz Oskar. Die Slawen in Deutschland. Braunschweig, F. Vieweg. 1902. 20, 520 p.

PRUSSIANS (ANCIENT)

Conybeare, Frederick. The paganism of the ancient Prussians. (Including a translation of "About the religion and sacrifices of the ancient Prussians: an epistle of John Meletius to George Sabine.") Folk-Lore. 12(1901): 293-302.

Łowmiański, Henryk. The ancient Prussians. Torun, Baltic Institute; London, J. B. Bergson. 1936. 109 p.

*Tetzner, Franz Oskar. Die Slawen in Deutschland. Braunschweig, F. Vieweg. 1902: 7-23.

Balys, Jonas. Lithuania and Lithuanians. A selected bibliography. New York, Praeger. 1961. 10, 190 p.

Lietuvos TSR Mokslu Akademija, Vilna. Centrine Biblioteka. LTM akademijc ir jos mokslo darbuotoju leidiniu bibliografija; knygos, 1941-1954. J. Basiulis, A. Bielinis, S. Kisieliene. Vil'nius, Centrine Biblioteka. 1956. 91 p. (A bibliography of the publications of the Academy of Sciences of the Lithuanian S.S.R. and its scientific collaborators; books, 1941-1954.)

Balčikonis, J., et al. Lietuvių liaudies menas. 1 kn. Audiniai. [Lithuanian folk art. Textiles. Book 1]. Vilnius, Valstybiné Grožinès Literatūros Leidykla. 1957. 17, 266 p., illus.

Baltrušaitis, Jurgis. Lithuanian folk art. Munich. 1948. 80 p., 82 plates, 256 illus.

Balys, Jonas. Über die Geheimbünde in Litauen. Acta Ethnologica (Kóbenhavn 2(1937): 131-132.

Balys, Jonas. Litauische Hochzeitsbräuche. Contributions of Baltic University, 9. Hamburg, Baltic University. 1946. 78 p.

Balys, Jonas. Volkscharakter und Volksbräuche der Litauer. Scholar (Heidelberg). 1(1947): 37-48.

Balys, Jonas. Fastnachtbräuche in Litauen. S.A.f.V. 45(1948): 40-69.

Balys, Jonas. Litauische Volksbräuche; volkskundliche Skizzen. Folk-Liv. 12-13(1948-1949): 112-140.

Balys, Jonas. Easter customs. The Marian (Chicago). 4, no. 3(1951): 16.

Balys, Jonas. Lithuanian folk songs in the U.S.A. Folkways Record FM4009. New York, Folkways Records. 1955, 1962. (One 12-in. LP record, with 11 pp. of texts, etc.)

Beliajus, Vytautas F. Traditional Lithuanian customs (Palm Sunday to the Feast of St. George). Viltis. 12(1946): 2.

Beliajus, Vytautas F. The skrupskai, a Lithuanian farm homestead. Viltis. 1948. 6(May 1948): 15.

Beliajus, Vytautas F. Spalis (The month of Shiving). Viltis. 17 (Summer Issue, 1958): 13.

Bezzenberger, Adalbert. Litauische Forschungen. Beiträge zur Kenntniss der Sprache und des Volkstumes der Litauer. Göttingen, Peppmüller. 1882. 15, 213 p.

LITHUANIANS

Bezzenberger, Adalbert. Über das litauische Haus. Altpreussische Monatsschrift. 23(1886): 34-79, 629-633, illus.

Bielinskis, F., et al. Lietuvių liaudies menas. 1 kn. Architektūra. [Lithuanian folk art. Architecture, Book 1]. Vilnius, Valstybinė Grožinės Literatūros Leidykla. 1957. 431 p., 597 illus.

Cappeller, Carl. Leben und Gebräuche der alten preussischen Litauer; Aufzeichnungen aus dem Kreise Stallupönen. 2d ed. Oberländer (Netherlands). 1925. 75 p.

Cibas, Daumantas. Kanklės, Lithuanian national musical instrument. Viltis. 23, no. 1(1964): 4-5.

Coxwell, Charles Fillingham. Siberian and other folktales. London, C. W. Daniel Co. 1925: 941-951.

Essen, Werner. Die ländlichen Siedlungen in Litauen. 2 vols. Leipzig, R. Voigtlander. 1931. 133 p., 4 plates, 1 vol. of maps.

Galaunė, Paulius, comp. Lietuvių liaudies menas. Medžio dirbiniai [Lithuanian folk art. Artifacts of wood]. 2 vols. Vilnius, Valstybinė Grožinės Literatūros Leidykla. 1956-1958. (Mostly illustrations.)

Gimbutas, Jurgis. Das Dach des litauischen Bauernhauses aus dem 19. Jahrhundert; ein Beitrag zur Geschichte des Holzbaues. Stuttgart, Mohr. 1948. 104 p., illus., 24 plates, maps.

Gimbutas, Marija. Ancient symbolism in Lithuanian folk art. Memoirs of the American Folklore Society. 49. Philadelphia. 1958. 8, 158 p.

Glemžaitė, Mikelina. Lietuvių tautiniai drabužiai [Lithuanian national costume]. Vilnius, Valstybinė Politinės ir Mokslinės Literatūros Leidykla. 1955. 205 p., illus., col. plates.

Jungfer, Victor. Alt-Litauen. Eine Darstellung von Land und Leuten, Sitten und Gebräuchen. Berlin, Leipzig, Neuner. 1926. 143 p.

Kessler, Otto. Die Baltenländer und Litauen. Beiträge zur Geschichte, Kultur und Volkswirtschaft. Berlin, Puttkammer & Mühlbrucht. 1916. 237 p.

Krikščiūnas, Jurgis. Die litauische Landwirtschaft. Kaunas, Verlag Žemės Ūkio Rūmai. 1933. 304 p., illus., diagr., map.

Krikščiūnas, Jurgis. Agriculture in Lithuania. Kaunas, Lithuanian Chamber of Agriculture. 1938. 155 p., plates.

Kurschat, Alexander. Haus und Hausrat im preussischen Litauen. Litauische Literarische Gesellschaft. Mitteilungen. 5(1907): 424-443.

Landsbergis, Algirdas, and Clark Mills, eds. The green linden. Selected Lithuanian folksongs. New York, Voyages Press. 1964. 135 p.

Lange, Erwin R. Sterben und Begräbnis im Volksglauben zwischen Weichsel und Memel. Beihefte zum Jahrbuch der Albertus Universität, Königsberg. 15. Würzburg, Holzner-Verlag. 1955. 176 p.

Leskien, August, und K. Brugman. Litauische Volkslieder und Märchen aus dem preussischen und dem russischen Litauen. Strassburg, K. J. Trübner. 1882. 8, 578 p.

Lingis, Juozas. Åkerns berdning i östra Litauen [The method of tilth in eastern Lithuania]. Folk-Liv. 7/8(1943-1944): 143-165. (English summary.)

Lingis, Juozas. The national character of Lithuanian people. Baltic Review. 1 (1946): 3-13.

*Lithuania. European conference on rural life, 1939. National monographs drawn up by governments. Lithuania. Series of League of Nations Publications. European Conference on Rural Life, 12. Geneva. 1939. 47 p., illus.

Lituanus; Lithuanian Quarterly. Brooklyn, N.Y., Lithuanian Student Association. 1 (1954):--

Maciuika, Benedict V., ed. Lithuania in the last 30 years. New Haven, printed by the Human Relations Area Files. 1955. 6, 411 p., illus., maps.

Mansikka, V. J. Litauische Zaubersprüche. Folklore Fellows Communications. 87. Helsinki, Suomalainen Tiedakatemia. 1929. 166 p.

Meulen, Reinder van der. Die Naturvergleiche in den Liedern und Totenklagen der Litauer. Leiden, A. W. Sijthoff. 1907. 14, 178 p.

Mortensen, Hans. Litauen; Grundzüge einer Landeskunde. Hamburg, L. Friederichsen. 1926. 14, 321 p., plates, maps.

Naumann, Hans. Bauernhaus und Kornkammer in Litauen. In Hans Naumann. Primitive Gemeinschaftskultur. Jena, Diederichs. 1921: 148-167, 8 plans.

Sachs, Curt. Die litauischen Musikinstrumente in der Kgl. Sammlung für Deutsche Volkskunde zu Berlin. International Archives of Ethnography. 23(1915): 1-7.

Salvatori, Giuseppe. Rustic and popular art in Lithuania. Milano, Casa Editrice Gea. 1925. 43 p., illus., plates, 2 col. plates.

Senn, Alfred. Christmas Eve in Lithuania. American Slavic and East European Review. 5(1946): 132-134.

Shallna, Susanne. Ruta. The Lithuanian national flower. Viltis. 5, no. 1 (1947): 6.

*Sirvaitis, Casimir Peter. Religious folkways in Lithuania and their conservation among the Lithuanian immigrants in the United States. Studies in Sociology. Abstract Series. 3. Washington, Catholic University of America Press. 1952. 49 p.

Tamošaitis, Antanas, ed. Sodžiaus menas [Rustic art]. 8 vols. Kaunas, Žemės Ūkio Rūmai. 1931-1939.

Tetzner, Franz Oskar. Haus und Hof der Litauer. Globus. 72(1897): 249-254, illus.

Tetzner, Franz Oskar. Feste und Spiele der Litauer. Globus. 73(1898): 317-323.

*Tetzner, Franz Oskar. Die Slawen in Deutschland. Braunschweig, F. Vieweg. 1902: 24-112.

Viltis. Hope. A Folklore and Lithuanistica Magazine. 1 (1942):--

Wagner, Gustav. Die Deutschen in Litauen--ihre kulturellen und wirtschaftlichen Gemeinschaften zwischen den beide Weltkriege. Marburg, Lahn, Herder-Institut. 1959. 312 p.

Witort, Jan. Kucya na Litwie [Christmas in Lithuania]. Lud. 3(1897): 1-6.

Woods, Ethel G. Skeat. The Baltic region; a study in physical and human geography. London, Methuen. 1932: 389-400.

Zobarskas, Stepas. Lithuanian folk tales. 2d ed. Brooklyn, G. J. Rickard. 1959. 240 p.

Zobarskas, Stepas. The maker of the gods. Ten Lithuanian stories. New York, Voyages Press. 1961. 131 p.

Zweck, Alb. Litauen: Landes- und Volkskunde. Stuttgart, Hobbing und Büchle. 1898. 8, 452 p., maps, illus.

Ozols, Zelma Aleksandra. Latvia; a selected bibliography. Washington, K. Karusa. 1963. 144 p. (Up to 1957 only.)

Anderson, Edgars, ed. Cross road country: Latvia. Waverly, Iowa, Latvju Grāmata. 1953. 387 p.

Balodis, Francis Aleksanders. Lettland; Landschaft, Volksleben, Baukunst und Museen; eine Folge von Bildern mit Einleitung und Erläuterungen . . . Riga Pagalms. 1938. 143 p., illus.

Bezzenberger, A. Die Kurische Nehrung und ihre Bewohner. Forschungen zur deutschen Landes- und Volkskunde, im Auftrage der Centralkommission für Wissenschaftliche. Landeskunde von Deutschland. 4(1888): 161-300.

Bielenstein, August J. G. Die Grenzen des lettischen Volksstammes und der lettischen Sprache in der Gegenwart und im 13. Jahrhundert. St. Petersburg, Commissionäre der Kaiserlichen Akademie der Wissenschaften. 1892. 16, 548 p., maps.

Bielenstein, August J. G. Die Holzbauten und Holzgeräte der Letten. 2 vols. Petrograd. 1907, 1918.

Bielenstein, Martha. Bast und Rinde an der Kleidung der alten Letten. Z.f.V., n.F. 3(1932): 147-156. 2 illus.

Bielenstein, Martha. Die altlettischen Färbmethoden. Veröffentlichungen der Volkskundlichen Forschungsstelle am Herderinstitut zu Riga. 2. Riga, Verlag Ernst Plates. 1935. 176 p., 5 plates (2 in color).

Biezais, H. Die Hauptgöttinnen der alten Letten. Uppsala, Almqvist & Wiksell 1955. 435 p.

Bogouschefsky, Baron de. Note on heathen ceremonies still practiced in Livonia, Russia. J.A.I. 3(1873): 275-276.

Böhm, Maximillian. Lettische Schwänke und Volksüberlieferungen. Reval, Kluge. 1911. 11, 125 p.

Bonne, Georg. Die Letten. Ein germanischer Bruderstamm. Berlin, F. Würtz. 1921. 58 p.

Bulmerincq, Ernest von. Die wirtschaftliche und soziale Lage der Landgemeinde Muremoix. Ein Beitrag zum Kenntniss der Agrarverhältnisse Livlands. Leipzig W. Schwanke. 1911. 112 p.

Chicago. University. Division of the Social Sciences. Latvia: an area study. George B. Carson, ed. New Haven, printed by the Human Relations Area Files. 1956. 13, 667 p., illus., maps.

LATVIANS

Coxwell, Charles Fillingham. Siberian and other folktales. London, C. W. Daniel Co. 1925: 909-940.

Dorofeev, V. L. Arkhitekturnoe nasledie narodnogo žilošča Latvii [The architectural heritage of the popular dwelling in Latvia]. Moskva, Mosk. Architek. Inst. 1956. 15 p., illus.

Dzērvītis, Arv., and V. Ģinters, eds. Ievads latviešu tautas tērpu vēsturē [An introduction to the history of the Latvian national costume]. Riga, J. Grīnbergs. 1936. 256 p., illus.

Grosberg, Oskar. Lettland. Land und Leute. Ein Plauderbuch. Riga, R. Ruetz. 1930. 84 p.

Jaunzems, Jānis. Der kurische Bauernhof, ethnographische Schilderung. Riga, V. Tepfers. 1944. 69 p., illus.

Johansons, Andrejs. Die Frau in der Fichte: zu einem synkretistischen Kult der Letten. Archiv für Völkerkunde. 16(1961): 49-54.

Johansons, Andrejs. Die Hüter der Schwelle im lettischen Volksglauben. Scando-Slavica (Copenhagen). 8(1962): 152-160.

Johansons, Andrejs. Der Kesselhaken im Volksglauben der Letten. Z.f.E. 87(1962): 63-76.

Johansons, Andrejs. Das Bauopfer der Letten. Tidskrift för Nordisk Folkminnesforskning (Uppsala). 18-19(1962-1963): 113-136.

Johansons, Andrejs. Das Schirmherr des Hofes im Volksglauben der Letten. Stockholm Studies in Comparative Religion. 5. Stockholm, Almqvist & Wiksell. 1964. 304 p., 3 plates.

Kanold, Johannes. Curieuse und nutzbare Anmerkungen von Natur- und Kunstgeschichte. Sitzungsberichte der Kurländischen Gesellschaft für Literatur und Kunst und Jahresbericht des Kurländischen Provinzialmuseums, 1905. Mitau. 1906: 71-87.

Kundzins, P. The Latvian rural architecture. Art and Archaeology. 32(1931): 169-174, 192, illus.

Kurtz, Edith. Heilzauber der Letten in Wort und Tat. 1. Allgemeines Siechtum magischen Ursprungs, innere Krankheit. Veröffentlichungen der Volkskundlichen Forschungsstelle am Herder-Institut zu Riga. 5. Riga, Ernst Plates. 1937. 185 p.

*Latvia. European conference on rural life, 1939. National monographs drawn up by governments. Latvia. Series of League of Nations Publications. European Conference on Rural Life, 11. Geneva. 1939. 92 p., illus.

LATVIANS

Latvju raksti; tautas māksla uzvalkas, a udumos, būvēs, podniecībā u. t. t.
pēc materialiem valsts un privatos krājumos. 3 vols. Rigā, Valstspapīru
spiestuves izdevums. 1924-1931. (Folk art, folk architecture, decoration,
and ornament.)

Die Letten. Aufsätze über Geschichte, Sprache und Kultur der alten Letten.
Riga, Valters & Rapa. 1930. 473 p.

Ligers, Ziedonis. Die Volkskultur der Letten. Ethnographische Forschungen.
1. Riga, the author. 1942. 381 p., 504 illus.

Ligers, Ziedonis. L'économie d'acquisition: la cuiellette, la chase et la
pêche en Lettonie. Paris, Presses Universitaires de France. 1953. 183 p.,
illus., 36 plates.

*Ligers, Ziedonis. Ethnographie Lettone. 1. Schriften der Schweizerischen
Gesellschaft für Volkskunde. 35. Basel. 1954. 622 p., illus.

Niedre, J. Die lettischen Handschuhe. Sammlungen des Staatlichen Historischen Museums Lettlands. 3. Riga, Valsts Vesturiskais Musejs. 1931.
32 p., 23 col. plates.

Paegle, Edvards. L'art populaire letton. Riga, Impr. Latvju Kultura. 1928.
26 p., 30 plates.

Paegle, Edvards. Latvian popular arts, a short history. Riga, Pagalms. 1935.
40 p., illus.

Paegle, Edvards. Lettische Volkskunst. Riga, Pagalms. 1935. 43 p., 55
plates.

Redlich, Friedrich Alexander. Sitte und Brauch des livländlichen Kaufmanns.
Veröffentlichungen der Volkskundlichen Forschungsstelle am Herderinstitut
zu Riga. 3. Riga, Ernst Plates. 1935. 110 p.

Straubergs, Karlis. Lettisk folktro om de Döda. Stockholm, Nordiska Museet.
1949. 149 p. (Folk beliefs about the dead.)

Tetzner, Franz Oskar. Die Slawen in Deutschland. Braunschweig, F. Vieweg.
1902: 113-178.

Tiesenberg, L. Einiges über die St. Johannis-Gilde zu Riga. Baltische
Monatshefte. 1936: 30-33.

Valters [Walters], Mikelis. Le peuple letton (The Latvian people). Riga,
Valters & Rapa. 1926. 407 p.

Williams, Maynard Owen. Latvia, home of the Letts. National Geographic
Magazine. 46 (1924): 401-443.

Woldemar, C. Die Lettenauswanderung nach Nowgorod im Jahre 1865.
Bautzen, Baltische Deutsche Presse; Leipzig, Schmaler & Peeh. 1867. 8,
45 p.

*Indiana. University. Graduate Program in Uralic and Asian Studies. The Livonians. By Felix J. Oinas. New Haven, printed by the Human Relations Area Files. 1955. 11, 61 p., maps.

Loorits, Oskar. Liivi ravha olevik [The contemporary status of the Livonians]. Eesti Kirjandus. 17(1923): 37-46, 73-82, 129-139, 166-182.

Loorits, Oskar. Livische Märchen und Sagenvarianten. Helsinki, Suomalainen Tiedeakatemia. 1926. 101 p.

Loorits, Oskar. Liivi ravha usund. 3 vols. Tartu, Tallinna Eesti Kirjastus-ühisuse Trükikoda. 1926-1928. (Folklore.)

Loorits, Oskar. Liivi usundi Kultuurilooline taust [Culture-historical background of Livonian religion]. Virittäjä (Helsinki). 1945: 248-259.

Loorits, Oskar. Eine Beschreibung der livischen Beerdungsbrauche. Z.f.V. 51(1955): 252-258.

Strobach, H. Ich bin ein livländischer Bauer. Zur Überlieferungsgeschichte einer Bauernklage. Deutsches Jahrbuch für Volkskunde. 6(1960): 293-329.

*Vuorela, Toivo. The Finno-Ugric peoples. Indiana University Publications, Uralic and Altaic Series, 39. Bloomington, Indiana University Press; The Hague, Mouton. 1964: 206-220, 385-386.

Hagar, Helmut. A bibliography of works published by Estonian ethnologists in exile 1945-1965. Stockholm, Institutum Litterarum Estonicum. 1965. 63 p.

Kuri, Salme. Estonia. A selected bibliography. Washington, Library of Congress. Slavic and Central European Division Publications. 1958. 74 p.

────────────

Anderson, W. Die Marspanik in Estland 1921. Z.d. V.f. V. 4(1925-1926): 229-252.

Boecler, Johann Wolfgang. Der einfältigen Ehsten abergläubische Gebräuche, Weisen und Gewohnheiten, derer sie sich so ins Gemein als insonderheit, bei ihren Kindtaufen, Hochzeiten, Begräbnissen, . . . Reval, zu finden bey C. Brendeken (1685?). In Scriptoria rerum Livonicarum. Riga and Leipzig. 2 vols. 1853: 665-684.

Coxwell, C. Fillingham. Siberian and other folktales. London, C. W. Daniel Co. 1925: 661-668.

Eesti Rahva Muuseum. Album de costumes nationaux Estoniens. Tartu, Eesti Rahva Muuseum. 1927. 6 p., 17 plates.

Hagar, Helmut. Två slädtyper i Estland [Two sledge types in Estonia]. Svio-Estonica. 8(1948): 105-124.

Haltenberger, Michael. Landeskunde von Eesti. Dorpat, J. G. Krüger. 1926. 204 p.

Hurt, J. Über estnische Himmelskunde. St. Petersburg, Eggers. 1900. 91 p., figs.

*Indiana. University. Graduate Program in Uralic and Asian Studies. The Estonians. By Linda Raun. New Haven, printed by the Human Relations Area Files. 1955. 10, 392 p., illus., maps.

Kalits, V. New features in the life of the peasants of Kihnu Island. Soviet Anthropology and Archaeology. 1 (1962): 27-36.

Kant, Edgar. Bevölkerung und Lebensraum Estlands; ein anthropoökologischer Beitrag zur Kunde Baltoskandias. Tartu, Akadeemiline Kooperatiiv. 1935. 7, 280 p., illus., maps.

Kirby, W. F. The hero of Estonia, and other studies in the romantic literature of that country. 2 vols. London, J. C. Nimmo. 1894.

Laid, Eerik. The origin and age of Estonian culture. Baltic Review. 1 (1945): 18-20.

Laugaste, Eduard. Die estnischen Vogelstimmendeutungen. Folklore Fellows Communications. 97. Helsinki, Suomalainen Tiedeakatemia. 1931. 96 p.

Leinbock, Ferdinand. Die materielle Kultur der Esten. Tartu, Akadeemiline Kooperatiiv. 1932. 112 p., 48 illus., 19 maps.

Linnus, H. Vysivka v estonskom narodom iskusstve. 1. Severnaia Estonija i ostrova [Needlework in Estonian art. 1. Northern Estonians and the islands]. Tallin, Estgosizdat, Gos. Hudož Inst. Eston. SSR. 1955. 122 p., illus., plates.

Loorits, Oskar. Estnische Volksdichtung und Mythologie. Dorpat, Akademiline Kooperatiiv. 1932. 107 p.

Loorits, Oskar. Estonian folklore today. Acta Ethnologica. 1(1935): 34-52.

Loorits, Oskar. Gedanken-, Tat- und Worttabu bei den estnischen Fischern. Acta et Commentationes Universitatis Tartuensis (Dorpatensis). B. Humaniora. 45, no. 2. Tartu. 1939. 127 p.

Loorits, Oskar. Eesti rahvausundi maailmavaade [The conception of life in ancient Estonian religion]. Stockholm, Eesti Raamat. 1948. 120 p.

Loorits, Oskar. Estnische Geistigkeit im Lichte des Volksglaubens. Scholar (Heidelberg). 2-3(1948): 53-59.

*Loorits, Oskar. Grundzüge des estnischen Volksglaubens. Skrifter Utgivna av Kunglige Gustav Adolfs Akademien för Folklivsforskning. 18(in 3 vols.) Lund, 1949-1960. 16, 591; 490; 690 p.

Looritis, Oskar. Die sogenannte Naturreden in der estnischen Volksüberlieferung. Arv. 7(1952): 96-128.

Loorits, Oskar. Insamlingen och ordnandet av Estlands folkminnen [Collection and systematization of Estonian popular tradition]. Svenska Landsmål och Svenskt Folkliv. 1952(1953): 87-104.

Loorits, Oskar. Estnische Volkserzählungen. Fabula. Supplement-Serie, Reihe A (Texte). 1. Berlin, 1959. 8, 227 p.

Manninen, I. Eesti rahvariiete ajalugu [History of Estonian folk costume]. Tartu, Eesti Rahva Muuseum. 1927. 516 p., 491 illus., 4 col. plates. (German summary: 486-514.)

Manninen, I. Die Sachkultur Estlands. 2 vols. Sonderabhandlungen der Gelehrten Estnischen Gesellschaft. 1-2. Tartu, J. G. Krüger. 1931-1933. 15, 275 p., 291 illus., map; 12, 357 p., 354 illus.

Mark, Julius. Über das Roggendreschen bei den Esten. Sitzungsberichte der Gelehrten Estonische Gesellschaft. 1931(1933): 315-374, 43 illus.

Mark, Julius. Neue Bemerkungen über das Dreschen und Ernten bei den Esten. Sitzungsberichte der Gelehrten Estonische Gesellschaft. 1932 (1935): 42-111, 82 illus., map.

Moora, H. A., ed. Estonskaia narodnaia odežda XIX i načala XX veka [Estonian folk clothing of the nineteenth and the beginning of the twentieth centuries]. Tallin, Estgosizdat. 1960. 248 p., illus.

*Moora, H. A., and A. Viires, eds. Abriss der estnischen Volkskunde. Tallinin, Estnischer Staatsverlag. 1964. 306 p., illus.

Petri, Johann Christoph. Ehstland und die Ehsten. 2 pts. Gotha. 1802.

Pullerits, Alb. Estland, Volk, Kultur, Wirtschaft. Reval, Kluge & Ströhm. 1931. 8, 356 p.

Pullerits, Alb. Estonia. Population, cultural and economic life. Tallinin. 1935. 4, 236 p., illus.

Ränk, Gustav. Das estnische Nationalmuseum und die ethnographische Arbeit in Eesti 1922-1927. Eurasia Septentrionalis Antiqua. 3(1928): 164-180, 5 illus.

Ränk, Gustav. Saarema taluehitised [Folk buildings on Saarema Island]. Ethnographische Forschung. 1. Tartu. 1939. 382 p.

Ränk, Gustav. Nagra korsningsformer mellan den Estniska boningsrian och Estlandssvensskkarnas bostadsbyggnadar [Some transitional forms between the Estonian combined dwelling and kiln houses and the dwelling houses of the Estonian Swedes]. Svio-Estonica. 8(1948): 72-93.

Ränk, Gustav. The Estonian dwelling house. Apophoreta Tartuensa. 1949: 95-107.

Ränk, Gustav. Vana Eesti rahvas ja kultuur [The people and culture of ancient Estonia]. Stockholm, Eesti Raamat. 1949. 223 p.

Ränk, Gustav. Öselska herrgårder vid utgangen av 1600-talet [The manorial estates of Saaremaa at the end of the 17th century]. Svio-Estonica. 12(1954): 31-59.

Ränk, Gustav. Die Hakenpflüge Estlands. Suomen Museo. 62(1955): 5-42.

Ränk, Gustav. Die estnische Volkskundeforschung in den Jahren 1945-1955. Zeitschrift für Ostforschung. 5(1956): 244-254.

Ränk, Gustav. Ostereier in Estland. S. A. f. V. 53(1957): 138-143.

Ränk, Gustav. Die Bauernhausformen im baltischen Raum. Marburger Ostforschungen. 17. Würzburg, Holzner Verlag. 1962. 16, 120 p., 58
illus., 4 maps.

Ränk, Gustav. Estniska folkdräkter från 1700-talets första halft [Estonian
peasant costumes in the first half of the eighteenth century]. Svio-Estonica.
16 (1962): 36-51.

Russwurm, Karl Fr. W. Sagen aus Hapsal, der Wick, Ösel und Runö. Reval,
Kluge. 1861. 20, 191 p.

Scheibe, Eva. Siedlungsgeographie der Inseln Osel und Moon. Schriften der
Deutschen Akademie in München. 17. München. 1934. 8, 150 p., 6
maps.

Schroeder, Leopold von. Die Hochzeitsbräuche der Esten und anderer
Finnisch-Ugrischer Volkerschaften in Vergleichung mit denen der Indoger-
manischen Völker. Berlin, Verlag von A. Asher. 1888. 265 p.

Soom, Arnold. Der Herrenhof in Estland im 17. Jahrhundert. Lund, n.p.
1954. 411 p. (Agriculture and economics.)

Talve, Ilmar. Virolainen sauna. (English summary: The Estonian sauna.)
Sananjalka. 2 (1960): 122-146. (Also published in: Scripta Ethnologica
[Turku]. 5. 1960. 27 p.)

Tampere, H. T. Estonskie narodnye pesni s melodijami [Estonian folk songs
with melodies]. Tallin, Estgosizdat, Akademiîa Nauk Estonskoĭ SSR Lit.
Muzeĭ im F. R. Krejcval'da. 1956. 1243 p.

Uustalu, Evald, ed. Aspects of Estonian culture. London, Boreas Publishing
Co. 1961. 332 p.

*Vuorela, Toivo. The Finno-Ugric peoples. Uralic and Altaic Studies. 39.
Bloomington, Indiana University Press; The Hague, Mouton. 1964: 170-
205, 384-385.

Washburne, Mrs. Marion Foster. A search for a happy country. Washington,
National Home Library Foundation. 1940. 17, 269 p.

Wiedemann, F. J. Aus dem inneren und äusseren Leben der Ehsten. Leipzig,
Voss. 1876. 18, 664 p.

*Aleksandrov, V. A., ed. Narody Evropeĭskoĭ chasti SSSR. 2 vols. Moskva, Nauka. 1964.

Diefenbach, Lor. Völkerkunde Osteuropas, insbesondere der Haemoshalbinsel und der unteren Donaugebiete. 2 vols. Darmstadt, Brill. 1880. 22, 318; 8, 414 p.

Fischer-Galati, Stephen A. Eastern Europe in the sixties. New York, Praeger. 1963. 13, 239 p.

Frolec, Vaclav. On the question of the origin of the irregular nucleated village. Národopisný Věstník Československý. 1(1966): 64-77.

Gasparini, Evel. Il matriarcato slavo: parte prima. Venezia, La Goliardica. 1961. 183 p.

Haase, Felix. Volksglaube und Brauchtum der Ostslaven. Breslau, Gerhard Märtin. 1939. 6, 428 p.

Jakobson, Roman. Slavic languages. A condensed survey. 2d ed. New York, King's Crown Press. 1955. 36 p.

Karcz, Jerzy, ed. Proceedings of the conference on Soviet and East European agriculture. Berkeley, University of California Press. 1967. 25, 445 p.

Latham, R. G. The native races of the Russian Empire. London, Hippolyte Baillière. 1854. 8, 340 p., map.

Piprek, Johannes. Slawische Brautwerbungs- und Hochzeitsbräuche. Z.f.Ö.V. Erg.-Bnd. 10. Stuttgart, Strecker und Schröder. 1914. 6, 192 p.

Rudy, Zvi. Ethnosoziologie sowjetischer Völker, Wege und Richtlinien. Bern und München, Franke Verlag. 1962. 244 p.

Sanders, Irwin T. The peasantries of eastern Europe. In Irwin T. Sanders, ed. Collectivization of agriculture in eastern Europe. Lexington, University of Kentucky Press. 1958: 24-48.

Sanders, Irwin T., ed. Collectivization of agriculture in eastern Europe. Lexington, University of Kentucky Press. 1958. 10, 214 p.

Summers, Montague. The Vampire in Europe. New Hyde Park, N. Y., University Books. 1961: 282-323.

Tetzner, Franz Oskar. Die Slawen in Deutschland. Braunschweig, F. Vieweg. 1902. 20, 520 p.

Tilke, Max. The costumes of eastern Europe. London, E. Benn; New York, E. Weyhe. 1926. 3, 32 p., 96 col. plates.

*Tokarev, S. A., and N. N. Cheboksarov, eds. Narody zarubezhnoĭ Evropy [The peoples of non-Russian Europe]. 2 vols. Moskva, Nauka. 1964-1965.

*Tomasić, Dinko. Personality and culture in eastern European politics. New York, George W. Stewart. 1948. 249 p. (Reprinted: Cambridge, Mass., M.I.T. Press. 1964.)

Tuckermann, Walther. Osteuropa. 2 vols. Breslau, Ferdinand Hirt. 1922. 116 p., 13 maps; 124 p., 6 maps.

Winkler, Heinrich. Zur Völkerkunde von Osteuropa. Breslau, Hirt'sche Buchhandlung. 1912. 40 p.

Wissenschaftliche Information zur Völkerkunde; Altertumskunde und Kultur-geographie aus dem östlichen Europa. 5 pts. München, Institut für Kultur- und Sozialforschung in München. 1958-1959.

Horecky, Paul L., ed. Basic Russian publications: an annotated bibliography on Russia and the Soviet Union. Chicago, University of Chicago Press. 1962. 26, 313 p.

König, W., and C. Kupfer. Ethnographische Bibliographie der Sowjetunion 1945-1953. Deutsches Jahrbuch für Volkskunde. 1 (1955): 323-375.

United States. Bureau of the Census. Bibliography of social science periodicals and monograph series—U.S.S.R., 1950-1963. Washington, Government Printing Office. 1965. 447 p.

Aksakov, Sergiei Timofieevich. Years of childhood. London, E. Arnold; New York, Longmans, Green. 1916. 11, 340 p.

Aksakov, Sergiei Timofieevich. Russian gentleman. London, E. Arnold. 1917. 9, 209.

Aksakov, Sergiei Timofieevich. Russian schoolboy. London, E. Arnold; New York, Longmans, Green. 1917. 216 p.

Aksakov, Sergiei Timofieevich. Chronicles of a Russian family. London, G. Routledge & Sons; New York, E. P. Dutton. 1924. 15, 398 p.

Arnaud, Charles A. de. New era in Russia. New York, J. S. Ogilvie. 1891. 166 p.

Baring, Maurice. A year in Russia. London, Methuen. 1907. 19, 319 p.

Baring, Maurice. Russian essays and stories. London, Methuen. 1908. 17, 295 p.

Baring, Maurice. Landmarks in Russian literature. London, Methuen. 1910. 17, 299 p. (National character studies.)

Baring, Maurice. Russian people. London, Methuen. 1911. 19, 366 p.

Baring, Maurice. What I saw in Russia. London and New York, T. Nelson & Sons. 1913. 381 p.

Beucler, André. Paysages et villes russes. Paris, Nouvelle Revue Française. 1929. 226 p.

*Blum, Jerome. Lord and peasant in Russia, from the ninth to the nineteenth century. Princeton, Princeton University Press. 1961. 10, 656 p.

Bobrinsky, Aleksiei Aleksandrovich. Volkstümliche russische Holzarbeiten, Hausindustrie, Haushalt und Küchengeräte. Leipzig, K. W. Hiersemann. 1913. 52 p.

Bobrinsky, Aleksiei Aleksandrovich. Russian peasant art; illustrating the specimens collected by Count A. A. Bobrinsky. New York, H. C. Perleberg. 1922. 2 p., 60 plates (3 col.). (In portfolio.)

Borders, Karl. Village life under the Soviets. New York, Vanguard Press. 1927. 22, 191 p.

Brandes, Georg Morris C. Impressions of Russia. New York, T. Y. Crowell. 1889. 10, 353 p. (Also: London, W. Scott. 1890. 10, 353 p.)

Brown, John Croumbie. Forests and forestry of northern Russia and the lands beyond. Edinburgh, Oliver and Boyd. 1884. 279 p.

Bury, Rev. Herbert. Russian life today. London, A. R. Mowbray; Milwaukee, Young Churchman Co. 1915. 7, 270 p.

Bury, Rev. Herbert. Russia from within—personal experiences of many years, and especially since 1923, with opinions and convictions formed in consequence. London, Churchman Publishing Co. 1927. 16, 231 p.

Buxton, Charles R. In a Russian village. London, Labour Publishing Co. 1922. 8, 96 p.

Calina, Josephine. Scenes of Russian life. London, Constable. 1918. 302 p.

Chaianov, Aleksandr V. The theory of peasant economy. Homewood, Ill., published for the American Economic Association by R. D. Irwin. 1966. 75, 317 p.

Cherniavsky, Michael. The old believers and the new religion. Slavic Review. 25(1966): 1-39.

Chicherov, V. I. Zimnii period russkogo zemledel'cheskogo kalendaria XVI-XIX vekov, cherki po istorii narodnykh verovanii [The winter period of the Russian agricultural calendar, 16th-19th centuries. Essay on the history of popular belief]. Moskva, Izdalelstvo Akademii Nauk SSSR, Trudy Instituta Etnografii imena N. N. Miklukho-Maklaia. Novaia seriia. 40. 1957. 236 p.

Chizhikova, L. N., and M. N. Shmeleva. Sovremennoe russkoe krestianskoe zhilishche. (Selo Virjatino, Tambovskoi obl) [Contemporary Russian peasant dwellings. (Village of Virjatina, Tambovsk region)]. Sovetskaia Etnografiia. 1955, no. 1 (1955): 54-71.

Chombart de Lauwe, J. Les paysans soviétiques. Paris, Éditions du Seuil. 1961. 7, 201 p.

Combes de Lestrade, Gaëtan. Present condition of the peasant in the Russian Empire . . . Annals of the American Academy of Political and Social Science. 2, no. 2(1892): 225-235.

Conybeare, Frederick Cornwallis. Russian dissenters. Cambridge, Harvard University Press. 1921. 10, 370 p.

Coxwell, Charles Fillingham. Through Russia in war-time. London, T. F. Unwin. 1917. 311 p.

Coxwell, Charles Fillingham. Siberian and other folktales. London, C. W. Daniel Co. 1925: 671-908.

Custine, Marquis de. The empire of the Czar; or, observations on the social, political, and religious state and prospects of Russia, made during a journey through that empire by the author. 3 vols. London, printed for Longman, Brown, Green, & Longmans. 1843.

Custine, Marquis de. La Russie en 1839. 4 vols. Paris, Amyot. 1843.

Debogorii-Mokrievich, Vladimir K. When I was a boy in Russia. Boston, Lothrop, Lee and Shepard. 1916. 173 p., plates.

Dicey, Edward. A month in Russia during the marriage of the czarevitch. London, Macmillan. 1867. 8, 248 p.

Dunn, Stephen P., and Ethel Dunn. The great Russian peasant: culture change or cultural development? Ethnology. 2(1963): 320-338.

*Dunn, Stephen P., and Ethel Dunn. The peasants of central Russia. New York, Holt, Rinehart & Winston. 1967. 16, 139 p., illus.

Edwards, Henry Sutherland. The Russians at home. London, W. H. Allen. 1861. 4, 432 p.

Elnett, E. Historic origin and social development of family life in Russia. New York, Columbia University Press. 1926. 11, 152 p.

*The Englishwoman in Russia; impressions of the society and manners of the Russians at home, by a lady, ten years resident in that country. London, J. Murray; New York, Scribners. 1855. 15, 350 p.

Fedorov, Mikhail. La Russie sous le régime communiste; réponse au rapport de la Délégation des Trades-unions Britanniques, basée sur la documentation officielle soviétique; avec une préface de Hubert Bourgin . . . Paris, Nouvelle Libraire Nationale. 1926. 12, 574 p.

Fedotov, Grigoriy Petrovich. The Russian church since the revolution. New York, Macmillan. 1928. 7, 95 p.

Fedotov, Grigoriy Petrovich. The Russian religious mind. Cambridge, Harvard University Press. 1946. 16, 438 p. (Kievan period.)

Fedotov, Grigoriy Petrovich. A treasury of Russian spirituality. New York, Sheed & Ward. 1948. 16, 501 p.

Fen, Elisaveta. A Russian childhood. London, Methuen. 1961. 286 p.

*Fenomenov, M. ĪA. Sovremennaĩa derevina. 2 vols. Moskva-Leningrad. 1925. (The classic early soviet village study.)

Fenomenov, M. ĪA. Folk songs and folk poetry in a contemporary Russian village. In Pitirim A. Sorokin, et al., eds. Systematic source book in rural sociology. Vol. 2. Minneapolis, University of Minnesota Press. 1931: 528-537.

Fenomenov, M. ĪA. Religion, magic, and ethics among the contemporary Russian peasants. In Pitirim A. Sorokin, et al., eds. Systematic source book in rural sociology. Vol. 2. Minneapolis, University of Minnesota Press. 1931: 424-431.

Fenomenov, M. ĪA. The size and fertility of the peasant family in relation to its economic well-being. In Pitirim A. Sorokin, et al., eds. Systematic source book in rural sociology. Vol. 2. Minneapolis, University of Minnesota Press. 1931: 114-118.

French, Reginald Michael, ed. The way of the pilgrim and the pilgrim continues his way. London, S.P.C.K. 1952. 10, 245 p. (An autobiographical spiritual account of the travels of a staretz in the 1860s.)

Garstin, Denis Norman. Friendly Russia. New York, McBride, Nast. 1915. 248 p.

Geiger, Kent. The soviet family. In M. F. Nimkoff. Comparative family systems. Boston, Houghton, Mifflin Co. 1965: 301-328.

Gorer, Geoffrey, and John Rickman. The people of Great Russia. New York, Chanticleer Press. 1950. 235 p.

Gorky [Gor'kiĭ], Maksim. My childhood. New York, The Century Co. 1915. 374 p. (Reprinted: Garden City, N.Y., Garden City Publishing Co. 1926.)

Gorky [Gor'kiĭ], Maksim. Childhood. Moscow, Foreign Languages Publishing House. 1950. 442 p.

Graham, Stephen. A vagabond in the Caucasus, with some notes of his experiences among the Russians. London and New York, J. Lane Co. 1911. 7, 311 p.

Graham, Stephen. Undiscovered Russia. London and New York, J. Lane Co. 1912. 16, 337 p.

Graham, Stephen. With the Russian pilgrims to Jerusalem. London, Macmillan. 1913. 10, 306 p.

Guthrie, Mrs. Katherine Blanche. Through Russia: from St. Petersburg to Astrakan and the Crimea. 2 vols. London, Hurst & Blackett. 1874.

Halle, Fannina W. Woman in Soviet Russia. (Translated from the German.) London, Routledge; New York, Viking Press. 1934. 13, 409 p.

Hapgood, Isabel Florence. Russian rambles. Boston and New York, Houghton, Mifflin. 1895. 11, 369 p.

Hapgood, Isabel Florence, comp. and tr. Service book of the Holy Orthodox-Catholic Apostolic (Graeco-Russian) Church. Boston and New York, Houghton. 1906. 38, 615 p. (Reprinted: Brooklyn, Syrian Archdiocese. 1956.)

*Haxthausen-Abbenburg, August Franz Ludwig Maria, Freiherr von. Studien über die inneren Zustände, das Volksleben und insbesondere die ländlichen Einrichtungen Russlands. 3 vols. Hannover, Hahn. 1847-1852.

Haxthausen-Abbenburg, August Franz Ludwig Maria, Freiherr von. Études sur la situation intérieure, la vie nationale et les institutions rurales de la Russie. 3 vols. Hanovre, Hahn. 1847-1853.

*Haxthausen-Abbenburg, August Franz Ludwig Maria, Freiherr von. The Russian empire, its people, institutions and resources. 2 vols. London, Chapman & Hall. 1856.

Haxthausen-Abbenburg, August Franz Ludwig Maria, Freiherr von. Die ländliche Verfassung Russlands. Ihre Entwicklungen und ihre Feststellung in der Gesetzgebung von 1861. Leipzig, F. A. Brockhaus. 1866. (Serfdom and land tenure.)

Hindus, Maurice G. The Russian peasant and the revolution. New York, H. Holt. 1920. 12, 327 p.

Hindus, Maurice G. Broken earth. New York, International Publishers. 1926. 287 p.

Hindus, Maurice G. Humanity uprooted. New York, J. Cape and H. Smith. 1929. 19, 369 p.

Holme, Charles. Peasant art in Russia. London and New York, The Studio. 1912. 10, 52 p., plates.

*Hourwich, Isaac Aaronovich. Economics of the Russian village. Studies in History, Economics and Public Law. 2. New York, Columbia College. 1892. 6, 182 p.

IAkushkin, Evgeny Ivanovich. Obychnoe Pravo [Customary law]. 4 vols. Iaroslav and Moscow. 1875-1909.

Jarintzov, Madame Nadine. Russia, the country of extremes. London, Sidgwick & Jackson. 1914. 14, 371 p.

Jarintzov, Madame Nadine. The Russians and their language. Oxford, B. H. Blackwell. 1916. 31, 222 p.

Karelin, Apollon Andreevich. Obshchinnoe vladĕnie i Rossii. St. Petersburg, A. S. Suvorina. 1893. 288 p. (Land tenure and village communities.)

*Kennard, Howard. The Russian peasant. Philadelphia, J. B. Lippincott. 1908. 15, 302 p.

Kohl, Johann Georg. Reisen im inneren von Russland und Polen. 3 vols. Dresden und Leipzig, Arnold. 1841.

Kohl, Johann Georg. Reisen in Südrussland. 2 vols. Dresden und Leipzig, Arnold. 1841.

Kohl, Johann Georg. Russia and the Russians in 1842. 2 vols. London, H. Colburn. 1842.

Kosa, John. Two generations of Soviet man. A study in the psychology of communism. Chapel Hill, University of North Carolina Press. 1962. 10, 214 p.

Kostomarov, Nikolai Ivanovich. Ocherk' domashnei zhizni i nravov veliko-russkago naroda. St. Petersburg, M. M. Stasulevicha. 1887. 428 p. (Social life and customs.)

Kovalevskii, Maksim Maksimovich. Tableau des origines et de l'évolution de la famille et de la propriété. Stockholm, Samson & Wallin. 1890. 202 p.

Kovalevskii, Maksim Maksimovich. Modern customs and ancient laws of Russia. London, David Nutt. 1891. 10, 260 p.

*Kovalevskii, Maksim Maksimovich. La régime économique de la Russie. Paris, V. Giard & E. Brière. 1898. 362 p.

Kovalevskii, Maksim Maksimovich. La crise russe; notes et impressions d'un témoin. Paris, V. Giard & E. Brière. 1906. 304 p.

Kovalevskii, Maksim Maksimovich. La Russie sociale. Paris, M. Giard & E. Brière. 1914. 178 p.

Krader, Lawrence. The transition from serf to peasant in eastern Europe. Anthropological Quarterly. 33 (1960): 76-90.

Kravchinskii, Sergiei Mikhailovich. Russia under the tzars. 2 vols. London, Ward & Downey. 1885.

Kravchinskii, Sergiei Mikhailovich. The Russian peasantry; their agrarian condition, social life and religion. 2d ed. New York, Harper and Brothers. 1888. 401 p. (There are many other one- and two-volume editions of this work.)

Kravchinskii, Sergiei Mikhailovich. The Russian peasantry . . . . London, G. Routledge & Sons. 1905. 651 p.

Krebel, Rudolf. Volksmedicin und Volksmittel der Völkerstämme Russlands. Leipzig-Heidelberg, C. F. Winter. 1858. 13, 194 p.

Kriukova, Irina Aleksandera. Russkaia narodnaia rez'ba po kosti [Russian folk carving on bone]. Moskva, Koiz Nauchnoissledov. Inst. Hudoz. Promijsl Rospromsoveta. 1956. 119 p., illus.

Le Play, Frédéric. Peasants of central Russia. In Pitirim A. Sorokin, et al., ed. Systematic source book in rural sociology. Vol. 2. Minneapolis, University of Minnesota Press. 1931: 84-94.

Lestrelin, Achille. Les paysans russes: leurs usages, moeurs, caractère, religion, superstitions, et les droits des nobles sur leurs serfs. Paris, E. Dentu. 1861. 8, 291 p.

Loukomski [Lukomskii], Georgii K. La vie et les moeurs en Russie. Paris, Librairie Ernst Leroux. 1928. 8, 45 p.

Luke, Louise E. Marxian woman: soviet variants. In Ernest J. Simmons, ed. Through the glass of soviet literature; views of Russian society. New York, Columbia University Press. 1953: 27-109.

Mace, David Robert, and Vera Mace. The soviet family. Garden City, Doubleday; London, Hutchinson. 1963. 367 p.

Maynard, Sir John. Russia in flux, before October. London, V. Gollancz. 1941. 301 p.

Maynard, Sir John. The Russian peasant; and other studies. London, V. Gollancz. 1942. 512 p. (Reprinted: New York, Collier Books. 1962.)

Mead, Margaret. Soviet attitudes toward authority. Santa Monica, Rand Corporation. 1951. 148 p.

Mitrany, David L. Marx against the peasant. A study in social dogmatism. London, Weidenfeld & Nicolson. 1951. 348 p.

Morley, Henry, ed. Sketches of Russian life before and after the emancipation of the serfs. London, Chapman and Hall. 1866. 298 p.

GREAT RUSSIANS

Munro-Butler-Johnstone, Henry Alexander. A trip up the Volga to the fair of
Nijni-Novgorod. Oxford and London, J. Parker. 1875. 8, 151 p.

Noble, Edmund. Russia and Russians. Boston and New York, Houghton,
Mifflin. 1900. 285 p.

Norman, Sir Henry. All the Russians, travels & studies in contemporary
European Russia, Finland, Siberia, the Caucasus, and central Asia. New
York, C. Scribner's Sons. 1902. 12, 476 p.

Oinas, Felix J. Folklore activities in Russia. In Richard M. Dorson, ed. Folk-
lore research around the world. Bloomington, Indiana University Press. 1961:
76-84.

Olearus [Oelschlager], Adam. The travels of Olearius in seventeenth-century
Russia. Stanford, Stanford University Press. 1968. 400 p., illus.

*Palmer, Francis H. E. Russian life in town and country. New York and Lon-
don, G. P. Putnam's Sons; London, George Newnes. 1901. 320 p.

Pavlovsky, George. Agricultural Russia on the eve of the revolution. London,
G. Routledge & Sons. 1930. 10, 340 p.

Pittard, Eugène. La castration chez l'homme. Recherches sur les adeptes
d'une secte d'eunuques mystiques, les Skoptzy. Archives Suisses d'Anthropologie Générale. 6(1934): 213-536, 70 illus., diagrs.

Pittard, Eugène. La castration chez l'homme, et les modifications morpholo-
giques qu'elle entraîne. Recherches sur les adeptes d'une secte d'eunuques
mystiques, les Skoptzy. Paris, the author. 1934. 327 p.

Poole, Ernest. "The dark people," Russia's crisis. New York, Macmillan.
1918. 11, 226 p.

Poole, Ernest. The village: Russian impressions. New York, Macmillan.
1918. 234 p.

Popova, Ol'ga S. Russkaia narodnaia keramika [Russian popular ceramics].
Moskva, KOIZ. 1957. 131 p., illus.

Prosvirkina, Sof'ia K. Russkaia dereviannaia posuda [Russian wooden plates
and dishes]. Moskva, Goskul'tprosvetizdat. Gosudarstvennyi Istoricheskii
Muzei. Trudy. Pamiatniki Kul'tury. 16. 1957. 56 p., illus.

Pushkarev, S. G. The political, social, and religious organization of the mir
of the peasants of northern Russia during the sixteenth and seventeenth centuries. In Pitirim A. Sorokin, et al., eds. Systematic source book in
rural sociology. Vol. 2. Minneapolis, University of Minnesota Press. 1931:
389-391.

Rabotnova, I. P. Russkoe narodnoe kruzhevo [Russian popular lace]. Moskva, Vses. Kooperativnoe Izd-vo. 1956. 113 p., illus.

Rabotnova, I. P., and V. ĨA. Jokovleva. Russkaia narodnaia vyšivka [Russian folk embroidery]. Moskva, KOIZ. 1957. 159 p., illus.

Ralston, William R. S. The songs of the Russian people, as illustrative of Slavonic mythology and Russian social life. 2d ed. London, Ellis & Green. 1872. 16, 447 p.

Ralston, William R. S. Russian folk-tales. London, Smith, Elder. 1873. 16, 382 p. (Especially see sections on magic, witchcraft, and demons.)

*Rappoport, Angelo S. Home life in Russia. New York, Macmillan. 1913. 10, 287 p., illus.

Reynolds, Rothay. My Russian year. London, Mills & Boon. 1913. 12, 304 p.

Reynolds, Rothay. My Slav friends. London, Mills & Boon. 1916. 7, 311 p., plates.

Robinson, G. T. Rural Russia under the old régime; a history of the landlord-peasant world and a prologue to the present revolution of 1917. New York, London, Longmans, Green. 1932. 10, 342 p.

Roskoschny, Hermann. Russland, Land und Leute. 2 vols. Leipzig, Gressner & Schramm. 1882-1884.

Rudy, Zvi. Ethnosoziologie Sowjetischer Völker, Wege und Richtlinien. Bern und München, Francke Verlag. 1962. 244 p.

Saltykov, A. B., comp. Russkoia narodnaia keramika [Russian folk ceramics]. Moskva, Sov. Hudožnik. 1960. 166 p., illus.

Sandklef, Albert A. Bee-keeping in the Government of Kazan, in Russia, in the early part of the 18th century; about an ethnologically valuable document from the time of Charles XII. Acta Ethnologica Anneé 1936 (1936): 139-164, 3 illus., map.

Schlesinger, Rudolf. The family in the USSR. Vol. 1. of Changing Attitudes in the Soviet Union. London, Routledge and Kegan Paul. 1949. 418 p.

Schneeweiss, Ed. Studien zum russischen Dorf in Alt-Novgoroder Ujezd. Z.f.Ö.V. 19 (1913): 1-15, 81-93.

*Shanin, T. Inheritance among the Russian peasantry. University of Birmingham Discussion Paper. Ser. RC/C, 3 (February 1966): 1-21.

Shcherbatov, Mikhail Mikhailovich. Über die Sittenverderbnis in Russland. Berlin, Neue Verlag. 1925. 39, 191 p.

Shchukin, Ivan Vasilevich. Le suicide collectif dans le Raskol russe. Paris. 1903. 129 p.

Sillitoe, Alan. The road to Volgograd. London, W. H. Allen. 1964. 176 p.

Smith, Jessica. Women in Soviet Russia. New York, Vanguard Press. 1928. 13, 216 p.

Smith, Robert E. F. The origins of farming in Russia. Paris, Mouton. 1959. 198 p., 12 plates, 2 maps.

Sokolov, Yury Matryeevich. Russian folklore. New York, Macmillan. 1950. 8, 760 p.

Solohov, M., et al. Poslovicy russkogo naroda. Sbornik V. Dalja [Proberbs of the Russian people. Collection of V. Dal]. Moskva, Goslitizdat. 1957. 28, 991 p.

Sorokin, Pitirim A. The essential characteristics of the Russian nation in the twentieth century. Annals of the American Academy of Political and Social Sciences. 370 (March 1967): 99-115.

Tereshchenko, Aleksandr V. Byty Russkogo naroda [Manners and customs of the Russian people]. 7 vols. St. Petersburg, Tip. Ministerstva Biutrenihi Dyeli. 1848.

Thut, I. N., and Don Adams. Educational patterns in contemporary societies. New York, McGraw-Hill. 1964: 172-201.

Tikhomirov, Mikhail Nikolaevich. The towns of ancient Rus. Moscow, Foreign Languages Publishing House. 1959. 502 p.

*Tolstoi, Lev [Leo] Nikolaevich. My life. As told by the peasant Anissia New York, Duffield. 1924. 136 p.

Troyat, Henri. Daily life in Russia under the last tsar. New York, Macmillan. 1962. 242 p.

Tschernenkoff, N. N. The size of peasant families and its factors. In Pitirim A. Sorokin, et al., eds. Systematic source book in rural sociology. Vol. 2. Minneapolis, University of Minnesota Press. 1931: 100-104.

Volin, Lazar. The peasant household under the mir and the kolkhoz in modern Russian history. In Caroline F. Ware, ed. The cultural approach to history. New York, Columbia University Press. 1940: 125-139.

Volin, Lazar. The Russian peasant household under the mir and the collective farm system. Foreign Agriculture. 4(1940): 133-146.

Volin, Lazar. A survey of Soviet agriculture. U.S. Department of Agriculture. Agriculture Monograph. 5. Washington, Government Printing Office. 1951. 8, 194 p.

*Vucinich, Wayne S., ed. The peasant in nineteenth-century Russia. Stanford, Stanford University Press. 1968. 22, 314 p.

Wallace, Sir Donald Mackenzie. Russia. New York, Henry Holt. 1877. 13, 620 p. (There are many other editions.)

Walter, Lavina Edna. Russia. London, A. & C. Black. 1910. 8, 87 p.

Wesson, Robert G. Soviet communes. New Brunswick, N.J., Rutgers University Press. 1963. 275 p.

Wiener, Leo. An interpretation of the Russian people. London, New York, McBride, Nast. 1915. 14, 247 p.

Wright, Richardson. The Russians, an interpretation. New York, Frederick A. Stokes Co. 1917. 13, 288 p.

Young, Pauline Vislick. The pilgrims of Russian town. Chicago, University of Chicago Press. 1932. 23, 296 p. (Mainly on the Molokans of Los Angeles, but some data on Russia.)

*Zelenin, Dmitrii K. Russische (ostslavische) Volkskunde. Berlin und Leipzig. W. E. de Gruyter. 1927. 26, 424 p., illus.

UKRAINIANS

(See also general works and bibliographies listed under Great Russians.)

Allen, W. E. D. The Ukraine. A history. New York, Russell and Russell. 1963. 404 p.

Anderson, Robert T., and Gallatin Anderson. Ukrainian night courting. Anthropological Quarterly. 35(1962): 29-32.

Chicago. University. Division of the Social Sciences. Aspects of contemporary Ukraine. New Haven, printed by the Human Relations Area Files. 1955. 11, 505 p., maps.

Coxwell, Charles Fillingham. Siberian and other folktales. London, C. W. Daniel Co. 1925. 1055 p.

*Dmytriw, Olya, comp. Ukrainian arts. New York, Ukrainian Youth's League of North America. 1955. 217 p., plates.

Kvitka, Grigorii F. Marusia. New York, E. P. Dutton. 1940. 217 p. (Fiction, but excellent on peasant life, 1820-1830.)

Michael, Louis G. The Soviet Ukraine—its people and agriculture. Foreign Agriculture. 3(1939): 281-306.

Orlow, Damon. Red wedding. Chicago, H. Regnery Co. 1952. 244 p.

Ossadcha-Janata, Natalia. Herbs used in Ukrainian folk medicine. East European Fund, Mimeograph Series. 21. New York, Research Program on the U.S.S.R. and the New York Botanical Garden. 1952. 114 p.

Rudnicki, Stephan. Ukraina, Land und Volk; eine gemeinfassliche Landeskunde. Wien, Bund zur Befreiung der Ukraina. 1916. 7, 416 p.

Rudnicki, Stephan. Ukraine, the land and its people; an introduction to its geography. New York, Rand McNally. 1918. 369 p.

Stechishin, Savella. Traditional Ukrainian cookery. 4th ed. Winnipeg, Trident Press. 1967. 497 p.

Tisserand, Roger. La vie d'un peuple: l'Ukraine. Paris, Maisonneuve. 1943. 4, 298 p.

*Ukraine. A concise encyclopedia. Vol. 1. Toronto, University of Toronto Press. 1963: 156-520 p.

Volkov, F. Rites et usages nuptiaux en Ukraine. L'Anthropologie. 2(1891): 160-184, 408-437, 537-587; 3(1892): 541-588.

UKRAINIANS

Volkov, F. Le traineau dans les rites funéraires de l'Ukraine. R. T. P.
    11 (1896): 114-128.

Winter, Nevin O. The Ukraine, past and present. National Geographic Maga-
    zine. 34(1918): 114-128.

Cresson, William Penn. The Cossacks; their history and country. New York, Brentano's. 1919. 5, 5, 239 p.

Czaplicka, Marie.A. The evolution of the Cossack communities. Journal of the Royal Central Asian Society. 5(1918): 42-58.

Eustafieff, Victor K. Cossack youth. Asia. 30(1930): 16-21, 73-74, illus.

Hindus, Maurice. The Cossack today and yesterday. Asia. 29(1929): 356-363, 414, 416, 419-420, illus.

Köppen, Peter Ivanovich. Statistische Reise in's Land der donischen Kosaken, durch die Gouvernments Tula, Orel und Woronesh im Jahre 1850. St. Petersburg, Kaiserliche Akademie der Wissenschaften. 1852. 4, 254 p.

Krasinski, Henryk. The Cossacks of the Ukraine; comprising biographical notices of the most celebrated Cossack chiefs. London, Partridge and Oakley. 1848. 14, 312 p.

Michael, Joseph. The Cossack "Dzhigit" festival. Geographical Magazine. 18 (1946): 531-534.

Simoleit, Gustav. Die Donkosaken und ihr Land. Koenigsberg, Otto Kümmel. 1930. 4, 154 p.

Wagner, Moritz. Der Kaukasus und das Land der Kosaken in den Jahren 1843 bis 1846. 2 vols. Dresden und Leipzig, Arnold. 1848. 12, 242; 4, 227 p.

Wagner, Moritz. Travels in Persia, Georgia and Koordistan; with sketches of the Cossacks and the Caucasus. 3 vols. London, Hurst and Blackett. 1856.

Chicago. University. Division of the Social Sciences. Aspects of contemporary Belorussia. New Haven, printed by the Human Relations Area Files. 1955. 11, 389 p., illus., maps.

Chubynskiĭ, Pavel P. Trudy etnografichesko-statisticheskoĭ ekspedit͡sii v Zapadno-Ruskiĭ kraĭ [Proceedings of the ethnographic-statistical expedition to West Russia]. 7 vols. St. Petersburg. 1871-1878.

Coxwell, Charles Fillingham. Siberian and other folktales. London, C. W. Daniel Co. 1925: 963-979.

Kaper, M. S. Belorusskaia arkhitektura. Istoricheskii ocherk [White Russian architecture. An historical essay]. Minsk, Gosizdat B. S. S. R. Inst. Litry. F. I. S. K. an B. S. S. R. 1956. 120 p.

Karskii, Evfimii Fedorovich. Geschichte der weisrussischen Volksdichtung und Literatur. Berlin und Leipzig, W. de Gruyter. 1926. 10, 202 p.

Nikol'skiĭ, N. M. Proishozhdenie i istoriia belorusskoĭ svadebnoĭ obriadisosti [The origin and history of the White Russian marriage ritual]. Minsk, Izd-vo Akad. Nauk S. S. S. R. 1956. 237 p.

Serbov, I. A. Belorussy-Sakuny. Kratkii etnograficheskii ocherk [The Belorussian Sakuns. A short ethnographic account]. Sbornik Otdeleniia Russkago I͡Azyka i Slovesnosti Imperatorskoĭ Akademii Nauk. 44, no. 1. 1915. 80 p.

Allodiatoris, Irma. A Kárpát-medence antropológiai bibliográfiája [Bibliography of the anthropology of the Carpathian Mountain range]. Budapest, Akadémiai Kiadó. 1958. 183 p.

Maas, W. Kritische Bibliographie zum Almwesen in den Karpathen. Karpathenland. 4(1931): 40-46, 94-95.

Bogatuirev, Petr. Actes magiques, rites et croyances en Russie subcarpathique. Travaux publiés par l'Institut d'Études Slaves. 11. Paris, Champion. 1929. 162 p.

Ch., M. In a village of the Carpathian Mountains. In Pitirim A. Sorokin, et al., eds. Systematic source book in rural sociology. Vol. 2. Minneapolis, University of Minnesota Press. 1931: 391-392.

Fischer, Adam. Rusini. Zarys etnografji Rusi [Ruthenia. Handbook of Ruthenian ethnography]. Lwów, Zakład Naukowy imienia Ossolínskich. 1928. 8, 192 p., 3 plates.

Franke, I. Eine ethnologische Expedition in das Bojkenland. Z. f. Ö. V. 11(1905): 17-32, 98-115.

Hodgson, M. L. Some notes on the Huculs (Ruthenians). Folk-Lore. 16(1905): 48-55. 6 plates.

*Kaindl, R. F. Die Huzulen. Ihr Leben, ihre Sitten und ihre Volksüberlieferung. Wien, A. Hölder. 1894. 4, 129 p.

Kaindl, R. F. Haus und Hof bei den Huzulen. M. A. G. W. 26(1896): 147-185.

Kaindl, R. F. Bei den Huzulen im Pruththal. Ein Beitrag zur Hausforschung in Österreich. M. A. G. W. 27(1897): 210-224.

Kochanowska, Auguste von. Der Schafhirt der Bukowinaer Karpathen. Z. f. Ö. V. 8(1902): 252-253.

Kochanowska, Auguste von. Aus dem Leben der Schafhirten in der Bukowina. Z. f. Ö. V. 20 (1914): 106-114.

Koenig, Samuel. The culture and institutions of the Ukrainians of eastern Galicia. New Haven. 1935. (Unpublished Ph. D. dissertation in Sociology. Yale University.)

*Koenig, Samuel. Magical beliefs and practices among the Galician Ukrainians. Folk-Lore. 48(1937): 59-91.

*Koenig, Samuel. Marriage and the family among the Galician Ukrainians. In George P. Murdock, ed. Studies in the science of society. New Haven, Yale University Press. 1937: 299-318.

*Koenig, Samuel. Beliefs regarding the soul and the future world among the Galician Ukrainians. Folk-Lore. 49(1938): 157-161.

*Koenig, Samuel. Supernatural beliefs among the Galician Ukrainians. Folk-Lore. 49(1938): 270-276.

*Koenig, Samuel. Beliefs and practices relating to birth and childhood among the Galician Ukrainians. Folk-Lore. 50(1939): 272-287.

Král, Jiři. Die Almwirtschaft in Karpathorussland. Mitteilungen der Geographischen Gesellschaft in Wien. 71 (1928): 112-122.

Makovskii, Sergiei Konstantinovich. Peasant art of subcarpathian Russia. Prague, Plamjaedition. 1926. 152 p., plates.

Simonjenko, I. Almenwirtschaftliche Schafzucht der ukrainischen Bevölkerung in den Waldkarpaten im 19. und zu Beginn des 20. Jahrhunderts. In László Földes, ed. Viehzucht und Hirtenleben in Ostmitteleuropa. Budapest, Akadémiai Kiadó. 1961: 363-388.

Szujski, Józef. Die Polen und Ruthenen in Galizien. Wien und Teschen, K. Prochaska. 1882. 282 p.

Vincenz, Stanislaw de. On the high uplands: sagas, songs, tales and legends of the Carpathians. New York, Roy Publishers. 1956. 344 p.

Belobanova, A. V., and V. I. Kijranen. Bibliograficheskii ukazatel' po tradicionnoma fol'kloru KASSR za sovetskoe vremia, 1917 g.-ijun' 1954 g. [Bibliographic index to the traditional folklore of the Karelian ASSR in soviet times, 1917 to June 1954]. Trudy Karelskogo Filîala Akademiiã Nauk SSSR. 8(1957): 81-156.

Gadolin, Axel von. Ostkarelien—das finnische Grenzland. München, Carl Röhrig Verlag. 1943.

Hämäläinen, Jouki. Lauli uudesta sammosta; runoja. Petroskoi, Valtion Kustannusliike. 1959. 187 p. (Folklore.)

Härkönen, Iivo, ed. Karjalan Kirja [The book on Karelia]. 2 vols. Porvoo, Werner Söderström. 1910.

Homén, Theodor, ed. East Karelia and Kola Lapmark. Described by Finnish scientists and philologists. London, Longmans, Green. 1921. 264 p.

*Indiana. University. Graduate Program in Uralic and Asian Studies. The Karelians. By Felix J. Oinas. New Haven, printed by the Human Relations Area Files. 1955. 14, 199 p., maps.

Kettunen, Lauri. Tieteen matkamiehen uusia elämyksiä [New experiences of a wandering scholar]. Porvoo and Helsinki, Werner Söderström. 1948.

Pettersson, Lars. Die kirchliche Holzbaukunst auf der Halbinsel Zaoneze in russisch Karelien; Herkunft und Werden. Helsinki, Suomen muinais muisstoyhdistyksen. 1950. 254 p.

Richter, D. Bemerkung über die tverischen Karelier. Journal de la Société Finno-Ougrienne. 22, no. 2(1904): 1-64.

Schvindt, T. Matkamiustaja Tverin Karjalasta [Diaries on travels in Tver-Karelia]. Helsinki, Suomen Muinaismuistoyhdistys. 1957. 62 p.

*Sheldon, Richard C. Socio-economic development in a Karelian village. Cambridge, Mass. 1952. 300 p. (Unpublished Ph.D. dissertation in Anthropology. Harvard University.) A study of the village of Hautavaara, just inside the pre-1940 Finnish border, north of Lake Ladoga. The author used informants [refugees] resettled in Finland.

Taroeva, Roza F. Material'naia kul'tura Karel [The material culture of the Karelians]. Leningrad, Nauka. 1965. 222 p., illus.

*Vuorela, Toivo. The Finno-Ugric peoples. Uralic and Altaic Studies. 39. Bloomington, Indiana University Press; The Hague, Mouton. 1964: 92-132, 380-381.

*Indiana. University. Graduate Program in Uralic and Asian Studies. The Votes. By Felix J. Oinas. New Haven, printed by the Human Relations Area Files. 1955. 13, 52 p., maps.

Pãss, E. Death, burial and life beyond the grave with the Estonians, Ingers and the Votes. Sitzungsberichte der Gelehrten Estnischen Gesellschaft. 2(1937): 193-259.

Rãnk, Gustav. Vatjalaisten oluenpanosta [Beer brewing among the Votes]. Kotiseuta. 1952: 130-132.

Rãnk, Gustav. Vatjalaisten riihi ja riihityöti [The kiln house and threshing procedure of the Votes]. Kalevalaseuran Vuosikirja. 35(1955): 279-295.

Rãnk, Gustav. Vatjalaiset. German summary: Die Wotan. Ein Volk und eine Kultur. Suomalaisen Kirjallisuuden Seuran Toimituksia. 267. Helsinki. 1960. 154 p.

Vuorela, Toivo. The Finno-Ugric peoples. Uralic and Altaic Series. 39. Bloomington, Indiana University Press; The Hague, Mouton. 1964: 145-169, 382-384.

*Indiana. University. Graduate Program in Uralic and Asian Studies. The Vepsians. By Felix J. Oinas. New Haven, printed by the Human Relations Area Files. 1955. 11, 61 p.

Vuorela, Toivo. The Finno-Ugric peoples. Uralic and Altaic Series. 39. Bloomington, Indiana University Press; The Hague, Mouton. 1964: 133-144, 381-382.

Weinreich, Uriel. Yiddish language and folklore, a selective bibliography for research. 's Gravenhage, Mouton. 1959. 66 p.

Adler, Cyrus, and I. M. Casanowicz. The collection of Jewish ceremonial objects in the United States National Museum. United States National Museum, Proceedings. 34(1908): 701-746, plates 60-105.

Anchel, Robert. Les Juifs de France. Paris, J. B. Janin. 1946. 291 p.

Andree, Richard. Zur Volkskunde der Juden. Leipzig, Velhagen & Klasing. 1881. 8, 296 p.

Ausubel, Nathan. A treasury of Jewish folklore: stories, traditions, legends, humor, wisdom, and folk songs of the Jewish people. New York, Crown Publishers. 1948. 24, 741 p.

Ausubel, Nathan. A treasury of Jewish humor. New York, Doubleday. 1951. 735 p.

Ayalti, Hanan J., ed. Yiddish proverbs. New York, Schocken Books. 1949. 127 p.

Berkowitz, Joseph. La question des Israélites en Roumanie. Étude de son histoire et des divers problèmes de droit qu'elle soulève. (Thèse.) Paris, Jouve. 1923. 798 p.

Bloch, Maurice. Les vertus militaires des Juifs. Paris, A. Durlacher. 1897. 56 p.

Bloch, Maurice. Quatre conferences sur les Juifs. Paris, Fischbacher. 1901. 261 p. (Jews in France.)

Cohen, Israel. Jewish life in modern times. New York, Dodd, Mead. 1914. 13, 374 p. (2d ed. London, Methuen. 16, 349 p.)

Cohen, Israel. Anti-Semitism in Germany. London, offices of the Jewish Chronicle and the Jewish World. 1918. 20 p.

Cohen, Israel. A ghetto gallery. London, E. Goldston. 1931. 351 p.

Freedman, Maurice, ed. A minority in Britain; social studies of the Anglo-Jewish community. London, Vallentine, Mitchell. 1955. 16, 279 p.

Gartner, L. P. The Jewish immigrant in England 1870-1914. London, Allen and Unwin. 1960. 320 p.

Ginzburgh, Natalia. Family sayings. New York, E. P. Dutton. 1967. 222 p. (Italian-Jewish life.)

Graeber, Isacque, ed. Jews in a Gentile world. New York, Macmillan. 1942. 10, 436 p.

Grunwald, Max, ed. Jahrbuch für jüdische Volkskunde. Berlin und Wien, Benjamin Harz. 1923. 480 p.

Haleiv, H. S. The demography of Jewish communities in western Europe. Jewish Journal of Sociology. 2(1960): 103-114.

Halévy, Mayer A. Comunitațiile Evreilor din Iași și București. București, Institutul de Istorie Evreo-Română. 1931. 112 p., illus., plates.

Jacobs, Melville. Jewish blood and culture. In Isacque Graeber, ed. Jews in a Gentile world. New York, Macmillan. 1942: 38-55.

Jewish Historical Society of England. Celebration of the 250th anniversary of the Whitehall Conference, 1655-1905. London, R. Tuck & Sons. 1906. 12 p.

Jewish Journal of Sociology (London). 1 (1959):--

Kahana, Rabbi K. The theory of marriage in Jewish law. Leiden, E. J. Brill. 1966. 11, 99 p.

Katz, J. Family, kinship and marriage among Ashkenazim in the sixteenth to the eighteenth centuries. Jewish Journal of Sociology. 1 (1959): 4-22.

Katz, Jacob. Tradition and crisis; Jewish society at the end of the Middle Ages. New York, The Free Press of Glencoe. 1961. 280 p.

Kertzler, Rabbi Morris Norman. What is a Jew? Cleveland, World Publishing Co. 1960. 217 p.

Krausz, E. Leeds Jewry. Cambridge, W. Heffer. 1964. 150 p.

Mace, David Robert. Hebrew marriage; a sociological study. London, Epworth Press; New York, Philosophical Library. 1953. 271 p.

Marie Thaddea de Sion, Sister. The economic and social conditions in the ghetto, together with the aspirations of the Jews as described by ghetto writers. Toronto, 1946. 200 p. (Unpublished Ph.D. dissertation in Sociology. University of Toronto.)

Mead, Margaret. Israel and problems of identity. New York, Herzl Institute. 1958. 27 p.

Meyer, Peter, et al. The Jews in the Soviet satellites. Syracuse, N.Y., Syracuse University Press. 1953. 637 p.

Mitteilungen zur Jüdischen Volkskunde. 32 vols. 1898-1929. Berlin, etc.

Morariu, Tiberiu. Noui contribuțiuni la păstoritul evreilor Maramureșeni [New contribution to Jewish herding life in Maramures]. Extras din Revista "Stâna." 1. No. 9 și 10. Sibiu, Tip Vestermean. 1934. 32 p., 2 plates.

Patai, Raphael, F. L. Utley, and Dov Noy. Studies in Biblical and Jewish folklore. Bloomington, Indiana University Press. 1961. 8, 374 p.

Pennell, Joseph. The Jew at home; impressions of a summer and autumn spent with him in Russia and Austria. New York, D. Appleton. 1892. 105 p.

Philipson, David. Old European Jewries. Philadelphia, Jewish Publication Society of America. 1894. 281 p.

Philipson, David. The Jew in English fiction. Cincinnati, Robert Clarke Co. 1911. 207 p.

Rappoport, Angelo Solomon. The folklore of the Jews. London, Soncino Press. 1937. 11, 276 p.

Roback, A. A. Psychological aspects of Jewish protective phrases. Bulletin of the Jewish Academy of Arts and Sciences. No. 4. New York. 1938. 18 p.

Roblin, Michel. Les Juifs de Paris, demographie, économie, culture. Paris, A. et J. Picard. 1952. 199 p., figs., maps, plans. (Thesis.)

Rosenau, William. Jewish ceremonial institutions and customs. Baltimore, Friedenwald Co. 1903. 193 p.

Rosenfeld, Morris. Songs from the ghettos. Boston, Small, Maynard. 1900. 10, 155 p.

Samuel, Maurice. The gentleman and the Jew. New York, Knopf. 1950. 8, 325 p.

*Schauss, Hayyim. The Jewish festivals from their beginnings to our own days. Cincinnati, Union of American Hebrew Congregations. 1938. 13, 320 p.

*Schauss, Hayyim. The lifetime of a Jew throughout the ages of Jewish history. Cincinnati, Union of American Hebrew Congregations. 1950. 13, 332 p.

Schön, Josef. Volksglaube und Brauch der Juden in Ungarn. Ethnologische Mitteilungen aus Ungarn. 5(1897): 215-216.

Schuster, Hans. Die Judenfrage in Rumänien. Leipzig, F. Meiner. 1939. 244 p. (Inaugural dissertation.)

Schwarz, Leo, ed. Memoirs of my people. Jewish self-portraits from the 11th to the 20th centuries. New York and Toronto, Farrar & Rinehart. 1943. 26, 597 p.

Silbermann, Jacob. Proccessul de la Ismail inaintea juratiloru din Buzeu.
Bucuresti, Typ. Thiel & Weiss. 1872. 53 p. (Jews in Rumania.)

Slang, Ignjat. Jevreji u Beogradu [The Jews in Belgrade]. Belgrade. 1926.
143 p.

Strizower, Schifra. Exotic Jewish communities. London, New York, T.
Yoseloff. 1963 (1962). 157 p.

Tietze, Hans. Die Juden Wiens: Geschichte-Wortschaft-Kultur. Leipzig und
Vienna, E. P. Tal. 1933. 301 p.

*Trachtenberg, Joshua. Jewish magic and superstition: a study in folk religion.
New York, Behrman's Jewish Book House. 1939. 12, 356 p. (Reprinted:
New York, Meridian Books. 1961. 12, 356 p.)

Trachtenberg, Joshua. The devil and the Jews, the medieval conception of
the Jew and its relation to modern anti-semitism. New Haven, Yale University Press; London, Oxford University Press, H. Milford. 1943. 14,
279 p.

*Wirth, Louis. The ghetto. Chicago, University of Chicago Press. 1928.
16, 306 p. (Many reprints.)

Ziderman, A. Leisure activities of Jewish teenagers in London. Jewish Journal of Sociology. 8(1966): 240-264.

Weinreich, Uriel. Yiddish language and folklore, a selective bibliography for research. 's Gravenhage, Mouton. 1959. 66 p.

Abramovitch, Hirsch. Rural Jewish occupations in Lithuania. Yivo. Annual of Jewish Social Science. 2-3(1947-1948): 205-221. New York, Yiddish Scientific Institute-Yivo.

Adler, Bruno. Die Krim-Karäer in geschichtlicher, demographischer und volkskundlicher Beziehung. Baessler Archiv. 17(1934): 103-133.

Ain, Abraham. Swislocz. Portrait of a Jewish community in eastern Europe. Yivo. Annual of Jewish Social Science. 4(1949): 86-114.

Andreski, S. An economic interpretation of antisemitism in eastern Europe. Jewish Journal of Sociology. 5(1963): 201-213.

Bienenstok, Theodore. Social life and authority in the East European shtetel community. S.W.J.A. 6(1950): 238-254.

Buber, Martin, ed. Tales of the Hasidim: the early masters. New York, Schocken Books. 1947. 18, 335 p.

Buber, Martin, ed. Tales of the Hasidim: the later masters. New York, Schocken Books. 1948. 7, 352 p.

Casanoewicz, I. M. The Jews of southern Russia. A.A. o.s. 9(1896): 143-145.

Chagall, Bella, and Marc Chagall. Burning Lights. New York, Schocken Books. 1946. 268 p. (Jewish life in Vitebsk.)

Dan, Demeter. Die Juden in der Bukowina. Z.f.Ö.V. 7(1901): 69-78, 117-125, 169-179.

Dawidowicz, Lucy S. The golden tradition. Jewish life and thought in eastern Europe. New York, Holt, Rinehart & Winston. 1967. 502 p.

Gini, Corrado. I Caraimi di Polonia e Lituania. Genus (Rome). 2(1936): 1-56, plates, table.

Hertz, A. Zydzi w kulturze polskiej [The Jews in Polish culture]. Paryz, Instytut Literacki. 1961. 284 p.

Herzog, Marvin I. The Yiddish language in northern Poland: its geography and history. Publications of the Indiana University Research Center in Anthropology, Folklore and Linguistics. 37; International Journal of American Linguistics. 31, no. 2, pt. 3. Bloomington, Indiana University Press. 1965. 29, 323 p.

*Heschel, Abraham Joshua. The earth is the Lord's: the inner world of the Jew in East Europe. New York, H. Schuman. 1950. 109 p.

Institute of Jewish Affairs. The position of Jewish communities in eastern Europe on the eve of 1958. New York, Institute of Jewish Affairs. 1958. 30 p.

Joffe, Natalie F. The dynamics of benefice among the East European Jews. Social Forces. 27(1949): 238-247.

Johnpoll, Bernard K. The politics of futility; the General Jewish Workers Bund of Poland 1917-1943. Ithaca, Cornell University Press. 1967. 19, 298 p.

Lapson, D. Jewish dances of eastern and central Europe. Journal of the International Folk Music Council. 15(1963): 58-61.

Levitats, Isaac. The Jewish community in Russia, 1772-1844. New York, Columbia University Press. 1943. 300 p.

Lew, Henri. Der Tod und die Beerdigungsgebräuche bei den polnischen Juden. M.A.G.W. 32(1902): 400-408.

Maurach, Reinhart. Die Karaimen in der russischen Judengesetzgebung. Zeitschrift für Rassenkunde. 10(1939): 163-175.

Meisl, Josef. Die Juden im Zarentum Polens; ein geschichtlicher Überblick. Bonn, A. Marcus und E. Weber. 1916. 78 p.

Meisl, Josef. Haskalah, Geschichte der Aufklärungsbewegung unter den Juden in Russland. Berlin, C. A. Schwetschke & Sohn. 1919. 7, 229 p.

Meisl, Josef. Geschichte der Juden in Polen und Russland. Berlin, C. A. Schwetschke & Sohn. 3 vols. 1921. 12, 342; 8, 217; 12, 420 p.

Melcer-Rutkowska, Wanda. Czarny lad [The black continent]. Warsaw, Dom Ksiazki Polskiej. 1936. (Jewish life in the Warsaw ghetto.)

Olšvanger, Immanuel. Aus der Volksliteratur der Ostjuden. Schwänke, Erzählungen, Volkslieder und Rätsel. Schriften zur jüdischen Volkskunde. 1. Basel. 1920. 38, 299 p.

Palmer, Francis H. E. Russian life in town and country. New York and London, G. P. Putnam's Sons. 1901: 138-165.

Rosenthal, Celia S. Deviation and social change in the Jewish community of a small Polish town. American Journal of Sociology. 60(1954): 177-181.

Rubinow, I. M. Economic conditions of the Jews in Russia. U.S. Department of Commerce and Labor. Bulletin of the Bureau of Labor No. 72: 487-583. Washington, Government Printing Office. 1907.

Samuel, Maurice. The world of Sholom Aleichem. New York, Alfred A. Knopf. 1943. 6, 331 p. (Many reprints.)

Samuel, Maurice. Prince of the ghetto. New York, Alfred A. Knopf. 1948. 6, 294 p. (Fiction, but useful.)

*Schauss, Hayyim. The Jewish festivals from their beginnings to our own days. Cincinnati, Union of American Hebrew Congregations. 1938. 13, 320 p.

*Schauss, Hayyim. The lifetime of a Jew throughout the ages of Jewish history. Cincinnati, Union of American Hebrew Congregations. 1950. 13, 332 p.

Singer, Israel Ioshua. Fun a welt vos iz nishto mer [Of a world that is no more]. New York, privately printed. 1946. 267 p.

Trachtenberg, Joshua. Jewish education in eastern Europe at the beginning of the seventeenth century. Easton, Penn., the author. 1939. 17 p.

Vetulani, A. The Jews in medieval Poland. Jewish Journal of Sociology. 4(1962): 274-294.

Wallenstein, Abraham. Jews and Germanism. New York, George H. Doran Co. 1918. 14 p.

Weinreich, Uriel. Culture geography at a distance: some problems in the study of East European Jewry. In Proceedings of the 1962 Annual Spring Meeting of the American Ethnological Society. Seattle, University of Washington Press. 1963: 27-39.

Weisenberg, S. Eine jüdische Hochzeit in Südrussland. Mitteilungen zur Jüdischen Volkskunde. 15(1905): 59-74.

Zajaczkowski, Ananiasz. Karaims in Poland: history, language, folklore, science. Warszawa, Państwowe Wydawn Naukowe. 1961. 115 p., 17 plates.

*Zborowski, Mark, and Elizabeth Herzog. Life is with people: the Jewish little town of eastern Europe. New York, International Universities Press. 1952. 7, 456 p. (Reprinted: New York, Schocken Books. 1962. 452 p.)

Zborowski, Mark, and Elizabeth Herzog. The place of book-learning in traditional Jewish culture. In Margaret Mead and Martha Wolfenstein, eds. Childhood in contemporary cultures. Chicago, University of Chicago Press. 1955: 118-141, 2 plates.

Adatto, Albert. Sephardim and the Seattle Sephardic community. Seattle. 1939. (Unpublished M. A. thesis. University of Washington.)

Algazi, L., comp. Chants Sephardis. n.p. 1958. 16, 63 p.

Benardete, Mair J. Hispanic culture and character of the Sephardic Jews. New York, Hispanic Institute of the United States. 1952. 186 p.

Caro Baroja, Julio. Los Judíos en la España moderna y contemporanea. 3 vols. Madrid, Ediciones Arion. 1961. 540, 462, 576 p.

Crews, Mrs. Cynthia Mary Jopson. Recherches sur le Judéo-espagnol dans les pays Balkaniques. Paris, E. Droz. 1935. 319 p.

Estrugo, José M. Los Sefardíes. Habana, Editorial Lex. 1958. 143 p.

Estrugo, José M. Datos y apuntes sobre los Sefardíes, para incorporar a mi libro "Los Sefardíes" en una posible secunda edición. Madrid. 1959. 54 p.

Firestone, Melvin M. Sephardic folk-curing in Seattle. J. A. F. L. 75(1962): 301-310.

Frankl, Ludwig August. The Jews of the East. 2 vols. London, Hurst and Blackett. 1859.

*Garnett, Lucy Mary Jane. The women of Turkey and their folk-lore. Vol. 2. The Jewish and Moslem women. London, David Nutt. 1891: 3-94.

Goodblatt, Moses S. Jewish life in Turkey in the XVIth century as reflected in the legal writings of Samuel de Medina. New York, Jewish Theological Seminary of America. 1952. 14, 240 p.

Hyamson, Albert M. The Sephardim of England, a history of the Spanish and Portuguese Jewish community, 1492-1951. London, Methuen. 1951. 12, 468 p.

Lacalle, J. M. Los Judíos Españoles. Barcelona, Sayma. 1961. 173 p.

Landschut, Siegfried. Jewish communities in the Muslim countries of the Middle East; a survey prepared for the Anglo-Jewish Committee and the Anglo-Jewish Association. London, Jewish Chronicle. 1950. 11, 102 p.

Loeb, Isidore. La situation des Israélites en Serbie et en Roumanie. Paris, Imprimerie Centrale de Chemins de Fer A. Chaix. 1876. 141 p.

Mendelssohn, Sidney. The Jews of Asia, especially in the sixteenth and seventeenth centuries. London, Kegan Paul, Trench, Trubner. 1920. 14, 242 p.

Mezan, Saül. Les Juifs Espagnols en Bulgarie. Vol. 1. Histoire, statistique, ethnographie. Sofia, Imprimerie "Amischpat." 1925. 150 p.

*Mohlo, Michael. Usos y costumbres de los Sephardíes de Salonica. Biblioteca Hebraecoespañola. 3. Madrid, Consejo Superior de Investigaciones Científicas, Instituto Arias Montana. 1950. 341 p.

Orano, Paolo. Gli Ebrei in Italia. Roma, Case Editrice Pinciana. 1930. 248 p.

Roth, Cecil. A history of the Marranos. Philadelphia, Jewish Publication Society of America. 1932. 12, 422 p.

Amador de los Rios, José. Historia social, política y religiosa de los Judíos de España y Portugal. Madrid, Aguilar. 1960. 20, 1109 p., illus.

*Caro Baroja, Julio. Los Judíos en la España moderna y contemporanea. 3 vols. Madrid, Ediciones Arion. 1961. 540, 462, 576 p.

Lacalle, José Maria. Los Judíos españoles. Barcelona, Sayma. 1961. 174 p., illus.

Machado, Casimiro de Morais. Mogadouro. Os Marranos de Vilarinho de Galegos. Douro-Litoral. Museu de Etnografia e Historia da Junta de Província. Quinta série. 1-2(1952): 17-49.

Paulo, Amílcar. Os Marranos em Trás-os-Montes (Reminiscências Judio-Portuguesas). Douro-Litoral. Museu de Etnografia e Historia da Junta de Província. Sétima série. 7-8(1956): 627-659.

Roth, Cecil. A history of the Marranos. Philadelphia, Jewish Publication Society of America. 1932. 12, 422 p.

Black, George Fraser. A Gypsy bibliography. London, printed by T. A. Constable at Edinburgh University Press for the members of the Gypsy Lore Society, and published by B. Quaritch. 1914. 7, 226 p.

Macfie, Robert Andrew Scott. In Memoriam Robert Andrew Scott Macfie. A catalogue of the Gypsy books collected by the late R. A. S. Macfie sometime sec. & editor of the Gypsy Lore Society. Liverpool, Liverpool University Press. 1936. 178 p.

Ratcliffe, Dorothy Una. Catalogue of the Romany Collection formed by D. U. McGrigor Phillips and presented to the University of Leeds. Containing a bibliography of over 1,000 printed works & much other material. Edinburgh, published for the Brotherton Collection by T. Nelson. 1962. 12, 227 p.

Adler, Marta. My life with the Gypsies. London, Souvenir Press; Toronto, Ryerson Press. 1960. 204 p.

Arnold, H. Die Zigeuner. Herkunft und Leben der Stämme im deutschen Sprachengebiet. Olten, Freiburg-im-Breisgau, Walter. 1965. 322 p.

Bartels, Erik Daniel, and G. S. K. Brun. Gipsies in Denmark. A social-biological study. Copenhagen, Munksgaard. 1943. 179 p.

Bercovici, Konrad. The story of the Gypsies. London, Jonathan Cape; New York, Cosmopolitan Book Co. 1928. 320 p.

Bloch, Jules. Les tsiganes. Paris, Presses Universitaires de France. 1953. 118 p.

Block, Martin. Die rumänischen Zigeuner. Versuch einer monographischen Darstellung der materiellen Kultur. Jena. 1923. 167 p., map, plates. (Thesis.)

Block, Martin. Zigeuner, ihr Leben und ihre Seele, dargestellt auf Grund eigener Reisen und Forschungen; mit Abbildungen auf 64 Kunstdrucktafeln. Leipzig, Bibliographisches Institut. 1936. 219 p.

*Block, Martin. Gypsies, their life and their customs. London, Methuen. 1938. 11, 247 p.

*Borrow, George. The Zincali, or an account of the Gypsies of Spain. 3d ed. 2 vols. in 1. London, J. Murray. 1843. (1st ed. 1841.) (Reprinted: London, John Murray. 1907. 23, 433 p.)

Borrow, George. Romany Lavo Lil: word-book of Romany; or, the Gypsy language. London, John Murray. 1874. 8, 331 p.

Brown, Irving. Nights & days on the Gypsy trail. Andalusia & other Mediterranean shores. New York, Harper. 1922. 16, 266 p.

Brown, Irving. Gypsy fires in America. Life among the Romanies of the U.S. & Canada. New York, Harper. 1924. 8, 244 p.

Brown, Irving. Deep song. Adventures in Andalusia & other lands with Gypsy songs and singers. New York, Harper. 1929. 12, 355 p.

Carew, F. W., ed. No. 747, being the autobiography of a Gypsy. Bristol, Arrowsmith. n.d. [1890]. 4, 459 p.

Chambers, William. Exploits & anecdotes of the Scottish Gypsies, with traits of their origin, character & manners. Edinburgh, Wm. Brown. 1886. 68 p. (Originally published in 1821.)

Charnock, R. S. Roumanian Gypsies. Anthropologia. 1 (1873-1875): 489-497.

Chatard, Joseph. Zanko, chef tribal chez les Chalderash. La tradition des tsiganes conserver par l'aristocratie de ce peuple, . . . Paris, La Colombe. 1959. 208 p.

Chelcea, Ion. Țiganii din Romînia. Monografie etnografică [The Gypsies of Romania. Ethnographic monograph]. București. 1944. 314 p.

*Clebert, Jean Paul. The Gypsies. London, Vista Books. 1963. 19, 234 p.

Coelho, Francisco Adolpho. Os ciganos de Portugal. Lisboa, Imprensa Nacional. 1892. 302 p.

Colocci, Adriano Amerigo, Marquis de. Gli Zingari, storia d'un popolo errante. Turin, E. Loescher. 1889. 419 p. (Italian Gypsies.)

Crabb, James. The Gipsies' advocate; or, observations on the origin, character, manners, and habits of the English Gipsies. 3d ed. London, Nisbet. 1832. 12, 199 p.

Croft-Cooke, Rupert. The moon in my pocket, life with the Romanies. London, S. Low. 1948. 9, 198 p.

*Cutriss, Frank [pseud. of F. R. Hinkins and R. Cutriss Hinkins]. Romany life experienced & observed during many years of friendly intercourse with the Gypsies. London, Mills & Boon. 1915. 12, 283 p. (English Gypsies.)

Dordević, Tikhomir R. Die Zigeuner in Serbien, ethnologische Forschungen. 2 pts. Mitteilungen zur Zigeunerkunde. 2; Ethnologische Mitteilungen aus Ungarn. 8. Budapest. 1903. 8, 80 p.

Dostal, W. Die Zigeuner in Österreich. Monographische Zusammenfassung der Ergebnisse meines Studienaufenthaltes unter Zigeunern, 1954. Archiv für Völkerkunde. 10 (1955): 1-15.

Duff, C. A Gypsy courtship and marriage in Spain. Journal of the Gypsy Lore Society. Third series. 44(1965): 2-11.

Erdős, Kamill. A classification of Gypsies in Hungary. Acta Ethnographica. 6(1958): 449-457, maps.

Evens, Eunice Thomas. Thro' the years with Romany. London, University of London Press. 1946. 8, 260 p.

Ficowski, Jerzy. Devils, corpses and bones and other magical properties (used by Polish Gypsy fortune tellers). Journal of the Gypsy Lore Society. Third series. 42(1963): 106-117.

Filipović, Milenko S. Visocki cigani. Zagreb, Izdaje Etnografski Muzej. 1932. 20 p.

Garnett, Lucy Mary Jane. The women of Turkey and their folk-lore. Vol. 2. The Jewish and Moslem women. London, David Nutt. 1891: 355-381.

Gerard, Emily. The land beyond the forest. Facts, figures and fancies from Transylvania. New York, Harper and Brothers. 1888: 236-278.

Gjorgjevic, Th. R. See Đordević, Tikhomir R.

Grellmann, Heinrich M. G. Dissertation on the Gypsies, being an historical enquiry, concerning the manners of life, economy, customs and conditions of these people in Europe, and their origin . . . (Translated into English.) London, printed for the editor by G. Bigg. 1787. 4, 1, 19, 255 p. (Reprinted: London, W. Ballantine. 1807. 13, 210 p.)

Groome, Francis H. In Gypsy tents. Edinburgh, W. P. Nimmo. 1880. 7, 387 p.

Groome, Francis H. Gypsy folk-tales. London, Hurst & Blackett. 1899. 83, 302 p. (Reprinted: Hatboro, Penn., Folklore Associates. 1963. 11, 83, 302 p.)

Gunda, Béla. Gypsy medical folklore in Hungary. J.A.F.L. 75 (1962): 131-146.

Gypsy Lore Society. Journal of the Gypsy Lore Society. 1-3, July 1888-April 1892. New series. 1-7, 1907-1916. Third series. 1 (1922)—

Heusch, Luc de. A la découverte des Tsiganes. Une expédition de reconnaissance (1961). Bruxelles, Institut de Sociologie. 1966. 208 p., 8 illus.

Horvãthovã, E. Cigáni na Slovensku. Bratislava, Vudavatel'stvo Slovenskej Akadémie Vied. 1964. 396 p.

Hughes, Cledwyn. West with the tinkers. A journey thro' Wales with the vagrants. London, Oldhams Press. 1954. 223 p.

Jockimson, L. Zigeuner heute. Untersuchung einer Aussenseitergruppe in einer deutschen Mittelstadt. Stuttgart, Enke. 1963. 11, 113 p.

Kenrick, D. Notes on the Gypsies in Bulgaria. Journal of the Gypsy Lore Society. Third series. 45(1966): 77-84.

Leland, Charles Godfrey. The English Gypsies and their language. New York, Hurd & Houghton. 1873. 13, 259 p.

Leland, Charles Godfrey. English-Gypsy songs. In Romany, with metrical English translations. London, Trübner. 1875. 12, 276 p.

Leland, Charles Godfrey. The Gypsies. Boston and New York, Houghton, Mifflin. 1882. 8, 372 p.

Leland, Charles Godfrey. Gypsy sorcery and fortune telling. New York, C. Scribner's Sons. 1891. 16, 271 p. (Reprinted: New Hyde Park, N. Y., University Books. 1962.)

Levy, Juliette de B. As Gypsies wander. Life with the Gypsies in England, Spain, Provence, Turkey & N. Africa. London, Faber & Faber. 1953. 300 p.

Levy, Juliette de B. Gypsies at Andalucian fairs. Journal of the Gypsy Lore Society. Third series. 40(1961): 45-52.

Liszt, Franz. Die Zigeuner und ihre Musik in Ungarn. Pesth, G. Heckenast. 1861. 259 p.

*Liszt, Franz. The Gypsy in music. 2 vols. London, William Reeves. 1926. 20, 208; 209-370 p.

McCormick, Andrew. The tinker Gypsies. Glasgow, John Menzies. 1907. 24, 538 p.

Macritchie, David. Scottish Gypsies under the Stewarts. Edinburgh, D. Douglas. 1894. 8, 123 p.

Madeen, G. Zigenarfragen i Finland [The problem of the Gypsies in Finland]. Sociala Meddelanden. 9(1956): 561-567.

Mandillo, E. Appunti sugi Zingari in Portogallo. Universo (Firenze). 37(1957): 453-464.

Miklosich, Franz Xaver von. Beiträge zur Kenntniss der Zigeunermundarten. 4 pts. Vienna, in Commission bei K. Gerold's Sohn. 1872-1881.

Morwood, Vernon S. Our Gypsies in city, tent & van. Origin & strange life, fortune telling practices, dialect etc. London, Sampson Low. 1885. 13, 350 p.

Paspates, Alexander Georgios. Études sur les Tchinghianén; ou Bohémiens de l'Empire Ottoman. Constantinople, Impr. A. Koroméla. 1870. 10, 652.

Peters, H. H. The Romanies in Austria today. Journal of the Gypsy Lore Society. Third series. 43(1964): 19-22.

Petulengro [Gypsy]. A Romany life. London, Methuen. 1948. 288 p. (English Gypsies.)

Phelan, Jim. Wagon-wheels. British Gypsy life and lore. London, G. G. Harrap. 1951. 224 p.

Pittard, E. Les Tziganes ou Bohémiens dans la péninsule des Balkans. Genève, Société Générale d'Imprimerie. 1932. 288 p.

Potra, George. Contribuţiuni la istoricul ţiganilor din România. Bucureşti, Fundaţia Regele Carol 1. 1939. 376 p., plates.

Reeve, Dominic. Smoke in the lanes. London, Constable. 1958. 302 p. (Romanys in southern England.)

Reeve, Dominic. No place like home. London, Phoenix House. 1960. 157 p.

Sampson, John. The dialect of the Gypsies of Wales. Being the older form of British Romani preserved in the speech of the clan of Abram Wood. London, Oxford University Press. 1926. 23, 230 p.

Schebeck, Bernhard, and Sigrid Bechmann. Ein Beschneidungsfest bei makedonischen Zigeunern. M. A. G. W. 88-89(1959): 154-157.

Schwicker, Johann Heinrich. Die Zigeuner in Ungarn und Siebenbürgen. Wien und Teschen, K. Prochaska. 1883. 187 p.

Smith, Hubert. Tent life with English Gypsies in Norway. 2d ed. London, H. S. King. 1874. 22, 540 p.

Starkie, Walter. Raggle-taggle: adventures with a fiddle in Hungary and Rumania. London, John Murray. 1933. 16, 390 p., illus.

Starkie, Walter. Gypsie fiddlers of the plains. Geographical Magazine. 13(1941): 146-155.

Starkie, Walter. The road to Santiago: pilgrims of Saint James. London, John Murray. 1957. 10, 339 p.

Starkie, Walter. A Gypsy tribe in Italy (1919). Journal of the Gypsy Lore Society. Third series. 43(1964): 12-19.

GYPSIES

Sweden. Zigenarutredningen, 1954. Zigenartrågan: betänkande. Malmö,
Tryckeriaktiebolaget. Framtiden. 1956. 153 p. (Gypsies in Sweden.)

*Thompson, T. W. English Gypsy death and burial customs. Journal of the
Gypsy Lore Society. Third series. 3(1924): 5-38, 60-93.

*Thompson, T. W. Gypsy marriage in England. Journal of the Gypsy Lore So-
ciety. Third series. 6(1927): 101-129, 151-182.

Tillhagen, C.-H. Married life and family life among Swedish Kalderaša
Gypsies. Journal of the Gypsy Lore Society. Third series. 33(1954):
129-150; 34(1955): 2-19.

Tillhagen, C.-H. The concept of justice among the Swedish Gypsies. Journal of the Gypsy Lore Society. Third series. 37(1958): 82-96; 38(1959):
18-31, 127-134.

Vessy-Fitzgerald, Brian Seymour. Gypsies of Britain. An introduction to their
history. London, Chapman & Hall. 1944. 16, 204 p.

Vessy-Fitzgerald, Brian Seymour. Gypsy Borrow. A biography. London, D.
Dobson. 1953. 161 p. (A biography of George Borrow, pioneer student
of Gypsy life.)

Ville, F. de. Les Tsiganes en Belgique. Études Tsiganes. 1(1956): 6-10.

Vukanović, T. P. The vampire. Journal of the Gypsy Lore Society. Third
series. 36(1957): 125-133.

Vukanović, T. P. The Gypsy population in Yugoslavia. Journal of the Gypsy
Lore Society. Third series. 42(1963): 10-27.

Vukanović, T. P. Ritual communion among Gypsies in Serbia. Journal of the
Gypsy Lore Society. Third series. 43(1964): 22-35.

Webb, Gadfrey Edward Cahrales. Gypsies; the secret people. London, H.
Jenkins. 1960. 189 p.

Wlislocki, Heinrich von. Haidebluten, Volkslieder der transsilvanischen
Zigeuner. Leipzig, W. Friedrich. 1880. 47 p.

*Wlislocki, Heinrich von. Vom wandernden Zigeunervolke. Bilder aus dem
Leben der siebenbürger Zigeuner. Geschichtliches, Ethnologisches, Sprache
und Poesie. Hamburg, Verlagsanstalt und Druckerei. 1890. 7, 390 p.

*Wlislocki, Heinrich von. Volksglaube und religiöser Brauch der Zigeuner.
Münster in Westfalen, Aschendorff. 1891. 16, 184 p.

GYPSIES

Wlislocki, Heinrich von. Aus dem inneren Leben der Zigeuner. Berlin, E.
    Felber. 1892. 220 p.

Wlislocki, Heinrich von. Seelenloskauf bei den mohammedanischen Zigeuner
    der Balkanländer. Ethnologische Mitteilungen aus Ungarn. 3(1893-1894):
    cols. 194-197.

Yates, Dora Esther. A book of Gypsy folk-tales. London, Phoenix House.
    1948. 17, 197 p.

Yoors, Jan. The Gypsies. New York, Simon and Schuster. 1967. 256 p.

CYPRUS

Cobham, Claude Delaval. An attempt at a bibliography of Cyprus. New ed. Nicosia, printed at the Government Printing Office. 1929. 4, 76 p.

Anderson, J. N. D. The family law of Turkish Cypriots. Welt der Islam. 5(1958): 161-187.

Balfour, Patrick. The orphaned realm: journeys in Cyprus. London, P. Marshall 1951. 221 p.

Beckingham, C. F. The Cypriot Turks. Royal Central Asian Journal. 43(1956): 126-130.

*Beckingham, C. F. The Turks of Cyprus. J.R.A.I. 87(1957): 165-174.

*Christodoulou, Demetrios. The evolution of the rural land use pattern in Cyprus. Monograph 2. Bude (Cornwall), Geographical Publications. 1959. 230 p., maps, illus.

Chrysanthis, Kypros. The personification of plague and cholera according to the Cypriots. Folk-Lore. 56(1945): 259-266.

Cobham, Claude Delaval. Excerpta Cypria: materials for a history of Cyprus. Cambridge, The University Press. 1908. 523 p.

Dixon, William Hepworth. British Cyprus. London, Chapman and Hall. 1879. 11, 368 p.

Durrell, Lawrence. Bitter lemons. London, Faber and Faber. 1957. 255 p.

George, V., and G. Millerson. The Cypriot community in London. Race. 8(1967): 277-292.

Gunnis, Rupert. Historic Cyprus: a guide to its towns and villages, monasteries and castles. London, Methuen. 1936. 495 p.

*Haji-Costa, Ismene. Some traditional customs of the people of Cyprus. Folk-Lore. 55(1944): 107-117.

Home, Gordon. Cyprus, then and now. London, J. M. Dent. 1960. 243 p.

Hornell, James. The Cypriot threshing sledge. Man. 30(1930): 135-139.

Hornell, James. Cylindrical beehives in Egypt and Cyprus. Man. 37(1937): 119-120. 2 illus.

Lang, Andrew. Medical superstitions in Cyprus. Folk-Lore. 11(1900): 120-125.

Lewis, Mrs. Agnes Smith. Through Cyprus. London, Hurst & Blackett. 1887. 9, 351 p.

CYPRUS

Melamid, Alexander. The geographical distribution of communities in Cyprus. Geographical Review. 46(1956): 355-374.

Meyer, Albert Julius. The economy of Cyprus. Harvard Middle East Studies. 6. Cambridge, Harvard University Press. 1962. 94 p.

*Ohnefalsch-Richter, Magda. Griechische Sitten und Gebräuche auf Cypern. Berlin, Reimer. 1913. 13, 369 p., illus., 80 plates, map.

*Peristiany, J. G. Honour and shame in a Cypriot highland village. In J. G. Peristiany, ed. Honour and shame. The values of Mediterranean society. London, Weidenfeld and Nicolson. 1965: 171-190.

Surridge, B. J. A survey of rural life in Cyprus based on reports of investigators who visited villages throughout the colony during 1927 and 1928, and amplified by statistical and other information from the records of government. Nicosia, printed at the Government Printing Office. 1930. 91 p.

*Tarsouli, Athena. Kypros. 2 vols. (Only Vol. 1 published.) Athens, "Alpha" I. M. Skaziki. 1955. 490 p., 21 plates, figures. (The basic work of Cypriot-Greek folk life.)

Barrow, Katherine M.   Three years in Tristan da Cunha. London, Skeffington & Son. 1910. 12, 280 p.

Brander, Jan. Tristan da Cunha 1506-1902. London, Allen and Unwin. 1940. 336 p.

Christopherson, Erling. Tristan da Cunha, the lonely isle. (Translated from the Norwegian.) London, Cassell. 1940. 8, 243 p.

Earle, Augustus. Narrative of a residence in New Zealand with journal of a residence in Tristan da Cunha. Oxford, The Clarendon Press. 1967. 304 p., plates.

Gane, Douglas Montague. Tristan da Cunha; an empire outpost and its keepers, with glimpses of its past and considerations of its future. London, Allen and Unwin. 1932. 173 p., plates.

Henricksen, Sverre Dick, and Per Oeding. Medical survey of Tristan da Cunha. Results of the Norwegian Scientific Expedition to Tristan da Cunha 1937-1938. No. 5. Oslo, Det Norske Videnskaps Akedemi i Oslo. 1940. 148 p.

*Munch, Peter A. Sociology of Tristan da Cunha. Results of the Norwegian Scientific Expedition to Tristan da Cunha 1937-1938. No. 13. Oslo, Det Norske Videnskaps Akademi i Oslo. 1945. 332 p.

Munch, Peter A. Culture and superculture in a displaced community: Tristan da Cunha. Ethnology. 3(1964): 369-376.